Español en marcha 1

Curso de español como lengua extranjera

Libro del alumno

Francisca Castro Viúdez
Pilar Díaz Ballesteros
Ignacio Rodero Díez
Carmen Sardinero Franco

SOCIEDAD GENERAL ESPAÑOLA DE LIBRERÍA, S. A.

Primera edición, 2005
Cuarta edición, 2007
Reimpresión, 2008

Produce SGEL – Educación
Avda. Valdelaparra, 29
28108 Alcobendas (MADRID)

© Salvador Dalí. Fundación Gala - Salvador Dalí. VEGAP. Madrid, 2006. Pág. 83.
© Sucesión Pablo Picasso. VEGAP. Madrid, 2006. Pág 83
© Wilfredo Lam. VEGAP. Madrid, 2006 Pág 83.
© Francisca Castro, Pilar Díaz, Carmen Sardinero, Ignacio Rodero.
© Sociedad General Española de Librería, S. A., 2004
   Avda. Valdelaparra, 29, 28108 ALCOBENDAS (MADRID).

Diseño de cubierta: Fragmenta comunicación S.L.
Diseño de interiores: Fragmenta comunicación S.L.
Maquetación: Verónica Sosa y Leticia Delgado
Ilustraciones: Maravillas Delgado
Fotografías: Héctor de Paz, Jesús García Bernardo, Birgitta Fröhlich, Archivo SGEL, Cordon Press, S. L.

ISBN: 978-84-9778-123-7
Depósito legal: M-10912-2008
Printed in Spain – Impreso en España.

Impresión: Orymu, S.A. - Ruiz de Alda, 1 - Pinto (Madrid)

Queda prohibida, salvo excepción prevista en la Ley, cualquier forma de reproducción, distribución, comunicación pública y transformación de esta obra sin contar con autorización de los titulares de propiedad intelectual. La infracción de los derechos mencionados puede ser constitutiva de delito contra la propiedad intelectual (Art. 270 y ss. Código Penal). El Centro Español de Derechos Reprográficos (www.cedro.org) vela por el respeto de los citados derechos.

Presentación

Español en marcha es un manual en cuatro niveles que abarca los contenidos correspondientes a los niveles A1, A2 y B1 del *Marco común europeo de referencia*. Al final de este primer tomo los estudiantes podrán comunicarse de forma elemental, pero correctamente, en pasado (pretérito indefinido), presente y futuro (*voy a* + infinitivo), y conocerán aproximadamente unas 1.000 palabras fundamentales. Además, podrán dar información básica sobre sí mismos y sobre los otros, así como desenvolverse en una serie de situaciones prácticas.

Cada una de las 10 unidades está compuesta de:
- Tres apartados (A, B y C) de dos páginas cada uno, en los que se presentan, desarrollan y practican los contenidos lingüísticos citados al inicio de cada uno de ellos. Cada apartado sigue una secuencia cuidadosamente graduada desde la presentación de las muestras de lengua hasta una actividad final de producción. A lo largo de cada unidad, el alumno tendrá la oportunidad de desarrollar todas las destrezas (leer, escuchar, escribir y hablar) así como de trabajar en profundidad la gramática, el vocabulario y la pronunciación, en una serie de tareas que van desde las más dirigidas a las más libres.
- Un apartado de *Autoevaluación,* con actividades destinadas a recapitular y consolidar los objetivos de la unidad, y donde se incluye un test con el que el alumno podrá evaluar su progreso según los descriptores del *Portfolio europeo de las lenguas.*
- El apartado *De acá y de allá,* que contiene información del mundo español e hispanoamericano y tiene como objetivo desarrollar la competencia tanto sociocultural como intercultural del estudiante.

Al final de las unidades se incluyen las transcripciones de las grabaciones de los CD, una referencia gramatical ordenada según ha ido apareciendo en las unidades, una tabla con los verbos regulares e irregulares más frecuentes y, lo más interesante, un conjunto de tareas de "vacío de información" para desarrollar la expresión oral en parejas.

Español en marcha puede ser utilizado tanto en clases intensivas (de tres o cuatro horas diarias), como en cursos impartidos a lo largo de todo un año.

contenidos

TEMA	A	B	C	CULTURA	PÁG.
Unidad 0 Presentación	**¡Hola! Me llamo Maribel** • Presentarse en clase.	**¿Cómo se escribe? ¿Cómo se pronuncia?** • Alfabeto. • Deletrear. • Recursos para la clase.	**Mapas de España y América**		7
Unidad 1 Saludos	**¡Encantado!** • Presentar y saludar. • Género de los adjetivos de nacionalidad.	**¿A qué te dedicas?** • Profesiones. • Género de las profesiones. • Verbos *ser* y *tener*. • Verbos regulares en presente.	**¿Cuál es tu número de teléfono?** • Números 0-20. **Pronunciación y ortografía:** Entonación interrogativa.	**Saludos** • Estilo formal e informal: *tú* o *usted*.	12
Unidad 2 Familias	**¿Estás casado?** • Describir a la familia. • Plural de los nombres.	**¿Dónde están mis gafas?** • Preposiciones de lugar: *debajo / encima / al lado / delante / detrás / entre / en*. • Adjetivos posesivos. • Demostrativos.	**¿Qué hora es?** • Decir la hora. • Horarios del mundo. • Números 21-5.000. **Pronunciación y ortografía:** Acentuación.	**La familia hispana**	20
Unidad 3 El trabajo	**Rosa se levanta a las siete** • Hablar de hábitos. • Verbos reflexivos. • Verbos irregulares: *empezar, volver, ir, venir*. • Preposiciones de tiempo.	**¿Estudias o trabajas?** • Los días de la semana. • Hablar de horarios de trabajo. • Lugares de trabajo.	**¿Qué desayunas?** • Hablar del desayuno. • Desayunos del mundo. **Pronunciación y ortografía:** /g/.	**Lenguaje gestual**	28
Unidad 4 La casa	**¿Dónde vives?** • Describir una casa. • Ordinales: 1.º - 10.º.	**Interiores** • Muebles y cosas de casa. • *Hay / está*.	**En el hotel** • Inscribirse en un hotel. • Patios. **Pronunciación y ortografía:** /k/	**Viviendas de España**	36
Unidad 5 Comer	**Comer fuera de casa** • Pedir comida en un restaurante. • Platos de cocina española. • Comer fuera.	**¿Te gusta el cine?** • Vocabulario de tiempo libre. • Verbo *gustar*. • Escribir un anuncio. • Imperativos regulares.	**Receta del Caribe** • Imperativo afirmativo. • Dar y entender instrucciones. • Productos de América. **Pronunciación y ortografía:** /b/ y /v/.	**Cocinas del mundo**	44
Unidad 6 El barrio	**¿Cómo se va a Plaza de España?** • Comprar un billete de metro. • Instrucciones para ir en metro.	**Cierra la ventana, por favor** • Imperativo irregular. • Pedir favores, dar órdenes. • ¿*Puede(s)* + infinitivo?	**Mi barrio es tranquilo** • *Ser* y *estar* **Pronunciación y ortografía:** La *r/rr*.	**Música latina**	52

TEMA	A	B	C	CULTURA	PÁG.
Unidad 7 Salir con los amigos	¿Dónde quedamos? • Recursos para concertar una cita por teléfono. • Verbo *quedar*.	¿Qué estás haciendo? • Hablar de acciones en desarrollo. *Estar* + gerundio + pronombres reflexivos. **Pronunciación y ortografía:** Entonación exclamativa.	¿Cómo es? • Descripción física y de carácter.	Los sábados por la noche	60
Unidad 8 De vacaciones	De vacaciones • Preguntar e indicar cómo se va a un lugar. • Vocabulario de la ciudad: farmacia, correos...	¿Qué hizo Rosa ayer? • Pret. indefinido de los verbos regulares. • Pret. indefinido *ir* y *estar*. **Pronunciación y ortografía:** acentuación.	¿Qué tiempo hace hoy? • Hablar del tiempo. • Los meses y estaciones del año.	Vacaciones en España	68
Unidad 9 Compras	¿Cuánto cuestan estos zapatos? • Recursos para comprar. • Demostrativos (adjetivos y pronombres). • Pronombres de objeto directo: *lo, la, los, las*.	Mi novio lleva corbata • Los colores. • Describir la ropa. • Concordancia nombre y adjetivo. **Pronunciación y ortografía:** *g* y *j*.	Buenos Aires es más grande que Toledo. • Comparar. • Adjetivos descriptivos de ciudades.	Pintura española e hispanoamericana Pablo Picasso, Diego Rivera, Salvador Dalí, Wifredo Lam.	76
Unidad 10 Salud y enfermedad	La salud • El cuerpo humano. • Hablar de enfermedades y remedios • Verbo *doler*. • Sugerencias: ¿*por qué no...?*	Antes salíamos mucho con los amigos • Hábitos en el pasado. • Pretérito imperfecto.	Voy a trabajar en un hotel • Hablar de planes e intenciones. • *Voy a* + infinitivo. **Pronunciación y ortografía:** Reglas de acentuación.	Los incas, pueblo del sol	84
Actividades en pareja					93
Apéndice gramatical					99
Verbos regulares e irregulares					111
Transcripciones					115

A. ¡Hola! Me llamo Maribel

1. Lee y escucha.

PROFESORA: ¡Hola!, me llamo Maribel y soy la profesora de español. Vamos a presentarnos. A ver, empieza tú, ¿cómo te llamas?
ESTUDIANTE 1: Me llamo Christian.
PROFESORA: ¿De dónde eres, Christian?
ESTUDIANTE 1: Soy alemán, de Berlín.
ESTUDIANTE 2: Yo me llamo Elaine y soy brasileña.

2. Practica con tus compañeros.

- ¡Hola!
- ¿Cómo te llamas?
- ¿De dónde eres?

- ¡Hola!
- *Me llamo* _____
- *Soy (de)* _____

3. Completa con el nombre de tu país y tu nacionalidad.

1. Alemania — alemán — alemana
2. Brasil — brasileño — brasileña
3. España — español — española
4. Francia — francés — francesa
5. _____ — _____ — _____

SALUDOS

¡Hola!

Buenos días

Buenas tardes

Buenas noches

B. ¿Cómo se escribe? ¿Cómo se pronuncia?

4. Escucha y repite.

VOCALES

A	E	I	O	U
a	e	i	o	u

CONSONANTES

Mayúscula	minúscula	nombre	sonido	ejemplos
B	b	(be)	/b/	abuelo, bien
C	c	(ce)	c + a, o, u = /k/	casa, cuatro
			c + e, i = /θ/	cine, cerrado
CH	ch	(che)	/tʃ/	chocolate
D	d	(de)	/d/	día, dos
F	f	(efe)	/f/	fumar
G	g	(ge)	g + a, o, u = /g/	gato, pago, agua
			gu + e, i = /g/	guerrero, guitarra
			g + e, i = /x/	genio, giro
H	h	(hache)	–	hotel, hospital
J	j	(jota)	/x/	jefe, jirafa
K	k	(ka)	/k/	kilogramo
L	l	(ele)	/l/	león, limón
Ll	ll	(elle)	/λ/	llave, camello, lluvia
M	m	(eme)	/m/	Madrid, mira
N	n	(ene)	/n/	nada, no
Ñ	ñ	(eñe)	/ɲ/	niña, año
P	p	(pe)	/p/	pan, pera
Q	q	(cu)	qu + e, i /k/	quince, queso
R	r	(ere, erre)	/r/	pera, Corea,
			/rr/	rosa, ramo, arroz
S	s	(ese)	/s/	casa, sol, paseo
T	t	(te)	/t/	tomate, tú
V	v	(uve)	/b/	vaca, ven, vino
W	w	(uve doble)	/u//b/	William, wolframio
X	x	(equis)	/ks/	examen, éxito
Y	y	(i griega)	/i/	(Juan) y (Luis)
			/y/	yogur, yo
Z	z	(zeta)	z + a, o, u = /θ/	zapato, cazo, azul

5. Escucha. 3

ca	casa	ga	gato	za	zapato	ja	jamón
que	queso	gue	guerra	ce	cerrado	je/ge	jefe/genio
qui	quiero	gui	guitarra	ci	cine	ji/gi	jirafa/gitano
co	color	go	agosto	zo	zoo	jo	jota
cu	cuatro	gu	agua	zu	azul	ju	julio

¿Con B o con V?
(En Latinoamérica: b = be larga; v = be corta)
Valencia, **B**ilbao, Isa**b**el, **V**icente.

¿Con G o con J?
Genio, ro**j**o, **j**irafa, **g**itana.

¿Con H o sin H?
Hotel, agua, **h**uevo, **h**elado.

Sílaba tónica

Si la palabra lleva tilde, ésta indica la sílaba tónica.

ca**fé**   **mé**dico   **ár**bol

Si no hay tilde, se pronuncia más fuerte la última cuando la palabra acaba en consonante (excepto **n** y **s**).

Ma**drid**   espa**ñol**   ha**blar**

Se pronuncia más fuerte la penúltima si la palabra termina en vocal, en **n** o **s**.

jefe   ven**ta**na   e**xa**men   **cri**sis

6. Escucha y señala la palabra que deletrean. 4

1. ROMERO ✓   RODERO ☐
2. DÍEZ ☐   DÍAZ ☐
3. GONZÁLEZ ☐   GONZALVO ☐
4. RIBERA ☐   RIVERA ☐
5. JIMÉNEZ ☐   GIMÉNEZ ☐
6. PADÍN ☐   BADÍN ☐

8. Subraya la sílaba tónica de las palabras del recuadro.

> alemán – alemana – japonés – profesor
> estudiante – profesora – brasileño
> hospital – estudiar – profesora – libro
> lección – compañero – madre

7. Piensa y escribe en tu cuaderno el nombre de un río, de una ciudad, de un cantante extranjero, de una montaña y de un océano. Deletrea esos nombres a tu compañero/a. Tu compañero/a los escribe.

A. *E-uve-e-ere-e-ese-te*
B. *EVEREST.*

9. Escucha, comprueba y repite. 5

Para la clase

¿Puede repetir, por favor?
¿Cómo se dice "orange" en español?
¿Cómo se escribe?
Perdone, no entiendo.
¿Qué significa "arroz"?

C. Mapas de España y América

El español o castellano es la lengua oficial de España y de 19 países latinoamericanos. Es la tercera lengua más hablada después del chino y del inglés; la hablan más de 300 millones de personas.

El español viene del latín, igual que el francés, el italiano, el portugués y el rumano. En España, también son lenguas oficiales el catalán, el gallego y el euskera.

GENTILICIOS ESPAÑOLES

andaluz / andaluza
aragonés / aragonesa
asturiano / asturiana
balear / balear
canario / canaria
cántabro / cántabra
catalán / catalana
castellanoleonés / castellanoleonesa
castellanomanchego / castellanomanchega

extremeño / extremeña
gallego / gallega
madrileño / madrileña
murciano / murciana
valenciano / valenciana
vasco / vasca

GENTILICIOS HISPANOAMERICANOS

argentino / argentina
boliviano / boliviana
colombiano / colombiana
costarricense / costarricense
cubano / cubana
chileno / chilena
dominicano / dominicana
ecuatoriano / ecuatoriana
guatemalteco / guatemalteca
hondureño / hondureña

mexicano / mexicana
nicaragüense / nicaragüense
panameño / panameña
paraguayo / paraguaya
peruano / peruana
puertorriqueño / puertorriqueña
salvadoreño / salvadoreña
uruguayo / uruguaya
venezolano / venezolana

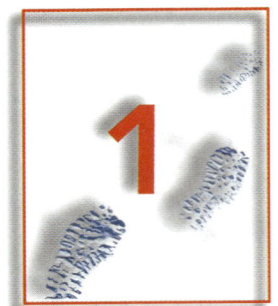

Presentar y saludar.

A. ¡Encantado!

1. Mira las fotos y señala dónde están.

a) En una cafetería _____
b) En clase _____
c) En una oficina _____

2. Lee y escucha.

A. RENATE: ¡Hola, Anil! ¿qué tal?
    ANIL: Bien, ¿y tú?
    RENATE: Muy bien. Mira, esta es Safiya, una nueva compañera, es nigeriana.
    ANIL: ¡Hola! ¡Encantado! ¿Eres de Lagos?
    SAFIYA: Sí, pero ahora vivo en Madrid.

B. DÍAZ: ¡Buenos días!, señor Álvarez, ¿qué tal está?
    ÁLVAREZ: Muy bien, gracias. Mire, le presento a Marta Rodríguez, la nueva directora.
    DÍAZ: Encantado de conocerla, yo me llamo Gerardo Díaz, y soy el responsable de administración.
    MARTA: Mucho gusto, Gerardo.

3. Completa.

LUIS: ¡Hola, Eva! ¿_____?
EVA: Bien, ¿_____?
LUIS: Muy bien. _____ este es Roberto, un compañero nuevo.
EVA: _____ . ¿De dónde_____?
ROBERTO: Soy cubano.

4. Escucha y comprueba.

COMUNICACIÓN

Informal

– ¡Hola!, ¿qué tal?
– Bien, ¿y tú?
– ¿Cómo te llamas?
– Esta es Celia. Este es Roberto.

Formal

– ¡Buenos días!, señor Jiménez, ¿cómo está usted?
– Muy bien, gracias.
– Le presento al señor Rodríguez.
– ¡Encantado/a! Mucho gusto.

HABLAR

5. Pregunta el nombre a dos compañeros formalmente.

   A. *¿Cómo se llama usted?*
   B. *Philip Schmidt.*
   A. *¿Y usted?*
   C. *Richard Burton.*

6. Presenta unos a otros.

   A. *Sr. Schmidt, este es el Sr. Burton.*
   B. *Mucho gusto.*
   C. *Encantado.*

GRAMÁTICA

Género de los adjetivos de nacionalidad	
Masculino	**Femenino**
italian**o**	italian**a**
español	español**a**
estadounidens**e**	estadounidens**e**
marroqu**í**	marroqu**í**

7. Completa.

1. chileno — *chilena*
2. _____ — española
3. inglés — _____
4. iraní — _____
5. _____ — sudafricana
6. estadounidense — _____
7. brasileño — _____

8. Mira las fotos y completa con la información de los recuadros.

> ~~Julio Iglesias~~ – Shirin Ebadi – Juan Carlos
> Pelé – Joanne K. Rowling – Nicole Kidman

> escritora – jurista – actriz
> ~~cantante~~ – futbolista – rey

> ~~español~~ – iraní – brasileño
> inglesa – australiana – español

Se llama Julio Iglesias.
Es cantante.
Es español.

Se llama _____

9. Comprueba con tu compañero.

Profesiones.

B. ¿A qué te dedicas?

VOCABULARIO

1. Escribe la letra correspondiente.

1. peluquera — a
2. profesor
3. médica
4. camarero
5. ama de casa
6. taxista
7. cartera
8. actriz

2. Escucha y repite. 8

3. Escoge una profesión. Pregunta a tres compañeros.

A. ¿A qué te dedicas?
B. Soy médico, ¿y tú?
A. Yo soy abogada.

GRAMÁTICA

Género de los nombres de profesión

Masculino	Femenino
camarero	camarera
profesor	profesora
estudiante	estudiante
presidente	presidenta
economista	economista

4. Escribe el femenino.

1. El vendedor — la *vendedora*
2. El secretario — la _____
3. El conductor — la _____
4. El cocinero — la _____
5. El futbolista — la _____

LEER

5. Escucha y lee. 9

Me llamo Manolo García. Soy médico. Soy sevillano, pero vivo en Barcelona. Trabajo en un hospital. Mi mujer se llama Amelia, es profesora y trabaja en un instituto. Ella es catalana. Tenemos dos hijos, Sergio y Elena; los dos son estudiantes. Sergio estudia en la universidad, y Elena, en el instituto.

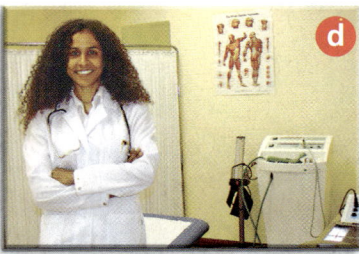

6. Responde.

1. ¿A qué se dedica Manolo? *Es médico.*
2. ¿De dónde es Manolo?
3. ¿Dónde viven?
4. ¿Dónde trabaja Amelia?
5. ¿De dónde es Amelia?
6. ¿Cuántos hijos tienen?
7. ¿Qué hacen los hijos?

GRAMÁTICA

Presente de verbos regulares

	Trabajar	Comer	Vivir
yo	trabaj**o**	com**o**	viv**o**
tú	trabaj**as**	com**es**	viv**es**
él/ella/usted	trabaj**a**	com**e**	viv**e**
nosotros/as	trabaj**amos**	com**emos**	viv**imos**
vosotros/as	trabaj**áis**	com**éis**	viv**ís**
ellos/ellas/ustedes	trabaj**an**	com**en**	viv**en**

Presente de verbos irregulares

	Ser	Tener
yo	soy	tengo
tú	eres	tienes
él/ella/usted	es	tiene
nosotros/as	somos	tenemos
vosotros/as	sois	tenéis
ellos/ellas/ustedes	son	tienen

7. Completa el texto siguiente con los verbos.

Me llamo Elaine Araujo y *soy* (1) arquitecta. (2)_____ brasileña, pero ahora (3)_____ en Madrid porque quiero bailar flamenco. (4)_____ en una escuela de danza y (5)_____ en un restaurante. Estoy soltera, pero tengo un novio español. Él (6)_____ en una compañía de seguros.

8. Escribe un párrafo sobre ti. Luego, léeselo a tus compañeros.

Me llamo _____ , soy _____ .

9. Completa las frases con la forma adecuada del verbo.

1. ¿Dónde (vivir) *viven* ustedes?
2. ¿Qué (estudiar) _____ Alicia?
3. Estos chicos no (estudiar) _____ nada.
4. ¿A qué hora (comer) _____ los españoles?
5. ¿Cuántos idiomas (hablar, usted) _____ ?
6. ¿Cómo (llamarse) _____ esa actriz?

10. Completa las frases con los verbos *tener* o *ser* en la forma adecuada.

1. Luisa no es madrileña, *es* valenciana.
2. Antonio Banderas _____ un actor español.
3. Yo _____ tres hijos.
4. Ellos _____ más ricos que nosotros, _____ más dinero.
5. Manolo _____ médico y _____ dos hijos.

PRONUNCIACIÓN

Entonación interrogativa

1. Escucha y repite.

1. ¿De dónde eres?
2. ¿De dónde son ustedes?
3. ¿Cómo te llamas?
4. ¿Quién es este?
5. ¿Dónde vives?
6. ¿Dónde trabaja usted?
7. ¿Dónde viven ustedes?
8. ¿Cómo se llama el marido de Ana?

Preguntar y decir números de teléfono.

c. ¿Cuál es tu número de teléfono?

1. Escribe los números.

> seis – uno – ocho – tres – nueve

0. cero
1. _____
2. dos
3. _____
4. cuatro
5. cinco
6. _____
7. siete
8. _____
9. _____
10. diez

2. Escucha y comprueba.

HABLAR

3. Practica con tu compañero.

2+3 = *cinco*
3+5 = _____
4+4 = _____
8-6 = _____
9-4 = _____
1-0 = _____

A. ¿Dos más tres?
B. *cinco.*
A. ¿Ocho menos seis?
B. *dos.*

4. Escucha y escribe los números de teléfono.

1. María: *936 547 832*
2. Jorge: _____
3. Marina: _____ , _____
4. Aeropuerto de Barajas: _____
5. Cruz Roja: _____
6. Radio-taxi: _____

5. Pregunta el número de teléfono a varios compañeros. Toma nota.

A. *Hans, ¿cuál es tu número de teléfono?*
B. *Es el 95 835 62 10.*
A. *Gracias.*

6. Escucha y aprende.

11. once	16. dieciséis
12. doce	17. diecisiete
13. trece	18. dieciocho
14. catorce	19. diecinueve
15. quince	20. veinte

7. Juega al bingo.

a. Escoge una de las dos cartas.
b. Escucha y señala lo que oyes. ¡Suerte!

B	I	N	G	O
1	4	8	7	3
11	5	6	14	18
19	2	13	16	15

B	I	N	G	O
20	4	8	17	14
9	10	7	5	11
7	13	15	16	3

GRAMÁTICA

Interrogativos

¿A **qué** te dedicas?
¿**Cómo** te llamas?
¿De **dónde** eres?

LEER

8. Lee, escucha y completa.

En el gimnasio

FELIPE: ¡Buenas tardes!
ROSA: ¡Hola!, ¿_Qué deseas?_.
FELIPE: Quiero apuntarme al gimnasio.
ROSA: Tienes que darme tus datos. A ver, ¿_Cómo te llamas_?
FELIPE: Felipe Martínez.
ROSA: ¿Y de segundo apellido?
FELIPE: Franco.
ROSA: ¿Dónde _vives_?
FELIPE: En la calle Goya, número ochenta y siete, tercero izquierda.
ROSA: ¿Teléfono?
FELIPE: _686 055 097_
ROSA: ¿Profesión?
FELIPE: _profesor_.
ROSA: Bueno, ya está; el precio es…

9. Completa la tarjeta con los datos de Felipe.

10. Completa las frases con *qué, dónde, cómo*.

1. A. ¿De *dónde* es Gloria Estefan?
   B. De Cuba.
2. A. ¿_Dónde_ trabajas?
   B. En un banco.
3. A. ¿_Cómo_ se llama tu compañero?
   B. Mariano.
4. A. ¿_Dónde_ vive Julio?
   B. En Miami.
5. A. ¿A _qué_ se dedica tu mujer?
   B. Es cantante.
6. A. ¿De _dónde_ son ustedes?
   B. Somos alemanes, de Bonn.

11. Prepara 5 preguntas para un compañero/a y luego pregúntale. Anota las respuestas.

¿Dónde vives?
¿Cómo se llama tu padre?
¿De dónde eres?…

ESTUDIO PRAGA
Gimnasio Club
Antonio López, 92 - 28019 MADRID
Tel.: (91) 560 94 08

DATOS PERSONALES

NOMBRE Y APELLIDOS _____
DOMICILIO ACTUAL _____
N.º _____ PISO _____ PUERTA _____
TELÉFONO _____ PROFESIÓN _____

Autoevaluación

1. Lee y completa las preguntas.

> **1.** Me llamo Peter Tuck. Soy profesor de inglés. Vivo en Madrid y trabajo en un colegio. Soy soltero.
>
> **2.** Yo me llamo Maria Rodrigues; soy brasileña, de Río de Janeiro. Mi marido se llama Bruno y también es brasileño. Somos profesores.
>
> **3.** Yo me llamo Yoshie Kikkawa y soy japonesa, de Tokio. Estoy casada. Mi marido se llama Mitsuo y tenemos dos hijos, Kimiko y Ken. Los dos estudian en el colegio.

1. A. ¿*Dónde* vive Peter?
   B. En Madrid.
2. A. ¿_____ Peter?
   B. En un colegio.
3. A. ¿_____ Maria?
   B. Es brasileña.
4. A. ¿_____ el marido de Maria?
   B. Bruno.
5. A. ¿_____ Yoshie?
   B. De Tokio.
6. A. ¿Qué _____ los hijos de Yoshie?
   B. Estudian en el colegio.

2. Completa los diálogos.

1. A. Hola, me *llamo* Manuel, y _____ español. ¿Cómo _____ tú?
   B. _____
2. A. Buenos días, señor Jiménez, ¿cómo _____ usted?
   B. Bien, gracias, ¿y _____?
3. A. Mire, señora Rodríguez, le _presento_ al señor Márquez.
   B. _____
   C. Mucho gusto.
4. A. Hola, Laura. ¿Qué _____?
   B. Hola, Manu, muy _____. Mira, _____ es Marina, una nueva _____.
   A. Hola, ¿qué _____?
   C. _____, ¿y tú?
   A. Muy bien.

3. Escucha los apellidos y escribe el número de orden. **16**

> Díaz (9), Martínez (1), Vargas ( ),
> Díez ( ), Marín (3), Martín (10),
> Serrano (4), López (5), Moreno (6),
> Romero (2), Jiménez (7), García (12),
> Pérez (8).

4. Lee y señala si hablan de "tú" o de "usted".

	tú	usted
1. ¿Cómo te llamas?	✓	
2. ¿Dónde vive usted?		✓
3. ¿De dónde es?		✓
4. ¿Dónde trabaja?		
5. ¿De dónde eres?	✓	
6. ¿Cuál es tu número de teléfono?	✓	
7. ¿A qué te dedicas?	✓	

Soy capaz de...

☐ ☐ ☐ Presentar a alguien y saludar.
☐ ☐ Decir algunas profesiones.
☐ ☐ Preguntar y decir números de teléfono.

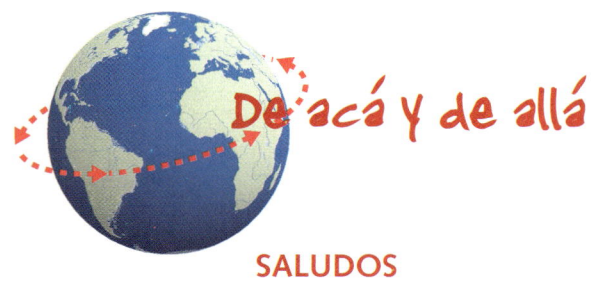

SALUDOS

SALUDOS

En español podemos hablar en estilo formal o informal. En estilo formal usamos **usted (Vd.)** y **ustedes (Vdes.)** para hablar con personas desconocidas, de mayor edad o superiores en rango: un jefe, un profesor, un médico. También en estilo formal utilizamos las fórmulas **señor (Sr.)** y **señora (Sra.)** con el apellido: Sr. Pérez.

En estilo informal usamos el nombre, y es muy habitual decir **¡hola!** para saludar y **¡hasta luego!** para despedirse.
En estilo formal e informal es normal saludar también con **¡buenos días!**, por la mañana; **¡buenas tardes!**, por la tarde, y **¡buenas noches!**, por la noche.

1. Señala lo adecuado.

1. Hablo con un camarero   tú / *usted*
2. Hablo con mi profesor   tú / usted
3. Hablo con mi tío   tú / usted
4. Hablo con la vendedora   tú / usted
5. Hablo con un desconocido   tú / usted

2. Relaciona cada diálogo con su foto.

1. A. ¡Hola!, ¿qué tal?
   B. ¡Hola!

2. A. ¡Hola!, me llamo Javier.
   B. ¡Hola!, yo soy Marisa.

3. A. ¡Adiós!
   B. ¡Adiós!, hasta luego.

4. A. Buenas tardes, ¿cómo está usted?
   B. Bien, ¿y usted?

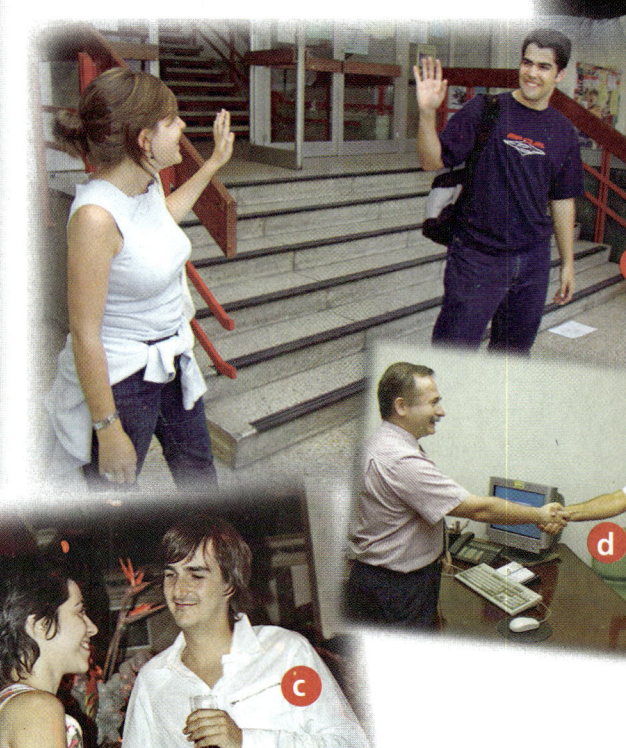

3. Escucha los diálogos y practica con tu compañero. **17**

Familias.

A. ¿Estás casado?

1. Relaciona.

1. ¿Estás casado/a?
2. ¿Tienes hijos?
3. ¿Tienes hermanos?

a) No, no tengo.
b) Sí, un hermano y una hermana.
c) No, estoy soltero/a.

2. Jorge y Luis hablan de sus familias. Lee y escucha. 18

Esta es mi familia. Mi mujer se llama Rosa y tenemos dos hijos, Isabel de 10 años y David de 12.

Yo vivo con mis padres, mi hermana y mi abuela. Mi padre se llama Manuel y tiene 58 años. Mi madre se llama Rocío y tiene 56 años. Mi hermana Laura es más pequeña que yo, tiene 14 años, y mi abuela, que se llama Carmen, tiene 75 años.

3. Escribe el nombre de cada uno en las fotos.

4. Completa las frases siguientes con las palabras del recuadro.

> ~~mujer~~ – hermana – padre – hijo
> abuela – madre – marido.

1. Rosa es la *mujer* de Jorge.
2. David es _____ de Jorge y Rosa.
3. Rosa es la _____ de Isabel.
4. Laura es _____ de Luis.
5. Manuel es el _____ de Luis.
6. Carmen es _____ de Laura.
7. Manuel es el _____ de Rocío.

HABLAR

5. Haz estas preguntas a varios compañeros y luego completa la ficha.

– ¿Estás casado/a o soltero/a?
– ¿Tienes hijos?
– ¿Tienes novio/a?
– ¿Cómo se llama tu padre/madre?
– ¿Cuántos hermanos tienes?
– ¿Tu hermano/a está casado/a?
– ¿Tienes abuelos?

	NOMBRE
– Está soltero/a	_____
– Está casado/a	_____
– Tiene hijos	_____
– Tiene novio/a	_____
– No tiene hermanos	_____
– Tiene abuelos	_____

ESCRIBIR

6. Escribe algunas frases sobre tu familia y léeselas a tu compañero.

Mi padre se llama _____ y tiene _____ años.
Mi hermana está casada y tiene _____ hijos.

GRAMÁTICA

Plural de los nombres	
un mapa	dos mapa**s**
un autobús	dos autobus**es**

7. Mira la imagen y señala si las frases son verdaderas (V) o falsas (F).

En esta clase hay:
a) una televisión ☐
b) dos mapas ☐
c) cinco sillas ☐
d) cinco libros ☐
e) dos diccionarios ☐
f) un teléfono ☐
g) tres mesas ☐
h) dos bolígrafos ☐

8. Escribe en plural.

1. Un coche — *Dos coches*
2. Un profesor — _____
3. Una ventana — _____
4. Una compañera — _____
5. Un lápiz — _____
6. Un cuaderno — _____
7. Un chico — _____
8. Un hotel — _____

9. Completa.

Singular	Plural
hermano / hermana	hermanos / hermanas
padre / _____	_____ / madres
_____ / hija	hijos / _____
abuelo / _____	abuelos / _____

2A

veintiuno 21

Lugar de los objetos.

B. ¿Dónde están mis gafas?

VOCABULARIO

1. Escribe la letra correspondiente.

1. reloj — b
2. paraguas ☐
3. zapatillas ☐
4. ordenador ☐
5. cuadro ☐
6. sofá ☐
7. silla ☐
8. mesita ☐
9. gafas ☐
10. teléfono ☐

GRAMÁTICA

Preposiciones de lugar

debajo   encima   entre
delante   detrás
al lado   en

*La planta está **debajo** de la ventana.*
*Los libros están **en** la cartera.*

A + el = **al**
De + el = **del**

*El sofá está **al** lado **del** sillón.*

2. Mira la habitación y completa las frases.

1. El reloj está *encima* de la mesita.
2. Las zapatillas están _____ de la mesita.
3. El teléfono está _____ del ordenador.
4. El sillón está _____ de la librería.
5. Las gafas están _____ el teléfono y el ordenador.
6. El gato está _____ de David.

ESCRIBIR

3. Mira tu clase o tu habitación. Escribe 5 frases.

El diccionario está al lado del cuaderno.
La silla está delante de la mesa.

GRAMÁTICA

Adjetivos posesivos

Sujeto	Singular		Plural	
yo	**mi**	hijo	**mis**	hijos
		hija		hijas
tú	**tu**	tío	**tus**	tíos
		tía		tías
él/ella/Vd.	**su**	hermano	**sus**	hermanos
		hermana		hermanas

4. Completa las frases con el posesivo correspondiente.

1. ¿Cuál es *tu* número de teléfono? (tú)
2. _____ gata se llama Bonita. (ella)
3. ¿Esta es _____ chaqueta? (tú)
4. ¿Dónde está _____ diccionario? (él)
5. ¿Tienes _____ gafas? (yo)
6. _____ casa está cerca de aquí. (yo)
7. _____ primos viven en Barcelona. (ella)
8. ¿Dónde viven _____ padres? (Vd.)
9. ¿Dónde vive _____ hermano? (tú)
10. ¿Dónde trabaja _____ madre? (él)

5. Completa la conversación con los adjetivos posesivos.

A. ¿Estos son (1) *tus* padres?
B. Sí, (2)_____ madre se llama Julia y (3)_____ padre, Miguel.
A. ¿Y éstos?
B. Son (4)_____ tíos, Carlos y Águeda.
A. ¿Esta es (5)_____ hija?
B. Sí, esa es (6)_____ prima Carolina.
A. Pues es muy guapa (7)_____ prima.

Demostrativos

Este es Pedro.
Esta es Elena.
Estos son Pablo y Amanda.
Estas son Lucía y Graciela.

6. Completa.

Mira, (1) *estos* son mis amigos.
(2)_____ es Celia, y (3)_____ es Gonzalo, su novio. (4)_____ de la derecha es Laura.
(5)_____ de aquí son las hermanas de Gonzalo, Marisa y Pilar.

7. Trae algunas fotos y presenta tus amigos y familia a tus compañeros.

*Decir la hora
y los números hasta 5.000.*

C. ¿Qué hora es?

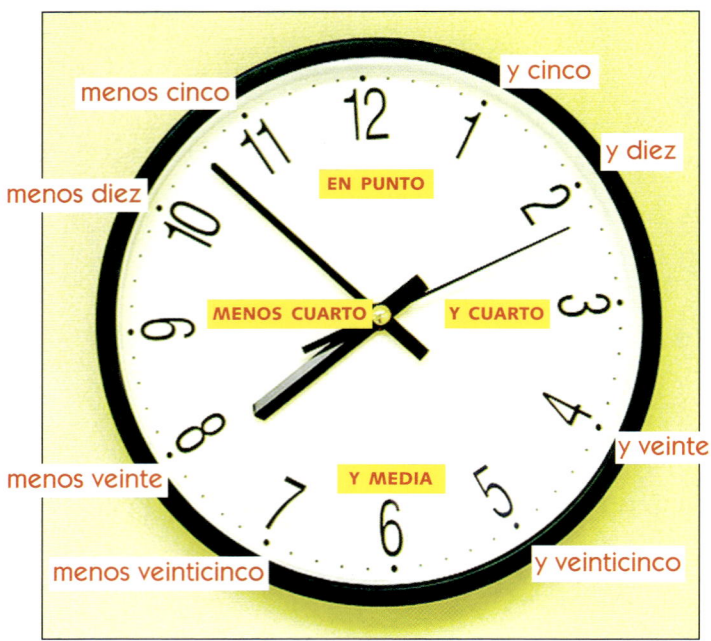

1. Mira los relojes. ¿Qué hora es?

las tres y media   las dos menos cuarto   las diez y cuarto

la una

2. Escucha y repite.

3. Dibuja tres horas diferentes en tu cuaderno. En parejas, pregunta y di las horas.

A. *Perdone, ¿qué hora es?*
B. *Son las siete y veinte.*

LEER Y HABLAR

4. Lee el texto y señala con *V* lo que es igual en tu país y con *X* lo que es diferente.

HORARIOS

1. En Noruega la gente come a las cinco de la tarde. ☐
2. En Senegal cenan a las 8 o las 8.30. ☐
3. En México los bancos no abren por la tarde. ☐
4. En los países árabes no trabajan los viernes. ☐
5. Los españoles cenan a las 10 de la noche. ☐
6. En Estados Unidos muchas tiendas abren por la noche. ☐
7. En China la escuela empieza a las 7.15. ☐
8. En Brasil los bancos abren a las 10. ☐

5. Habla con tu compañero/a y compara las afirmaciones anteriores con lo que ocurre en tu país.

En Noruega comen a las cinco de la tarde y en mi país también.

En Noruega comen a las cinco de la tarde, pero en mi país comemos a la una.

VOCABULARIO

6. Relaciona.

1. Sesenta segundos — a) una hora
2. Veinticuatro horas — b) una semana
3. Siete días — c) un minuto
4. Doce meses — d) un día
5. Sesenta minutos — e) un año

NÚMEROS

7. Escucha y completa. **20**

21	veintiuno	80	ochenta
22	veintidós	90	_____
23	veintitrés	100	cien
24	_____	103	ciento tres
30	treinta	200	doscientos/as
31	treinta y uno	300	_____
40	_____	400	_____
50	cincuenta	500	quinientos/as
60	sesenta	1.000	mil
70	_____	5.000	cinco mil

8. Escucha y señala el número que oyes. **21**

a. _2_ / 12   f. 135 / 125
b. 25 / 35   g. 830 / 850
c. 90 / 50   h. 1.589 / 1.389
d. 37 / 67   i. 1.988 / 1.998
e. 226 / 323   j. 1.975 / 1.985

9. Escucha y escribe el número. **22**

1. Edad de la niña: *12 años.*
2. Precio de las naranjas: _____.
3. Precio del paquete de café: _____.
4. Año de nacimiento: _____.
5. Distancia entre Madrid y Barcelona: _____ km.
6. Precio del café y la cerveza: _____.

PRONUNCIACIÓN Y ORTOGRAFÍA

1. Escucha. **23**

> te**lé**fono – **lá**piz – ven**ta**na – ho**tel**
> profe**sor** – her**ma**no – fa**mi**lia – **mú**sica

2. Escucha otra vez y repite. Observa las sílabas fuertes. **23**

3. Escucha estas palabras y subraya la sílaba fuerte. **24**

> profe**so**ra – español – café – gramática
> mesa – vivir – hablar – médico
> autobús – Pilar – alemán – brasileña
> familia – libro – examen

4. Escribe las palabras del ejercicio anterior en la columna correspondiente.

música	ven**ta**na	ho**tel**

Autoevaluación

1. Relaciona.

1. ¿Dónde está mi bolígrafo? [c]
2. ¿Estás casado? [ ]
3. ¿Tienes hijos? [ ]
4. ¿Cuántos hermanos tienes? [ ]
5. ¿Qué hora es? [ ]
6. ¿A qué hora comen en tu país? [ ]

a) No, estoy soltero.
b) Tres.
c) Encima de la mesa.
d) Sí, una niña de tres años.
e) A la una.
f) Las dos menos cuarto.

2. Escribe los números.

a) 27 — *veintisiete*
b) 52 — _____
c) 116 — _____
d) 238 — _____
e) 456 — _____
f) 510 — _____
g) 1.987 — _____
h) 2.003 — _____
i) 2.999 — _____

3. Escribe en plural.

1. Este hotel es muy caro.
   Estos hoteles son muy caros.
2. Mi hermana está casada.
   _____.
3. Mi hermano tiene un hijo.
   _____ dos _____.
4. Mi compañero es japonés.
   _____.
5. Esta profesora es simpática.
   _____.
6. Este libro es interesante.
   _____.
7. Este profesor no es español.
   _____.

4. Completa con los verbos *estar* o *tener*.

1. Las zapatillas *están* debajo de la silla.
2. Marieli _____ dos hijos.
3. Mi hermano _____ casado.
4. Yo no _____ abuelos.
5. ¿_____ hermanos?
6. ¿Dónde _____ la carpeta roja?
7. Mi marido no _____ en casa.

5. Escucha y escribe las horas de salida y llegada de los trenes de la estación. [25]

Salidas

Tren	Andén	Destino	Hora
Altaria	3	Zaragoza	____
Talgo	6	Málaga	____
AVE	2	Sevilla	____

Llegadas

Tren	Andén	Procedencia	Hora
AVE	11	Sevilla	____
Alaris	8	Valencia	____
Talgo	4	Vigo	____

Soy capaz de...

☐ ☐ ☐ *Hablar de la familia.*
☐ ☐ ☐ *Decir dónde están las cosas.*
☐ ☐ ☐ *Decir la hora y los números hasta 5.000.*

De acá y de allá

LA FAMILIA

1. Lee y señala verdadero (V) o falso (F).

LA FAMILIA HISPANA

Cuando una persona de España o Hispanoamérica habla de su familia, no habla solamente de sus padres y de sus hermanos, habla también de sus abuelos, de sus tíos, de sus primos y de otros parientes.

Además, las reuniones familiares son frecuentes. Todos se juntan para celebrar las fiestas más importantes, como los cumpleaños, la Navidad, el día del padre y de la madre. Ese día comen todos en una casa o en un restaurante.

Por otro lado, en algunos países de Hispanoamérica es normal celebrar el día que las chicas cumplen quince años. Les hacen muchos regalos y toda la familia y amigos van a comer a un restaurante.

DOS APELLIDOS

En la mayoría de los países hispanoamericanos, todas las personas tienen dos apellidos. El primero es el apellido del padre y el segundo es el de la madre. Estos dos apellidos aparecen en todos los documentos y no cambian al casarse, son para toda la vida.

Me llamo Santiago. Mi padre se llama Enrique Lozano Linares y mi madre Luisa Pardo Pérez.

a) La familia hispana está compuesta de padres e hijos. **F**

b) Las familias españolas e hispanoamericanas se reúnen muchas veces. ☐

c) En el día del padre y de la madre comen todos en casa o en un restaurante. ☐

d) Las chicas hispanoamericanas se casan a los quince años. ☐

2. Según lo leído, ¿cuáles son los apellidos de Santiago?

Santiago _____ _____

3. Comenta con tus compañeros.

¿Cuántos apellidos tienes?
¿Cambia tu apellido al casarte?
¿Te parece bien la costumbre de los españoles e hispanoamericanos?

veintisiete

*Hablar de hábitos.
Verbos reflexivos.*

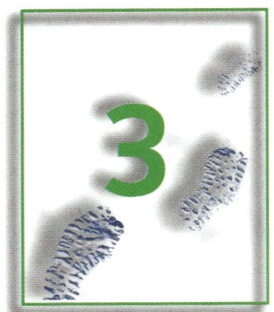

A. Rosa se levanta a las siete

GRAMÁTICA

Verbos reflexivos		
	Levantarse	**Acostarse**
yo	me levanto	me acuesto
tú	te levantas	te acuestas
él/ella/Vd.	se levanta	se acuesta
nosotros/as	nos levantamos	nos acostamos
vosotros/as	os levantáis	os acostáis
ellos/ellas/Vds.	se levantan	se acuestan

1. Responde.

a) ¿A qué hora te levantas?
b) ¿Cuántas horas duermes?

2. Relaciona las frases con los dibujos.

1. Rosa se levanta a las siete. — e
2. José se ducha. — ☐
3. Mercedes se baña. — ☐
4. Carlos y Ana se casan. — ☐
5. Mis vecinos se acuestan temprano. — ☐
6. Roberto se afeita todos los días. — ☐

3. Completa con los verbos del recuadro.

> levantarse – acostarse – ducharse

A. Y tú, Juan, ¿a qué hora *te levantas*?
B. Bueno, yo ___ _____ pronto, a las 7, más o menos, ___ _____ rápidamente, tomo un café y salgo de casa.
A. Y tu mujer, ¿a qué hora ___ _____?
B. Pues, a las 7.30.
A. ¿Y tus hijos?
B. Bueno, ellos ___ _____ a las ocho, ___ _____, desayunan y se van al colegio, porque entran a las 9.
A. ¿Y los días de fiesta también ___ _____ todos temprano?
B. ¡Ah, no!, ni hablar, los domingos ___ ___ _____ a las 10, porque, claro, el sábado___ _____ más tarde.

4. Escucha y comprueba. **26**

LEER

5. Lee el artículo y contesta las preguntas.

ESCUELA PROVINCIAL DE BALLET ALEJO CARPENTIER (LA HABANA, CUBA)

En esta escuela estudian los alumnos desde los 9 hasta los 14 años. El ritmo de trabajo es muy duro, tienen clase por la mañana y por la tarde. Por la mañana, las clases empiezan a las 7.15 todos los días, y algunos alumnos se levantan a las 5 de la mañana. Las clases de baile terminan a las 12, y a esa hora los alumnos van a otra escuela que está cerca. Allí estudian las mismas asignaturas (lengua, matemáticas, geografía, etc.) que los demás niños de su edad. Terminan las clases a las 6 de la tarde y a veces vuelven otra vez a la escuela de ballet, hasta las 8.

1. ¿Cuántas horas de ballet tienen cada día?
2. ¿Estudian en la misma escuela otras asignaturas?

6. Lee el texto otra vez y completa las frases con las preposiciones del recuadro.

> a – de – desde – hasta – por

1. En esta escuela estudian los niños _____ los 9 _____ los 14 años.
2. Algunos alumnos se levantan muy pronto, _____ las 5 _____ la mañana.
3. _____ la mañana, los niños están en la escuela de ballet _____ las 7.15 _____ las 12.
4. En la escuela de ballet los alumnos tienen clase _____ la mañana y _____ la tarde.

GRAMÁTICA

Verbos irregulares en presente

	Empezar	Volver	Ir
yo	emp**ie**zo	v**ue**lvo	voy
tú	emp**ie**zas	v**ue**lves	vas
él/ella/Vd.	emp**ie**za	v**ue**lve	va
nosotros/as	empezamos	volvemos	vamos
vosotros/as	empezáis	volvéis	vais
ellos/ellas/Vds.	emp**ie**zan	v**ue**lven	van

7. Forma frases.

1. Carmen / empezar a trabajar / a las 8.
   Carmen empieza a trabajar a las 8.
2. ¿A qué hora / empezar / la película?
   _____
3. Mi padre / ir a trabajar / en autobús.
   _____
4. Yo / volver / a mi casa / a las 7.
   _____
5. ¿Cuándo / volver / de vacaciones tus hermanos?
   _____
6. ¿Ir (nosotros) / a dar una vuelta?
   _____
7. ¿Cómo / ir (tú) / a trabajar?
   _____

Preposiciones de tiempo

Días

El lunes		la mañana
Ayer	**por**	la tarde
El sábado		la noche

*Yo sólo trabajo **por** la mañana.*

Horas

Son las 10		la mañana
A las 5	**de**	la tarde
A las 3		la noche
		la madrugada

*Se levanta **a** las 6 **de** la mañana.*
*Ella trabaja **desde** las 8 **hasta** las 3.*
*Ella trabaja **de** 8 **a** 3.*

Hablar de hábitos y horarios de trabajo.

B. ¿Estudias o trabajas?

1. ¿Qué día de la semana te gusta más?
¿Qué día de la semana te gusta menos?

| lunes | martes | miércoles | jueves | viernes | sábado | domingo |

A mí me gusta más el sábado porque no trabajo.
A mí me gusta menos el lunes.

LEER

2. Lee y escucha. 27

Carlos es bombero. Trabaja en el ayuntamiento de Toledo. Vive en un pueblo cerca de Toledo y va al trabajo en tren. Tiene 34 años, está casado y no tiene hijos. Trabaja en turnos de 24 horas, un día sí y otro no. Si trabaja el sábado o el domingo, después tiene dos días libres. Siempre se levanta muy temprano, a las 7 o las 8 de la mañana, por eso normalmente no sale por las noches, cena a las diez, después ve la tele y a las once y media se acuesta.

Lucía es técnico de sonido y trabaja en una emisora de radio, la Cadena Día. Tiene 29 años y no está casada. Vive en Valencia, y habla inglés y francés perfectamente.
Todos los días trabaja de 8 a 3, menos los sábados y domingos. Los días laborables se levanta a las 7 y sale de casa a las 7.30. Va al trabajo en autobús. Los sábados por la noche siempre sale con sus amigos a cenar y a bailar, por eso se acuesta muy tarde, a las 3 o las 4 de la madrugada.

3. Completa las frases.

1. Lucía *es* técnico de sonido.
2. Trabaja _____ 8 _____ 3.
3. Normalmente _____ a las 7.
4. _____ al trabajo _____ autobús.
5. Los sábados _____ la noche _____ con sus amigos.

4. Completa las frases.

1. Carlos *vive* en un pueblo pequeño.
2. No _____ hijos.
3. Se levanta muy _____ .
4. Carlos normalmente no _____ por la noche y _____ a las once y media.

HABLAR Y ESCRIBIR

5. Prepara estas preguntas para tu compañero y házselas. Toma nota.

1. ¿Hora / levantarse?
   ¿A qué hora te levantas?
2. ¿Hora / empezar clases o trabajo?
   _____

3. ¿Hora / terminar el trabajo?
_____

4. ¿Hora / de llegar a casa?
_____

5. ¿Hacer / después de cenar?
_____

6. ¿Hora / acostarse?
_____

6. Escribe un párrafo sobre la vida de tu compañero.

Michael es _____ , trabaja en _____ .
Va al trabajo en _____ .

VOCABULARIO

7. Escribe cada profesión en la columna correspondiente.

médico/a – estudiante – enfermero/a
informático/a – dependiente/a – cajero/a
secretario/a – profesor/a

HOSPITAL	UNIVERSIDAD	OFICINA	SUPERMERCADO

8. ¿Qué hace? Relaciona las dos columnas.

1. La dependienta   a) hace la comida.
2. El recepcionista   b) cuida enfermos.
3. La azafata   c) fabrica muebles.
4. La enfermera   d) atiende pasajeros.
5. El carpintero   e) recibe a turistas.
6. El cocinero   f) vende ropa.

ESCRIBIR

9. Piensa en tres o cuatro personas conocidas y explica a qué se dedican, dónde trabajan, qué hacen.

Mi amigo Ángel es dependiente, trabaja en unos grandes almacenes, vende muebles.

HABLAR

10. En grupos de cuatro. Uno representa con mímica una profesión y el resto adivina de qué profesión se trata.

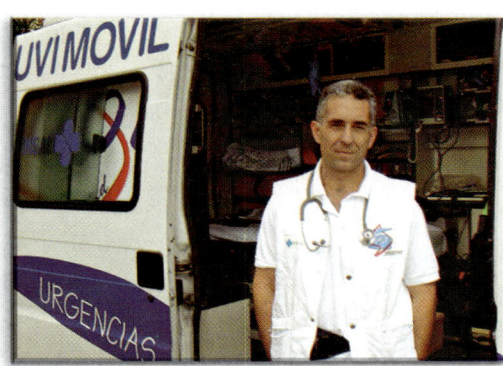

Pedir un desayuno.

C. ¿Qué desayunas?

1. ¿Qué bebes para desayunar?

a) café con leche
b) té
c) leche con cacao
d) _____

2. Mira estos desayunos. ¿Alguno se parece al tuyo?

VOCABULARIO

3. Escribe la letra correspondiente.

1. té — f
2. café con leche — ☐
3. zumo de naranja — ☐
4. magdalenas — ☐
5. müesli — ☐
6. leche — ☐
7. huevo — ☐
8. queso — ☐

4. Escucha a estas personas de diferentes países hablar de su desayuno. Completa la tabla. 28

	País	Desayuno
1. Olga	*rusa*	*un bocadillo, mantequilla y queso*
2. Rabah	_____	_____
3. Yi	_____	_____
4. Philip	_____	_____

HABLAR

5. En grupos. Cada uno cuenta qué desayuna normalmente y qué los domingos.

Yo, normalmente, sólo tomo un café con leche y una magdalena, pero los domingos tomo un bocadillo de jamón y zumo de naranja, además del café con leche, claro.

Cafetería Teide

Desayunos (Hasta las 12)   Meriendas (Desde las 17 hasta las 19)

Continental
Café + bollería o tostada
con mantequilla y mermelada   **1,75** euros

Europa
Supersandwich mixto caliente
+ café…   **2,35** euros

Andaluz
Tostada de pan con tomate y aceite
de oliva + café o refresco…   **2** euros

ESCUCHAR

6. Ordena el siguiente diálogo.

CAMARERA:	Buenos días, ¿qué desean?	1
HIJO:	Yo sólo quiero un zumo.	☐
MADRE:	Yo quiero un desayuno andaluz, ¿y tú, hijo?	☐
HIJO:	No, mamá, sólo quiero un zumo de naranja.	☐
MADRE:	Toma algo más, un bollo, o una tostada.	☐
MADRE:	Bueno, pues un andaluz y un zumo de naranja.	☐
CAMARERA:	Muy bien.	☐

7. Escucha y comprueba. **29**

HABLAR

8. En grupos de tres. Practica otras conversaciones. Uno es el camarero y los otros dos van a desayunar o merendar.

A. ¿Qué desean?
B. *Un desayuno continental, por favor.*
C. *Yo un café con leche y una tostada con mantequilla y mermelada.*

PRONUNCIACIÓN Y ORTOGRAFÍA

1. Escucha y repite. **30**

> gato – agua – gota – guerra – guión

¿Qué sonido se repite en todas las palabras?

> El sonido **g** se escribe **g** antes de **a, o** y se escribe **gu** antes de **e, i**.

2. Completa con *g* o *gu*.

1. g_uapo.
2. ci g_arrillos.
3. g_itarra.
4. g_afas.
5. pa g_ar.
6. g_erra.
7. g_uatemala.
8. g_oma.

3. Escucha y repite. **31**

treinta y tres   **33**

Autoevaluación

1. Completa con el verbo entre paréntesis en presente de indicativo.

1. Pepe *se ducha* con agua fría. (Ducharse)
2. Celia ___ _____ a las once y media. (Acostarse)
3. A. ¿Tú ___ _____ todos los días? (Afeitarse)
   B. No, sólo los domingos.
4. Yo no ___ _____ en la piscina, prefiero la playa. (Bañarse)
5. Mi hija tiene seis años y ya ___ _____ sola. (Vestirse)
6. ¿A qué hora ___ _____ vosotros? (Acostarse)
7. Luis y Rosa ___ _____ muy temprano. (Levantarse)
8. ¿A qué hora ___ _____ tú? (Levantarse)
9. Yo ___ _____ por la noche. (Ducharse)

2. Completa con la preposición adecuada.

1. Yo empiezo a trabajar *a* las 8 *de* la mañana.
2. José no trabaja _____ la tarde.
3. Paloma trabaja _____ las 8 _____ las 3.
4. Los domingos _____ la mañana voy al Rastro.
5. Los sábados ____ la noche voy ____ la discoteca.
6. Mi marido vuelve ____ casa ____ las 8 ____ la tarde.
7. Mi hija va ____ la escuela ____ la mañana y ____ la tarde.

3. Relaciona.

1. ¿A qué te dedicas? _____   a) Soy bombero.
2. ¿Qué horario tienes?   b) En el Ayuntamiento.
3. ¿Tienes algún día libre?   c) Sí, los domingos.
4. ¿Dónde trabajas?   d) No, soy soltero.
5. ¿Cómo vas al trabajo?   e) Trabajo de 9 a 5.
6. ¿Estás casado?   f) 37.
7. ¿Cuántos años tienes?   g) Voy en tren.

4. Escribe el verbo.

1. Empezar, él *empieza.*
2. Volver, yo _____.
3. Ir, nosotros _____.
4. Empezar, vosotros _____.
5. Ir, ellos _____.
6. Volver, Vd. _____.
7. Volver, tú _____.

5. Escribe un párrafo sobre tu rutina diaria. Utiliza los verbos del recuadro.

> levantarse – ducharse – desayunar – salir
> empezar – terminar – comer – volver
> cenar – acostarse

Yo me levanto a las _____ . Me ducho _____ .
Salgo de casa _____ .

6. Adriana es argentina y nos habla de la vida en Buenos Aires. Escucha y contesta a las preguntas. **32**

1. ¿A qué hora se levantan en Buenos Aires?
2. ¿A qué hora comen normalmente?
3. ¿Qué horario tienen las tiendas?
4. ¿Abren los bancos por la tarde?
5. ¿A qué hora cenan?
6. ¿Estudian los niños por la mañana y por la tarde?

Soy capaz de…

☐ ☐ ☐ *Hablar de mis hábitos.*

☐ ☐ ☐ *Hablar de horarios.*

☐ ☐ ☐ *Pedir un desayuno.*

De acá y de allá

GESTOS

1. A continuación tienes algunos gestos que se usan con frecuencia en España e Hispanoamérica. Relaciónalos con su significado.

1. Hay mucha gente — d
2. Poco
3. Dinero
4. Silencio
5. Dormir

LENGUAJE GESTUAL
Cada cultura tiene su propio lenguaje gestual, pero los habitantes de unos países son más expresivos que otros.

2. Comenta con tus compañeros.

¿En tu país utilizan también estos gestos?
¿Crees que los hispanos hablan demasiado alto?
¿Y demasiado cerca?

Describir una casa.

A. ¿Dónde vives?

1. ¿Dónde vives?

a) En un piso. ☐
b) En un chalé con jardín. ☐
c) En una casa. ☐

2. Lee y escucha.

> Esta es la casa de Rosa y Miguel, un chalé adosado con dos plantas.
>
> En la planta baja hay un recibidor, una cocina, un salón comedor grande y un servicio.
>
> En la planta de arriba hay tres dormitorios y un cuarto de baño. La casa tiene también un jardín pequeño.

3. Lee las frases y escribe verdadero (V) o falso (F).

1. La cocina está en la planta baja. **V**
2. El salón es muy grande. ☐
3. Hay un garaje. ☐
4. Hay tres dormitorios. ☐
5. Los dormitorios están en el piso de arriba. ☐
6. No hay jardín. ☐
7. Hay un pequeño servicio en la planta baja. ☐
8. El salón está en la planta de arriba. ☐

ESCUCHAR

4. Escucha a Manuel hablar de su casa. Contesta las preguntas.

1. ¿Cómo es el piso de Manu?
2. ¿Cuántos dormitorios tiene?
3. ¿Dónde está el cuarto de baño?
4. ¿Tiene terraza? ¿Cómo es?

HABLAR

5. En parejas. Habla con tu compañero sobre tu casa: cuántas habitaciones tiene, dónde están. Dibuja el plano.

6. Escribe la descripción de la casa de tu compañero utilizando el vocabulario del recuadro.

> salón – comedor – cocina – jardín
> cuarto de baño – dormitorio – garaje

*La casa de _____ es pequeña / grande.
Tiene _____ dormitorios.*

VOCABULARIO

Números ordinales

7. Escucha y repite. 35

1.º / 1.ª	Primero/a	6.º / 6.ª	Sexto/a
2.º / 2.ª	Segundo/a	7.º / 7.ª	Séptimo/a
3.º / 3.ª	Tercero/a	8.º / 8.ª	Octavo/a
4.º / 4.ª	Cuarto/a	9.º / 9.ª	Noveno/a
5.º / 5.ª	Quinto/a	10.º / 10.ª	Décimo/a

Los ordinales **primero** y **tercero** pierden la **-o** delante de un nombre masculino singular.

8. Completa las frases con un adjetivo del recuadro.

> primera – tercera – quinta
> segundo – ~~primer~~

1. El ascensor está en el *primer* piso.
2. A. ¿Luis, tú qué estudias?
   B. _____ de Económicas.
3. ¡Qué impresionante! Es la _____ vez que veo el mar.
4. Nosotras somos tres hermanas, yo soy la _____ .
5. El departamento de contabilidad está en la _____ planta.

ESCUCHAR

9. Escucha y completa. 36

	PISO	PUERTA
1. Sr. González	4.º	derecha.
2. Sra. Rodríguez	___	___
3. Srta. Herrero	___	___
4. D. David Acedo	___	___
5. Sr. de la Fuente	___	___
6. Sres. Barroso	___	___

HABLAR

10. Pregunta y contesta a cuatro compañeros, según el modelo.

*¿En qué piso vives?
En el cuarto derecha.*

Hay y está.

B. Interiores

VOCABULARIO

1. vitrocerámica
2. lavavajillas
3. fregadero
4. lavadora
5. armario
6. frigorífico
7. horno
8. horno microondas
9. mesa
10. silla

1. sofá
2. sillón
3. mesita
4. librería
5. equipo de música
6. televisión (TV)
7. lámpara
8. cojín

1. lavabo
2. armario
3. espejo
4. toalla
5. bañera

1. Completa.

Mi cocina es grande y luminosa y tenemos un (1) *frigorífico* nuevo. También hay un (2)_____ y un (3)_____ . Hay muchos (4)_____ y una (5)_____ con (6)_____ para desayunar.

En el salón-comedor tenemos dos (7) *sofás* muy cómodos y dos (8)_____ pequeños. Los libros están en una (9)_____ de madera, junto a la (10)_____ .
Entre los dos sofás hay una mesa pequeña con una (11)_____ encima.

El cuarto de baño es bastante grande también. Hay una (12) *bañera* y un armario. El (13)_____ está encima del (14)_____.

2. Completa las frases con la forma correcta de los verbos del recuadro.

> escuchar – ver – ducharse – dormir
> comer – ~~hacer~~

1. La cocina es donde tú *haces* la comida.
2. El cuarto de baño es donde tú _____.
3. El salón es donde tú _____ la TV.
4. El comedor es donde tú _____.
5. El dormitorio es donde tú _____.
6. El salón es donde tú _____ música.

GRAMÁTICA

Artículos

Determinados: el / la / los / las
Para algo que conocemos.
¿Dónde está el gato?

Indeterminados: un / una / unos / unas
Para algo que mencionamos por primera vez.
Hay un gato en el jardín.

3. Señala el artículo más adecuado.

1. *El / Un* ordenador está en mi dormitorio.
2. En mi clase hay *un / el* mapa del mundo.
3. *Los / Unos* amigos de Pablo son muy simpáticos.
4. ¿Hay *la / una* película buena en la tele?
5. *Los / Unos* libros están en mi mochila.
6. En el patio hay *unos / los* niños.
7. *Las / Unas* llaves están en la mesa de la cocina.

Hay – Está

Hay + un, una, unos, unas (+ nombre).
Hay un lavavajillas.
Hay una bañera.

Hay + muchos, pocas, algunos… (+ nombre).
Hay muchos armarios.

Hay + dos, tres, cuatro… (+ nombre).
Hay dos sillones.

Hay + nombre común.
¿Hay espejo en el cuarto de baño?

Está(n) + el, la, los, las (+ nombre).
En la cocina está el frigorífico.

Está(n) + preposición + nombre.
El espejo está encima del lavabo.

Está + nombre propio.
¿Está Juan?

4. Completa las frases con *hay/está/están*.

1. Perdone, ¿*hay* un supermercado cerca de aquí?
2. Por favor, ¿dónde _____ los cines Ideal?
3. Mañana no _____ clase, es fiesta.
4. No _____ agua en la botella.
5. El comedor _____ al lado de la cocina.
6. ¿Dónde _____ las llaves?
7. Mi coche _____ en el taller.
8. ¿_____ Jesús en la oficina?
9. ¿_____ leche en la nevera?
10. En esta casa sólo _____ un cuarto de baño.

HABLAR

5. Describe qué hay en tu cocina, tu cuarto de baño y tu salón. Compara la descripción con la de tu compañero.

ESCUCHAR

6. Escucha la información sobre las casas en venta y completa la tabla. **37**

	METROS	DORMITORIOS	BAÑOS
1.			
2.			
3.			
4.			

Reservar una habitación.

C. En el hotel

1. Relaciona las siguientes palabras con los símbolos de las instalaciones del hotel.

1. Piscina — e
2. Habitación individual
3. Habitación doble
4. Restaurante
5. Tarjetas de crédito
6. Garaje

2. Escucha y completa el siguiente diálogo. 38

RECEPCIONISTA: Parador de Córdoba, ¿dígame?
CARLOS: Buenas tardes. ¿Puede decirme si hay habitaciones libres para el próximo fin de semana?
RECEPCIONISTA: Sí. ¿Qué desea, una habitación ___individual___ o ___doble___?
CARLOS: Una doble, por favor. ¿Qué precio tiene?
RECEPCIONISTA: ___Tiene___ por noche más IVA.
CARLOS: De acuerdo. Hágame la reserva, por favor.
RECEPCIONISTA: ¿Cuántas noches?

CARLOS: ___Viernes___ y ___Sábado___, si es posible.
RECEPCIONISTA: No hay problema.
CARLOS: ¿Hay ___piscina___?
RECEPCIONISTA: Sí, señor, hay una.
CARLOS: ¿Admiten tarjetas de crédito?
RECEPCIONISTA: Sí, por supuesto.

3. Practica este diálogo con tu compañero.

4. Escucha el final del diálogo anterior y completa la ficha de reserva. 39

NOMBRE: *Carlos*   APELLIDOS: _____
DIRECCIÓN: ___Mc_____
CIUDAD: ___Madrid___   TELF.: ___91579 8647___
SENCILLA O DOBLE: ____   N.º DE NOCHES: ____

LEER

5. Lee y escucha. 40

Los patios

Los patios son lugares comunes para encontrarse, para jugar, para charlar, para descansar. Hay muchos tipos de patios. Está el patio del colegio, donde los niños pasan el recreo. Está el patio andaluz, lleno de macetas con flores, que en verano protegen del calor, y es un lugar de descanso y conversación.

En las ciudades tenemos el patio de vecinos, donde la gente tiende la ropa y habla con los vecinos de enfrente.

En Hispanoamérica muchas casas coloniales conservan bellos patios llenos de plantas tropicales que ayudan a pasar las horas más calurosas del día.

En Córdoba (España), el segundo fin de semana de mayo se celebra el Festival de los Patios. Los vecinos abren sus casas y todo el mundo puede visitar sus hermosos patios.

6. ¿Verdadero (V) o falso (F)?

1. En los colegios hay un patio. ☑ V
2. En las ciudades no hay patios. ☐
3. En los patios coloniales hay plantas tropicales. ☐
4. El Festival de los Patios de Córdoba es el 1 de mayo. ☐
5. Los turistas siempre pueden visitar los patios cordobeses. ☐

PRONUNCIACIÓN Y ORTOGRAFÍA

1. Escucha y repite. 41

> queso – cuarto – cuanto
> quinto – casa – comedor

2. ¿Qué sonido se repite en todas las palabras?

> El sonido **k** se escribe **qu** antes de **e, i,** y se escribe **c** antes de **a, o, u.**

3. Completa con *qu* o *c*.

1. _c_ uando.
2. _qu_ ién.
3. _c_ uatro.
4. tran _qu_ ilo.
5. médi _c_ o.
6. E _c_ uador.
7. pe _qu_ eño.
8. _qu_ inientos.

Autoevaluación

1. ¿En qué parte de la casa están las siguientes cosas?
1. cama: *en el dormitorio.*
2. microondas: _____ .
3. sillones: _____ .
4. equipo de música: _____ .
5. espejo: _____ .
6. lavavajillas: _____ .
7. bañera: _____ .
8. televisión: _____ .

2. ¿Qué hay en cada habitación?
1. Salón-comedor: *sillones,* _____
_____
2. Cocina: _____
_____
3. Dormitorio: _____
_____
4. Cuarto de baño: _____
_____

3. Completa la siguiente serie de ordinales.
Primero, _____ , tercero, _____ , _____ , sexto, _____ , octavo, noveno, _____ .

4. Escribe una carta a tu familia, describiendo la casa en la que pasas tus vacaciones.

Queridos _____ :
    Estoy de vacaciones en _____
con _____ . Estoy en un / una _____ .
Está cerca de _____ . La casa es grande /
pequeña / luminosa…Tiene _____
habitaciones, _____ , _____ ,
_____ y _____ .
En este momento, estoy en _____ .
¡Hasta pronto!
                            Muchos besos.

5. Elige la forma correcta.
1. En la clase *hay / están* muchos estudiantes.
2. En mi casa no *hay / está* la televisión en el salón.
3. *Hay / está* una cafetería aquí cerca.
4. ¿Dónde *hay / están* las llaves?
5. En la nevera *hay / está* carne.
6. La información *hay / está* en Internet.
7. ¿Dónde *hay / está* un bolígrafo rojo?

6. Relaciona cada pregunta con su respuesta.
1. ¿Qué tipo de habitación desea? ☐
2. Buenas tardes, ¿hay habitaciones libres? ☐
3. ¿Admiten tarjetas de crédito? ☐
4. ¿Para cuántas noches? ☐
5. ¿Cuál es el precio de la habitación? ☐

a) Para el fin de semana.
b) Sí, por supuesto.
c) Una doble.
d) Con desayuno, 90 euros.
e) Sí, tenemos una individual y dos dobles.

7. Ordena el diálogo del ejercicio anterior.

Soy capaz de…

☐ ☐ ☐ *Describir una casa.*
☐ ☐ ☐ *Hablar de muebles y cosas de la casa.*
☐ ☐ ☐ *Reservar una habitación en un hotel.*

LA VIVIENDA

1. Mira estas fotos de viviendas.

1. ¿Cuál te gusta más para vivir?
2. ¿Cuál te gusta más para pasar las vacaciones?
3. ¿Cuál te gusta menos?

2. Lee los textos y relaciónalos con las fotos.

1. En el sur de España, en Andalucía, las casas son blancas y con terrazas. Muchas tienen un patio interior y están decoradas con plantas y flores.

2. En el norte, la mayoría de las casas son de piedra, con gruesos muros para protegerlas del frío y tejados inclinados para evitar la acumulación de nieve y agua. La mayoría tiene una huerta para cultivar los productos de la tierra.

3. En la costa mediterránea hay muchas viviendas destinadas al turismo, pequeñas urbanizaciones de chalés y apartamentos y grandes hoteles se mezclan con las viviendas tradicionales.

4. Una gran parte de la población vive en las ciudades. En ellas encontramos bloques de pisos y apartamentos. Las urbanizaciones de chalés adosados son cada vez más frecuentes a las afueras de la ciudad.

3. Contesta las siguientes preguntas:

1. ¿En qué zona de España tienen patio las casas?
2. ¿De qué material son las casas del norte de España?
3. ¿Dónde hay muchos apartamentos, chalés y hoteles?
4. ¿Dónde vive la mayoría de la población?
5. ¿Dónde se encuentran los chalés adosados?

HABLAR

4. Imagina que estás de vacaciones en alguna de las diferentes zonas de España. Contesta a las preguntas de tu compañero.

¿En qué parte de España estás?
¿En qué tipo de casa?
Describe la casa.

cuarenta y tres 43

5. Pedir en un restaurante.

A. Comer fuera de casa

1. ¿Conoces algún plato hispano? Escribe los nombres junto a la fotografía correspondiente.

> gazpacho – tortilla de patatas
> arroz a la cubana

ESCUCHAR

2. Mira la carta del restaurante LA MORENITA; escucha el diálogo y completa la tabla. **42**

	Teresa	Juan
Primer plato	ensalada	_____
Segundo plato	_____	_____
Bebida	_____	_____
Postre	_____	_____

MESÓN RESTAURANTE LA MORENITA
PATIO CORDOBÉS

PRIMEROS
- Sopa de picadillo
- Gazpacho
- Judías verdes
- Ensalada mixta

SEGUNDOS
- Huevos con chorizo
- Carne con tomate
- Chuletas de cordero
- Fritura de pescado

POSTRES
- Fruta del tiempo
- Flan
- Arroz con leche
- Natillas

BEBIDAS
Vino blanco, vino tinto, cerveza, agua

CARDENAL GONZÁLEZ, 63 - TEL. 957 487 099

HABLAR

3. Mira la carta y elige qué quieres comer.

Primer plato:
Segundo plato:
Bebida:
Postre:

4. En grupos de tres. Uno es el camarero y los otros dos son clientes. Representad el siguiente diálogo:

CAMARERO: ¿Qué van a tomar de primero?
CLIENTE 1: Yo, de primero, quiero _____ .
CLIENTE 2: Pues yo, _____ .
CAMARERO: ¿Y de segundo?
CLIENTE 1: _____ .
CLIENTE 2: _____ .
CAMARERO: ¿Qué quieren para beber?
CLIENTE 1: _____ .
CLIENTE 2: _____ .
CAMARERO: ¿Y de postre?
CLIENTE 1: _____ .
CLIENTE 2: _____ .

VOCABULARIO

vaso   copa   taza
jarra   jarra   jarrón

5. Completa con la palabra adecuada.

1. Una *copa* de vino.
2. Una _____ de cerveza.
3. Una _____ de café.
4. Un _____ de agua.
5. Un _____ de flores.
6. Una _____ de agua.

LEER

6. Lee y escucha.

Hoy comemos fuera

En España, comer es algo que nos gusta compartir con amigos, familiares, compañeros de trabajo o estudio. Para la mayoría de los españoles es más importante la compañía que el tipo de restaurante. Al escoger un restaurante preocupa la higiene, la calidad de los alimentos y la dieta equilibrada. En un país como España, con un clima agradable, de largos días con luz, el comer o cenar fuera de casa es un hábito muy extendido.
Es durante los días festivos cuando más se visitan bares y restaurantes.

7. Di si estas afirmaciones son verdaderas (V) o falsas (F).

1. A los españoles les gusta comer solos. **F**
2. Cuando comen fuera de casa les gusta hacerlo con familiares y amigos.
3. Para los españoles lo más importante es el tipo de restaurante.
4. Los restaurantes están más llenos los días laborables.
5. Los españoles con frecuencia cenan fuera de casa.

Hablar de gustos.

B. ¿Te gusta el cine?

1. ¿Te gusta el cine? ¿Qué tipo de películas te gustan? Coméntalo con tus compañeros.

a) comedia   b) drama   c) policíaca
d) de terror   e) de ciencia-ficción

VOCABULARIO

2. Relaciona las palabras siguientes con las dibujos.

1. el fútbol — d
2. ir de compras
3. montar en bicicleta
4. leer
5. andar
6. ir a la discoteca
7. la música rock
8. ir al cine
9. viajar
10. nadar
11. bailar
12. pintar

ESCUCHAR

3. Escucha a Elena hablar de sus gustos y de los de su marido. Señala en el cuadro. 44

	Elena		Luis	
	SÍ	NO	SÍ	NO
El cine				
Andar por el campo				
Ir de compras				
Los deportes				
Navegar por Internet				
Leer				
El fútbol				
La música				

4. En parejas. Pregunta a tu compañero sobre sus gustos.

A. *Peter, ¿(a ti) te gusta el cine?*
B. *No, me gusta más leer.*

5. Escribe unas frases sobre tu compañero.

A Peter no le gusta mucho el cine, pero le gusta leer.

GRAMÁTICA

Verbo Gustar

(A mí)	me	
(A ti)	te	gusta/n
(A él/ella/Vd.)	le	
(A nosotros/as)	nos	
(A vosotros/as)	os	gusta/n
(A ellos/ellas/Vds.)	les	

A Elena **le gusta** viajar.
A Jaime **le gustan** los deportes.
A nosotros no **nos gusta** el fútbol.

6. Completa las frases con un pronombre (*me, te, le...*) y *gusta* o *gustan*.

1. A María *le gusta* mucho nadar.
2. A mi marido ___ _____ ir al cine.
3. A mí no ___ _____ las películas de terror.
4. A los españoles ___ _____ mucho salir y hablar con los amigos.
5. A nosotros ___ _____ los animales.
6. ¿A vosotros ___ _____ la música tecno? A mí, no.
7. ¿A Vd. ___ _____ la paella?
8. ¿A ti ___ _____ los niños?

LEER Y ESCRIBIR

7. Lee estos anuncios.

8. Responde las preguntas.

1. ¿De dónde es Olga?
   _____
2. ¿Qué deporte le gusta a Tiago?
   _____
3. ¿Cuántos años tiene Miguel?
   _____
4. ¿Cómo se llama la chica sevillana?
   _____
5. ¿Qué baile le gusta a Olga?
   _____
6. ¿Qué le gusta a Marisol?
   _____

9. Ahora escribe un anuncio, pero no pongas tu nombre. Dáselo a tu profesor/a. Él/ella leerá todos los anuncios y la clase tendrá que adivinar de quién son.

Me llamo Marisol, soy soltera. Me gusta viajar, hacer deporte y leer. Busco amigos para salir. SEVILLA.

Me llamo Miguel, tengo 25 años. Me gusta jugar al fútbol, nadar y montar en bicicleta, busco chicos y chicas con aficiones similares. MADRID.

Me llamo Tiago, soy brasileño, de Río de Janeiro. Me gusta salir con chicas, ir a la playa, navegar por Internet. También me gusta ver partidos de baloncesto en la tele. ¿Por qué no me escribes?

Me llamo Olga, tengo 32 años, me gusta el cine, salir de copas, bailar tango y nadar. Escríbeme. BUENOS AIRES.

> *Comprender instrucciones de recetas.*

C. Receta del Caribe

1. ¿Te gusta cocinar? ¿Qué sabes hacer?

2. Completa la lista de ingredientes con las palabras del recuadro.

> azúcar – hielo – limón
> leche – vainilla – plátanos

BATIDO DE PLÁTANO
Ingredientes:
3 _____
1 taza de _____
1/4 de taza de _____
1/4 de taza de zumo de _____
1/2 cucharadita de _____
8 cubitos de _____

ESCUCHAR

3. Ordena las instrucciones para su preparación.

a) Añade los cubitos de hielo y mézclalos con los otros ingredientes. ☐

b) Pela los plátanos y córtalos en rodajas. [1]

c) Reparte la mezcla en cuatro vasos. ☐

d) Mezcla los plátanos, la leche, el azúcar, el zumo de limón y la vainilla en una batidora. ☐

e) Ofrece el refresco a tus amigos. ☐

4. Escucha y comprueba. 45

GRAMÁTICA

Imperativo			
	Cortar	**Comer**	**Abrir**
tú	cort**a**	com**e**	abr**e**
usted	cort**e**	com**a**	abr**a**

5. Completa las siguientes instrucciones para llevar una vida sana. Utiliza los verbos del recuadro en imperativo.

> caminar – tomar – descansar
> comer – evitar – ~~beber~~

TODOS LOS DÍAS:
1. *Bebe* más de un litro de agua.
2. _____ tres piezas de fruta.
3. _____ durante media hora.
4. _____ más de siete horas.
5. _____ fumar.
6. _____ bebidas sin alcohol.

6. ¿De dónde crees que son originalmente estos productos?

PRODUCTOS DE AMÉRICA

1. la piña
   - [ ] Hawai
   - [ ] Cuba y Puerto Rico
2. el maní
   - [ ] Georgia
   - [ ] Bolivia y Perú
3. la patata
   - [ ] Perú y Ecuador
   - [ ] Irlanda
4. el tomate
   - [ ] México
   - [ ] Italia
5. los plátanos
   - [ ] Ecuador
   - [ ] África
6. el café
   - [ ] África
   - [ ] Brasil

> Casi todas las piñas de los supermercados son de Hawai, pero sus cultivadores originales son los indios de Cuba y Puerto Rico.
>
> Los italianos preparan una deliciosa salsa de tomate, pero los cultivadores originales del tomate son los indios de México.

7. Escucha y comprueba. 46

PRONUNCIACIÓN Y ORTOGRAFÍA

> La **b** y la **v** se pronuncian igual.

1. Escucha y repite. 47

> Isa**b**el – **v**i**v**ir – **v**ino – **b**ueno – Á**v**ila
> **v**iajar – **b**otella – a**b**uelo – ha**b**lar
> muy **b**ien – **b**eber

2. Escucha y repite. 48

1. ¿Dónde vive Isabel?
2. Cuba es una isla preciosa.
3. Vicente es abogado y trabaja en Sevilla.
4. Las bebidas están en la nevera.
5. Este vino es muy bueno.
6. Valeriano viaja mucho en avión.
7. Beatriz es de Venezuela.
8. Esta bicicleta es muy barata.

3. Completa con *b* o *v*.

1. Yo __i__o en __arcelona.
2. Este __atido tiene __ainilla.
3. Camarero, un __aso de agua, por favor.
4. A Isa__el le gusta __iajar y __ailar tangos.
5. __e__er agua es muy __ueno.

4. Escucha otra vez y repite. 49

Autoevaluación

1. Con estos ingredientes vamos a elaborar un menú. ¿Qué lleva cada plato?

> huevos – ~~tomates~~ – arroz – pollo – leche
> gambas – pepinos – calamares – azúcar
> aceite – sal – ajo

MENÚ

1.er plato, gazpacho: *tomates*, _____,
_____, _____, _____.

2.º plato, paella: _____, _____,
_____, _____, _____,
_____.

Postre, flan: _____, _____, _____.

2. Elabora un menú con platos típicos de tu país y haz la lista de ingredientes que necesitas para su elaboración.

3. Escribe el pronombre correcto (*me, te, le, nos, os, les*).

1. A ellos *les* gusta la música clásica.
2. A nosotros _____ gusta salir de noche.
3. A su hermana _____ gusta la paella.
4. A mí no _____ gustan los toros.
5. ¿A ti _____ gusta el fútbol?
6. ¿A vosotros _____ gustan las gambas?
7. A Luisa no _____ gusta viajar.

4. Haz frases como en el ejemplo.

1. Rosa / no gustar / animales
   A Rosa no le gustan los animales.
2. Ellos / gustar / salir
   _____
3. Nosotros / gustar / ver la tele
   _____
4. Yo / no gustar / fútbol
   _____

5. ¿Tú / gustar / flan?
   _____
6. Pepe / no gustar / la fruta
   _____
7. ¿Vosotros / gustar / nadar?
   _____

5. Escribe en imperativo las órdenes que da Maribel a su hijo.

1. ¡*Baja* la tele! (bajar)
2. ¡_____ más verdura! (comer)
3. ¡_____ la ventana de tu dormitorio! (abrir)
4. ¡_____ una nota para tu profesor! (escribir)
5. ¡_____ cuando te hablo! (escuchar)
6. ¡_____ a tu hermana! (ayudar)
7. ¡_____ más leche! (beber)

6. Relaciona cada pregunta con su respuesta.

1. ¿Qué desea para beber?   [d]
2. ¿Y de segundo?   [ ]
3. ¿Me deja la carta, por favor?   [ ]
4. ¿Y de postre?   [ ]
5. ¿Qué quiere el señor de primero?   [ ]
6. ¿Desea algo más?   [ ]

a) Sí, ahora mismo. Un momento.
b) Una sopa de fideos, por favor.
c) Un helado de vainilla.
d) Agua mineral.
e) No, muchas gracias.
f) Pollo con patatas.

7. Ordena el diálogo anterior.
_____

 *Soy capaz de…*

 *Pedir en un restaurante.*

 *Hablar de gustos.*

 *Comprender y dar instrucciones sencillas.*

De acá y de allá

COCINAS DEL MUNDO

LEER

1. Lee estos anuncios de los restaurantes y después contesta las preguntas.

Probablemente la mejor comida peruana, en Madrid.
Menús de la casa.

RESTAURANTE PERUANO
La Llama
SABROSOS PLATOS PERUANOS

San Francisco, 12. (Detrás Hotel Sol). Metro Sol
Teléfonos 916 542 082 · 916 542 083 · 28005

Taberna • Restaurante
El Rincón del Café
Cocina Tradicional Casera
Menú especial diario: 9 €
C/ Infanta, 54 – Tel. 913 578 453

RESTAURANTE LA ALPUJARRA
- Pescaditos fritos
- Pescados al horno y a la sal
- Carnes rojas

Pza. Granada, 4
Tel.: 913 455 512
913 455 513
(Aparcacoches)

GAMBRINUS CERVECERÍA
TAPAS DE:
Mejillones
Berberechos
Gambas
Pulpo con verduras naturales.

Príncipe de Viana, 20 Tel.: 913 502 864

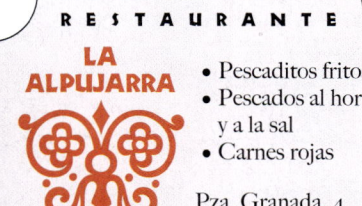

EL PÁDEL — COCINA MEDITERRÁNEA
- MENÚ DEGUSTACIÓN • PINCHOS • TAPAS
- MENÚS DIARIOS PARA EMPRESAS
- SALONES PARA REUNIONES FAMILIARES Y DE NEGOCIOS

C/ MARQUESA DE TOLEDO, 5 (RECOLETOS). PARKING A 50 METROS
TEL.: 914 323 320 / 914 323 321

LA ESTANCIA
Único asador criollo en España
Carnes elaboradas al estilo autóctono de la campiña argentina
Asador Restaurante
Cabrito - Lechón - Carnes argentinas
Carnes gallegas - Pescados a la brasa
APARCACOCHES
C/ Petunias, 66 - Tel.: 914 506 142

1. ¿En qué estación de metro está el restaurante peruano?
2. ¿En qué restaurante podemos celebrar una reunión con nuestra familia o de negocios?
3. ¿Qué tipo de comida ofrece El Rincón del Café?
4. ¿Dónde podemos comer comida argentina?
5. ¿Dónde podemos tomar tapas?
6. ¿Dónde podemos comer pescado?
7. ¿Qué restaurantes ofrecen aparcacoches?
8. ¿Cuánto cuesta el menú en El Rincón del Café?
9. ¿Dónde podemos tomar gambas?

2. ¿Con qué países hispanos relacionas las siguientes comidas y bebidas?

> café – naranjas – frijoles – chorizo – mate
> ron – paella – tequila – churrasco – tortilla

3. ¿Conoces otras comidas y bebidas hispanas? Coméntalo con tus compañeros.

Instrucciones para ir en metro.

6

A. ¿Cómo se va a Plaza de España?

1. Mira el dibujo y responde. ¿Qué están haciendo Sergio y Beatriz?

a) Están llamando a un taxi.
b) Están comprando un billete de metro.
c) Están recogiendo su coche.

2. Completa la conversación con las expresiones del recuadro.

> ¿Cuánto es? – cómo se va
> dos billetes de metro – sexta estación
> ¿Puede darme

SERGIO: Perdone, queremos _____ (1)_____ , por favor.

TAQUILLERO: ¿Sencillos o de diez viajes?

SERGIO: Bueno, mejor uno de 10 viajes. (2)_____

TAQUILLERO: 6 euros.

SERGIO: Perdone, ¿puede decirme (3)_____ _____ a Plaza de España?

TAQUILLERO: Pues desde aquí es muy fácil, coja usted la línea 8 hasta Nuevos Ministerios y cambie a la línea 10 en dirección Puerta del Sur. La (4)_____ es Plaza de España.

SERGIO: Muchas gracias. ¿ (5)_____ un plano del metro?

TAQUILLERO: Sí, claro, tome.

3. Escucha y comprueba. 50

4. Escucha otra vez y marca el recorrido en el plano del metro de Madrid. 50

COMUNICACIÓN

5. Completa el cuadro.

> **Formal (Vd.)**
> - *Perdone, ¿cómo se va a la Plaza de España?*
> - *Coja la línea 8 hasta Nuevos Ministerios, allí cambie a la línea 10 en dirección Puerta del Sur.*
>
> **Informal (tú)**
> _____ *, ¿cómo voy / se va a la Plaza de España?*
> _____ *la línea 8 hasta Nuevos Ministerios, allí* _____ *a la línea 10 en dirección Puerta del Sur.*

HABLAR

6. Mira otra vez el plano y practica con tu compañero, uno pregunta y el otro responde, para ir de… a…

De Aeropuerto a Arturo Soria
De Cuatro Caminos a Fuencarral
De Cuatro Caminos a Callao
De Sol a Avenida de América
De Avenida de América al Aeropuerto

A. *Perdona, ¿cómo se va de Barajas a Arturo Soria?*
B. *Coge la línea 8 hasta Mar de Cristal, allí cambia a la línea 4 en dirección Argüelles. Es la tercera parada.*

LEER

7. Lee el texto y responde a las preguntas.

MADRID EN METRO

El metro de Madrid tiene unos 170 kilómetros. En total hay 11 líneas y 158 estaciones. El horario de servicio al público es de 6:00 h de la mañana a 1:30 h de la madrugada, todos los días del año. Durante las horas de cierre del metro existe un servicio de autobuses nocturnos que salen de la plaza de Cibeles.

Hay dos tipos de billetes, además del abono transportes: el billete sencillo, que sólo tiene un viaje, y el metrobús o billete de diez viajes, que también puede utilizarse en el autobús.

Los billetes se pueden comprar en las taquillas o en las máquinas del metro. El metrobús también se puede comprar en quioscos y estancos.

www.ctm-madrid.es
www.metrodemadrid.es

1. Son las 6.30 h, tienes que ir al trabajo, ¿está abierto ya el metro? ¿Desde qué hora?
2. Son las dos de la madrugada, ¿puedes volver a casa en metro? ¿Por qué? ¿Puedes volver en autobús?
3. ¿Cuántas veces puedes usar el billete sencillo?
4. ¿Cómo se llama el billete de 10 viajes?
5. ¿Puedes usar el metrobús en el autobús?
6. ¿Dónde se compra el metrobús?

Dar instrucciones y pedir favores.

B. Cierra la ventana, por favor

1. Escucha y relaciona los dibujos con las frases.

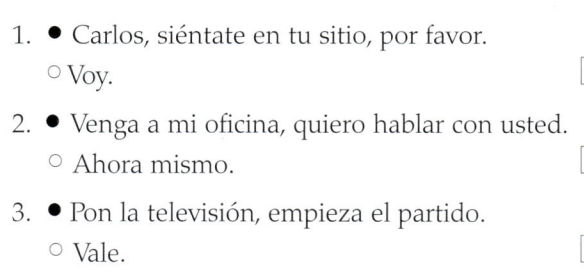

1. ● Carlos, siéntate en tu sitio, por favor.
   ○ Voy.   `a`

2. ● Venga a mi oficina, quiero hablar con usted.
   ○ Ahora mismo.

3. ● Pon la televisión, empieza el partido.
   ○ Vale.

4. ● Cierra la ventana, por favor, tengo frío.
   ○ Sí, claro.

5. ● Tuerce a la derecha, esa es la calle.
   ○ Ah, sí, tienes razón.

6. ● Coja la primera a la derecha y después siga recto.
   ○ Muchas gracias.

7. ● Haz los deberes antes de cenar.
   ○ Vale, mamá.

GRAMÁTICA

Imperativo irregular

Hacer	Poner	Venir	Coger
haz	pon	ven	coge
haga	ponga	venga	coja

Torcer	Cerrar	Sentarse	Decir
tuerce	cierra	siéntate	di(me)
tuerza	cierre	siéntese	diga(me)

2. Completa con el verbo en imperativo.

1. El hospital está muy cerca, (torcer, tú) *tuerce* a la derecha por esa calle y luego (seguir, tú) _____ todo recto.
2. (Hacer, tú) _____ tú la ensalada, mientras yo pongo la mesa.
3. ¡Carlos! (venir, tú) _____ a tu habitación ahora mismo.
4. (Cerrar, tú) _____ la puerta, por favor, hay mucho ruido.

3. Completa con los verbos del recuadro.

> cerrar – sentarse – poner – ~~pasar~~ – hacer

JEFE: Sr. Hernández, ¿puede venir a mi oficina, por favor?
HERNÁNDEZ: Sí, claro.
HERNÁNDEZ: ¿Se puede?
JEFE: Sí, sí, (1) *pase* y (2) _____ la puerta, por favor… (3) _____ . Tengo una reunión en el banco el próximo lunes y necesito la información de su departamento.
HERNÁNDEZ: No hay problema, está todo preparado.
JEFE: Bien, (4) _____ el informe antes del lunes y (5) _____ todos los datos de este año.

4. Escucha y comprueba.

COMUNICACIÓN

+ directo	– directo
¡Ven un momento!	¿Puedes venir un momento?
¡Haga ya la comida!	¿Puede hacer ya la comida?

5. Transforma las frases como en el ejemplo.

1. Venga a mi oficina.
   ¿Puede venir a mi oficina?
2. Pon la televisión, empieza la película.
   ¿Puedes _____?
3. Cierra la ventana, por favor.
   ¿_____?
4. Hoy haz tú la cena.
   ¿_____?
5. Dime la hora, por favor.
   ¿_____?

HABLAR

6. Piensa en un compañero sentado lejos de ti en la clase y escribe una petición en un papel. Luego léelo en voz alta.

> Para Svieta:
> Déjame tu diccionario.
>   Olga.

Puedes pedirle:
– Abrir / cerrar la ventana.
– Prestar dinero / un bolígrafo / un lápiz / un diccionario.
– Esperar a la salida de clase.
– Encender / apagar la luz.
– Sentarse más cerca de ti.

Describir el barrio.

C. Mi barrio es tranquilo

1. ¿Cómo es tu barrio? ¿Es tranquilo o ruidoso? ¿Está cerca de tu trabajo o está lejos?

2. Lee los mensajes.

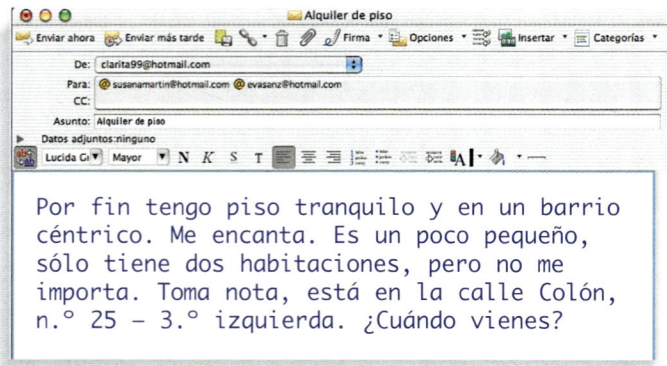

Por fin tengo piso tranquilo y en un barrio céntrico. Me encanta. Es un poco pequeño, sólo tiene dos habitaciones, pero no me importa. Toma nota, está en la calle Colón, n.º 25 – 3.º izquierda. ¿Cuándo vienes?

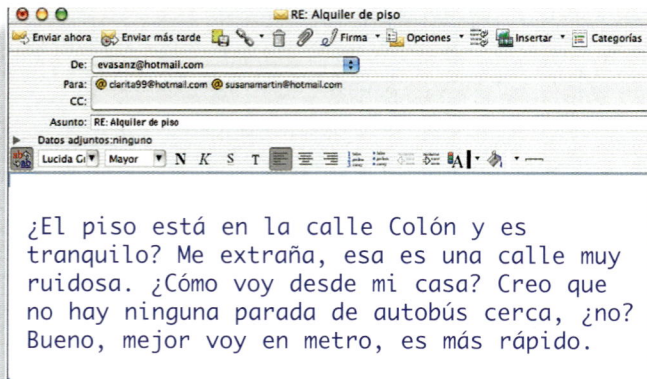

¿El piso está en la calle Colón y es tranquilo? Me extraña, esa es una calle muy ruidosa. ¿Cómo voy desde mi casa? Creo que no hay ninguna parada de autobús cerca, ¿no? Bueno, mejor voy en metro, es más rápido.

3. Contesta las preguntas.

1. ¿Es grande el piso de Clara?
2. ¿Eva conoce el piso de Clara?
3. ¿Cómo se va a casa de Clara?

GRAMÁTICA

Ser / Estar	
Es / son	
	grande (s) – pequeño (s)
	tranquilo (s) – ruidoso (s)
	rápido (s) – lento (s)
Es	bueno/malo
Está / están	
	cerca – lejos
	en la calle…
	enfrente de…
Está	bien/mal

4. Subraya la forma adecuada.

1. El piso *es / está* en un barrio céntrico y *es / está* pequeño, sólo tiene dos habitaciones.
2. Su casa *es / está* en la calle Goya, enfrente de la estación del metro.
3. El metro *es / está* más rápido que el autobús.
4. Fumar no *es / está* bueno.
5. El hospital *es / está* lejos de mi casa, en un barrio que *es / está* muy tranquilo porque *es / está* a las afueras de la ciudad.
6. Este ejercicio *es / está* mal.
7. Esta escuela *es / está* al lado de la parada del autobús.

5. Haz frases con los elementos de cada columna.

Los coches	es	baratos
Esta calle	está	lejos
Los billetes de metro	están	ruidosa
La parada de autobús	son	cerca
La estación de metro		muy tranquila
		en el garaje

HABLAR

6. En parejas. Habla con tu compañero sobre tu barrio. ¿Te gusta? ¿Es grande o pequeño? ¿Tiene mucho tráfico? ¿Está bien comunicado (autobús, metro, etc.)?

PRONUNCIACIÓN Y ORTOGRAFÍA

1. Escucha y repite. 53

> rey – arroz – perro – reloj – rojo – arriba
> caro – pero – diario – soltera – para

El sonido **r (fuerte)** se escribe simple (r) a principio de palabra y doble (rr) en medio de dos vocales. El sonido **r (suave)** se escribe siempre simple (r).

2. Escucha y completa con *r* o *rr*. 54

1. ____oma.
2. Ingle____a.
3. Pe____ú.
4. carte____o.
5. compañe____o.
6. ____osa.
7. piza____a.
8. te____aza.
9. arma____io.

3. Dicta a tu compañero.

El perro de San Roque no tiene rabo porque Ramón Rodríguez se lo ha cortado.

Autoevaluación

1. Completa esta nota que Juan escribe para un compañero del trabajo. Utiliza los verbos del cuadro.

> guardar – ~~hacer~~ – conectar
> apagar – cerrar

Carlos:
Me marcho dentro de 10 minutos. El informe está en mi mesa, por favor (1) haz las fotocopias y (2) _____ todo en el primer cajón.
Después (3) _____ el despacho con llave y (4) _____ la alarma. Ah, antes de salir (5) _____ todas las luces.

Gracias por todo.
                                  Juan

2. Relaciona los adjetivos contrarios.

1. ruidoso   a) bajo
2. ancho   b) corto
3. largo   c) tranquilo
4. bonito   d) pequeño
5. rápido   e) estrecho
6. alto   f) lento
7. grande   g) feo

3. Completa las frases con *ser* o *estar*.

1. Mi piso nuevo *es* bastante grande.
2. Esa oficina _____ bastante lejos de aquí.
3. Las fotocopias no _____ bien.
4. La catedral _____ en el centro.
5. Mi barrio _____ antiguo.
6. Este restaurante _____ muy ruidoso, no me gusta nada.
7. Las llaves _____ en el cajón.

4. Lee este correo y contesta verdadero (V) o falso (F).

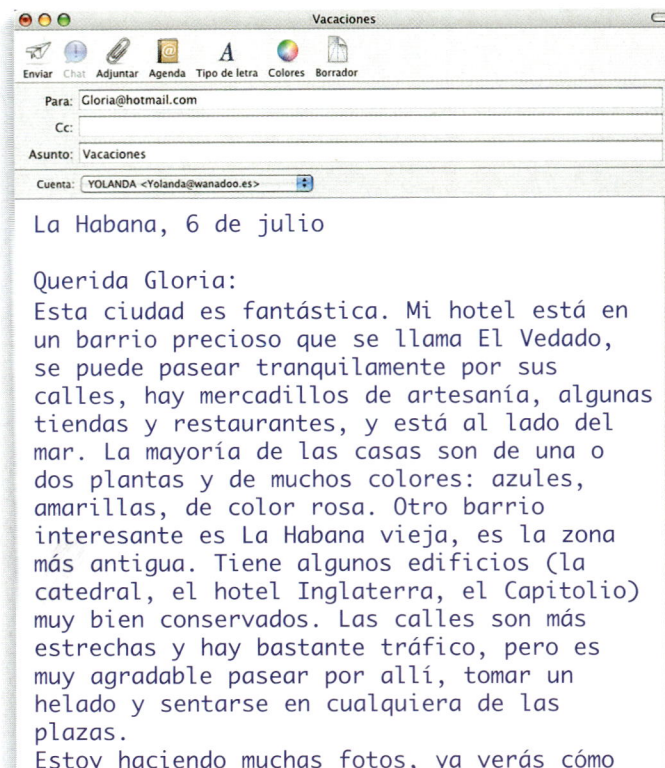

1. El hotel de Yolanda está en La Habana vieja. ☐
2. El Vedado está al lado del mar. ☐
3. En El Vedado hay muchos edificios altos. ☐
4. La catedral está en La Habana vieja. ☐
5. En la zona antigua no hay tráfico. ☐

5. Escribe un párrafo sobre tu barrio.

¿Es grande / pequeño / no muy grande?
¿Tiene mucho / poco tráfico?
¿Hay muchas / pocas / bastantes tiendas?
¿Cómo son los edificios, altos / bajos?

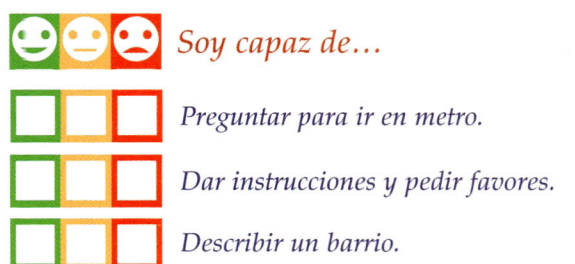

De acá y de allá

MÚSICA LATINA

1. ¿Sabes qué significan estas palabras?

guitarra – flamenco – salsa – tango – fiesta

Dentro de la cultura hispana encontramos una gran variedad de estilos y ritmos musicales: unos son para bailar en fiestas y otros para escuchar con más tranquilidad.

2. A continuación vas a escuchar cuatro ritmos musicales diferentes. ¿Puedes relacionarlos con estos nombres? 55

a) Tango   b) Ranchera   c) Flamenco   d) Salsa

3. Relaciona la foto con la información correspondiente.

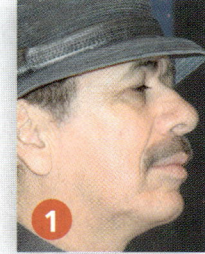  

Carlos Santana   **Jennifer López**   **Enrique Iglesias**

a (España, 1975) hijo de Julio Iglesias. Es uno de los artistas jóvenes con más premios internacionales. "Bailamos"

b (México, 1947) es guitarrista y cantante. Compone música de fusión entre el rock y los ritmos latinos y afrocubanos. "Oye cómo va"

c (EE UU, 1970) es cantante y actriz. Le encanta bailar salsa. "Una noche más"

TANGO

RANCHERA

FLAMENCO

SALSA

4. ¿Alguien tiene un CD de música latina? ¿Qué tipo de música es? ¿Puede traerla a clase?

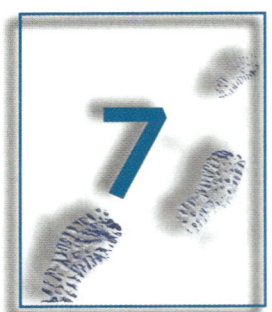

Concertar una cita.
Verbo quedar.

A. ¿Dónde quedamos?

1. ¿Te gusta salir con los amigos? ¿Adónde vas?

   a) al cine
   b) al fútbol
   c) a la discoteca
   d) a casa de otros amigos

2. Lee y escucha. Después contesta las preguntas.

MADRE: ¿Sí, dígame?
PEDRO: ¿Está Antonio?
MADRE: Sí, ¿de parte de quién?
PEDRO: Soy Pedro.
MADRE: Enseguida se pone.
ANTONIO: ¿Pedro?
PEDRO: ¡Hola, Antonio! ¿Qué haces?
ANTONIO: Nada, estoy viendo la tele.
PEDRO: ¿Vamos al cine esta tarde?
ANTONIO: Venga, vale, ¿y qué ponen?
PEDRO: Podemos ver la última película de Almodóvar, ¿no?
ANTONIO: ¡Estupendo! ¿Cómo quedamos?
PEDRO: ¿A las siete en la puerta del metro?
ANTONIO: No, mejor a las ocho. ¿De acuerdo?
PEDRO: Vale. ¡Hasta luego!

1. ¿Qué van a hacer Antonio y Pedro?
2. ¿Dónde quedan?
3. ¿A qué hora?

3. Completa el diálogo. Utiliza las expresiones siguientes.

> Mejor mañana – Lo siento – Te parece bien
> Vienes conmigo – no puedo

A. ¿Sí?
B. ¿Está Alicia?
A. Sí, soy yo.
B. ¡Hola! Soy Begoña.
A. ¡Hola! ¿Qué hay?
B. Voy a salir de compras esta tarde.
   ¿(1)_____?
A. (2)_____, hoy (3)_____,
   tengo mucho trabajo. (4)_____.
B. Bueno, vale. ¿A qué hora? ¿(5)_____ a las seis?
A. Sí, de acuerdo.
B. Hasta mañana.

4. Escucha y comprueba.

COMUNICACIÓN

5. Completa el recuadro.

Invitar	Aceptar
¿Por qué no te vienes?	Venga, vale.
¿Vamos a cenar después?	_____
¿Vienes conmigo?	_____

Rechazar y proponer alternativa
–Lo siento, no puedo, tengo mucho trabajo.
–No puedo, ¿te parece bien mañana?
–No, mejor a las ocho.

HABLAR

6. Imagina que vives en Madrid. Practica con tus compañeros/as con estos datos.

Propuesta	¿Cuándo?
a) ir al teatro.	mañana
b) comer.	el sábado
c) tomar una copa.	esta noche
d) jugar al billar.	esta tarde
e) ir al cine.	este domingo

¿Dónde?	¿Hora?
a) Plaza Mayor.	18:00 h
b) Mesón Madrid.	14:30 h
c) Cine Ideal.	23:15 h
d) Metro Callao.	20:30 h
e) Cine Princesa.	17:45 h

Ejemplo:
A. *¿Vamos al teatro mañana?*
B. *Vale. ¿Dónde quedamos?*
A. *En la plaza Mayor. ¿Te parece bien?*
B. *Sí, ¿a qué hora?*
A. *A las seis.*
B. *Vale. ¡Hasta luego!*
A. *¡Hasta luego!*

ESCUCHAR

7. Ordena la siguiente conversación telefónica.

B. No está en este momento. ¿Quiere dejarle un recado? ☐
B. Muy bien, le dejo una nota. ☐
B. Inmobiliaria Miramar. Buenos días. [1]
A. Muchas gracias. Adiós. ☐
B. Adiós. ☐
A. Sí, por favor, dígale que la Sra. García va mañana a las once y media para hablar con él. ☐
A. Buenos días. ¿Puedo hablar con el Sr. Álvarez? ☐

8. Escucha y comprueba. [3]

HABLAR

9. Practica con tu compañero/a las siguientes conversaciones telefónicas.

Estudiante A:
1. Llamas a Pepe para ir al cine.
2. Llamas a Julia para quedar para ir al cine.
3. Llamas a Borja y quedas para ir al cine.

Estudiante B:
1. Eres el padre de Pepe, y Pepe no está en su casa.
2. Eres Julia, no puedes ir al cine.
3. Eres Borja, te apetece ir al cine y quedas con tu compañero.

Hablar de acciones en desarrollo.

B. ¿Qué estás haciendo?

1. Mira el dibujo y señala si las siguientes frases son verdaderas (V) o falsas (F).

1. El chico del bañador amarillo está duchándose. — V
2. El señor con gafas de sol está leyendo el periódico. ☐
3. La señora del bañador verde está abriendo la sombrilla. ☐
4. Los niños de la toalla blanca están jugando a las cartas. ☐
5. La chica del sombrero rojo está paseando. ☐
6. Una señora está durmiendo sobre la tumbona. ☐
7. Dos señoras están hablando en la orilla. ☐
8. Un grupo de niñas está jugando a la pelota. ☐
9. La chica del bañador rosa está secándose la cabeza. ☐
10. La señora pelirroja está peinándose. ☐

GRAMÁTICA

Estar + gerundio

Estoy
Estás
Está   hablando
Estamos
Estáis
Están

Infinitivo   **Gerundio**

Llorar   llorando
Comer   comiendo
Escribir   escribiendo

Irregulares

Leer   leyendo
Dormir   durmiendo

2. Mira los dibujos y di qué están haciendo los personajes, como en el ejemplo.

dormir / escuchar
No está durmiendo; está escuchando música.

1. escribir / pintar
2. hablar / cantar
3. estudiar / ver la tele
4. leer / navegar en Internet
5. discutir / hablar

Estar + gerundio + verbos reflexivos

Estoy lavándo**me** o **me** estoy lavando.
Estás lavándo**te** o **te** estás lavando.
Está lavándo**se** o **se** está lavando.
Estamos lavándo**nos** o **nos** estamos lavando.
Estáis lavándo**os** u **os** estáis lavando.
Están lavándo**se** o **se** están lavando.

---

3. Completa las frases con el pronombre reflexivo adecuado.

1. A. Rosa, ¿qué estás haciendo?
   B. Ahora mismo estoy peinándo*me* porque voy a salir.
2. A. ¡Luis, al teléfono!
   B. No puedo, estoy duchándo____ .
3. A. Niños, ¿qué hacéis?
   B. Nada, mamá, ____ estamos lavando las manos.
4. A. ¡Qué ruido hacen los vecinos!
   B. Sí, están levantándo____ ahora porque salen de viaje.
5. A. ¡Hola!, ¿está Roberto?
   B. Sí, pero está afeitándo____ , llama más tarde.
6. A. ¿Y Clara?, ¿dónde está?
   B. En el baño, está duchándo____ .
7. A. Joana, ¿qué haces?
   B. ____ estoy pintando para salir.

4. Escucha y comprueba.

PRONUNCIACIÓN Y ORTOGRAFÍA

Entonación exclamativa

1. Escucha y repite.

a) ¡Vale!   e) ¡Qué bonito!
b) ¡Hasta luego!   f) ¡Es horrible!
c) ¡Qué bien!   g) ¡Estupendo!
d) ¡Qué va!

2. Escucha las afirmaciones y reacciona con una de las exclamaciones anteriores.

1. ¡Qué va! *d*   5. ☐
2. ☐   6. ☐
3. ☐   7. ☐
4. ☐

3. Escucha otra vez y comprueba.

sesenta y tres 63

> *Descripción física y de carácter.*

c. ¿Cómo es?

VOCABULARIO

3. Escucha las descripciones y señala quiénes son. 9

1. _____ .   3. _____ .
2. _____ .   4. _____ .

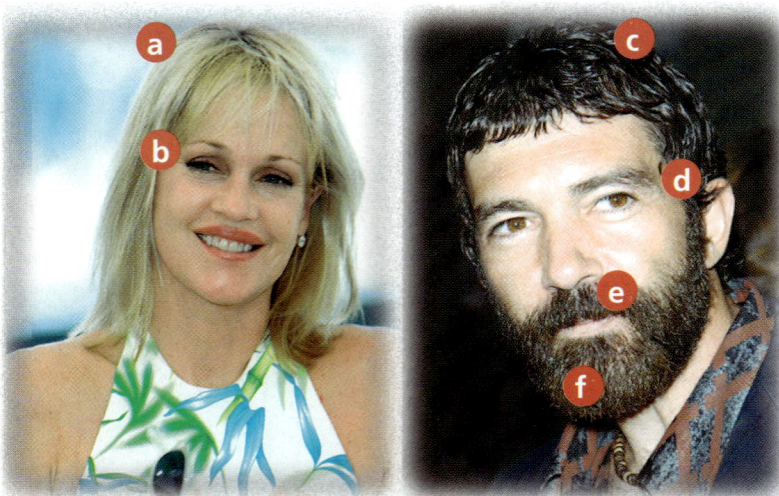

1. Señala en estos personajes las siguientes características físicas.

1. Pelo largo y rubio. ☐
2. Pelo corto y moreno. ☐
3. Ojos claros.   ☐
4. Ojos oscuros.   ☐
5. Bigote.   ☐
6. Barba.   ☐

2. Escucha y completa las siguientes descripciones y adivina a qué personaje se refiere cada una de ellas. 8

1. Tiene el _____ largo y rubio. Tiene los _____ verdes. ¡No tiene _____!
2. Tiene los _____ oscuros. Tiene el _____ corto y la _____ negra.

COMUNICACIÓN

Es { Joven ≠ mayor
     Alto/a ≠ bajo/a
     Delgado/a ≠ gordo/a
     Calvo

Tiene { el pelo largo, corto, rubio, moreno
        el pelo liso, rizado
        los ojos azules, marrones, oscuros ≠ claros

Lleva { gafas
        barba
        bigote

ESCRIBIR

4. Describe a estas dos personas.

HABLAR

5. Describe a una persona de la clase sin decir el nombre. ¿Saben tus compañeros quién es?

Es alta y delgada…   *Tiene los ojos…*
Tiene el pelo…

VOCABULARIO

6. Relaciona.

1. tacaño   a) alegre
2. antipático   b) generoso
3. maleducado   c) simpático
4. serio   d) educado
5. hablador   e) callado

LEER

7. Completa el párrafo con los verbos del recuadro.

> gusta – gustan – es – beber – Odia

Dolores Fuentes es poetisa. Ella dice que (1) *es* simpática y alegre. Le (2)_____ los hombres y las mujeres generosos. En su tiempo libre lo que más le gusta es mirar al mar. Además, le (3)_____ comer cocido madrileño y (4)_____ vino tinto. (5)_____ las guerras y, por otro lado, le gusta mucho la música clásica. Su película favorita es *Tiempos modernos*, de Charlie Chaplin.

HABLAR Y ESCRIBIR

8. Primero lee las preguntas y luego haz la encuesta a tu compañero/a. Utiliza los adjetivos del vocabulario.

1. ¿Cómo eres tú? *Simpático y hablador.*
2. ¿Cómo te gustan los hombres? _____ y _____.
3. ¿Cómo te gustan las mujeres? _____ y _____.
4. ¿Qué prefieres hacer en tu tiempo libre? _____.
5. ¿Cuál es tu comida preferida? _____.
6. ¿Cuál es tu bebida preferida? _____.
7. ¿Cuál es tu deporte favorito? _____.
8. ¿Qué tipo de música prefieres? _____.
9. ¿Cuál es tu película favorita? _____.

9. Escribe un párrafo parecido al de la actividad 7 sobre tu compañero/a.

10. ¿Sabes qué es un hombre sincero? En la canción *Guantanamera* está la respuesta. Escúchala. **10**

Autoevaluación

1. Mira la sección de espectáculos del periódico y busca la información siguiente.

a) ¿Qué ponen en la tele el viernes?

b) ¿Dónde ponen *El fantasma de la Ópera*?

c) ¿Qué podemos ver en Casa Patas?

d) ¿A qué hora empieza la película de Almodóvar?

e) ¿Qué equipos juegan al fútbol el domingo por la tarde?

f) ¿Qué película podemos ver el domingo?

g) ¿Qué obra ponen en el teatro Fígaro?

h) ¿Quién canta el domingo en el Palacio de Congresos?

ESPECTÁCULOS

VIERNES
TELEVISIÓN
La 2, 22 h: Documental *Exiliados*.
CINE
Cine Ideal, 22.30 h: *Pasos de baile*.
TEATRO
Teatro Lope de Vega, 23 h: *El fantasma de la Ópera* (musical).
MÚSICA
Palacio de Vistalegre, 21.30 h: *Nabucco*, de Verdi.

SÁBADO
TELEVISIÓN
Canal +, 22.30 h: *Todo sobre mi madre*, de Almodóvar.
CINE
Cinema Azul, 20 h: *Arrebato*, de Iván Zulueta.
TEATRO
Teatro Albéniz, 22.30 h: *La Gaviota*, de Chejov.
MÚSICA
Casa Patas, 24 h: *Concierto flamenco*.

DOMINGO
TELEVISIÓN
Antena 3, 20.30 h: *Fútbol*, Real Madrid-Barcelona.
CINE
Cines Princesa, 20.15 h: *Te doy mis ojos*, de Icíar Bollaín.
TEATRO
Fígaro, 22.30 h: *Bodas de sangre*, de García Lorca.
MÚSICA
Palacio de Congresos, 21 h: Concierto de Alejandro Sanz.

2. ¿Qué palabra utilizarías para describir a estas personas?

1. Nunca gasta dinero: _____
2. Nunca habla: _____
3. Está siempre hablando: _____
4. Siempre está sonriendo: _____
5. Actúa con mucha educación: _____
6. Hace muchos regalos: _____

3. Describe lo que están haciendo los personajes del dibujo. Utiliza los verbos del recuadro.

> ~~reír~~ – comer – discutir
> escuchar – hablar

Ana se está riendo.

😊😐☹️ *Soy capaz de…*

☐☐☐ *Concertar una cita.*

☐☐☐ *Hablar de acciones en desarrollo.*

☐☐☐ *Describir personas.*

De acá y de allá

LOS SÁBADOS

LOS SÁBADOS POR LA NOCHE

Para los jóvenes la noche del sábado es muy especial. No tienen que estudiar, no tienen que trabajar, no tienen que aprender los verbos irregulares… Entonces, ¿qué hacen los sábados por la noche? Depende. No todos tienen los mismos gustos.

Tomás (dieciocho años, Costa Rica) Conozco a muchas chicas de mi edad, pero normalmente prefiero salir con mis amigos. Hay muchas cosas que nos gusta hacer juntos. Cuando tenemos suficiente dinero vamos al cine o a una cafetería. Si no, vamos a la casa de otro amigo y escuchamos música.

Carolina (diecisiete años, Perú) Yo no salgo mucho. Mis padres son muy estrictos. Casi nunca me dan permiso para salir de noche. Así que me quedo en casa viendo la televisión.

1. Señala verdadero (V) o falso (F).

1. Los jóvenes tienen que estudiar los sábados por la noche. **F**
2. No todos los jóvenes tienen los mismos gustos. ☐
3. Rafael sale sólo con sus amigos. ☐
4. Carolina se queda en casa, viendo la televisión. ☐
5. Tomás, algunas veces, va al cine. ☐

2. En grupos de cuatro, habla con tus compañeros.

¿Sales a menudo los sábados por la noche?
¿Con quién sales?
¿Adónde te gusta ir?
¿Sales los domingos?
¿Sales solo/a o con tus amigos?

Rafael (veintitrés años, Alicante) Yo siempre salgo con mi novia y mis amigos. Normalmente vamos al cine y a tomar algo.

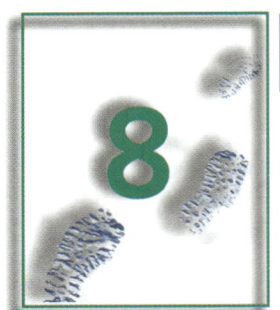

Preguntar e indicar cómo se va a un lugar.

COMUNICACIÓN

sigue (siga) todo recto | gira (gire) a la izquierda | gira (gire) a la derecha | toma (tome) la 2.ª a la derecha

A. De vacaciones

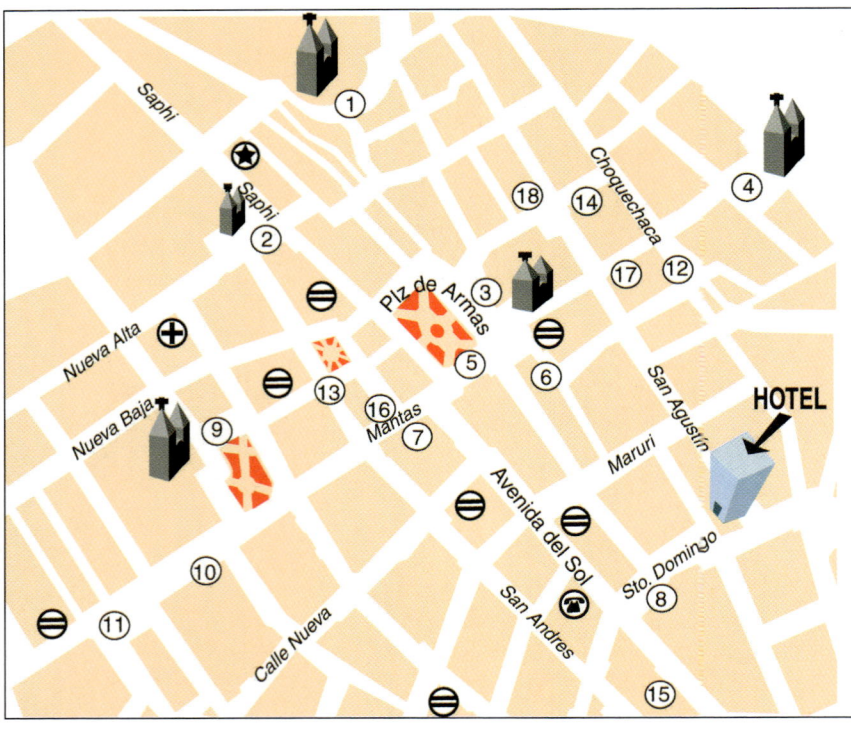

1. San Cristóbal
2. Santa Teresa
3. Catedral
4. San Blas
5. La Compañía
6. Santa Catalina
7. La Merced
8. Santo Domingo
9. San Francisco
10. Santa Clara
11. San Pedro
12. Piedra de los 12 Ángulos
13. Casa de Garcilaso
14. Monasterio de Nazarenas
15. Centro de Arte Nativo
16. Oficina de Correos
17. Museo de Arte
18. Museo Arqueológico

Farmacia
Central telefónica
Posta sanitaria
Estación de policía

1. Mira el mapa de Cuzco y encuentra: una farmacia, la iglesia de San Francisco, una posta sanitaria, el Museo de Arte, una estación de policía y la oficina de correos.

2. Escribe frases como en el ejemplo.

Hay una farmacia en la calle…
La iglesia de San Francisco está en la calle…

3. Lee y escucha el diálogo. Sigue el recorrido en el plano. **11**

LUIS: Buenos días, perdone, ¿puede decirme cómo se va a la plaza de Armas?

RECEPCIONISTA: Sí, ¡cómo no! Es muy sencillo. Salga del hotel hacia la derecha y siga todo recto hasta el final de la calle. Entonces gire a la izquierda. Siga recto y tome la tercera calle a la derecha, la avenida del Sol, y al final de la avenida, girando a la derecha, se encuentra la plaza de Armas.

LUIS: Entonces, giro en la primera a la izquierda y en la avenida del Sol a la derecha. ¿No es así?

RECEPCIONISTA: Así es, señor. En quince minutos puede estar allí.

LUIS: Muchas gracias. ¡Hasta luego!

4. Mira el mapa y completa el diálogo.

a) Desde el hotel:
  A. Perdone, ¿puede decirme dónde está la farmacia más cercana?
  B. _____ por la calle Santo Domingo; gire la primera _____ y, después, la primera _____ .

b) Desde la iglesia de San Francisco:
  A. Por favor, ¿puede decirme cómo se va a la iglesia de Santa Teresa?
  B. Siga todo recto y gire la segunda _____ _____ y después tome la calle _____ .

5. Escucha y comprueba.

HABLAR

6. En parejas, mirando el plano de Cuzco, A pregunta y B responde. Estamos en la iglesia de Santa Teresa.

1. Perdone, por favor, ¿para ir a la catedral?
2. ¿Puede decirme cómo se va a la plaza de Armas, por favor?
3. ¿La iglesia de San Francisco, por favor?
4. Disculpe, ¿la posta sanitaria, por favor?

Plaza de Armas

VOCABULARIO

7. Escribe la letra correspondiente.

1. medicinas — c
2. fruta y carne
3. periódico
4. sellos y tabaco
5. cartas
6. policía

8. Relaciona los establecimientos con el vocabulario anterior.

1. Correos — e
2. Quiosco
3. Farmacia
4. Mercado
5. Estanco
6. Comisaría

Hablar del pasado (ayer).

B. ¿Qué hizo Rosa ayer?

1. ¿Adónde fuiste el sábado?

Yo fui a _____ .
Yo no salí, me quedé en casa.

2. Relaciona las frases con las imágenes.

1. Salió de casa a las ocho de la mañana. [d]
2. Empezó a trabajar a las ocho y media. [ ]
3. Comió en la cafetería del hospital. [ ]
4. Terminó de trabajar a las cinco de la tarde. [ ]
5. Por la tarde, fue al supermercado. [ ]
6. Compró algo de fruta para la cena. [ ]

a

b

c

d

e

f

GRAMÁTICA

Pretérito indefinido

	Trabajar	Comer	Salir
yo	trabajé	comí	salí
tú	trabajaste	comiste	saliste
él/ella/Vd.	trabajó	comió	salió
nosotros/as	trabajamos	comimos	salimos
vosotros/as	trabajasteis	comisteis	salisteis
ellos/ellas/Vds.	trabajaron	comieron	salieron

3. Escribe las siguientes frases en pretérito indefinido.

1. Ayer / no leer / el periódico. (yo)
   Ayer no leí el periódico.
2. El lunes / Juan y yo / comer / en un restaurante nuevo.
   _____
3. Anoche / cenar / con María. (nosotros)
   _____
4. Mis amigos / no trabajar / el sábado.
   _____
5. ¿Comprar / ayer / el periódico? (tú)
   _____
6. Eduardo / llevar / al niño al colegio.
   _____
7. ¿Salir / el viernes por la noche? (vosotros)
   _____

ESCUCHAR

4. ¿Qué hizo Rosa ayer? Completa los huecos con el pretérito indefinido de los verbos.

> acabar – cenar – visitar – pasar
> llegar – atender – invitar

Ayer, como todos los días, me levanté a las siete de la mañana y me preparé para ir a trabajar. Al llegar al hospital, como todos los días, (1) atendí a los enfermos de la consulta y (2)_____ a los pacientes de las habitaciones. A las cinco de la tarde, como todos los días, (3)_____ de trabajar y (4)_____ por el supermercado a comprar algo para la cena. A las seis de la tarde (5)_____ por fin a casa, muy cansada, como todos los días. Pero ayer fue diferente: mi marido me (6)_____ a un concierto y después (7)_____ en mi restaurante favorito.

5. Escucha y comprueba. 13

GRAMÁTICA

Pretérito indefinido

verbos irregulares

	Ir	Estar
yo	fui	estuve
tú	fuiste	estuviste
él/ella/Vd.	fue	estuvo
nosotros/as	fuimos	estuvimos
vosotros/as	fuisteis	estuvisteis
ellos/ellas/Vds.	fueron	estuvieron

ESCUCHAR

6. Soledad y Federico son dos ejecutivos argentinos. Escúchalos y completa el cuadro con las ciudades en las que estuvieron la semana pasada. 14

Lima – Madrid – Buenos Aires
Río de Janeiro – Caracas

	Soledad	Federico
Lunes	_____	_____
Martes	_____	_____
Miércoles	_____	_____
Jueves	_____	_____
Viernes	_____	_____

HABLAR

7. Completa las preguntas con el pretérito indefinido.

1. ¿A qué hora *te levantaste* ayer?
2. ¿A qué hora (empezar) _____ a trabajar?
3. ¿Dónde (ir) _____ a comer?
4. ¿Con quién (comer) _____?
5. ¿Dónde (estar) _____ después de comer?
6. ¿A qué hora te (acostar) _____?

8. Haz las preguntas anteriores a tu compañero/a y luego escribe sobre él/ella.

Ayer mi compañero se levantó a las…

PRONUNCIACIÓN Y ORTOGRAFÍA

Acentuación

1. Escucha y señala lo que oyes. 15

1. a) Llevo gafas ☐
   b) Llevó gafas ☐
2. a) Como mucho ☐
   b) Comió mucho ☐
3. a) ¿Abro la puerta? ☐
   b) ¿Abrió la puerta? ☐
4. a) ¿Hablo más alto? ☐
   b) ¿Habló más alto? ☐
5. a) Entro a las ocho. ☐
   b) Entró a las ocho. ☐
6. a) Trabajo por la mañana. ☐
   b) Trabajó por la mañana. ☐
7. a) Estudio Geografía. ☐
   b) Estudió Geografía. ☐

2. Escucha otra vez y repite. 15

*Hablar del tiempo.
Meses y estaciones del año.*

c. ¿Qué tiempo hace hoy?

1. Relaciona las siguientes expresiones con las fotos.

1. hace frío — e
2. hace calor — ☐
3. hace viento — ☐
4. está nublado — ☐
5. está lloviendo — ☐
6. hay nieve — ☐

2. Contesta las siguientes preguntas.

1. ¿Qué tiempo hace hoy?
2. ¿Qué tiempo te gusta más?
   Me gusta cuando…

3. Completa el siguiente calendario con el tiempo que suele hacer en tu ciudad en los distintos meses del año.

enero	_____	julio	_____
febrero	_____	agosto	_____
marzo	_____	septiembre	_____
abril	_____	octubre	_____
mayo	_____	noviembre	_____
junio	_____	diciembre	_____

HABLAR

4. Pregunta a tu compañero/a.

1. ¿Cuándo es tu cumpleaños?
   Mi cumpleaños es el…
2. ¿Cuándo es el cumpleaños de tu madre?
3. ¿Cuándo es el cumpleaños de tu padre?
4. ¿Cuándo es el cumpleaños de tu mejor amigo?

5. Completa el texto con las palabras del recuadro.

> veces – mucho – hace (2) – primavera
> altas – enero – noviembre – julio

En Toledo, durante los meses de invierno (diciembre, (1)_____ y febrero) (2)_____ mucho frío y algunas (3)_____ nieva. Durante la (4)_____ (marzo, abril y mayo), suben las temperaturas y empieza a hacer buen tiempo. En verano (junio, (5)_____ y agosto), hace (6)_____ calor. Todos los días hace mucho sol y las temperaturas son muy (7)_____ . En otoño (septiembre, octubre y (8)_____), los días son más cortos, el cielo está nublado y a veces llueve y (9)_____ viento.

6. Escucha y comprueba. 16

7. Escribe un párrafo sobre el tiempo en tu país.

ESCUCHAR

8. Escucha el informe meteorológico y completa la tabla. 17

	Brasil	Caribe	México
Tiempo			
Temperatura			

LEER

9. Lee el texto y contesta a las preguntas.

¿En qué festividades:
1. reciben regalos los niños?
2. las celebraciones duran dos semanas?
3. se encienden velas?
4. se utilizan trajes regionales?
5. se baila en las calles?
6. se representa la muerte de Jesucristo?

VEN A DISFRUTAR DE TUS VACACIONES EN MÉXICO Y PARTICIPA CON NOSOTROS EN NUESTRAS FIESTAS TRADICIONALES

CARNAVAL: Los festejos de Carnaval se celebran en febrero. Empiezan en viernes y terminan el martes de la semana siguiente. Durante estos días la gente baila en las calles, en los hoteles y en las casas de la ciudad, en un ambiente muy alegre. Las mujeres se visten con hermosos trajes regionales y bailan sus danzas tradicionales.

SEMANA SANTA: La Semana Santa se celebra en marzo o en abril. Los habitantes de los pueblos hacen procesiones, llevan velas y ofrecen flores. También se realizan representaciones de los principales hechos de la pasión y muerte de Jesucristo.

DÍA DE LOS MUERTOS: El 1 de noviembre pueblos enteros van a las tumbas de sus muertos, llevándoles dulces, comida y flores. El espectáculo es impresionante por la noche cuando se encienden las velas en los cementerios.

FIESTAS DE NAVIDAD Y AÑO NUEVO: Estas fiestas empiezan el 24 de diciembre y terminan el 6 de enero, cuando los tres Reyes Magos dejan juguetes y golosinas en los zapatos de los niños.

Autoevaluación

1. ¿Dónde se puede/n encontrar…
 1. sellos? *en el estanco.*
 2. revistas? _____
 3. aspirinas? _____
 4. carne y pescado? _____
 5. un cartero? _____
 6. un policía? _____

2. ¿Verdadero o falso?

 1. En el desierto llueve mucho. F
 2. Cuando hace calor no llevo abrigo. ☐
 3. Siempre nieva en verano. ☐
 4. En otoño caen las hojas de los árboles. ☐
 5. Cuando hace mucho viento es difícil abrir el paraguas. ☐
 6. Cuando llueve está nublado. ☐

3. Ordena los párrafos de la postal que Carolina escribe a Rosa.

Rosa García Iglesias
C. Príncipe, 15 - 1º izda.
28080 Madrid

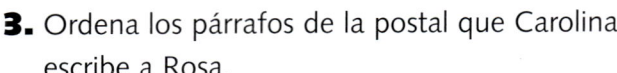

Querida Rosa:

a) Después ellos fueron a la plaza Mayor a tomar un aperitivo y yo me fui de compras con Ana, mi compañera de piso.
b) Segovia es una ciudad preciosa. Ayer estuve allí de excursión con unos amigos.
c) Al final del día, Ana y yo hicimos unas fotos del acueducto. El tiempo se pasó muy rápido, pero fueron unas horas inolvidables.
d) Por la mañana visitamos la catedral y el alcázar.
e) Por la tarde, todos bajamos al río. Dimos un paseo muy agradable.

¡Hasta pronto!
Carolina

4. Completa el siguiente texto con el pretérito indefinido de los verbos.

Ayer me (levantar) (1) **levanté** a las 6.30 de la mañana. Mi marido y yo (desayunar) (2)_____ juntos y después él se (3)_____ (ir) a trabajar en tren y yo me (4)_____ (ir) en coche. Mis hijos (5)_____ (estar) en el colegio hasta las 3. Luego, todos (6)_____ (comer) juntos. Por la tarde, mi marido (7)_____ (preparar) la cena mientras yo (8)_____ (ayudar) a mi hijo pequeño con los deberes. A las 11.30 nos (9)_____ (ir) todos a dormir.

5. Escucha a Sara, Lucía y Carlos hablando de sus últimas vacaciones y completa la tabla.

	Sara	Lucía	Carlos
1. ¿Dónde estuvieron?			
2. ¿Qué transporte utilizaron?			
3. ¿Con quién estuvieron?			
4. ¿Cuánto tiempo estuvieron?			

😊 😐 ☹ *Soy capaz de…*

☐ ☐ ☐ Preguntar e indicar cómo se va a un lugar.
☐ ☐ ☐ Hablar del pasado.
☐ ☐ ☐ Hablar del tiempo.

De acá y de allá

DE VACACIONES

1. Con tus compañeros/as elabora una lista de ciudades y monumentos españoles que conozcáis.

2. Lee y escucha. 19

VACACIONES EN ESPAÑA

Hay tantas cosas que ver en España que es difícil seleccionar las más interesantes. Si empezamos por el Noroeste, podemos visitar Galicia y allí pararnos a ver Santiago de Compostela y su catedral. Siguiendo por la costa cantábrica, el viajero descubre paisajes inolvidables de praderas suaves y pequeñas playas entre acantilados. Desde el País Vasco nos dirigimos a Cataluña, que mira al Mediterráneo. La ciudad catalana más importante es Barcelona, puerto de mar y punto de partida y llegada de barcos de todo el mundo. Podemos seguir nuestro viaje por la costa mediterránea para disfrutar de las ciudades y playas que llegan hasta Almería y Málaga, en Andalucía. También la comunidad andaluza merece una atención especial por los restos de cultura árabe que se pueden ver en Córdoba, Sevilla y Granada, especialmente. Desde Córdoba podemos ir a Madrid, atravesando la Mancha, la tierra de Don Quijote, el héroe de Cervantes. Aquí acaba nuestro viaje por esta vez, pero aún nos quedan por ver muchos otros paisajes y ciudades.

3. Señala verdadero (V) o falso (F).

1. La catedral de Santiago está en Galicia. ☐
2. Barcelona está en la costa cantábrica. ☐
3. En Córdoba hay restos árabes. ☐
4. Almería no tiene playa. ☐
5. La Mancha está al sur de Madrid. ☐

4. Señala en el mapa el recorrido del viaje propuesto en el texto.

*Recursos para comprar.
Pronombres de objeto directo.*

A. ¿Cuánto cuestan estos zapatos?

1. Comenta con tus compañeros y compañeras.

¿Te gusta ir de compras?
¿Dónde compras, en tiendas pequeñas o en grandes almacenes?

2. Celia y Álvaro van de compras. Completa el diálogo con las palabras del recuadro.

> ¿cuánto cuestan – No están mal
> Gracias – preciosos

CHICA: Mira estos zapatos, Álvaro, son (1)_____ .
CHICO: (2)_____ , pero a mí me gustan más aquellos marrones.
CHICA: Oiga, ¿(3)_____ estos zapatos negros?
DEPENDIENTE: 90 euros.
CHICA: ¿Y aquellos marrones?
DEPENDIENTE: 115 euros.
CHICA: ¿115 euros? (4)_____ , tengo que pensarlo.

3. Escucha el resto de la conversación. ¿Qué otras cosas miran Celia y Álvaro? ¿Lo compran o no? **20**

¿Qué miran?	¿Cuánto cuesta?	¿Lo compran?

4. Ordena la conversación siguiente:

DEPENDIENTE:	180 euros.	☐
CLIENTE:	¿Puedo probármelas?	☐
DEPENDIENTE:	Buenos días, ¿puedo ayudarla?	1
CLIENTE:	Me gustan, me las llevo.	☐
DEPENDIENTE:	Sí, éstas están rebajadas, cuestan 120 euros.	☐
CLIENTE:	Sí, ¿cuánto cuestan estas gafas de sol?	☐
DEPENDIENTE:	¿Cómo paga, con tarjeta o en efectivo?	☐
CLIENTE:	¿No tiene otras más baratas?	☐
DEPENDIENTE:	Sí, claro.	☐
CLIENTE:	Con tarjeta.	☐

5. Escucha y comprueba. **21**

HABLAR

6. En parejas. Practica la conversación anterior. *A* es el vendedor y *B* es el cliente. Podéis comprar un bolso, unos vaqueros, un anillo...

 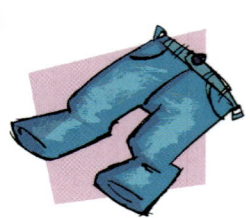 

estos zapatos
aquellos zapatos
esos zapatos

GRAMÁTICA

Demostrativos (adjetivos y pronombres)			
Singular		Plural	
Masculino	Femenino	Masculino	Femenino
este	esta	estos	estas
ese	esa	esos	esas
aquel	aquella	aquellos	aquellas

Pronombres demostrativos

esto   eso   aquello

7. Subraya el demostrativo adecuado.

1. ¿Te gustan *estos / estas* gafas de sol?
2. ¿Cuánto cuesta *este / esto* anillo?
3. ¿De quién es *esta / esto*?
4. ¿De quién es *esta / este* cartera?
5. Luis, trae *aquel / aquello* bolso.
6. ¿Cuánto cuestan *estos / esto* vaqueros?
7. ¿Qué es *aquellos / aquello*?
8. Dame *esa / ese* caja de ahí.
9. *Eso / esos* no me gusta.

Pronombres de objeto directo

Me gusta **este jersey**, ¿puedo probárme**lo**?
Me gusta **esta camisa**, ¿puedo probárme**la**?
Me gustan **estos pantalones**, ¿puedo probárme**los**?
Me gustan **estas gafas** de sol, ¿puedo probárme**las**?

8. Completa las frases con los pronombres *lo, la, los, las*.

1. Me gusta mucho este jersey, me *lo* llevo.
2. ¿Sabes dónde están mis gafas?, no _____ veo.
3. A. ¿Quién es ése?
   B. No lo sé, no _____ conozco.
   A. ¿Y aquella morena?
   B. Tampoco _____ conozco.
4. A. Y tus amigos Pepa y Jaime, ¿qué tal están?
   B. No sé, hace tiempo que no _____ veo.
5. A. ¿Te quedan bien los vaqueros?
   B. Sí, me _____ llevo.
6. A. ¿Conoces a mis padres?
   B. Sí, _____ vi en tu boda.

¿Qué es esto?
Es un regalo para ti.

> *Describir la ropa.*

B. Mi novio lleva corbata

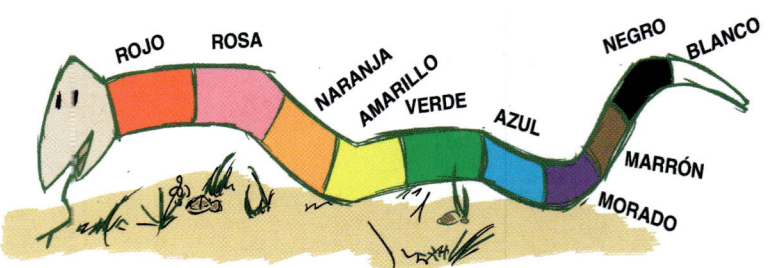

1. Responde.

a) ¿De qué color llevas hoy la camiseta/camisa?

b) ¿De qué color son los autobuses en tu ciudad?

2. Escribe el nombre debajo de cada descripción.

1. Lleva una falda negra, una camiseta morada y unas medias negras también.

   _____

2. Lleva unos pantalones vaqueros, una camisa azul y unas playeras marrones.

   _____

3. Lleva una camisa marrón, muy elegante, y una corbata amarilla. También lleva una chaqueta marrón más oscuro.

   _____

4. Lleva unos pantalones negros, una camiseta roja y un collar a juego con los pendientes.

   _____

3. Escucha y comprueba. **22**

GRAMÁTICA

Adjetivos			
Singular		Plural	
Masculino	Femenino	Masculino	Femenino
blanc**o**	blanc**a**	blanc**os**	blanc**as**
verd**e**	verd**e**	verd**es**	verd**es**
azul	azul	azul**es**	azul**es**

Los adjetivos de color terminados en **-a** (*rosa, naranja, fucsia*) no cambian:
Me gusta ese coche (de color) **naranja**.

ESCRIBIR

4. Describe la ropa de dos compañeros/as, léelo en voz alta. Los demás tienen que adivinar quiénes son.

LEER Y HABLAR

5. Responde al cuestionario.

> ### TU ROPA Y TÚ
>
> 1. ¿Cómo prefieres la ropa?
>   a) cómoda ☐
>   b) elegante ☐
>   c) moderna ☐
>
> 2. ¿Con quién vas a comprarla?
>   a) con mi madre ☐
>   b) solo/a ☐
>   c) con un amigo/a ☐
>
> 3. ¿Cuándo compras ropa?
>   a) todos los meses ☐
>   b) una vez al año ☐
>   c) cuando necesito algo ☐
>
> 4. Si vas a una entrevista de trabajo, ¿qué te pones?
>   a) algo formal: un traje, por ejemplo. ☐
>   b) algo cómodo: pantalones vaqueros. ☐
>   c) algo informal, pero elegante: una falda bonita / una americana moderna. ☐
>
> 5. Cuando vas a la fiesta de cumpleaños de un/a amigo/a, ¿qué llevas?
>   a) algo cómodo: camiseta y vaqueros. ☐
>   b) algo elegante: un vestido largo / camisa y pantalón negros. ☐
>   c) me da igual: lo primero que encuentro. ☐
>
> 6. ¿Qué color es el más elegante?
>   a) negro ☐
>   b) rojo ☐
>   c) blanco ☐
>   d) otro: _____
>
> 7. ¿Cuál es tu color preferido para la ropa?
>   _____

6. Compara tus respuestas con las de tu compañero o compañera.

VOCABULARIO

7. Relaciona los adjetivos contrarios.

1. caro   a) oscuro
2. cómodo   b) estrecho
3. claro   c) incómodo
4. ancho   d) grande
5. corto   e) sucio
6. limpio   f) antiguo
7. moderno   g) barato
8. pequeño   h) largo

8. Escribe cinco frases utilizando estos adjetivos.

Rosa lleva una falda larga.

9. Lee las frases a tus compañeros/as.

PRONUNCIACIÓN Y ORTOGRAFÍA

> **g / j**
>
> /x/ ja, je, ji, jo, ju
>   ge, gi
>
> /g/ ga, go, gu
>   gue, gui

1. Escucha y repite.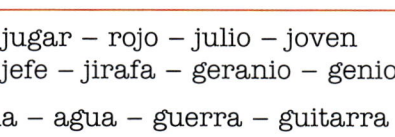

> jamón – jugar – rojo – julio – joven
> gimnasia – jefe – jirafa – geranio – genio
>
> gato – goma – agua – guerra – guitarra
> guapo – águila – Guadalajara – gota

2. Escucha y señala lo que oyes.

> gusto/justo – gabón/jabón – higo/hijo
> hago/ajo – pagar/pajar

Comparar.

C. Buenos Aires es más grande que Toledo

1. ¿Vives en un pueblo o en una ciudad? Señala los adjetivos que describen tu pueblo o ciudad.

- moderno/a ☐
- tranquilo/a ☐
- antiguo/a ☐
- pequeño/a ☐
- ruidoso/a ☐
- grande ☐
- limpio/a ☐

2. Mira las fotos de Buenos Aires y Toledo, lee las frases y señala si las afirmaciones son verdaderas (V) o falsas (F).

1. Buenos Aires es más antigua que Toledo. **F**
2. Toledo es más pequeña que Buenos Aires. ☐
3. Toledo no tiene tantos habitantes como Buenos Aires. ☐
4. Las calles de Buenos Aires son más anchas que las calles de Toledo. ☐
5. Toledo es más ruidosa que Buenos Aires. ☐
6. Buenos Aires está más contaminada que Toledo. ☐

3. Completa las frases con *más, menos, que, tan, como.*

1. Tu coche no es *tan* rápido *como* el mío.
2. Ese vestido es más caro _____ este.
3. Vuestra habitación no es tan grande _____ la nuestra.
4. El avión es _____ rápido _____ el coche.
5. La bicicleta es _____ ruidosa _____ el tren.
6. El taxi no es _____ barato _____ el metro.
7. Un traje siempre es _____ elegante _____ unos pantalones vaqueros.

GRAMÁTICA

Comparativos

más + adjetivo + que
Juan es más simpático que Pedro.

menos + adjetivo + que
Pedro es menos simpático que Juan.

tan + adjetivo + como
Juan (no) es tan alto como Pedro.

Comparativos irregulares

bueno   **mejor / mejores + que**
Esta película es **mejor que** esa.

malo   **peor / peores + que**
Esos pasteles son **peores que** estos.

grande   **mayor / mayores + que**
Yo soy **mayor que** ella.

pequeño   **menor / menores + que**
Sus hijos son **menores que** los míos.

6. Observa el dibujo y elige la opción correcta.

1. Carlos es (*mayor / menor*) que Clara.
2. Clara es (*mayor / menor*) que Carlos.
3. Clarita es (*mayor / menor*) que Carlitos.
4. Carlitos es (*mayor / menor*) que Clarita.

CARLOS 40 AÑOS
CLARA 42 AÑOS
CLARITA 5 AÑOS
CARLITOS 3 AÑOS

VOCABULARIO

7. Relaciona.

1. Música   a) rica
2. Playas   b) clásica
3. Canción   c) inteligente
4. Comida   d) alta
5. Montaña   e) caro
6. Persona   f) desiertas
7. Restaurante   g) bonita

4. Completa el diálogo con los comparativos *peor/es*, *mejor/es*, *mayor/es*.

ÉL: Voy a preparar mi maleta para el viaje, a ver… ¿qué llevo? Mira, estos zapatos están bien, ¿no?

ELLA: No, para ir a la montaña, las botas son (1)_____ _____ los zapatos.

ÉL: Tienes razón. ¿Llevo los vaqueros?

ELLA: No, para el frío son (2)_____ los pantalones de pana.

ÉL: Bueno, llevo los dos y ya está.

ELLA: ¿Por qué llevas la maleta azul?

ÉL: Pues porque es (3)_____ _____ la gris, tiene ruedas.

ELLA: Yo prefiero la gris, caben más cosas. Toma el paraguas, guárdalo.

ÉL: ¿El rojo? No, este es (4)_____ _____ el negro y más pequeño.

ELLA: Lo siento, el negro ya está en mi maleta.

5. Escucha y comprueba.

8. Escribe frases comparando.

1. El tren y el avión (*rápido / lento*).
   El avión es más rápido que el tren.
3. Nueva York y París (*grande / pequeño*).
4. La comida italiana y la comida japonesa (*rica / mala*).
5. Los coches y las motos (*seguros / inseguros*).
6. Vivir en el campo y vivir en la ciudad (*aburrido / divertido*).
7. La comida casera y la comida rápida (*buena / mala*).
8. La música clásica y la música moderna (*relajante / estresante*).
9. Isaac Newton y Albert Einstein (*inteligente*).

HABLAR

9. Compara tus frases con las de tu compañero/a.

ochenta y uno   81

Autoevaluación

1. Completa las descripciones con los adjetivos del recuadro.

> negra – negros – ~~marrones~~
> blanca – marrón

Rafael viene hoy muy elegante. Lleva unos pantalones (1) *marrones*, una camisa (2)_____ y una corbata a rayas. La chaqueta es de color (3)_____, pero más oscuro que los pantalones y los zapatos, (4)_____. También lleva una cartera (5)_____.

> moderno – negras – negros
> azules – roja – negra

Marina viene hoy a clase con ropa deportiva. Lleva unos pantalones (6)_____, una camiseta (7)_____ con un estampado muy (8)_____, unas zapatillas deportivas (9)_____, unos calcetines (10)_____ y, en el pelo, una cinta también (11)_____.

2. Relaciona.

1. Buenos días, ¿puedo ayudarle? — **f**
2. ¿Puedo probarme estos pantalones?
3. ¿Cómo paga, con tarjeta o en efectivo?
4. Álvaro, ¿te gustan estos zapatos?
5. ¿No tiene otro más barato?
6. ¿Cómo le queda la falda?

a) Bien, me la llevo.
b) No mucho, me gustan más aquellos.
c) Sí, claro, allí están los probadores.
d) Con tarjeta.
e) Sí, este sólo cuesta 30 euros.
f) Sí, ¿cuánto cuestan estas gafas?

3. Completa con los pronombres *lo, la, los, las*.

JULIA: ¿Qué llevas en esa bolsa?
CRISTINA: Los regalos de Navidad.
JULIA: ¿Puedo (1) ver*los*?
CRISTINA: Bueno, estos paquetes son para los abuelos: una corbata y un pañuelo.
JULIA: ¿Y esas cajas blancas?
CRISTINA: Son para mamá y papá.
JULIA: ¿Puedo (2) abrir____?
CRISTINA: No, es una sorpresa.
JULIA: ¿Y ese coche rojo? ¿Es para Raúl?
CRISTINA: Sí, tengo que (3) envolver____ primero. ¿Tienes papel de regalo?
JULIA: Sí, (4)____ tengo en el primer cajón de la mesa. ¿Para quién es esta raqueta? ¿Para mí?
CRISTINA: No, es para Raúl, (5)____ voy a envolver también.
JULIA: ¿Y para mí?
CRISTINA: Es este paquete, ¿(6)____ quieres ver ahora? ¿No prefieres esperar?
JULIA: No, ahora, (7) ábre____, por favor.
CRISTINA: ¡Un cinturón negro! Me encanta. ¿Puedo (8) ponérme____ hoy?

4. Selecciona la opción correcta.

1. A. ¿Qué es *esto* / *este*?
   B. Es un cuaderno, ¿te gusta?
2. A. ¿Quién es *eso* / *ese* chico?
   B. Es mi hermano *mayor* / *más grande*.
3. A. ¡Mira! Están robando una moto del garaje.
   B. ¿Cuál?
   A. *Esta* / *Aquella* moto del fondo, la azul.
4. A. ¿Cuánto valen *estas* / *aquellas* bolsas de caramelos, las de allí?
   B. 3 euros, pero *estas* / *esas* otras de aquí son *más* / *menos* baratas, valen 1,50.

5. Escribe el adjetivo contrario.

1. Antiguo — *moderno*
2. Sucio — _____
3. Tranquilo — _____
4. Claro — _____
5. Barato — _____
6. Largo — _____

Soy capaz de…

☐ ☐ ☐ *Hacer algunas compras.*
☐ ☐ ☐ *Describir la ropa.*
☐ ☐ ☐ *Hacer comparaciones.*

De acá y de allá

PINTURA ESPAÑOLA E HISPANOAMERICANA

1. ¿Conoces algún cuadro o pintor español o hispanoamericano?

2. Mira los cuadros y relaciona los títulos con sus autores.

1. *Guernica.* ___ 2. *Murales de la Alameda.* ___
3. *La jungla.* ___ 4. *Muchacha de espaldas.* ___

a) Wifredo Lam (1902-1982) b) Pablo Picasso (1881-1973)
c) Diego Rivera (1886-1957) d) Salvador Dalí (1904-1989)

LEER

3. Lee el texto.

BREVE HISTORIA DEL *GUERNICA* DE PICASSO

En 1937, en plena Guerra Civil española, el gobierno de la República española encargó a Pablo Picasso un cuadro para exponerlo en el pabellón de España de la Exposición Universal de París. En esos días se produjo un ataque de la aviación alemana contra Guernica, un pueblo de Euskadi, en el norte de España.

Picasso, en recuerdo de ese bombardeo, pintó su cuadro, en el que reflejó el dolor y el sufrimiento de la gente en la guerra.

Durante la II Guerra Mundial el cuadro fue trasladado al Museo de Arte Moderno de Nueva York (MOMA).

El cuadro está en Madrid desde 1981, cuando España era ya una democracia, como soñaba Picasso.

Actualmente se expone en el Museo Nacional de Arte Contemporáneo Reina Sofía, de la capital española, y cada año lo ven millones de personas.

4. ¿Verdadero (V) o falso (F)?

1. El gobierno español encargó un cuadro a Picasso. **V**
2. En París se celebró una Exposición Universal. ☐
3. En París hubo un bombardeo. ☐
4. El cuadro estuvo en Nueva York más de 30 años. ☐
5. Ahora el cuadro está en Madrid. ☐

5. Comenta con tus compañeros.

¿Qué cuadro te gusta más?
¿Cuál te gusta menos?
¿Te gusta la pintura?
¿Vas a los museos con frecuencia?

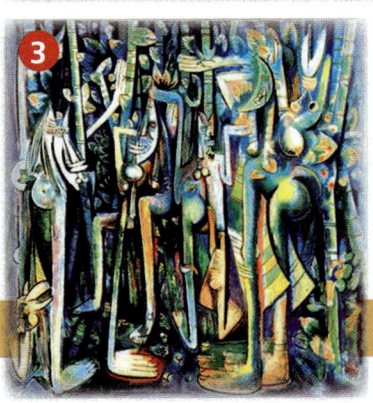

Hablar de enfermedades.
Verbo doler.

A. La salud

1. ¿Vas mucho al médico? ¿Cuándo? ¿En verano, en invierno, en primavera...?

2. Mira el dibujo, escucha y repite. 26

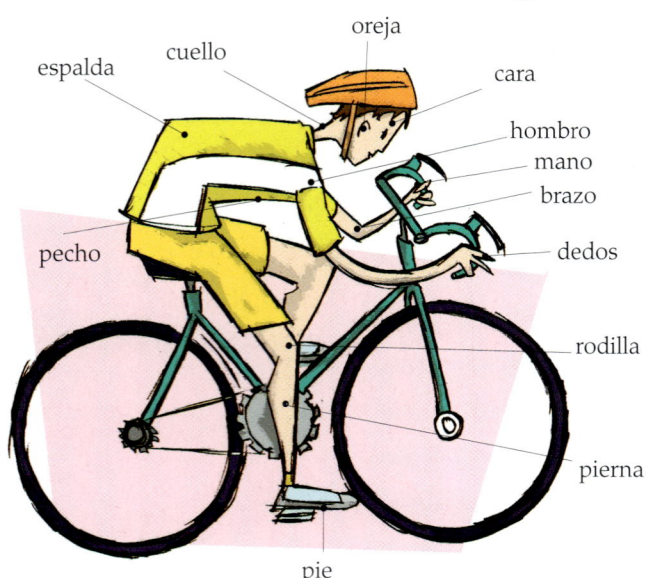

espalda, cuello, oreja, cara, hombro, mano, brazo, dedos, pecho, rodilla, pierna, pie

4. Lee y escucha los siguientes diálogos y contesta las preguntas. 28

1.
SARA: ¡Hola, Ángel!, ¿qué tal estás?
ÁNGEL: No muy bien.
SARA: ¿Qué te pasa?
ÁNGEL: Tengo una gripe muy fuerte.
SARA: ¿Y qué tomas cuando estás así?
ÁNGEL: De momento, nada.
SARA: ¿Por qué no tomas una aspirina y un vaso de leche con miel y te vas a la cama?
ÁNGEL: Sí, creo que es mejor.

2.
RAÚL: ¡Qué mala cara tienes! ¿Qué te pasa?
LUISA: Me duele muchísimo el estómago.
RAÚL: ¿Por qué no vas al médico?
LUISA: Sí, voy a ir mañana.
RAÚL: Mira, tómate un té y acuéstate sin cenar.
LUISA: Sí, creo que es lo mejor. Mañana voy al médico.

1. ¿Qué le pasa a Ángel?
2. ¿Qué le aconseja Sara?
3. ¿Qué le pasa a Luisa?
4. ¿Qué le aconseja Raúl?

ESCUCHAR

3. Escucha y relaciona cada personaje con su problema de salud. 27

1. A Rosa
2. A Daniel — le duele
3. A Ramón
4. A Julia — le duelen
5. A Andrés
6. Ana — tiene
7. A Ricardo

a) los oídos
b) el estómago
c) la espalda
d) la cabeza
e) la garganta
f) las muelas
g) fiebre

Ana — Ramón — Julia

Andrés — Rosa — Ricardo — Daniel

GRAMÁTICA

Verbo Doler

(A mí)	me		
(A ti)	te		
(A él/ella/Vd.)	le	**duele**	la cabeza
(A nosotros/as)	nos	**duelen**	los oídos
(A vosotros/as)	os		
(A ellos/ellas/Vds.)	les		

5. Completa con el pronombre y la forma adecuada del verbo *doler*.

1. A mi hermano *le duelen* las piernas.
2. A mí _____ las muelas.
3. Carmen y Chus son peluqueras y _____ la espalda.
4. ¿A ti _____ algo?
5. ¡No hagáis tanto ruido! Al abuelo y a mí _____ la cabeza.
6. ¿A usted no _____ el estómago con esa comida tan fuerte?

6. Relaciona estos problemas de salud con su remedio.

1. dolor de cabeza — a
2. dolor de garganta ☐
3. dolor de espalda ☐
4. dolor de muelas ☐
5. fiebre ☐
6. dolor de oídos ☐

a) tomar una aspirina.
b) ir a un gimnasio.
c) ir al médico.
d) ir al dentista.
e) tomar miel con limón.
f) acostarse y descansar.

ESCUCHAR

7. Escucha y completa las siguientes conversaciones. 29

a) El paciente n.º 1 tiene *la gripe*.
   Consejo del médico: tomar _____ y _____ .
b) Al paciente n.º 2 le duele _____ .
   Consejo del médico: tomar _____ y _____ .
c) Al paciente n.º 3 le duele _____ .
   Consejo del médico: no tomar _____ ni _____ , comer _____ y _____ y tomar _____ .

HABLAR

8. En parejas, practica diálogos como en el ejemplo, dando consejos para los problemas de salud de tu compañero (mira la actividad 6).

— ¿Qué te pasa?
— Me duele la cabeza.
— ¿Por qué no te tomas una aspirina?

10 A

Hábitos en el pasado.

B. Antes salíamos con los amigos

1. "Antes la gente era más feliz que ahora". ¿Estás de acuerdo?

No estoy de acuerdo porque antes no había televisión.

2. Lee y escucha el siguiente texto.

Elena y Emilio ya son padres. Su vida cambió cuando, de repente, se encontraron con... dos bebés en los brazos.

ELENA: Antes de ser padres teníamos una vida social muy activa: viajábamos, íbamos al cine, salíamos con los amigos, teníamos mucho tiempo libre. Emilio jugaba al hockey, yo estudiaba alemán...

EMILIO: Ahora todo es distinto. Dedicamos todo nuestro tiempo a Álvaro y Adrián, que son maravillosos.

3. ¿Verdadero (V) o falso (F)?

1. Elena y Emilio tienen un bebé. ☐
2. Antes viajaban mucho. ☐
3. Emilio no practicaba deportes. ☐
4. Ahora están muy ocupados con sus hijos. ☐

GRAMÁTICA

Pretérito imperfecto de los verbos regulares

	Viajar	Tener	Salir
yo	viaja**ba**	ten**ía**	sal**ía**
tú	viaja**bas**	ten**ías**	sal**ías**
él/ella/Vd.	viaja**ba**	ten**ía**	sal**ía**
nosotros/as	viajá**bamos**	ten**íamos**	sal**íamos**
vosotros/as	viaja**bais**	ten**íais**	sal**íais**
ellos/ellas/Vds.	viaja**ban**	ten**ían**	sal**ían**

4. Elige la forma correcta del verbo en las siguientes frases:

1. Antes Elena y Emilio no *tenían* / *tienen* hijos.
2. Cuando no tenían hijos, Elena y Emilio *viajan* / *viajaban* por todo el mundo.
3. Ahora Elena no *estudiaba* / *estudia* alemán.
4. Emilio ya no *juega* / *jugaba* al hockey.
5. Antes de ser padres, *salían* / *salen* los fines de semana con sus amigos.

Pretérito imperfecto de los verbos irregulares

	Ir	Ser	Ver
yo	iba	era	veía
tú	ibas	eras	veías
él/ella/Vd.	iba	era	veía
nosotros/as	íbamos	éramos	veíamos
vosotros/as	ibais	erais	veíais
ellos/ellas/Vds.	iban	eran	veían

5. Completa el siguiente texto sobre la vida de Emilio.

> Yo antes (1) *era* jugador de un equipo de hockey. (2)_____ (entrenar) tres días a la semana. Los domingos mis compañeros y yo (3)_____ (jugar) un partido de liga. Cada dos semanas nos (4)_____ (ir) en autocar al campo del equipo contrario. A veces, Elena me (5)_____ (acompañar) y después de los partidos (6)_____ (ir) a cenar todos juntos. Todo (7)_____ (ser) estupendo. ¡Pero ahora es más divertido porque somos cuatro!

HABLAR

6. ¿Cómo era tu vida cuando tenías 10 o 12 años? En parejas, pregunta y responde a tu compañero/a.

1. ¿Cómo era tu colegio?
2. ¿A qué hora entrabas y a qué hora salías?
3. ¿Qué hacías cuando salías del colegio?
4. ¿Comías en el colegio o en tu casa?
5. ¿Qué hacías los domingos por la mañana?, ¿y por la tarde?
6. ¿Cómo era tu profesor o profesora favorito?
7. ¿Qué hacías durante las vacaciones de verano?

7. ¡A Federico le tocó la lotería! Comenta con tu compañero qué cosas son ahora diferentes en su vida. Utiliza los verbos del recuadro.

> tener – desayunar – regalar
> navegar – comer – ~~vivir~~

Antes no vivía en un chalé.

ESCUCHAR

8. Escucha la historia de Martina y elige la respuesta correcta.

1. Martina tiene:
   a) casi cien años.
   b) menos de ochenta años.

2. Cuando era pequeña, vivía:
   a) con sus padres.
   b) con sus hermanos y su madre.

3. Trabajaba en el campo:
   a) cuando era una niña.
   b) después de terminar sus estudios.

4. Trabajaba:
   a) ocho horas diarias.
   b) doce horas diarias.

5. A los diecinueve años tenía:
   a) dos hijos.
   b) un hijo.

6. Los sábados y domingos:
   a) compraba en el mercadillo.
   b) trabajaba en el mercadillo.

> Hablar de planes e intenciones.
> Voy a + *infinitivo*.

C. Voy a trabajar en un hotel

1. Lee este correo.

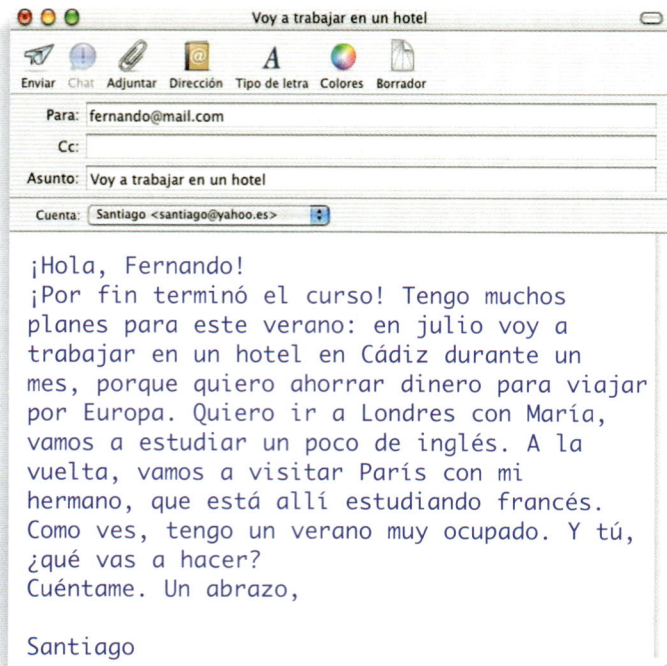

¡Hola, Fernando!
¡Por fin terminó el curso! Tengo muchos planes para este verano: en julio voy a trabajar en un hotel en Cádiz durante un mes, porque quiero ahorrar dinero para viajar por Europa. Quiero ir a Londres con María, vamos a estudiar un poco de inglés. A la vuelta, vamos a visitar París con mi hermano, que está allí estudiando francés. Como ves, tengo un verano muy ocupado. Y tú, ¿qué vas a hacer?
Cuéntame. Un abrazo,

Santiago

2. Relaciona los planes de Santiago con las siguientes situaciones, como en el ejemplo.

Santiago va a trabajar en un hotel porque quiere ahorrar dinero.

1. Santiago va a trabajar en un hotel.   c
2. Va a viajar por Europa.
3. Él y María van a ir a Londres.
4. Van a visitar París.
5. Su hermano está en París.

a) quiere aprender francés.
b) quieren mejorar su inglés.
c) quiere ahorrar dinero.
d) tiene un mes de vacaciones.
e) quiere estar unos días con su hermano.

3. ¿Qué van a hacer? Utiliza los verbos del recuadro.

> ver una obra de teatro – comprar un coche
> besarse – tener un hijo – casarse – ~~bañarse~~

Va a bañarse.

HABLAR

4. En parejas, di lo que vas a hacer este fin de semana. Utiliza las siguientes ideas:

a) levantarme tarde
b) limpiar la casa
c) hacer deporte
d) salir a cenar
e) leer el periódico
f) reunirme con amigos
g) ver la televisión
h) ir a pasear

5. ¿Qué va a hacer Federico con el dinero que ganó en la lotería? Relaciona las preguntas con las respuestas.

1. ¡Felicidades, Federico! ¿Cómo te sientes?
2. ¿Vas a organizar una fiesta?
3. ¿Qué es lo primero que te vas a comprar?
4. ¿Te vas a comprar un barco?
5. ¿Te vas a ir de vacaciones?
6. ¿Qué le vas a regalar a tu mujer?

a) No, no sé navegar.
b) Sí, voy a dar una vuelta alrededor del mundo.
c) Muchas joyas.
d) ¡De maravilla! ¡Como nunca!
e) Sí, con todos mis amigos.
f) Una casa muy grande en el campo.

ESCRIBIR

6. Imagina que eres periodista. Escribe una pequeña noticia sobre los planes de Federico.

Federico tiene grandes planes para el futuro.
Dice que va a...
Dice que no va a...

PRONUNCIACIÓN Y ORTOGRAFÍA

Reglas de acentuación

1. Escucha las palabras siguientes y escríbelas en la columna correspondiente según el acento. **32**

> alemán – café – teléfono – cantante
> árbol – canción – examen – estudiar
> ordenador – ventana – periódico
> móvil – pintura – música

Esdrújulas	Llanas	Agudas
tel**é**fono	can**tan**te	ale**mán**
___	___	___
___	___	___
___	___	___

Reglas de acentuación

a) Las palabras **agudas** llevan tilde cuando terminan en vocal, *n* o *s*.

b) Las palabras **llanas** llevan tilde cuando terminan en consonante diferente de *n* o *s*.

c) Las palabras **esdrújulas** llevan tilde siempre.

2. Escucha y escribe las tildes que faltan. **33**

1. Andres me llamo por telefono para saludarme.
2. Barbara trabaja en una empresa de informatica en Mexico.
3. Yo estudie decoracion en Milan.
4. Antes Raul vivia cerca de aqui, pero ahora esta viviendo en Valencia.
5. Aqui hace mas calor que alli.
6. Ella es mas guapa que el.
7. Los telefonos moviles son muy comodos.
8. Esta casa es mas centrica que tu piso.

Autoevaluación

1. Relaciona.

1. Estos zapatos son nuevos, por eso — c
2. Juan lleva dos pendientes
3. Los futbolistas cuidan especialmente
4. Uso guantes
5. Ana lleva varios anillos
6. Cuando cojo mucho peso

a) me duelen los brazos
b) sus piernas
c) me duelen los pies
d) porque tengo frío en las manos
e) en cada oreja
f) en los dedos

2. Completa el texto con el pretérito imperfecto de los verbos entre paréntesis.

Marisa y Alfredo se casaron la semana pasada. Ahora viven juntos en Madrid, pero antes de conocerse, cuando ellos (1) *eran* (ser) jóvenes, los dos (2) _____ (vivir) en distintas ciudades. Marisa (3) _____ (trabajar) con un grupo de teatro infantil y (4) _____ (estudiar) en la universidad. Alfredo (5) _____ (hacer) películas con un grupo de aficionados y (6) _____ (escribir) magníficos guiones. Un día, cuando los dos (7) _____ (ir) a un festival de cine, se conocieron y, desde entonces, ya no se separan nunca.

3. Subraya el verbo más adecuado.

1. Ayer *fui / iba* a ver a Jacinto.
2. Cuando Luis *tenía / tuvo* diez años, *jugaba / jugó* al fútbol todos los sábados.
3. Antes me *gustaba / gustó* la música rock, pero ahora me *gustaba / gusta* la música romántica.
4. Elena y Emilio antes no *tuvieron / tenían* hijos y ahora tienen dos.
5. Elena y Emilio *iban / fueron* a París el año 2002.
6. Mi marido *jugó / jugaba* al baloncesto cuando *era / fue* joven.
7. Yo no fumo, pero antes *fumé / fumaba* mucho.

4. Escribe las preguntas sobre planes para el próximo fin de semana.

1. ¿Tú / estudiar?
   ¿Vas a estudiar?
2. ¿Vosotros / ir al cine?
   _____
3. ¿Lorenzo / escuchar música?
   _____
4. ¿Tu novio / comprar ropa?
   _____
5. ¿Tú / navegar por Internet?
   _____
6. ¿Vosotros / hacer los ejercicios de español?
   _____
7. ¿Ellos / ir al fútbol?
   _____

5. Escucha al grupo de música *Los Escorpiones* hablando con su *manager* y contesta las preguntas. **34**

1. ¿Cuándo va a estar el nuevo disco de *Los Escorpiones* en el mercado?
2. ¿Cuándo van a empezar la gira?
3. ¿Van a hacer su propia página web?
4. ¿Qué van a hacer en septiembre?
5. ¿Quién va a cantar con ellos en el concierto?

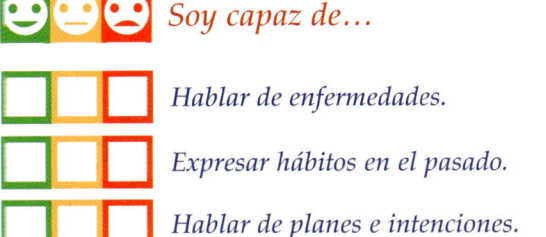

Soy capaz de…

Hablar de enfermedades.
Expresar hábitos en el pasado.
Hablar de planes e intenciones.

De acá y de allá

LOS INCAS, PUEBLO DEL SOL

A. En el siglo xv, los incas vivían en la montaña, en el corazón de los Andes. Hablaban una lengua llamada quechua y tenían un gran imperio.

B. Cuzco, la capital del imperio, se levantaba a 3.200 m de altitud. Estaba rodeada de montañas y protegida por una fortaleza. Para los incas, Cuzco era el centro del mundo.

C. Los incas creían en dioses como el Sol, la Luna y el Trueno. Pero también adoraban montañas, lagos o plantas.

D. Las casas eran de piedra, con tejados de hierba seca y una sola habitación. Dentro, los incas comían en cuclillas. Por la noche dormían envueltos en mantas.

E. Los incas construyeron una importante red de caminos empedrados. En las laderas abruptas tallaban escalones en la roca. Y para cruzar los precipicios, hacían puentes colgantes con cuerdas vegetales.

F. Se calcula que en el imperio vivían ocho millones de personas. Los campesinos cultivaban la tierra y cuidaban rebaños de llamas. Los artesanos fabricaban objetos de cerámica y tejidos.

Reportero Doc n.º 41, Bayard Revistas

10 D

1. Relaciona los siguientes títulos con los párrafos A-F.

El imperio inca.	A
Un pueblo religioso.	☐
La ciudad imperial.	☐
Casas sencillas.	☐
Constructores de carreteras hábiles.	☐
Campesinos y artesanos.	☐

2. Corrige las siguientes afirmaciones.

1. Los incas hablaban español.
   Los incas hablaban quechua.
2. Los campesinos vivían del comercio.
3. Los incas adoraban a un solo dios.
4. Vivían en grandes casas de madera.
5. En la época de los incas, no había vías de comunicación.
6. Cuzco está al nivel del mar.

Actividades en pareja
Estudiante A

1. GENTE FAMOSA (U. 1)

A. Pregunta a B la información sobre los números 1, 3, 5, 7, 9.

¿Cómo se llama el número 1? ¿De dónde es? ¿A qué se dedica?

Ricky Martin.
Puertorriqueño.
Cantante.

Nelson Mandela.
Surafricano.
Presidente.

Sara Baras.
Española.
Bailaora.

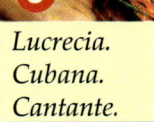

Lucrecia.
Cubana.
Cantante.

B. Responde a B la información sobre los números 2, 4, 6 y 8.

Se llama Ricky Martin. Es puertorriqueño. Es cantante.

2. DATOS PERSONALES (U. 1)

A. Pregunta a B para completar la ficha.

```
Nombre _____
Apellido _____
Domicilio _____
Ciudad _____
Teléfono _____
```

B. Lee esta información y responde a las preguntas de B.

Me llamo Julia Rodríguez y vivo en Valencia, en la calle del Mar, 12. Mi número de teléfono es el 693 568 220

3. ¿DÓNDE ESTÁN LAS LLAVES? (U. 2)

A. Pregunta a B dónde están los objetos de los recuadros.

¿Dónde están las gafas?

 gafas
 zapatillas deportivas
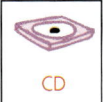 CD
 bolígrafo
 cuaderno
 agenda

B. Responde a B dónde están sus objetos.

El móvil está al lado del ordenador.

4. GUSTOS (U. 5)

A. Pregunta a B sobre sus gustos.

¿Te gusta el chocolate?
¿Te gustan los deportes?

	Mucho	Bastante	No mucho	Nada
El chocolate				
Tomar el sol				
Los deportes				
Los gatos				
Los coches				
Ver la tele				
Leer				
La fruta				

B. Responde a B las preguntas sobre tus gustos.

Sí, mucho / Sí, bastante / No mucho / No, nada.

5. EN EL HOTEL (U. 4)

A. Pregunta a B la información sobre el hotel Miramar y completa el cuadro.

a) ¿En qué planta está:
  – la peluquería
  – la discoteca
  – la boutique
  – la piscina
  – el comedor para desayunar?

¿En qué planta está la peluquería?

b) Pregunta los precios de las habitaciones.
  ¿Cuánto cuesta la habitación doble/individual?

c) Pregunta el horario de las comidas.
  ¿A qué hora se puede desayunar?

HOTEL MIRAMAR

Quinta planta _____
Cuarta planta _____
Tercera planta _____
Segunda planta _____
Primera planta _____
Planta baja   **RECEPCIÓN**
Sótano   **PARKING**

PRECIOS:
Habitación individual: ____
Habitación doble: ____

COMIDAS:
Desayunos: de ____ a 11 h
Comidas: de ____ a ____ h
Cenas: de ____ a ____ h

B. Responde a las preguntas de B sobre el hotel Embajador.

HOTEL EMBAJADOR

Quinta planta   **CAFETERÍA**
Cuarta planta   **SALÓN DE BAILE**
Tercera planta **SAUNA Y GIMNASIO**
Segunda planta **RESTAURANTE**
Primera planta **SALÓN DE CONFERENCIAS**
Planta baja   **RECEPCIÓN**
Sótano   **PARKING**

PRECIOS:
Habituación individual: 100 €
Habitación doble: 145 €

COMIDAS:
Desayunos: de 7.30 a 10.30 h
Comidas: de 13 a 15 h
Cenas: de 20 a 23 h

6. ¿HAY UNA FARMACIA? (U. 8)

A. Explica a B dónde está cada establecimiento.

La farmacia está en la calle Colombia, al lado del quiosco.

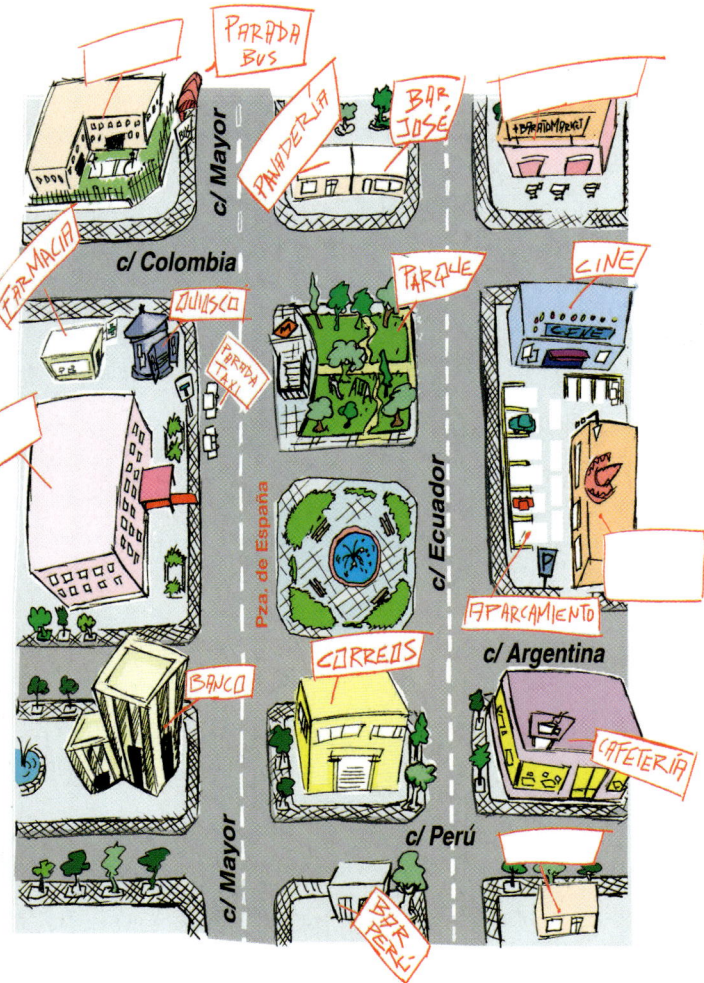

B. Escucha a B y señala dónde están los establecimientos en su plano.

7. ¿QUÉ HICISTE AYER? (U. 8)

A. Encuentra en la clase a alguien que hizo ayer estas cosas. Pregunta a varios compañeros.

¿Te levantaste antes de las 8?
¿Desayunaste café con leche?
¿Fuiste al supermercado?

1. Se levantó antes de las 8 _____
2. Desayunó café con leche _____
3. Fue al supermercado _____
4. Leyó un periódico _____
5. Comió fuera de su casa _____
6. Fue al gimnasio _____
7. Vio un partido de fútbol _____
8. Vio una película _____
9. Vio las noticias de la tele _____
10. Navegó por Internet _____
11. Habló por teléfono con sus padres _____
12. Cenó una ensalada _____
13. Se acostó antes de las once _____

8. HÁBITOS DE SALUD (U. 9)

A. Dicta y escucha el dictado de tu compañero para completar el texto sobre la salud.

Para tener buena ____ ____ _____ cuidarse.
Todos sabemos cuáles _____ ____ _____ _____
saludables: comer frutas y _____, _____ ____
_____ carne, no fumar ni beber _____,
____ _____ _____ __ días, beber mucha
_____, _____ ____ ____, _____.
Por otro lado, también es _____ ____ ____
____ con la gente: salir __ __ _____, ____
_____, sobre todo, reírse mucho.

9. TRABALENGUAS

A. Dicta estos trabalenguas a B.

a) *Si Pancha plancha con cuatro planchas, con cuatro planchas, Pancha plancha.*

b) *Pablito clavó un clavito. ¿Qué clavito clavó Pablito?*

c) *Si cien cenicientas encienden cien cirios, cien mil cenicientas encenderán cien mil cirios.*

B. Apréndelos de memoria y dilos rápidamente.

Actividades en pareja
Estudiante B

1. GENTE FAMOSA (U. 1)

A. Responde a A la información sobre los números 1, 3, 5, 7, 9.

El número 1 se llama Isabel Allende.
Es chilena. Es escritora.

1 Isabel Allende. Chilena. Escritora.

2

3 Ronaldo. Brasileño. Futbolista.

4

5 Belmonte. Español. Torero.

6

7 Gloria Estefan. Cubana. Cantante.

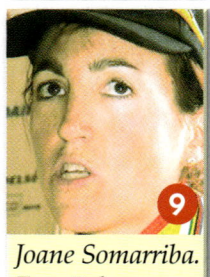
8

9 Joane Somarriba. Española. Ciclista.

B. Pregunta a A la información sobre los números 2, 4, 6 y 8.

¿Cómo se llama el número 2?

2. DATOS PERSONALES (U. 1)

A. Lee esta información y responde a las preguntas de A.

> Me llamo Ernesto Domínguez y vivo en Barcelona, en la calle Balmes, 18. Mi número de teléfono es el 933 672 895.

B. Pregunta a A para completar la ficha.

Nombre _____
Apellido _____
Domicilio _____
Ciudad _____
Teléfono _____

3. ¿DÓNDE ESTÁN LAS LLAVES? (U. 2)

A. Responde a A dónde están los objetos.

Las gafas están encima de la silla.

 móvil calcetines  diccionario  flauta  caja  llaves

B. Pregunta a A dónde están los objetos de los recuadros.

¿Dónde está el móvil?

4. GUSTOS (U. 5)

A. Responde a A.

Sí, mucho / Sí, bastante / No mucho / No, nada.

B. Pregunta a A sobre sus gustos:

¿Te gusta viajar? / ¿Te gustan los perros?

	Mucho	Bastante	No mucho	Nada
Viajar				
La música clásica				
Los perros				
Las motos				
Navegar en Internet				
Jugar al fútbol				
Andar				
Hablar				
Los niños				

5. EN EL HOTEL (U. 4)

HOTEL MIRAMAR

Quinta planta   **PISCINA**
Cuarta planta   **PELUQUERÍA**
Tercera planta   **BOUTIQUE**
Segunda planta   **COMEDOR DESAYUNOS**
Primera planta   **DISCOTECA**
Planta baja   **RECEPCIÓN**
Sótano   **PARKING**

PRECIOS:
Habitación individual: 45 €
Habitación doble: 60 €

COMIDAS:
Desayunos: de 8 a 11 h
Comidas: de 2 a 4 h
Cenas: de 8 a 11 h

A. Responde a las preguntas de A sobre el hotel Miramar.

B. Pregunta a A la información sobre el hotel Embajador y completa el cuadro.

a) ¿Dónde está…
  – el salón de baile
  – la sauna y el gimnasio
  – el restaurante
  – la cafetería
  – el salón de conferencias?

¿En qué planta está el salón de baile?

b) Pregunta los precios de las habitaciones.
  ¿Cuánto cuesta la habitación individual / doble?

c) Pregunta los horarios de las comidas.
  ¿A qué hora se puede desayunar / comer / cenar?

HOTEL EMBAJADOR

Quinta planta   _____
Cuarta planta   _____
Tercera planta   _____
Segunda planta   _____
Primera planta   _____
Planta baja   _____
Sótano   _____

PRECIOS:
Habituación individual: ____
Habitación doble: ____

COMIDAS:
Desayunos: de ____ a ____ h
Comidas: de ____ a ____ h
Cenas: de ____ a ____ h

6. ¿HAY UNA FARMACIA? (U. 8)

A. Escucha a A y señala donde están los establecimientos en el plano.

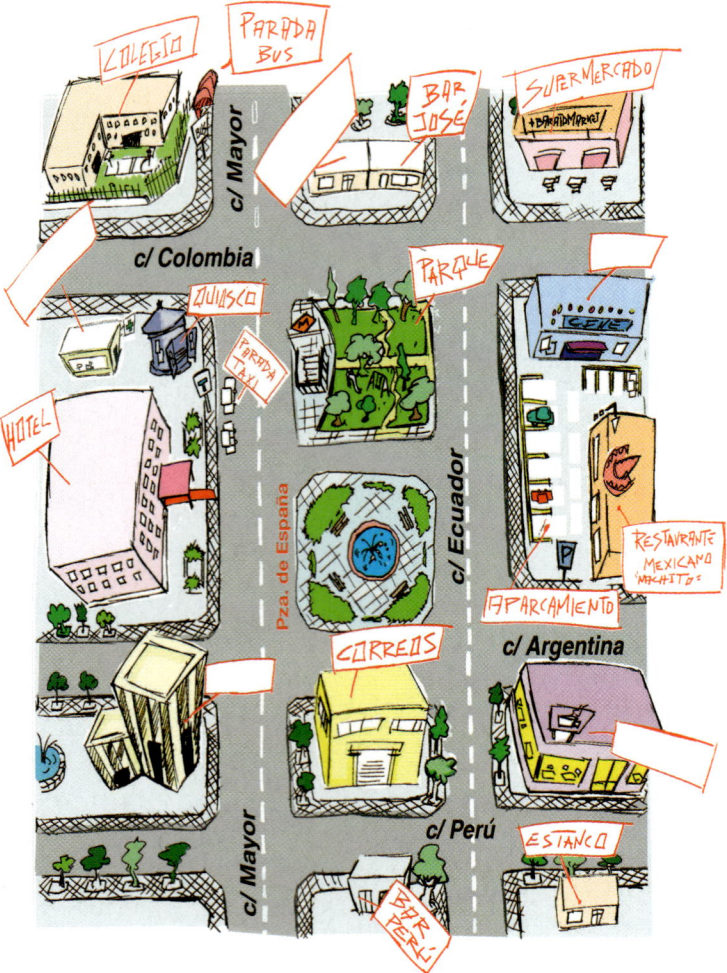

B. Explica a B dónde están los establecimientos en tu plano.

El supermercado está en la calle Colombia, enfrente del cine.

7. ¿QUÉ HICISTE AYER? (U. 8)

A. Encuentra en la clase a alguien que hizo ayer estas cosas. Pregunta a varios compañeros.

¿Te levantaste antes de las 8?
¿Desayunaste café con leche?
¿Fuiste al supermercado?

1. Se levantó antes de las 8 _____
2. Desayunó café con leche _____
3. Fue al supermercado _____
4. Leyó un periódico _____
5. Comió fuera de su casa _____
6. Fue al gimnasio _____
7. Vio un partido de fútbol _____
8. Vio una película _____
9. Vio las noticias de la tele _____
10. Navegó por Internet _____
11. Habló por teléfono con sus padres _____
12. Cenó una ensalada _____
13. Se acostó antes de las once _____

8. HÁBITOS DE SALUD (U. 9)

A. Dicta y escucha el dictado de tu compañero para completar el texto sobre salud.

_____ _____ _____ salud es necesario _____. _____ _____ _____ son los hábitos más _____: _____ _____ __ verduras, no comer mucha _____, __ _____ __ _____ alcohol, hacer ejercicio todos los _____, _____ _____ agua, dormir la siesta, etcétera. _____ _____ _____, _____ ____ importante tener buenas relaciones ____ __ _____: _____ con los amigos, hablar y, _____ _____, reírse mucho.

9. TRABALENGUAS

A. Dicta estos trabalenguas a A.

a) *Pedro Pérez Pacheco, pintor, pinta preciosos paisajes por poco precio para personas pobres.*

b) *Perejil comí, perejil cené, y de tanto perejil, me emperejilé.*

c) *En un plato plano de plata con la pata un pato aplasta la pasta.*

B. Apréndelos de memoria y dilos rápidamente.

Referencia gramatical y léxico útil

UNIDAD 1

GRAMÁTICA

1. Verbo *ser*.

Presente del verbo Ser	
yo	soy
tú	eres
él/ella/Vd.	es
nosotros/as	somos
vosotros/as	sois
ellos/ellas/Vdes.	son

▶ Usamos el verbo **ser** para identificarnos, hablar de la nacionalidad y de la profesión.

Esta es Pilar
Pilar es española
Pilar es azafata

2. Género de los nombres.

▶ Los nombres de las cosas tienen género masculino o femenino:

el libro   la ventana

▶ Los nombres de las personas y animales tienen género masculino y femenino.

el gato   la gata
el profesor   la profesora
el hombre   la mujer

▶ En el caso de los nombres de profesión:

a) Si el masculino termina en **-o**, cambia por **-a**:
   abogado   abogada

b) Si el masculino termina en consonante, añade **-a**:
   pintor   pintora

c) Si el masculino termina en **-e**, puede quedar igual o cambiar por **-a**.
   el estudiante   la estudiante
   el presidente   la presidenta

d) Si el masculino termina en **-ista**, no cambia.
   el taxista   la taxista

3. Género de los adjetivos.

▶ Los adjetivos tienen el mismo género que el nombre al que se refieren:

El profesor es simpático.   La profesora es simpática.

▶ En el caso de los adjetivos de nacionalidad:

a) Si el masculino termina en **-o**, el femenino termina en **-a**:
   brasileño   brasileña

b) Si el masculino termina en **consonante**, el femenino añade **-a**:
   alemán   alemana

c) Si el masculino termina en **-a, -e, -í**, no cambia:
   belga / belga, canadiense / canadiense, marroquí / marroquí.

4. Verbos regulares. Presente.

Tenemos tres conjugaciones (1.ª, 2.ª, 3.ª), según la terminación del infinitivo: **-ar, -er, -ir**.

Trabajar	Comer	Vivir
trabaj**o**	com**o**	viv**o**
trabaj**as**	com**es**	viv**es**
trabaj**a**	com**e**	viv**e**
trabaj**amos**	com**emos**	viv**imos**
trabaj**áis**	com**éis**	viv**ís**
trabaj**an**	com**en**	viv**en**

5. Pronombres personales sujeto.

▶ Tenemos 10 pronombres personales sujeto:

> yo, tú, él, ella, usted (Vd.), nosotros, nosotras, vosotros, vosotras, ellos, ellas, ustedes (Vdes.).

▶ Estos pronombres no se utilizan siempre, sólo cuando queremos distinguir bien entre diferentes sujetos.

¿De dónde sois (vosotros)?

Yo soy chileno y ella es peruana.

6. Tú / usted, vosotros / ustedes.

▶ Usamos **tú** y **vosotros** cuando hablamos con conocidos, amigos y personas de igual o inferior rango.

▶ Usamos **usted** y **ustedes** cuando hablamos con desconocidos, personas mayores y de mayor rango.

▶ En América Latina se usa **ustedes** en lugar de **vosotros** y en algunos países **vos** en lugar de **tú**.

LÉXICO ÚTIL

Gentilicios

> alemán/a – andaluz/a – brasileño/a
> catalán/a – estadounidense – francés/a
> inglés/a – japonés/a – marroquí
> mexicano/a

Profesiones

> ama de casa – actriz – camarero/a
> cantante – cartero/a – ciclista – escritor/a
> estudiante – futbolista – médico/a
> policía – peluquero/a – profesor/a
> secretario/a – taxista – torero

Cantante

Cartera

Albañil

Médica

Números

0 cero	7 siete	14 catorce
1 uno	8 ocho	15 quince
2 dos	9 nueve	16 dieciséis
3 tres	10 diez	17 diecisiete
4 cuatro	11 once	18 dieciocho
5 cinco	12 doce	19 diecinueve
6 seis	13 trece	20 veinte

UNIDAD 2

GRAMÁTICA

1. Plural de los nombres.

▶ Si el singular termina en vocal (excepto *í*), el plural se forma añadiendo una **-s**:

Un libro   dos libros

▶ Si el singular termina en consonante, se añade **-es**:

un hotel   dos hoteles
un lápiz   dos lápices

2. Adjetivos posesivos.

Sujeto	Posesivos	
	Singular	Plural
yo	mi	mis
tú	tu	tus
él/ella/Vd.	su	sus

Los adjetivos posesivos concuerdan en número con el nombre al que acompañan.
*Esta es **mi** hermana y estos son **mis** padres.*

3. Verbo *estar*.

Presente del verbo Estar

yo	estoy
tú	estás
él/ella/Vd.	está
nosotros/as	estamos
vosotros/as	estáis
ellos/ellas/Vds.	están

LÉXICO ÚTIL

Preposiciones de lugar

El móvil está…

al lado del libro — debajo del libro — encima del libro

delante de los libros — detrás de los libros — entre el libro y la lámpara

Familia

abuelo/a/os/as – padre/s – madre
hijo/a/os/as – primo/a/os/as – tío/a/os/as
marido – mujer – hermano/a/os/as

Estado civil

soltero/a/os/as – casado/a/os/as
divorciado/a/os/as

La clase

bolígrafo – cuaderno – diccionario
lápiz – libro – mapa – mesa – silla
televisión – ventana

Números

20 veinte	90 noventa
21 veintiuno	100 cien
22 veintidós	101 ciento uno
23 veintitrés	200 doscientos/as
24 veinticuatro	300 trescientos/as
25 veinticinco	400 cuatrocientos/as
26 veintiséis	500 quinientos/as
27 veintisiete	600 seiscientos/as
28 veintiocho	700 setecientos/as
29 veintinueve	800 ochocientos/as
30 treinta	900 novecientos/as
31 treinta y uno	1.000 mil
40 cuarenta	1.105 mil ciento cinco
50 cincuenta	1.500 mil quinientos
60 sesenta	1.940 mil novecientos cuarenta
70 setenta	2.001 dos mil uno
80 ochenta	5.000 cinco mil

UNIDAD 3

GRAMÁTICA

1. Verbos reflexivos.

Levantar(se)

yo	**me**	levanto
tú	**te**	levantas
él/ella/Vd.	**se**	levanta
nosotros/as	**nos**	levantamos
vosotros/as	**os**	levantáis
ellos/ellas/Vds.	**se**	levantan

▶ Los pronombres reflexivos se usan con verbos que expresan acciones que el sujeto realiza sobre sí mismo: *lavarse, ducharse, peinarse, afeitarse*, etcétera.

▶ Cuando la acción del sujeto no se realiza sobre sí mismos estos verbos no llevan pronombre:

María se lava la cara.
María lava la ropa.

▶ Tenemos otros verbos que se utilizan con estos pronombres, aunque no son reflexivos: *llamarse, quedarse, casarse,* etcétera.

2. Verbos irregulares en presente.

Verbos con irregularidades vocálicas

Empezar	Volver	Acostarse
e>ie	o>ue	o>ue
emp**ie**zo	v**ue**lvo	me ac**ue**sto
emp**ie**zas	v**ue**lves	te ac**ue**stas
emp**ie**za	v**ue**lve	se ac**ue**sta
empezamos	volvemos	nos acostamos
empezáis	volvéis	os acostáis
emp**ie**zan	v**ue**lven	se ac**ue**stan

Otros verbos irregulares

Ir	Venir
voy	vengo
vas	vienes
va	viene
vamos	venimos
vais	venís
van	vienen

3. Preposiciones.

Rosa se levanta a las 7.
Carlos sale de casa a las 8.
Yo trabajo desde las 8 hasta las 3.
Yo no trabajo por la tarde.
Ella termina su trabajo a las 5 de la tarde.
Ellos van a trabajar en autobús.
Rosa vuelve a su casa a las 4.
Mi jefe trabaja de 8 de la mañana a 8 de la tarde.

LÉXICO ÚTIL

Verbos de acciones cotidianas

> levantarse – desayunar – ducharse
> afeitarse – empezar – estudiar – terminar
> trabajar – peinarse – comer
> cenar – acostarse

Verbos de movimiento

> salir – ir – venir – entrar – llegar – volver

Desayunos

> café – leche – té – mantequilla
> mermelada – zumo – huevo – queso – bollos
> bocadillo – tostada

tostada con mantequilla y mermelada — café — zumo de naranja — bocadillo

UNIDAD 4

GRAMÁTICA

1. Ordinales.

1.º / 1.ª	primero/a	6.º / 6.ª	sexto/a
2.º / 2.ª	segundo/a	7.º / 7.ª	séptimo/a
3.º / 3.ª	tercero/a	8.º / 8.ª	octavo/a
4.º / 4.ª	cuarto/a	9.º / 9.ª	noveno/a
5.º / 5.ª	quinto/a	10.º / 10.ª	décimo/a

▶ Los ordinales se usan, por ejemplo, para nombrar los pisos de una casa y el número de orden en un grupo:

*Mi amigo vive en el **cuarto** piso.*
*Luis siempre llega el **primero**.*

▶ Los ordinales concuerdan en género y número con el sustantivo al que acompañan:

*Mi clase está en la **segunda** planta.*
*Mañana salen los **primeros** discos de este grupo.*

▶ Los ordinales **primero** y **tercero** pierden la **-o** delante de un nombre masculino singular:

*Estudio **tercer**(o) curso de Inglés.*
*Vivo en el **primer**(o) piso.*

2. Artículos.

	Determinados		Indeterminados	
	Para algo que conocemos		Para algo que mencionamos por primera vez	
	Masc.	Fem.	Masc.	Fem.
Sing.	el	la	un	una
Pl.	los	las	unos	unas

▶ Los artículos determinados se usan:
- Cuando hablamos de algo que conocemos:
  *Cierra **la** ventana.*
- Con la hora:
  *Son **las** cinco.*
- Con los días de la semana:
  ***Los** viernes vamos al cine.*

▶ Los artículos indeterminados se usan:
- Cuando mencionamos algo por primera vez:
  *Tengo **un** coche nuevo.*
- Con el verbo **haber**:
  *¿Dónde hay **una** silla?*

3. Hay / está(n).

▶ Se utiliza *hay* para hablar de la existencia o no de personas, animales, lugares y objetos.

***Hay** vasos en la cocina.*

▶ Con *hay*, a los nombres nunca les pueden acompañar los artículos determinados.

*En mi pueblo no **hay** (la) universidad.*

▶ Se utiliza *está(n)* para indicar un lugar.

*La leche **está** en la nevera.*
*¿Dónde **están** mis libros?*

Mamá, no hay leche.

LÉXICO ÚTIL

Cosas de la casa

armario – ascensor – espejo
frigorífico/nevera – sillón – lavabo
lámpara – microondas – llave
cocina – cuarto de baño
dormitorio/habitación – salón/comedor
garaje – jardín – piscina – patio

¿Dónde?

derecha – izquierda – arriba – abajo

UNIDAD 5

GRAMÁTICA

1. Verbo *gustar*.

(A mí)	me	**gusta**	el cine
(A ti)	te		la música
(A él/ella/Vd.)	le		viajar
(A nosotros/as)	nos		
(A vosotros/as)	os	**gustan**	los deportes
(A ellos/ellas/Vds.)	les		las plantas

▶ El verbo *gustar* se utiliza en la tercera persona del singular o del plural, dependiendo del sujeto gramatical.

*Me **gustan** tus ojos.*
*No les **gusta** el gazpacho.*

2. Imperativo (verbos regulares).

	Cortar	Comer	Abrir
tú	cort**a**	com**e**	abr**e**
Vd.	cort**e**	com**a**	abr**a**

▸ El imperativo se usa para dar instrucciones y órdenes.

Corta la lechuga en trozos pequeños.
Abre la puerta, por favor.
Abre el libro, Peter.

LÉXICO ÚTIL

Comida básica

arroz – pan – carne – ensalada
pescado – fruta – huevos – queso
patatas – sal – azúcar

Bebidas

agua – cerveza – refresco – vino – zumo

Actividades de tiempo libre

bailar – escuchar música – hacer deportes
navegar en Internet – ir al teatro – andar
ir de compras – ir a la discoteca
montar en bicicleta – viajar

UNIDAD 6

GRAMÁTICA

1. Imperativos irregulares.

▸ Los verbos en imperativo tienen la misma irregularidad que en presente.

Infinitivo	Presente	Imperativo
cerrar	c**ie**rro	c**ie**rra, c**ie**rre
dormir	d**ue**rmo	d**ue**rme, d**ue**rma
sentarse	me s**ie**nto	s**ié**ntate, s**ié**ntese

Otros irregulares

poner	pongo	pon, ponga
decir	digo	di, diga
venir	vengo	ven, venga
hacer	hago	haz, haga
ir(se)	voy	vete, váyase
salir	salgo	sal, salga

▸ Se usa el imperativo:

- Para dar instrucciones o consejos:

  *Primero **eche** una cucharada de sal, luego **hierva** el arroz durante…*
  *Si te duele la cabeza, **toma** una pastilla y **acuéstate**.*

- Hacer peticiones o dar órdenes, especialmente seguido de "por favor".

  ***Habla** más despacio, por favor.*
  ***Siéntese**, por favor.*
  *¡**Ven** aquí ahora mismo!*

Toma este vaso de leche y acuéstate.

2. Ser/Estar.

Ser

▸ Se usa para describir características o cualidades de algo o de alguien: tamaño, color, carácter, etcétera.

*Luis **es** alto y delgado.*
*Su casa **es** pequeña.*
*Su coche **es** rojo.*
*Luis **es** muy simpático.*

▸ Expresa también nacionalidad, profesión, posesión:

*Mary **es** inglesa.*
*¿Ellos **son** médicos?*
*Ese libro no **es** mío.*

Estar

▶ Expresa lugar o posición:

*El colegio **está** en la C/ Velázquez.*
*La parada de autobús **está** enfrente de mi casa.*

▶ Sirve para expresar también estados de salud o de ánimo:

*Clara **está** enferma, tiene gripe.*
*Hoy **estoy** muy contenta.*

▶ Con los adverbios **bien** y **mal** siempre usamos **estar**.

*Este ejercicio **está** ~~(es)~~ mal.*

LÉXICO ÚTIL

Transportes

> billete – autobús – metro – tren
> línea de metro – viaje – estación – parada

Adjetivos

> tranquilo – ruidoso – céntrico
> rápido – frío – lento – malo – pequeño
> fácil – difícil – bueno

Adverbios

> cerca – lejos – bien – mal

UNIDAD 7

GRAMÁTICA

1. Gerundio de verbos regulares.

Infinitivo	Gerundio
llorar	llor**ando**
comer	com**iendo**
escribir	escrib**iendo**

2. Gerundio de verbos irregulares.

leer	leyendo
dormir	durmiendo

3. *Estar* + gerundio.

estoy	
estás	
está	
estamos	hablando
estáis	
están	

Estar + **gerundio** suele expresar acciones que se están desarrollando en el momento en que se habla.

¿Qué estás haciendo?
Estoy leyendo el periódico.

4. *Estar* + gerundio (verbos reflexivos).

Estoy lavándome o me estoy lavando.
Estás lavándote o te estás lavando.
Está lavándose o se está lavando.
Estamos lavándonos o nos estamos lavando.
Estáis lavándoos u os estáis lavando.
Están lavándose o se están lavando.

LÉXICO ÚTIL

Verbos de actividades

leer el periódico

jugar a las cartas

lavarse

dormir

pintar

bañarse

Descripción de personas

> Pelo: rubio – moreno – largo – corto.
> Ojos: claros – oscuros – marrones – verdes.
> Es: mayor – joven – alto – bajo
> delgado – gordo.
> Lleva: barba – bigote – gafas.

Carácter

> simpático – antipático – tacaño
> generoso – hablador – serio – alegre
> educado – callado

UNIDAD 8

GRAMÁTICA

1. Pretérito indefinido.

	Trabajar	Comer	Salir
yo	trabaj**é**	com**í**	sal**í**
tú	trabaj**aste**	com**iste**	sal**iste**
él/ella/Vd.	trabaj**ó**	com**ió**	sal**ió**
nosotros/as	trabaj**amos**	com**imos**	sal**imos**
vosotros/as	trabaj**asteis**	com**isteis**	sal**isteis**
ellos/ellas/Vds.	trabaj**aron**	com**ieron**	sal**ieron**

2. Pretérito indefinido de los verbos *ir* y *estar*.

	Ir	Estar
yo	fui	estuve
tú	fuiste	estuviste
él/ella/Vd.	fue	estuvo
nosotros/as	fuimos	estuvimos
vosotros/as	fuisteis	estuvisteis
ellos/ellas/Vds.	fueron	estuvieron

▶ El pretérito indefinido expresa acciones acabadas en un momento determinado del pasado.

*Ayer **trabajé** mucho.*
*El verano pasado **estuve** en Cancún.*

LÉXICO ÚTIL

Establecimientos

> farmacia – iglesia – museo – comisaría
> oficina de correos – quiosco – mercado
> estanco

Objetos

> medicinas – cartas – periódico
> sellos – tabaco

Estaciones del año

> la primavera – el verano
> el otoño – el invierno

Meses del año

> enero – febrero – marzo – abril – mayo
> junio – julio – agosto – septiembre – octubre
> noviembre – diciembre

El tiempo

> llover – llueve – está lloviendo
> nevar – nieva – está nevando
> hace frío – hace (mucho) calor
> hace viento – está nublado

está lloviendo   está nublado   está nevando

hace viento

hace mucho calor

hace frío

UNIDAD 9

GRAMÁTICA

1. Demostrativos (adjetivos y pronombres).

Demostrativos (adjetivos y pronombres)

Singular		Plural	
Masculino	**Femenino**	**Masculino**	**Femenino**
este	esta	estos	estas
ese	esa	esos	esas
aquel	aquella	aquellos	aquellas

Pronombres demostrativos (neutro)

esto	eso	aquello

▸ Los adjetivos demostrativos van delante del nombre y concuerdan con él en género y número:

Este coche es de mi vecino.
Esas chicas son muy simpáticas.

▸ Los pronombres demostrativos *esto, eso, aquello* nunca van con el nombre. Se refieren a una idea o a algo de lo que no sabemos el género:

Esto no me gusta nada.
¿Qué es aquello que se ve en el cielo?

▸ El uso de uno u otro pronombre nos indica la cercanía o lejanía del objeto señalado:

Este coche (cerca del hablante, aquí)
Ese coche (cerca del oyente, ahí)
Aquel coche (lejos de los dos, allí)

2. Pronombres de complemento directo.

Sujeto	Objeto
yo	me
tú	te
él/ella/Vd.	lo/la/le
nosotros/as	nos
vosotros/as	os
ellos/ellas/Vds.	los/las/les

¿Compramos las flores? = ¿Las compramos?
Hoy no he visto a tu padre. = Hoy no lo/le he visto.
¿Sabes que vendo mi casa? = ¿Sabes que la vendo?

▸ Normalmente, los pronombres personales de objeto directo van delante del verbo y separados:

Te quiero.

▸ Pero con el imperativo afirmativo van detrás y unidos al verbo:

¡Mírame!
Cómpralo, por favor.

▸ Con algunas construcciones pueden ir delante o detrás.

La puerta está abierta,
¿puedes cerrarla? = ¿la puedes cerrar?

3. Concordancia del nombre y los adjetivos de color.

▸ Los adjetivos concuerdan en género y número con el nombre al que se refieren.

¿Puedo coger el bolígrafo rojo?
Tengo unos pantalones marrones.

Singular		Plural	
masc.	**fem.**	**masc.**	**fem.**
blanco	blanca	blancos	blancas
verde	verde	verdes	verdes
azul	azul	azules	azules

▸ Los adjetivos de color terminados en **-a** (**rosa, naranja, fucsia**) no cambian.

Me gusta el vestido (de color) fucsia.
Me gusta mucho ese abrigo naranja.

4. Comparativos.

Comparativos

más + adjetivo + **que**
Juan es más simpático que Pedro.

menos + adjetivo + **que**
Pedro es menos simpático que Juan.

tan + adjetivo + **como**
Juan (no) es tan alto como Pedro.

Comparativos irregulares

bueno	**mejor / mejores** + que

Esta película es mejor que esa.

malo	**peor / peores** + que

Esos pasteles son **peores** que estos.

grande	**mayor / mayores** + que

Yo soy mayor que ella.

pequeño	**menor / menores** + que

Sus hijos son menores que los míos.

Mayor y **menor** se refieren sobre todo a la edad, no al tamaño.

Mi hermano **mayor** es arquitecto.
Él es el **menor** de sus hermanos.
Su casa es **más grande** que la mía.
Mi ciudad es **más pequeña** que la tuya.

Adjetivos

blanco – negro – verde – rojo – rosa amarillo – morado – azul – naranja

caro – barato – formal – informal práctico – incómodo – limpio – sucio elegante

UNIDAD 10

GRAMÁTICA

1. Verbo *doler*.

(A mí)	me	
(A ti)	te	
(A él/ella/Vd.)	le	**duele** la cabeza
(A nosotros/as)	nos	**duelen** los oídos
(A vosotros/as)	os	
(A ellos/ellas/Vds.)	les	

El verbo **doler**, al igual que el verbo **gustar**, se utiliza en la tercera persona del singular o del plural, según sea el sujeto.

¿Te duele la cabeza?
A Ana le duelen los oídos.

2. Pretérito imperfecto de los verbos regulares.

	Viajar	Tener	Salir
yo	viaj**aba**	ten**ía**	sal**ía**
tú	viaj**abas**	ten**ías**	sal**ías**
él/ella/Vd.	viaj**aba**	ten**ía**	sal**ía**
nosotros/as	viaj**ábamos**	ten**íamos**	sal**íamos**
vosotros/as	viaj**abais**	ten**íais**	sal**íais**
ellos/ellas/Vds.	viaj**aban**	ten**ían**	sal**ían**

LÉXICO ÚTIL

Ropa y complementos

Anillo

Camiseta — Cartera

Collar

Camisa

Corbata

Falda — Gafas

Jersey

Medias

Pendientes — Vaqueros

Zapatillas deportivas

Zapatos

3. Pretérito imperfecto de los verbos irregulares.

	Ir	Ser	Ver
yo	iba	era	veía
tú	ibas	eras	veías
él/ella/Vd.	iba	era	veía
nosotros/as	íbamos	éramos	veíamos
vosotros/as	ibais	erais	veíais
ellos/ellas/Vds.	iban	eran	veían

▶ Usamos el pretérito imperfecto para expresar acciones habituales en el pasado.

*Cuando **éramos** jóvenes, **íbamos** a la discoteca.
Ahora no salimos, pero antes **salíamos** mucho.*

▶ También se usa para describir en el pasado:

Mi profesor de matemáticas era simpático y nunca nos castigaba.

4. Ir a + infinitivo.

yo	voy a	
tú	vas a	
él/ella/Vd.	va a	
nosotros/as	vamos a	estudiar
vosotros/as	vais a	
ellos/ellas/Vds.	van a	

Con **ir a** + infinitivo expresamos planes e intenciones.

*Este fin de semana **vamos a ir** al teatro.*

LÉXICO ÚTIL

El cuerpo humano

> brazo – cabeza – cara – cuello – dedos
> espalda – estómago – garganta – hombro
> mano – oído – oreja – pecho – pie
> pierna – rodilla

Cuando éramos jóvenes salíamos todos los fines de semana, pero ahora no salimos tanto.

Verbos regulares e irregulares

VERBOS REGULARES

TRABAJAR

Presente	Pretérito indefinido	Pretérito imperfecto	Imperativo	Gerundio
trabajo	trabajé	trabajaba		trabajando
trabajas	trabajaste	trabajabas	trabaja	
trabaja	trabajó	trabajaba	trabaje	
trabajamos	trabajamos	trabajábamos		
trabajáis	trabajasteis	trabajabais	trabajad	
trabajan	trabajaron	trabajaban	trabajen	

BEBER

bebo	bebí	bebía		bebiendo
bebes	bebiste	bebías	bebe	
bebe	bebió	bebía	beba	
bebemos	bebimos	bebíamos		
bebéis	bebisteis	bebíais	bebed	
beben	bebieron	bebían	beban	

ESCRIBIR

escribo	escribí	escribía		escribiendo
escribes	escribiste	escribías	escribe	
escribe	escribió	escribía	escriba	
escribimos	escribimos	escribíamos		
escribís	escribisteis	escribíais	escribid	
escriben	escribieron	escribían	escriban	

VERBOS IRREGULARES

CERRAR

Presente	Pretérito indefinido	Pretérito imperfecto	Imperativo	Gerundio
cierro	cerré	cerraba		cerrando
cierras	cerraste	cerrabas	cierra	
cierra	cerró	cerraba	cierre	
cerramos	cerramos	cerrábamos		
cerráis	cerrasteis	cerrabais	cerrad	
cierran	cerraron	cerraban	cierren	

DAR

Presente	Pretérito indefinido	Pretérito imperfecto	Imperativo	Gerundio
doy	di	daba		dando
das	diste	dabas	da	
da	dio	daba	dé	
damos	dimos	dábamos		
dais	disteis	dabais	dad	
dan	dieron	daban	den	

DECIR

Presente	Pretérito indefinido	Pretérito imperfecto	Imperativo	Gerundio
digo	dije	decía		diciendo
dices	dijiste	decías	di	
dice	dijo	decía	diga	
decimos	dijimos	decíamos		
decís	dijisteis	decíais	decid	
dicen	dijeron	decían	digan	

ESTAR

Presente	Pretérito indefinido	Pretérito imperfecto	Imperativo	Gerundio
estoy	estuve	estaba		estando
estás	estuviste	estabas	está	
está	estuvo	estaba	esté	
estamos	estuvimos	estábamos		
estáis	estuvisteis	estabais	estad	
están	estuvieron	estaban	estén	

HACER

Presente	Pretérito indefinido	Pretérito imperfecto	Imperativo	Gerundio
hago	hice	hacía		haciendo
haces	hiciste	hacías	haz	
hace	hizo	hacía	haga	
hacemos	hicimos	hacíamos		
hacéis	hicisteis	hacíais	haced	
hacen	hicieron	hacían	hagan	

IR

Presente	Pretérito indefinido	Pretérito imperfecto	Imperativo	Gerundio
voy	fui	iba		yendo
vas	fuiste	ibas	ve	
va	fue	iba	vaya	
vamos	fuimos	íbamos		
vais	fuisteis	ibais	id	
van	fueron	iban	vayan	

OÍR

Presente	Pretérito indefinido	Pretérito imperfecto	Imperativo	Gerundio
oigo	oí	oía		oyendo
oyes	oíste	oías	oye	
oye	oyó	oía	oiga	
oímos	oímos	oíamos		
oís	oísteis	oíais	oíd	
oyen	oyeron	oían	oigan	

PEDIR

Presente	Pretérito indefinido	Pretérito imperfecto	Imperativo	Gerundio
pido	pedí	pedía		pidiendo
pides	pediste	pedías	pide	
pide	pidió	pedía	pida	
pedimos	pedimos	pedíamos		
pedís	pedisteis	pedíais	pedid	
piden	pidieron	pedían	pidan	

PODER

Presente	Pretérito indefinido	Pretérito imperfecto	Imperativo	Gerundio
puedo	pude	podía		pudiendo
puedes	pudiste	podías	puede	
puede	pudo	podía	pueda	
podemos	pudimos	podíamos		
podéis	pudisteis	podíais	poded	
pueden	pudieron	podían	puedan	

PONER

Presente	Pretérito indefinido	Pretérito imperfecto	Imperativo	Gerundio
pongo	puse	ponía		poniendo
pones	pusiste	ponías	pon	
pone	puso	ponía	ponga	
ponemos	pusimos	poníamos		
ponéis	pusisteis	poníais	poned	
ponen	pusieron	ponían	pongan	

QUERER

Presente	Pretérito indefinido	Pretérito imperfecto	Imperativo	Gerundio
quiero	quise	quería		queriendo
quieres	quisiste	querías	quiere	
quiere	quiso	quería	quiera	
queremos	quisimos	queríamos		
queréis	quisisteis	queríais	quered	
quieren	quisieron	querían	quieran	

SABER

Presente	Pretérito indefinido	Pretérito imperfecto	Imperativo	Gerundio
sé	supe	sabía		sabiendo
sabes	supiste	sabías	sabe	
sabe	supo	sabía	sepa	
sabemos	supimos	sabíamos		
sabéis	supisteis	sabíais	sabed	
saben	supieron	sabían	sepan	

SALIR

Presente	Pretérito indefinido	Pretérito imperfecto	Imperativo	Gerundio
salgo	salí	salía		saliendo
sales	saliste	salías	sal	
sale	salió	salía	salga	
salimos	salimos	salíamos		
salís	salisteis	salíais	salid	
salen	salieron	salían	salgan	

SEGUIR

Presente	Pretérito indefinido	Pretérito imperfecto	Imperativo	Gerundio
sigo	seguí	seguía		siguiendo
sigues	seguiste	seguías	sigue	
sigue	siguió	seguía	siga	
seguimos	seguimos	seguíamos		
seguís	seguisteis	seguíais	seguid	
siguen	siguieron	seguían	sigan	

SER

Presente	Pretérito indefinido	Pretérito imperfecto	Imperativo	Gerundio
soy	fui	era		siendo
eres	fuiste	eras	sé	
es	fue	erais	sea	
somos	fuimos	éramos		
sois	fuisteis	erais	sed	
son	fueron	eran	sean	

TENER

Presente	Pretérito indefinido	Pretérito imperfecto	Imperativo	Gerundio
tengo	tuve	tenía		teniendo
tienes	tuviste	tenías	ten	
tiene	tuvo	tenía	tenga	
tenemos	tuvimos	teníamos		
tenéis	tuvisteis	teníais	tened	
tienen	tuvieron	tenían	tengan	

VENIR

Presente	Pretérito indefinido	Pretérito imperfecto	Imperativo	Gerundio
vengo	vine	venía		viniendo
vienes	viniste	venías	ven	
viene	vino	venía	venga	
venimos	vinimos	veníamos		
venís	vinisteis	veníais	venid	
vienen	vinieron	venían	vengan	

VER

Presente	Pretérito indefinido	Pretérito imperfecto	Imperativo	Gerundio
veo	vi	veía		viendo
ves	viste	veías	ve	
ve	vio	veía	vea	
vemos	vimos	veíamos		
veis	visteis	veíais	ved	
ven	vieron	veían	vean	

VOLVER

Presente	Pretérito indefinido	Pretérito imperfecto	Imperativo	Gerundio
vuelvo	volví	volvía		volviendo
vuelves	volviste	volvías	vuelve	
vuelve	volvió	volvía	vuelva	
volvemos	volvimos	volvíamos		
volvéis	volvisteis	volvíais	volved	
vuelven	volvieron	volvían	vuevan	

Transcripciones

UNIDAD 0

6. Pista 4

R-O-M-E-R-O
D-Í-A-Z
G-O-N-Z-A-L-V-O
R-I-B-E-R-A
G-I-M-É-N-E-Z
P-A-D-Í-N

UNIDAD 1

A. ¡Encantado!

4. Pista 7

Luis: ¡Hola, Eva!, ¿qué tal?
Eva: Bien, ¿y tú?
Luis: Muy bien. Mira, este es Roberto, un compañero nuevo.
Eva: ¡Hola! ¡Encantada! ¿De dónde eres?
Roberto: Soy cubano.

C. ¿Cuál es tu número de teléfono?

2. Pista 11

1. uno / 3. tres / 6. seis / 8. ocho / 9. nueve.

4. Pista 12

UNO
A. María, ¿cuál es tu número de teléfono?
B. El 936 547 832
A. ¿Puedes repetir?
B. 9 3 6 5 4 7 8 3 2.
A. Gracias.

DOS
A. Jorge, ¿me das tu teléfono?
B. Sí, es el 945 401 832.
A. Gracias.

TRES
A. Marina, ¿cuál es tu número de teléfono?
B. Mi móvil es el 686 52 61 36
A. ¿Y el de tu casa?
B. Sí, es el 91 539 82 67.
A. Vale, gracias.

CUATRO
A. Información, dígame.
B. ¿Puede decirme el teléfono del aeropuerto de Barajas?
A. Sí, tome nota, es el 902 353 570
B. ¿Puede repetir?
A. Sí, 9 0 2 3 5 3 5 7 0.
B. Gracias.

CINCO
A. Información, dígame.
B. ¿Puede decirme el teléfono de la Cruz Roja?
A. Sí, tome nota, es el 9 1 5 3 3 6 6 6 5.
B. ¿Puede repetir?
A. Sí, 9 1 5 3 3 6 6 6 5.

SEIS
A. Información, dígame.
B. Buenos días, ¿puede decirme el teléfono de Radio-taxi?
A. Tome nota, por favor.
El número solicitado es: 9 1 4 0 5 1 2 1 3. El número solicitado es 9 1 4 0 5 1 2 1 3.

7. Pista 14

15	1	4	20	8	7
3	11	5	6	14	9
18	19	2	13	16	

8. Pista 15

FELIPE:	¡Buenas tardes!
ROSA:	¡Hola!, ¿qué deseas?
FELIPE:	Quiero apuntarme al gimnasio.
ROSA:	Tienes que darme tus datos. A ver, ¿cómo te llamas?
FELIPE:	Felipe Martínez.
ROSA:	¿Y de segundo apellido?
FELIPE:	Franco.
ROSA:	¿Dónde vives?
FELIPE:	En la calle Goya, número ochenta y siete, tercero izquierda.
ROSA:	¿Teléfono?
FELIPE:	686 055 097
ROSA:	¿Profesión?
FELIPE:	Profesor.
ROSA:	Bueno, ya está; el precio es…

D. Autoevaluación

3. Pista 16

Uno: Martínez; dos: Romero; tres: Marín; cuatro: Serrano; cinco: López; seis: Moreno; siete: Jiménez; ocho: Pérez; nueve: Díaz; diez: Martín; once: Vargas; doce: García; trece: Díez.

UNIDAD 2

C. ¿Qué hora es?

2. Pista 19

Las doce y cinco
Las ocho menos veinte
Las doce y diez
Las cinco y media
La una menos cuarto

7. Pista 20

24. veinticuatro / 40. cuarenta / 70. setenta / 90. noventa / 300. trescientos/as / 400. cuatrocientos/as.

8. Pista 21

2. Dos
25. Veinticinco
50. Cincuenta
37. Treinta y siete
323. Trescientos veintitrés
135. Ciento treinta y cinco
850. Ochocientos cincuenta
1.589 Mil quinientos ochenta y nueve
1.998 Mil novecientos noventa y ocho
1.985 Mil novecientos ochenta y cinco

9. Pista 22

DIÁLOGO 1

PROFESORA:	¡Hola!, Clara, ¿cuántos años tienes?
CLARA:	Doce.

DIÁLOGO 2

CLIENTE:	¿Cuánto son las naranjas?
DEPENDIENTE:	Uno con diez.

DIÁLOGO 3

CLIENTE:	¿Cuánto es el paquete de café?
DEPENDIENTE:	Uno treinta.

DIÁLOGO 4

MUJER:	¿En qué año nació usted?
HOMBRE:	En mil novecientos cuarenta y siete.

DIÁLOGO 5

1ª PERSONA:	¿Por favor, cuántos kilómetros hay entre Madrid y Barcelona?
2ª PERSONA:	Seiscientos cincuenta.

DIÁLOGO 6

CLIENTE:	Por favor, ¿cuánto es el café y la cerveza?
CAMARERO:	Tres euros.

D. Autoevaluación

5. Pista 25

SALIDAS:
– El tren Altaria exprés, situado en el andén n.º 3 con destino Zaragoza, efectuará su salida a las 15.35.

– El tren Talgo con destino Málaga, situado en el andén n.º 6 saldrá dentro de 15 minutos, a las 14.30.
– El AVE con destino Sevilla sale a las diez en punto del andén n.º 2.

Llegadas:
– El AVE procedente de Sevilla tiene su llegada a las 20 horas en el andén n.º 11.
– El Alaris procedente de Valencia efectuará su entrada por el andén n.º 8 a las 16.45 horas.
– El tren Talgo procedente de Vigo hará su entrada en el andén n.º 4 a las 17 horas.

UNIDAD 3

A. Rosa se levanta a las siete

4. Pista 26

A. Y tú, Juan, ¿a qué hora te levantas?
B. Bueno, yo me levanto pronto, a las siete, más o menos, me ducho rápidamente, tomo un café y salgo de casa.
A. Y tu mujer, ¿a qué hora se levanta?
B. Pues a las siete y media.
A. ¿Y tus hijos?
B. Bueno, ellos se levantan a las ocho, se duchan, desayunan y se van al colegio, porque entran a las nueve.
A. ¿Y los días de fiesta también os levantáis todos temprano?
B. ¡Ah, no, ni hablar, los domingos nos levantamos a las diez, porque claro, el sábado nos acostamos más tarde.

C. ¿Qué desayunas?

4. Pista 28

1. A: Olga, ¿qué se desayuna en Rusia?
   Olga: Bueno, generalmente tomamos un bocadillo de pan negro, mantequilla y queso. Y para beber, té, café o café con leche.

2. A: Rabah, ¿qué se desayuna en Siria?
   Rabah: La gente toma té verde y pan con aceite y aceitunas negras. También toman mucho queso fresco con aceite. Algunos toman café con leche, claro.

3. A: Yi, ¿qué desayuna la gente en China?
   Yi: China es muy grande, pero en el sur se toma una sopa de arroz con algo parecido a los churros. Los niños toman leche de soja. En el norte algunas personas toman leche de vaca o yogur, sobre todo los jóvenes. También se toman unas empanadas al vapor.

4. A: Philip, ¿qué se toma en Alemania para desayunar?
   Philipp: Hay muchas cosas. Algunos toman pan con mantequilla y salami y un huevo. Otros toman müesli con yogur. Y té, mucha gente toma té. Algunos toman café, claro

4. Pista 31

guapo
cigarrillos
guitarra
gafas
pagar
guerra
Guatemala
goma

D. Autoevaluación

6. Pista 32

A: Adriana, tú eres argentina, ¿no?
Adriana: Sí, claro.

A: ¿Y de qué ciudad?
ADRIANA: De Buenos Aires
A: Cuéntame un poco los horarios habituales… por ejemplo, ¿a qué hora os levantáis?
ADRIANA: Pues mira, nos levantamos muy temprano, a las cinco y media o las seis, porque el trabajo está lejos... y, bueno, normalmente empezamos a trabajar a las ocho...
A: ¿Y hasta qué hora trabajáis?
ADRIANA: Hasta las seis... sí, en las oficinas hasta las seis de la tarde, paramos una hora para comer, entre las doce y las dos, comemos algo rápido y, ya, volvemos al trabajo.
A: ¿Y en las tiendas?
ADRIANA: Bueno, el horario de las tiendas es distinto, abren también sobre las ocho de la mañana y cierran a las ocho o las nueve de la noche, y no cierran a mediodía, ¿eh?, no es como en España. Ah, y los bancos también tienen otro horario, abren a las diez y cierran a las tres, y por la tarde ya no abren.
A: Y una cosa, Adriana, cuando la gente sale del trabajo, ¿va directamente a su casa?
ADRIANA: Sí, sí, eso es lo normal, vamos a casa, tenemos otra hora más para volver, claro, cenamos entre las ocho y las nueve y media, y no nos acostamos tarde, sobre las once más o menos.
A: Oye, ¿y los niños? ¿Qué horario tienen en el colegio?
ADRIANA: Pues, mira, estudian sólo o por la mañana o por la tarde, creo que es de ocho a doce en el turno de la mañana y de una a cinco los que estudian por la tarde.

UNIDAD 4

A. ¿Dónde vives?

4. Pista 34

A: Manu, ¿cómo es tu piso?
MANU: Mi piso es muy pequeño, porque vivo solo. Tiene un dormitorio, un salón comedor pequeño, una cocina y un cuarto de baño, que está al lado del dormitorio.
A: ¿Nada más?
MANU: Bueno, tengo una terraza grande y ahí tengo muchas plantas.

9. Pista 36

A: ¿Sería tan amable de indicarme dónde vive el Sr. González?
B: En el 4.º derecha.
A: Muchas gracias.

A: ¿Me podría decir dónde vive doña Manuela Rodríguez?
B: En el 2.º izquierda.
A: Gracias.

A: ¿En qué piso vive la señorita Herrero?
B: En el 3.º A

A: ¿Me podría enviar este paquete a mi domicilio en la Avda. del Mediterráneo, 5, 6.º B?
B: Por supuesto, señor Acedo.

A: ¿El señor de la Fuente, por favor?
B: Es el inquilino del ático.
A: Muchas gracias.

A: ¿Vive aquí la señorita Laura Barroso?
B: Sí, es la hija de los vecinos del 5.º E.

B. Interiores

6. Pista 37

A: Inverpiso, ¿Dígame?
B: Buenos días. Llamo para informarme sobre los chalés anunciados en el periódico de ayer.
A: Con mucho gusto. Mire, el primero está en la calle Alonso Cano. Tiene 138 metros cuadrados. Hay cuatro dormitorios en la planta de arriba y dos baños, calefacción individual y ascensor. El segundo es una casa de tres plantas en

Torrelodones. Tiene 311 metros cuadrados, con jardín y piscina. Hay un salón comedor y un baño en la planta baja, y 5 dormitorios y otros 2 cuartos de baño en la planta superior. El garaje es para 2 coches.

El tercer chalé está en una urbanización en Pozuelo. Tiene 300 metros cuadrados construidos en 2 plantas. Tiene un amplio salón y 4 dormitorios. Hay un cuarto de baño en cada planta. Los materiales son de primera calidad. Hay piscina comunitaria.

El último es un piso en Moratalaz de 70 metros cuadrados con 3 dormitorios. La cocina está en el salón y hay un baño completo.

C. En el hotel

2. Pista 38

Escucha y completa el diálogo:

RECEPCIONISTA: Parador de Córdoba, ¿dígame?
CARLOS: Buenas tardes. ¿Puede decirme si hay habitaciones libres para el próximo fin de semana?
RECEPCIONISTA: Sí. ¿Qué desea, una habitación individual o doble?
CARLOS: Una doble, por favor. ¿Qué precio tiene?
RECEPCIONISTA: 100 euros por noche más IVA.
CARLOS: De acuerdo. Hágame la reserva, por favor.
RECEPCIONISTA: ¿Cuántas noches?
CARLOS: Viernes y sábado, si es posible.
RECEPCIONISTA: No hay problema.
CARLOS: ¿Hay piscina?
RECEPCIONISTA: Sí, señor, hay una.
CARLOS: ¿Admiten tarjetas de crédito?
RECEPCIONISTA: Sí, por supuesto.

4. Pista 39

RECEPCIONISTA: ¿Me dice su nombre y apellidos, por favor?
CARLOS: Carlos López Ruiz.
RECEPCIONISTA: ¿Dirección?
CARLOS: Calle de Velázquez n.º 66, en Madrid.
RECEPCIONISTA: ¿Número de teléfono, por favor?
CARLOS: 91 569 88 47
RECEPCIONISTA: Entonces, una habitación doble para las noches del viernes y sábado, ¿no es así?
CARLOS: Sí, correcto, muchas gracias. Hasta el viernes.
RECEPCIONISTA: ¡Hasta el viernes! Buenas tardes.

UNIDAD 5

A. Comer fuera de casa

2. Pista 42

CAMARERO: Buenos días, señores, ¿qué quieren comer?
JUAN: De primer plato nos pone un gazpacho para mí y una ensalada para la señora.
CAMARERO: ¿Y de segundo?
TERESA: ¿La carne es de ternera?
CAMARERO: Sí, señora. Es muy buena.
TERESA: Entonces, me pone carne con tomate. ¿Y tú, Juan?
JUAN: Yo prefiero unos huevos con chorizo.
CAMARERO: ¿Y para beber?
JUAN: El vino de la casa y una botella de agua, por favor.
CAMARERO: Muy bien, muchas gracias.
CAMARERO: Y de postre, ¿qué desean?
JUAN: Para mí, unas natillas.
TERESA: Pues, yo quiero arroz con leche.
CAMARERO: Enseguida se lo traigo, muchas gracias.

B. ¿Te gusta el cine?

3. Pista 44

Mi marido y yo siempre tenemos problemas para decidir qué hacer durante el fin de semana. A mí me gusta ir al cine los viernes, y el sábado por la mañana ir de compras. Por el contrario, a mi marido le gusta pasar el fin de semana en el campo: andar, hacer deporte... El domingo por la tarde, lo que más le gusta es ver un partido de fútbol por la tele, mientras yo navego por Internet. Durante la semana lo tenemos más fácil: a los dos nos gusta leer y oír música en nuestro tiempo libre.

C. Receta del Caribe

4. Pista 45

Queridos amigos y amigas, hoy vamos a hacer un delicioso refresco de plátano. Bueno, ¿estáis preparados? Aquí van los ingredientes: en primer lugar vamos a necesitar 3 plátanos y una taza de leche. Como el refresco será sólo para cuatro personas, vamos a utilizar únicamente un cuarto de taza de azúcar y un cuarto de taza de zumo de limón y, por último, media cucharadita de vainilla y ocho cubitos de hielo. Y ahora, para su elaboración, sigue las siguientes instrucciones:
Primero, pela los plátanos y córtalos en rodajas.
A continuación, mezcla los plátanos, la leche, el azúcar, el zumo de limón y la vainilla en una batidora.
Añade los cubitos de hielo y mézclalos con los otros ingredientes.
Reparte la mezcla en cuatro vasos.
Finalmente, invita a tus amigos.

7. Pista 46

Casi todas las piñas de los supermercados son de Hawai, pero los cultivadores originales son los indios de Cuba y Puerto Rico.

Es cierto que hay una variedad de maní que procede de Georgia, pero sus cultivadores originales son los indios de Bolivia y Perú.

Los italianos preparan una deliciosa salsa de tomate, pero los cultivadores originarios del tomate son los indios de México.

El Ecuador es el mayor productor de plátanos del mundo, pero los plátanos son de origen africano. Llegaron a América porque los españoles los introdujeron.

El Brasil es el mayor productor de café del mundo, pero el café es también de origen africano y también llegó a América porque los españoles lo introdujeron.
Las patatas son muy populares en Irlanda, pero proceden originalmente de Perú y Ecuador.

Pronunciación y ortografía

4. Pista 49

Yo vivo en Barcelona.
Este batido tiene vainilla.
Camarero, un vaso de agua, por favor.
A Isabel le gusta viajar y bailar tangos.
Beber agua es muy bueno.

UNIDAD 6

A. ¿Cómo se va a Plaza de España?

3. Pista 50

SERGIO: Perdone, queremos dos billetes de metro, por favor.
TAQUILLERO: ¿Sencillos o de diez viajes?
SERGIO: Bueno, mejor uno de 10 viajes. ¿Cuánto es?
TAQUILLERO: 6 euros.
SERGIO: Perdone, ¿puede decirme cómo se va a Plaza de España?
TAQUILLERO: Pues desde aquí es muy fácil, coja usted la línea 8 hasta Nuevos Ministerios y cambie a la línea 10 en dirección Puerta del Sur. La sexta estación es Plaza de España.
SERGIO: Muchas gracias. ¿Puede darme un plano del metro?
TAQUILLERO: Sí, claro, tome.

B. Cierra la ventana, por favor

4. Pista 52

JEFE: Sr. Hernández, puede venir a mi oficina, por favor?
HERNÁNDEZ: Sí, claro.
HERNÁNDEZ: ¿Se puede?
JEFE: Sí, sí, pase y cierre la puerta, por favor... Siéntese. Tengo una reunión en el banco el próximo lunes y necesito la información de su departamento.
HERNANDEZ: No hay problema, está todo preparado.
JEFE: Bien, haga el informe antes del lunes y ponga todos los datos de este año.

C. Mi barrio es tranquilo

Pronunciación y ortografía

2. Pista 54

1. Roma, 2. Inglaterra, 3. Perú, 4. cartero, 5. compañero, 6. rosa, 7. pizarra, 8. terraza, 9. armario.

UNIDAD 7

A. ¿Dónde quedamos?

4. Pista 2

ALICIA: ¿Sí?
BEGOÑA: ¿Está Alicia?
ALICIA: Sí, soy yo.
BEGOÑA: ¡Hola! Soy Begoña.
ALICIA: ¡Hola! ¿Qué hay?
BEGOÑA: Voy a salir de compras esta tarde. ¿Vienes conmigo?
ALICIA: Lo siento, hoy no puedo, tengo mucho trabajo. Mejor mañana.
BEGOÑA: Bueno, vale. ¿A qué hora? ¿Te parece bien a las seis?
ALICIA: Sí, de acuerdo.
BEGOÑA: Hasta mañana.

B. ¿Qué estás haciendo?

4. Pista 4

1. A. Rosa, ¿qué estás haciendo?
   B. Ahora mismo estoy peinándome porque voy a salir.

2. A. ¡Luis, al teléfono!
   B. No puedo, estoy duchándome.

3. A. Niños, ¿qué hacéis?
   B. Nada, mamá, nos estamos lavando las manos.

4. A. ¡Qué ruido hacen los vecinos!
   B. Sí, están levantándose ahora porque salen de viaje.

5. A. ¡Hola!, ¿está Roberto?
   B. Sí, pero está afeitándose, llama más tarde.

6. A. ¿Y clara?, ¿dónde está?
   B. En el baño, está duchándose.

7. A. Joana, ¿qué haces?
   B. Me estoy pintando para salir.

Pronunciación y ortografía

2. Pista 6

1. Claudia Schiffer es bastante fea, ¿verdad?
2. ¿Vamos al cine?
3. Mira qué bolso me he comprado.
4. Tengo un piso nuevo.
5. Bueno, me voy, ¡hasta luego!
6. Hay paella para comer.
7. Mira la tele, cuántas noticias malas.

3. Pista 7

1. Claudia Schiffer es bastante fea, ¿verdad?
   ¡Qué va!

2. ¿Vamos al cine?
   Vale, estupendo.

3. Mira qué bolso me he comprado.
   ¡Qué bonito!

4. Tengo un piso nuevo.
   ¡Qué bien!

5. Bueno, me voy, ¡hasta luego!
   ¡Hasta luego!

6. Hay paella para comer.
   ¡Qué bien! ¡Estupendo!

7. Mira la tele, cuántas noticias malas.
   ¡Es horrible!

c. ¿Cómo es?

2. Pista 8

1. Tiene el pelo largo y rubio. Tiene los ojos verdes y la piel clara. ¡No tiene bigote!

2. Tiene los ojos oscuros. Tiene el pelo corto y la barba negra.

3. Pista 9

Tiene el pelo largo y moreno, los ojos oscuros y la piel clara. No lleva gafas.
Es un famoso tenista mallorquín.

Tiene el pelo corto y moreno. Tiene los ojos oscuros y la piel morena.
No tiene barba. Juega al fútbol en el Real Madrid.

Tiene el pelo corto y rubio. Tiene los ojos azules y la piel clara.
Es la reina de España.

Tiene el pelo largo y rubio, los ojos oscuros y la piel clara.
También es futbolista.

10. Pista 10

Guantanamera

Guantanamera,
Guajira guantanamera
Guantanamera,
Guajira guantanamera

Yo soy un hombre sincero
De donde crece la palma
Yo soy un hombre sincero
De donde crece la palma
Y antes de morirme quiero
Echar mis versos del alma

Guantanamera,
Guajira guantanamera
Guantanamera,
Guajira guantanamera

Mi verso es de un verde claro
Y de un jazmín encendido
Mi verso es de un verde claro
Y de un jazmín encendido
Mi verso es un ciervo herido
Que busca en el monte amparo

Guantanamera,
Guajira guantanamera
Guantanamera,
Guajira guantanamera

Por los pobres de la tierra
Quiero yo mi suerte echar
Por los pobres de la tierra
Quiero yo mi suerte echar
El arrullo de la tierra
Me complace más que el mar

Guantanamera,
Guajira guantanamera
Guantanamera,
Guajira guantanamera

Guantanamera,
Guajira guantanamera
Guantanamera,
Guajira guantanamera

UNIDAD 8

A. De vacaciones

5. Pista 12

a) Desde el hotel:
  A. Perdone, ¿puede decirme dónde está la farmacia más cercana?
  B. Salga por la calle de Santo Domingo, gire la primera a la izquierda y, después, la primera a la izquierda.

b) Desde la iglesia de San Francisco:
  A. Por favor, ¿puede decirme cómo se va a la iglesia de Santa Teresa?
  B. Siga todo recto y gire la segunda a la derecha, y después tome la calle Nueva Alta.

B. ¿Qué hizo Rosa ayer?

5. Pista 13

Ayer, como todos los días, me levanté a las siete de la mañana y me preparé para ir a trabajar.
Al llegar al hospital, como todos los días, atendí a los enfermos de la consulta y visité a los pacientes de las habitaciones.
A las cinco de la tarde, como todos los días, acabé de trabajar y pasé por el supermercado a comprar algo para la cena.
A las seis de la tarde llegué por fin a casa, muy cansada, como todos los días.
Pero ayer fue diferente: mi marido me invitó a un concierto y después cenamos en mi restaurante favorito.

6. Pista 14

SOLEDAD: ¡Oh, qué semana tan terrible! Por fin de vuelta a casa.
FEDERICO: ¿Dónde estuviste?
SOLEDAD: El lunes fui a Caracas para visitar a un cliente, y el martes volamos, mi jefe y yo, a Madrid, para firmar un contrato. Estuvimos dos días de conversaciones y, al fin, lo logramos. El jueves nos fuimos a Río de Janeiro para cerrar unos asuntos pendientes y hoy por fin vuelvo a casa. Y a ti, ¿cómo te fue?
FEDERICO: Hasta el martes estuve aquí, en Buenos Aires, preparando cosas para irme al día siguiente a Lima, donde estuve trabajando dos días y aproveché para conocer esa linda ciudad. Hoy fui al aeropuerto a primera hora y terminé mi semana de trabajo. ¿Qué te parece si cenamos juntos?
SOLEDAD: Estupendo. Me parece muy buena idea.

C. ¿Qué tiempo hace hoy?

6. Pista 16

En Toledo, durante los meses de invierno (diciembre, enero y febrero) hace mucho frío y algunas veces nieva. Durante la primavera (marzo, abril y mayo), suben las temperaturas y empieza a hacer buen tiempo. En verano (junio, julio y agosto), hace mucho calor. Todos los días hace mucho sol y las temperaturas son muy altas. En otoño (septiembre, octubre y noviembre), los días son más cortos, el cielo está nublado y a veces llueve y hace viento.

8. Pista 17

Estas son las condiciones meteorológicas para el día de hoy en algunas zonas de Sudamérica. Tenemos tiempo inestable en Brasil, con fuertes lluvias y bajas temperaturas, sobre todo en el interior, donde tenemos 8 grados centígrados en estos momentos. En la zona del Caribe, por el contrario, hace muy buen tiempo, con mucho sol y una temperatura de 22 grados centígrados. Tiempo inestable en la República de México, con fuerte viento y cielo nublado. La temperatura en la capital es de 15 grados centígrados. Próximo parte meteorológico en una hora.

D. Autoevaluación

5. Pista 18

SARA: El pasado mes de mayo, después de un año de mucho trabajo, tuve 15 días de vacaciones. Fui en tren a Galicia y me alojé en un hotel maravilloso. Pasé unos días estupendos yo sola, sin salir prácticamente de la playa.

LUCÍA: Mi sitio favorito para pasar las vacaciones es la Isla de Capri. Hace veinte años que fui por primera vez. Este verano llegué a la isla en barco, como siempre, para pasar mi mes de vacaciones con un grupo de amigos. Capri no es la misma de hace 20 años, pero sigue siendo única.

CARLOS: Tengo muy buen recuerdo de las últimas vacaciones que pasé con mi familia en Atacama, al norte de Chile; está a unos 4.000 metros de altura. Alquilamos un coche para recorrer toda la zona, uno de los desiertos más secos del mundo, con unas salinas impresionantes. Fueron unas vacaciones memorables.

UNIDAD 9

A. ¿Cuánto cuestan estos zapatos?

3. Pista 20

ÁLVARO: Celia, ¿qué te parece esta camisa para mí?
CELIA: Bien. ¿Cuánto cuesta?
ÁLVARO: Sólo 60 Euros. Voy a probármela.
CELIA: Vale.
CELIA: A ver… pues no te queda bien, ¿eh?
ÁLVARO: No, no, a mí tampoco me gusta.
CELIA: Toma, pruébate esta chaqueta, es muy bonita.
ÁLVARO: A ver… pues sí, parece que me queda bien, ¿no?
CELIA: Muy bien, es tu talla.
ÁLVARO: ¿Cuánto cuesta?
CELIA: 120 euros, es un poco cara.
ÁLVARO: Bueno, me la llevo.
CELIA: Mira, ¿qué te parece este gorro? ¿Cómo me queda?
ÁLVARO: Bien, muy bien.
CELIA: Pues me lo llevo, sólo cuesta 5 euros.
DEPENDIENTE: Una chaqueta y un gorro de lana… muy bien… son 125 euros. ¿Pagan en efectivo o con tarjeta?
ÁLVARO: En efectivo.

5. Pista 25

ÉL: Voy a preparar mi maleta para el viaje, a ver… ¿qué llevo? Mira estos zapatos están bien, ¿no?
ELLA: No, para ir a la montaña, las botas son mejores que los zapatos.
ÉL: Tienes razón. ¿Llevo los vaqueros?
ELLA: No, para el frío son mejores los pantalones de pana.
ÉL: Bueno, llevo los dos y ya está.
ELLA: ¿Por qué llevas la maleta azul?
ÉL: Pues porque es mejor que la gris, tiene ruedas.
ELLA: Yo prefiero la gris, caben más cosas. Toma el paraguas, guárdalo.
ÉL: ¿El rojo? No, este es peor que el negro.
ELLA: Lo siento, el negro ya está en mi maleta.

UNIDAD 10

A. La salud

7. Pista 29

PACIENTE 1
DOCTOR: Buenos días, ¿qué le ocurre?
PACIENTE: No me siento muy bien. Creo que tengo la gripe.

DOCTOR:	Tome una aspirina cada ocho horas y beba mucho zumo de naranja.

PACIENTE 2

DOCTOR:	Buenas tardes, ¿qué problema tiene?
PACIENTE:	Me duele la garganta cuando hablo.
DOCTOR:	A ver… No está muy mal, pero tome leche con miel y no hable mucho.

PACIENTE 3

DOCTOR:	Buenos días, ¿qué le pasa?
PACIENTE:	Mire, doctor, me duele mucho el estómago desde hace días.
DOCTOR:	Vaya, pues no tome café, ni fume. Coma frutas y ensaladas. Y tome estas pastillas.

ESCORPIÓN 2:	¿Y cuándo nos vamos de gira?
MANAGER:	En diciembre vamos a dar unos conciertos por toda España y, si todo va bien, nos vamos a Sudamérica.
ESCORPIÓN 3:	¿Y vamos a salir en televisión?
MANAGER:	Claro, y también tengo preparada nuestra propia página web.
ESCORPIÓN 1:	¿Cuándo vamos a ir a Barcelona?
MANAGER:	En septiembre, antes de empezar la gira. ¿A que no sabéis quién va a cantar con vosotros?
ESCORPIÓN 2:	Ni idea.
MANAGER:	Jennifer López.
ESCORPIÓN 3:	¡Vaya sorpresa!

B. Antes salíamos con los amigos

8. Pista 31

Martina tiene 92 años. Cuando era pequeña no iba a la escuela. Vivía con su madre y sus cuatro hermanos en un pueblo pequeño del sur de España. A los ocho años, ya trabajaba en el campo con su familia. Empezaba a las seis de la mañana y acababa a las seis de la tarde. No sabía leer, ni escribir, pero tenía muchas ilusiones y planes para el futuro. A los 19 años se casó y tuvo su primer hijo.
Los fines de semana iba con su marido a vender las verduras de su huerta en los mercadillos de los pueblos vecinos. Sólo los domingos por la tarde descansaban y se reunían con sus vecinos en la plaza del pueblo.

D. Autoevaluación

5. Pista 34

MANAGER:	Este disco suena muy bien, es mejor que el otro.
ESCORPIÓN 1:	Sí, estoy de acuerdo.
MANAGER:	Va a estar en las tiendas en la próxima semana y creo, amigos míos, que va a tener gran futuro.

Modern Foraminifera

Modern Foraminifera

edited by

Barun K. Sen Gupta
Louisiana State University

KLUWER ACADEMIC PUBLISHERS
Dordrecht/Boston/London

Library of Congress Cataloging-in-Publication Data is available.

ISBN 0-412-82430-2 (hardback)
ISBN 1-4020-0598-9 (paperback)

Published by Kluwer Academic Publishers,
P.O. Box 17, 3300 AA Dordrecht, The Netherlands.

Sold and distributed in North, Central and South America
by Kluwer Academic Publishers,
101 Philip Drive, Norwell, MA 02061, U.S.A.

In all other countries, sold and distributed
by Kluwer Academic Publishers,
P.O. Box 322, 3300 AH Dordrecht, The Netherlands

COVER: *Foraminifera*, from Ernst Haeckel, *Kunstformen der Natur*, 1904, redrawn and arranged by Mary Lee Eggart, Louisiana State University.

The quotation from E.O. Wilson is printed with permission from *Naturalist*, © Island Press, 1994. Published by Island Press, Shearwater Books, Washington, DC, and Covelo, California.

Printed on acid-free paper

First published 1999
Reprinted with corrections 2002
First published in paperback 2002

All rights reserved
© 1999, 2002 Kluwer Academic Publishers
No part of the material protected by this copyright notice may be reproduced or utilized in any form or by any means, electronic or mechanical, including photocopying, recording or by any information storage and retrieval system, without prior permission from the copyright owners.

Printed and bound in Great Britain by MPG Books, Bodmin, Cornwall.

Nous disons qu'elle est à la portée de tout le monde, en ce sens que, placé n'importe où, sur les côtes des diverses portions du globe terrestre ou sur les parties des continents recouvertes par des terrains tertiaires, crétacés ou oolithiques, partout disons-nous, l'observateur trouve sous ses pieds, et dans une seule pincée de sable, une grande quantité de Foraminifères qu'il peut étudier avec le seul secours d'une loupe. Pour l'importance réelle de leur étude, nous croyons qu'il n'est pas de série animale offrant plus de facilités et d'avantages au géologue et au zoologiste: au premier, pour déterminer la température des lieux où vivaient les espèces perdues, par la comparaison avec ce que nous voyons maintenant dans les mers, et pour expliquer la formation des couches (questions de la plus haute importance dans l'histoire de notre planète); au second, par leur admirable diversité, par l'élégance de leurs formes, par la singularité de leur organisation, et enfin en ce qu'ils constituent une classe des plus nombreuses du règne animal, et jouent, malgré leur petitesse, un rôle immense dans la nature.

Alcide d'Orbigny, 1839, in Ramon de la Sagra, *Histoire Physique, Politique et Naturelle de l'Ile de Cuba*

Love the organisms for themselves first, then strain for general explanations, and, with good fortune, discoveries will follow. If they don't, the love and pleasure will have been enough.

Edward O. Wilson, 1994, *Naturalist*.

Contents

Contributors ix

Preface and Acknowledgments xi

PART I: BASIC CONSIDERATIONS 3

1. **Introduction to Modern Foraminifera** 7
   Barun K. Sen Gupta

2. **Systematics of Modern Foraminifera** 37
   Barun K. Sen Gupta

3. **Foraminifera: A Biological Overview** 57
   Susan T. Goldstein

4. **Shell Construction in Modern Calcareous Foraminifera** 71
   Hans Jorgen Hansen

5. **Quantitative Methods of Data Analysis in Foraminiferal Ecology** 93
   William C. Parker and Anthony J. Arnold

PART II: FEATURES OF DISTRIBUTION

6. **Biogeography of Neritic Benthic Foraminifera** 103
   Stephen J. Culver and Martin A. Buzas

7. **Biogeography of Planktonic Foraminifera** 123
   Anthony J. Arnold and William C. Parker

8. **Symbiont-Bearing Foraminifera**
   Pamela Hallock

viii　Contents

9 **Foraminifera in Marginal Marine Environments** 141
Barun K. Sen Gupta

10 **Benthic Foraminiferal Microhabitats below the Sediment-Water Interface** 161
Frans Jorissen

11 **Benthic Foraminifera and the Flux of Organic Carbon to the Seabed** 181
Paul Loubere and Mohammad Fariduddin

12 **Foraminifera of Oxygen-Depleted Environments** 201
Joan M. Bernhard and Barun K. Sen Gupta

13 **Effects of Marine Pollution on Benthic Foraminifera** 217
Valentina Yanko, Anthony J. Arnold, and William C. Parker

PART III: GEOCHEMISTRY OF SHELLS

14 **Stable Oxygen and Carbon Isotopes in Foraminiferal Carbonate Shells** 239
Eelco J. Rohling and Steve Cooke

15 **Trace Elements in Foraminiferal Calcite** 259
David W. Lea

PART IV: PRESERVATION OF RECORD

16 **Taphonomy and Temporal Resolution of Foraminiferal Assemblages** 281
Ronald E. Martin

References 299

General Index 353

Taxonomic Index 361

Contributors

Anthony J. Arnold
Department of Geology
Florida State University
Tallahassee, FL 32306
U.S.A.

Joan M. Bernhard
Department of Environmental Health Sciences
and Marine Science Program
University of South Carolina
Columbia, SC 29208
U.S.A.

Martin A. Buzas
Department of Paleobiology
National Museum of Natural History
Smithsonian Institution
Washington, DC 20560
U.S.A.

Steve Cooke
School of Ocean and Earth Science
University of Southampton
Southampton Oceanography Centre
Southampton SO14 3ZH
U.K.

Stephen J. Culver
Department of Geology
East Carolina University
Greenville, NC 27858
U.S.A.

Mohammad Fariduddin
Department of Earth Sciences
Northeastern Illinois University
5500 North St. Louis Avenue
Chicago, IL 60625
U.S.A.

Susan T. Goldstein
Department of Geology
University of Georgia
Athens, GA 30602
U.S.A.

Pamela Hallock
Department of Marine Science
University of South Florida
140 7th Ave. S
St. Petersburg, FL 33701
U.S.A.

Hans Jørgen Hansen
Geological Institute
Oster Voldgade 10
1350 Copenhagen
Denmark

Frans Jorissen
Laboratoire de Géologie
Université d'Angers
2 Boulevard Lavoisier
49045 Angers Cedex
France

David W. Lea
Department of Geological Sciences
University of California, Santa Barbara
Santa Barbara, CA 93106
U.S.A.

Paul Loubere
Department of Geology and Environmental Geosciences
Northern Illinois University
De Kalb, IL 60115
U.S.A.

Ronald E. Martin
Department of Geology
University of Delaware
Newark, DE 19716
U.S.A.

William C. Parker
Department of Geology
Florida State University
Tallahassee, FL 32306
U.S.A.

Eelco J. Rohling
School of Ocean and Earth Science
University of Southampton
Southampton Oceanography Centre
Southampton SO14 3ZH
U.K.

Barun K. Sen Gupta
Department of Geology and Geophysics
Louisiana State University
Baton Rouge, LA 70803
U.S.A.

Valentina Yanko
Avalon Institute of Applied Science
Charleston Technology Centre
3227 Roblin Boulevard
Winnipeg, MB R3R OC2
Canada

Preface and Acknowledgments

Modern Foraminifera started with a simple idea: to write an advanced text for university students that would also serve as a reference book for professionals. Being keenly aware of the boundaries of my competence, I invited fourteen colleagues to write most of the chapters. The chapters were designed to be balanced reviews, but, with the lone exception of chapter two, they had to be written under a rather stringent space limitation. Thus, although the list of references is long, it surely does not include every single significant article on every topic covered in the book. Both the subject matters of the chapters and the selection of authors were entirely my responsibity, and no other author can be accused of a personal bias in the structure of the book. I have assumed that the reader will have an elementary knowledge of foraminiferal shell morphology, as found in undergraduate paleontology texts.

I am deeply indebted to the reviewers who helped shape the chapters into their final form. They are: Paul Aharon, Elisabeth Alve, Laurie Anderson, Anthony Arnold, William Berggren, Joan Bernhard, Samuel Bowser, Kevin Carman, Robert Carney, Lui-Heung Chan, Bruce Corliss, Robert Douglas, Thomas Gibson, Susan Goldstein, Andrew Gooday, Pamela Hallock, Jeffrey Hanor, John Haynes, Johann Hohenegger, Scott Ishman, Frans Jorissen, Susan Kidwell, Martin Langer, David Lea, Richard Norris, William Parker, Nancy Rabalais, Charles Ramcharan, Charles Schafer, Scott Snyder, Kenneth Towe, Bert van der Zwaan, and two others who chose to remain anonymous. Jessica Schreyer assisted in editorial tasks. In the final stages of putting the book together, my burden was lightened by the cheerful cooperation of Petra van Steenbergen, our publishing editor at Kluwer. In addition, I was helped by Ian Francis at the planning stage of the book.

Two people deserve special acknowledgment. I am grateful to Mary Lee Eggart for the art on the cover and in several chapters, and to Poree Sen Gupta, my wife, for her tolerance of my obsessive preoccupation with the book for the past two years.

Finally, I thank the Cushman Foundation for its very special role in publishing and promoting foraminiferal research. In appreciation of this service, the royalty for the book has been transferred to this organization.

Baton Rouge   Barun K. Sen Gupta
December, 1998

PART I: BASIC CONSIDERATIONS

1

Introduction to modern Foraminifera

Barun K. Sen Gupta

'These minute animals are interesting objects of study, geologically and biologically as well as esthetically. As objects of beauty they arrest the attention of even the casual observer by the delicacy of their structure as well as the symmetry and variety of their forms. Geologically they are of interest because they are among the most ancient and abundant of fossils and also the most efficient of rock builders. Biologically they are instructive examples of the powers and possibilities of an individualized bit of protoplasm.'

James M. Flint, 1899, *Recent Foraminifera: A Descriptive Catalogue of Specimens Dredged by the U.S. Fish Commission Steamer Albatross.*

Foraminifers are better known for their spectacular fossil record than for their variety or abundance in modern marine environments. They, however, constitute the most diverse group of shelled microorganisms in modern oceans. In 1846, Alcide d'Orbigny counted 68 modern foraminiferal genera, and estimated that there are 1,000 modern species. In the latest taxonomic *magnum opus* on the class, Alfred R. Loeblich and Helen Tappan (1987) described 878 modern genera. The number of extant foraminiferal species is now estimated to be about 10,000 (Vickerman, 1992), that is, about one-eighth of the estimated number of modern species within the Kingdom Protoctista (Hammond *et al.*, 1995). The overwhelming majority of modern Foraminifera are benthic; there are only about 40–50 planktonic species. In addition to their much greater diversity, the benthic species have a much longer geological record. Their oldest fossils are Cambrian in age, whereas those of the planktonic species are Jurassic.

Shells (usually called 'tests') of extant Foraminifera have been noticed in shore sands since the 17th century (see Cifelli, 1990). An unusual early find was by the great microscopist Antonie van Leeuwenhoek, who, in 1700, wrote about foraminifer shells 'no bigger than a coarse sand grain' in stomachs of shrimps, and described the specimens as 'very little snail shells, which

Barun K. Sen Gupta (ed.), Modern Foraminifera, 3–6
© 1999 Kluwer Academic Publishers. Printed in Great Britain.

because of their roundness, I called little cockles' (Dobell, 1932). Leeuwenhoek's drawing of one of these shells (Fig. 1.1) is detailed enough to be recognized as that of an *Elphidium*. It is an interesting but not a surprising coincidence that after foraminifers were identified as shelled protists (chapters 2, 3), the early studies of their life cycle were focused on *Elphidium* (e.g. Lister, 1895; chapter 3). This genus is easily collected from nearshore environments, where large populations are common (chapter 9). Overall, a relative ease of collection is reflected in the much greater body of literature that exists on continental-shelf foraminifers, compared to that on deeper-water species.

The biology of foraminifers has not been examined as intensively as that of some protistan cousins (e.g. ciliates); apparently, the shell has been somewhat of a problem in cellular studies. The biological feature that has drawn the most attention is the alternation between a sexual and an asexual generation (and the variations of this cycle; chapter 3), because this explains the distinct morphological dimorphism that is seen in the shells of many species, including, especially, some relatively large fossil forms. In addition, from the very beginning of biological studies of foraminifers in the 19th century, the reticulate pseudopodia ('reticulopodia') have been regarded as a special feature of this group, and recent studies have shed light on their diverse functions (chapter 3). To most students and researchers, however, the most significant aspect of foraminiferal biology is the production of an amazing variety of shells (chapter 2), matched in no other class of organisms. On the basis of the morphology of these shells, one can recognize 15 extant foraminiferal orders. In seven orders, the shell is made of secreted calcite; in others, the species secrete aragonite or opaline silica, or make their shells with organic matter or foreign particles (chapter 2). The mechanics of chamber formation in some calcareous species has been studied in great detail (chapters 3, 4), and used in the recognition of supragenetic taxa (chapter 2). Genetic research on Foraminifera is a new and sparsely populated field, but judging by the effect of this research on species-level taxonomy (e.g. Pawlowski *et al.*, 1995), a major impact on foraminiferal systematics is expected in the future.

The ecology of Foraminifera became a major area of study in the second half of the 20th century, and the first text on this subject was by Fred B Phleger (1960a). In the the past 30 years, research in this field has increased greatly, mainly because of the realization that modern foraminiferal distributions are likely to provide reliable clues ('analogs') for the understanding of marine environmental changes in the geological (and, in some cases, historical) past. The advantage of using foraminifers in paleoecology lies in their significant numerical density in diverse marine sediments and in the excellent preservation of their shells. Both of these factors are partly related to their small size. Some species, however, are better preserved than others, causing a taphonomic bias even in relatively recent sedimentary records (chapter 16).

Traditionally, the focus of foraminiferal distribution studies has been on water depth (relevant to paleodepth research on sedimentary rocks), except for marginal marine species, which are strongly influenced by salinity changes (chapter 9). In waters of normal marine salinity, placing a foraminiferal zone boundary at the shelf-slope break is common practice. Furthermore,

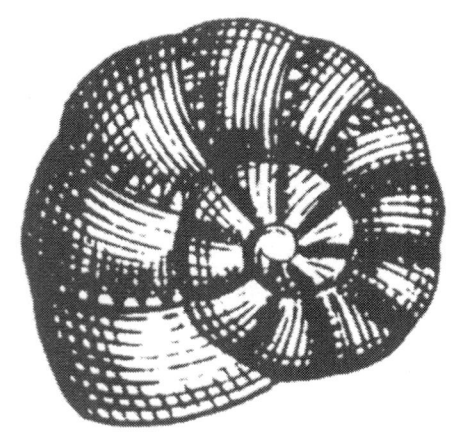

Figure 1.1 Leeuwenhoek's drawing of *Elphidium* in a letter dated June 2, 1700. From Dobell (1932), where the genus is reported as *Polystomella*.

Introduction to modern Foraminifera

numerous investigators have followed Phleger (e.g. 1964a) in recognizing distinctive foraminiferal assemblages on the 'inner continental shelf, outer continental shelf, upper continental slope, lower continental slope and deep sea.' Application of numerical techniques of data analysis (chapter 5) to relative abundances of species has led to finer groupings in many areas. With a different perspective, latitudinally extensive biogeographic provinces of benthic Foraminifera have been recognized on various continental shelves and slopes. In many of these provinces, the proportion of endemic species in the foraminiferal community is very high (chapter 6).

Recognition of patterns (and their causes) in the distribution of deep-sea benthic Foraminifera has remained a problem since the *Challenger* report of 1884, because many species of this 'cold-water sphere' are ubiquitous. They, however, are not equally abundant everywhere, and the dominance of certain species seems to be connected with particular deep-bathyal or abyssal water masses, although invariant associations are hard to establish. Two associations that have been verified in multiple deep basins relate to well-oxygenated waters: *Cibicides wuellerstorfi* is a dominant species in North Atlantic Deep Water (or its remnant in Caribbean basins), and *Nuttallides umbonifera* in Antarctic Bottom Water (e.g. Streeter, 1973; Schnitker, 1974b; Douglas and Woodruff, 1981; Sen Gupta, 1988). In many correlations between a benthic foraminiferal species or assemblage and a water mass (defined by the combination of temperature and salinity), causality is elusive. On the other hand, there is compelling evidence that the variable input of labile organic matter (a reflection of surface-ocean productivity) affects abundances of deep-sea foraminiferal species (chapter 11). Thus, *Epistominella exigua*, once thought to be a foraminiferal marker of some deep-water masses, is now known to be a species whose population density is dependent on phytodetritus falls (e.g. Gooday, 1993). In bathyal depths, the correlation between a benthic foraminiferal association and the oxygen-minimum water mass has been clearly demonstrated (e.g. Hermelin and Shimmield, 1990; Denne and Sen Gupta, 1993), but the controlling factor may be the organic-rich sediment on the seafloor (Hermelin and Shimmield, 1990). This book does not include a chapter on the connection between water masses and foraminiferal assemblages on the deep-sea floor, but the point of view that there is a connection is expressed succinctly by Schnitker (1994): 'Benthic foraminifers are unequivocal indicators of productivity in areas where productivity is high. In areas of low or very uniform productivity the composition of the benthic fauna clearly carries the imprint of deep water mass structure as the dominant feature.' An additional difficulty is posed by the probability that all species in the same deep-sea assemblage may not be equally dependent on food falls. A recent study in eastern South Atlantic Ocean provides an illustration. Schmiedl and Mackensen (1997) studied the variations in the Quaternary benthic foraminiferal record of two cores taken from the same depth (about 3,000 m), but under surface waters of sharply different productivities. They concluded that fluctuations in the abundances of *Cibicides wuellerstorfi* and *Bulimina alazanensis* are related to temporal changes in the advection of North Atlantic Deep Water, whereas those of *Cassidulina laevigata*, *Melonis barleeanus*, and *M. zaandami* are linked to shifts in productivity.

At the sediment-water interface, many Foraminifera are neither obligate epibenthos (living *on* the sediment) nor obligate endobenthos (living *within* the sediment), because they can move up or down the sediment column in search of food, and thus have variable microhabitats (Linke and Lutze, 1993). Some truly epibenthic species (free or attached) live on substrates *above* the sediment surface, whereas some truly endobenthic species live several centimeters down in the sediment (chapter 10). Such deep endobenthic species may have to cope with a severe shortage of oxygen in the sediment pore water, but as recent research has shown, many foraminiferal species can live in extremely oxygen-poor water in varying depths of the sea (chapter 12). Because of the paucity of observations on the preferred depths of living individuals within the substrate, microhabitats of most sediment-dwelling species are unknown. Some researchers use the shell shape ('morphotype') to infer the microhabitat, but this practice has an inherent uncertainty (chapter 10).

In many coastal areas, especially in industrialized countries, pollution has severely affected foraminiferal microhabitats. Studies on the effects of various forms of pollution on Foraminifera show that many species can serve as indicators in pollution monitoring programs (chapter 13). Many foraminiferal species have adapted to extreme natural environments, such as habitats of very high salinity (chapter 9), areas near hydrothermal vents (e.g. Jonasson et al., 1995), bacterial mats at hydrocarbon vents (e.g. Sen Gupta et al., 1997) or in silled basins (e.g. Bernhard et al., 1997), and pack ice (planktonic species, chapter 7). These are not exotic species, however; they are recruited from the surrounding areas where the environment is 'normal' for the water depth and distance from the shore.

Modern planktonic Foraminifera, because of their enormous population sizes, produce a significant amount of oceanic carbonate. There is a much larger proportion of taxa with algal symbionts within this group than within the benthic group (chapter 8). The environmental controls on planktonic species are much better understood than those on benthic species, because the only major variables are the temperature, salinity, and productivity of the surface layer of seawater (mainly in the upper 100 m). The species are distributed in a few large latitudinal provinces, with some showing bipolar distributions; many species can be used as tracers of ocean currents (e.g. Oberhänsli, 1992). The present-day temperature limits of the biogeographic provinces have been of great use in estimating Quaternary sea-surface paleotemperatures from the fossil record of extant species (chapter 7).

The extraordinary progress of foraminiferal shell geochemistry in recent years has been in the context of major questions of paleoceanography that relate to the nature and movement of past water masses, at the sea surface and in the water column. The principles behind these inquiries have to be established by analyses of modern foraminiferal shells – both planktonic and benthic. Culturing studies have become especially significant in this research, because of the necessity of understanding the species-specific 'vital effect' in the incorporation of trace elements and the acquiring of the oxygen and carbon isotope signatures in the shell (chapters 14 and 15).

In summary, much of this book is about patterns of foraminiferal distribution in seafloor sediments and in seawater, and about the processes that govern this distribution. In spite of prolific research since Phleger's days, many questions about processes remain unresolved. On matters of speculative interpretation, there may be disagreement even among authors of this book. We hope such issues will generate thought and discussion, not frustration.

Acknowledgment. I thank Anthony Arnold and Joan Bernhard for reviewing this chapter.

2
Systematics of modern Foraminifera

Barun K. Sen Gupta

2.1 INTRODUCTION: THE EARLY PHASE OF SUPRAGENERIC TAXONOMY

As J.J. Lister wrote, 'the Foraminifera received their name before their nature was understood' (Lister, 1903). In fact, numerous foraminiferal species had been described under a linnaean binomial before this understanding. In the latter half of the 18th century, most foraminifers were described as cephalopods, particularly as *Nautilus*. The original descriptions of about 140 such false nautiluses named between 1758 and 1819 are given in the *Catalogue of Foraminifera* (Ellis and Messina, 1940 and later). Many of the species and varieties were well illustrated by their authors, and it is possible to place them under currently accepted generic labels. The best known example of this phase of foraminiferal taxonomy is the *Testacea Microscopica* of Fichtel and Moll (1798) in which 47 extant and fossil taxa (putatively, distinct species or varieties) were given linnaean names under the single generic heading of *Nautilus*; 18 separate genera (Fig. 2.1), all extant, are now recognized within this group (Rögl and Hansen, 1984).

The identification and separation of foraminiferal species, genera, and higher taxa solely by aspects of test morphology, especially chamber arrangement, did not change with the recognition by Felix Dujardin (1835a–c; spelt 'Desjardins' in 1835a) that the foraminiferal body was simply a jelly-like mass ('sarcode') with pseudopodia (Fig. 2.2; see also chapter 3). The classification in vogue at this time (d'Orbigny, 1826) underwent only minor modifications after d'Orbigny's acceptance of Dujardin's conclusion that foraminifers were unicellular organisms, and not cephalopods. In d'Orbigny's 1826 classification, the Foraminifera, as a foramina-bearing (as opposed to siphon-bearing) class of cephalopods, was split into five orders; his 1852 classification of the Foraminifera (as sarcodines), included all of these orders, plus an order for single-chambered forms (Monostègues) and one in which chambers were arranged in annuli (Cyclostègues; Fig. 2.3). At this stage, d'Orbigny had recognized a total of 72 foraminiferal genera. Although wall characters were considered a significant criterion in generic taxonomy, d'Orbigny (1852) placed both calcareous and agglutinated genera in the same family, because of some similarity in chamber arrangement. For example, the agglutinated form *Clavulina* and the calcareous forms *Bulimina* and *Globigerina*

Figure 2.1 Foraminiferal genera (all extant) considered as micromolluscs and placed under *Nautilus* by Leopold von Fichtel and Johann Paul Carl von Moll (1798). Redrawn from Fichtel and Moll (plates in Rögl and Hansen, 1984); j, l, m, p, ventral views; q, dorsal view; c, r, sectional views. Currently accepted generic nomenclature (Rögl and Hansen, 1984) and ordinal and superfamilial affiliations (Loeblich and Tappan, 1987, 1992) are as follows: a, *Dendritina* (Miliolida, Soritacea); b, *Peneroplis* (Miliolida, Soritacea); c, *Archaias* (Miliolida, Soritacea); d, *Borelis* (Miliolida, Soritacea); e, *Lenticulina* (Lagenida, Nodosariacea); f, *Planularia* (Lagenida, Nodosariacea); g, *Astacolus* (Lagenida, Nodosariacea); h, *Nonion* (Lagenida, Nonionacea); i, *Melonis* (Lagenida, Nonionacea); j, *Eponides* (Rotaliida, Discorbacea); k, *Cancris* (Rotaliida, Discorbacea); l, *Hanzawaia* (Rotaliida, Chilostomellacea); m, *Anomalinoides* (Rotaliida, Chilostomellacea); n, *Elphidium* (Rotaliida, Rotaliacea); o, *Calcarina* (Rotaliida, Rotaliacea); p, *Cibicides* (Rotaliida, Planorbulinacea); q, *Amphistegina* (Rotaliida, Asterigerinacea); r, *Nummulites* (Rotaliida, Nummulitacea); a–d are porcelaneous genera, e–r hyaline.

Introduction: The early phase of suprageneric taxonomy

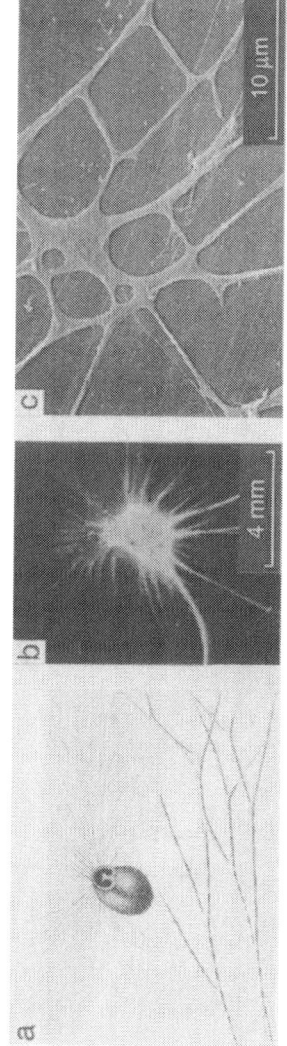

Figure 2.2 Pseudopodial network (reticulopodia) in Foraminifera; a, top (8×) and bottom (250×), miliolaceans (reduced from drawings in Dujardin, 1835c); b and c, *Astrammina rara*, an astrorhizacean (scanning electron micrographs by Samuel Bowser, reprinted with permission).

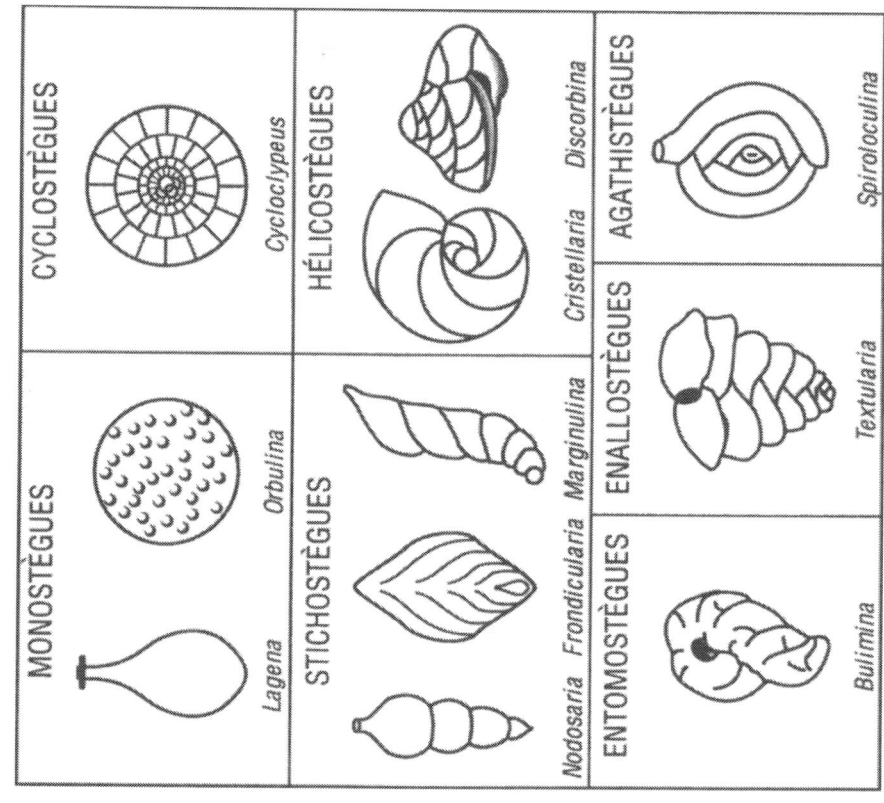

Figure 2.3 The seven foraminiferal orders of Alcide d'Orbigny (1852). Redrawn from Chapman (1902).

were all placed under Tubinoidaea (Order Heli-costègues). This practice of placing agglutinated and calcareous genera (especially those with serial chamber arrangements) within one family continued well into the 20th century. At the highest level of taxonomic discrimination, however, the shift in the primary emphasis from chamber arrangement to wall characters is clear in many schemes of foraminiferal classification developed in Europe and the U.S. (see, e.g. Galloway, 1933; Glaessner, 1945; Loeblich and Tappan, 1964a, b). The most significant transitions are discussed below. An elegant summary of all major classifications from d'Orbigny (1826) to Galloway (1933), their philosophical bases, and their relevance in an evolutionary context are given in Cifelli (1990).

The hierarchical base of d'Orbigny's classification was severely criticized by a number of researchers in Great Britain in the 1850s and 1860s (W.K. Parker, T.R. Jones, W.C. Williamson, W.B. Carpenter, and H.B. Brady; see Cifelli, 1990), because they concluded that these unicellular organisms are so variable that clear distinctions, whether among species or among orders, are unattainable (Carpenter et al., 1862). Nevertheless, attempts at classification, by these critics and others, continued, culminating in two hierarchical schemes of great significance (Reuss, 1861; Carpenter et al., 1862). Although they were considerably different in details, wall structure was used as the feature of primary importance in both of these schemes, and two major divisions were recognized, one with perforate families, the other with imperforate families. The scheme was significantly modified by Jones (1876) when he separated the porcelaneous group from the arenaceous, thus recognizing three major divisions.

One of the greatest works on modern Foraminifera was H.B. Brady's magnificent monograph (1884) on the material collected during the Challenger expedition of 1873–1876. Brady's illustrations are still used extensively for species identifications; names may have changed because of questions of priority, but by and large, the internal consistency of nomenclature is impressive (see Barker, 1960; Jones, 1994).

Brady's views on foraminiferal systematics, forcefully expressed in the Challenger monograph, strongly influenced researchers in the next five decades. Brady included both modern and ancient (including Paleozoic) genera in his 10 families and 29 subfamilies, but placed no importance on stratigraphic distributions, occasionally grouping Paleozoic genera together with very different Cenozoic ones. In Brady's view, even the largest taxa within the Foraminifera (to him, an order) had to be recognized on the basis of multiple characters, and no single character (e.g. wall composition or texture) could be used as the sole basis for the separation of these taxa. Thus, he kept all known genera with serially arranged chambers within a single family, the Textularidae (Textularidae of later workers), because he considered the wall composition to span the range between agglutinated or calcareous, warranting no more than a recognition of two subfamilies, Textularinae (Textularinae of later workers) for the former, and Bulimininae for the latter. On the whole, however, the value of wall structure is reflected in Brady's classification. Of the other nine families, the largest taxonomic groups in his scheme, one (Gromidae) is characterized by organic walls, two (Astrorhizidae and Lituolidae) by agglutinated walls, one (Miliolidae) by calcareous imperforate walls, and five (Chilostomellidae, Lagenidae, Globigerinidae, Rotaliidae, Nummulinidae) by calcareous perforate walls. Furthermore, the practice of placing all planktonic foraminifers into a distinct major taxon was firmly established with Brady's classification, although currently this group has the status of an order (Globigerinida as in Loeblich and Tappan, 1992) rather than that of a family (Globigerinidae as in Brady, 1884). About two decades later, Lister (1903), while keeping the basic hierarchy of Brady, elevated his 10 foraminiferal families to superfamilies (with a suffix change from -idae to -idea), and the order Foraminifera to a class. Lister categorically rejected Carpenter's extreme view (Carpenter et al., 1862) that morphological variability and intergradation among foraminifers are so strong that separation of species is impossible. He clarified the issue by stating that the question 'appears to be not whether all intermediate forms do or do not exist between dissimilar forms, but whether the whole body of forms, as they occur in nature, tend to group themselves or are aggregated about certain centres. ... In a very large number of cases, ... such centres do exist among the Foraminifera, as among other organised beings, and the characters of the middle individuals of them are those of the species' (Lister, 1903).

2.2 THE AGE OF CUSHMAN

Joseph A. Cushman, the most notable foraminiferal taxonomist in the first half of the 20th century, was strongly influenced by Brady's view of suprageneric groupings. Cushman's first classification (1925) was simply an adaptation of Brady's 10 families with some changes in the naming of subfamilies. Although he argued against keeping genera with the same chamber arrangement but different wall structures (e.g. the coiled-tubular *Ammodiscus*, *Cornuspira*, and *Spirillina*) within one family, he retained Brady's concept of the Textulariidae, with both agglutinated and calcareous genera. The big expansion came with his 1927 and 1928 classifications, in which he increased the number of families to 45, without proposing superfamilies or orders. Apart from test morphology, Cushman's new classification was 'based upon the known geological history of the genera, upon the phylogenetic characters through a study of very much fossil material from all the continents, and finally by a study of the ontogeny in very many microspheric specimens, which show the relationships much more definitely than do megalospheric specimens of the same species' (Cushman, 1933; see Fig. 2.4). In the final version of this classification (Cushman, 1948), the number of families (without any suprafamilial groupings) was 50. Galloway's classification, apparently ready in 1927, and the cause of a private and public dispute between Galloway and Cushman regarding claims to priority (see Cifelli, 1990), was published in 1933. As in Cushman (1927), (1) the number of families was greatly expanded (to 35, from Brady's 10), without the recognition of superfamilies or suborders, and (2) the agglutinated textulariids were separated from the calcareous-hyaline buliminids, but the phylogenetic concepts of Cushman and Galloway and their family and subfamily groupings were substantially different. With Cushman's expanded classification of 1927, the role of wall structure was firmly established as the primary basis for first-level splitting. Although Cushman did not propose any suprafamilial taxon within the Order Foraminifera, he arranged the families in a wall-structure sequence, beginning with membranous and single-chambered agglutinated families, which he considererd the most primitive, and ending with calcareous, perforate, trochospiral families, which he considered the most advanced. The morphological separation of families and genera was unambiguous, permitting Cushman to produce identification keys (1928, 1933, 1940, 1948). An abbreviated version of his last identification key to foraminiferal families (1948) is given below (Table 2.1). Cushman did not identify any suprafamilial, subordinal taxa, but the identities of several of the morphological groups in his key match the orders proposed in the most widely accepted classification of later decades (Loeblich and Tappan, 1964a).

Within about twenty years after its publication, Cushman's 1927 classification became the standard classification, 'adopted by workers on the Foraminifera throughout the world' (Cushman, 1948). A contributing factor was Cushman's reputation as the foremost specialist in the use of fossil Foraminifera in petroleum exploration. Biological research on the Foraminifera, however, had not progressed much beyond what it was at the beginning of the 20th century. Thus, according to a distinguished protozoologist, not enough information was available on living organisms to warrant a complete revision of the classification, and Cushman's monumental work was subject to some derision because it was 'plain that some of Cushman's splitting of groups' was not 'biologically sound.' An allowance was made that such a classification, based purely on shell morphology, 'may

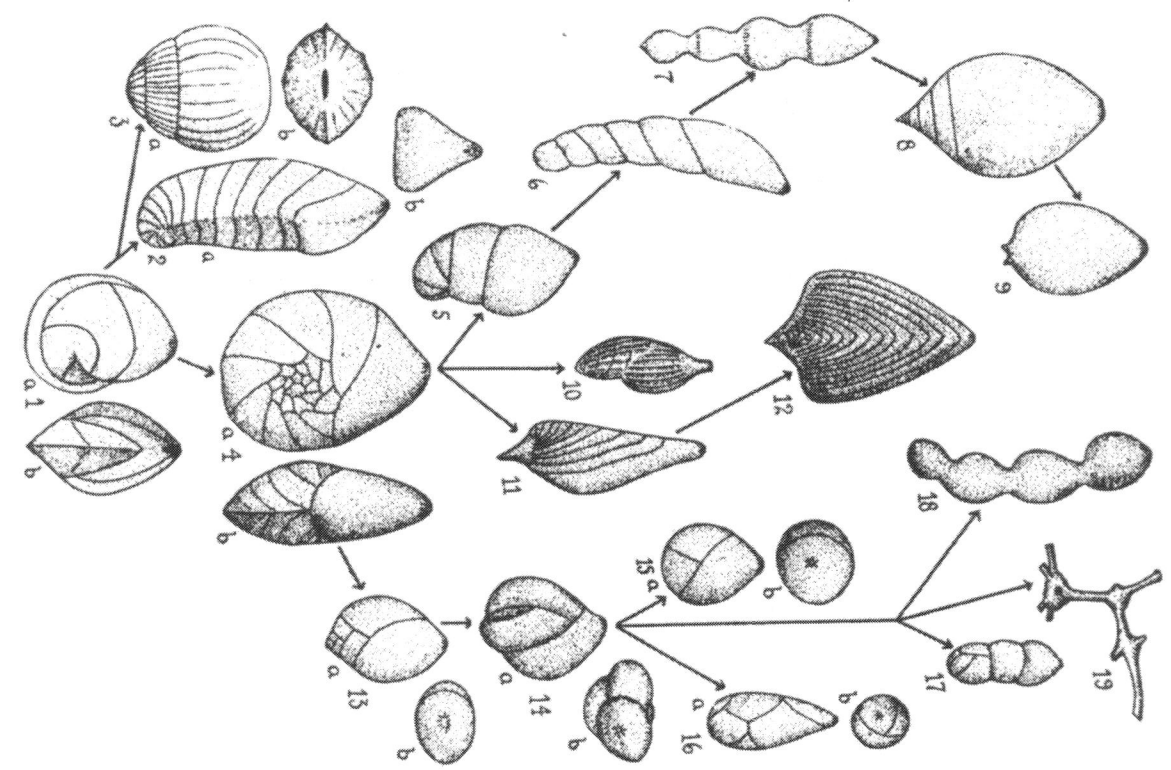

Figure 2.4 Evolutionary relationships envisaged by Cushman (1927) among the genera he placed in the Lagenidae and Polymorphinidae. 1, *Robulus*; 2, *Saracenaria*; 3, *Lingulina*; 4, *Cristellaria*; 5, *Marginulina*; 6, *Dentalina*; 7, *Nodosaria*; 8, *Glandulina*; 9, *Lagena*; 10, *Amphicoryne*; 11, *Vaginulina*; 12, *Frondicularia*; 13, *Polymorphina*; 14, *Guttulina*; 15, *Globulina*; 16, *Pyrulina*; 17, *Dimorphina*; 18, *Vitrewebbina*; 19, *Ramulina*. From Cushman (1927), with the generic names used by him.

serve the commercial purpose for which it was in fact designed,' but zoologists were admonished to 'adhere to Brady's simpler classification' (Jepps, 1956). A reticence still exists among some biologists in accepting shell morphology, especially wall structure, as a basis for elaborate, hierarchical, foraminiferal classifications (e.g. Cavalier-Smith, 1993, discussed later).

Several classifications developed in the two decades following Cushman's last major taxo-

The age of Cushman

Table 2.1 Outline of Cushman's identification key (1948) to foraminiferal families. The complete version includes a key to each family, followed by keys to the genera. The informal morphological group and subgroup numbers and the family numbers are from Cushman. Asterisks indicate extinct families. The Paleozoic families Fusulinidae and Neoschwagerinidae are misplaced in the key. Their calcareous wall is correctly noted in the text descriptions of the families (written by C.O. Dunbar).

Group	Wall structure	Subgroup	Chamber arrangement and other key characters	Families
I	Membranous			1. Allogromiidae
II	Agglutinated	II A	Single chamber or irregular cluster	2. Astrorhizidae
				3. Rhizamminidae
				4. Saccamminidae
				5. Hyperamminidae
				7. Ammodiscidae
				16. Silicinidae
		II B	Two chambered, coiled	6. Reophacidae
		II C	Multichambered	8. Lituolidae
				12. Fusulinidae*
				13. Neoschwagerinidae*
				14. Loftusiidae*
				9. Textulariidae
				10. Verneuilinidae
				11. Valvulinidae
				15. Neusinidae
				20. Trochamminidae
				21. Placopsilinidae
				22. Orbitolinidae*
III	Calcareous imperforate	III A	Coiled in multiple planes	17. Miliolidae
		III B	Trochospiral	19. Fischerinidae
		III C	Planispiral, at least in early part	18. Ophthalmididae
				27. Peneroplidae
		III D	Globular test	28. Alveolinellidae
IV	Calcareous perforate	IV A	Not trochospiral; vitreous lustre; radiate aperture	29. Keramosphaeridae
				23. Lagenidae
		IV B (Types 1–6)	Planispiral, serial, or crudely trochospiral; no vitreous lustre; no radiate aperture	24. Polymorphinidae
				25. Nonionidae
				26. Camerinidae
				30. Heterohelicidae
				41. Hantkeninidae*
				31. Buliminidae
				32. Ellipsoidinidae
		IV B (Type 7)	Trochospiral, at least in early stage; no vitreous lustre; no radiate aperture	34. Pegididae
				33. Rotaliidae
				35. Amphisteginidae
				36. Calcarinidae
				37. Cymbaloporidae
				38. Cassidulinidae
				39. Chilostomellidae
				40. Globigerinidae
				42. Globorotaliidae
				43. Anomalinidae
				44. Planorbulinidae
				45. Rupertiidae
				46. Victoriellidae*
				47. Homotremidae
				48. Orbitoididae*
				49. Discocyclinidae*
				50. Miogypsinidae*

nomic work (1948) introduced a suprafamilial hierarchy within the order Foraminifera, but other than a scheme developed in the Soviet Union (Rauzer-Chernousova and Fursenko, 1959, 1962; Grigelis, 1978; see later), none received a wide acceptance. This scene changed with the appearance of Loeblich and Tappan's first book on foraminiferal systematics (1964a). Meanwhile, a landmark paper on foraminiferal wall structure (Wood, 1949) focused attention on optical characters of calcitic foraminiferal walls that had been more or less ignored until this time.

2.3 CRYSTAL ORIENTATION IN CALCAREOUS WALLS

As already explained, the wall structure had been considered as a basis for foraminiferal taxonomy since its early days. However, little attention had been paid to the details of the wall characters of calcareous taxa, other than the simple distinction between perforate and imperforate groups, and the related hyaline and porcelaneous surface textures observed in reflected light under the microscope. Although several studies of the optical phenomena observed in calcareous walls of Foraminifera had been published in late 19th and early 20th centuries, and the presence of an extinction cross had been reported in polarized-light studies of certain species (e.g. Ehrenberg, 1854; Sollas, 1921), the careful documentation by Wood (1949) demonstrated clearly the difference between two interference patterns produced by polarized light when viewed between crossed nicols: (1) a 'radial' pattern, in which a black cross and concentric color bands are observed in single chambers or fragments of chambers (Fig. 2.5, 2.6a) and (2) a 'granular' pattern, characterized by randomly distributed flecks of color (Fig. 2.6b). The radial pattern, a mimic of the uniaxial negative interference figure, is caused by the perpendicular orientation of the c-axis of calcite crystals in relation to the curvature of the test wall. The granular pattern reflects the lack of any such preferred orientation.

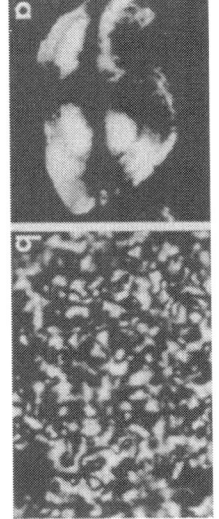

Figure 2.6 Optically radial wall of *Islandiella algida* (a, 290×) and granular wall of *Cassidulina crassa* (b, 470×). From French (1979, reprinted with permission).

Figure 2.5 Black-and-white image of pseudoextinction cross and concentric color bands in a radial-walled foraminiferal test (*Globigerina*), 150×. Original color photograph by Manfred Kage, 1980 Zeiss calendar (reprinted with permission).

documentation of the optical characters of numerous calcareous hyaline genera by Wood (1964a) to place a new emphasis on crystal orientation in their first suprageneric classification (see next section). Electron-microscopic studies of crystal orientation (e.g. Towe and Cifelli, 1967; Stapleton, 1973; Bellemo, 1974a, 1976) later showed that calcite crystals in optically granular walls are not randomly put together but arranged in oblique orientation or in bundles of several preferred orientations, but the optical distinction between radial and granular walls has been retained as a taxonomic guide at some level, especially in the schemes proposed by Alfred R. Loeblich and Helen Tappan.

2.4 EARLIER CLASSIFICATIONS OF LOEBLICH AND TAPPAN

New suprafamilial taxonomic entities were proposed within the Foraminifera by several workers in the 1950s (see Loeblich and Tappan, 1964a), including one in which the nature of lamellae in the foraminiferal wall was used as the basis for the recognition of superfamilies (Reiss, 1958). The most elaborate of these post-Cushman classifications was organized by a team of Soviet paleontologists (Rauzer-Chernousova and Fursenko, 1959; 1962). It contained 13 orders (within the subclass Foraminifera), 14 superfamilies, and 72 families. In contrast, Loeblich and Tappan's 1964 classification, which soon became the most widely used taxonomic guide to the Foraminifera, included 5 suborders (within the order Foraminiferida), 17 superfamilies, and 94 families (see Grigelis, 1978, for a comparison of the two systems). Loeblich and Tappan (1964a) recognized about 1200 extant and extinct genera as valid, about a three-fold increase since the last revision of Cushman's taxonomy (1948), but still the outcome of a conservative approach (Berggren, 1965).

Following Galloway (1933) and Cushman (1945), Loeblich and Tappan (1964a) argued that 'the same chamber arrangement and form of test may have developed in independent lineages by parallel evolution, without indicating interrelationship of the similarly shaped shells.' Thus, in the descending hierarchy of classification, the starting point was the nature of the test wall. The wall composition and texture formed the basis for the separation of the five suborders: (1) organic wall for the Allogromiina, (2) agglutinated wall for the Textulariina, (3) calcareous microgranular wall for the extinct Fusulinina, (4) calcareous, porcelaneous wall for the Miliolina, and (5) calcareous, hyaline wall for the Rotaliina.

Within the Rotaliina, the suborder with the most variety (10 superfamilies), eight superfamilies were partially or completely segregated on the basis of various combinations of wall layering (monolamellar, bilamellar with primarily doubled septa, and bilamellar with secondarily doubled septa; see chapter 4) and optical orientation of crystals (single crystal, radial arrangement, and granular crystal arrangement). These distinctions sufficed for the Discorbacea, Spirillinacea, Rotaliacea, and Cassidulinacea. Additional features were needed for distinguishing superfamilies that could not be segregated on the basis of the observed wall characters: (a) apertural characteristics (terminal radiate vs. loop-shaped aperture with internal toothplate) for Nodosariacea and Buliminacea; and (b) environmental adaptation (benthic vs. planktonic) for Orbitoidacea and Globigerinacea. Apparently, the optical properties were considered more significant in superfamily distinctions than the wall layering. Cassidulinacea, the only superfamily with granular test wall, included both monolamellar and bilamellar taxa. Single properties were used to distinguish Carterinacea and Robertinacea: a wall with secreted calcite spicules for the former, an aragonitic wall for the latter. Within the suborders Textulariina and Fusulinina ('lower groups'), the number of chambers was used for the separation of superfamilies. Thus, in the Textulariina, an essentially non-septate test was considered typical of the Ammodiscacea, whereas multiple-chambered forms were placed within the Lituolacea.

Several modifications to their 1964 classification were proposed by Loeblich and Tappan in later years (e.g. Loeblich and Tappan, 1974, 1984; Tappan and Loeblich, 1982), culminating in a large compendium (Loeblich and Tappan, 1987; not 1988, as in some citations in the literature; see Loeblich and Tappan, 1989) with descriptions of 2,446 genera (Haman, 1988), including 878 extant genera (Tappan and Loeblich, 1988). A brief, but significant, revision of the taxonomic hierarchy (orders to subfamilies) was published in 1992. The 1987 classification included 12 suborders (Fig. 2.7). In the 1992 revision, 10 of these were changed to orders, 4 new orders were recognized, and the taxon Foraminifera (labeled 'Foraminiferea' after Lee, 1990a) was raised to the rank of class.

2.5 PRESENT CLASSIFICATION

2.5.1

The classification adapted in this chapter is a modified version of Loeblich and Tappan (1992), with morphological criteria taken from Loeblich and Tappan (1987), and, for one order (Globigerinida), also from Simmons *et al.* (1997). The 1987 monograph of Loeblich and Tappan does not include a hierarchical summary of the classification, but outlines are given in Ross and Haman (1989) and Decrouez (1989). At infraordinal levels, there are many inconsistencies and inadequate explanations; these have been noted and discussed in an illuminating review by Haynes (1990). Loeblich and Tappan (1992) includes some discussion of the wall structure, as used in that final revision of the 1964 classification, but not all new taxonomic groups are defined. Perhaps the most serious lag is in the non-definition of the new order, Buliminida (Fursenko, 1958). In the modified version of Loeblich and Tappan's 1992 classification proposed in this chapter, the distinction between Rotaliida and Buliminida (split from Rotaliina of Loeblich and Tappan, 1987) is partly taken from Grigelis (1978) and

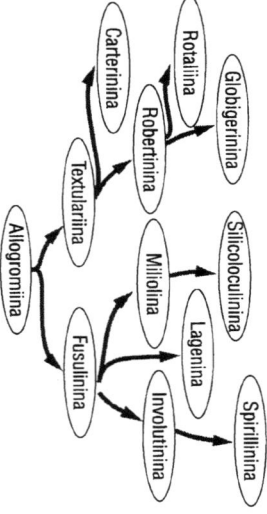

Figure 2.7 Foraminiferal suborders in Loeblich and Tappan (1987) and their envisaged phylogeny. Redrawn from Tappan and Loeblich (1988). Among the suborders in this scheme, only the Fusulinina is extinct.

Haynes (1981), but since the inclusion of infraordinal taxa in either Buliminida or Rotaliida follows the practice in Loeblich and Tappan (1992), the distinction is equivocal. The separation, based on multiple characters, is easy in typical cases, for instance between a high-trochospiral test with a loop-shaped aperture that projects internally as a toothplate (Buliminida) and a low-trochospiral test with a slit-like aperture and no toothplate (Rotaliida), but there are many taxa whose placement in one of these two orders (using the 1992 scheme for suprageneric taxa, and the 1987 scheme for genera) appears to be highly subjective. The term 'toothplate' has been used by various authors for several internal structures that differ in detail (Revets, 1993); a restricted definition (an internal structure descending from an apertural lip and 'composed of a single piece of inner lining,' Revets, 1993) would apply to the Buliminida. In Loeblich and Tappan (1992), however, this order includes taxa such as Loxostomatacea that possess no toothplate. Clearly, a major taxonomic and phylogenetic study is needed to resolve the ambiguities and contradictions in this part of the foraminiferal classification.

Table 2.2 gives a comparison of the orders in the present classification with those in two relatively recent classifications in which the Foraminifera are considered a class (Haynes, 1981; Lee, 1990a). The total number of orders in the present classification is 16, and it differs from Loeblich and Tappan (1992) in the status of two orders.

(1) Order Silicoloculinida. The primary character for the separation of the orders in the 1992 classification is the shell composition, including mineralogy. However, Silicoloculinina, separated from Miliolina in 1987, was made part of the Miliolida, the new porcelaneous order. Loeblich and Tappan (1992) did not clearly explain this shift, except to say that 'mineralized particles of the wall in the abyssal-dwelling suborder Silicoloculinina also are randomly oriented rodlike crystals, although consisting of silica rather than calcite' (as is the case with typical Miliolida). Although not articulated, the

Present classification

Table 2.2 Comparison of the ordinal nomenclature in the present adaptation of Loeblich and Tappan (1992) with those in Lee (1990a) and Haynes (1981), showing approximate matches. Unless indicated otherwise, the named orders are extant.

Loeblich and Tappan (1992), present adaptation, Class Foraminifera	Lee (1990a), Class Foraminiferea	Haynes (1981), Class Foraminifera
Allogromiida	Allogromiida	Allogromiida
Textulariida	Textulariida, part	Textulariida, part
Astrorhizida	Textulariida, part	Astrorhizida
Lituolida	Textulariida, part	Lituolida
Trochamminida	Textulariida, part	Textulariida, part
Fusulinida (*Paleozoic*)	Fusulinida (*Paleozoic*)	Fusulinida (*Paleozoic*)
Spirillinida	Spirillinida	Rotaliida, part
Involutinida	Involutinida (*only Mesozoic*)	Rotaliida, part
Carterinida	Carterinida	None
Miliolida	Miliolida	Miliolida
Silicoloculinida	Silicoloculinida	None
Lagenida	Lagenida	Nodosariida
Robertinida	Robertinida	Robertinida
Globigerinida	Globigerinida	Globigerinida
Buliminida	Rotaliida, part	Buliminida
Rotaliida	Rotaliida, part	Rotaliida, part

milioline chamber arrangement of *Miliammellus*, the single genus within the silicic group, was probably a factor in this taxonomic placement. In the present adaptation, the Silicoloculinida (silicic wall) is retained as a distinct entity and not placed under the Miliolida (calcitic wall). The available information on the wall structure (Resig *et al.*, 1980) shows that the opaline silica is secreted, not agglutinated. Furthermore, the interpretable phylogeny of Miliolida is unaffected by the recognition of silicic foraminifers as a separate suborder or a separate order. Thus, in spite of test isomorphism with miliolids, the placement of silicic foraminifers in a separate major taxon, the order Silicoloculinida (as in Lee, 1990a), is justified.

(2) Order Involutinida. In Loeblich and Tappan (1992), the calcite-aragonite distinction was not used as an invariant basis for ordinal separation among calcareous Foraminifera. The aragonitic Involutinina was placed under the otherwise calcitic Spirillinida, whereas the aragonitic Robertinina of the 1987 classification was given the status of a separate order, Robertinida, and thus separated from the calcitic Buliminida and Rotaliida. The present adaptation reverts to the hierarchy in Loeblich and Tappan (1987), with a rank elevation, thus retaining both the Involutinida and Spirillinida as orders. The family Planispirillinidae (aragonitic wall) is retained within the Involutinida as the only extant family within this order, and not transferred to Spirillinida (calcitic wall).

There are many ambiguities in the superfamily and family designations in Loeblich and Tappan (1987). The problems are mainly of two kinds: (1) the defining characters of a larger taxon being inadequate for the inclusion of all subordinate taxa listed under it, and (2) the defining characters of two taxa of the same rank being inadequate for their separation. An example of the first problem is the inclusion of the Notodendrodidae (bulbous central region and tubular arms) within the Hippocrepinacea (proloculus followed by tubular or flaring second chamber); that of the second problem is the distinction between the Cornuspiridae and Hemigordiopsidae, a streptospiral to planispiral coiling being the characteristic of both (Haynes, 1990). Conflicts of these kinds are not resolved in Loeblich and Tappan (1992), because although a complete outline classification (down to the subfamily level) is given there, the infraordinal taxa are not defined. Other than the assignment of the Planispirillinidae to the Involutinina, the classification summarized later in this chapter retains the placement of superfamilies and families as in Loeblich and Tappan (1992), notwithstanding unreconciled contradictions.

2.5.2 Supraordinal taxa

Kingdom PROTOCTISTA. Foraminifers, as eukaryotic unicellular organisms, belong to the Kingdom Protoctista, which includes all such organisms and some multicellular ones, i.e. 'the entire motley and unruly group of non-plant, non-animal, non-fungal organisms representative of lineages of the early descendants of eukaryotes' (Margulis, 1990). To avoid confusion, the recommended practice is to restrict an informal designation of Protista to only microscopic protoctists (Margulis, 1990). Following this usage, all foraminifers are protoctists, but not all are protists.

A contrary practice, the recognition of a subkingdom or phylum of single-celled animals, Protozoa (under Kingdom Animalia), is still in vogue. Margulis (1990) takes strong exception to this taxonomy: 'Even today, many scientists (e.g. especially cell biologists, plankton ecologists and geologists) routinely write about Protozoa and Algae as if they were phyla in the Animal and Plant kingdoms, respectively. These organisms are no more "one-celled animals and one-celled plants" than people are shell-less multicellular amoebas.' To most foraminiferal systematists, however, Protoctista/Protista vs. Protozoa is not a major controversy. Ever since the publication of Loeblich and Tappan (1964a), most of them have placed the foraminifers in the Protista (in the traditional sense, i.e. same as the current Protoctista) rather than in the Protozoa (see Hart and Williams, 1993, for a recent exception).

Phylum GRANULORETICULOSA. The phylum includes heterotrophic protoctists characterized by granular reticulopods (pseudopodial networks) with two-way streaming. Complex sexual cycles are present in this group (Lee, 1990a).

Class FORAMINIFERA. The taxonomic rank of foraminifers was raised from order to class by Loeblich and Tappan (1992) because of the following characteristics of the organisms: (1) granuloreticulose pseudopodia, (2) outer cover (usually a test), (3) alternation of haploid and diploid generations, and (4) 'a test wall in some that is constructed of non-oriented calcareous or siliceous crystals (Textulariida, Fusulinida, Miliolida, Carterinida), such crystalline disorder being unknown elsewhere in the animal kingdom.' Accompanying this rank change was a change in nomenclature, from Foraminiferida to Foraminiferea, although the International Commission of Zoological Nomenclature (International Code of Zoological Nomenclature, 1985) does not require or suggest such a change, being silent on the nomenclature of orders or classes. Loeblich and Tappan (1992) chose 'Foraminiferea' because d'Orbigny's 'Foraminifères' (1826) was not a latinized name, and the 'earliest formal Latinized citation as a class' they found was the Foraminiferea of Lee (1990a). In fact, however, the usage of the latinized class name Foraminifera goes back to 1903 (Lister, p. 47), but more importantly, the rightful author of the class name Foraminifera is d'Orbigny, because the change from Foraminifères to Foraminifera is simply an emendation that calls for the retention of the original author and date. This is fitting. Regardless of later harsh opinions on d'Orbigny's approach to foraminiferal systematics, a consensus exists that in the world of foraminiferologists 'one name must always be held in an esteem which may be described as affectionate, and that is the name of Alcide d'Orbigny' (Heron-Allen, 1917).

2.5.3 Morphologic basis of present classification

The overwhelming importance of the chemistry, mineralogy, and structure of the foraminiferal test wall in the ordinal classification is obvious in Loeblich and Tappan (1992). In the present adaptation, the sole use of these features leads

Present classification

to the following separations: (a) organic wall, Order Allogromiida; (b) agglutinated, with proteinaceous or mineralized matrix, Orders Astrorhizida, Lituolida, Trochamminida; (c) agglutinated, with low-Mg calcitic cement, Order Textulariida, (d) microgranular calcite, Order Fusulinida (extinct); (e) elongate, high-Mg calcite, Order Miliolida; (f) elongate, low-Mg calcite forming large spicules, Order Carterinida; (g) one or a few crystals of elongate, low-Mg calcite, Order Spirillinida; (h) numerous crystals of elongate, low-Mg calcite, forming monolamellar wall, Order Lagenida; (i) numerous crystals of elongate, low-Mg calcite, forming bilamellar wall, Orders Buliminida, Rotaliida, and Globigerinida (all extant and most extinct genera); (j) aragonite, Orders Involutinida, Robertinida, and Globigerinida (a few extinct genera); (k) silica, Order Silicoloculinida. A significant difference between the present classification and those of Loeblich and Tappan is the placement of the sole planktonic order, Globigerinida, under a calcitic group, as well as under the aragonitic group. This is because of the recognition by Simmons et al. (1997) that in the most primitive planktonic superfamily, the Favusellacea (Jurassic and early Cretaceous), the test wall is aragonitic, in contrast to the calcitic wall in all other planktonic groups, including the three modern superfamilies (Heterohelicacea, Globorotaliacea, and Globigerinacea).

Further distinctions of orders within groups b, i, and j are based on the number (one, two, or many) and arrangement of chambers, presence of toothplates, and benthic vs planktonic adaptations. Subordinal distinctions within most orders are based on numerous combinations of diverse morphological features, including wall pores, wall passages, and principal apertural features for superfamilies, and free or fixed nature of the test, mode of chamber addition, simple or divided nature of chamber interior, and apertural modifications for families (Loeblich and Tappan, 1987; Haman 1988). In one remarkable exception, a non-test character, biflagellate vs amoeboid gametes, has been used to separate two families of Allogromiida – Lagynidae and Allogromiidae (Loeblich and Tappan, 1987).

2.5.4 Identification key to orders

The present classification of 16 orders does not lend itself to the construction of a simple ordinal key, based on just two or three morphological features. The system designed by Loeblich and Tappan is complex, and takes into account not just the morphology but the long geological history and an interpreted phylogeny of the Foraminifera. In this context, it is hard to dispute that 'the fundamental purpose of classification ... is to provide an orderly hierarchical array of taxa reflecting the genetic lines of descent, not simply to provide a convenient pigeon-holing' and that a natural classification must not be confused with 'an artificial identification key or retrieval system' (Haynes, 1990). On the other hand, even a perfectly natural classification (a hypothetical construct for the Foraminifera, given the guesswork involved in determining lines of descent) is useless if we are unable to place major taxa into clearly marked compartments in that classification. With this practical aspect of taxonomy in mind, a key to the identification of foraminiferal orders (Loeblich and Tappan, 1992, modified) is given below. A simplified graphic version of this morphological key is given in Fig. 2.8. Representative genera (one per order) are illustrated in Fig. 2.9.

Class FORAMINIFERA

Group 1 Test or outer membrane made of organic material, in some cases with a few particles picked up from the environment: Order 1, ALLOGROMIIDA.

Group 2 Test agglutinated, i.e. made of particles picked up from the environment ('foreign particles'), 4 orders.

2.1 Test particles attached to a proteinaceous or mineralized matrix: 3 orders.

2.1.1 Test shape irregular; typically single-chambered or branching tubular; septa incomplete in multichambered forms: Order 2, ASTRORHIZIDA.

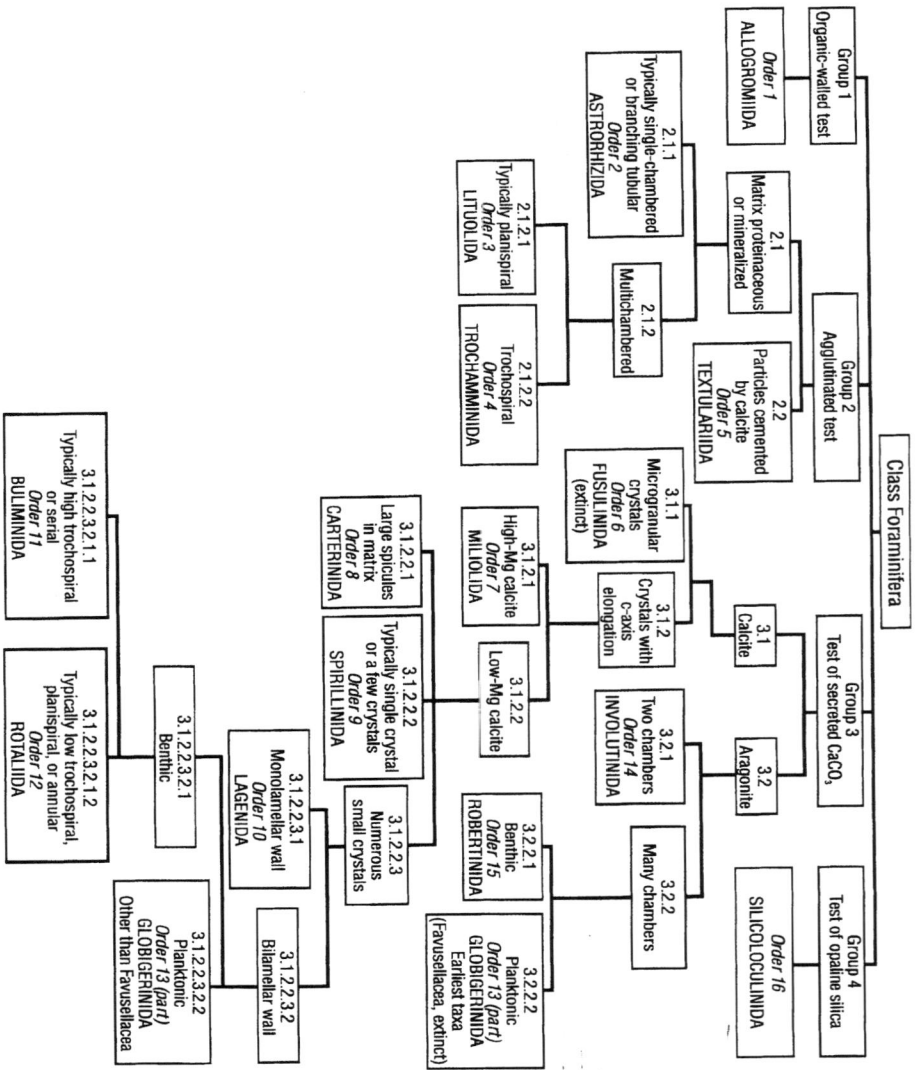

Figure 2.8 Simplified morphological key to foraminiferal orders. See text for further explanations.

Figure 2.9 Representative genera, foraminiferal orders; 1, photomicrograph; 2–21, scanning electron micrographs. Scale bars: 500 μm in 2, 7, and 13; 10 μm in 11; 100 μm in others. 1, *Allogromia* (Allogromiida); 2, *Saccammina* (Astrorhizida); 3, *Ammodiscus* (Lituolida); 4, 5, *Trochammina* (Trochamminida); 6, *Siphotextularia* (Textulariida); 7, *Triticites* (Fusulinida); 8, *Miliolinella* (Miliolida); 9–11, *Carterina* (Carterinida), dorsal and ventral views, and arrangement of large and small spicules; 12, *Spirillina* (Spirillinida); 13, *Dentalina* (Lagenida), dorsal view, ventral view, and arrangement (Rotaliida), dorsal and ventral views; 17, 18, *Globigerinoides* (Globigerinida), dorsal and ventral views; 19, *Planispirillina* (Involutinida); 20, *Robertinoides* (Robertinida); 21, *Miliammellus* (Silicoloculinida). Species illustrated: 1, *A. laticollaris* (Arnold); 2, *S. comprima* (Parker); 3, *A.* sp.; 4, 5, *T. nana* (Brady); 6, *S. affinis* (Fornasini); 7, *T. secalicus* (Say); 8, *M. warreni* (Andersen); 9–11, *C. spiculotesta* (Carter); 12, *S.* sp.; 13, *D. albatrossi* (Cushman); 14, *B. lowmani* (Parker); 15, 16, *A. beccarii* (Linné); 17, 18, *G. ruber* (d'Orbigny); 19, *P. papillosa* (Cushman); 20, *R. charlottensis* (Cushman); 21, *M. legis* (Saidova and Burmistrova). All species are extant, except *Triticites secalicus* (Late Carboniferous). [Sources: 1, S.T. Goldstein (reprinted with permission); 2, 8, 14, E. Platon (reprinted with permission); 6, M.H. Jones (1997, reprinted with publisher's permission); 19, W.E. Piller (1983, reprinted with publisher's permission); 3–5, 7, 12, 13, 15–18, 20, specimens collected by S. Deutsch and J.H. Lipps (1976, reprinted with publisher's permission); 21, J.M. Resig et al. (1980, reprinted with publisher's permission, micrographs by E. Platon.]

Present classification

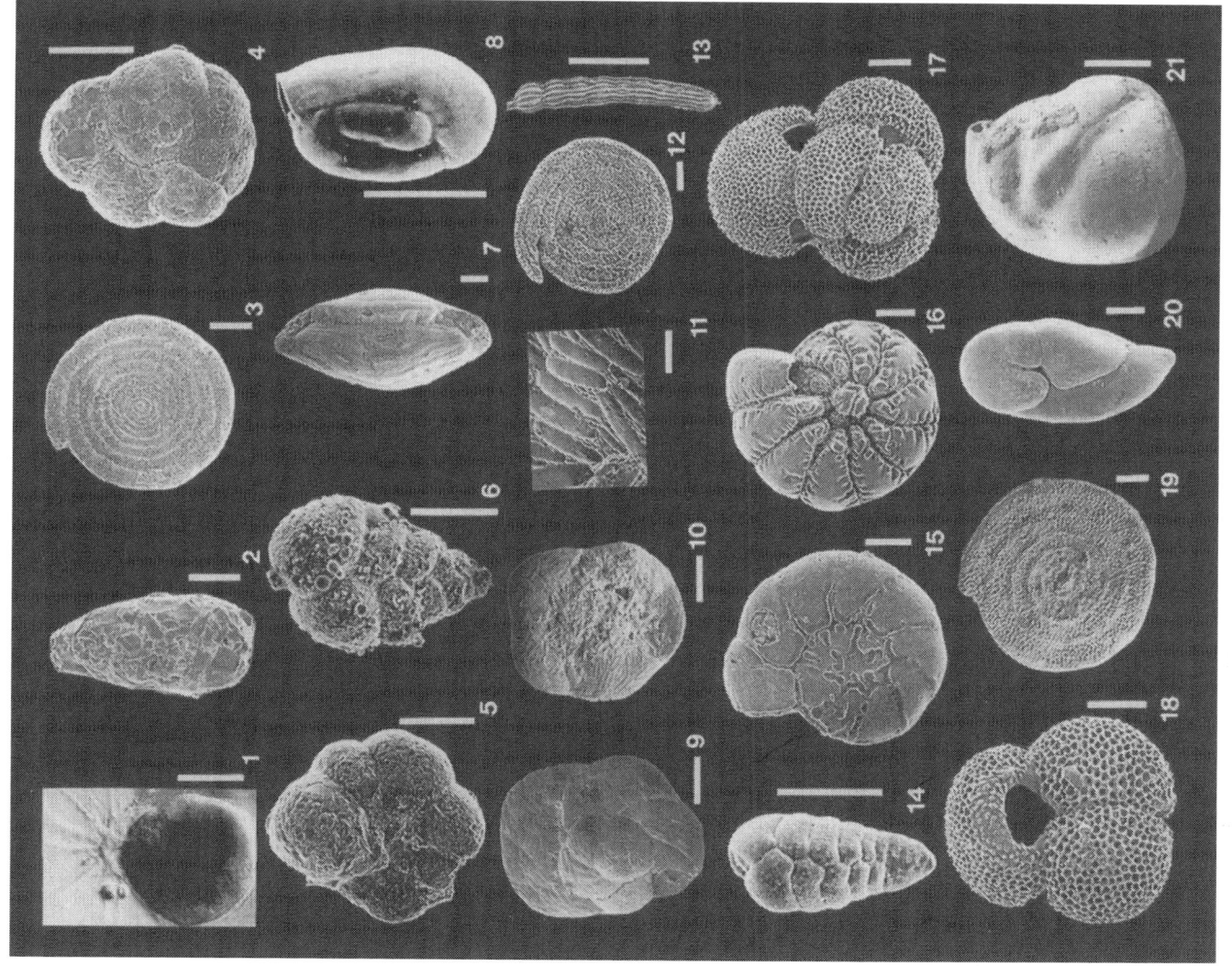

2.1.2 Multichambered, i.e. septa present: 2 orders.
2.1.2.1 Coiling usually planispiral, but in some cases streptospiral or trochospiral: Order 3, LITUOLIDA.
2.1.2.2 Coiling trochospiral: Order 4, TROCHAMMINIDA.
2.2 Test particles cemented by low-Mg calcite: Order 5, TEXTULARIIDA.

Group 3 Test wall made of secreted calcium carbonate: 9 orders.

3.1 Calcite: 8 orders.
3.1.1 Crystals microgranular, i.e. very small and nearly equidimensional; no preferred crystal orientation: Order 6, FUSULINIDA (Extinct).
3.1.2 Crystals elongate along the c-axis: 7 orders.
3.1.2.1 High-Mg calcite: Order 7, MILIOLIDA.
3.1.2.2 Low-Mg calcite: 6 orders.
3.1.2.2.1 Large spicules (unusually large crystals) in a matrix of fine spicules: Order 8, CARTERINIDA.
3.1.2.2.2 Optically, a single crystal or a few crystals (or, rarely, a mosaic of crystals): Order 9, SPIRILLINIDA.
3.1.2.2.3 Numerous small crystals; lamellar wall: 4 orders.
3.1.2.2.3.1 Monolamellar. Single-chambered or multichambered, but no complexly coiled forms beyond planispiral: Order 10, LAGENIDA.
3.1.2.2.3.2 Bilamellar. Multichambered: 3 orders.
3.1.2.2.3.2.1 Environmental adaptation benthic: 2 orders.
3.1.2.2.3.2.1.1 Chamber arrangement trochospiral (typically, high-trochospiral), triserial, biserial, or uniserial; aperture typically comma-shaped ot loop-shaped, typically with toothplate: Order 11, BULIMINIDA.
3.1.2.2.3.2.1.2 Chamber arrangement trochospiral (typically, low trochospiral), planispiral, annular, or irregular: Order 12, ROTALIIDA.
3.1.2.2.3.2.2 Environmental adaptation planktonic: Order 13, GLOBIGERINIDA, part (all modern and most fossil taxa).
3.2 Aragonite: 3 orders.
3.2.1 Two chambers: Order 14, INVOLUTINIDA.
3.2.2 Many chambers: 2 orders.
3.2.2.1 Environmental adaptation benthic: Order 15, ROBERTINIDA.
3.2.1.2 Environmental adaptation planktonic: Order 13, GLOBIGERINIDA, part (only Favusellacea, extinct).

Group 4 Test wall made of silica: Order 16, SILICOLOCULINIDA.

2.5.5 Superfamilies and families

The characteristic features of Holocene superfamilies and representative families are briefly summarized below, with examples of extant genera. The listing does not include subfamilies and some minor families. Only essential descriptions are given here, summarized from Loeblich and Tappan (1987) and corrected for contradictions or ambiguities, especially in cases (e.g. Spiroplectamminacea) where superfamily characters, as reported by Loeblich and Tappan, do not accommodate those of all constituent families. Unfortunately, some uncertainties still remain in the distinction between closely related superfamilies or families, because the present modification of Loeblich and Tappan (1992) leaves the subordinal hierarchy untouched. For full descriptions of the taxa, and for generic descriptions, see Loeblich and Tappan (1987). Only 283 genera are mentioned below as examples, out of a total of 878 extant genera described in Loeblich and Tappan (1987). For a complete listing of genera and suprageneric taxa under the Loeblich and Tappan (1987) hierarchy, see Decrouez (1989), but the status and placement of some subfamilies, families, and superfamilies are different in Loeblich and Tappan (1992), and thus in the present adaptation.

Most morphological terms used in the following brief descriptions are simple, and require no further explanation. A few are defined

Present classification

when they first appear. One frequently used apertural term, 'interiomarginal', refers to an opening at the basal margin of the final chamber (Loeblich and Tappan, 1964a). The principal types of chamber arrangement and aperture are sketched in Figs. 2.10 and 2.11.

Order 1, ALLOGROMIIDA. Organic wall. Includes freshwater forms. No superfamily named. Examples of extant families and genera:

Family Lagynidae. Single-chambered or colonial; agglutinated matter rare; biflagellate gametes. *Myxotheca, Ophiotuba.*

Family Allogromiidae. Single-chambered; agglutinated matter common; amoeboid gametes. *Allogromia* (Fig. 2.9), *Dendrotuba, Hospitella.*

Order 2, ASTRORHIZIDA. Agglutinated wall with particles attached to a proteinaceous or mineralized matrix; single-chambered, branching tubular, or irregularly multichambered with incomplete septa.

(1) Superfamily Astrorhizacea. Test of various shapes, including branching; no septa, although the single chamber may be partially divided. Examples of extant families and genera:

Family Astrorhizidae. Branching test, branches diverging from the central part of the test. *Astrorhiza, Pelosina.*

Family Bathysiphonidae. Test a straight or slightly curved tube. *Bathysiphon.*

Family Rhabdamminidae. Test a branching or twisted tube. *Psammatodendron, Rhabdammina, Rhizammina.*

Family Psammosphaeridae. Test globular or irregular; several may be joined together. With large pores, but no distinct apertures. *Psammosphaera.*

Family Saccamminidae. Test globular or elongate. Single or multiple apertures. *Lagenammina, Saccammina* (Fig. 2.9), *Technitella.*

Family Hemisphaeramminidae. Test with subglobular or discoidal chambers. *Crithionina, Iridia.*

(2) Superfamily Komokiacea. Test formed of multiple branching tubules. With pores, but no distinct aperture. Examples of extant families and genera:

Family Komokiidae. Bushlike or tree-like arrangement of tubules. *Komokia, Normanina.*

(3) Superfamily Hippocrepinacea. Test tubular with one closed end, or two-chambered, with rounded or irregular first chamber and tubular or flaring second chamber. Examples of extant families and genera:

Family Hippocrepinidae. Test typically tubular; terminal aperture slightly constricted. *Hippocrepina, Hyperammina, Jaculella, Saccorhiza.*

Family Notodendrodidae. Test with a bulbous center, an arborescent upper part, and a branching lower part serving as anchor. With small pores but no distinct aperture. *Notodendrodes.*

Order 3, LITUOLIDA. Agglutinated wall with particles attached to a proteinaceous or mineralized matrix; planispirally (or in some cases, streptospirally or trochospirally) coiled throughout, or uncoiled in the later stage; also, arranged in series throughout.

(1) Superfamily Ammodiscacea. Two-chambered test, with a globular initial chamber and a tubular (coiled or uncoiled) second chamber with terminal aperture.

Family Ammodiscidae. The only family under Ammodiscacea; defining characters same as those of the superfamily. Examples: *Ammodiscus* (Fig. 2.9), *Ammolagena, Glomospira.*

(2) Superfamily Rzehakinacea. Test planispiral or with milioline coiling (chambers arranged in various planes); imperforate.

Family Rzehakinidae. The only family under Rzehakinacea; defining characters same as those of the superfamily. Examples: *Ammoflintina, Miliammina.*

(3) Superfamily Hormosinacea. Test with uniserial chambers. Examples of extant families and genera:

Family Reophacidae. Test with asymetrical chambers (made of a single layer of agglutinated material) arranged in a slightly arcuate series; terminal aperture on a neck. *Nodulina, Reophax.*

Family Hormosinidae. Thick-walled test with symmetrical chambers arranged in a rectilinear

Systematics of modern Foraminifera

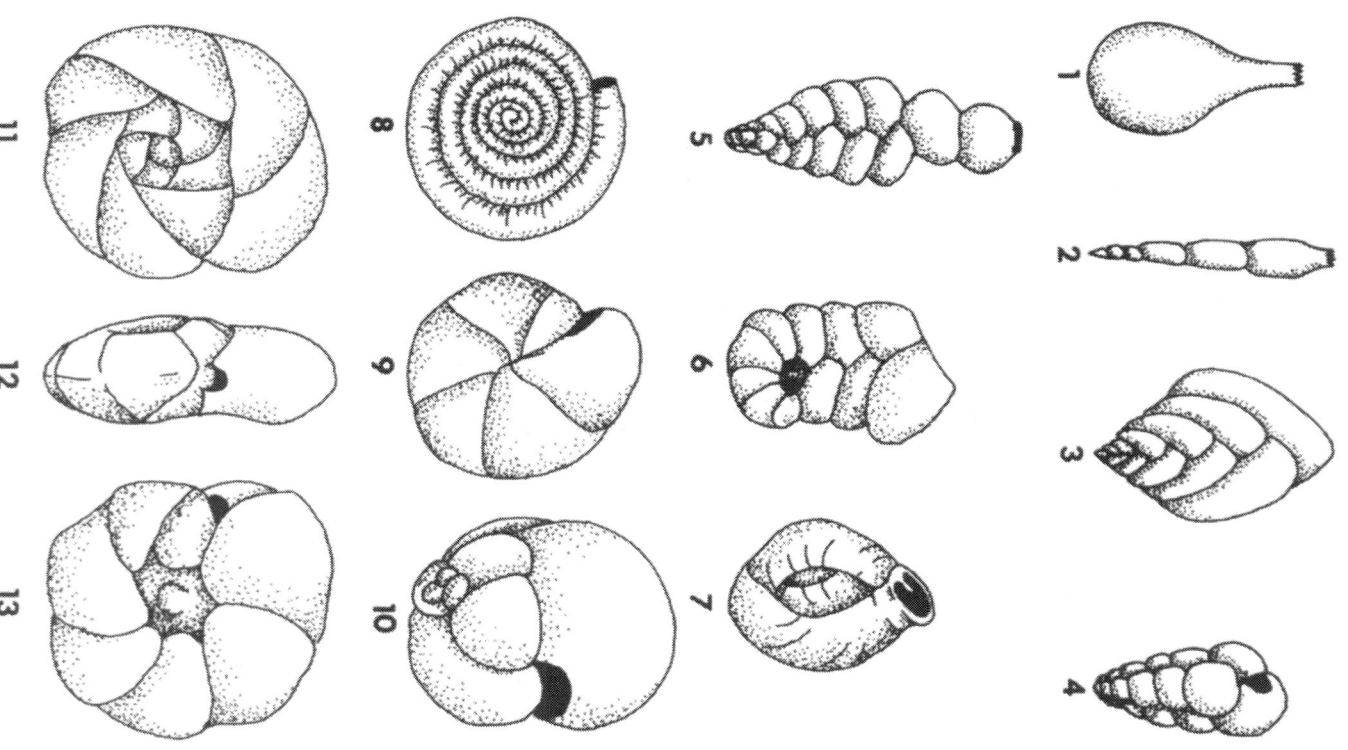

Figure 2.10 Principal types of chamber arrangement. 1, single-chambered; 2, uniserial; 3, biserial; 4, triserial; 5, triserial to biserial to uniserial; 6, planispiral to biserial; 7, miliolinc; 8, planispiral evolute; 9, planispiral involute; 10, streptospiral; 11–13, trochospiral (11, dorsal view; 12, edge view; 13, ventral view). 2–13 redrawn from Loeblich and Tappan, 1964a.

Present classification

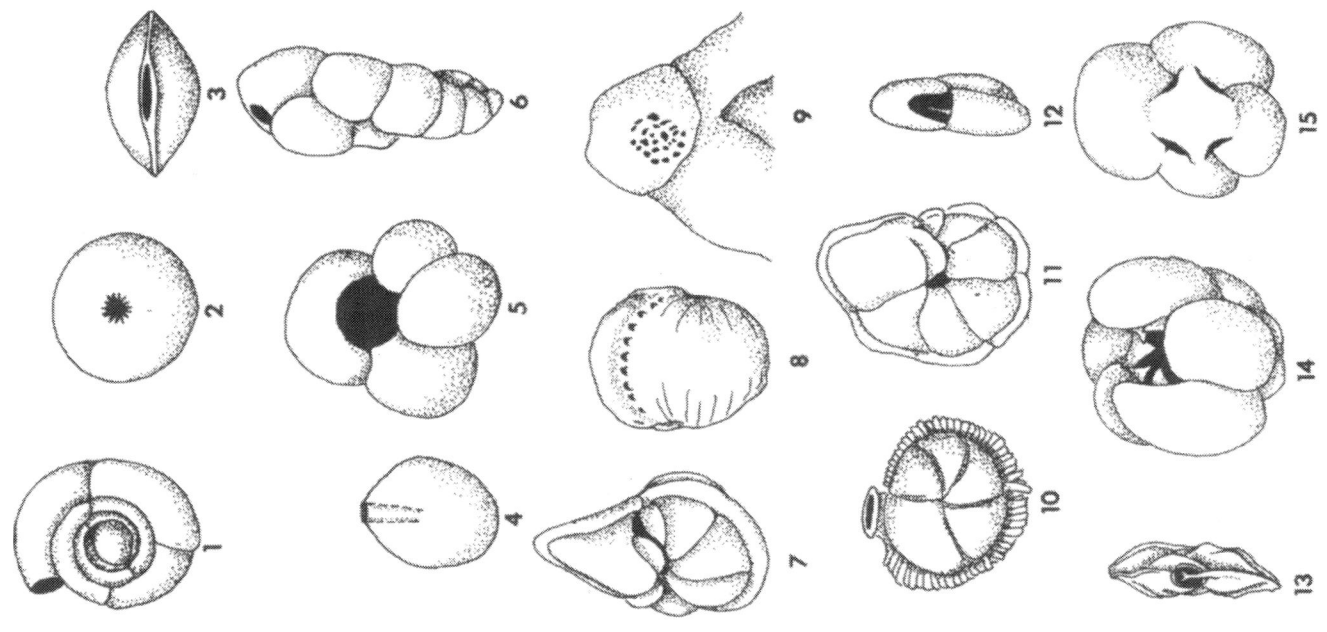

Figure 2.11 Principal types of aperture. 1, open end of tube; 2, terminal radiate; 3, terminal slit; 4, terminal with entosolenian tube; 5, umbilical; 6, loop-shaped; 7, interiomarginal; 8, interiomarginal multiple; 9, areal, cribrate; 10, with phialine lip; 11, with simple apertural lip; 12, with simple tooth; 13, with bifid tooth; 14, with umbilical teeth; 15, with umbilical bulla. 1–3, 5–11, 13–15 redrawn from Loeblich and Tappan, 1964a.

series; terminal aperture on a neck. *Hormosina, Pseudonodosinella.*

(4) Superfamily Lituolacea. Imperforate test with multiple chambers; planispirally coiled throughout or in early stage. Examples of extant families and genera:

Family Haplophragmoididae. Chambers in a fully or partially involute coil. Aperture single or multiple, interiomarginal or areal. *Cribrostomoides, Haplophragmoides.*

Family Lituotubidae. Initial chamber followed by a coiled, tubular second chamber, and then by a series of coiled or uncoiled adult chambers with interiomarginal or terminal aperture. *Lituotuba, Trochamminoides.*

Family Lituolidae. Coiled throughout, or later chambers in a linear series, with terminal aperture. *Ammoastuta, Ammobaculites, Ammomarginulina, Ammotium, Lituola.*

Family Placopsilinidae. Attached test, with streptospirally coiled throughout or in the initial part, with interiomarginal or areal aperture. Examples of extant families and genera: *Ammocibicides, Placopsilina.*

(5) Superfamily Haplophragmiacea. Test streptospirally coiled throughout or in the initial part, with interiomarginal or areal aperture. Examples of extant families and genera:

Family Ammosphaeroidinidae. Streptospiral, with a small number of chambers. *Adercotryma, Recurvoides.*

(6) Superfamily Coscinophragmataceae. Test attached, uniserial or branching, but initial part may be coiled; coarsely perforate. Examples of extant families and genera:

Family Coscinophragmatidae. Test with alveolar wall, aperture terminal. *Bdelloidina.*

(7) Superfamily Loftusiacea. Test with planispiral, streptospiral, or trochospiral coil; wall with an imperforate outer layer and an alveolar inner layer. Examples of extant families and genera:

Family Cyclamminidae. Test planispiral involute, with interiomarginal or areal aperture. *Alveophragmium, Cyclammina.*

(8) Superfamily Spiroplectamminacea. Chamber arrangement variable: (a) planispiral or streptospiral in early part, and biserial or uniserial in later part, (b) biserial to uniserial, (c) high spiral. Examples of extant families and genera:

Family Spiroplectamminidae. Planispiral or streptospiral in early part, and biserial or uniserial in later part. *Spiroplectammina, Vulvulina.*

Family Nouriidae. Chambers arranged biserially or in a high spiral, with terminal aperture. *Nouria.*

(9) Superfamily Verneuilinacea. Test trochospiral, triserial, or biserial; last part may be uniserial. Examples of extant families and genera:

Family Verneuilinidae. Triserial throughout or in the early part, with biserial or uniserial later part. *Gaudryina.*

(10) Superfamily Ataxophragmiacea. Trochospiral throughout or in the early part, with triserial, biserial, or uniserial later part. Examples of extant families and genera:

Family Globotextulariidae. Test high trochospiral throughout or with triserial or biserial later part; aperture interiomarginal or areal. *Globotextularia, Liebusella.*

Family Textulariellidae. Test trochospiral in early part, later triserial, biserial, or uniserial; wall alveolar. *Guppyella, Textulariella.*

Order 4, TROCHAMMINIDA. Agglutinated wall with particles attached to a proteinaceous or mineralized matrix; trochospirally coiled throughout or uncoiled in later part.

(1) Superfamily Trochamminacea. Trochospirally coiled throughout or uncoiled in later part. Examples of extant families and genera:

Family Trochamminidae. Test with low trochospiral coil; with interiomarginally or areally located single or multiple apertures. *Ammoglobigerina, Arenoparrella, Jadammina, Tiptotrocha, Tritaxis, Trochammina* (Fig. 2.9).

(2) Superfamily Remaneicacea. Test with low trochospiral coil; chambers subdivided by secondary partitions.

Family Remaneicidae. The only family under Remaneicacea; defining characters same as those of the superfamily. Example: *Remaneica.*

Order 5, TEXTULARIIDA. Agglutinated wall, with particles cemented by low-Mg calcite. Superfamily Textulariacea. Test trochospiral,

Present classification

triserial, or biserial throughout, or with biserial or uniserial later part; wall with canals. Examples of extant families and genera:

Family Eggerellidae. Test trochospiral or triserial throughout, or with biserial or uniserial later part, with interiomarginally or areally located single or multiple apertures. *Eggerella, Karreriella, Martinottiella.*

Family Textulariidae. Test biserial throughout or uniserial in later part, with interiomarginally or areally located single or multiple apertures. *Bigenerina, Cribrobigenerina, Siphotextularia* (Fig. 2.9), *Tawitawia, Textularia.*

Family Pseudogaudryinidae. Test triserial in early part, later biserial or uniserial, with interiomarginal aperture. *Pseudogaudryina.*

Family Valvulinidae. Test trochospiral, triserial, or biserial throughout, or with uniserial later part; aperture single (with tooth) or multiple. *Clavulina, Goesella.*

Order 6, FUSULINIDA. Extinct. Microgranular, calcitic test wall. Example: *Triticites* (Fig. 2.9).

Order 7, MILIOLIDA. Test of high-Mg calcite; surface texture porcelaneous; adult chambers imperforate, except in a few fossil genera; surface pitted in some genera.

(1) Superfamily Squamulinacea. Test imperforate, single-chambered.

Family Squamulinidae. The only family under Squamulinacea; defining characters same as those of the superfamily. Example: *Squamulina.*

(2) Superfamily Cornuspiracea. Test imperforate, two-chambered. Initial chamber rounded; second chamber tubular, and planispirally, streptospirally, or irregularly coiled, or uncoiled in later part.

Family Cornuspiridae. The only family under Cornuspiracea; defining characters same as those of the superfamily. Examples: *Cornuspira, Meandrospira.*

(3) Superfamily Hemigordiopsacea. Test imperforate, two-chambered. Initial chamber rounded; second chamber streptospiral throughout or planispiral in later part.

Family Hemigordiopsidae. The only family under Hemigordiopsacea; defining characters same as those of the superfamily. Example: *Gordiospira.*

(4) Superfamily Nubeculariacea. Test imperforate, multichambered, coiled planispirally, streptospirally, trochospirally, or irregularly. Examples of extant families and genera:

Family Fischerinidae. Test coiled planispirally; initial chamber rounded, second chamber coiled tubular, succeeding chambers arranged in a spiral. *Fischerina, Nodobaculariella, Planispirina, Vertebralina, Wiesnerella.*

Family Nubeculariidae. Test planispiral, trochospiral, or irregularly coiled throughout, or uncoiled in later part. *Calcituba, Nodophthalmidium, Nubecularia.*

Family Ophthalmidiidae. Chambers arranged planispirally or in various planes. Initial chamber and coiled tubular second chamber succeeded by chambers one-half to one coil in length. *Cornuloculina, Edentostomina.*

(5) Superfamily Discospirinacea. Test imperforate, multichambered, planispiral, discoid; first chamber rounded, second chamber coiled tubular, later chambers one-half coil in extent or annular.

Family Discospirinidae. The only family under Discospirinacea; defining characters same as those of the superfamily. Example: *Discospirina.*

(6) Superfamily Miliolacea. Test imperforate, multichambered; chambers arranged in various planes. Examples of extant families and genera:

Family Spiroloculinidae. Initial chamber rounded, second chamber coiled tubular, adult chambers one-half coil in extent; aperture terminal, toothed or partly covered. *Spiroloculina, Cribrospiroloculina.*

Family Hauerinidae. Initial chamber rounded, succeeding chambers arranged in one or several planes, each chamber covering one-half coil or less; later part of test may be uncoiled; aperture terminal, toothed or partly covered. The test may have an outer agglutinated layer. *Ammomassilina, Biloculinella, Cruciloculina, Hauerina, Massilina, Miliolinella* (Fig. 2.9), *Pyrgo, Quinqueloculina, Siphonaperta, Sigmoilina, Sigmoilopsis, Triloculina.*

Family Tubinellidae. Test coiled in early part, with chambers arranged in one or several planes, but uncoiled in later part.

Family Miliolidae. Test with pitted surface, coiled in one or several planes; aperture terminal, open or partly blocked. *Ruperlianella.*

(7) Superfamily Alveolinacea. Test imperforate, wall thickened, with passages and pillars; chambers (with chamberlets in some genera) arranged planispirally, streptospirally, or in various planes; aperture multiple. Examples of extant families and genera:

Family Alveolinidae. Test coiled around the long axis; initial chamber rounded, second chamber coiled tubular, adult chambers in a planispiral coil and divided into chamberlets. Examples of extant families and genera: *Borelis, Alveolinella.*

Family Keramosphaeridae. Globular test with concentric chambers and chamberlets. *Keramosphaera.*

(8) Superfamily Soritacea. Adult chambers imperforate, except in a few fossil genera. Early chambers pitted or perforate; chamber arrangement planispiral, multispiral, annular, or serial. Examples of extant families and genera:

Family Peneroplidae. Chamber arrangement planispiral in early part, multispiral, serial, or annular in later part; chambers undivided. *Dendritina, Monalysidium, Peneroplis.*

Family Soritidae. Chamber arrangement planispiral throughout, or multispiral, annular, or serial in later part; chambers subdivided into chamberlets. *Amphisorus, Archaias, Cyclorbiculina, Marginopora, Parasorites, Sorites.*

Order 8, CARTERINIDA. Wall of secreted low-Mg calcite, with large spicules in a matrix of small spicules; imperforate. No superfamily designated.

Family Carterinidae. Test trochospiral, attached; later chambers may be subdivided by septula. *Carterina* (Fig. 2.9).

Order 9, SPIRILLINIDA. Test with wall of low-Mg calcite, optically a single crystal, a few crystals, or a mosaic of crystals; imperforate or perforate; coiling planispiral or trochospiral. No superfamily designated. Examples of extant families and genera:

Family Spirillinidae. Test coiled, with two chambers; first chamber globular, second chamber tubular. *Spirillina* (Fig. 2.9).

Family Patellinidae. Test conical, multichambered; first chamber globular, second chamber spiral tubular, two chambers in each later whorl. *Patellina.*

Order 10, LAGENIDA. Test of low-Mg calcite; wall monolamellar; perforate; single-chambered or multichambered with serial or planispiral chamber arrangement.

(1) Superfamily Nodosariacea. Test single-chambered or multichambered, with serial or spiral chamber arrangement; aperture terminal. Examples of extant families and genera:

Family Nodosariidae. Test (a) multichambered with uniserial or biserial chamber arrangement, or (b) single-chambered, with a long slitlike aperture. *Dentalina* (Fig. 2.9), *Frondicularia, Lingulina, Nodosaria, Rimulina.*

Family Vaginulinidae. Test coiled throughout or in early stage. *Amphicoryna, Astacolus, Lenticulina, Marginulina, Saracenaria, Vaginulina.*

Family Lagenidae. Test single-chambered; aperture round or radiate. *Lagena.*

(2) Superfamily Polymorphinacea. Test single-chambered or multichambered with serial or elongate spiral chamber arrangement; apertural modifications include the presence of an internal tube (entosolenian tube). Examples of extant families and genera:

Family Polymorphinidae. Test multichambered; chamber arrangement serial or elongate spiral, with round, radiate, or slitlike terminal aperture. *Globulina, Guttulina, Polymorphina, Ramulina, Sigmomorphina, Webbinella.*

Family Ellipsolagenidae. Test single-chambered, aperture with an internal tubular extension. *Oolina, Fissurina.*

Family Glandulinidae. Test multichambered, uniserial, biserial, or elongate spiral; aperture terminal, with an internal tubular extension. *Glandulina, Laryngosigma, Seabrookia, Tappanella.*

Order 11, BULIMINIDA. Test of low-Mg calcite; wall bilamellar, perforate, multichambered, with high trochospiral, triserial, biserial,

Present classification

or uniserial chamber arrangement; aperture in many advanced forms with internal toothplate.

(1) Superfamily Bolivinacea. Test biserial throughout, or uniserial in later part; aperture elongate, with a toothplate. Wall optically radial. Examples of extant families and genera:

Family Bolivinidae. Aperture loop-shaped, interiomarginal or areal. *Bolivina* (Fig. 2.9).

(2) Superfamily Loxostomatacea. Aperture interiomarginal or terminal, without toothplate. Wall optically radial or granular. Examples of extant families and genera:

Family Bolivinellidae. Test biserial, palmate; aperture cribrate. *Bolivinella*.

(3) Superfamily Bolivinitacea. Test biserial; aperture interiomarginal, rounded, with toothplate. Wall optically radial.

Family Bolivinitidae. The only family under Bolivinitacea; defining characters same as those of the superfamily. Example: *Bolivinita*.

(4) Superfamily Cassidulinacea. Test biserial, coiled planispirally or trochospirally throughout or in early part; aperture interiomarginal or terminal, with or without toothplate; wall optically radial or granular. Examples of extant families and genera:

Family Cassidulinidae. Coiling planispiral. *Cassidulina, Cassidulinoides, Ehrenbergina, Globocassidulina, Islandiella*.

(5) Superfamily Turrilinacea. Test high trochospiral, triserial, or biserial throughout, or changing to biserial or uniserial in later part; aperture with or without toothplate; wall optically radial or granular. Examples of extant families and genera:

Family Stainforthiidae. Test (a) triserial in early part and twisted biserial in later part, or (b) twisted biserial throughout; aperture large, elongate; rimmed or lipped apertural margin, partly infolded and linked with internal toothplate. *Hopkinsina, Stainforthia*.

(6) Superfamily Buliminacea. Test high trochospiral throughout, or modified to biserial or uniserial in later part. Aperture interiomarginal, loop-shaped, with internal toothplate; wall optically radial. Examples of extant families and genera:

Family Siphogenerinoididae. Test triserial or biserial in early part, biserial or uniserial in later part. *Rectobolivina, Rectuvigerina, Sagrina, Siphogenerina*.

Family Buliminidae. Test triserial. *Bulimina, Globobulimina*.

Family Buliminellidae. Test high trochospiral, with numerous chambers in a whorl. *Buliminella*.

Family Uvigerinidae. Test triserial throughout or in early stages; aperture terminal, extended into a neck, with internal toothplate. *Angulogerina, Trifarina, Uvigerina*.

Family Reussellidae. Test triserial throughout, or changing to biserial or uniserial in later part; periphery angular; aperture interiomarginal or terminal, slitlike or cribrate. *Reussella*.

Family Pavoninidae. Test biserial in early part, uniserial later; fan-shaped. *Pavonina*.

(7) Superfamily Fursenkoinacea. Test twisted or flat biserial, or triserial. Aperture loop-shaped, with internal toothplate. wall optically granular. Examples of extant families and genera:

Family Fursenkoinidae. Test twisted biserial throughout, or uniserial in later part. *Fursenkoina, Sigmavirgulina*.

Family Virgulinellidae. Test triserial or biserial, with partly covered sutural apertures. *Virgulinella*.

(8) Superfamily Delosinacea. Test trochospiral or triserial throughout, or biserial in later part. Aperture areal, elongate, or in the form of sutural pores. Wall optically granular. Examples of extant families and genera:

Family Delosinidae. Test high triserial; with sutural pores, but no primary aperture. *Delosina*.

(9) Superfamily Pleurostomellacea. Test triserial or biserial, changing to uniserial, or uniserial throughout; aperture areal, slitlike (and partly covered) or cribrate; aperture and foramina connected by internal siphon; wall optically granular.

Family Pleurostomellidae. The only family under Pleurostomellacea; defining characters same as those of the superfamily. Examples: *Ellipsoglandulina, Pleurostomella*.

(10) Superfamily Stilostomellacea. Test uniserial; aperture terminal, with phialine lip and small tooth.

Family Stilostomellidae. The only family under Stilostomellacea; defining characters same as those of the superfamily. Examples: *Nodogenerina, Siphonodosaria, Stilostomella.*

(11) Superfamily Annulopatellinacea. Test low conical; round initial chamber enclosed by second chamber; succeeding uniseriate chambers arranged in annuli on the convex side, but overlapping on concave or flat side, and subdivided by small tubules (internal extensions of surface pores); no aperture, but conspicuous pores.

Family Annulopatellinidae. The only family under Annulopatellinacea; defining characters same as those of the superfamily. Example: *Annulopatellina.*

Order 12, ROTALIIDA. Test of low-Mg calcite; wall bilamellar, perforate; chamber arrangement low or (rarely) high trochospiral, planispiral, annular, or irregular.

(1) Superfamily Discorbacea. Chamber arrangement low trochospiral; aperture umbilical, interiomarginal, with or without supplementary apertures; wall structure optically radial. Examples of extant families and genera:

Family Bagginidae. Test wall finely perforate overall, but imperforate in a part of ventral side. *Baggina, Cancris.*

Family Eponididae. Aperture interiomarginal and slitlike (or a narrow arch) or areal and cribrate. *Eponides, Ioanella, Paumotua, Poroeponides.*

Family Heleninidae. Primary aperture interiomarginal; secondary apertures sutural. *Helenina.*

Family Mississippinidae. With distinct, translucent or opaque bands near periphery on one or both sides. *Mississippina, Stomatorbina.*

Family Pegidiidae. Coiling modified trochospiral, with resorbed early chambers; apertures open ends of tubes on ventral side. *Pegidia.*

Family Discorbidae. Umbilical area partly covered by chamber extensions; each chamber partly divided by an imperforate wall. *Discorbis, Neoeponides.*

Family Rosalinidae. Aperture a low interiomarginal arch; chamber interiors simple; umbilicus partly covered by chamber extensions or closed. *Gavelinopsis, Neoconorbina, Rosalina.*

Family Sphaeroidinidae. Chambers strongly overlapping, arranged trochospirally or in different planes; aperture areal and slitlike or sutural and multiple. *Sphaeroidina.*

(2) Superfamily Glabratellacea. Aperture umbilical, interiomarginal. Umbilicus depressed, surrounded by radial sutures or ornamentation; wall structure optically radial. Examples of extant families and genera:

Family Glabratellidae. Test low trochospiral; radially aligned striations or granules around umbilicus. *Glabratella.*

Family Heronallenidae. Test low trochospiral, planoconvex; aperture closed by a plate; radial striations around umbilicus. *Heronallenia.*

(3) Superfamily Siphoninacea. Test low trochospiral throughout or in early part; aperture interiomarginal or areal, with a lip (usually on a short neck); wall structure optically radial or granular.

Family Siphoninidae. The only family under Siphoninacea; defining characters same as those of the superfamily. Example: *Siphonina.*

(4) Superfamily Discorbinellacea. Test low trochospiral or nearly planispiral; aperture wholly or partly interiomarginal, arch-like or slitlike; wall structure optically radial. Examples of extant families and genera:

Family Pseudoparrellidae. Test low trochospiral; aperture partly interiomarginal and partly an almost vertical slit on the terminal chamber face. *Eilohedra, Epistominella, Stetsonia.*

Family Discorbinellidae. Test flat trochospiral or nearly planispiral; primary aperture interiomarginal, with or without secondary apertures under umbilical flaps. *Laticarinina, Discorbinella.*

(5) Superfamily Planorbulinacea. Test low trochospiral throughout or in the early part, with planispiral, uniserial, biserial, or irregular arrangement in the later part; coarsely perforate; primary aperture interiomarginal in coiled forms, with or without secondary apertures; wall structure optically radial or intermediate. Examples of extant families and genera:

Family Planulinidae. Test evolute or partly evolute on both sides; chamber arrangement

Present classification

trochospiral throughout or planispiral in the later part. *Hyalinea, Planulina.*

Family Cibicididae. Test attached; chamber arrangement (a) low trochospiral throughout, or uniserial or biserial in the later part, or (b) planispiral or annular. Aperture interiomarginal in trochospiral forms, usually extending from ventral to dorsal side. *Cibicides, Cibicidoides, Cyclocibicides, Dyocibicides.*

Family Planorbulinidae. Chamber arrangement trochospiral throughout, or planispiral, annular, or irregularly multispiral in the later part. Aperture in adult forms peripheral and multiple. *Caribeanella, Planorbulina.*

Family Cymbaloporidae. Chamber arrangement trochospiral in early part, annular in later part; numerous apertures, usually as large pores. *Cymbaloporetta.*

(6) Superfamily Acervulinacea. Earliest chambers may be coiled; adult chambers numerous and irregularly arranged, producing diverse test forms; aperture present only as mural pores; test coarsely perforate; wall structure optically radial. Examples of extant families and genera:

Family Acervulinidae. Chambers spirally arranged in early part, and spreading irregularly in layers in later part. Test attached or free. *Acervulina, Gypsina.*

Family Homotrematidae. Chambers arranged spirally in early part, and forming a massive or branching structure in the later part. Test attached. *Homotrema, Miniacina.*

(7) Superfamily Asterigerinacea. Test trochospiral; chamber arrangement trochospiral to nearly planispiral; chambers fully or partly subdivided by internal partitions; primary aperture interiomarginal or areal; secondary apertures sutural or areal; wall structure optically radial. Examples of extant families and genera:

Family Epistomariidae. Test trochospiral; chambers with complete or incomplete chamberlets. *Nuttallides, Palmerinella.*

Family Asterigerinidae. Test trochospiral; alternating larger and smaller chamberlets in a stellate arrangement on the ventral side. *Asterigerina.*

Family Amphisteginidae. Test trochospiral; numerous chambers and chamberlets with sinuous sutures. *Amphistegina.*

(8) Superfamily Nonionacea. Test fully or nearly planispiral; aperture distinct or pore-like, with interiomarginal, areal, sutural, or peripheral location; wall structure optically granular or radial. Examples of extant families and genera:

Family Nonionidae. Test fully planispiral throughout or in early part; aperture slitlike or a series of pores. *Astrononion, Haynesina, Melonis, Nonion, Nonionella, Nonionellina, Pullenia.*

(9) Superfamily Chilostomellacea. Test trochospiral to planispiral throughout, or in the early part, with uncoiled later part; aperture interiomarginal in coiled forms, terminal in uncoiled forms; wall structure optically granular. Examples of extant families and genera:

Family Chilostomellidae. Test low trochospiral to planispiral; later chambers enveloping earlier ones; chambers without internal partitions. *Allomorphina, Chilostomella.*

Family Quadrimorphinidae. Test low trochospiral; chambers not enveloping, with internal partitions. *Quadrimorphina.*

Family Osangulariidae. Test low trochospiral; aperture (a) partly interiomarginal, partly areal oblique, or (b) wholly areal. *Osangularia.*

Family Oridorsalidae. Test low trochospiral; primary aperture interiomarginal; secondary apertures sutural, on both sides of test. *Oridorsalis.*

Family Gavelinellidae. Test low to high trochospiral; aperture interiomarginal, usually bordered by a narrow or wide extension of chamber wall. *Gyroidina, Gyroidinoides, Hansenisca, Hanzawaia.*

Family Karreriidae. Test attached. Chamber arrangement low trochospiral in early part, serial later. *Karreria.*

(10) Superfamily Rotaliacea. Test typically low trochospiral or planispiral, with numerous chambers; intercameral septa doubled by the addition of a lamina during new chamber formation, usually with various internal passages; aperture interiomarginal or areal, single or multiple; wall structure optically radial, with a few granular exceptions. Examples of extant families and genera:

Family Rotaliidae. Test low trochospiral

throughout, usually with radial, intraseptal, or sutural canals or fissures. *Ammonia* (Fig. 2.9), *Asterorotalia, Pararotalia.*

Family Calcarinidae. Test low trochospiral to planispiral; symmetrical or nearly so; usually spinose. *Baculogypsina, Calcarina.*

Family Elphidiidae. Test planispiral to low trochospiral; with sutural canal system and pores. *Cribroelphidium, Elphidium, Elphidiella, Ozawaia, Parrellina.*

(11) Superfamily Nummulitacea. Chamber arrangement planispiral or annular; numerous chambers, with or without chamberlets; spiral or interseptal canals present. Examples of extant families and genera:

Family Nummulitidae. Test form lenticular, discoidal, or stellate; numerous chambers on the equatorial plane; with a complex canal system. *Cycloclypeus, Operculina, Heterostegina.*

Order 13, GLOBIGERINIDA. The only planktonic order of the Foraminifera. Test of low-Mg calcite in all extant and most extinct taxa, but aragonitic in the Favusellacea (Jurassic to early Cretaceous); wall bilamellar, perforate; chamber arrangement trochospiral, planispiral, or serial; wall structure optically radial.

(1) Superfamily Heterohelicacea. Chamber arrangement biserial or triserial throughout, or in the early part (with fewer or more series in the later part). Examples of extant families and genera:

Family Guembelitriidae. Test triserial throughout or in the early part. *Gallitella.*

Family Chiloguembelinidae. Test biserial; aperture with a rim. *Laterostomella.*

(2) Superfamily Globorotaliacea. Chamber arrangement trochospiral or streptospiral; surface nonspinose; primary aperture interiomarginal. Examples of extant families and genera:

Family Globorotaliidae. Chamber arrangement low trochospiral; wall smooth or pustulose; aperture with rim. *Berggrenia, Clavatorella, Globorotalia, Neogloboquadrina, Turborotalia.*

Family Pulleniatinidae. Chamber arrangement streptospiral in the adult stage; chambers inflated. *Pulleniatina.*

Family Candeinidae. Chamber arrangement trochospiral; primary aperture interiomarginal and single, or sutural and multiple, in some forms covered by bullae. *Candeina, Tenuitella, Tinophodella.*

(3) Superfamily Globigerinacea. Chamber arrangement trochospiral to planispiral; test surface characteristically spinose; primary aperture usually interiomarginal, secondary apertures sutural; aperture may be replaced by surface pores. Examples of extant families and genera:

Family Globigerinidae. Chamber arrangement trochospiral throughout or changing to planispiral in later part; test partially or completely enclosed by the final chamber in some genera. Spines loosely attached *Beella, Bolliella, Globigerina, Globigerinella, Globigerinoides* (Fig. 2.9), *Orbulina, Sphaeroidinella.*

Family Hastigerinidae. Chamber arrangement trochospiral in early part, planispiral or streptospiral in later part. Spines growing from collar-like projections. *Hastigerina, Hastigerinopsis, Orcadia.*

Order 14, INVOLUTINIDA. Test made of aragonite. Two chambered test; initial chamber enclosed by coiled, tubular second chamber. No designated superfamily.

Family Planispirillinidae. The only extant family in this suborder. Asymmetrical test, coiling planispiral or trochospiral; umbilical area, at least on one side, filled by lamellar growth; aperture terminal. Examples: *Alanwoodia, Conicospirillinoides, Planispirillina* (Fig. 2.9), *Trocholinopsis.*

Order 15, ROBERTINIDA. Test made of aragonite, perforate, multichambered.

(1) Superfamily Ceratobuliminacea. Chambers with internal partitions and arranged in a trochospiral coil; aperture areal or interiomarginal. Examples of extant families and genera:

Family Ceratobuliminidae. Primary aperture entirely interiomarginal or with areal extension. *Ceratobulimina.*

Family Epistominidae. Primary aperture a slit on the test margin. *Hoeglundina.*

(2) Superfamily Robertinacea. Chambers

with double internal partitions; secondary chambers clearly distinguishable from primary chambers.

Family Robertinidae. The only family under Robertinacea; defining characters same as those of the superfamily. Examples: *Alliatina*, *Cushmanella*, *Robertina*, *Robertinoides* (Fig. 2.9), *Sidebottomina*.

Order 16, SILICOLOCULINIDA. Test made of opaline silica; imperforate. No superfamily designated.

Family Silicoloculinidae. Multichambered coiled test; chambers arranged in various planes; aperture terminal, partly blocked. Example: *Miliammellus* (Fig. 2.9).

2.6 GEOLOGICAL RECORD OF EXTANT FORAMINIFERAL TAXA

Many foraminiferal species and genera were first reported as fossils rather than as living organisms. Any massive compilation of geological ranges of such taxa is likely to miss a few later reports of their occurrence in modern sediments. Thus, some genera continuing into the Holocene (e.g. *Loxostomum*, *Suggrunda*) are listed as extinct in Loeblich and Tappan (1987). On the other hand, about half of the nearly 900 extant foraminiferal genera mentioned in Loeblich and Tappan (1987) have no pre-Holocene record (Tappan and Loeblich, 1988). This does not necessarily mean that the earliest species of all these genera actually evolved in the last 10,000 years; the earlier history may be lost, because of taphonomic processes (see chapter 16) and diagenesis, and by the destruction of the sedimentary record by diverse geological processes. Organic-walled tests (Allogromiida) are preserved only under exceptionally favorable conditions; they have a very poor and erratic fossil record. Agglutinated tests with loosely attached grains or with organic cement frequently disintegrate in many sedimentary environments, and during diagenesis. Aragonitic tests (Robertinida and Involutinida) are destroyed in diagenesis more readily than calcitic tests. Compared to low-Mg calcitic tests, both aragonitic and high-Mg calcitic tests (Miliolida) are preferentially dissolved in the deep sea. Apparently, tests made of calcite spicules (Carterinida) are also poorly preserved; they are known from the Eocene and Holocene, but not from the intervening epochs.

The geological record of extant families is given in Table 2.3. About three-fourths of these 164 families have a pre-Holocene record. Eleven can be traced as far back as early Paleozoic (Cambrian and Ordovician); all of these taxa are organic-walled or agglutinated (orders Allogromiida, Astrorhizida, and Lituolida. The most specialized calcareous order of the Paleozoic (Fusulinida) is extinct. Among modern families with secreted calcareous tests, only two can be traced to the Paleozoic (early Carboniferous); both of these are characterized by imperforate walls (Miliolida). A few extant hyaline families (calcareous perforate tests) extend back to the Triassic, but for the two most diverse groups of Holocene calcareous Foraminifera, the record of modern families begins in the Cretaceous; 27% of extant families of the Buliminida and 37% of extant families of the Rotaliida started in this 78-my-long period. The effect of the mass extinction at the Cretaceous-Paleogene boundary was much more severe on planktonic Foraminifera. All seven extant families of the Globigerinida were present in the Miocene, but only one family, Guembelitriidae (with a single Holocene genus, *Gallitellia*), can be traced back to the Cretaceous. Overall, the stratigraphic record shows that 62 benthic families originated in the Cretaceous, of which 22 are extinct. For planktonic families, the numbers are 10 and 9, respectively.

2.7 CONCLUDING REMARKS

The Loeblich and Tappan classification of 1987, emended by them in 1992, and further modified for ordinal taxa in this chapter, is the most

Table 2.3 Origination record of extant families. The number of extant families beginning in a given period or epoch is shown under each order. The total number of extant families within each order is in parentheses after the order number. Data on geological ranges from Loeblich and Tappan (1987). Order numbers (as in fig. 2.8): 1, Allogromiida; 2, Astrorhizida; 3, Lituolida; 4, Trochamminida; 5, Textulariida; 6, Fusulinida (extinct, not in table); 7, Miliolida; 8, Carterinida; 9, Spirillinida; 10, Lagenida; 11, Buliminida; 12, Rotaliida; 13, Globigerinida; 14, Involutinida; 15, Robertinida; 16, Silicoloculinida.

Period/Epoch	Order 1 (4)	Order 2 (15)	Order 3 (28)	Order 4 (2)	Order 5 (5)	Order 7 (15)	Order 8 (1)	Order 9 (2)	Order 10 (6)	Order 11 (22)	Order 12 (52)	Order 13 (7)	Order 14 (1)	Order 15 (3)	Order 16 (1)	All orders (164)
Holocene	2	5	6	1	1	1				4	5		1			26
Pleistocene																
Pliocene											1					1
Miocene			1			1				3	2	2			1	10
Oligocene											6					6
Eocene	1		2			2	1			5	14	2				27
Paleocene					2					4	5	2		1		14
Cretaceous		1	6		1	5		1		6	19	1		2		40
Jurassic			4		1	3			2							12
Triassic			3			1		1	4							9
Permian																
Carboniferous		2	3	1		2										8
Devonian																
Silurian																
Ordovician	1	6	2													9
Cambrian		1	1													2

Concluding remarks

elaborate hierarchical classification of the Foraminifera ever produced. Although the 1987 classification was not as well-received as their simpler 1964 classification (Haman, 1988), it is the current standard, at least for the placement of genera into families and superfamilies. Hierarchical biological classifications are inherently subjective, especially where a large part of the data is derived from the fossil record. There is disagreement between Loeblich and Tappan (1987, 1992) and other taxonomists even on some well-known foraminiferal taxa, e.g. (a) about the recognition of superfamilies, families, subfamilies, and their constituent genera within the Buliminida (Revets, 1996), (b) about the inclusion of *Discorbis*, *Rosalina*, *Eponides*, and *Gavelinopsis* in the Discorbacea, rather than in the Rotaliacea or Eponidacea, a superfamily not recognized by Loeblich and Tappan (Hansen and Revets, 1992), and (c) about the placement of the Elphidiidae in the Rotaliacea, rather than in the Nonionacea (Haynes, 1990). In the context of the entire classification, however, these problems are not overwhelming.

On the positive side, the major improvement over the 1964 version is the de-emphasizing of the optical property of hyaline walls in the 1987 expansion. The use of the radial and granular wall structures (as seen in polarized light) for superfamily distinctions has been considered an 'unnecessarily rigid constraint' for a long time (e.g. Cifelli, 1976). This constraint was removed by Loeblich and Tappan in 1987. For example, *Cassidulina* and *Islandiella*, two similar genera, were placed in two different superfamilies (Cassidulinacea and Buliminacea) in Loeblich and Tappan (1964a); they are now in the same family (Cassidulinidae). The problem is not fully resolved, however. In view of the fact that both radial and granular structures have been observed within a single genus (*Elphidium*), the usefulness of this optical property at any level of taxonomic hierarchy needs reexamination. At the ordinal level, the status of the Silicoloculinida and the placement of the extant members of the Involutinida are uncertain; the decisions in Loeblich and Tappan (1992) are different from those in Loeblich and Tappan (1987).

Foraminiferal classifications are largely the outcome of paleontological research. Those reported in relatively recent protozoological literature (e.g. Levine *et al.*, 1980; Lee, 1990a) generally agree in concept and overall structure, if not in the ranks of taxa, with one of the Loeblich and Tappan schemes. However, a startling regression to chamber count as the chosen primary criterion is observed in one classification (Cavalier-Smith, 1993). In this, the Foraminifera (as a subphylum within the Kingdom Protozoa) is split into two classes, one with single-chambered forms (Monothalamea), the other with multichambered forms (Polythalamea). The Monothalamea, reminiscent of d'Orbigny's Monostègues, is not split further into lower suprageneric categories. The included genera are not named, but by definition, this group would include *Myxotheca* (organic-walled), *Saccammina* (agglutinated), *Squamulina* (calcareous imperforate), and *Lagena* (calcareous perforate), i.e. genera representing four separate orders (three of them with numerous multichambered genera) in the schemes of Haynes (1981), Lee (1990a), and Loeblich and Tappan (1992). Such taxonomy is a denial of the enormous body of extant information on foraminiferal wall compositions, stratigraphic distributions, and probable phylogenies.

On the other hand, it is almost axiomatic that scientific classification of the Foraminifera must not be based on skeletal morphology alone. The geological record of fossils and the DNA signatures of living species, both providing significant clues to phylogenetic connections, must support any logical scheme of classification. The geological history of the Foraminifera has been taken into consideration by most systematists, starting with Cushman, but the genetic study is still in its infancy (see, e.g. Pawlowski *et al.*, 1994a, b, 1996; Wray *et al.*, 1995; Holzmann and Pawlowski, 1997), and has not yet become a cause for restructuring the suprageneric classification. In any case, the half-century old statement of Alan Wood is still true: "If classifications of the future are to be "natural," reflecting the evolutionary history of the group, they will be not less but more complicated than those at present in favour' (Wood, 1949).

2.8 ACKNOWLEDGMENTS

I thank Laurie Anderson, Anthony Arnold, William Berggren, and John Haynes for their helpful suggestions regarding the manuscript, Johanna Resig for sharing her current thoughts on the Silicoloculinida, and Samuel Bowser, Leanne French, Susan Goldstein, Megan Jones, Manfred Kage, and Emil Platon for contributing illustrations to this chapter. I am indebted to Mary Lee Eggart for art work and to Emil Platon for scanning electron micrography of my foraminiferal specimens.

3
Foraminifera: A biological overview

Susan T. Goldstein

3.1 INTRODUCTION: FORAMINIFERA AS LIVING ORGANISMS

The Foraminifera are an enormously successful group of amoeboid protists. Branching very deeply within the eukaryotic evolutionary tree (Pawlowski et al., 1998b), they first appeared in the Cambrian, and, over the course of the Phanerozoic, invaded most marginal to fully marine environments and diversified to exploit a wide variety of modes of life. Foraminifera are abundant and diverse in modern oceans where they occur from coastal settings to both planktonic and benthic habitats of the deep sea. They occupy tiered epibenthic to deep infaunal microhabitats and utilize a diversity of trophic mechanisms.

Some representatives have attained gigantic proportions. The extinct *Lepidocyclina elephantina*, for example, at over 14 cm is among the largest reported (Grell, 1973). The Foraminifera, although exclusively unicellular, accomplish nearly all of the fundamental functions of life performed by the myriad of multicellular animals. Foraminifera eat, defecate, move, grow, reproduce, and respond to a variety of environmental stimuli. Whereas metazoans evolved organs and other specialized features through multicellularity, Foraminifera and other protists specialized by diversifying subcellular components or organelles to perform these various functions.

Two broad morphological features distinguish the Foraminifera from other protists. First, all Foraminifera possess granuloreticulopodia (Figs. 3.1, 3.2), which are fine, thread-like, pseudopodia that anastomose (split and rejoin) and have a granular texture when viewed with the light microscope. Second, nearly all Foraminifera possess a test or shell that encompasses the organism and separates it from the surrounding milieu. The test may be organic (not mineralized), agglutinated (constructed of foreign particles cemented together by the foraminifer), composed of calcium carbonate or, in rare cases, silica (see chapter 2). In addition, the Foraminifera are united by a life cycle characterized by a fundamental alternation of sexual and asexual generations that has become secondarily modified in some groups. Having made these generalizations, it is interesting to note that the freshwater rhizopod *Reticulomyxa* has pseudopodia that are strikingly similar to those of the Foraminifera (Orokos et al., 1997), though it lacks a shell. Genetically, this protist is a foraminiferan (Pawlowski et al., 1998a).

Our understanding of the Foraminifera dates to Dujardin's (1835a,b,d) observations on several living shallow-water Foraminifera (*Triloculina*, *Elphidium*, *Ammonia*, *Peneroplis*) which he obtained by washing fucoid and coralline algae collected from the Mediterranean into glass vessels. He also observed *Gromia oviformis*, a protistan relative of the Foraminifera that superficially resembles the foraminifer *Allogromia* (*Gromia*'s pseudopodia and life cycle differ from those characteristic of the Foraminifera; see Arnold, 1972). Watching live miliolione Foraminifera climb the walls of his vessels, Dujardin (1835b) described granule-filled, anastomosing 'filaments' (pseudopodia) which slowly extended and retracted as the Foraminifera adhered to the vessel walls and slowly moved. Dujardin coined the term 'sarcode' to describe amoeboidal cytoplasm, and established the 'Rhizopodes', suggesting a relationship between the Foraminifera and other amoebae.

3.2 PSEUDOPODIA

The key to Dujardin's (1835a,b,d) correct identification of the Foraminifera as amoeboid organisms, thus removing them from the cephalopods where d'Orbigny (1826) had previously placed them (see Cole, 1926; Lipps, 1981), were his observations on the undifferentiated body ('sarcode') of the Foraminifera and on the anastomosing, granular pseudopodia which all Foraminifera possess (see Fig. 2.2). We now know that pseudopodia accomplish many essential life functions for the Foraminifera and are, therefore, of fundamental importance (Travis and Bowser, 1991). Pseudopodia are essential not only for motility and attachment, as recognized by Dujardin (1835a,b,d), but also for feeding, building and structuring tests, protection, and some aspects of respiration and reproduction. Pseudopodia provide the mechanism by which Foraminifera interact with their surroundings.

Foraminifera extrude pseudopodia through one or more apertural openings in the test. The first pseudopodia extruded commonly are fine filaments or 'filopodia' that are often straight. As this process continues, the pseudopodial trunk or 'peduncle' thickens and virtually fills the apertural opening(s), branching into numerous finer pseudopodia that often anastomose. The result, if the foraminifer is provided a hard, smooth surface, is an intricate, sticky pseudopodial network of 'reticulopodia' that rivals the complexity of a spider's web (Carpenter et al., 1862; Leidy, 1879). Unlike a spider's web, however, reticulopodia are continuously remodeled and transport a variety of materials. Particle movement, as many early observers remarked, is bidirectional, even within a single pseudopodial strand (Allen, 1964).

The intricacy and function of reticulopodia captivated many of the early foraminiferal biologists who provided detailed and sometimes poetic accounts of their observations (Dujardin, 1835a,b,d; Carpenter et al., 1862; Leidy, 1879 [though his descriptions were based largely on freshwater protists included in '*Gromia*']; Lister, 1903; Winter, 1907; Sandon, 1934; Jepps, 1942). Contemporary cell biologists have found foraminiferal pseudopodia excellent experimental systems for a number of processes including cell motility and the assembly and disassembly of microtubules (e.g. Jahn and Rinaldi, 1959; Allen, 1964; Travis and Allen, 1981; Bowser and Reider, 1985; Bowser et al., 1986; Travis and Bowser, 1986a,b; Bowser et al., 1988; Travis and Bowser, 1988; Welnhofer and Travis, 1996).

Though some benthic Foraminifera do indeed live attached to hard or firm surfaces such as seagrasses, macroscopic algae, shells, sponges, or rocks (Lutze and Altenbach, 1988; Lutze and Thiel, 1989; Langer, 1993), and probably extend reticulopodial nets in the field much as they do on glass slides, most live associated with fine-grained sediments through which they actively migrate (Severin and Erskian, 1981; Severin, 1987b; Wetmore, 1988; Weinburg, 1991; Hemleben and Kitazato, 1995; Bornmalm et al., 1997). When offered abundant fine-grained sediment, most Foraminifera use their pseudopodia to collect a variety of materials, including sediment, algal cells, bacteria, and organic detritus (see Goldstein and Corliss, 1994). Such collections are formed into mounds that may be large enough to completely encompass the test and are riddled with a three-dimensional reticulopodial array. Though commonly associated with feeding, many benthic Foraminifera construct somewhat similar mounds or cysts during the formation of a new chamber or prior to reproduction.

Structurally, foraminiferal pseudopodia are encased by a cell membrane and contain a cytoskeletal core of microtubules which may occur singly, but more typically as loosely organized bundles (Fig. 3.3) (reviewed in Travis and Bowser, 1991). These loosely arranged microtubules in the Foraminifera lack the intricate microtubular patterns found in cross sections of the 'axopodia' of such amoeboid protists as the heliozoans (Kitching, 1964; Smith and Patterson, 1986) and radiolarians (Cachon and Cachon, 1971, 1972; Anderson, 1983). However, perhaps not unlike the heliozoans, the Foraminifera have developed specialized mechanisms for rapid assembly and disassembly of microtubules, which allow rapid retraction of reticulopodia and their redeployment when needed (Welnhofer and Travis, 1996, and references therein).

Ultrastructural studies show that the characteristic granular appearance of foraminiferal pseudopodia is due to the presence of several organelles or structures that include mitochondria, 'dense bodies', phagosomes, defecation vacuoles, and a variety of other smaller structures (Fig. 3.3) (reviewed in Travis and Bowser, 1991). Mitochondria are the most prominent pseudopodial granules. They move bidirectionally, and are probably responsible for transporting metabolic energy (ATP) within the reticulopodial network. 'Dense bodies' are membrane-bound vesicles that appear refractile under the light microscope and opaque with TEM (transmission electron microscopy). Their function has not yet been determined, though Travis and Bowser (1991) suggest that they may serve as storage vesicles for phospholipids (building blocks of membranes). Phagosomes are vacuoles that contain materials captured for ingestion, and their content varies widely, depending on the diet of the foraminifer. Xanthosomes, packets of undigested materials along with metabolic wastes, are transported out and away from the foraminifer along pseudopodia in defecation vacuoles (illustrated in Bowser et al., 1985). For more information on pseudopodial structure and function, see Travis and Bowser (1991).

3.3 TROPHIC MECHANISMS

As a group, the Foraminifera utilize a broad range of feeding mechanisms and nutritional resources, including grazing, suspension feeding, deposit feeding, carnivory, parasitism, the direct uptake of DOC, and symbiosis. Many smaller Foraminifera that live within the photic zone commonly feed on selected species of algae (Fig. 3.4) (see reviews by Arnold, 1974, and Anderson et al., 1991), but are also known to ingest bacteria, yeasts, fungi, and in some cases, small animals (Lee et al., 1966; Lipps, 1983; Lee, 1980; Bernhard and Bowser, 1992). Bacteria appear to play an indispensable role in the nutrition of many Foraminifera (Lee, 1980). Though the diet of most Foraminifera may be quite varied, feeding experiments have shown that many species feed selectively (Lee et al., 1966; Lee, 1980). Pseudopodia play an indispensable role in feeding in that they function to gather food (e.g. Jepps, 1942), subdue prey (Bowser et al., 1992), and, in at least some species, may also function in extrathalamous digestion (Jepps, 1942; Meyer-Reil and Köster, 1991; Lee et al., 1991b; Faber and Lee, 1991b).

Foraminifera that live below the photic zone cannot rely on living algal cells as a food source. However, the influx of phytodetritus to the seafloor from the plankton provides important primary and secondary food resources for Foraminifera and other members of the benthos. Gooday (1988) documented the selective exploitation of phytodetritus by several small species that appear to reproduce very rapidly, thus colonizing fresh phytodetritus as it arrives on the seafloor. A number of subsequent investigations support these findings (Thiel et al., 1989; Gooday and Lambshead, 1989; Lambshead and Gooday, 1990; Gooday and Turley, 1990; Gooday, 1993). More degraded forms of organic detritus, and, especially, the microbiotas (largely bacteria) associated with this material provide important food resources for shallow (Heeger, 1990) to deeper infaunal taxa (Goldstein and Corliss, 1994).

Grazing, found in some shallow-water Foraminifera, is accomplished by feeding largely on algal cells while moving over a surface such as a seagrass blade, kelp, or coralline algae. This process can be observed easily in culture. Jepps (1942), for example, described individuals of '*Polystomella*' (= *Elphidium*) *crispum* feeding on lawns of cultured diatoms. The foraminifers would use their pseudopodia to collect mounds of diatoms so extensive that they completely covered the test. After feeding within one mound for some time (usually hours), the foraminifer would discard it, move on, then construct a fresh mound. Discarded mounds, or 'feeding cysts' contained small orange xanthosomes (waste particles) that were shed by the foraminifer.

Suspension feeding Foraminifera make use of the small organisms and detritus that are suspended in the water column. This mode of feeding occurs in Foraminifera that occupy elevated epibenthic substrates as well as some of those that live in association with soft sediments.

Lipps (1983) suggested that suspension feeding is widespread in Foraminifera that elevate their aperture(s) above the sediment–water interface and extrude their pseudopodia directly into the water column. Because Foraminifera lack a mechanism for creating water currents as do many suspension-feeding invertebrates and ciliated protists, the suspension-feeding Foraminifera are most likely 'passive' suspension feeders (Lipps, 1983).

Suspension feeding occurs in both agglutinated and calcareous taxa. *Astrorhiza limicola*, for example, is a biconvex, agglutinated, monothalamous foraminifer with multiple apertures, each positioned at the end of a tube. In life position, this foraminifer rises up on its edge, positioning some apertures into the sediment and others into the overlying water column. Pseudopodia extend from all apertures. Those protruding into the sediment serve to anchor the foraminifer while those protruding from elevated apertures extend into the water column, and trap food particles (Cedhagen, 1988). *Pelosina arborescens*, another monothalamous agglutinated foraminifer that lives in soft sediments, similarly utilizes suspension feeding as a trophic mechanism (Fig. 3.5, 3.6) (Cedhagen, 1993). Suspension feeding also occurs in several calcareous species that occupy elevated habitats: *Rupertina stabilis*, *Cibicides wuellerstorfi*, and *Planulina ariminensis* (Lutze and Altenbach, 1988; Lutze and Thiel, 1989) as well as the agglu-

Figure 3.1 Juvenile *Cribrothalammina alba* with reticulopodia extended. Scale bar approximately 50 μm.

Figure 3.2 Higher magnification of apertural region of *Cribrothalammina alba* in Fig. 3.1. Note large pennate diatom near aperture. Scale bar approximately 10 μm.

Figure 3.3 TEM micrograph of a single pseudopodial strand from *Spiroloculina hyalina*, illustrating some of the various 'granules' found in foraminiferal pseudopodia: mitochondria (m), microtubules (mt), dense bodies (arrow). Scale bar = 1 μm. Micrograph provided by Samuel S. Bowser.

Figure 3.4 TEM micrograph of a partially digested diatom in a large food vacuole in *Cribrothalammina alba*. Chloroplasts and lipid vesicles appear to be the most persistent components within the diatom. Scale bar = 2 μm.

Figure 3.5 The large agglutinated species *Pelosina arborescens*. This foraminifer utilizes suspension feeding as a trophic mechanism. Micrograph provided by Tomas Cedhagen.

Figure 3.6 A reticulopodial net extended by *Pelosina arborescens* (see Fig. 3.5) that functions in suspension feeding. Micrograph provided by Tomas Cedhagen.

Figure 3.7 TEM micrograph of a food vacuole which contains sediment and a bacterium in the deposit-feeding foraminifer *Globobulimina pacifica*. Scale bar = 0.5 μm.

Trophic mechanisms

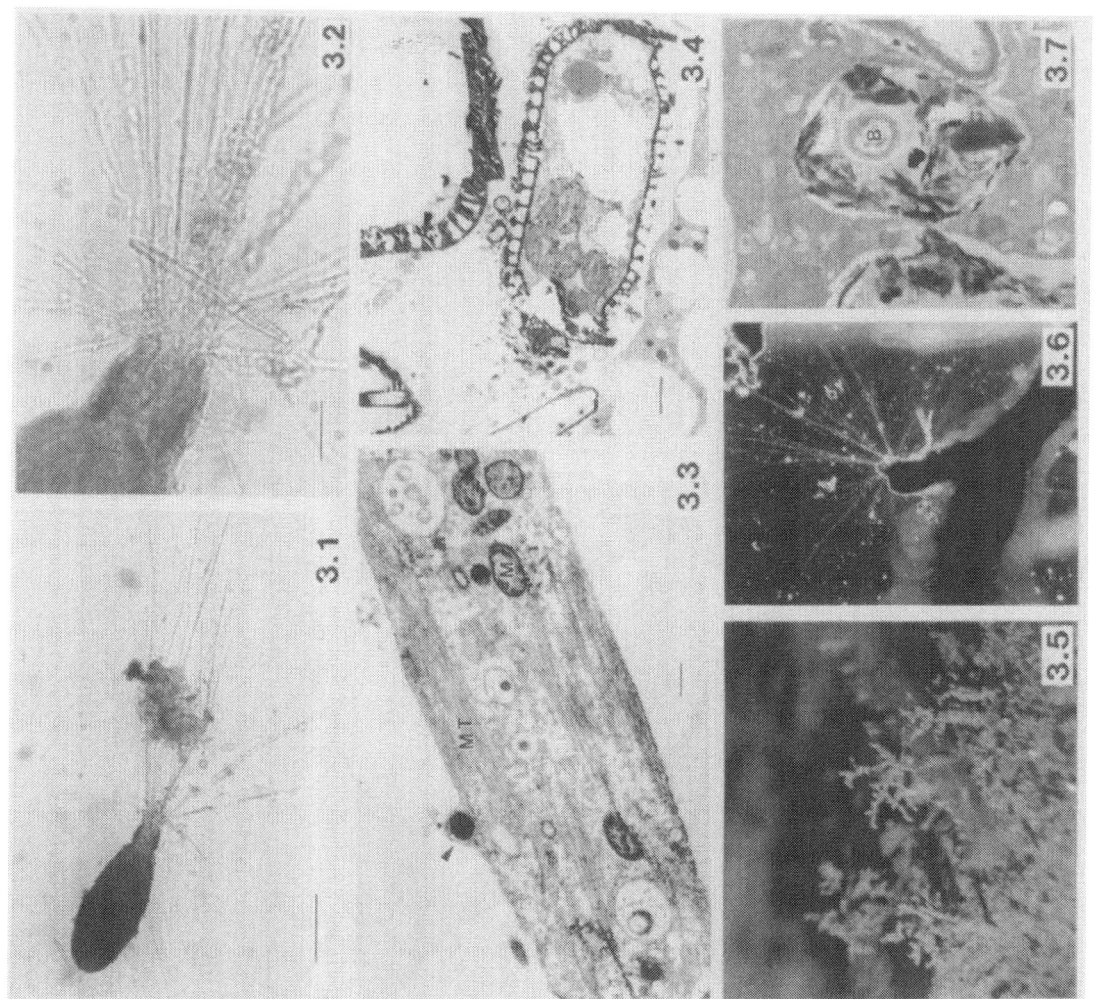

tinated *Saccorhiza ramosa* (Altenbach et al., 1988). Epizoic Foraminifera that reside on the shells of living brachiopods may also utilize suspension feeding and benefit from brachiopod feeding currents (Zumwalt and DeLaca, 1980).

The construction of feeding cysts, as in *Elphidium crispum*, is not limited to grazing, but is also an integral part of *deposit feeding*. Many benthic Foraminifera that live in muddy sediments, both within and below the photic zone, use their pseudopodia to construct feeding cysts (Hofker, 1927; Nyholm, 1957; Goldstein and Corliss, 1994) with sediment, algal cells (or their remains in the form of phytodetritus), bacteria, and organic detritus (Goldstein and Corliss, 1994). Some of the material gathered by the pseudopodia is partitioned into small parcels which the foraminifer ingests by phagotrophy within the terminal chamber (Fig 3.7). Deposit feeding Foraminifera, such as the deep-sea dwellers *Globobulimina pacifica* and *Uvigerina peregrina* and the shallow-water *Ammonia beccarii*, ingest a surprisingly large amount of sediment as well as algal cells, bacteria, and organic detritus. Bacteria appear to constitute an important element in the diet of deposit-feeding Foraminifera (Goldstein and Corliss, 1994).

Carnivory is utilized by some Foraminifera, including both benthic and planktonic species and both symbiont-bearing and non-symbiont-bearing forms. The large symbiont-bearing foraminifer *Peneroplis pertusus*, for example, feeds on copepods, but ingests only portions of the prey, leaving the empty carapace behind (Winter, 1907). The large non-symbiont-bearing agglutinated foraminifer *Astrorhiza limicola* is at least partly carnivorous, and captures prey as large as 2–3 cm, including several types of small crustaceans (cumaceans, caprellids), and echinoid larvae (Buchanan and Hedley, 1960). Some carnivorous Foraminifera are quite small. Hallock and Talge (1994) described a small predatory foraminifer (*Floresina amphiphaga*) that attacks the larger foraminifer, *Amphistegina gibbosa*. *F. amphiphaga* attaches to the test of its prey and drills up to 10 holes per attachment site, often killing its prey. Carnivory has been reported in several additional benthic species (see Boltovskoy and Wright, 1976).

Carnivory also occurs in some planktonic Foraminifera. Anderson and Bé (1976) and Bé et al. (1977a) found the remains of copepods and other small crustaceans within the bubble capsule of *Hastigerina pelagica* and among the spines and pseudopodia of *Globigerinella aequilateralis*. These and several other planktonic taxa (*Orbulina universa*, *Globigerinoides ruber*, *Globorotalia menardii*, and *Pulleniatina obliquiloculata*) would prey on copepods and nauplii of the brine shrimp, *Artemia*, in laboratory cultures.

The pseudopodia of carnivorous Foraminifera may be specially adapted for capturing prey. In the large agglutinated foraminifer *Astrammina rara*, pseudopodia secrete an extracellular matrix material that functions to strengthen pseudopodia and maintain their integrity as prey resist capture. Non-carnivorous Foraminifera lack this material and have pseudopodia that are many times weaker than those from carnivorous Foraminifera (Bowser et al., 1992). In addition, some carnivorous Foraminifera may have the ability to secrete an adhesive material in the area where prey contact pseudopodia (Anderson and Bé, 1976; Bowser et al., 1992).

Many carnivorous Foraminifera, however, are not strictly carnivorous, but utilize carnivory in addition to at least one other trophic mechanism. Cedhagen (1988), for example, reported suspension feeding in *Astrorhiza limicola*, a carnivorous planktonic Foraminifera also ingest diatoms (Bé et al., 1977a). Some species, both benthic and planktonic, utilize carnivory in conjunction with algal endosymbiosis.

Though the vast majority of Foraminifera are free-living, a few species show *parasitism*, primarily infesting other foraminifers, bivalve molluscs, sponges, or stone corals. Le Calvez (1947) first documented parasitism in the Foraminifera by reporting the ectoparasitic existence of the uniolocular '*Entosolenia*' (= *Fissurina*) *marginata* on the foraminifer *Discorbis vilardeboanus*. *F. marginata* attaches to the spiral side of the

Trophic mechanisms

host and uses its pseudopodia to capture granules from the host's extrathalamous cytoplasm. This species could be cultured only in association with *D. vilardeboanus* and not when offered alternative foods such as algae or other species of Foraminifera. The small foraminifer *Metarotaliella tuvaluensis* may potentially parasitize several miliolid species (Collen, 1998). *M. tuvaluensis* attaches to the surface of juvenile miliolids, and causes deformations of the host test as the host overgrows this small foraminifer; living material, however, was not observed. The foraminifer *Cibicides refulgens* parasitizes the Antarctic scallop *Adamussium colbecki* by eroding through the scallop's shell and feeding on the nutrient-rich fluids in the extrapallial cavity; this species also feeds by grazing and suspension feeding (Alexander and DeLaca, 1987). Unlike other parasitic Foraminifera, *Hyrrokkin sarcophaga* infests multiple hosts (selected bivalves, sponges, and stone corals). This foraminifer penetrates the body wall of the hosts and feeds on soft tissues (Cedhagen, 1994).

Pawlowski (1989) and Pawlowski and Lee (1992) described an unusual association between the small foraminifer *Rotaliella elatiana* and the macrophytic alga *Enteromorpha*. The foraminifer lives inside the filaments of the alga and will not grow in culture unless the alga is present. Pawlowski (1989), therefore, suggests that this foraminifer is nutritionally dependent on the alga.

The large arborescent foraminifer *Notodendrodes antarctikos* is capable of utilizing *dissolved organic carbon* (DOC) (DeLaca et al., 1981; DeLaca, 1982). Labeled amino acids and glucose introduced into sterile seawater were taken up by the foraminifer and rapidly metabolized. Given the opportunity, however, this foraminifer also ingests bacteria and particulate organic matter, and thus, does not rely exclusively on the uptake of DOC. Reservoirs of DOC present in sediments may provide an important nutritional resource during particularly oligotrophic seasons in the Antarctic (DeLaca, 1982). This potentially widespread trophic mechanism, however, has received little attention.

Symbiotic relationships, discussed in detail in chapter 8, are quite varied in the Foraminifera, and include algal endosymbiosis (Lee and Anderson, 1991a), chloroplast husbandry (Lopez, 1979; Lee et al., 1988; Bernhard, 1996), and bacterial endosymbiosis (Bernhard, 1996). Of these, algal endosymbiosis, which occurs in larger calcareous benthic Foraminifera (Fig. 3.8) and many planktonic species, is the best known. Chloroplast husbandry, the process by which Foraminifera sequester and house chloroplasts but not the entire algal cell, occurs in some benthic Foraminifera from both shallow-water habitats (Lopez, 1979; Leutenegger, 1984; Lee et al., 1988; Lee and Anderson, 1991a) and low-oxygen microhabitats located well below the photic zone (Bernhard, 1996). In addition, bacterial endosymbionts have been identified in some benthic Foraminifera that live in anoxic or very low-oxygen microhabitats, though the actual mechanisms involved in this relationship have not yet been determined (Bernhard, 1996).

Algal endosymbiosis occurs in some representatives from three Foraminiferal orders: Miliolida, Rotaliida, and Globigerinida. Symbiont-bearing members of the Rotaliida (Amphisteginidae, Calcarinidae, Nummulitidae). Planktonic Foraminifera (Globigerinida) may host either dinoflagellate or chrysophyte symbionts (see chapter 8, and reviews by Leutenegger, 1984, and Lee and Anderson, 1991a).

This broad array of potential algal endosymbionts allows different foraminiferal hosts to thrive at different depths within the photic zone (Leutenegger, 1984; Hallock, 1988a, 1988b; see chapter 8). The shallowest-water habitats are home to benthic Foraminifera with all types of symbionts. Those bearing chlorophytes, however, are limited to the shallowest depths (~ 30 m), whereas those with rhodophytes or

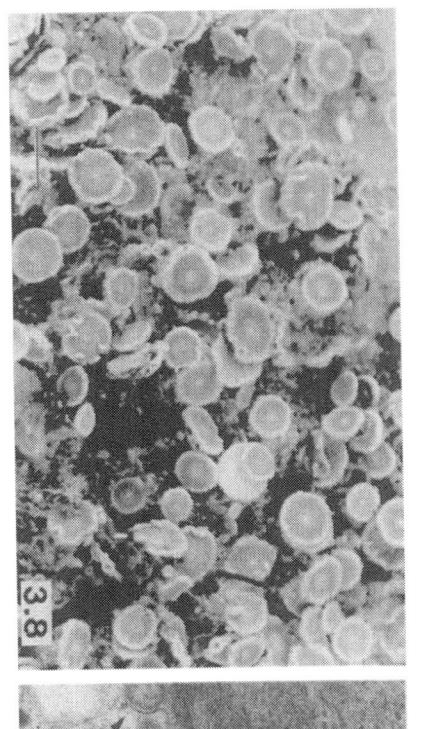

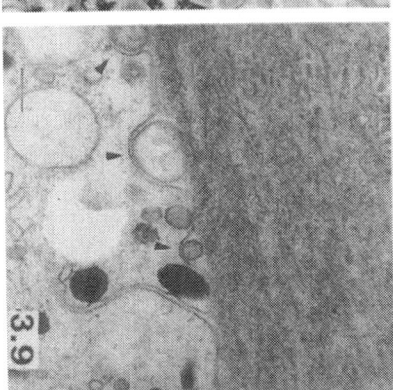

Figure 3.8 Live individuals of *Marginopora vertebralis* collected at the Lizard Island Research Station, northern Great Barrier Reef (ICOP Foram Biology Workshop, July, 1997). Scale bar approximately 1 cm.

Figure 3.9 TEM micrograph of a section across the contact between the test and cytoplasm in *Myxotheca* sp. The test is characterized by a fine meshlike structure (see also Angell, 1971). This foraminifer adds material to its test (vesicles at arrows) at regions distant from the aperture. Specimen prepared by high pressure freezing and freeze substitution. Scale bar = 0.25 µm. Micrograph by E.A. Richardson and S.T. Goldstein.

dinoflagellates extend to deeper habitats (60–70 m). Those with diatoms are found as deep as ~130 m. The photosynthetic pigments of different algal groups are activated by light of different wavelengths. Diatoms utilize light in the blue to green range, allowing them to exploit the deepest habitats (Leutenegger, 1984). Though diatom-bearing Foraminifera occur at all depths, those in shallow-water habitats may protect themselves behaviorally by avoiding direct sunlight (*Heterostegina depressa*) or possessing a test that morphologically prevents overexposure (calcarinids) (Leutenegger, 1984; Hallock et al., 1991b; Lee and Anderson, 1991a).

Relationships between Foraminifera and their algal endosymbionts are often not specific. A single foraminiferal species may host different species of symbionts, particularly if they are diatoms (Lee et al., 1989, 1992; Lee and Anderson, 1991a). In addition, the same species of symbiont may occur in more than one species of Foraminifera. The dinoflagellate *Gymnodinium béii*, for example, has been reported from four different species of planktonic Foraminifera (see review by Lee and Anderson, 1991a). Relationships between the foraminiferal host and symbiont are varied and complex. In general, however, symbionts release exudates to the host, and can in some cases supply the foraminifer with all the organic carbon it requires (Jørgensen et al., 1985). Algal symbionts also promote calcification in some planktonic and benthic hosts (Bé et al., 1982; Duguay, 1983). The foraminifer, in return, provides the symbiont with a fairly stable microenvironment in addition to dissolved nitrogen, phosphorus, and potentially other nutritional requirements (see Lee and Anderson, 1991a). Carnivory plays an important dietary role in some symbiont-bearing Foraminifera by providing a source for nitrogen and phosphorus for the host-algal system (Jørgensen et al., 1985).

Foraminifera that host algal symbionts are quite dependent on their presence and well being. Hosts do not grow well in the dark or where the symbionts have been experimentally removed. Most symbionts, however, can be grown in culture quite readily without their foraminiferal host, and this is perhaps an essential feature of the relationship. Though symbionts are transmitted to offspring during asexual reproduction (multiple fission), gametes and (presumably) zygotes are symbiont-free. How and when the developing zygotes acquire symbionts in not known.

Some benthic Foraminifera belonging to the families Nonionidae, Elphidiidae, and Rotalielldae sequester and house chloroplasts obtained from algal food sources (Lopez, 1979; Lee and Anderson, 1991a). Such chloroplasts retain their ability to photosynthesize in some hosts that reside within the photic zone. Over time, however, the foraminiferal host digests its chloroplasts, suggesting that the foraminifer must constantly replenish its supply (Lee and Anderson, 1991a). Interestingly, Bernhard (1996) identified a similar relationship in a nonionid that lives well below the photic zone in low-oxygen, benthic microenvironments of the Santa Barbara Basin.

3.4 GROWTH AND TEST MORPHOGENESIS

Growth in the Foraminifera is accomplished by either increasing the size of a single chamber (unilocular forms) or, more commonly, by intermittently adding a new chamber. Details of the former process are sketchy for agglutinated taxa and unknown in unilocular calcareous ones; the latter is better known in both calcareous and agglutinated representatives.

In allogromid Foraminifera, new shell material appears to be added near the aperture (Angell, 1980), and this may also be the case for many members of the Astrorhizida. In addition, however, single-chambered agglutinated Foraminifera, such as *Cribrothalammina alba*, add material to the inner organic lining of the test at sites distant from the aperture (Goldstein and Barker, 1988). Figure 3.9, for example, illustrates the addition of vesicles (probably containing glycosaminoglycans; see Langer, 1992) to the base of the inner organic lining of *Myxotheca* sp.

Astrammina rara is a large single-chambered, coarsely agglutinated foraminifer that occurs abundantly in shallow-water habitats of the Antarctic. This astrorhizid is perhaps unusual in that it frequently sheds its test, and after a brief shell-less existence, stops and builds a new one (Bowser et al., 1995). The interior of the test is characterized by a fibrous inner organic lining that is continuous with cables of bioadhesive (organic cement of other authors) that anchor sediment grains in place. Finer sediment grains fill the spaces between larger grains along the distal surface of the test and are also bound with bioadhesive (Bowser and Bernhard, 1993). As the foraminifer rebuilds its test, it initially gathers sediment of a variety of sizes, then appears to separate it by size by extending and retracting its pseudopodia. This concentrates the larger sediment grains to the interior of the forming test (Kinoshita et al., 1996).

Many pioneers of foraminiferal biology observed and described the process of chamber formation in calcareous Foraminifera at the level of the light microscope (see comments in: Bé et al., 1979; Hemleben et al., 1986; 1989). Angell (1967b), however, provided the first ultrastructural account of chamber formation in a calcareous perforate foraminifer, *Rosalina floridana* (Order Rotaliida). This benthic species begins the process by forming a translucent algal cyst that is cemented to the substrate and extends over the entire spiral surface of the test. Next, pseudopodia coalesce within the cyst to form a template or anlage in the shape of the new chamber. This anlage is highly vesicular, and contains mitochondria, fibrillar material, electron-dense vesicles, and vesicles that appear to be empty. The inner organic lining (IOL) of the new chamber forms by the activities of pseudopodia over the surface of the anlage. Once the IOL is complete, cytoplasm from within the test floods the interior of the forming chamber and forces the vesicular material of the anlage out through the new aperture, thus forming a sheath over the entire test surface. A layer of calcite is then deposited over both the new chamber and the entire test. The sheath breaks up as the foraminifer frees itself from its cyst and resumes feeding. This process produces a 'monolamellar' test (terminal chamber is one layer thick) which, overall, is multilayered (see chapter 4). Figure 3.10 illustrates a very similar sequence of events during chamber formation in the calcareous perforate foraminifer *Ammonia tepida* (Order Rotaliida). Older chambers of the test consist of layers of calcite separated by organic linings that are continuous with the organic materials that fill the pores (Fig. 3.11 and 3.12) (Angell, 1967a).

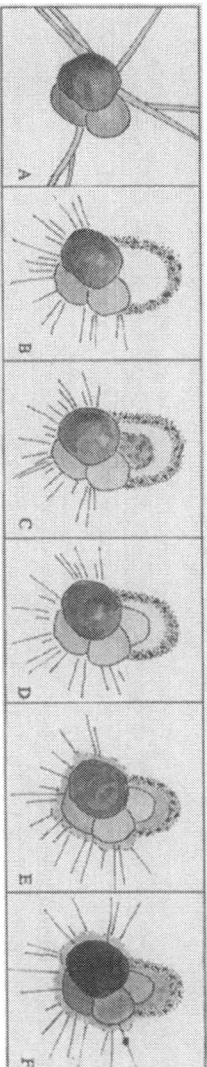

Figure 3.10 The sequence of chamber formation in the calcareous perforate species *Ammonia tepida*. A. Juvenile with three chambers. B. Construction of a cyst that includes foreign materials over the region where the fourth chamber will form (cyst does not cover the entire test). C. Anlage constructed of cytoplasm. D. Organic lining constructed on the outside of the anlage cytoplasm. E. Sheath of 'frothy' cytoplasm extruded to cover the entire test. F. Calcification occurring over the surface of the new chamber and the entire test. Illustration by Elizabeth Gardiner.

In subsequent tracer studies using Ca^{45} and C^{14}, Angell (1979) showed that *R. floridana* (calcareous perforate species) does not pool either calcium or carbonate ions in the cytoplasm, but rather extracts them from the surrounding seawater during calcification. This, however, is not universal among calcareous perforate Foraminifera. The symbiont-bearing, calcareous perforate foraminifer *Amphistegina lobifera* indeed pools fairly large reserves of carbonate in the cytoplasm for use during calcification. The symbiont-bearing, calcareous imperforate *Amphisorus hemprichii*, however, does not pool carbonate, but obtains it directly from seawater during calcification (ter Kuile and Erez, 1987; ter Kuile, 1991).

Chamber formation in planktonic Foraminifera, also calcareous and perforate, shows broad similarities to the process in *R. floridana*, as well as significant differences. In the non-spinose *Globorotalia truncatulinoides*, *G. hirsuta*, and *G. menardii*, a protective organic envelope is formed (Hemleben et al., 1977, 1986), comparable to the translucent cyst described by Angell (1967b). A cytoplasmic bulge ultimately fills the envelope and forms a 'primary organic lining' (POM) between the envelope and the cytoplasmic bulge. The POM and the envelope collectively comprise the anlage for the new chamber (a slightly different usage than that of Angell, 1967b), and calcification occurs as patches of calcite are deposited on both sides of the POM, thus forming a bilamellar shell (Hemleben et al., 1977; Bé et al., 1979; Hemleben et al.,

1989). Chamber formation is generally similar in spinose and non-spinose taxa with spines being added once the chamber is otherwise complete (Hemleben et al., 1986).

In the planktonic, non-spinose taxa, the newly formed chamber undergoes subsequent modification. Pores form secondarily by pseudopodia that pass through the wall and form rudimentary pores. Further, additional calcite is added to the surface of the chamber, thus thickening the test (Hemleben et al., 1977, 1986). This differs significantly from the formation of a monolamellar, multilayered shell in *Rosalina floridana*.

Among the Miliolida (calcareous imperforate Foraminifera), chamber formation at the ultrastructural level has been described in *Calcituba polymorpha* (Berthold, 1976a; Hemleben et al., 1986) and in *Spiroloculina hyalina* (Angell, 1980). *C. polymorpha* is an unusual miliolid in that its shell is cemented to a substrate and consists of somewhat randomly arranged, bifurcating calcareous tubes that are partially subdivided by constrictions. Occasionally, these individuals reproduce by what appears to be multiple fission, forming numerous young with miolioline coiling that grow by forming long branching tubes (Arnold, 1967). *C. polymorpha* adds a new tube or chamber by forming an 'outer organic lining,' then transporting vesicles of preformed calcite needles to the site of calcification where they are released to form the shell. An inner organic lining is the last element added

Growth and test morphogenesis

to the shell (Berthold, 1976a; Hemleben et al., 1986).

Chamber formation in *Spiroloculina hyalina*, reported by Angell (1980), begins with the construction of a cyst that surrounds the entire test and is composed of algal cells and detritus bound by a transparent membrane, similar to the process in *Rosalina floridana*. Fine pseudopodia anchor the foraminifer within the cyst and remain active throughout the process. Cytoplasm begins to flow from the test, and starting near the aperture, forms the shape of the new chamber which is being simultaneously secreted and calcified. Calcification occurs beneath a cytoplasmic sheath (probably comparable to the outer organic lining in *C. polymorpha*), beginning near the aperture of the last chamber and progressing from the base to the new aperture of the forming chamber. The interior of the chamber is formed and calcified by pseudopodia. The aperture and apertural tooth are the last to form. The resulting new chamber wall in miliolids consists of calcite needles randomly oriented in an organic matrix (Fig. 3.13), both of which are preformed within the cytoplasm and transported in vesicles to the developing wall where they are released. Older chambers are thicker than younger ones, but are 'nonlamellar.' Angell (1980) suggests that additional calcite is added to older portions of the test during chamber formation.

Chamber formation in the miliolid *Spiroloculina hyalina* differs from that in the rotaliid *Rosalina floridana* and globigerinids in two important regards. First, *S. hyalina* does not form an anlage of membranes or organic linings as does *R. floridana* and the planktonic Foraminifera, and calcification does not occur on the template of an organic lining. Rather, calcite needles and their associated organic matrix are preformed within the cytoplasm and transported to the forming chamber where they are released into the wall. Second, calcification occurs as cytoplasm is being extruded from the last complete chamber, proceeding from the base of the new chamber to the aperture and tooth. That is, extruded cytoplasm does not first form the shape of the new chamber and then the wall.

The agglutinated foraminifer *Textularia candeiana* utilizes both organic and calcitic cements in the construction of its test (Bender, 1992). Chamber formation begins with the foraminifer

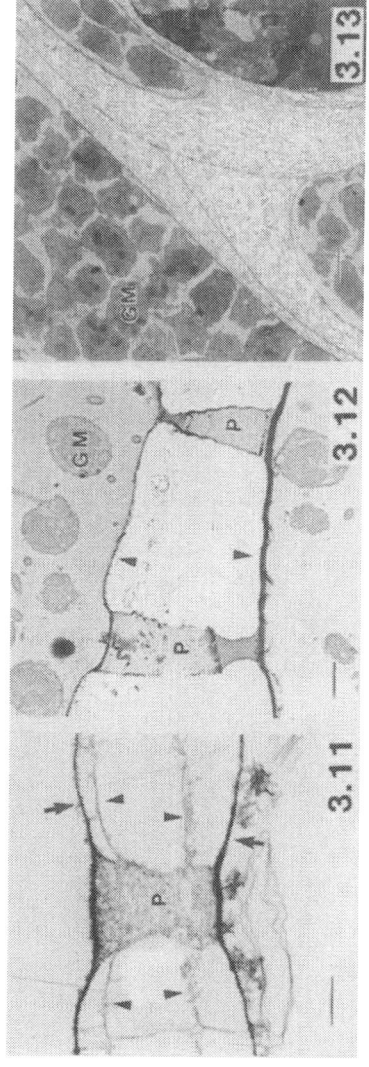

Figure 3.11 TEM micrograph of a decalcified test of the foraminifer *Chilostomella* sp. showing the continuity of the organic linings (large arrow), organic layers (small arrow), and pore material (p). Scale bar = 0.5 µm.

Figure 3.12 TEM micrograph of a an internal chamber from a decalcified test of *Ammonia tepida*, illustrating the organic linings and pore material. Organic layers between the organic linings, however, are absent, probably because the chamber was internal. The foraminifer was in the process of releasing gametes (GM). Scale bar = 1 µm.

Figure 3.13 TEM micrograph of the juncture of several internal chambers in the miliolid *Triloculina oblonga*. The test wall is composed of calcite needles (white linear structures) embedded in organic material (gray component of shell). The shell was decalcified during sample preparation using EDTA (see Goldstein, 1997). The foraminifer was in the process of releasing gametes (GM). Scale bar = 2 µm.

gathering sediment grains into a mound near the aperture. Once a cavity is formed within this mound of sediment, the foraminifer begins constructing a chamber by first coating grains with a thin organic envelope, and then cementing them together with a small amount of organic cement, beginning on the surface of the penultimate chamber and working outward toward the aperture. Calcite is then added primarily to the external surface of the chamber in the form of calcite bundles that fill in the open spaces in the test and further cement the agglutinated materials together. Pores, characteristic of the test of *T. candeiana*, appear during calcification, with their position depending on the orientation of the agglutinated grains and the position of the calcite bundles (Bender, 1992).

It should also be noted that many Foraminifera are capable of repairing their shells. Angell (1967c) showed that *Rosalina floridana*, decalcified with HCl, recalcified their shells, though the laminated wall structure was not restored. The planktonic foraminifer *Globigerinoides sacculifer* can reconstruct its shell after major injury, though extensive shell repair often results in very aberrant morphologies (Bé and Spero, 1981). The large nummulitid *Cycloclypeus carpenteri* can also repair a damaged shell (Song et al., 1994) within about four months (Krüger et al., 1996). Shell repair has also been reported in *Heterostegina depressa* (Rötger, 1978; Rötger and Hallock, 1982), the miliolid *Triloculina barnardi* (Collen, 1998), and a number of fusulinids (e.g. Kahler, 1942; Wilde, 1965). The ability to repair damaged shells appears to have evolved in the Paleozoic and is widespread among Foraminifera. It imparts obvious advantages to individuals subjected to attacks by predators or to mechanical damage.

3.5 REPRODUCTION AND THE FORAMINIFERAL LIFE CYCLE

3.5.1

The typical foraminiferal life cycle is characterized by a heterophasic alternation of sexual and asexual generations (Fig. 3.14). Though 'species pairs' (now recognized as dimorphic tests) had been identified as early as the mid-1800s (Lister, 1895), the fundamental outline of the life cycle was first presented by Lister (1895), with additional comments supplied by Schaudinn (1895). The foraminifer *Polystomella* (= *Elphidium*) *crispum*, a fairly large, regionally abundant, shallow-water dweller, was the subject of both studies.

The life cycle of *Elphidium crispum* includes a number of features that are shared by numerous other taxa, and it is perhaps fortuitous that Lister and Schaudinn selected this foraminifer as the subject of their observations. Had they studied any of a number of other species (e.g. *Allogromia laticollaris*, *Spirillina vivipara*, *Patellina corrugata*, or any of the 'microforaminifera' studied by Grell; see Grell, 1979), these early accounts of the life cycle might have taken a very different form.

Elphidium crispum is a dimorphic foraminifer (Lister, 1895, 1903; Schaudinn, 1895; Jepps, 1942). The adult gamont, which produces gametes, has a single nucleus and a megalospheric test characterized by a relatively large proloculus but a relatively small overall test diameter. The adult agamont, which produces numerous young by multiple fission, is multinucleate and has a microspheric test characterized by a tiny proloculus but a relatively large overall test diameter. The terms megalospheric and microspheric, therefore, refer to the size of the proloculus, not the size of the entire test.

E. crispum produces biflagellated gametes and is gametogamous (gametes liberated directly into the surrounding seawater; see below), which is the case for most species of Foraminifera (see Goldstein, 1997). Fertilization then takes place by the fusion of two gametes, generally from different parents. Flagellated foraminiferal gametes typically are quite small (~1–4 µm), and the resulting zygote is also small. In gametogamous species, the zygote may spend a brief phase as a naked (shell-less) amoeba during which it feeds and grows before it calcifies, forming the microspheric proloculus.

In higher animals, meiosis typically occurs as

Reproduction and the foraminiferal life cycle

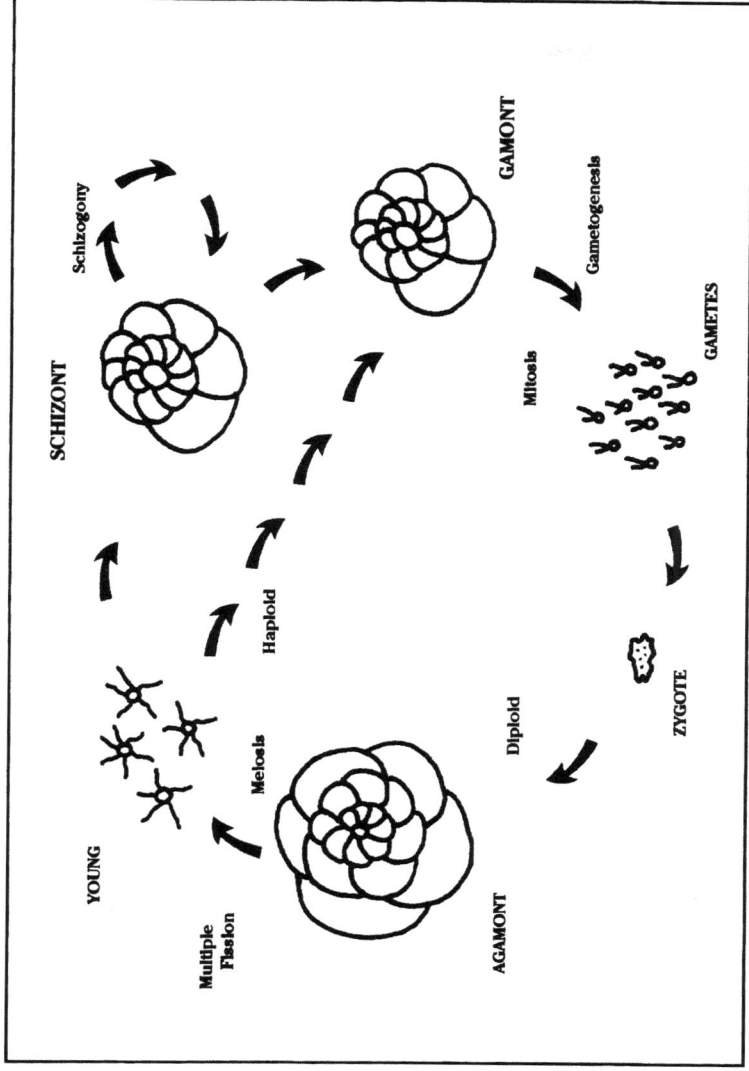

Figure 3.14 Outline of the foraminiferal life cycle which classically includes a regular alternation between a haploid, uninucleate, megalospheric gamont, and a diploid, multinucleate, microspheric agamont. Meiosis occurs in the agamont as part of multiple fission, and gametes are produced by mitosis. In some species, the life cycle also includes a schizont which is produced from the agamont and reproduces asexually. It can interject numerous successive asexual cycles. Meiosis typically occurs in the schizont in the agamont. However, the type of nuclear divisions in the schizont have not been documented for any species. See text for discussion.

an integral part of gametogenesis. Meiosis is a reduction division in that it halves the diploid number of chromosomes and produces haploid daughter cells. In the Foraminifera, however, meiosis occupies an intermediate position in the life cycle, occurring in the agamont as an integral part of multiple fission. The resulting young are haploid individuals that typically grow to become adult, uninucleate gamonts. Gametogenesis then occurs in haploid individuals and involves only mitotic nuclear divisions.

Perhaps limited by technology or the small size of nuclei in *E. crispum*, none of these pioneers in foraminiferal biology (J.J. Lister, F. Schaudinn, M.W. Jepps) were able to document the correct position of meiosis. This element of the life cycle was first documented by Le Calvez (1946, 1950) who reexamined the life cycles of *Patellina corrugata* and *Discorbis vilardeboanus* and recognized meiotic division figures that preceded multiple fission in the agamont. Grell (1954) and Arnold (1955) soon verified Le Calvez's findings by documenting the intermediate position of meiosis in *Rotaliella heterocaryotica* and *Allogromia laticollaris*, respectively.

3.5.2 Variations on the general theme

Today, reasonably complete life cycles are known for fewer than 30 of the >10,000 extant species of Foraminifera. In spite of this limitation, these relatively few well-documented life cycles illustrate a significant range of variation in the life cycle and in the corresponding morphological variation imparted to the test (Table 3.1). These variations relate to the

Foraminifera: A biological overview

Table 3.1 List of selected features of Foraminifera for which reasonably complete life cycles are known. Partial life cycles are known for a number of other taxa (see Lee et al., 1991a, Goldstein, 1997).

Species	Alteration of generations	Morphology	Gametes	Fertilization	Nuclear dimorphism	References
Allogromia laticollaris	facultative; budding, plasmotomy	variable	amoeboid	autogamous	no	Arnold, 1954; McEnery and Lee, 1976
Heterotheca lobata	obligatory	gamonts generally larger than agamonts	biflagellated	gametogamous	no	Grell, 1988
Myxotheca arenilega	? obligatory	agamont larger than gamont	biflagellated	gametogamous	no	Grell, 1958c
Iridia lucida	? obligatory	no morphological difference between gamont and agamont	biflagellated	gametogamous	unknown	LeCalvez, 1936a, 1938
Nemogullmia longevariabilis	unknown	no morphological difference between gamont and agamont	biflagellated	gametogamous	unknown	Nyholm, 1956
Saccammina alba	facultative; budding, plasmotomy	gamont larger than agamont	biflagellated	gametogamous	possibly	Goldstein, 1988a
Ovammina opaca	facultative; budding, plasmotomy	secondary pores form in circumapertural ring in test of gamont prior to release of gametes	biflagellated	gametogamous	unknown	Dahlgren, 1962, 1964; Goldstein, unpublished observations
Cribrothalammina alba	facultative; budding	secondary pores form in test of gamont prior to release of gametes	biflagellated	gametogamous	unknown	Goldstein and Barker, 1988, 1990; Goldstein, unpublished observations
Patellina corrugata	obligatory	reversed test dimorphism	amoeboid	gamontogamous	no	Myers, 1935; Grell, 1958c; Myers, 1936
Spirillina vivipara	obligatory	reversed test dimorphism	amoeboid	gamontogamous	no	Myers, 1936
Spiroloculina hyalina	apogamic	not applicable	not applicable	not applicable	only uninucleate individuals known	Arnold, 1964
Fissurina marginata	apogamic	not applicable	not applicable	not applicable	unknown	Le Calvez, 1947
Elphidium crispum	obligatory	classically dimorphic	biflagellated	gamontogamous	unknown	Lister, 1895; Schaudinn, 1895; Jepps, 1942; Bradshaw, 1957; Schnitker, 1974a; Goldstein and Moodley, 1993
Ammonia tepida	facultative	variable	biflagellated	gamontogamous	unknown	Le Calvez, 1936; Myers, 1943a
'Tretomphalus' bulloides (= *Rosalina globularis*)	obligatory	classically dimorphic, but a terminal float chamber occurs in mature gamonts	biflagellated	gametogamous	unknown	Myers, 1940
Discorbis patelliformis	obligatory	classically dimorphic	triflagellated	gamontogamous	unknown	Le Calvez, 1950
Discorbis mediterranensis	?obligatory	classically dimorphic	triflagellated	gamontogamous	unknown	Føyn, 1936; Le Calvez, 1950
Glabratella sulcata	obligatory	gamont larger than agamont	triflagellated	gamontogamous	yes; number variable	Grell, 1958b, 1979

Reproduction and the foraminiferal life cycle

Table 1 (Continued).

Species	Alteration of generations	Morphology	Gametes	Fertilization	Nuclear dimorphism	References
Rubratella intermedia	obligatory	not dimorphic	amoeboid	gamontogamous	yes; 1 somatic, 5 generative	Grell, 1958a, 1979
Metarotaliella simplex	obligatory	not dimorphic	amoeboid	gamontogamous	yes; 1 somatic, 3 generative	Grell, 1973, 1979
Metarotaliella parva	obligatory	not dimorphic	amoeboid	gamontogamous	yes; 1 somatic, 3 generative	Grell, 1973, 1979
Rotaliella roscoffensis	obligatory	not dimorphic	amoeboid	autogamous	yes; 1 somatic, 3 generative	Grell, 1957, 1979
Rotaliella heterocaryotica	obligatory	not dimorphic	amoeboid	autogamous	yes; 1 somatic, 3 generative	Grell, 1954, 1979
Rotaliella elatiana	?facultative	gamont generally smaller	amoeboid	mostly autogamous	yes; number variable from 1-4	Pawlowski and Lee, 1992
Heterostegina depressa	biologically trimorphic	?trimorphic	biflagellated	gametogamous	no	Röttger et al., 1990
Amphistegina gibbosa	biologically tripmorphic	trimorphic	biflagellated	gametogamous	unknown	Harney et al., 1998; Dettmering et al., 1998
Planktonic taxa	?gamic	unknown	biflagellated	gametogamous	unknown	see review in Hemleben et al., 1989

sequence of 'alternating' generations, trimorphism, apogamic and possibly gamic life cycles, binary fission and various forms of budding, type of gametes, mode of fertilization, occurrence of nuclear dimorphism, and test dimorphism. Overall, the life cycle is more varied in the Foraminifera than in virtually any other group of protists.

The *alternation of generations* in the Foraminifera may be *obligatory* in some species, and *facultative* in others. In the obligatory alternation of generations, reproduction in the agamont always includes meiosis as a precedent to multiple fission. The resulting young are always haploid and uninucleate, and they grow to form mature gamonts. With the possible exception of *Iridia lucida* in which both gamonts and agamonts are uninucleate (Le Calvez, 1936a, 1938), the uninucleate forms are gamonts that produce gametes which ultimately form zygotes and mature into agamonts. This type of life cycle does not deviate from this regular alternation of generations. Examples include *Elphidium crispum* (Lister, 1895, 1903; Jepps, 1942), *Glabratella sulcata* (Grell, 1958b), *Rotaliella heterocaryotica* (Grell, 1954), and *Patellina corrugata* (Myers, 1935; Grell, 1958c).

Alternatively, the life cycle may be characterized by a facultative alternation of generations. In some species, the life cycle includes successive asexual cycles that include reproduction by multiple fission (e.g. *Ammonia tepida* – Bradshaw, 1957; Schnitker, 1974a; Goldstein and Moodley, 1993). In this case, the agamont (B) begins as a zygote, and is diploid. The agamont may undergo meiosis and multiple fission to produce haploid young that mature into uninucleate gamonts (A_2). Alternatively, the agamont (B) may produce, by multiple fission, a second asexual generation, the schizont (A_1), which in turn may produce a number of successive asexual divisions. The type of nuclear divisions that occurs in schizonts, however, has not been documented.

This facultative alternation of generations is referred to as biological trimorphism, and has been documented in the living nummulitid *Heterostegina depressa* by Röttger et al. (1990) and in the amphisteginid *Amphistegina gibbosa* by Harney et al. (1998) and Dettmering et al. (1998). This type of life cycle includes one microspheric generation (B) and two megalospheric generations, the gamont (A_2) and the schizont (A_1). A number of foraminiferologists have reported biological trimorphism, particularly in regard to the larger, algal symbiont-bearing Foraminifera (see Röttger et al., 1986, 1990; Harney et al., 1998; Dettmering et al., 1998).

Does biological trimorphism extend to trimorphism of the test? The validity of this hypothesis requires two observations: (a) the presence of three morphologically distinct types of tests based on the diameter of the proloculus, and (b) the correlation of each of these distinct morphologies to a specific phase of the life cycle (gamont, agamont, schizont) (Röttger et al., 1986, 1990). Most studies on test trimorphism, however, have relied almost exclusively on morphological observations.

Rather than adding alternative cycles to the life cycle as in biological trimorphism, some taxa are apogamic and appear to have reduced the complexity of the life cycle by omitting one of the generations. At least two species, *Fissurina marginata* and *Spiroloculina hyalina*, have apparently lost the sexual phase of the life cycle (the gamont and gametogenesis) (Le Calvez, 1947; Arnold, 1964). Only successive asexual generations were observed in these species, and in *S. hyalina*, asexual reproduction occurs in uninucleate individuals (Arnold, 1964).

Only sexual reproduction has been observed in planktonic Foraminifera, in spite of numerous investigations. As a result, Hemleben et al. (1989) proposed a possible 'gamic' life cycle for planktonic Foraminifera in which the agamont form as gametes from separate parents fuse. It is possible then that zygotes mature to adult gamonts and that meiosis occurs in the zygote, and multiple fission have been lost. Gamonts, which are uninucleate, undergo gametogenesis, producing thousands of free-swimming, biflagellated gametes that are released directly into the surrounding seawater. Zygotes presumably form as gametes from separate parents fuse. It is possible then that zygotes mature to adult gamonts and that meiosis occurs in the zygote, immature gamont, or adult gamont, though this has yet to be demonstrated.

The life cycle of some allogromiids and astrorhizids appears to be more plastic or variable than in other Foraminifera. In addition to multiple fission, several other forms of asexual reproduction have been observed, including binary fission in *Allogromia laticollaris* (McEnery and Lee, 1976); budding in *Saccammina sphaerica* (Rhumbler, 1894), *S. alba* (Goldstein, 1988a), *Allogromia laticollaris* (Arnold, 1954, 1955), *Halyphysema tumanowiczii* (Hedley, 1958), *Technitella legumen* (Haman, 1971), *Astrammina rara* (DeLaca, 1986a), *Ovammina opaca* (Goldstein, unpublished observations), and *Psammophaga simplora* (Goldstein, unpublished observations); serial budding in *Nemogullmia longevariabilis* (Nyholm, 1956) and *Cylindrogullmia alba* (Nyholm, 1974); and plasmotomy or multiple budding in *Allogromia laticollaris* (Arnold, 1955) and *Saccammina alba* (Goldstein, 1988a). In addition, fragmentation occurs in the miliolid *Calcituba polymorpha* (Arnold, 1967), and *Spiroloculina hyalina* and *Floresina amphiphaga* are capable of producing multiple broods (Arnold, 1964; Hallock and Talge, 1994).

Gametes in the Foraminifera may be biflagellated, triflagellated, or amoeboid. Of these, biflagellated gametes (Fig. 3.15) are by far the most common, and occur in many extant groups, including planktonic taxa and the most diverse benthic suborders. The sequence of events by which biflagellated gametes are produced is remarkably similar, even in distantly related taxa, suggesting that this mode of gametogenesis is probably primitive within the Foraminifera (Goldstein, 1997). The other types of gametes and the processes that produce them, therefore, are most likely derived from the more primitive biflagellated type (Grell, 1967; Goldstein, 1997).

Triflagellated and amoeboid gametes have evolved on more than one occasion and independently in different groups of Foraminifera. Triflagellated gametes are best known in a few plastogamic (forms in which the gamonts fuse before gamete release, see below) discorbids and glabratellids (e.g. *Discorbis patelliformis*, *D. mediterranensis*, *Glabratella sulcata* – Myers, 1940; Le Calvez, 1950; Grell, 1958b). However, they also occur in at least one (*Nummulites venosus* – Röttger et al., 1998), but not all of the few extant nummulitids. It is noteworthy that *N. venosus* is gametogamous (see below) and not plastogamic. Amoeboid gametes occur in the

Reproduction and the foraminiferal life cycle

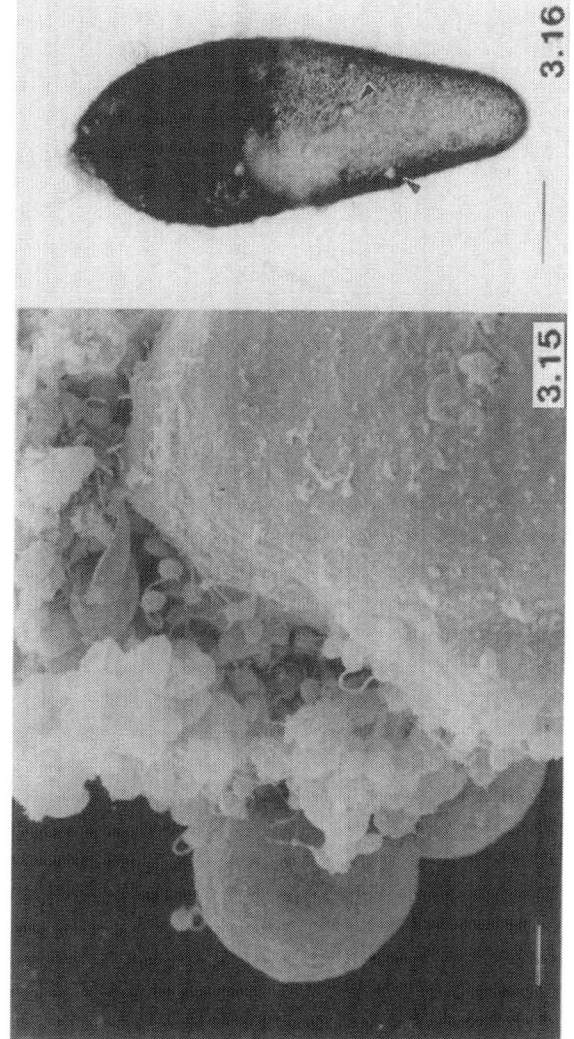

Figure 3.15 SEM micrograph of gamete release in the miliolid *Triloculina oblonga*. Gametes in this and most (but not all) gametogamous Foraminifera are biflagellated. Scale bar = 5 μm.

Figure 3.16 Light micrograph of gamete release in *Cribrothalammina alba*. Note the secondary pores scattered over the surface of the test. Pores form just prior to gamete release in the species and provide an example of 'heterothalamy.' Scale bar approximately 100 μm.

allogromiid *Allogromia laticollaris* (Arnold, 1955), but are also known in several of the small rotaliellids (e.g. *Rotaliella heterocaryotica*, *R. roscoffensis*, *Metarotaliella simplex*, *M. parva*, *Rubratella intermedia* – Grell, 1973, 1979) and in the spirillinids *Patellina corrugata* (Myers, 1935) and *Spirillina vivipara* (Myers, 1936). Amoeboid gametes may also occur in the saccamminid *Psammophaga simplora*. However, although Arnold (1984) reported the formation of amoeboid structures during gametogenesis, he also reported that they may become flagellated before their release from the shell. Triflagellated and amoeboid gametes generally are larger than biflagellated ones and are produced in fewer numbers.

Fertilization in the Foraminifera may be gametogamous, gamontogamous, or autogamous (Grell, 1973). Gametogamy is the most common mode found in the Foraminifera and involves the release of numerous gametes directly into the surrounding seawater where fertilization occurs. Gametogamy is generally associated with the production of numerous (often thousands), small (∼1–4 μm), biflagellated gametes. However, although rare, gametogamy may also occur in Foraminifera with triflagellated gametes, as in the nummulitid *Nummulites venosus* (Röttger et al., 1998).

Alternatively, rather than simply broadcasting gametes, gamonts can associate in pairs or groups (e.g. *Spirillina vivipara*, *Patellina corrugata*, *Metarotaliella parva*, *M. simplex*) prior to the release of gametes. This mode of fertilization is referred to as gamontogamy, and most gamontogamous Foraminifera produce either triflagellated or amoeboid gametes. Plastogamy is a specific type of gamontogamy in which two gamonts attach to each other along the umbilical margins of the tests. Gametes are then released within the shared space of the joined tests (internal septa are generally removed during gametogenesis). Examples of plastogamic Foraminifera include: *Discorbis patelliformis*, *D.*

pulvinata, *D. ornatissima* (Myers, 1940), *D. mediterranensis* (Le Calvez, 1950), and *Glabratella sulcata* (Grell, 1958b).

The gamonts of some gamontogamous species are differentiated into 'sexes' or mating types. No morphological features distinguish conspecific gametes or gamonts. However, gamonts of *Discorbis mediterranensis* from one mating type will pair only with those from another (Le Calvez, 1950). In species that associate in groups (e.g. *Patellina corrugata*), both mating types must be present for reproduction to occur (Grell, 1958c). It is not known whether or not mating types occur in gametogamous species as well.

Autogamy (self fertilization) is known in some taxa. Amoeboid gametes are produced, but are not released from the parental test. Rather, fertilization occurs within the parental test from which the resulting young then escape. Autogamy occurs in *Allogromia laticollaris* (Arnold, 1955), *Rotaliella heterocaryotica* (Grell, 1954), and *R. roscoffensis* (Grell, 1957). In culture, this mode of fertilization can be very difficult to distinguish from multiple fission (asexual reproduction), although the size of offspring may provide a clue for some species. Arnold (1955) reported that sexually produced young are generally smaller than those produced by multiple fission in *Allogromia laticollaris*.

Nuclear dimorphism is perhaps best known in ciliated protozoans, but also occurs in some small calcareous perforate Foraminifera, particularly *Glabratella sulcata* and members of the Family Rotaliellidae (see Grell, 1973, 1979). In Foraminifera with nuclear dimorphism, different types of nuclei occur simultaneously in the agamont. Generally, there is one somatic nucleus and one to five generative nuclei. The generative nuclei remain in the proloculus until the agamont reproduces, at which time all undergo meiosis. The somatic nucleus resides in an intermediate chamber, is generally larger, and contains more DNA than the generative nuclei; it is involved in the cell's metabolic functions. The onset of meiosis in the generative nuclei (Grell, 1973). Zech (1964) showed that nuclear dimorphism does not occur in the foraminifer *Patellina corrugata*. Whether this phenomenon occurs elsewhere in the Foraminifera, however, remains to be demonstrated.

The classical form of test dimorphism in which the gamont (and schizont if it occurs) is relatively small and megalospheric, and the agamont is relatively large and microspheric, has been identified in numerous modern and fossil taxa. However, not all Foraminifera that show an alternation of generations also display classical test dimorphism. *Patellina corrugata* and *Spirillina vivipara*, for example, have reversed test dimorphism (Myers, 1935, 1936). The agamonts are smaller and 'megalospheric,' whereas the gamonts are larger and 'microspheric.' This foraminifer produces fairly large amoeboid gametes, and the resulting zygotes are generally larger than the young produced by multiple fission.

Test dimorphism in *Glabratella sulcata* also deviates from the norm. In this species, the gamont typically is larger than the agamont, and no significant differences in size identify the proloculus as either megalo- or microspheric. In many of the tiny Foraminifera studied by Grell (see Grell, 1973, 1979), the gamonts and agamonts are morphologically indistinguishable.

Some Foraminifera are characterized by a wide range of morphological variability which may extend to the size of the proloculus. Gamonts of *Ammonia tepida*, for example, have a wide range of prolocular diameters (Goldstein and Moodley, 1993), making it difficult to distinguish gamonts from agamonts by the morphology of empty shells.

What causes test dimorphism? Early workers on the foraminiferal life cycle explained test dimorphism as the result of the small size of the proloculus formed by amoeba-form zygotes that had resulted from the fusion of two very small biflagellated gametes, and observations on *Elphidium crispum* seemed to support this view (Myers, 1935). Myers (1935), however, proposed that the controlling factor more likely was the size of the nucleus, and not the size of the zygote. This, he believed, better explained why in some species, the shape and form of the proloculus were similar in tests of both generations (though not in *Patellina corrugata*, the subject of his 1935 paper). Similarly, Le Calvez (1938) proposed that the number of nuclei in the young agamont determined the size of the proloculus. This may also provide a reasonable explanation for the size of proloculi in the small heterocaryotic foraminifer *Rotaliella elatiana* (Lee et al., 1991a).

Test dimorphism was defined with regard to multilocular taxa, and application of this term should therefore be restricted to these forms. However, morphological differences may also occur in unilocular taxa for which Grell (1988) coined the term heterothalamy. In some cases the distinction occurs only with regard to size. Gamonts of *Heterotheca lobata* (Grell, 1988) and *Saccammina alba* (Goldstein, 1988a) are significantly larger than the corresponding agamonts. In *S. sphaerica* (Føyn, 1954) and *Myxotheca arenilega* (Grell, 1958c), however, the agamonts are larger. Because all four of these species liberate numerous, small, biflagellated, free-swimming gametes, the size of gametes does not explain this form of heterothalamy.

Ovammina opaca and *Cribrothalammina alba* exhibit another variation. The gamonts of both species form secondary pores during gametogenesis that serve as the sole avenue for the release of numerous biflagellated gametes (Fig. 3.16). In *O. opaca*, pores form in a ring just behind the aperture (Dahlgren, 1962, 1964), whereas in the larger *C. alba*, pores are distributed over the entire test, with the exception of the abapertural tip (Goldstein and Barker, 1988, 1990).

3.6 ACKNOWLEDGMENTS

I thank Pamela Hallock, Rudolf Röttger, and Samuel Bowser for their formal and informal comments on this paper. Samuel Bowser provided the TEM micrograph of a pseudopodium from *Spiroloculina hyalina* (Fig. 3.3), and Tomas Cedhagen provided the micrographs of *Pelosina arborescens* (Figs. 3.5 and 3.6). Beth Richardson collaborated on the TEM micrograph, prepared by high pressure freezing and freeze substitution, of *Myxotheca* sp. (Fig. 3.9). I also thank Elizabeth Gardiner and Daniel Hunter, graduate students at the University of Georgia, for providing the results of their 1998 micropaleontology class project on shell morphogenesis in *Ammonia tepida* (Fig. 3.10).

4

Shell construction in modern calcareous Foraminifera

Hans Jørgen Hansen

4.1 INTRODUCTION

The majority of foraminiferal species build their shells (or 'tests') with $CaCO_3$. Such calcareous species constitute 11 out the 15 extant orders of the class Foraminifera (see chapter 2). The present chapter is focused on the modes in which various types of walls are built by modern calcareous taxa.

4.2 WALL OF SECRETED CALCITE SPICULES (CARTERINIDA)

The order Carterinida is represented by a single genus, *Carterina*, which constructs its shell with concentrically laminated, ovoid spicules (Figs. 2.9, 4.1) that are held in place by organic material (Hansen and Grønlund, 1977). To test the possibility that the shell may be agglutinated, Deutsch and Lipps (1976) searched for loose spicules in the sediments of Eniwetok atoll, from where they had collected specimens of *C. spiculotesta*, but did not find any. In addition, adult specimens were found attached to hard substrate where sedi-

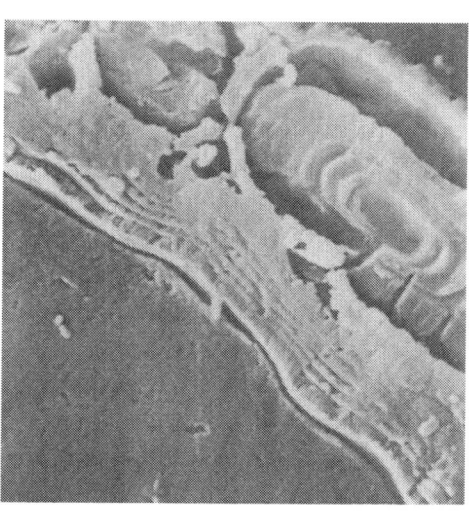

Figure 4.1 Concentric lamellae in sectioned and etched spicules of *Carterina*. Note the laminated inner organic lining. Reprinted from Hansen and Grønlund (1977), with the permission of the publisher.

mentary particles do not accumulate. Such evidence led to the suggestion that the spicules in the test of *Carterina* were secreted. The spicules are made of calcite (with c-axis parallel to elongation) which contains blebs of organic matter. They come in two size groups, with the smaller spicules packed tightly between the larger ones (Fig. 2.9), and reported as a 'ground mass' by earlier observers (e.g. Brady, 1884; Loeblich and Tappan, 1964a). The rounded shapes of the spicules and the lack of connections between adjacent spicules show that they are not formed *in situ* in the shell (Hansen and Grønlund, 1977).

4.3 PORCELANEOUS, IMPERFORATE WALLS (MILIOLIDA)

The non-lamellar porcelaneous wall is constructed of rods/laths of high magnesium calcite (Blackmon and Todd, 1959). The calcite units of the wall are arranged in a disorderly manner in the embedding organic material. On the basis of ultrastructural studies, Berthold (1976a) reported that in *Calcituba polymorpha*, calcite rods are present in cytoplasmatic vesicles formed during chamber construction. Similar observations were made by Angell (1980) in a study of chamber formation in *Spiroloculina hyalina*. Some porcelaneous forms possess a smoothly finished outermost layer of well crystallized calcite, with rhombohedral crystal faces arranged parallel to the surface ('tile roof pattern'). It is difficult to imagine how these crystallites could have formed away from their position, since many show an interlocking pattern (see also Debenay *et al.*, 1996). Haake (1971) recorded a 'cobble pattern' on the surface of porcelaneous forms in which calcite crystals are more or less perpendicular to the shell surface in the outermost layer. It may be concluded that the porcelaneous wall in this case is mainly constructed of calcitic units that are secreted by the foraminifer away from their final locations in the shell; the smoothly finished surface layer, however, is most likely formed *in situ*.

4.4 MONOCRYSTALLINE WALLS (SPIRILLINIDA)

The optically monocrystalline wall of *Patellina* has an a-axis-preferred orientation (Towe *et al.*, 1977). As observed by Berthold (1976c), new chamber material is added by lateral apposition. Growth is initiated in the apertural region of the preceding chamber where nearby structures, such as radial septa grow faster than distant structures. Berthold (1976b) also found that during growth of the septa in the spiral (dorsal) wall, small spaces are formed, and they are not closed in the course of shell development, thus becoming rounded pores. The reason for the suppression of calcification in the pore regions may be linked to the filling of pores by granular organic material. The pores and both sides of the shell wall are covered by a delicate organic layer. At the inner entrance to a pore, this covering organic layer is finely perforated by openings of about 0.01 μm diameter. In contrast, the exterior pore opening apparently remains uncovered.

4.5 LAMELLAR WALLS

4.5.1

The lamellar shells are constructed of either calcite or aragonite. As a new chamber is added, one new layer of shell material is secreted, covering the exposed earlier part of the shell (which does not happen in non-lamellar walls). This leads to an increase in wall thickness from later to earlier chambers (Fig. 4.2). In non-lamellar Foraminifera the addition of a new chamber does not lead to the deposition of a layer of shell material onto the earlier exposed part of the shell.

4.5.2 Optical orientation of the wall material

Following the pioneering work of Wood (1949) on the optical orientation of the carbonate material of foraminiferal shells, Loeblich and Tappan (1964a) introduced the radial-granular distinction in foraminiferal classification (see chapter 2 and Figs. 2.5, 2.6). This was a very attractive feature of this classification, because major taxonomic groups could be distinguished by a simple optical character. The crystallographic orienta-

Lamellar walls

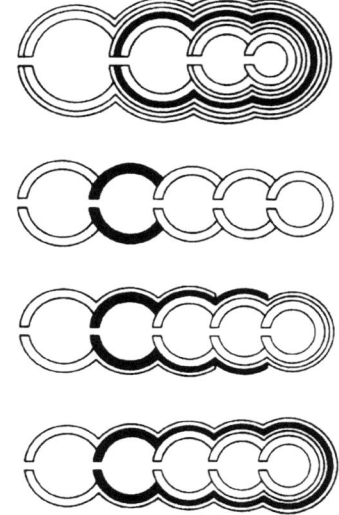

Figure 4.2 Monolamellar constructional designs: **a**, basic plan in which the one-layered wall material of the ultimate chamber continues uninterrupted to cover (as a secondary lamella) the exposed surfaces of earlier chambers; **b**, secondary lamella covering only two earlier chambers (*Dentalina pauperata* d'Orbigny); **c**, no addition of secondary lamella to earlier chambers (*Nodosaria subsoluta* Cushman); **d**, one to six secondary lamellae enveloping earlier chambers. From Grønlund and Hansen (1976), reproduced with permission.

tion of optically radial and granular walls has been studied by several authors (e.g. Towe and Cifelli, 1967; Hansen, 1968), and the terms 'radiate' and 'granulate' have also been used for the two optical properties. Their determination, however, is not necessarily easy under a polarizing microscope. For example, the presence of very narrow pores may give the impression of a radial optical structure in thin sections.

Both radial and granular optical properties have been observed within the same genus. Hansen (1972a) demonstrated a granular wall structure in an Eocene species of *Turrilina*, and a radial structure in an Oligocene species. Within the 26 species of elphidiids studied by Hansen and Lykke-Andersen (1976), 19 were radial and 7 were granular, thereby corroborating an earlier report of a granular elphidiid (Buzas, 1966). Thus, the optical orientation of shell material is not an infallible character for taxonomic distinctions above the species level. Ultrastructures of both radial and granular walls show considerable variability; several structural types have been identified (Bellemo, 1974a, b; 1976).

4.5.3 Monolamellar, hyaline, perforate walls (Lagenida)

In this group of hyaline Foraminifera, the latest added chamber is constructed of a single layer of shell material (Grønlund and Hansen, 1976). When this new chamber is added, the layer that forms that chamber also covers the exposed exterior walls of earlier chambers. Thus, the ultimate chamber wall consists of one layer, the penultimate chamber of two layers, and so on (Fig. 4.2). Partial deviations from this mode of wall construction exist within the group. Secondary lamellae may cover only the two previous chambers or only part of the penultimate chamber, or as in *Lingulina*, the final chamber may be composed of one to six lamellae, all of which extend over the exposed earlier part of the shell (Fig. 4.2). Where one curved chamber meets another, the columnar morphology of calcite in the wall leads to a somewhat irregular structural arrangement. The pores in monolamellar walls (and those in aragonitic bilamellar walls) are all of small diameter. Present data show that monolamellar walls in modern species are constructed with only optically radial calcite.

4.5.4 Bilamellar, hyaline, perforate walls (Buliminida, Rotalida, Globigerinida)

In the bilamellar group, the wall of the final chamber consists of two carbonate layers separated by an organic 'median layer.' Traditionally, the outside calcareous layer is termed the 'outer lamella,' while the inside calcareous layer is termed the 'inner lining' (Fig. 4.3); the latter is not to be confused with the inner organic lining of the calcareous wall. In some taxa, the

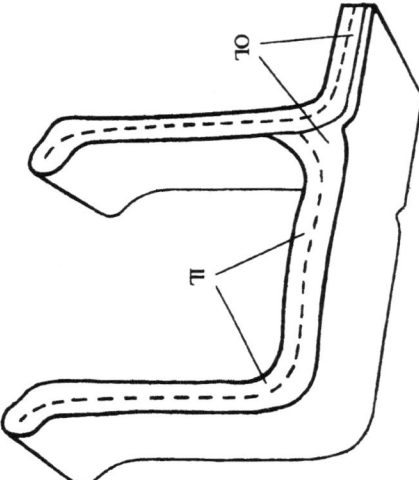

Figure 4.3 Bilamellar wall construction. IL, inner calcareous lining; OL, outer calcareous lamella; dashed line: median layer.

scanning electron microscope (SEM) studies of embedded, sectioned, polished, and etched specimens may be necessary.

The basic bilamellar mode of wall construction was first explained by Reiss (1957) as a modification of the mode suggested by Smout (1954). The inner lining stops at the junction with the previous chamber, while the outer lamella continues over the exposed parts of the earlier chambers to form a secondary lamella. The septum of the previous chamber becomes isolated from the surface, and does not receive the secondary lamination, thus becoming the shell interior (Fig. 4.3). The result is a shell where all septa (including the ultimate one) have two calcareous layers. In a variant of this constructional design, the inner lining does not stop at the junction with the previous apertural face but continues as a calcareous layer deposited onto the penultimate septum (former apertural face), leading to a three-layered septum (Fig. 4.4). In this model, the ultimate septum is two-layered while the penultimate and earlier septa are three-layered. The calcareous layer covering the penultimate septum is termed a 'septal flap.' Septal flaps have not been found in monolamellar forms and appear to be confined to the bilamellar group.

median layer is thin and well defined; in others, it may not be sharply delineated between the two carbonate lamellae. In *Cibicides* and *Stomatorbina*, the median layer contains particles (fine sedimentary grains, e.g. quartz) that are not secreted by the foraminifer. In *Stomatorbina*, these particles are absent in porous regions of the shell, but are clearly seen through the shell in non-porous areas. In *Cibicides*, they appear to be distributed randomly in the median layer. It is unclear if these particles in the median layer should be regarded as being truly agglutinated or as contaminations, but their distribution in *Stomatorbina* points to some degree of organization. The median layer apparently plays a significant role in the chamber forming process and calcification. In thin section under the light microscope, it may be seen as a dark line or a dark diffuse band that is usually most conspicuous in the septal part closest to the aperture and foramina. Sometimes the median layer and the boundaries between secondary lamellae are difficult to observe, but a parallel alignment of the two polarizers in the microscope improves the visibility of the lamellar boundaries, their planar orientation being at right angles to the plane of polarization. The thickness of each lamella may be only a few microns, or even less than a micron. In such cases, observations with a light microscope may not be adequate, and

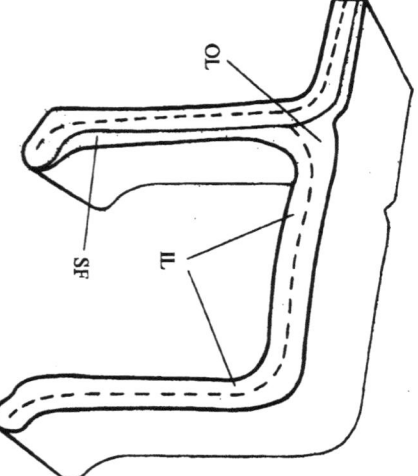

Figure 4.4 Bilamellar construction with septal flap. IL, inner calcareous lining; OL, outer calcareous lamella; SF, septal flap; dashed line, median layer.

Lamellar walls

4.5.5 Interlocular spaces and subsutural canals

The presence of a septal flap is often, but not always, connected with interlocular spaces, i.e. spaces between adjacent chambers. *Melonis pompilioides* has a septal flap, but no interlocular space (Fig. 4.5). It does, however, possess an umbilical spiral canal system (Fig. 4.6). *Nonion labradoricum* has septal flaps, but no interlocular spaces or umbilical canal system (Hansen and Lykke-Andersen, 1976). When an interlocular space is present, the attachment of one chamber to another is very fragile, and the weak shell architecture leads to breakage of the last chamber(s). In *Pseudorotalia*, interlocular spaces are present, but secondary lamellae build protrusions in both anterior and posterior directions from the sutures; after the addition of two or three chambers, pillars bridge the interlocular spaces, and thereby prevent breakage (Fig 4.7). The interlocular walls receive secondary lamina- tion, showing that these walls are functional shell surfaces.

An alternative constructional design is seen in the presence of posterior extensions (retral processes) of the chamber lumen and surrounding walls (ponticuli); these are attached to the exterior-most part of the preceding apertural face when a new chamber is added (e.g. in *Elphidium*, Fig. 4.8). This leads to the formation of a well-anchored final chamber with little chance of mechanical damage, in spite of the presence of a deep interlocular space. Thus, both *Pseudorotalia* and *Elphidium* have deep interlocular spaces crossed by small bridges, but of different origin.

In *Asterigerina*, the addition of a new chamber produces a chamber lumen that is primarily divided into two sub-chambers. The peripheral part is termed the 'main chamber,' while the part with a rhombohedral outline found closest

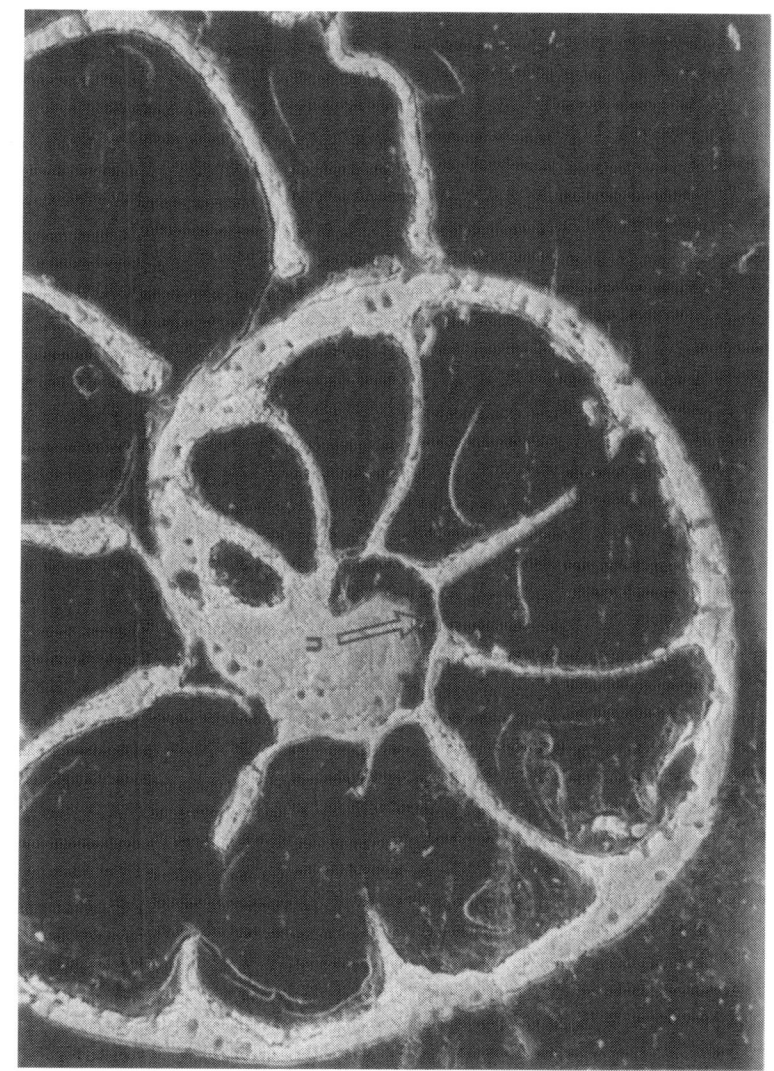

Figure 4.5 *Melonis pompilioides*. Section showing umbilical cover plates (u); scale bar = 0.1 mm.

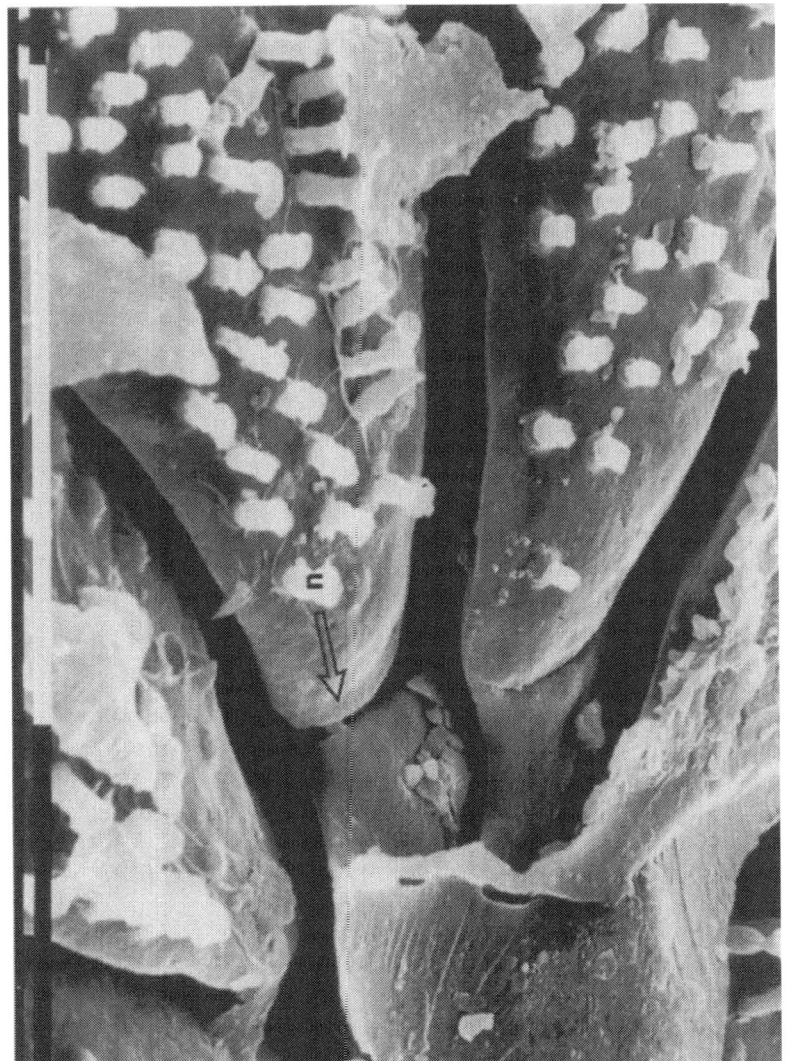

Figure 4.6 *Melonis pompilioides.* Internal mold showing position of umbilical cover plate (u); scale bar = 0.1 mm.

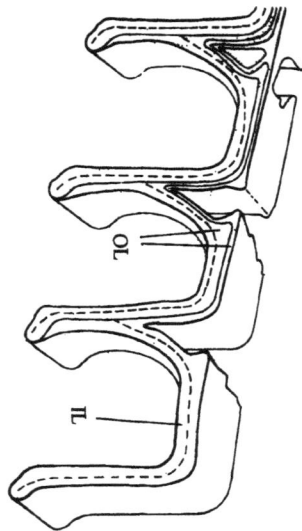

Figure 4.7 *Pseudorotalia.* Constructional design of secondary bridges spanning the interlocular spaces; IL, inner calcareous lining; OL, outer calcareous lamella; dashed line, median layer.

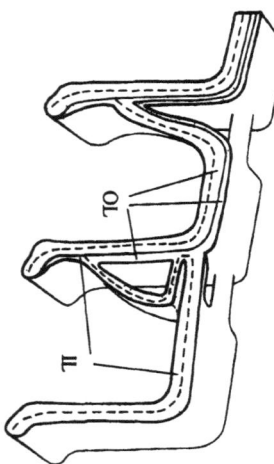

Figure 4.8 *Elphidium.* Bridging of interlocular spaces by ponticuli with retral processes; IL, inner calcareous lining; OL, outer calcareous lamella; dashed line, median layer.

to the umbilicus is the 'chamberlet.' These two units are separated from each other by a two-layered partition which bridges the previous aperture with an arch. Their development represents an 'instar,' i.e. a single episode in the formation of the shell (see next section). When the two-layered partition is followed to the outer chamber wall, it is seen to be constructed by a doubled inner lining (Fig 4.9). In this case, the construction of the inner lining does not involve a simultaneous construc-

Lamellar walls

formation of a chamber and the associated deposition of a secondary lamella as one instar. This concept is useful in explaining the development of several shell structures. A chamber-forming instar in *Ammonia* also involves the deposition of structural elements in the penultimate chamber (Hansen and Reiss, 1971). The umbilical part of the final chamber in *Ammonia* is open to the umbilicus. However, the main umbilical opening in the penultimate chamber is closed by the deposition of a cover plate that is continuous with a folded, almost vertical, foraminal plate protruding in the proximal direction. In section, the folded plate is seen as a two-layered hook extending from the umbilical cover plate of the preceding chamber. These umbilical cover plates and the exposed parts of the hooks are secondarily laminated. The folded plate represents the site of attachment of the succeeding cover plate. These structures show up in a shell section as a continuous series of hooks and plates (Figs. 4.12, 4.13). This constructional pattern is characteristic of many trochospirally and planispirally coiled forms. Even in apparently simple forms such as *Astrononion* in which hooks (foraminal plates) are absent, the deposition of a cover plate in the penultimate chamber is easy to recognize in shell molds (Fig. 4.14).

The deposition of umbilical cover plates in the earlier chambers leads to the formation of the so-called umbilical spiral canal systems (shown by Carpenter *et al.*, 1862, in a natural mold of *Elphidium craticulatum*). The origin of this conspicuous canal system is in parts of the shell that are closest to the umbilicus. In *Elphidium*, the single umbilical chamber tip embraces the previous chamber tip and covers its proximal umbilical part, allowing the presence of a passage (aperture) into the final chamber. Along with this, a plate is deposited in such a way that it seals off the communication between the main part of the preceding chamber lumen and the part closest to the umbilicus (Figs. 4.15, 4.16). The plate, deposited through one of the multiple interiomarginal apertures (the one closest to the umbilicus) of the preceding chamber, is a two-layered structure consisting of an outer lamella

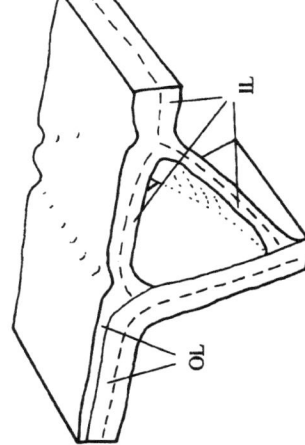

Figure 4.9 Constructional detail showing doubled inner lining separating chamber and chamberlet in *Asterigerina*; IL, inner calcareous lining; OL, outer calcareous lamella; dashed line, median layer.

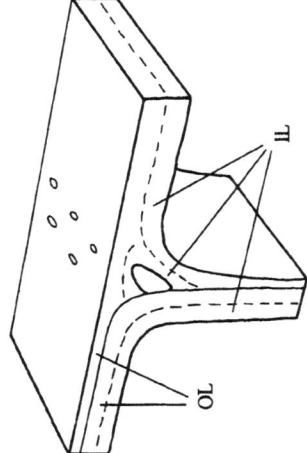

Figure 4.10 Constructional organization of subsutural canals in *Elphidiella*. The canals are delimited by double inner lining towards the chamber lumen, but by inner and outer lamella towards the shell surface; IL, inner calcareous lining; OL, outer calcareous lamella; dashed line, median layer.

tion of an outer lamella (Hansen and Reiss, 1972). Exactly the same plan of lamellar construction is found in *Elphidiella*, where the space between the ultimate and the penultimate chamber is delimited by the double inner lining of the ultimate chamber against the penultimate septum. (Fig. 4.11) Several openings in the roof (Fig. 4.11) connect the chamber interior with shell surface, thereby becoming true multiple apertures of the ultimate chamber (Hansen and Lykke-Andersen, 1976). Such openings in the sutures are sometimes misleadingly called 'sutural pores.'

4.5.6 Umbilical cover plates and foraminal plates

The concept of instars in shell formation was introduced by Smout (1954) who regarded the

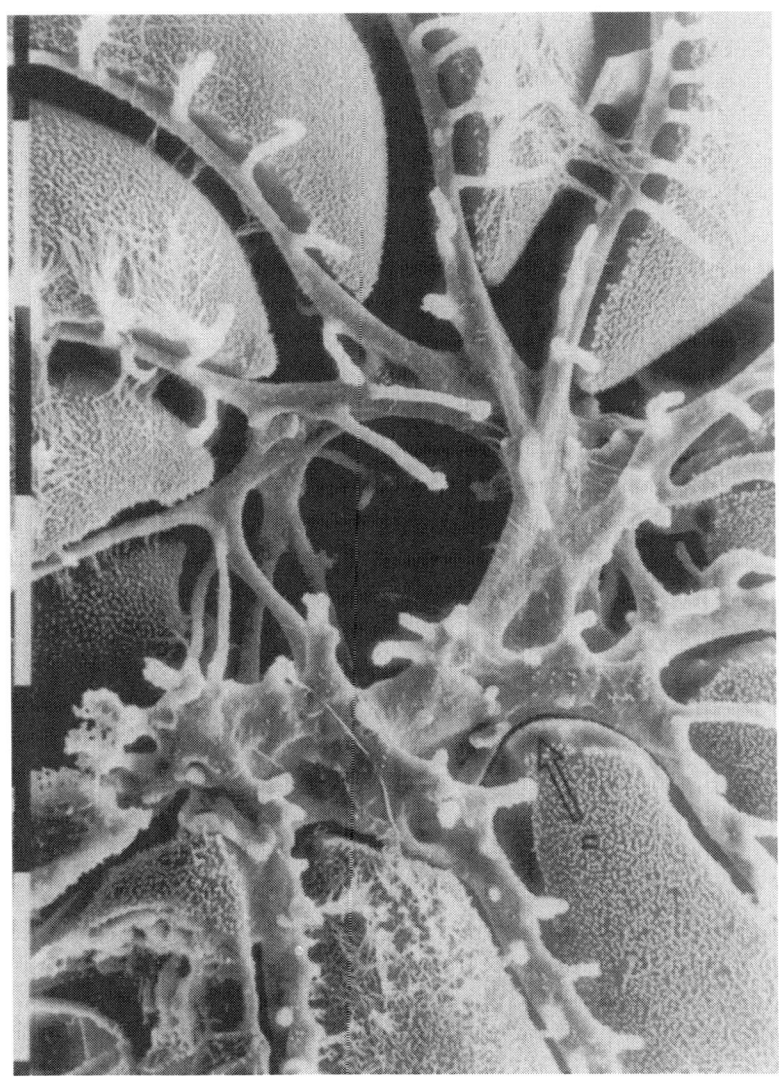

Figure 4.11 Detail of internal mold of *Elphidiella arctica*, showing connection of subsutural canals to shell surface and positions of umbilical cover plates (u); scale bar = 0.1 mm.

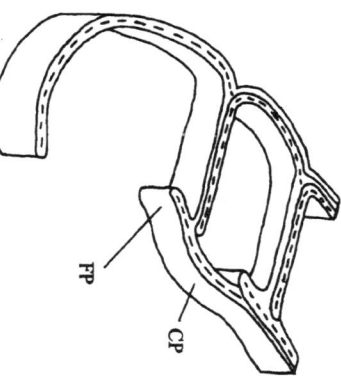

Figure 4.12 Constructional design of umbilical cover plates (CP) and associated foraminal plates (FP) in *Ammonia*; dashed line: median layer.

space retains an opening into the small space (closest to the umbilicus) now isolated by the umbilical cover plate. With the addition of new chambers, openings between adjacent chamber tips gradually form a spiral canal system in the umbilical region. When the umbilical chamber tip is not attached to the umbilicus (e.g. in *Ammonia*), the umbilical spiral canal remains open, demonstrating that the spiral canal is a functional surface, since it receives secondary lamination.

The cytoplasm leaves the chamber lumen in *Elphidium* through the interiomarginal multiple apertures or, posteriorly, through the opening constituted by a former aperture (closest to the umbilicus) of the penultimate chamber. Thus, it moves inside the umbilical spiral canal system, which is a functional surface, and then into interlocular spaces through openings in the spiral

and an inner lining. The inner lining faces the chamber lumen and is covered by the outer lamella in the umbilical direction. In between chambers, the umbilical part of the interlocular

Lamellar walls

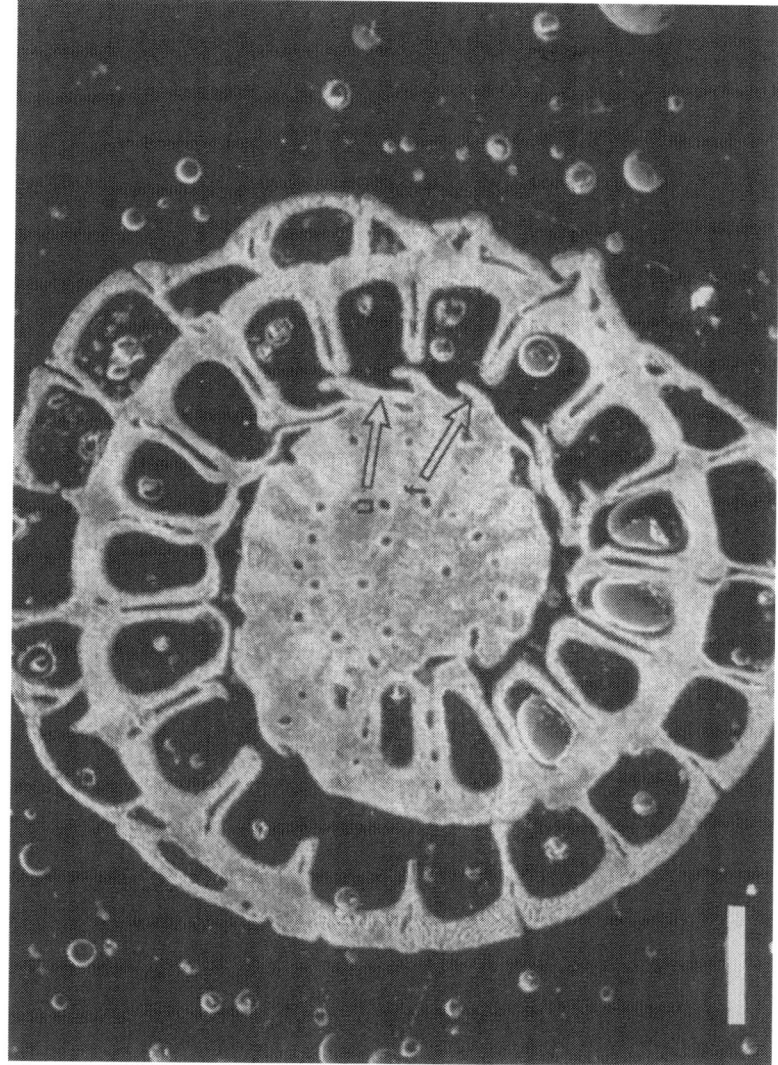

Figure 4.13 Detail of horizontal section through *Pseudorotalia* showing hooks (foraminal plates = f) and umbilical cover plates (u); scale bar = 0.2 mm.

canal. This allows the cytoplasm to emerge everywhere on the foraminiferal shell, between the ponticuli that bridge the interlocular spaces, as well as into interlocular spaces of previous whorls.

The nummulitids, in addition to possessing an umbilical spiral canal system, have developed a so-called marginal cord. This is a system of elongate 'islands' or ridges in the peripheral part of the final chamber, which, with the addition of secondary lamination, is gradually converted into a multi-pipe marginal channel. This channel communicates with all interlocular spaces, which are formed between the primary ridges of the septa and the septal flaps.

'Toothplates' are a special feature of some calcareous bilamellar Foraminifera. True toothplates are found within the Buliminida, and seem confined to that group. A buliminid toothplate is constructed of a single inner lining (Revets, 1993). Following the construction principles outlined above, the toothplate, if it were a functional surface, would have received secondary lamination. That has never been observed.

All planktonic Foraminifera are known or assumed to construct bilamellar shells. Although a monolamellar structure was reported in *Hastigerina pelagica* (Hemleben *et al.*, 1989), the scanning electron micrograph of a wall section shows it to be bilamellar (Fig. 4.17). This wall is only about 2 μm thick, rendering observation of the lamellarity difficult.

4.5.7 Aragonitic walls (Robertinida)

The study of several taxa belonging to the aragonitic order Robertinida shows that the shell con-

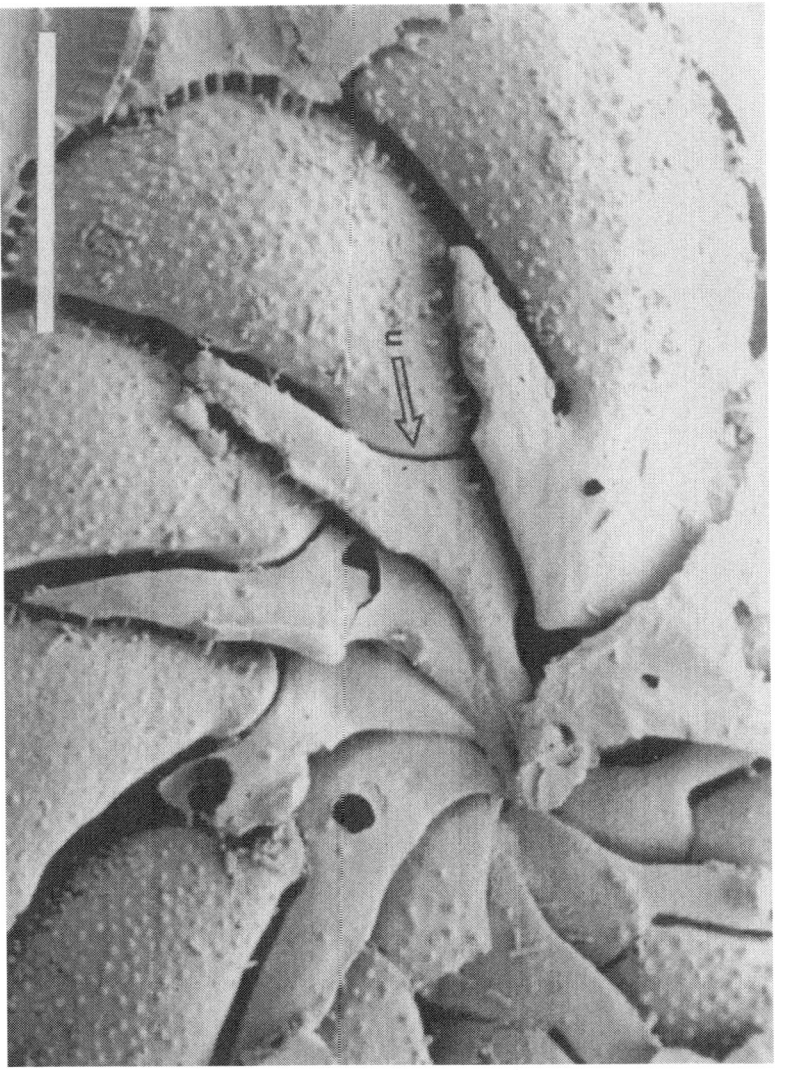

Figure 4.14 Detail of mold of *Astrononion* showing positions of umbilical cover plates (u); scale bar = 0.1 mm.

struction is bilamellar, although there is no obvious difference between the median layer and the boundary between the secondary lamellae. For example, the ultimate chamber wall in *Hoeglundina* is bilamellar, but in contrast to calcitic bilamellar walls, the aperture is not converted into a foramen with the addition of a new chamber. The aperture in *Hoeglundina* is positioned in the peripheral region of the final chamber; as a new chamber is added, this peripheral aperture is closed in the penultimate chamber by the deposition of a two-layered plate, while an opening is resorbed in the penultimate septal face, thereby creating a secondary foramen. Along with the formation of the outer chamber wall, *Hoeglundina* deposits a folded two-layered plate as a prolongation of the wall on the spiral side. This structure is often referred to as a toothplate, but it is not a true toothplate, which is a single-layered feature so far found only in the buliminids (see earlier). The two-layered plate ends in a folded extension, and is attached to the previous septum where the inner lining continues as a septal flap. The inner plate extends in the anterior direction for about half the length of the chamber. The entry of the cytoplasm into a chamber interior and earlier chambers of *Hoeglundina* takes place over the free folded part and through a foramen on the spiral side of the plate, and then from one foramen into the next (see illustrations in Hansen, 1979). A Jurassic *Epistomina* has exactly the same construction pattern. Ceratobuliminid shells have identical two-layered plates with a folded edge, and show the resorption of a foramen in the penultimate chamber. *Cushmanella* and related genera are extremely delicate, and their inner structures are more complicated than those of *Hoeglundina* and *Ceratobulimina*, and some species have several apertures associated

Lamellar walls

Figure 4.15 Mold of *Elphidium craticulatum* showing umbilical spiral canal; scale bar = 0.1 mm.

with partially closed inner pipes. The more complicated aragonitic shells appear to have evolved in the Jurassic, but the study of fossil aragonitic forms is hampered by the frequent recrystallization of their wall material. The record of simpler aragonitic forms goes back to the Permian (Loeblich and Tappan, 1987), but early involutinids may be unrelated to the structurally advanced forms of the Jurassic and later times (Piller, 1983).

4.5.8 The carbonate units of bilamellar forms

The shells of bilamellar forms are often described as being constructed of platelets of calcite. The platelets (0.1–0.2 μm thick) are arranged in stacks with identical orientation, but are apparently separated from each other by very thin organic layers. These organic layers are much thinner than those separating adjacent secondary lamellae, which, in turn, are thinner than the median layer.

There has been much speculation on the calcification process in bilamellar walls, but few direct observations have been made; such observations are hampered by the limited resolution of the light microscope. Angell (1979) made a study of shell formation in *Rosalina floridana*, but he had to clean various parts of the shell with chlorine; the effect of this procedure is uncertain, and some of the observed structures may be artifacts. Some speculative models of calcification are in poor agreement with the available ultrastructural evidence. In essence, explanations are needed for (a) the formation of stacks of platelets with the same orientation across spongy organic layers that separate adjacent secondary lamellae, and (b) the presence of pairs of euhedral calcite rhombohedrons that sandwich the median layer.

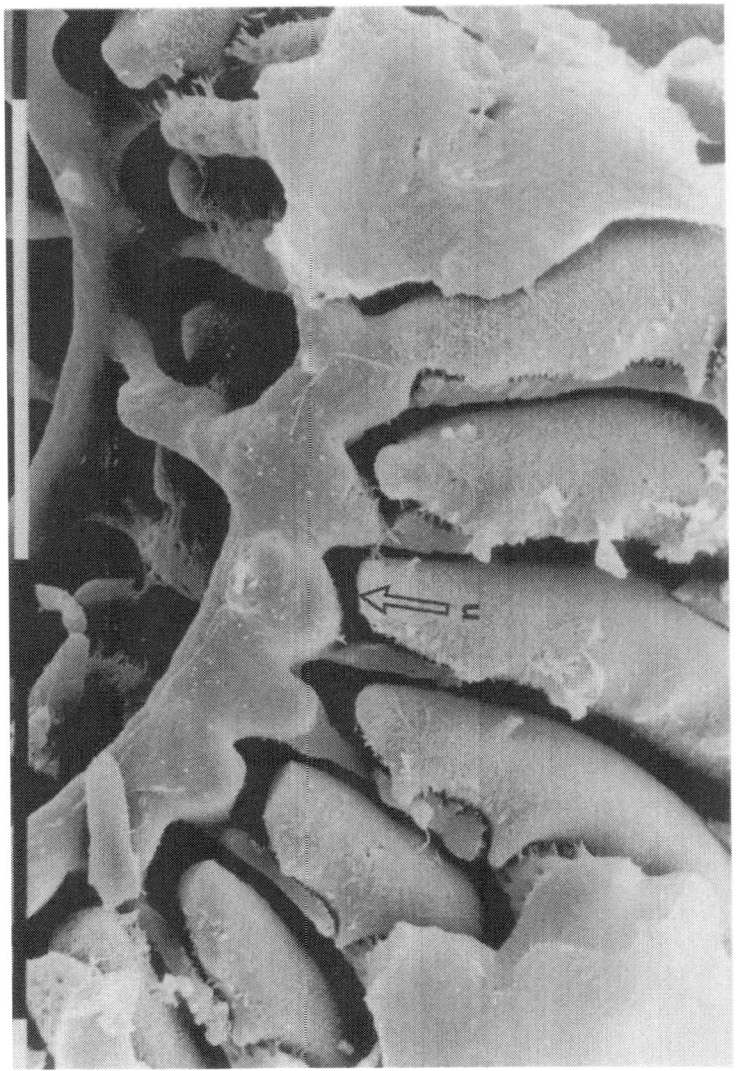

Figure 4.16 Detail of Fig. 4.15 showing positions of umbilical cover plates (u); scale bar = 0.1 mm. Note the absence of cover plate in the final chamber.

The difference between secondary lamellar boundaries and the median layer was noted by Hansen and Reiss (1971). In forms such as *Ammonia* and *Pseudorotalia*, the median layer was found to be composed of an organic sponge-like mat, sandwiched between calcite rhombohedrons whose obtuse angles protrude in the direction of the shell surface and the shell interior. Thus, from pure morphology, the optical axis is oriented perpendicular to the shell surface of this base pair of calcite crystallites. The rhombohedrons appear almost perfect, indicating that they formed without interference. The stacks of overlying platelets continue the orientation of the base-pair crystal faces. On etched shell sections, such stacks are separated by concentrations of organic material, which were regarded by Hansen (1970) as delimiters of 'crystal units.'

Debenay *et al.* (1996) illustrated two important features from the surface of a naturally corroded specimen of *Helenina anderseni*. The first concerns the nature of crystal units. The platelets around a pore are steep, indicating that platelets in *H. anderseni* may be oriented according to a more acute crystallographic form than {10$\bar{1}$1}, with the pore oriented along the c-axis. The other observation is on the detail of the boundary between crystal units, which shows an almost whisker-like pattern, and points to uninhibited growth, with neighboring crystal units in identical crystallographical orientation.

Debenay *et al.* (1996) suggested a calcification model for calcareous Foraminifera in which the primary elements are globular crystallites. The existence of such globular units, however, has not been satisfactorily documented. The possibility exists that they are artifacts, because similar globules can be produced in the laboratory by etching a foraminiferal wall, from which they

Lamellar walls

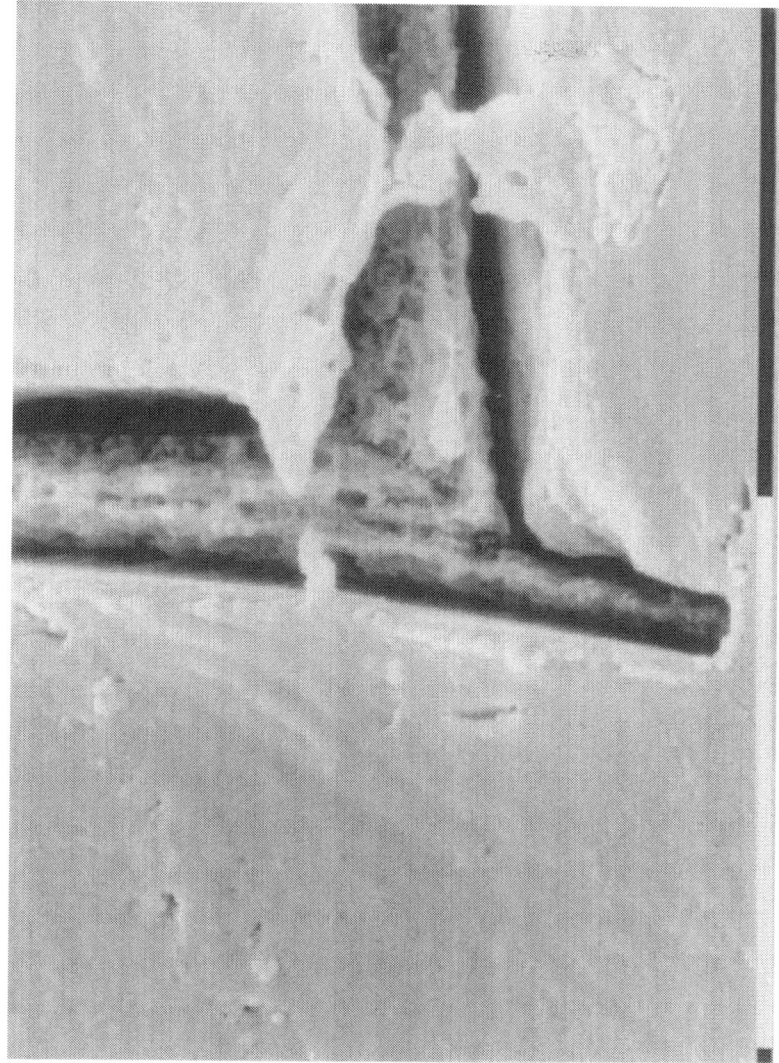

Figure 4.17 *Hastigerina pelagica*, junction between ultimate and penultimate chambers, detail of embedded, polished, and etched horizontal section; scale bar = 10 μm. Note the bilamellar construction.

can be completely or partially removed by extraction peels. Angell (1979) illustrated globular units of about 600 Å diameter on the surface of a *Rosalina floridana*, and there is a hint of a layered arrangement in these globules. However, Angell had removed organic material from the shell surface with sodium hypochlorite, and therefore there is a possibilty that these globules too may be etching artifacts.

4.6 THE PORES

Details of pore structures have been studied in just a few calcareous species. The pores in the monocrystalline *Patellina* were described by Berthold (1976b), who found an organic tubule and granular organic material filling the interior of the tubule, and demonstrated the uptake of the neutral red dye through the pores. The construction of the pores in the bilamellar *Amphistegina* was described by Leutenegger (1977b). These pores have an organic tubule that is subdivided by organic plates; each plate corresponds to a boundary between secondary lamellae. The median layer also crosses the pore tubule, and carries calcite crystallites that may represent the crystal base pairs of the median layer, indicating a late time of formation of the pores. In contrast to the pores of *Amphistegina*, those in genera such as *Heterostegina*, *Cycloclypeus*, and *Operculina* are not lined with organic tubules (Leutenegger, 1977b). Leutenegger and Hansen (1979) demonstrated the uptake of radioactive CO_2 through the pores of symbiont-bearing *Amphistegina*, but neither ^{14}C-labeled glucose nor the neutral red dye passed in appreciable amounts. This is not surprising, because it has been known for a long time that the Rose Bengal dye used for staining living Foraminifera generally produces coloration in only the youngest two or three chambers, while the remaining shell, in spite of the presence of cytoplasm, does not take up any dye, showing the impermeability of the pores for larger fluid molecules. Hemleben et al. (1989) found that the pores in some planktonic species originate through resorption in the late state of chamber formation. The pore tubules in planktonic Foraminifera apparently cross the median layer, but the boundary layers between secondary lamellae do not correspond to any structures crossing the pores.

So far, the presence of pore plates has been demonstrated only in lamellar forms. It appears that the so-called sieve plates of the pores in *Amphistegina* are nothing but a continuation of the organic material that separates adjacent lamellae (Hansen, 1972b). The extremely complicated pore-plate pattern illustrated by Jahn (1953) has not been found by other workers, and unfortunately, the species studied has never been identified.

A concentration of mitochondria in cytoplasmic material at the inner end of pores has been observed by Leutenegger and Hansen (1979) in some shells collected from low-oxygen environments. They interpreted this as an indication that pores serve as conduits for the passage of dissolved oxygen and carbon dioxide. This interpretation, however, is controversial, because of later observation that mitochondria are also concentrated in apertural cytoplasm (Bernhard and Alve, 1996) and that they move through pseudopodia (see chapter 12). Thin, thread-like structures emerging from pore plates in *Amphistegina* have been interpreted as extrusions of pseudopodial material (Hansen, 1972b). This has been challenged by Berthold (1976b) and Leutenegger (1977b), because the passage of cytoplasm could not be confirmed by TEM studies of pores. According to Berthold, the strands were most likely produced by fungi that invaded the pores in the laboratory culture.

Pore-like pits ('pseudopores' of authors) occur in some porcelaneous forms. They do not have an organic pore tubule, and a thin calcareous wall (about 10 µm thick) separates the bottom of the pits from the shell interior. In radio-tracer experiments, Hansen and Dalberg (1979) found uptake of labeled CO_2 directly through the thin lateral walls of living symbiont-bearing *Amphisorus*. They explained the uptake as being caused by CO_2 diffusion directly through the organic material of the shell wall, and considered the pits (pseudopores) as an adaptation to obligate algal symbiosis.

5
Quantitative methods of data analysis in foraminiferal ecology

William C. Parker and Anthony J. Arnold

5.1 INTRODUCTION

Undeniably, the Foraminifera offer a wealth of ecological information. Rarely, the data are sufficiently uncomplicated that knowledgeable observation is all that is required to reveal the critical ecological relationships. The desired information is most often camouflaged by aspects of the data involving undesired synecologic and autecologic factors, historical factors, sampling effects, etc. This is where quantitative analytical methods become necessary. The appropriate method can enhance the desired ecological signal in the data while suppressing the unwanted noise; it may simplify or condense the complicated structure of the data, making it easier to explore relationships; and it can facilitate testing an apparent relationship against the standard of chance occurrence. Additionally, the results of commonly used analytical techniques may be more convincing and more easily explained than an intuitive understanding of the data. Even when the relationship seems obvious, confirmatory analyses are a good idea.

With the proliferation in the 1980s and 1990s of desktop microcomputers and packaged analytical software, most foraminiferal researchers now use some form of quantitative analysis, ranging from simple spreadsheet or database operations to complex multivariate statistical techniques. However, most workers have a limited background in statistics and, when faced with the prospect of choosing an analytical method, can make inappropriate choices. When using the techniques described here as exploratory devices to increase understanding of a complex and confusing array of data, there are no right or wrong techniques. Some are certainly more efficient or appropriate 'signal-enhancing' filters, depending on the nature of the data and the questions of the researcher. For most of these methods, evaluation of success or failure of the analysis depends on whether the results offer a meaningful view of the data in the context of the research focus. The purpose of this chapter is to explore the variety of available and commonly used techniques, and to comment on their characteristics and applicability, so as to (1) aid in understanding the choice, application, and interpretation of methods employed by other researchers, and (2) provide an introduction to the selection of techniques for the reader's research. We will assume an understanding of simple statistical concepts (mean, standard deviation, etc.) and will focus on the more complicated multivariate techniques. The interested reader is referred to sources such as Shi (1993), Davis (1986), and Dillion and Goldstein (1984) for more general coverage of the methods discussed.

As an explanatory aid we will include analyses of a set of benthic foraminiferal assemblages collected from the Georgia–South Carolina continental slope. This data set includes counts of 183 species present in 38 samples of bottom sediment. The data and some analyses are discussed in Arnold (1977, 1983), Arnold and Sen Gupta (1981), and Sen Gupta and Hayes (1979). The data are available in Arnold (1977) or from the chapter authors at http://quartz.gly.fsu.edu/~parker/data.html.

5.2 DATA

Stevens' classic paper (1946) on scales of measurement provides valuable insights into types of measurements and the operations that can be performed on them. Foraminiferal data can be (1) *nominal* (using numbers as labels, e.g. 0 = smooth, 1 = spined, etc.), (2) *ordinal* (numerical values record monotonically increasing states, but not necessarily with equivalent intervals, e.g. 0 = absent, 1 = rare, 2 = common, etc.), (3) *interval* (numbers indicating equal measurement intervals, but with no true zero, e.g. distance from a geographic point or depth/time from a stratigraphic marker), and (4) *ratio* (like interval, but with a fixed zero, e.g. counts of specimens in a sample). Note that calculation of means, standard deviations, and correlations are technically valid only with interval and ratio data. Calculations involving alteration of variance (e.g. log calculations or standardizations) are only appropriate for true ratio data.

Some foraminiferal studies may include types of data that require special coding. For example, angular data, such as angular morphometric or latitudinal/longitudinal measures can present problems due to the apparent numerical discontinuity at the limits of the scale (e.g. 360°). This problem is best handled by orienting the measurement scale (in most senses an interval scale) such that the recorded observations fall only in the continuous portion. Quantitative chemical measurements, often used with environmental studies, present problems at the low end of the scale. A chemical constituent can rarely be said to be truly absent from a sample, even when the analytical technique fails to detect it. Such 'false zeroes' are more appropriately recorded as 'below detection limit,' reflecting a possible concentration somewhere between the analytical lower limit and true zero. Under these circumstances, a recorded value of some fraction of the detection limit (e.g. 1/2) is more appropriate. Finally, most data have a few samples for which all desired measurements are not possible. While in some cases it may be most desirable to simply discard the samples (or variables) concerned, this may also result in serious reduction in the study's coverage. Although the missing values can be estimated using a variety of techniques (e.g. regression, kriging, etc.), the resulting analysis utilizing the estimated values may be biased by the estimation process. A better approach is to code the missing values with some label or value designated as 'missing.' Most packaged analytical programs include the option of using missing value codes, and will provide options for dealing with such values that are most appropriate for the techniques available in the package.

Since many numerical techniques are sensitive to the relative sizes of the recorded values (e.g. variables recorded with 'big numbers' may dominate an analysis) or to the way in which the values are distributed (e.g. a normal distribution), it is often desirable to transform the data to make it numerically more suitable (see Davis, 1986, for a discussion, and Table 5.1 for the most common data transformation types). However, these recalculations can hide or distort some of the information originally present. For example, recalculation of species abundance as a percent of the sample is a common practice, but may disguise the presence of very depauperate samples, and hide major differences in variance. Some measurements, like species abundance in

Data

Table 5.1 Types of data transformations.

Translations		*	Comments
Minimum → 0	$X'_i = X_i - [\min(X_1 \ldots X_N)]$	V	sensitive to extremes
Mean → 0	$X'_i = X_i - [\sum X)/N]$	V	sensitive to extremes
Scaling transforms			
Percent maximum	$X'_i = (X_i * 100/[\max(X_1 \ldots X_N)]$	V	sensitive to extremes
Percent total	$X'_i = (X_i * 100/\sum X)$	S	most often used to transform samples to be of equal size, generates closure problem because one degree of freedom is lost
Percent range	$X'_i = \dfrac{[\max(X_1 \ldots X_N) - X_i] * 100}{[\max(X_1 \ldots X_N) - \min(X_1 \ldots X_N)]}$	V	changes ratio data to interval
Standardization	$X'_i = X_i - [(\sum X)/N]/\text{STD}(X)$ where **STD** = standard deviation	V	each variable becomes a standard normal deviate
Algebraic transforms			
Log	$X'_i = \log_e(X_i)$ or $X'_i = \log_{10}(X_i)$	V	will 'pull in' a right-skewed tail, recall that log(0) is undefined
Root	$X'_i = (X_i)^a$	V	especially useful if variables include measurements of different dimensionality, e.g. lengths, areas, and volumes
Arcsin	$X'_i = \text{Arcsin}(p^{-0.5})$ where $p = X_i/\sum X$	S	transforms samples so as to emphasize very rare and very dominant components
Normalization	$X'_i = X_i/[\sum (X)^2]^{0.5}]$	S	generally used to transform samples into vectors of unit length

*Column indicates whether the transform is primarily used on variables (V) or samples (S)

a pool of samples, may be distinctly 'non-normal' (e.g. skewed) and benefit from a variance-altering transformation (e.g. log transform or power transform). Additionally, species present as no more than a minor faunal element may have little impact on the analysis, unless species numbers or proportions are standardized (for each variable, recalculating the value by subtracting its mean and dividing by its standard deviation).

Because many foraminiferal data sets are sparse (e.g. having many species present in low abundances in a few samples), researchers often eliminate rare species from the analysis to improve the analytical response. Traditionally, species present at abundances of less than 1 or 2% (sometimes only when low in more than 50% of the samples) are eliminated. Keep in mind that the analytical results will then say nothing about the eliminated taxa, or the portion of the fauna they represent.

Outliers are data elements which, for one or more reasons, seem at odds with the rest of the data (i.e. they do not fit the expected trend). Outliers exist for a variety of reasons: (1) errors in sampling, measuring, and recording of data, (2) greater than expected variability in a sampled value, (3) inclusion of one or more members of a 'different population,' and (4) incorrect expectations of relationships within the data. It is principally because they differ from the majority of the data that outliers are so often viewed as troublesome hindrances. Their variance from the data mean often gives the outliers unexpected influence in the outcome of analytical techniques. While the researcher may be inclined (and sometimes justified) in discarding such distracting elements, this is a potentially dangerous course. The outliers, by virtue of their difference, contain more 'information' than their counterparts, and to eliminate them is to discard this information. If a good case can be made that the outliers are different because of some *a priori* condition, then they may be discarded, *along with all other entities that meet the same criteria*. Otherwise, they should remain in the analysis (with attempts made to minimize their distracting effects), or the analysis should be continued without them and their relationship to the final results stated.

One potentially confusing aspect of multivariate analytical techniques is the use of the terms 'sample' and 'variable'. As used here, 'samples' refer to entities which are conceptually composed of or described by other entities, the 'variables.' Thus, for a biogeographic study of foraminiferal assemblages, a sample might be the collection of recorded abundances of various species at a given location, and the variables would be the species. For a morphometric study of a single species, the sample might be a single specimen (or a population of specimens), and the variables would be the morphometric measurements. In our example data set, we have 38 foraminiferal assemblages from splits of washed, sieved, and floated sediment (containing at least 300 individual foraminiferal specimens, where possible) as samples. The 138 species present in these samples are the variables, and their values are recorded as counts of individual specimens for each species in each sample (ratio data). Due to the large and unwieldy nature of a 138-element variable list (many packaged programs have restrictions on the number of variables used in some analyses), and the observation that many of the species occur sparsely and have little correlation with any other species, we have reduced the variable list to the 77 species which show significant associations with at least one other species (following Arnold, 1983). Log transformation of data was chosen because species abundances are generally log-normal and because, philosophically, the difference between 0 and 1 individuals should be more significant than the difference between 100 and 101. Note that since the data set contained 0 values (for which the log transform is undefined), a constant, small value (smaller than the minimum positive value, e.g. 0.5) was added to each entry in the data set prior to log transformation. Thus a 0.0 value becomes −0.69. In addition to species abundances, we also have data on the depth, location, and sediment type at each sampling locality. These latter variables will be used to interpret the results of multivariate analyses of the species assemblages.

5.3 CLUSTER ANALYSIS

Cluster analysis (CA) is one of the most widely used and commonly understood multivariate analytical techniques in the foraminiferal literature. It segregates entities (samples, species, measurements) into 'naturally occurring' groups and quantifies the between-group relationships. It is difficult to peruse a copy of *Journal of Foraminiferal Research* or *Marine Micropaleontology* without seeing at least one example of the characteristic dendrogram (see Fig. 5.1) generated by most packaged cluster analysis programs. The spindles of the dendrogram track the entities in the clusters, while the linkage bars reflect the similarity of the clustered entities. Cluster analysis has been used to delineate biofacies (e.g. Ishman, 1996), species associations (e.g. Ishman and Domack, 1994), and morphometric associations (e.g. Saraswati, 1995). One caveat which must be remembered is that cluster analysis *always* produces clusters, whether or not any naturally distinct groupings occur in the data. It is most often used as an exploratory technique, to see what groupings might be present. To confirm the presence of any clusters observed, researchers resort to the quantification techniques discussed at the end of this section, or a comparison ('mapping') of the cluster analysis results with results of other multivariate techniques (e.g. factor analysis, principal components analysis, correspondence analysis, multidimensional scaling).

Almost exclusively, the varieties of clustering used with foraminiferal data fall under the heading of 'hierarchical agglomerative' clustering, meaning that they start with all entities in separate groups and proceed to cluster iteratively, by merging pairs of groups from previous iterations, until all entities are grouped into a single cluster. Analyses are referred to as Q-mode for clustering of samples (i.e. entities composed of several measurable parameters), or R-mode for clustering of variables (the measurable parame-

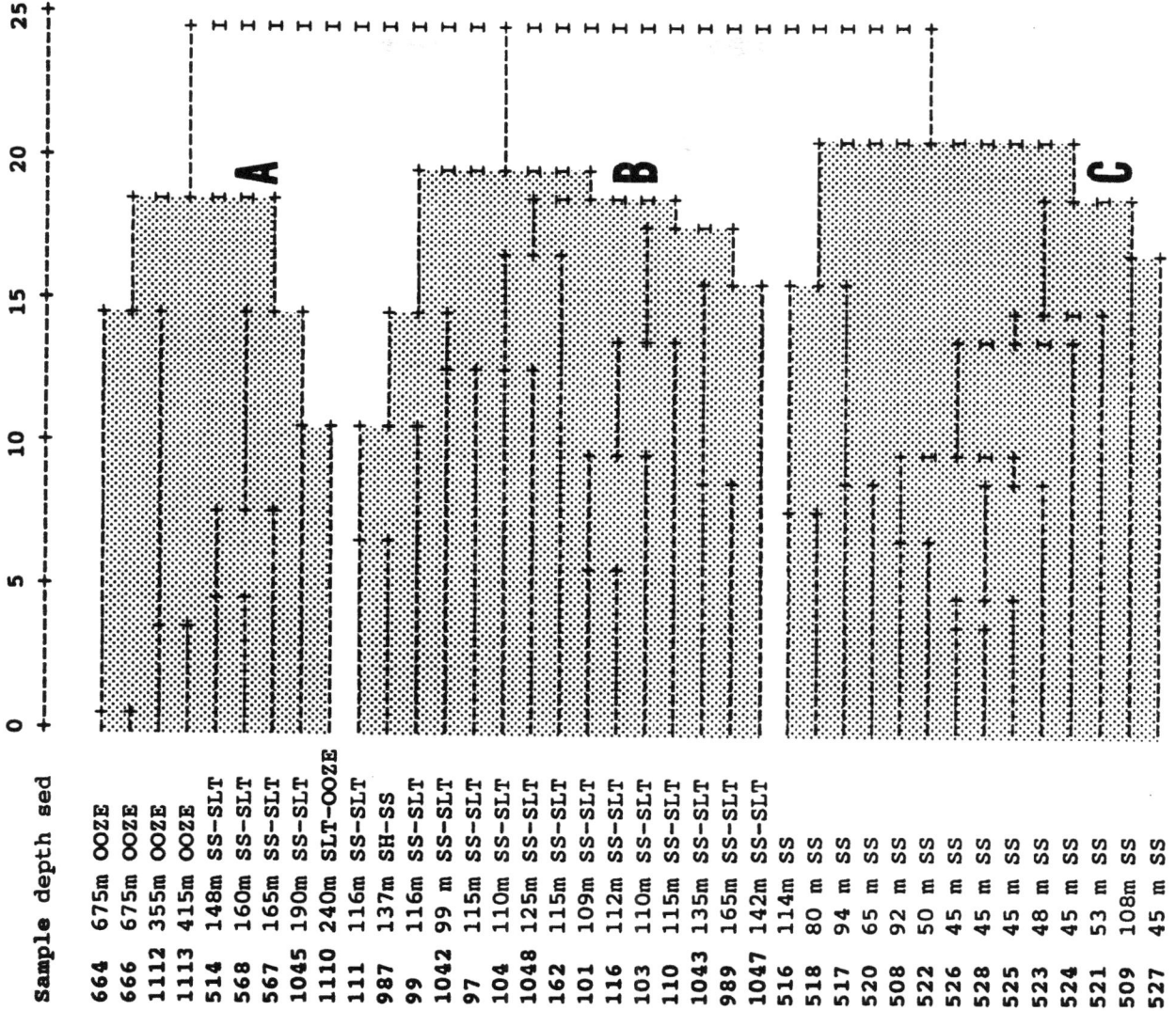

Figure 5.1 Dendrogram from Q-mode cluster analysis of samples from the Georgia–South Carolina continental slope using Pearson's coefficient and UWPGA method. Based on relative separation, three clusters (shaded) have been recognized. Note the relationship of the clusters to sample depth (A, deep; B, intermediate; C, shallow) and sediment type (A and B, finer-grained; C, coarse-grained).

ters). The choice of R- or Q-mode is a logical result of the kind of question being 'asked' of the data. If your interest is in similarity/dissimilarity among samples, then a Q-mode clustering of samples is indicated. Most implementations begin with conversion of the data to a matrix of similarities (or dissimilarities) among the entities to be clustered, and end with the production of the descriptive dendrogram. Variations on the basic format arise from differences in (1) the similarity (or dissimilarity) calculation used, (2) the means of choosing which entities to cluster at each step, and (3) the means of calculating similarities of entities to newly fused clusters.

Commonly chosen similarity measures include the Pearson's correlation coefficient (0–1.0) and euclidean distance (0-infinity). This choice can be important due to interaction between the nature of the data and the way similarity is calculated. Some indices of similarity, such as Pearson's correlation, are relatively immune to differences in the 'numerical size' of the entities being clustered, (i.e. whether the values are numerically larger or smaller than for other entities). Others, such as euclidean distance, change similarity values with changes in scale of measurement. Additionally, some data sets may produce similarity values between entities that have such small numerical ranges that interpretation of the dendrogram becomes difficult. Unless the worker is interested in exploring the numerical nuances of the various similarity measures, it is advisable to run several analyses with different indices, and discard, or at least distrust, any result that is fundamentally different from the others. Davis (1986), Sneath and Sokal (1973), and Sepkoski (1974) discuss various similarity measures available.

Most of the common clustering methods simply join the two entities with the highest mutual similarity at each iteration. One popular variant is Ward's minimum variance clustering method, which does not involve a similarity measure as such, but uses the data to calculate a sums-of-squares index E for all entities. At each step, a potential new cluster that yields the lowest total E value (for all the entities present at that step) is formed. This continues until a single cluster remains. Ward's method is often preferred because the dendrogram, when scaled to E, produces what appears to be exceptionally well defined clusters. This is primarily because E is a function of squared differences and is, therefore, nonlinear. A dendrogram scaled against the square root of E would be more comparable to the other methods. Note that Ward's method, because it uses no similarity measure (other than E, surrogate for variance), is susceptible to scale and measurement changes.

Among the variety of methods for calculating similarities for newly fused clusters, two methods, Unweighted Pair Group Method with Arithmetic averaging (UPGMA) and single linkage (SLINK), appear most popular. The former averages similarities of entities to new clusters (adjusting for the number of entities in each cluster), while the other takes the maximum similarity between the entity and any member of the new cluster. As expected, these different methods can produce dramatically different dendrograms, especially with regard to the levels of linkage between clusters.

Recognition of 'significant' clusters within a dendrogram is largely a subjective process. Practitioners most commonly attempt to define clusters based on relative spacing of linkages in the dendrogram. Clusters can be graphically designated by shading or by construction, on the dendrogram, of a 'phenon line,' marking a level of similarity (or dissimilarity) at which the clusters are presumed to represent meaningful aggregations.

If the aim of clustering is to explore or illustrate group structure in the data, then the appropriateness of the specific choice of method can be judged subjectively (i.e. do you see what you were looking for?). However, if the goal is to objectively quantify the 'success' of a given analysis, we require more rigor. Two quantification techniques are available. The cophenetic correlation value compares the between-entity similarity values in the original matrix with a similar set derived from the clustered results (described in detail in Davis, 1986). Values approaching 1.0 indicate less distortion of the original similarities by the clustering process. More involved techniques use a Monte Carlo process (described in Milligan, 1996) to generate artificial, random data sets from the original data. Analysis of the artificial data provides a basis for quantitative comparison of the results of a given cluster analysis. Comparisons of various techniques (Milligan, 1996; Milligan and Cooper, 1986; Hubert and Arabie, 1985) suggest that the correlation coefficient generally outperforms euclidean distance and that Ward's method may show some superiority to UPGMA. SLINK methods, in general, fare poorly.

Recent examples of CA include delineation of species assemblages (Ishman and Domack, 1994; Chang and Yoon, 1995) and environmentally related biofacies (Whitehead and McMinn, 1997). A dendrogram for Q-mode CA (SPSS for Windows 7.5.1) of the example data set is shown in Fig. 5.1 with the clusters (shaded for identification) chosen on the basis of relative separation. Arnold (1983) presents both R- and Q-mode clusters of this data, using the data in presence/absence (1 or 0) form, and demonstrates that the Q-mode clusters thus formed are strongly related to sample depth. The analysis shown here uses fully quantitative data (counts rather than presence/absence) converted to natural logs and subsequently standardized. Sample similarites were calculated using Pearson's coefficient and the clusters formed using the UWPGA method. As you can see, the clusters display a relationship, albeit an imperfect one, with sample depth. The selection of the options presented here is based on approximately 15 different runs with a variety of data treatments, similarity coefficients, and clustering strategies, with varying success in producing depth-related clusters. While the results shown illustrate that the assemblages are related by their depths, the manipulation of the methodology necessary to achieve even moderately strong depth-related clusters suggests that depth is not the only factor influencing groupings in the data. For example, note that the clusters also tend to separate groups related by sediment type. We also note that those techniques which tend to minimize the range of the variables, and make them numerically comparable, produce results most similar to that of Arnold (1983), perhaps because the presence or absence of a species indicates the environment better than its abundance.

5.4 EIGENVECTOR TECHNIQUES

5.4.1

Eigenvector techniques embrace a variety of analytical methods, including Principal Components Analysis, Factor Analysis, and Correspondence Analysis. All of these techniques attempt to portray/resolve the similarities or differences between entities (samples, species, etc.) in terms of placement in a multidimensional space. The dimensions of this new space are determined by converting the original or transformed data into some measurement of similarity between entities, and factoring the matrix of similarities into eigenvectors (mutually perpendicular axes defining the coordinate system of the new space) and eigenvalues (a measure of how 'important' each new axis is to the data). This factoring process is used to reduce the dimensionality of a multivariate data set, without losing important information, to the point that researchers can easily work with it. Although some of the techniques are most often used with species, and others with samples, all of these methods can be used in both R- and Q-modes (see discussion in David et al., 1974; Klovan and Imbrie, 1971); the choice is less restrictive than for CA. With the calculation of loadings and scores, it is possible to derive information from the analytical results about the roles of samples and variables in the reduced dimensional space. Keep in mind that loadings address the relationships between the entities being factored and the new axes (e.g. for R-mode, loadings ⇔ variables; for Q-mode, loadings ⇔ samples), while scores represent the 'alternate entities' (R-mode, scores ⇔ samples; Q-mode, scores ⇔ variables). The differences between the various techniques discussed here are primarily due to the different assumptions

5.4.2 Principal Components Analysis

Principal Components Analysis (PCA) is the simplest of the eigenvector analytical techniques. In PCA a variance/covariance matrix or a correlation matrix is factored, thus making this technique most suitable for R-mode investigations (note that calculation of an R-mode correlation matrix involves standardization of the variables). The process ideally will extract as many new dimensions as there were original entities in the data (e.g. factoring a matrix with 10 entities, you get 10 principal coordinates or factors). These new dimensions are mutually independent and each accounts for a decreasing share of the information in the original data (reflected by monotonically decreasing eigenvalues).

Most commonly, researchers are not interested in all of the new dimensions. The decision about how many dimensions to consider can be made in many ways. A common method is to plot the eigenvalue (or its log) versus its order (see Fig. 5.2 for an example, also known as a 'scree plot') and look for a 'natural break' in the decrease in eigenvalues with increasing rank.

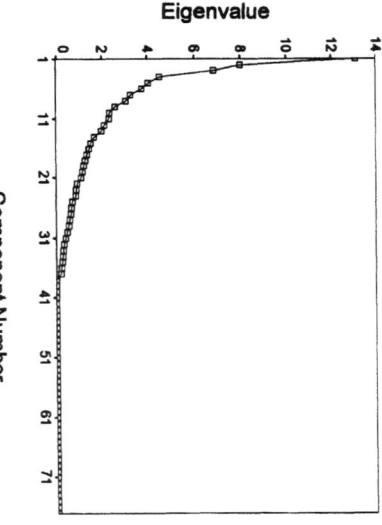

Figure 5.2 Scree plot showing eigenvalue against relative order of eigenvector (component) for principal components analysis of data discussed in text. Here, the first three PC's have substantially higher eigenvalues than the rest, suggesting that they hold more explanatory value.

Others choose to retain only those eigenvalues accounting for more variance than any original entity would have, if variance were distributed evenly (e.g. when factoring 20 species, only keep dimensions with 5% or more of the total variance). Keep in mind that as you reduce dimensionality, you lose information. Communality values (square root of sums of squares of loadings for retained dimensions) will help indicate when reducing dimensionality has effectively eliminated an entity from the analysis.

The new axes can be rotated in multidimensional space to increase their explanatory value. Rotations can be either orthogonal (maintaining the axes as independent) or oblique (allowing for inter-correlation). The only commonly used rotation is VARIMAX, an orthogonal rotation which maximizes the variance in factor loadings, thus having the effect of leaving each factor characterized by a few entities with high loadings.

There are a variety of ways in which PCA results can be interpreted. The principal components or factors can be viewed as new, 'synthetic' variables (R-mode), or new, 'endmember' associations of variables (Q-mode). Sometimes significant members of the original variables or samples have sufficiently strong loadings on a certain factor that the factor can be 'named' (e.g. the first factor in morphometric analyses often contains strong loadings from size-dependent variables, and is called the growth or size axis).

One advantage of the new synthetic variables is their orthogonality; they are independent (i.e. uncorrelated) to each other. Thus, if one axis describes size, the other axes are size-independent. The loadings can be used to characterize the original entities, or to explore relationships between subsets of entities. Naturally occurring groups of entities can be picked out on plots of loadings or scores. Lines or arcs of entities on loading or score plots reveal gradients of change. Often, plots of PCA loadings may display a highly curved or horseshoe-shaped arc. This is 'Kendall's horseshoe,' an artifact in the analytical process that can distort a simple (e.g. one-dimensional) gradient of change into a higher dimensional curve.

Eigenvector techniques

Recent examples of PCA in foraminiferal research include Mackensen et al. (1993b) and Harloff and Mackensen (1997); these use Q-mode PCA to differentiate ecologically significant benthic foraminiferal associations. Loubere (1996) uses PCA of benthic species abundance data to illustrate the differences between factoring correlation versus variance/covariance matrices (correlation equally weights all taxa, variance/covariance favors abundant taxa). Speijer et al. (1996) present results of both an R-mode CA and a PCA of Egyptian Paleogene benthic foraminiferal assemblages, giving a comparative view of the two techniques and showing how to incorporate the results of one in the other. Fig. 5.3 (after Speijer et al., 1996) shows the stratigraphic distribution of sample scores, using the scores as synthetic sample descriptors which the authors have related to environmental variables.

Table 5.2 Eigenvalues extracted using principal components analysis (example data).

Component	Eigen value	% of variance	Cumulative %
1	13.893	17.812	17.812
2	8.031	10.296	28.107
3	6.850	8.782	36.889
4	4.590	5.885	42.774
5	4.055	5.199	47.973
6	3.763	4.824	52.797
7	3.280	4.205	57.003
8	3.066	3.931	60.933
9	2.610	3.346	64.279
10	2.363	3.029	67.309
11	2.315	2.968	70.276
12	2.113	2.710	72.986
13	1.992	2.554	75.540
14	1.658	2.126	77.666
15	1.512	1.939	79.605
16	1.444	1.851	81.456
17	1.348	1.728	83.183
18	1.269	1.627	84.810
19	1.228	1.574	86.384
20	1.170	1.499	87.883
21	1.086	1.392	89.276

Note: components with eigenvalues < 1.0 omitted.

An R-mode PCA carried out on the example data set (using log transformed variables) yielded eigenvalues (and associated percentages of the total variance each accounts for) shown in Table 5.2. A scree plot of these eigenvalues (Fig. 5.2) shows a distinct drop after the first three components, suggesting that these three have substantially more explanatory power than the rest. A condensed table of VARIMAX rotated loadings (containing only those variables with high loadings on one of these first three components) is shown in Table 5.3. Note that many species, especially *Textularia conica* (TXT_CONI), *Textularia agglutinans* (TXT_AGGL), *Siphonaperta sabulosa* (SIPHON_S), *Reophax curtus* (REOPX_CU), *Eponides antillarum* (EPON_ANT), and *Calcituba decorata* (CATLUB_D) have high loadings on component one, the species *Amphistegina lessonii* (AMPHIS), *Cassidulina laevigata* (CASS_LAE), *Cibicides floridanus* (CIB_PSEU), *Glabratella laurieri* (GLAB_LAU), *Quinqueloculina jugosa* (Q_JUGOS), and *Rosalina bertheloti* (ROSA_

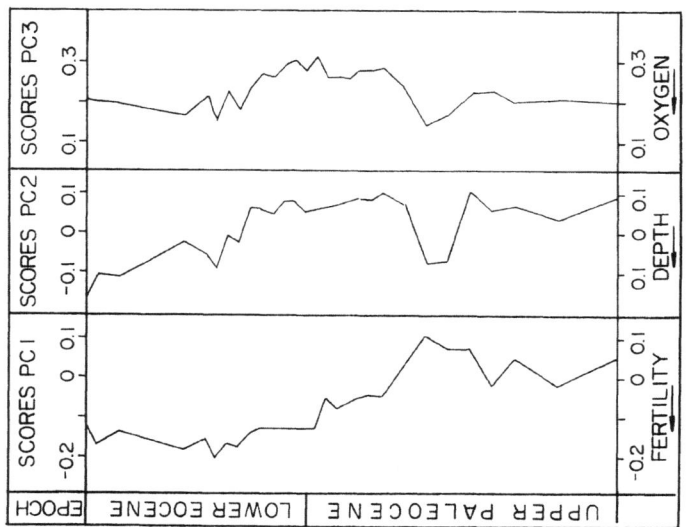

Figure 5.3 Plot of sample scores (after Speijer et al., 1996) for the first three PC's from an R-mode PCA of benthic foraminiferal species versus sample stratigraphic position. The PC's are being used as 'synthetic variables' with suggested environmental associations.

Table 5.3 Rotated principal component matrix (example data).

Species	Component 1	2	3
ACERV_IN	0.638	−0.375	−4.630E-02
AMPHIST	−1.623E-02	0.621	0.169
ASTRLINA	−0.581	−0.322	0.264
BIGEN_IR	0.595	−4.628E-02	6.716E-02
BOL_LOWM	−0.625	−0.461	4.297E-02
BUL_ACUL	−0.565	−0.337	−0.278
CALTUB_D	0.718	−0.504	7.535E-03
CASS_L_C	−0.579	0.189	−0.180
CASS_IAE	6.824E-02	0.529	−0.394
CIB_PSEU	3.803E-04	0.580	−0.547
CIB_RFLG	−0.133	−7.125E-02	−0.819
EPON_ANT	0.690	−9.299E-02	−2.276E-02
FISS_MAR	−0.512	−4.053E-02	4.325E-02
GLAB_LAU	0.105	0.604	−0.130
HANZ_CON	0.413	0.263	0.533
MELON_ZA	−0.273	0.334	−0.522
MIL_CIRC	0.360	−9.843E-02	0.503
NODOBC_A	0.563	0.296	0.328
NONLLA_A	5.480E-02	0.211	0.539
PLACPS_C	0.584	−0.447	8.983E-02
Q_JUGOS	6.614E-03	0.656	4.143E-02
REOPX_CU	0.701	0.142	5.469E-02
REUSSLA	0.289	1.515E-02	0.542
ROSA_BRT	−0.153	0.668	0.123
ROSA_FLD	−0.408	8.491E-02	0.578
SIPHON_S	0.739	−0.285	−1.543E-03
STILOSTO	−0.148	−8.637E-02	−0.815
MARTNOT	−0.104	4.071E-02	−0.791
TXT_AGGL	0.678	−0.171	0.392
TXT_CAND	0.643	−0.372	9.147E-02
TXT_CONI	0.836	2.850E-02	0.310
UVIG_PER	−0.372	0.405	−0.538
WEBNIA_C	0.671	−0.454	−4.151E-03

Extraction method: Principal Components Analysis.
Rotation method: Varimax with Kaiser normalization.

plot of PC1 versus depth, shown in Fig. 5.5 shows a positive correlation, so that PC1 may be thought of as a depth component. The circles in Fig. 5.4a surround the cluster locations (Arnold, 1983) reveals that the clusters A and C break up a continuum, while cluster B represents something different. Referral to a map of sample locations (Arnold, 1983) reveals that the samples scoring high on PC2 are substantially farther northeast along the slope than other samples at similar depths, and are typified by finer grained sediments. Thus, the analysis has picked up differences due to a variety of causes.

5.4.3 Factor analysis

Factor analysis (FA), *sensu stricto*, differs from PCA primarily in conceptualization of the data. In contrast to PCA, FA assumes that the information in the data is composed of a few factors common to all entities, mixed with factors unique to individual entities. The underlying common factors are not directly observable but are reflected in the observable entities. One implication of the factor analytic approach is that the number of underlying common factors may be known *a priori*, rather than approximated by looking at scree plots, loadings, or communalities.

A variety of methods exist for extraction of factors: principal components, principal factor, maximum likelihood, alpha, etc. Dillon and Goldstein (1984) conclude that (1) with communalities ~ = 1.0, all methods produce nearly identical results, and (2) with more variables, method choice is less important. Various studies (cited in Dillon and Goldstein, 1984) have suggested that the maximum likelihood method may be superior for very large numbers of samples (>1500), while the alpha and image methods may be better for small data sets.

Like PCA, FA can be done in Q- or R-mode, the factors can be rotated either orthogonally or obliquely, and the results interpreted as discussed for PCA above. Recent examples of FA include an R-mode analysis of biometric data by Saraswati (1995), analyses of benthic species distribution data in relation to environment by

BRT), on component two, and especially, *Cibicides* sp. cf. *C. refulgens* (CIB_RFLG), *Rosalina floridana* (ROSA_FLD), *Stilostomella antillea* (STILOSTO), and *Martinottiella communis* (MARTNOT) on component three (a negative sign on the loading indicates that the species decreases as the component increases). A plot of sample scores in Fig. 5.4 shows a gradation of points high on PC1 with a separate grouping of samples along PC2. PC3 primarily accounts for two samples (1112 and 1113). A

Eigenvector techniques

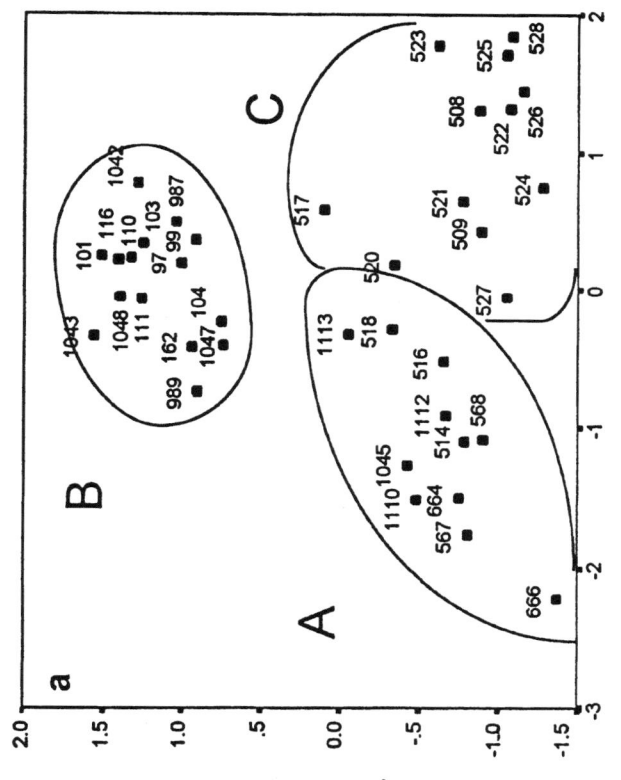

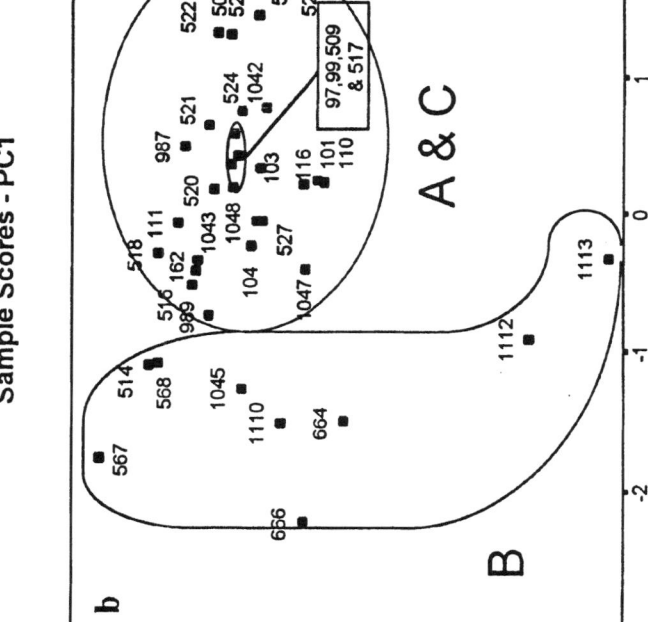

Figure 5.4 Bivariate plots of sample scores (first 3 PC's) form an R-mode PCA of the data discussed in the text. The circles enclosing groups of points map the three clusters shown in Fig. 5.1 onto the PCA. Note that PC1 contains a gradation of samples, with PC2 and PC3, separating out different subgroups.

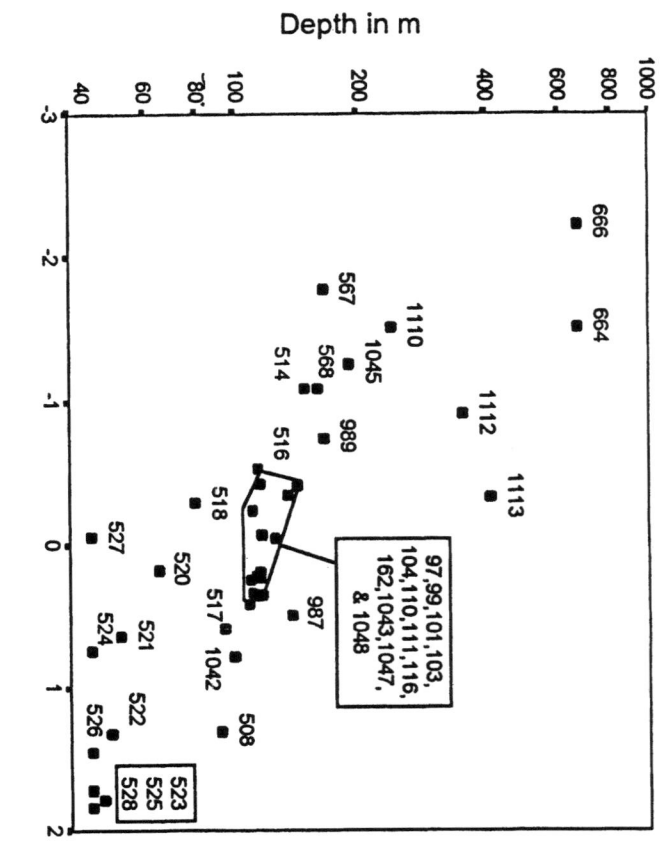

Figure 5.5 A comparison of PCA sample scores from PC1, as shown in Fig. 5.4, with sample depth. The obvious strong correlation suggests that PC1 may be thought of as a surrogate for depth.

Nigam (1987) and Jayaraju and Reddeppa Reddi (1996a), and an R-mode factor analysis of benthic foraminiferal assemblages in the northwestern Gulf of Mexico by Denne and Sen Gupta (1993).

5.4.4 Correspondence analysis

Correspondence Analysis, described by Davis (1986) and David et al. (1974), is similar to FA except that the data matrix is transformed into a matrix of conditional probabilities. This process allows for the use of data that are not ratio or interval type (e.g. enumerative data such as the counts of specimens in various species). The transformation is such that relationships between rows and columns in the transformed matrix are the same as in the original data; thus R- and Q-mode solutions are equivalent and are obtained simultaneously. Published results of correspondence analysis often show samples and variables plotted on the same set of axes, thus enhancing interpretation of the results (provided the plots remain comprehensible) and reducing the number of figures necessary to illustrate the analysis. Recent examples of correspondence analysis include Widmark (1995) and Hermelin and Shimmield (1990).

5.5 MULTIDIMENSIONAL SCALING

Multidimensional scaling (MDS) is another data reduction technique that attempts to uncover 'hidden structure' in data. It requires a matrix of similarities (or dissimilarities), and can be used in either Q- or R-mode. Unlike eigenvalue techniques, MDS attempts to 'map' entities into a limited dimensional space such that the proximities between entities reflect their similarities. The process is iterative, involving changing the mapped locations of entities, and checking a calculated value of mismatch (between distances in the map and similarities) called 'stress.' Most packaged varieties of MDS require specification of the number of dimensions for the map and a starting configuration. MDS can be either metric (assuming ratio or interval data and a precise function relating similarities to mapped distances) or nonmetric (assuming nominal or ordinal data and an unspecifiable monotonic relationship between similarity and mapped distance). Nonmetric MDS can be superior to eigenvector techniques when relationships between entities are not linear, because nonmetric MDS does not assume linearity. Interpretation of the results is superficially similar to that for PCA, with mapped coordinates for the entities in each requested dimension (~ loadings) and correlations between map axes and entity characteristics (~ scores).

A good general description of MDS can be found in Dillon and Goldstein (1984), while discussions of applicability to paleontological data are in Shi (1993), Hazel (1977), and Millendorf *et al.* (1978). Despite its many advantages for foraminiferal research, MDS has seen less use than eigenvector techniques. Ishman (1996) uses a Q-mode MDS, CA, and PCA to analyze foraminiferal assemblages as indicators of North Atlantic deep water circulation patterns.

Application of Q-mode MDS to the sample data (log transformed) yields the two dimensional map shown in Fig. 5.6. The routine used was ALSCAL (SPSS for Windows 7.5.1), and the matrix of scaled distances was calculated from the data by the program using euclidean distance. A two dimensional solution was chosen for comparison to the results from PCA. Note that the pattern of sample locations is very similar to that from the PCA scores. The envelopes drawn are the clusters generated from CA. Again, MDS axis one seems highly correlated with depth while axis two separates geographically distinct groups of samples.

5.6 DISCRIMINANT FUNCTION ANALYSIS

Discriminant function analysis (DFA) is a technique for classifying entities into mutually exclusive *a priori* groups based on a set of independent variables. The technique operates by deriving linear combinations (discriminant functions) of the variables such that misclassification of the entities into the groups is minimized. Entities of unknown group affinity can then be classified using the discriminant function and a probability calculated for membership in each of the groups. This technique works best when the groups are well known and at least some of their members can be identified unequivocally. DFA shares many similarities with multiple linear regression, and it should be remembered that if the variables are highly intercorrelated, the list of 'discriminator' variables used in the discriminant function many not include all those expected.

Recent examples of DFA include Jennings and Nelson (1992), in which the technique is used to discriminate foraminiferal assemblage zones in Oregon tidal marshes. Martin *et al.* (1995) use DFA, along with CA and FA, to distinguish species assemblages in Gulf of California tidal flats. Ishman and Domack (1994) use DFA, CA, and PCA to identify benthic foraminiferal assemblages from the Antarctic Peninsula. For the sample data set, we have used DFA to distinguish between samples associated with coarse sandy sediment and those from finer grained sediments. Fifteen samples with obvious coarse sandy sediment were coded 1.0, and thirteen obviously fine-grained samples were coded 2.0. The remaining samples were left uncoded and were classified by the analysis. As shown in Table 5.4 the DFA achieved 100% correct classification of the coded samples with a function using only six of the species abundances (*Melonis zaandami* [MELON_ZA], *Quinqueloculina jugosa* [Q._JUGOS], *Rosalina bertheloti* [ROSA_BRT], *Rosalina floridensis* [ROSA_FLE], *Spiroloculina atlantica* [SPIROL_A], and *Martinottiella communis* [MARTNOT]). Figure 5.7 illustrates the distribution of all the samples on a plot comparing the sample discriminant scores with their depths. Note that the discriminant axis divided the samples into two groups, sand to the left, fine-grained to the right, and both groups falling in the 0–200 m range (possibly explaining why attempts to sep-

84 Quantitative methods of data analysis in foraminiferal ecology

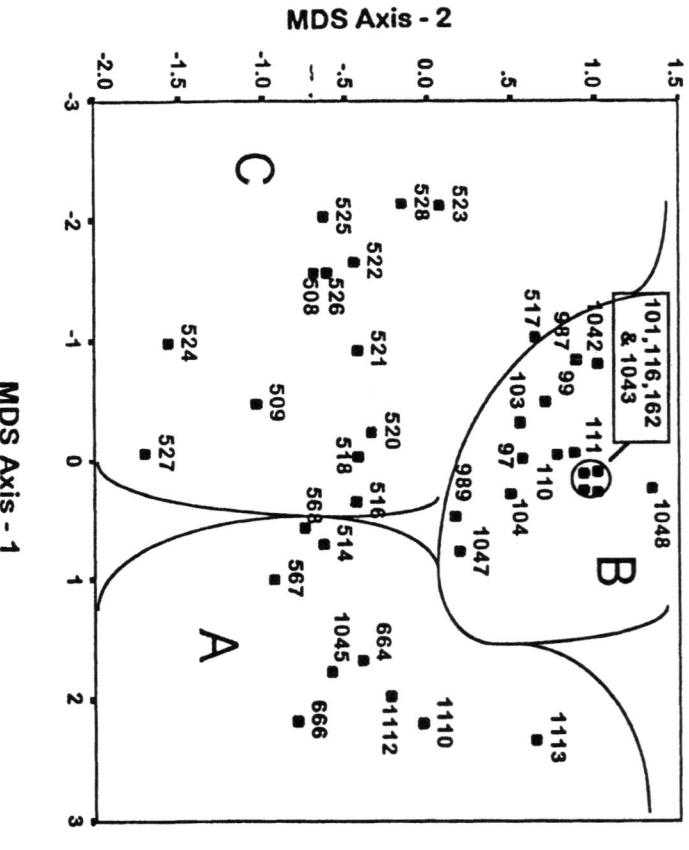

Figure 5.6 A two dimensional sample map of the data described in the text, produced by Q-mode MDS. The pattern of sample positions is very similar to that seen in Fig. 5.4 for PCA. The envelopes drawn map the clusters defined in Fig. 5.1.

Table 5.4 Discriminant function coefficients and classification results (example data).

Variable name	Standarized discriminant function coefficients
MELON_ZA	1.015
Q_JUGOS	1.056
ROSA_BRT	1.636
ROSA_FLE	1.097
SPIROL_A	0.512
MARTNOT	0.889

		Code	Predicted group membership		Total
			1.00	2.00	
Count	1.00		15	0	15
	2.00		0	13	13
	Ungrouped cases		8	2	10
%	1.00		100.0	0.0	100.0
	2.00		0.0	100.0	100.0
	Ungrouped cases		80.0	20.0	100.0

arate these samples by depth alone were not successful). The deeper samples (not originally coded), although primarily classified by the DFA as sandy, do include one intermediate and one fine-grained sample.

5.7 REGRESSION ANALYSIS

Regression analysis is principally concerned with predicting the mean expected value of one variable ('dependent variable') from one or more explanatory variables ('independent variables'). The model for the predictive relationship is a linear function of the independent variables as shown below:

$$Y = b_0 + b_1 X_1 + b_2 X_2 + \cdots + b_p X_p + e,$$

where Y = dependent variable, X = independent variable, b = regression coefficient (b_0 is intercept), e = error or residual.

Note that although the form of the regression model is linear, the relationship between the

Regression analysis

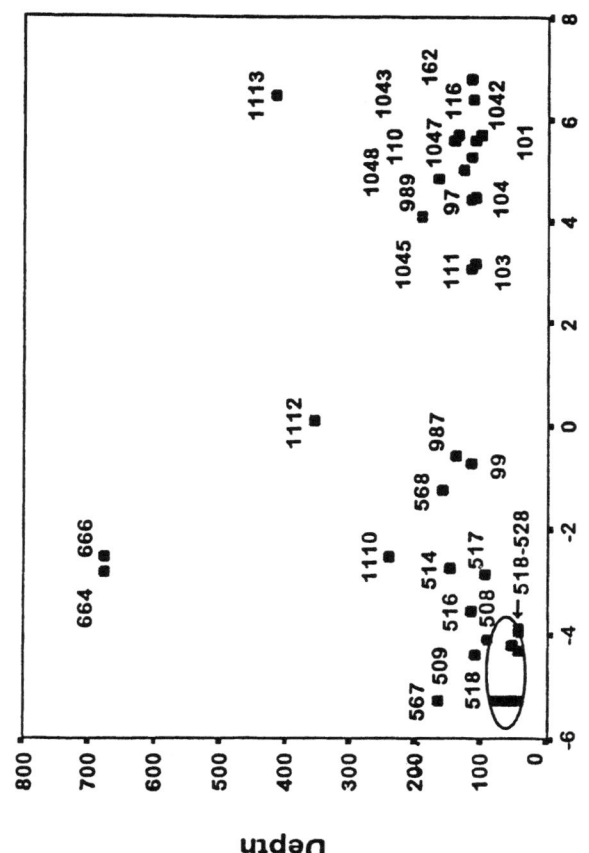

Discriminant Scores from Function 1

Figure 5.7 A plot of discriminant function scores versus sample depth for the data described in the text (see Table 5.4 for coefficients and classification results). The samples were discriminated using sediment texture (coarse- vs. fine-grained), yielding two groups of samples at opposite ends of the function axis. Note that both these groups fall into the 0–200 m depth range (possibly explaining why attempts to separate the samples purely on depth were unsuccessful).

independent and dependent variables may be nonlinear. For example, any independent variable X_i can be replaced with X_i^2 or $\ln(X_i)$. The values of independent variables are assumed to be known precisely and the dependent variable is assumed to be normally distributed for any set of independent variables. In the common Ordinary Least Squares (OLS) approach, the coefficients (b's) are chosen so as to minimize the sums of squares of the error terms (e's). Packaged regression analysis routines not only estimate the coefficient terms (b's) but also the standard errors of the coefficients. Coefficients with large standard errors may be insignificantly different from 0.0 (checked with a t-test), and therefore contribute little to the prediction. In addition, an analysis of variance (ANOVA) for the entire regression will indicate whether the predictive equation represents a significant partitioning of variance in the dependent variable. The residuals (differences between the predicted and observed values of the dependent variable) should be inspected for heteroscedasticity (a pattern in their variance) which would suggest an inappropriate choice in the form of the regression model. Because all of the coefficients have standard errors, the confidence limits for the equation as a predictor of the dependent variable are notably 'vase-shaped,' with 'tightest' confidence limits near the mean of each independent and larger limits near the extremes (i.e. the predicted values will be most precise near the means of the predictors).

If the independent variables are highly correlated (multicollinearity), then fewer than the expected number of independents is needed for an efficient prediction equation. Calculation of a regression equation with correlated independents can lead to instability in the coefficients (e.g. coefficients may change radically with the addition or subtraction of a single datum). Stepwise regression, a process that sequentially adds or deletes independents to produce the most efficient regression equation, solves the dilemma of selecting the most efficient subset of independent predictors.

Quantitative methods of data analysis in foraminiferal ecology

Interpretation of regression results can take many forms. For example, the regression can be used to specify a trend, which can then be analyzed separately from the deviations (residuals). In foraminiferal research, multiple regression analysis is commonly used to predict physical and chemical environmental parameters from sample loadings in Q-mode PCA or FA (e.g. Giraudeau and Rogers, 1994; Mudie et al., 1984), the regression equations then becoming transfer functions. This use of the procedure benefits from the orthogonal nature of the PC's such that no multicollinearity should occur. Other possible uses include trend surface analysis, where the independent variables record dimensions of a 'space' (e.g. map coordinates and/or depth and/or time), in which the dependent variable records the values of a presumably continuous function (e.g. an environmental variable or species density). The regression equation specifies a multidimensional 'surface' describing the regional trend in the dependent variable, while the residuals indicate local deviations from the trend. Both the regional trend and the pattern of local deviations may be of interest. Table 5.5 shows the results of regression

(SPSS for Windows 7.5.1) of sample scores for the previous sample data PCA against natural log of depth (regression against linear depth was also significant, but with substantially smaller R^2). The adjusted R^2 values show that almost 80% of the variance in depth can be predicted or explained using a 'transfer function' consisting of PC1 and PC3. The form of the transfer function is

$$\ln depth = 4.751 - 0.554 * PC1 \text{ score} - 0.274 * PC3 \text{ score}$$

A comparison of true and predicted depth is shown in Fig. 5.8. Samples plotting above and to the left of a diagonal through the graph have positive residuals and have predicted depths higher than real, those to the lower right have negative residuals and under-predicted depths. Table 5.6 shows the results of a stepwise regression of the species abundance data against log depth. Here six independent variables (species) are included, yielding an adjusted R^2 of 0.939, and almost 94% of depth variance explained. Fig. 5.9 shows a comparison of true versus predicted depths with much smaller residuals. Note that

Table 5.5 Transfer function regression model summary (example data).

Model summary

Model	R	R^2	Adjusted R^2	Std. error of the estimate
1	0.804	0.647	0.637	0.4149
2	0.897	0.805	0.794	0.3127

Dependent variable: LNDEPTH.

Coefficients

Model		Unstandardized coefficients		Standardized coefficients	t	Sig.
		B	Std. error	Beta		
1	(Constant)	4.751	0.067		70.588	0.000
	PC 1 scores	−0.554	0.068	−0.804	−0.8124	0.000
2	(Constant)	4.751	0.051		93.643	0.000
	PC 1 scores	−0.554	0.051	−0.804	−10.777	0.000
	PC 3 scores	−0.274	0.051	−0.397	−5.325	0.000

Dependent variable: LNDEPTH.

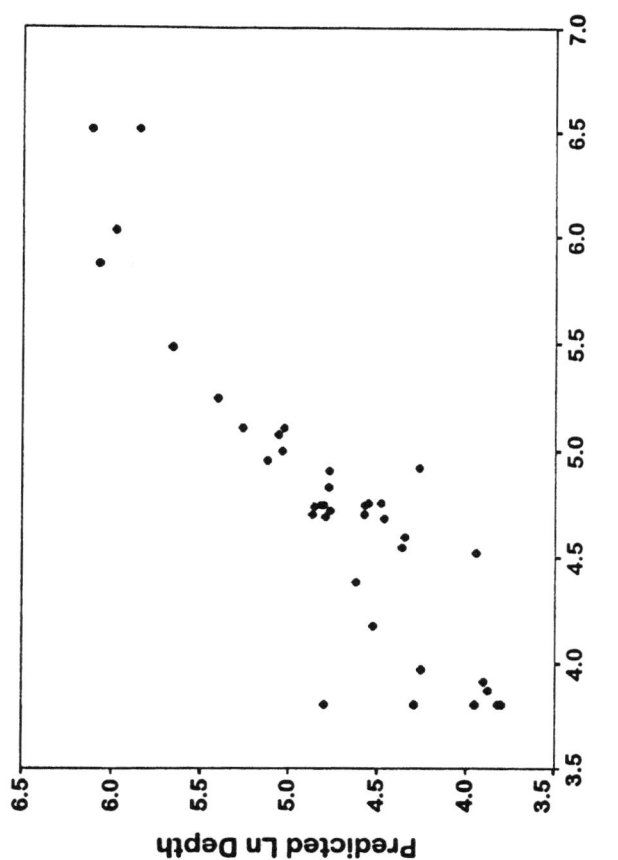

Figure 5.8 A plot of true sample depth versus depth predicted by a transfer function for the data discussed in the text. The transfer function was generated through linear regression of the natural log of sample depth on PCA scores. Adjusted R^2 = 0.794 (see Table 5.5).

although only six species' abundances were deemed sufficient for prediction of depth, other species may also be strongly depth-dependent.

5.8 ROADS LESS TRAVELED

There are a number of techniques in use in other areas of earth and life sciences which have potential for application to foraminiferal studies, but have yet to be commonly employed by researchers. Some of these methods suffer from a lack of inclusion in software packages, others from obscure backgrounds. Since they are not in common use, we will mention them only briefly, but the interested researcher may find value in some of these techniques.

Polar ordination is a data reduction technique developed by plant ecologists (Orloci, 1978; applied to fossil assemblages by Cisne and Rabe, 1978) which places entities in a limited dimensional space, the axes of which are defined by select entities from the original data. It can be operated in either Q- or R-mode, and interpreted much like PCA or MDS. It has the advantage of being less perturbed by outlier entities (those with little in common with the rest of the data), but is handicapped by a limited number of non-orthogonal axes. However, it has produced excellent results with ecological data, and has the distinct advantage that the endpoints of the axes are represented by 'real' entities, rather than by calculated associations.

Recurrent group analysis (Sen Gupta and Hayes, 1979) attempts to define groups of species which co-occur in a statistically significant number of samples. Working with presence/absence, it is somewhat similar to cluster analysis. Unavailable in common statistical packages, it has seen limited usage. Sen Gupta and Hayes (1979) used it for groups of species on the Georgia shelf and Grand Banks, and compared it to cluster analysis, finding that recurrent group analysis gave a better fit to species diversity

Table 5.6 Results of step-wise regression (example data).

Model summary

Model	R	R^2	Adjusted R^2	Std. error of the estimate
1	0.869	0.755	0.749	0.3453
2	0.920	0.846	0.837	0.2784
3	0.946	0.895	0.886	0.2327
4	0.957	0.917	0.906	0.2107
5	0.969	0.939	0.930	0.1823
6	0.974	0.949	0.939	0.1703

Coefficients

Model 6	Unstandardized coefficients B	Unstandardized coefficients Std. error	Standardized coefficients Beta	t	Sig.
(Constant)	5.109	0.073		70.224	0.000
MDS 1	0.349	0.046	0.608	7.530	0.000
EPON_TUM	0.484	0.052	0.440	9.218	0.000
NODOBC_A	0.101	0.029	0.206	3.516	0.001
STILOSTO	0.318	0.068	0.230	4.676	0.000
PLACPS_C	−8.340E-02	0.021	−0.216	−3.942	0.000
RCTOBOL	6.099E-02	0.026	0.107	2.384	0.023

Dependent variable: LNDEPTH.
Models 1–5 omitted for brevity.

gradients and identified patterns of group distribution that correlated with water depth and sediment type.

Kriging, developed in geology, is a method of analyzing regionalized data (data sampled at discrete locations, but with a continuous distribution over a spatial region). It can be used to estimate values of regionalized variates at unsampled locations, or to analyze the pattern of increase in variance between two observations with increasing separation distance. Having many of the same applications as regression (specifically, trend surface analysis), it differs in that the regionalized variate need not be modeled as a specific linear function. In addition, confidence limits are not as sensitive to the position within the region. Described in Isaaks and Srivastava (1989), kriging has seen little application in paleontological research.

5.9 CONCLUSION

For a researcher approaching quantitative analysis for the first time, or for one considering the expansion of a limited repertoire of techniques, the variety of different techniques and options available may initially seem overwhelming and undecipherable. In general, if the researcher believes that the data set contains natural groupings, and wishes to define these numerically, then cluster analysis or recurrent group analysis are recommended. If some or all of the members of the groups are known *a priori*, and the researcher wishes to classify unknowns or quantify the differences between the groups, then DFA is recommended. If the researcher is investigating underlying structure independent of groupings, then PCA, FA, correspondence analysis, MDS, or polar ordination are recommended. If the

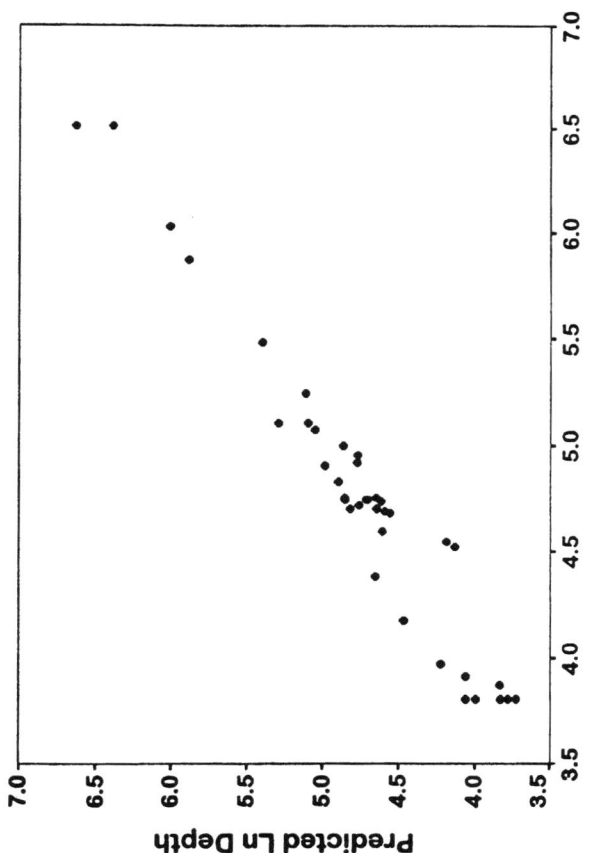

Figure 5.9 A plot of true sample depth versus depth predicted by a step-wise linear regression for the data discussed in the text. The procedure regressed the natural log of sample depth on species abundances, yielding a model involving six variables (species). Adjusted $R^2 = 0.939$ (see Table 5.6).

researcher wishes to use underlying relationships to predict values or compare prediction models with observed values, then regression analysis or kriging is recommended.

This chapter has provided only the briefest introduction to what techniques are available and in use in the field of foraminiferal research. The references cited, along with the software packages available, will give more detailed descriptions of specific methods. In closing, we leave the reader with a single caveat: Remember that no statistical technique or software routine, no matter how complex or expensive, can take the place of a deep understanding of the data and the processes being studied.

PART II: FEATURES OF DISTRIBUTION

6

Biogeography of neritic benthic Foraminifera

Stephen J. Culver and Martin A. Buzas

6.1 INTRODUCTION

Biogeographical studies (the distribution of organisms, present and past, and the historical and ecological processes that cause these distributions) are a natural extension of systematics. At the highest level of the systematic hierarchy, Kingdom, we recognize a ubiquitous geographic distribution of organisms. As we proceed downward to the lower members of the systematic hierarchy, discrete geographic distributions emerge. Recognizing patterns of distribution and attempting to explain them is the domain of the biogeographer. However, the recognition of pattern depends upon our definition of what constitutes pattern(s), what systematic level we are examining, and at what geographic scale. Likewise, explanation requires a historical as well as an ecological perspective. These considerations, coupled with the vast variety and numbers of organisms, insure a lack of simplicity or unification of the subject.

At the species level, differences in distribution with depth and latitude are readily apparent for most benthic marine organisms, including the Foraminifera. If we were to list desirable attributes for an organism at the Class or Order level that would ideally suit it for biogeographic studies at the species level, we might list: 1, ubiquitous distribution; 2, easily sampled; 3, high density; 4, many species; 5, good preservation providing an excellent fossil record; 6, large number of researchers; and 7, many years of study. Curiously, the benthic Foraminifera have all of these attributes and yet they have received very little attention for biogeographic studies. North America is the exception in that Culver and Buzas (1980, 1981a, 1982a, 1985, 1986, 1987) compiled and taxonomically standardized all the existing data on the distribution of benthic Foraminifera around the margins of the North American continent. We will use this data set to gain some understanding of the biogeography of neritic benthic Foraminifera, but first we will briefly review two worldwide provincial schemes.

6.2 GLOBAL BIOGEOGRAPHY

6.2.1 Cushman's faunas

Joseph Cushman's knowledge and experience with Foraminifera led him to recognize general distribution patterns for different groups (Cushman, 1948). For example, he noted that lagenids characterize continental shelves, miliolids (with some deep water exceptions such as *Pyrgo*) are most abundant in shallow warm-water, coral reef regions, while larger benthic foraminifera are essentially restricted to tropical waters less than 60 m deep. Cushman considered that temperature is the predominant controlling factor of benthic foraminiferal distributions. This led him to a global subdivision into cold-water and warm-water faunas (Fig. 6.1a, b; Cushman, 1948, map dated 1921).

The distribution of cold-water faunas is obviously relatable to cold oceanic currents (e.g. southern extension of cold faunas on the western sides of the North Atlantic and North Pacific; Fig. 6.1a). Cushman noted that although the Antarctic region has its own characteristic species, faunas there are very similar to those in the Arctic (species lists given in Murray, 1991b, suggest this is an over-simplification). Cushman also recognized the extension of cold-water faunas into the ocean basins, most of the information for this conclusion deriving from Brady's (1884) *Challenger* Report.

Warm-water faunas were recognized by Cushman (1948) to be less cosmopolitan; he drew four subdivisions but noted that there could be more (Fig. 6.1b). These are essentially shallow-water faunas as indicated by the extension of the West Indian fauna from Florida to Bermuda and across the Atlantic to the coast of Ireland. The Mediterranean fauna extends into the shallow margins of the Red Sea, and the Atlantic and Indian Ocean margins of Africa. Warm-water faunas around the islands of the Indian Ocean (East African fauna) were distinguished by Cushman from the generally more diverse East Indian fauna of the Pacific Ocean (Fig. 6.1b).

Cushman (1948) believed that although temperature controls benthic foraminiferal distributions, historical factors, such as Tertiary migrations, are of great importance in explaining modern distribution patterns. Cushman noted that the faunas of the Caribbean region are much more like those of Australia than of other tropical regions. Similarly, he pointed out that the cold-water fauna of the west coast of South America is more like that of northern Europe than of the much closer Pacific island groups. These patterns were attributed to earlier migrations rather than modern oceanographic conditions.

6.2.2 Boltovskoy and Wright's provinces

Boltovskoy and Wright (1976) concurred with Cushman's ideas concerning the importance of temperature and migrations in explaining the biogeography of neritic benthic foraminifera. They refined Cushman's map using the data published in many papers during the 1950s to 1970s and recognized 17 provinces, seven characterized by warm-water species, two by cold-water species, and eight by temperate-water species (Fig. 6.2). Boltovskoy and Wright (1976) noted that where enough data were available, division into subprovinces was possible but a subprovincial scheme was given only for South America (subsequently elaborated upon in Boltovskoy et al., 1980).

There is great similarity between Cushman's and Boltovskoy and Wright's provincial schemes. West Indian, Mediterranean, East African, and Indo-Pacific provinces are recognized in both, but Boltovskoy and Wright distinguished Lusitanian and West African faunas from those of the Mediterranean. Similarly, they distinguished Panamanian and West Indian provinces. Cushman and Boltovskoy and Wright also recognized Arctic and Antarctic provinces but the greatest difference between the two schemes is in the temperate regions where Boltovskoy and Wright (1976) recognized eight distinct provinces. The pattern of shading on Cushman's map (Fig. 6.1a) suggests that he considered these temperate regions to be transitional between cold- and warm-water provinces (Cushman, 1948).

6.3 BIOGEOGRAPHY OF NORTH AND CENTRAL AMERICA

6.3.1 Background

Like Cushman (1948), Boltovskoy and Wright (1976) did not indicate in detail the criteria used

Biogeography of North and Central America

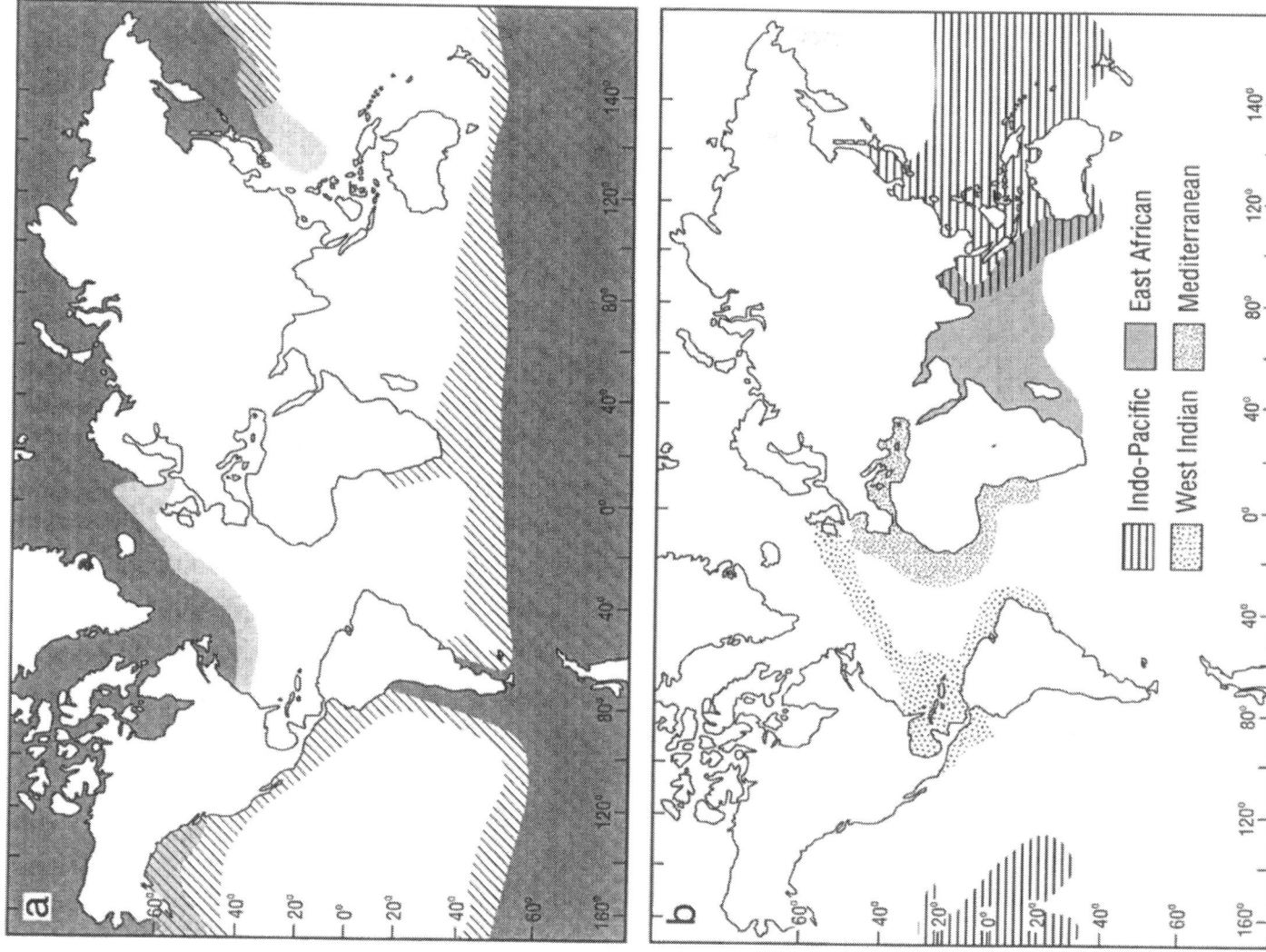

Figure 6.1 Distribution of (a) cold-water and (b) warm-water benthic foraminiferal faunas (after Cushman, 1948).

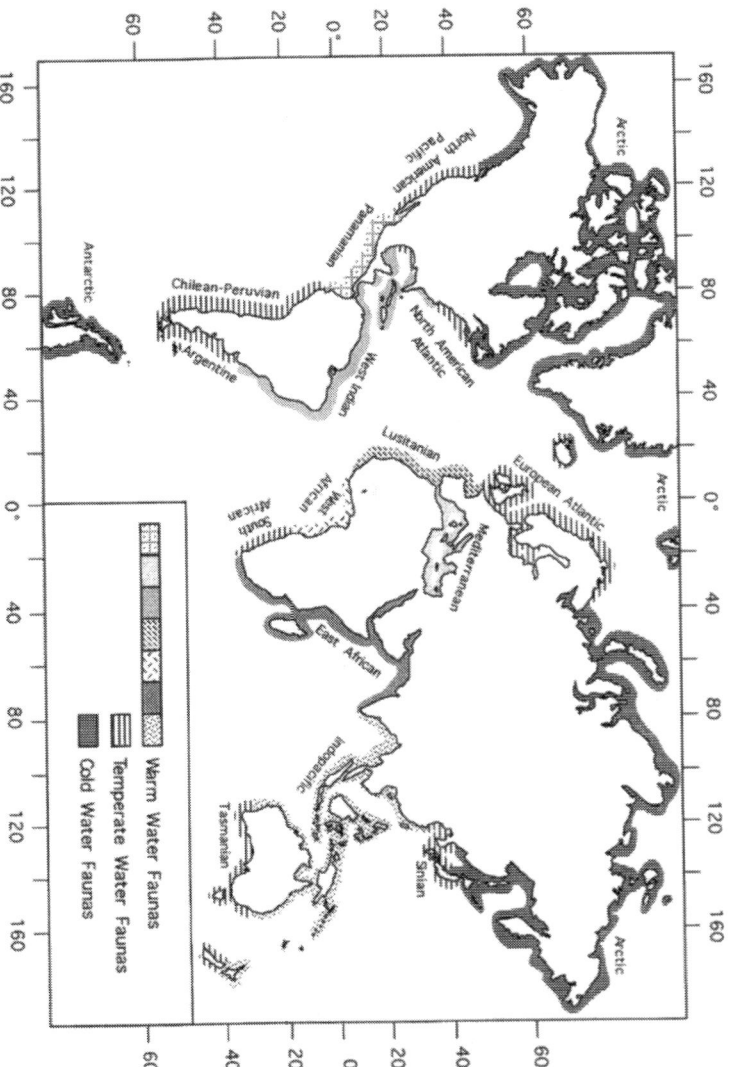

Figure 6.2 Benthic foraminiferal zoogeography of continental shelves (after Boltovskoy and Wright, 1976).

to distinguish provinces and subprovinces or to define the location of provincial and subprovincial boundaries. However, their provincial scheme is very similar to that produced by Hedgpeth (1957b) for macroorganisms of the littoral zones of the world. Boltovskoy and Wright (1976) did not consider this to be surprising, given the fact that similar controlling factors were involved. They did note, however, that differences could be best explained by differences in regional geological history.

Hedgpeth (1957b) was following the lead given by famous predecessors in the field of marine macrofaunal biogeography (e.g. Milne-Edwards, 1838; Dana, 1853; Woodward, 1856; Ekman, 1953). These workers classified the shallow seas of the world into realms and provinces based on the degree of endemism within the species inhabiting a province. But the amount of endemism necessary to recognize a province has varied greatly. Woodward (1856) considered a province to be characterized by greater than 50% endemic species. Later workers (e.g. Kauffman and Scott, 1976) reduced this figure to 25 to 50% endemism (as low as 20% in practice), while Briggs (1974) considered 10% endemism to be sufficient.

When Culver and Buzas embarked on a project in 1978 to study the biogeography of modern benthic Foraminifera from the continental margins of North and Central America, they chose to identify provinces using the more flexible definition of provinces proposed by Valentine (1968, p. 257) namely, '... collections of communities associated in space and time.' They also chose to recognize provinces using the numerical technique of cluster analysis rather than relying on experience and/or visual examination of distributional data.

The amount of information on the distribution of modern benthic Foraminifera around North America is vast. Several hundred publications (Culver, 1980) contain relevant material, and the database has continued to grow. The majority of these data were compiled during the 1950s and 1960s in response to the pressure to locate oil and gas. It was realized that a knowledge of the distribution of modern Foraminifera would help interpretation of foraminiferal assemblages recovered from well-cuttings. Studies such as those by Phleger and Parker (1951), Parker (1954), and many others fulfilled this need.

Culver and Buzas constructed databases containing all of the published distributional data for all benthic foraminiferal species names ever recorded from the continental margins of North America. These data were published in volumes for the Atlantic continental margin (Culver and Buzas, 1980), the Gulf of Mexico (Culver and Buzas, 1981a), the Caribbean (Culver and Buzas, 1982a), and the Pacific continental margin from Alaska to Panama (Culver and Buzas, 1985, 1986, 1987). Data were also compiled for the Arctic margin of North America but remain unpublished.

Because the methodologies employed by authors over the years were quite variable (e.g. sampling equipment, sieve size, live or dead, absolute abundances or percent or presence-absence data, etc.), Culver and Buzas' compilations utilized presence-absence data. No information points were deleted. Some geographic locations were represented by only one species whereas others had scores of species. Where small areas had been intensively sampled, the data were combined so that a single locality represented all of those stations.

The problem with compilations is the inconsistency of the incorporated data. Utilizing a presence-absence approach ameliorates this problem but, without doubt, the most significant problem is taxonomic inconsistency. To address this problem, Culver and Buzas conducted an exhaustive process of taxonomic standardization. For example, by using the literature and extensive collections in the Smithsonian Institution, Washington, D.C., The Natural History Museum, London, and several other institutions, the 1303 species names used by authors for species found on the Atlantic continental margin were reduced to 876. Similar reductions were made on the other continental margins. It is likely that no other foraminiferologist would agree with all of the taxonomic decisions that were made (all taxonomic changes were documented in the publications), but the resulting data set was standardized and, indeed, if errors were included (and they undoubtedly were), the scale of the data set meant that it, and the patterns that were subsequently recognized, were robust.

In addition to distributional data, Culver and Buzas (1980, 1981a, 1982a, 1985, 1986, 1987) provided maps showing the geographic and bathymetric distribution of the most commonly occurring species on the various continental margins. Cluster analysis (more elegant statistical procedures were not appropriate for such a heterogeneous database) resulted in the recognition of several provinces on each continental margin (Buzas and Culver 1980, 1990; Culver and Buzas, 1981b,c, 1982b, 1983).

Shallow-water provinces were similar to those recognized for other organisms, but depth-related provinces were also evident (e.g. Culver and Buzas, 1982b). Indeed, the faunal differences between shallow (<200 m) and deep (>200 m) provinces at the same latitude were greater than between adjacent shallow-water provinces (Culver and Buzas, 1981b, 1982b).

This succession of provinces with increasing depth was most evident on the passive continental margins of the Atlantic and the Gulf of Mexico. A similar pattern was present on the active Pacific margin but was less well developed, probably due to the relative narrowness of the continental margin and the more patchy distribution of data points. Culver and Buzas (1981b, 1983) related the depth-related provincial boundaries to water-mass boundaries and speculated (Buzas and Culver, 1982) that there may be as many provinces in the marine world as there are water masses impinging on the seafloor.

The next section will deal only with provinces on the continental shelves around North and Central America and will compare their config-

6.3.2 Neritic provinces

Figure 6.3 diagrammatically indicates the eleven provinces that Culver and Buzas recognized in the shelf waters of North and Central America. Clear boundaries are evident along the generally north–south Pacific and Atlantic margins but the boundaries between the Arctic Province (1) and the Aleutian (2) and Atlantic Northern Inner Shelf Province (10) are not clearly defined. The southern extensions of the Panamanian Province (5) and Caribbean Province (= West Indian Province, 6) are detailed in Boltovskoy and Wright (1976). The entire width of the open continental shelf is the site of a single province around most of the continental margins, but on the broad shelves of the Gulf of Mexico, and on the Atlantic margin north of Cape Hatteras, outer shelf or upper slope provinces are present on the Atlantic margin north of Cape Hatteras, where slope waters impinge on the outer shelf (Culver and Buzas, 1981b, 1983).

The characteristic faunas of the eleven provinces are given in the various Culver and Buzas papers and, for the Arctic, in Vilks (1989), and need not be repeated here. However, it is interesting to compare the benthic foraminiferal provinces with those recognized for the benthic macrofauna around North and Central America. Valentine (1966) summarized the provincial schemes proposed by various mollusc workers for the Pacific shelf of North and Central America. Despite differences, all workers, including Valentine, recognized important provincial boundaries at the Strait of Juan de Fuca, Point Conception, and Cabo San Lucas (Fig. 6.3). In their study of isopods, Brusca and Wallerstein (1979) noted the same important boundaries, but also recognized a Cortez Province (in the Gulf of California) and a Mexican Province from Tangola Tangola to Cabo San Lucas (Fig. 6.3). They also recognized a transitional zone between Cabo San Lucas and Punta Eugenio, a region recognized as the Surian Province by Valentine (1976) in a study of ostracod biogeography. Valentine (1976) also recognized Oregonian, Californian, and Panamanian provinces and subprovinces within them. Major changes in foraminiferal faunas also occur at the Strait of Juan de Fuca, Point Conception and Cabo San Lucas (Fig. 6.3), but subprovinces recognized by Valentine (1976) and Brusca and Wallerstein (1979) are not evident in the foraminiferal data (Lankford and Phleger, 1973; Crouch and Poag, 1987; Buzas and Culver, 1990).

The Caribbean and Gulf of Mexico regions have also been subject to various provincial classifications based on macrofaunal data. Hall (1964), working with molluscs, included both areas in a single Caribbean Province, whereas other mollusc workers (Rehder, 1954; Warmke and Abbott, 1961) included the southern tip of Florida and the southern half of the Gulf of Mexico together with the Caribbean region in a Caribbean Province. The benthic Foraminifera of the shallow waters around the Caribbean islands and along the northern coast of south and Central America cannot be subdivided at this scale (Culver and Buzas, 1982a). Together with the carbonate substrate faunas of the Yucatan, southern Florida, and the Bahamas, they constitute a Caribbean Province. This is distinct in foraminiferal composition from the Gulf of Mexico Inner Shelf Province (Culver and Buzas, 1982b; Buzas and Culver, 1982).

Some macrofaunal workers have distinguished northern and southern shelf areas in the Gulf of Mexico and have assigned them to Carolinian and Caribbean provinces, respectively, with a boundary at Cabo Rojo (Fig. 6.3) (Hedgpeth, 1953). Foraminiferal distribution patterns in the Gulf of Mexico are largely concentric (Culver and Buzas, 1981c; Poag, 1981) and the faunas of the Gulf of Mexico Inner Shelf Province are as distinct from faunas south of Cape Hatteras (Fig. 6.3) (the macrofaunal Carolinian Province) as they are from those of the Caribbean Province (Culver and Buzas, 1982b; Buzas and Culver 1982).

The foraminiferal data agree with those for macrofauna in placing the carbonate substrate southern tip of Florida, between Cape Romano

Biogeography of North and Central America

Figure 6.3 Benthic foraminiferal shelf provinces around North and Central America 1, Arctic Province; 2, Aleutian Province; 3, Oregonian Province; 4, Californian Province; 5, Panamanian Province; 6, Caribbean Province; 7, Gulf of Mexico Inner Shelf Province; 8, Gulf of Mexico Outer Shelf and Slope Province; 9, Atlantic Southern Shelf Province; 10, Atlantic Northern Inner Shelf Province; 11, Atlantic Northern Outer Shelf and Slope Province. Geographic locations: a, Strait of Juan de Fuca; b, Cape Mendocino; c, Point Conception; d, Punta Eugenio; e, Cabo San Lucas; f, Tangola Tangola (Puerta Angel); g, Yucatan; h, Cabo Rojo; i, Cape Romano; j, Cape Canaveral; k, Cape Hatteras; l, Cape Cod; m, Grand Banks; n, Axel Heiberg shelf; o, Beaufort Sea

and south of Cape Canaveral (Fig. 6.3), in a Caribbean Province. Between Cape Canaveral and Cape Hatteras, the distinctive foraminiferal assemblage comprises the Atlantic Southern Shelf Province (Fig. 6.3), equivalent to the Atlantic portion of the macrofaunal Carolinian Province (Hedgpeth, 1953). The shelf macrofaunas north of Cape Hatteras have been subdivided into Virginian and Acadian (= Nova Scotian) Provinces with the boundary at Cape Cod (e.g. Dana, 1853; Hall, 1864; Maturo, 1968). Several foraminiferal workers followed this scheme (e.g. Cushman, 1948; Parker, 1948; Murray, 1973), but Culver and Buzas (1981b) did not make this distinction and recognized a single Atlantic Northern Inner Shelf Province stretching from Cape Hatteras to the Grand Banks off Newfoundland (Fig. 6.3). Several mollusc workers concur with this provincial classification (Coomans, 1962; Franz and Merrill, 1980).

The neritic environments of the Canadian Arctic Archipelago and northern Alaska are placed within the Arctic Province (Fig. 6.3). In review papers, Lagoe (1979) and Vilks (1989) noted that the foraminiferal faunas from water depths of less than 200 m were generally dominated by agglutinated Foraminifera, thus distinguishing them from faunas of the Aleutian Province and the Atlantic Northern Shelf Province. This pattern is not ubiquitous, however, and some regions, e.g. the Beaufort shelf (Fig. 6.3; Vilks, 1989) and the Axel Heiberg shelf (Schröder-Adams et al., 1990) are dominated by calcareous species, and may exhibit quite high diversity.

At the beginning of this chapter, we described Cushman's (1948) and Boltovskoy and Wright's (1976) global provincial schemes for shelf Foraminifera which indicated temperature as the major controlling factor for species distributions, an opinion shared by Hedgpeth (1957b) and Murray (1991b). While acknowledging the important role of temperature as an environmental variable, it is worth noting that many provincial boundaries are located at headlands (Fig. 6.3) associated with oceanographic boundaries. Thus, many workers have related the large-scale distribution of shelf Foraminifera to water-mass distributions (e.g. Lankford and Phleger, 1973; Buzas and Culver, 1980, 1990; Culver and Buzas, 1981c; Crouch and Poag, 1987).

Figure 6.4 illustrates the relationship between water masses and benthic foraminiferal provinces from shelf to abyssal depths in the Gulf of Mexico and on the Atlantic continental margin. The Gulf of Mexico Inner Shelf Province (Fig. 6.4) is associated with the surface mixed layer whose transitional boundary with the underlying Subtropical Underwater lies at 100 to 200 m, the depth limit of seasonal effects on water-mass characteristics (Phleger and Parker, 1954; Nowlin and Parker, 1974). The Gulf of Mexico Outer Shelf and Slope Province is related to several layered water masses (Fig. 6.4). Where these impinge upon the outer shelf and upper slope, changes in foraminiferal assemblages occur (Culver, 1988), but these are considered to represent biofacies variations within a province (Culver and Buzas, 1983).

On the Atlantic continental margin, the Atlantic Southern Shelf Province is related to Southern Shelf Water (Fig. 6.4). North of Cape Hatteras, the shelf is overlain by the much cooler Northern Shelf Water, and this is reflected in the significant change to the neritic foraminiferal assemblages of the Atlantic Northern Inner Shelf Province. Slope water overlies the slope but impinges on the outer shelf, and this overlies the Atlantic Northern Outer Shelf and Slope Province (Culver and Buzas, 1981b).

6.4 CENTERS OF ORIGIN AND DISPERSAL OF BENTHIC FORAMINIFERA

The concept of centers of origin for species has been extensively discussed in the literature of biogeography and evolution (e.g. McCoy and Heck, 1983) and the Antarctic (Zinsmeister and Feldmann, 1984) have been proposed as possible centers of origin, the tropics usually have this characteristic attributed to them (e.g. Durazzi and Stehli, 1972; Briggs, 1974; Pielou, 1979), with newly evolved species dispersing to the higher latitudes. Thus, on the Atlantic continental margin of North America one could hypothesise enhanced origination of benthic foraminiferal species in the Caribbean Province. Buzas and Culver (1986; 1989) examined this hypothesis by documenting the worldwide dis-

Centers of origin and dispersal of benthic Foraminifera

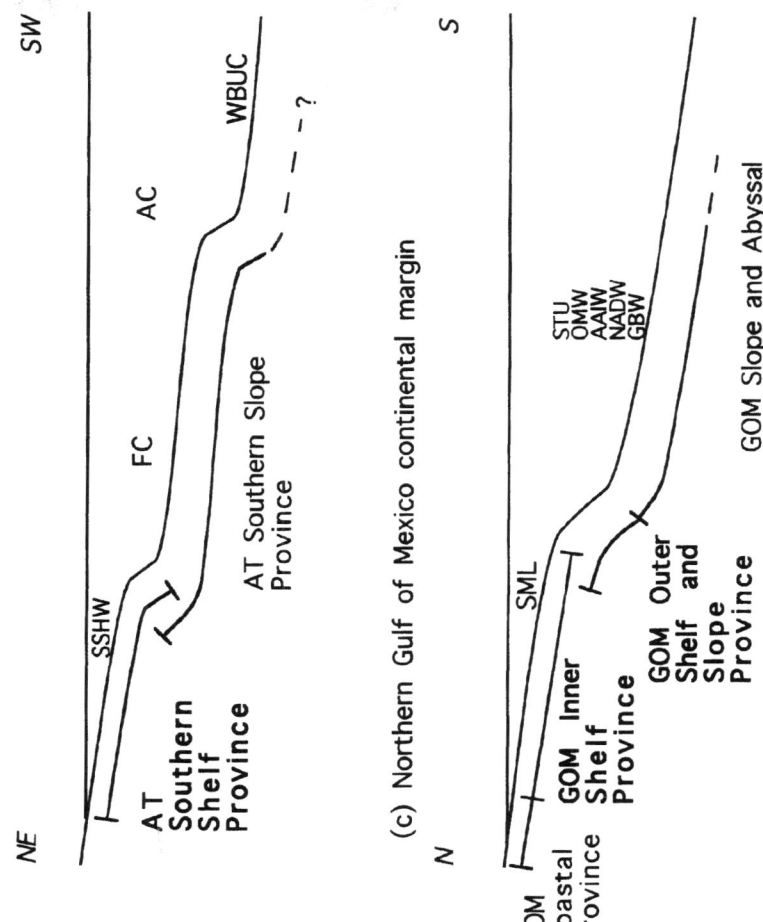

Figure 6.4 Profiles across continental margins of eastern North America, (a) northern Atlantic, (b) southern Atlantic, and (c) the northern Gulf of Mexico, showing the relationship between water masses and benthic foraminiferal provinces (not to scale); provinces in bold discussed in text. Water masses and currents: (a) CW, Coastal Water; NSHW, Northern Shelf water; SW, Slope Water; GS, Gulf Stream; SAW, Sargasso Water; ABW, Arctic Bottom Water; AABW, Antarctic Bottom Water; GOM, Gulf of Mexico; AT, Atlantic; (b) SSHW, Southern Shelf Water; FC, Florida Current; AC, Antilles Current; WBUC, Western Boundary Undercurrent; (c) SML, Surface Mixed Layer; STU, Subtropical Underwater; OMW, Oxygen Minimum Water; AIW, Antarctic Intermediate Water; NADW, North American Deep Water; GBW, Gulf Basin Water.

tribution of first reliable stratigraphic occurrences of all modern species recorded on the North American Atlantic continental margin. They found that modern species of benthic Foraminifera have originated in all parts of the world's oceans from the Cretaceous to the Pleistocene (Buzas and Culver, 1989). Possible concentrations of first occurrences in the Miocene of the Caribbean region were considered to be monographic effects. The Pleistocene was characterized by many more high-latitude occurrences but this, again, was considered to be due to one significant paper. Further, the apparent trend of more high latitude originations as climatic cooling occurred during the Neogene was believed to be the result of the distribution of outcrops of that age. Buzas and Culver (1989) concluded that the available data do not support a simple concept of a center of origin for modern benthic foraminiferal species from the North American Atlantic continental margin.

The data used to investigate centers of origin showed that first occurrences were often recorded in more than one place. This could be explained by poor stratigraphic control, but in the Pleistocene, where greater resolution is possible, several species were first recorded in Alaska and Maine in deposits of the same age. Buzas and Culver (1989) considered this to be the result of rapid dispersal, instantaneous in terms of our powers of resolution. Thus, this dispersal ability means that vicariance events, although important in some instances, such as the formation of the Isthmus of Panama, are probably factors of little importance to benthic foraminiferal biogeography.

The dispersal ability of continental margin benthic Foraminifera was further investigated by Buzas and Culver (1991). They showed that 53 of 878 species that currently occur on the North American Atlantic continental margin are ubiquitous around North and Central America even though they have no fossil record. Most of these are abundant and would have been found in the well-documented Cenozoic deposits around the North American margins if they had existed in the past. Buzas and Culver (1991) concluded that these taxa must have evolved recently and dispersed rapidly.

6.5 SUMMARY

Large-scale biogeographic distributions of benthic Foraminifera of the world's shelves exhibit a pattern that indicates a major controlling role for temperature at this scale. Cold-, temperate-, and warm-water groupings of provinces have been recognized around the world, with a greater number of provinces delineated in warmer regions. Modern provincial patterns, however, have also been influenced by differences in regional geological histories.

The continental margins of North and Central America have been subject to the most intensive biogeographic investigations, and eleven benthic foraminiferal provinces have been recognized in the neritic zone. Their distribution and boundaries can be closely related to the distribution and boundaries of major water masses. Thus, the provincial scheme for modern benthic Foraminifera is similar to that for modern shallow marine macroorganisms. The differences suggest that benthic Foraminifera may be somewhat less sensitive to the changes in the marine climate than other benthic organisms of the neritic zone.

No center or centers of origin can be identified for the modern benthic Foraminifera of the North American Atlantic continental margin. First stratigraphic occurrences are both temporally and geographically widespread, and suggest rapid dispersal.

6.6 ACKNOWLEDGMENTS

We thank J. Jett, J. Swallow, and P. Christopher for their help. This paper is a contribution from the Natural History Museum-University College London research program in 'Global Change in the Biosphere.'

7 Biogeography of planktonic Foraminifera

Anthony J. Arnold and William C. Parker

7.1 INTRODUCTION

7.1.1 A historical perspective

It is often said that nothing makes sense in biology except in the light of evolution (Dobzhansky, 1973). It could equally well be said that little makes sense in biogeography except in the context of its historical development, since modern biogeography reflects both organismal habitat preferences and the historical processes that have culminated in modern distribution patterns.

Research on most modern plankton groups has resulted in broad agreement among many plankton biogeographers as to the disposition of large scale provinces (e.g. Backus 1986; McGowan, 1986). The frontal systems that sometimes separate these provinces often show steep environmental gradients that can correspond to faunal transitions. However, even these most conspicuous biogeographic provinces do not always show a clearly-defined relationship to physicochemical variables, and the search for the factor(s) that explain the distribution of a species or a group of species is rarely successful (Backus, 1986). Such difficulties of finding connections are usually attributed to the complexity of interaction between controlling factors, but historical considerations can also play a significant role. Work on the planktonic Foraminifera has made it increasingly clear that large scale biogeographic features such as the global diversity gradient and the latitudinally arrayed major provinces owe their existence at least partly to differential rates of speciation and extinction – processes that are inherently historical in the sense that they involve adaptation to antecedent rather than present-day conditions. It is in precisely this sense that modern biogeography cannot be separated from its evolutionary past.

Nonetheless, with rare exceptions, research on plankton biogeography has focused primarily on the relationship between species distribution patterns and the physicochemical environment they inhabit. Usually, delineating a modern biogeographic province involves quantifying species distributions along plankton tow transects, then using physicochemical properties of the environment to extrapolate over larger areas. However, when readily fossilized organisms such as the planktonic Foraminifera are involved, their stratigraphic record adds both historical dimension and complexity to the analysis; as a consequence, it becomes even more essential to develop an understanding of the issue of scale – both spatial and temporal.

For example, it is often smaller-scale factors that mediate the evolutionary origins of species, even though larger-scale considerations may constrain their distribution. To the extent that allopatry and peripheral isolation play a role in the origin of planktonic species, the present-day provincial-scale geographic range of a given species is likely to be much larger than its range at its time of origin – and yet the adaptive circumstances of that species' time and place of origin may well dictate (and explain) its present distribution. Further, if the conditions for speciation arise only rarely – say, on a geological (rather than ecological) time scale – then the full diversity potential of a given province may not yet have been reached, and the question of equilibration time arises. For reasons like these, temporal and spatial scale are central issues and fundamental organizing principles in this chapter.

Before beginning any discussion of biogeography, it is important to be aware of the taphonomic and methodological factors that can influence basic data.

7.1.2 Taphonomy and methodology
7.1.2.1

Our perceptions of foraminiferal distribution and diversity are necessarily dependent on taxonomic philosophy, which can vary considerably. There are currently approximately forty-four recognized species of Recent planktonic Foraminifera, of which twenty-one are common in the world's oceans (Hemleben *et al.*, 1989), although some specialists recognize up to sixty-four for the total number (e.g. Saito *et al.*, 1981). Data on the patterns of distribution of living planktonic Foraminifera come from three main sources: plankton tows, sediment traps, and sediment-surface samples. Data derived from plankton tows are vulnerable to methodological difficulties relating to the mesh size used in plankton nets. Berger (1969) showed that there is an inverse relationship between the cube of the mesh size and the number of planktonic Foraminifera trapped in the mesh, and provided a methodology for correcting samples to a nominal mesh size. The fact that reported abundances can vary by eight orders of magnitude, depending largely on the sampling gear used, indicates that care must be taken when making biogeographic abundance comparisons between plankton tow studies. In addition to absolute abundances, relative abundances and seasonal abundance variability also show a strong size dependency in plankton tows, which is reflected in diversity indices, multivariate statistical treatments, and even presence/absence data (Ottens, 1991).

In general, the cold water aspect of a living fauna tends to be enhanced in the sediments for two reasons. The first is an artifact of the dissimilar mesh sizes used in plankton tows versus the smaller size ranges commonly included when examining coretop samples, since the smaller size fractions tend to have a cooler aspect (Berger, 1971). The second reason stems from differential dissolution susceptibilities between species and the resulting biases thereby introduced into our perceptions of fossil biogeography (useful summaries can be found in Ruddimann, 1977, and Vincent and Berger, 1981).

Many tropical species (as well as those that are enriched in the sediments due to spring upwelling) are relatively susceptible to dissolution; the differential removal of these species increases the cold water aspect of sediment-surface assemblages (Rudimann, 1977). The effects of differential dissolution are further complicated by variations in bottom topography in relation to the position of the lysocline.

Vertical mixing, current winnowing and sorting, and displacement by turbidites, among other taphonomic effects, can introduce additional bias into the biogeographic record; these are discussed in more detail by Bé (1977), Rudimann (1977), Orr and Jenkins (1977) and in chapter 16 of this book.

The relationship between abundance in the sediments and standing abundance in the water column is distorted significantly by a number of factors, not all of them taphonomic. Species with shorter generation times have proportionally greater representation in underlying sediments (Berger and Soutar, 1967; Berger, 1970a, Berger, 1971). Current transport can displace living adult individuals outside the limits of their normal reproductive range (McGowran et al., 1997).

7.1.2.2 Transfer functions

One of the most powerful tools used in the investigation of biogeographic and paleobiogeographic patterns is the transfer function. These functions relate species abundances to their life habitats (usually abundances in sediments are related to habitat conditions in the overlying waters), and the functions are normally applied to the problem of estimating environmental characteristics from species abundance data. Subject to several assumptions, any environmental parameter, say, temperature, can be predicted. Perhaps the simplest and most direct predictive equation was proposed by Berger (1969):

$$T_{est} = \frac{\sum P_i t_i}{\sum P_i}$$

where t_i, the optimum temperature preference of the ith species, is weighted by the species' proportional representation, P_i, yielding an average optimum temperature for the assemblage. This equation has been further refined (see Berger and Gardner, 1975; Vincent and Berger, 1981), but even in its simplest form it can yield surprisingly accurate results when used to predict average sea surface temperatures. However, this approach alone cannot account for complex interaction between temperature and other parameters that influence distribution, and requires an *a priori* understanding of the optimum temperature preferences of species.

A more widely used transfer function is based on empirically derived relationships between a spectrum of environmental parameters and species abundance data; it takes the form:

$$P_{est} = k_0 + k_1 A + k_2 B + k_3 C + k_4 D + \ldots$$

where the k's are predictive coefficients (usually regression coefficients), P is an environmental parameter, say, temperature, and A,B,C, etc. are variables, which may be actual species proportions, synthetic variables consisting of grouped proportions (e.g. characteristic polar, tropical, etc. species), or variables derived from multivariate analysis of species proportions. In this case, knowledge of the optimum environmental conditions for the species is replaced by a relationship usually derived from statistical regression.

Imbrie and Kipp's (1971) classic work on Caribbean temperature fluctuation, for example, used factor analysis to extract synthetic variables consisting of tropical, subtropical, subpolar, and 'gyre margin' assemblages, which show a partial correspondence to the large-scale latitudinal provinces discussed below. It is possible to apply these synthetic variables to the derivation of any environmental variable associated with the samples; they can also be used to estimate past environmental conditions (Imbrie and Kipp, 1971; CLIMAP 1976, 1981; Thunell et al., 1994, among others). Useful reviews of the technique can be found in Hutson (1977), Sachs et al. (1977), and Vincent and Berger (1981).

Although the use of transfer functions has yielded excellent results, the technique must be used with caution. The predictive value of transfer functions based on recent sediment surface samples in a particular area is high when applied to recent environments in the same region, but complications arise when the function is applied to spatially or temporally distant samples. Relevant considerations include the following:

(1) The environmental preferences of extant species may not be the same wherever and whenever they occur. For example, some bipolar species can show different environmental preferences in different hemispheres. This could be because different limiting factors may act to control abundance in different settings. Additionally, species habitat preferences may have evolved through time, thereby diminishing the predictive power of transfer functions used to calculate past conditions based on present-day distributions.

(2) Present-day distributions may not have equilibrated. If they are still in a state of recovery

from recent environmental changes (e.g. a recent glacial phase or other shorter-term climatic pulse), then modern foraminiferal distributions (and their derived transfer functions) may not fully reflect either their historical habitat preferences, or their modern preferences. For example, the limiting factor in recovery time may be the presence of geographic barriers to repopulation rather than the ecological responsiveness of the species. Thus, continental positions (see below) can exclude species from occupying areas to which they would otherwise be adapted.

(3) Since these functions tend to be based on sea surface measurements and sediment samples recovered from depth, factors like changing seasonality and vertical depth distributions are not taken into account.

(4) Taphonomic effects such as preferential dissolution, winnowing, and diagenesis must be assumed to be negligible. To whatever extent these effects show temporal and spatial variation, it is not accounted for in transfer functions based on the distribution of modern faunas in surficial sediments (Vincent and Berger, 1981).

(5) In principle, there is nothing in the transfer methodology that prevents the prediction of an unlimited number of environmental variables from a limited amount of paleontological information ('transfer dilemma' of Vincent and Berger, 1981). This is partly due to covariation between environmental variables. Transfer function predictions may not be based on direct causal relationship between species distributions and the environmental variable being predicted. If the causal relationship is secondary or indirect, then that indirect linkage may change geographically or temporally even when the species' actual habitat preference is unchanged. This dilemma is a direct result of the methodology and is ultimately a reflection of the fact that correlation does not demonstrate causality.

(6) There may be some ancient environments for which there are no modern analogs, and which are therefore not predicted by transfer functions based on modern faunas ('transfer paradox' of Vincent and Berger, 1981). In particular, it is not valid to extrapolate beyond the limits of the parameters used to initially establish the transfer function.

(7) The modern species upon which the transfer function is based may not have sufficient historical range to allow application of the function to older samples, particularly samples that predate the first appearance of the most recently-evolved modern species that contribute to the transfer function.

Despite these problems, transfer functions remain a valuable tool in environmental reconstruction. However, it should not be forgotten that they are formulated to predict environmental characteristics from biogeographic distribution patterns rather than to address the reverse problem of explaining biogeographic distributions in terms of environmental parameters.

7.2 ECOLOGICAL FACTORS CONTROLLING THE DISTRIBUTION OF PLANKTONIC FORAMINIFERA

7.2.1

The tolerance limits of most species are not sharply defined. Instead, departure from optimal conditions causes a gradational reduction of organismal functionality, resulting in inhibition of reproduction, nutrient uptake, and growth, eventually leading to death. These effects can be both interdependent and nonlinear; for example, an organism may require optimal temperatures in order to tolerate extremes of hypersalinity (Odum, 1971; Hedgpeth, 1957a). For a general discussion of models dealing with the coupling between plankton and their physical environment, see Eckman (1994) and references therein. For specific correlations of modern species abundances with CLIMAP data on specific environmental factors, see Hilbrecht (1996).

7.2.2 Temperature

7.2.2.1 Direct control

As a result of the general observation that the most conspicuous planktonic foraminiferal distribution patterns are latitudinal, more research effort has focused on the influence of temperature than on any other single variable.

Some of the most convincing evidence for direct control of temperature over distribution comes from the experimental work of Bijma et al. (1990). Their results showed a correspondence between in vitro temperature tolerance limits and the known natural limits of their experimental species. Vital functions like food acceptance, growth, and reproduction were inhibited when natural temperature limits were exceeded, providing compelling evidence that temperature may be an important factor in controlling individual species distributions.

7.2.2.2 Temperature and the biogeography of coiling directions

Some species show a change in the dominance of coiling direction that appears to be temperature-dependent, although there is no known kinetic reason that one handedness should be preferred over another. Work on coiling direction has touched on such interrelated topics as stratigraphic applications (Cosijn, 1938; Vasicec, 1953; Nagappa, 1957; Bandy 1960), biogeography (Gandolfi, 1942; Ericson et al., 1954; Bandy, 1959, 1960; Ericson, 1959), correlation (Ericson and Wollin, 1968; Robinson, 1969; Olsson, 1970; Hofker, 1972), evolution (Bolli, 1950, 1951, 1971), ecology and paleoecology (Vasicec, 1953; Ericson, 1959; Bandy, 1959, 1960; Loeblich and Tappan, 1964a; Bé, 1977; Boltovskoy, 1966b, 1969), and life history (Vella, 1974; Lipps, 1976, 1979) without explaining the nature of the relationship between temperature and coiling direction. The history of this literature is summarized in Bolli (1950, 1951), Loeblich and Tappan (1964a), Thiede (1971), Malmgren (1974), Kennett (1976), Boltovskoy and Wright (1976), Srinivasan and Azmi (1978), Lipps (1979), Vincent and Berger (1981), and Hemleben et al. (1989).

Recent work by Lohmann and Schweitzer (1990) provided concrete evidence that Lipps' (1976, 1979) focus on reproductive strategy might be appropriate, at least in the case of Globorotalia truncatulinoides. They discussed handedness-correlated variation with two factors in G. truncatulinoides: (1) the timing of descent from surface waters, and (2) the consequent depth (especially in relation to the thermocline) at the time of gametogenetic calcification and reproduction. Specifically, a shallow thermocline seems to have a negative effect on the reproductive success of G. truncatulinoides, possibly due to interference from a correlated hydrographic gradient such as the pycnocline. Since sinistral individuals descend from the surface waters earlier in their life cycle, they are likely to descend to greater depths and, if the thermocline is too shallow, may find themselves below the depth at which seasonal overturn will return juveniles to the surface for another reproductive cycle. This selects against sinistral individuals, leaving an increase in the relative frequency of dextral individuals. Lohmann and Schweitzer point out that this is not a full explanation of the relationship between temperature and handedness, since the effect shows size-dependence even within samples (Thiede, 1971). Schweitzer and Lohmann (1991) showed a similar relationship between reproductive success and the depth of the pycnocline in menardiform globorotalids.

Lohmann (1992) suggested that the apparent biogeographic relationship between coiling direction and sea surface temperature may be an indirect result of the fact that the deepest mixing generally happens in late winter in most parts of the ocean, and is intensified at higher latitudes where temperatures are lower. He supports this hypothesis with the observation that handedness dependency persists in the Mediterranean where temperature and deep mixing are decoupled.

7.2.2.3 Temperature and the biogeography of pore size

Bé (1968) reported that porosity was highest in tropical and surface-dwelling species (Fig. 7.1). Scott (1972) suggests that this might imply a hydromechanical function for pores, since the reduced density and increased buoyancy that accompany increased porosity would retard settling rates in high-temperature low-density habitats; this inference is supported by experimental results of Bijma et al. (1990); also see

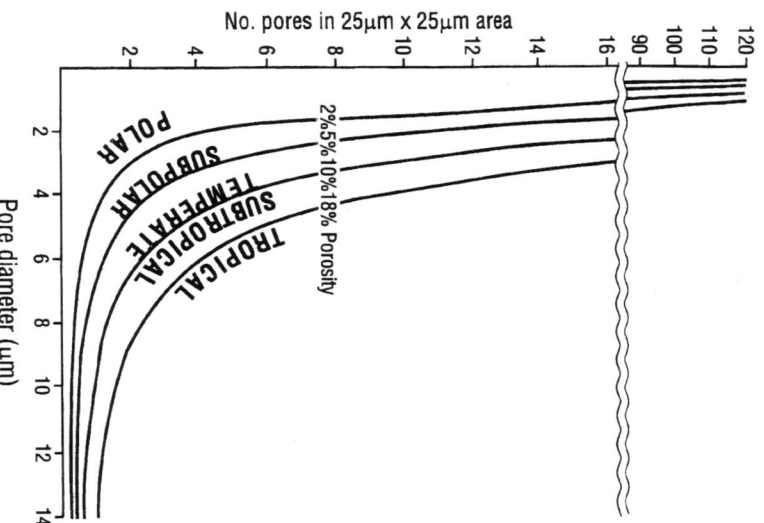

Figure 7.1 Pore concentration plotted against pore diameter for 22 living planktonic taxa. Horizontal lines indicate ranges of pore diameters (from Scott, 1972, after Bé, 1968).

Kennett (1976) for additional discussion. Furbish and Arnold (1997) have investigated the functional morphology of hydrodynamical properties in spinose planktonic Foraminifera with specific attention to the determinants of settling velocity. Since there is a constructional constraint relating pore size and spacing to spine number, it follows that these characters may have a functional or constructional interrelationship. This possibility has not been investigated.

It is clear that temperature is not the only factor controlling species distributions. For example, even though temperatures in the deep sea are uniformly low, deep sea benthic taxonomic diversity is comparable to diversity levels on tropical shelves. Other factors must be considered.

7.2.3 Salinity

Planktonic Foraminifera are intolerant of brackish water. The lowest salinity in which living specimens have been captured is about 30‰ (Boltovskoy, 1976). The species most tolerant of hyposaline conditions in nature are reported to be *Globigerina bulloides*, *G. quinqueloba*, *Globigerinita uvula*, *Globigerinoides ruber*, *Neogloboquadrina pachyderma* (f. *superficiaria*), and *Orbulina universa*; these species have been recovered from waters having salinities of 30.5 to 31‰ (Bé and Tolderlund, 1971). *Neogloboquadrina dutertrei* is also associated with relatively low salinities, and shows abundance peaks during late Cenozoic episodes of Mediterranean sapropel deposition, which were probably caused by stagnation-induced glacial meltwater spillover from the Black Sea (Thunell et al., 1977). Bijma et al. (1990) studied salinity tolerances of some planktonic species in laboratory culture and found that the *in vitro* salinity tolerance limits are greater than those found in nature, with *Globigerinoides ruber* showing the greatest tolerance range (22 to 49‰). They concluded that natural salinity variation in the open ocean is unlikely to exert significant control over the distribution of modern planktonic Foraminifera.

7.2.4 Nutrients and geographic variation in abundance

In general, foraminiferal abundance patterns are similar to those of other groups that are believed to reflect primary productivity (Bé and Tolderlund, 1971; McGowan, 1971). Productivity is largely determined by photic levels and nutrient salts, especially phosphate, available to phytoplankton (Parker, 1960; Ryther, 1963; Berger, 1969). Although most research on planktonic foraminiferal abundance has shown correlations with phytoplankton productivity and nutrient levels (e.g. Hemleben et al., 1989; Fairbanks and Wiebe, 1980; Ravelo and Fairbanks, 1995), there is evidence that the relationship may not be a simple one. For example, Oberhänsli et al. (1990) have shown that standing stocks can be highest where primary production is intermediate.

ate, suggesting the correlation may be nonlinear. Additionally, small-mesh tows correlate with phosphate levels while larger-mesh tows do not (Berger, 1969).

Quantitative comparisons of absolute abundances between studies are often problematic due to the variation introduced by sampling gear (see section 7.1.2.1). For these reasons, it is best to discuss abundances in relative terms. Abundances tend to be relatively lower in oligotrophic high-salinity central basin waters with weak circulation, such as are found in the North and South Atlantic and Indian Oceans; higher abundances tend, in general, to be found in major current gyres, equatorial and West Wind Drift, currents, upwellings, and frontal systems. Numerically, planktonic Foraminifera can range from 1.3 to 9.9% of the total zooplankton, ranking sixth in winter (after copepods, chaetognaths, tunicates, krill, and siphonophores, respectively) and third in summer, and sometimes achieving local dominance even over copepods. However, their small body size means the foraminiferal biomass contribution is less significant than their numerical abundance (Boltovskoy and Wright, 1976).

Some of the highest concentrations of Foraminifera are found in the North Pacific, north of the central water mass (Bradshaw, 1959; Berger, 1969; Bé and Tolderlund, 1971; Spindler and Dickmann, 1986), where plankton abundances are three orders of magnitude greater than those in the Sargasso Sea. Indo-Pacific abundances are a factor of two greater than those of the Atlantic ocean, although the relative pattern of accumulation rates are reversed, so that there appears to be a negative correlation between standing stock and shell deposition rates (Berger, 1969). Berger also noted that concentration maxima for small-mesh tows are found in high latitudes, while large-mesh tows show their concentration maxima at low latitudes, and suggested that this may be due to accelerated reproductive rates in areas of high productivity, which results in steeper size-frequency distributions. Regardless of the steepness of the size-frequency distribution, its exponential nature implies that there are many more juveniles than adults, and is consistent with the general expectation of high juvenile mortality and concave-upward survivorship curves.

The highest measured oceanic abundances (greater than 10^4 specimens per 1000 m^3) occur in major current systems, boundary currents, divergences, and upwellings. Depauperate standing stocks (less than 10^3 specimens per 1000 m^3) are found in central waters of oceanic basins and over continental shelves (Bé, 1977), although slope waters have been reported with 10^4–10^5 specimens per 1000 m^3 (Cifelli and Smith, 1969). Some of the highest abundances reported (4.7×10^8 per 1000 m^3) have been of small, juvenile *Neogloboquadrina pachyderma*, probably living, recovered from melted Antarctic annual sea ice (Lipps and Krebs, 1974; Lipps, 1979; Spindler and Dickmann, 1986), and by Berger (1969) who reported abundances as high as 10^8 per 1000 m^3 for small-mesh tows, although these abundances should not be compared due to differences in sampling technique discussed by Berger (1969). Berger (*op. cit.*), and Boltovskoy and Wright (1976) provide useful discussions of abundance variation.

7.2.5 Water depth and biogeography

Although there is considerable literature on the depth distribution of planktonic Foraminifera, the following discussion focuses on those aspects of depth distribution that influence biogeography of the group. Living planktonic Foraminifera have their maximum abundance in euphotic near-surface waters between 10 and 50 meters (Fig. 7.2), below which depth they show an approximately exponential decline in abundance (Bé, 1977). This pattern correlates with the abundance of nutrients, prey, and (for those with photosymbionts, e.g. *Globigerinoides sacculifer*) sunlight (Bijma and Hemleben, 1994). The depth habitats of individual species can seldom be defined within narrow limits because they show diurnal, ontogenetic, seasonal, and long-term variation that is beyond the scope of most studies to fully document. Bé (1977) considered three broad groups on the basis of their depth distribution. The first consists of shallow-water

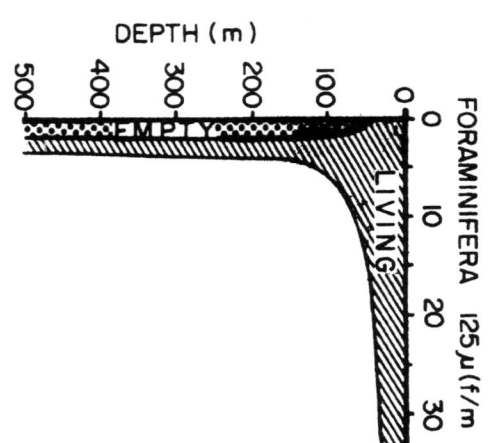

Figure 7.2 Abundance profile of planktonic Foraminifera in the Santa Barbara Basin, August, 1966 (after Berger, 1971).

species, primarily spinose forms including all species of *Globigerinoides* and several of *Globigerina*. These species tend to be thinner-walled and smaller than deeper-dwelling forms. Bé's intermediate water depth assemblage, whose species live predominantly in the 50 to 100 meter depth range, consists of both spinose (*Globigerina bulloides*, *Hastigerina pelagica*, *Orbulina universa*, *Globigerinella aequilateralis*, and spinose *Hastigerinella digitata*, which possibly is unique in that it may spend its entire life cycle below 1000 m. The remaining 12 species in Bé's deep water assemblage all live in the euphotic zone as juveniles but are found mainly below 100 meters as adults. These include two additional spinose forms, *Globigerinella adamsi* and *Sphaeroidinella dehiscens*, the non-spinose *Neogloboquadrina pachyderma* and *G. conglomerata*, and all the species of *Globorotalia*.

Depth often shows a relationship to the distribution patterns of living planktonic Foraminifera, but depth-correlated factors such as temperature, salinity, dissolved oxygen, photic conditions, and nutrient levels are probably the direct controls over foraminiferal depth habitats. In nearshore environments, however, the influence of depth can persist even when physicochemical conditions are equivalent to an open marine setting. Planktonic Foraminifera are often undersized, and usually sparsely distributed in shelf waters; this is especially true of inner shelf environments on broad continental shelves where they may be entirely absent (Saidova, 1957; Lipps and Warme, 1966; Boltovskoy, 1976; Wang et al. 1985).

Bandy (1956) pointed out that the characteristic depth habitat of some species may preclude their survival in shallow waters. This could be due to a relationship between the life cycle and environmental gradients like the thermocline (Lohmann and Schweitzer, 1990; Schweitzer and Lohmann, 1991), the pycnocline, or the chlorophyll maximum (Hemleben and Bijma, 1994), rather than to the absolute magnitudes of temperature, salinity, and productivity in nearshore environments. In species that depend on seasonal overturn above the thermocline for successful completion of their life cycle, the depth of the thermocline — or even its existence where bathymetry intervenes in the shelf environment — may play a role in determining vertical and horizontal abundance and distribution. This is supported by Orr's (1967) finding that the intraspecific proportion of adult pregametogenic specimens of some species found in surficial sediments shows a discontinuity at depths that can be related to the species' life cycle.

If Orr's finding is the general case, then interspecific variations in shoreward distribution may be understood in terms of the bathymetry of their respective reproductive cycles. As Hemleben et al. (1989) have pointed out, historical changes in biogeographic distribution patterns cannot be fully understood until a fuller knowledge of foraminiferal depth habitats is developed. Of course, for extinct species, such knowledge must rely on the indirect evidence of bathymetry and light isotopes.

Although it is possible in principle to infer the vertical habitat distribution of planktonic Foraminifera from their light isotope composition (Savin and Douglas, 1973; Grazzini, 1976; Fairbanks et al., 1980; Fairbanks, 1982; Deuser,

1987; Spero et al., 1991; Sautter and Thunell, 1991; Spero and Lea, 1993; Ravelo and Fairbanks, 1992, 1995; Hemleben and Bijma, 1994; van Eijden, 1995), and ranked depth stratifications have been developed on that basis, it is also clear that ontogenetic changes in depth habitat and vital effects (including those of photosymbionts and gametogenic calcification) complicate the interpretation of isotopic data – a complication that is compounded when extrapolated into the fossil record (e.g. Shackleton et al., 1985; Lohmann and Schweitzer, 1990; Corfield and Cartilidge, 1991; D'Hondt et al., 1994; Kelly et al., 1996; see also chapter 14).

Having enumerated the main factors influencing planktonic foraminiferal distributions, we will now discuss the effects they have on biogeographic patterns. This discussion is (somewhat arbitrarily) divided into large, meso-, and small-scale patterns.

7.3 LARGE-SCALE DISTRIBUTION PATTERNS

7.3.1 The global diversity gradient and latitudinal provinciality

7.3.1.1

Perhaps the single most conspicuous aspect of the Earth's biosphere is the global latitudinal diversity gradient, a gradient that embraces virtually all taxonomic levels. Wallace (1878) drew attention to the phenomenon, and Murray (1897) became the first to discuss latitudinal gradients in the planktonic Foraminifera. Since that time, eight large-scale biogeographic provinces have been identified that are symmetrically disposed about a ninth tropical province (Figs. 7.3, 7.4). Although various authors differ on the exact positions of provincial boundaries, and some have added details that reflect smaller-scale hydrography (e.g. McGowan, 1974; Hemleben et al., 1989), the overall picture of latitudinal provinces and the diversity gradient that spans them is consistent with patterns seen in the remainder of the world's biota (McGowan, 1971). These large-scale patterns have been the central theme in most surveys of planktonic foraminiferal biogeography. The reader is referred to Bradshaw (1959), Bandy (1964), Belyaeva (1969), Bé and Tolderlund (1971), Boltovskoy and Wright (1976), Bé (1977), Bé and Hutson (1977), Lipps (1979), Olsson (1982), and Hemleben et. al (1989) for useful summaries. Pianka (1966) provides a useful general discussion of the phenomenon.

7.3.1.2 General features of latitudinal provinces

These nine large-scale provinces do not map systematically onto clearly defined physicochemical oceanographic properties (Williams et al., 1968; Backus, 1986), or onto planktonic surface-water distributions (Ottens, 1991), with the result that provinces are easier to describe than explain. Diversity shows a monotonic decrease from about 20 species (ten indigenous) in the tropical province to about 5 (one indigenous) in the polar regions, with few species being restricted to a single province (Fig. 7.3). Cold-water faunas are somewhat less diverse in the north than in the south, possibly because of the relatively restricted circulation in the Arctic (Bé, 1977).

The high-latitude provinces tend to be longitudinally continuous and faunally uniform due to a relative lack of continental barriers, but lower latitude provinces are interrupted, most conspicuously by the Americas, with the result that faunal differences are most pronounced between the low-latitude provinces of the Atlantic and the Eastern Pacific (Fig. 7.4).

Bé (1977) has drawn attention to the fact that the ratio of indigenous to total species found in these nine provinces is lowest in the transitional zone where only *Globorotalia inflata* is considered to be indigenous. This observation tends to characterize the transitional zone as an area of overlap between higher and lower latitude species distributions, and suggests that the number of large-scale functional ecosystems may be smaller than the number of provinces that can be delineated on the basis of foraminiferal distribution patterns.

Biogeography of planktonic Foraminifera

Superimposed on this first-order provinciality is a second-order pattern that correlates most strongly with currents, frontal systems, and upwellings (e.g. Ottens, 1991), effects that are most strongly developed in the temperate through tropical provinces. Subtropical provinciality is most strongly developed along western boundaries (Gulf Stream, and Kuroshio current in the north, Brazil Current, Mozambique-Agulhas Current, and East-Australian Current in the south) and it is in these areas that provincial distortion is most apparent (e.g. McGowran

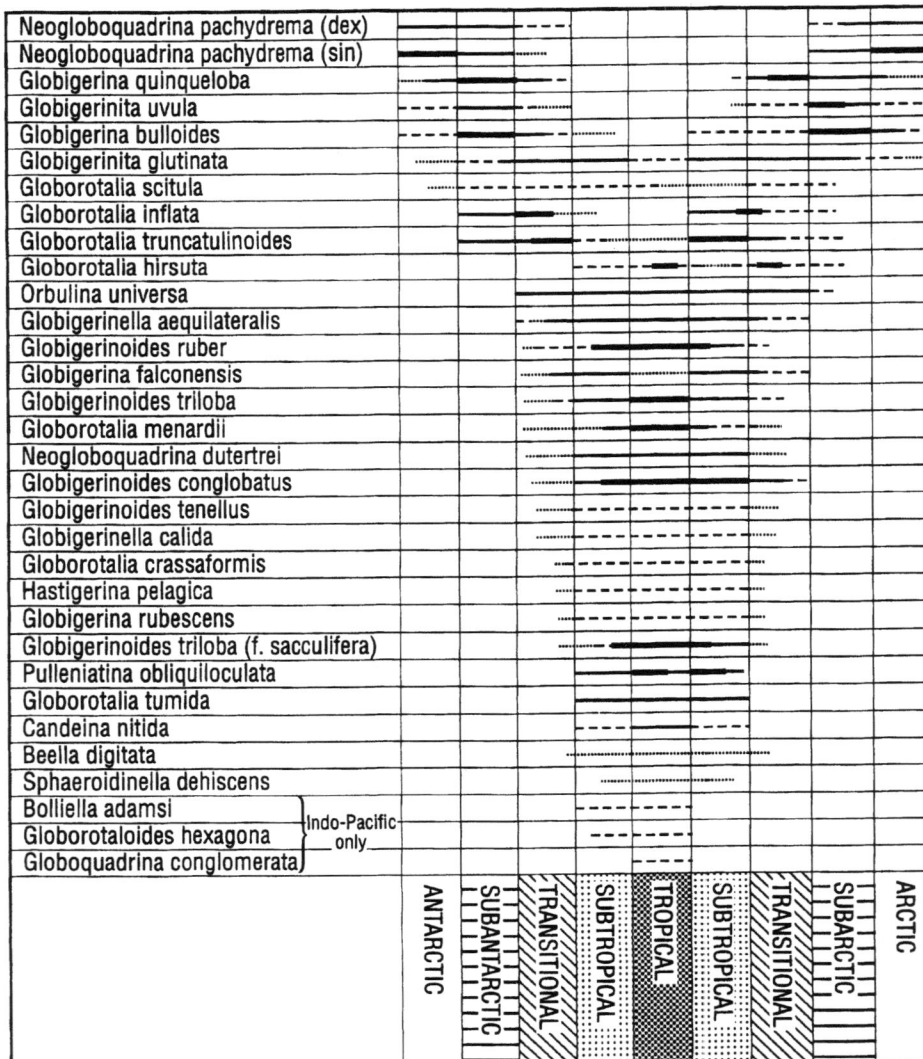

Figure 7.3 Latitudinal summary of planktonic foraminiferal species distributions. After Bolovskoy and Wright (1979) and Bé (1977).

inces, for example, tend to include a significant number of species (four of twelve) associated with upwellings and boundary currents. Current gyres also distort the latitudinal orientation of low-latitude faunal provinces by transporting equatorial species poleward in clockwise northern hemisphere gyres and in counterclockwise southern hemisphere gyres. These currents are

et al., 1997). Similarly, high latitude species are carried equatorward by the Labrador, Portugal-Canaries, Oyashio, Benguela, and California Currents (Fig. 7.5).

The geographic disposition and species composition of these provinces have been characterized in contexts ranging from broad latitudinal and provincial summaries (Figs. 7.3,

Large-scale distribution patterns

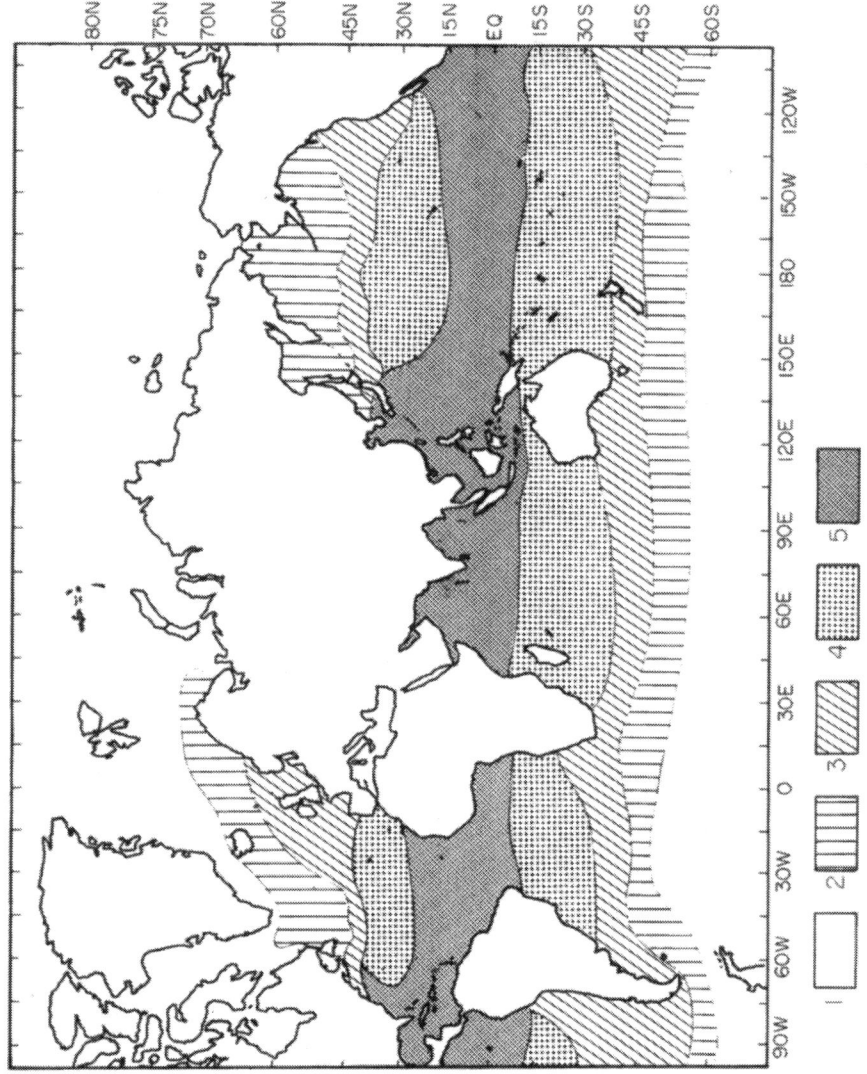

Figure 7.4 Biogeographic provinciality in modern planktonic Foraminifera. (1) Polar, (2) sub-polar, (3) transitional, (4) subtropical, and (5) tropical provinces. Note correspondence to Figs. 7.3 and 7.5. After Bé (1977).

7.4) to more detailed species-by-species documentation (e.g. Bé, 1977; Hilbrecht, 1996). The latitudinal character of these provinces and of the diversity gradient implies that temperature plays a dominant role in their disposition, although that role is probably indirect (Cifelli, 1971, but see Stehli et al., 1969, 1972). Likely candidates for more direct influence would include temperature-correlated phenomena like productivity (Ortiz et al., 1995) and the latitudinal distribution of hydrographic barriers to gene flow. Lipps (1979) listed six hypotheses that relate temperature, salinity, circulation patterns, water masses, ecosystem cores/ecotones, and environmental stability/predictability to planktonic foraminiferal provinciality, but concluded that these hypotheses are more useful as tools in paleoecological inference than as explanations for foraminiferal distribution patterns.

7.3.2 The historical development of the global diversity gradient

7.3.2.1

Early classic works like those of Stehli et al. (1969) and Stehli et al. (1972) analyzed large scale biogeographic patterns from relatively restricted data bases. Recent workers such as Wei and Kennett (1983, 1986), Stanley et al. (1988), Norris (1991a), and Parker et al. (in press), have taken advantage of global compendia like Kennett and Srinivasan (1983), Blow (1979), and Olsson et al. (1999) to relate paleobiogeography to macroevolutionary patterns of speciation and extinction as well as to morphology, life history, abundance, taxonomic affiliation, and paleoceanographic change.

It is clear that the well-developed global latitudinal diversity gradient seen in the Globigerinida has not been a static feature throughout the Cenozoic; rather, it is the continuing culmination of the last great iterative phase of the group's evolutionary history (Cifelli, 1969; Norris, 1991a). Latitudinal environmental gradients, and their consequent foraminiferal diversity gradients, were clearly much less steep in the early Paleogene (Olsson, 1982; Boersma and Premoli Silva, 1983, 1991; Olsson et al. 1999) but the speciation/extinction patterns that accompany this transition are not well understood.

7.3.2.2 The ecological role of temperature

Stehli et al. (1972) advanced the hypothesis that the latitudinal diversity gradient is driven by thermal control of two factors: greater ease of entry into low-latitude niches, and an equatorward increase in niche space. The latter factor could be related to intensified vertical stratification at low latitudes (Lipps, 1970), an equatorward increase in local upwelling (Stanley et al., 1988), or to an equatorward gradient in the trophic resource continuum (Hallock, 1987). The effect of historical changes in temperature will be discussed in section 7.3.2.5.

7.3.2.3 Speciation and extinction rates

Stehli et al. (1969) discussed taxonomic survivorship, endemicity, and latitudinal diversity trends in Permian brachiopods, modern Bivalvia, and Cretaceous planktonic Foraminifera, and noted two striking patterns:

(1) a lack of endemic taxa at high latitudes (cold-water assemblages tend to be comprised almost exclusively of cosmopolitan species; Fig. 7.6); and

(2) turnover rates among low-latitude groups are higher than among high-latitude taxa (suggested by patterns of taxonomic survivorship).

In foraminiferal studies Stanley et al. (1988), Norris (1991a), Feldman et al. (1998), and Parker et al. (in press) confirmed the geographic pattern (1, above) in Neogene planktonic Foraminifera. Stehli et al. (1972) found indirect generic-level evidence of high turnover among low latitude Foraminifera, but was unable to find similar evidence at the species level, possibly because of a decoupling between species and higher-level taxic behavior (Arnold, 1982). Stanley et al. (1988), Norris (1991a), Feldman et al. (1998), and Parker et al. (in press) later confirmed a pattern (2 above) of higher species turnover among low-latitude Foraminifera.

The causes of these patterns were subsequently pursued by Wei and Kennett, (1986), Stanley et al. (1988), Norris (1991b, 1992), and Parker et al. (in press), who, in various combinations, examined the relationship between diversity and factors such as morphology (keeled vs. unkeeled, spinose vs. non-spinose), taxonomic affiliation (within-clade species turnover), geographic range (cosmopolitan vs. endemic), population size (dominance), patchiness (occurrence in upwelling), depth distribution, biology (symbiont relationships and life cycle), latitudinal occurrence (most poleward extent), and latitudinal variation in provinciality. Tracing patterns of causality among these factors despite extensive covariation has been a central issue in these works. The results tend to support Stehli's earlier work, and are further consistent with the expectation (Fisher, 1930; Wright, 1942) that the limited possibilities for genetic isolation in widespread, abundant cosmopolitan panmictic populations may retard microevolutionary rates and suppress speciation at high latitude.

7.3.2.4 Biogeographic change during speciation

Superficially, it would seem reasonable to expect that during lineage diversification, species would originate locally and then expand their biogeographic ranges into increasingly broad biogeographic provinces. However, on the average, Neogene speciation events tend to result in a

Large-scale distribution patterns

Figure 7.5 Generalized major surface circulation systems. Current abbreviations are Ag = Agulhas Current; As = Alaska Current; Bg = Benguela Current; Br = Brazil Current; Ca = Canary Current; Cf = California Current; Ea = East Australia Current; Ec = Equatorial Countercurrent; Eg = East Greenland Current; Fa = Falkland Current; Fl = Florida Current; Gf = Gulf Stream; Gu = Guinea Current; Ks = Kuroshio; La = Labrador Current; Ne = North Equatorial Current; Np = North Pacific Current; Os = Oyashio; Pr = Peru Current; Se = South Equatorial Current; Wa = West Australia Current; Wd = Westwind Drift; The circum-Antarctic Polar Current, flowing from east to west along the coast of Antarctica, is not shown. After Kennett (1982) and Parker (1971).

statistically significant *reduction* in geographic range (Parker *et al.*, in press). This observation implies that the development of biogeographic patterns may proceed from relatively cosmopolitan ancestors that speciate by specializing and exploring increasingly geographically restricted niches. Indeed, it is established that the Cenozoic iterative diversifications did originate from relatively cosmopolitan, 'primitive' globigerine ancestors (Cifelli, 1969; Norris, 1991a). A tendency toward geographic specialization might be verified by examining changes in distribution patterns over the geologic history of species, but the existing comprehensive compendia on foraminiferal distribution patterns do not provide sufficient stratigraphic and geographic detail. However, Jenkins (1992) examined a restricted data set and found a pattern of retreat toward the tropics prior to extinction; if this pattern holds for pseudoextinctions, then Jenkins' pattern has general implications for the biogeography of evolution as well as extinction (see also Vermeij, 1989). Note that Hunter (1985), Hansard (1994), and Lazarus *et al.* (1995) have found cladogenesis to be accompanied by reduced abundances, although the generality of this observation and its biogeographic implications have not been assessed.

116   Biogeography of planktonic Foraminifera

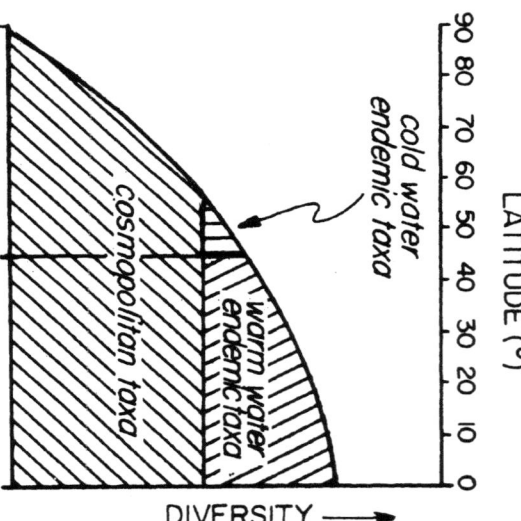

Figure 7.6 Diagrammatic depiction of the composition of warm and cold assemblages. Note that endemic assemblages are virtually absent at high latitudes, where assemblages consist almost entirely of cosmopolitan elements. This is true not only of planktonic Foraminifera, but of many other taxa as well. After Stehli et al. (1969).

7.3.2.5 Late Cenozoic cooling and latitudinal species distributions

For most of geologic time, global climates have been warmer than they are at present; the modern widespread cold-temperate and arctic regions developed as a result of Late Cenozoic cooling. If the world has been warm nearly everywhere for much of its history, then Darlington's (1959) classical view of low latitudes as centers of radiation may lose its meaning (Stanley, 1979). This suggests that an examination of Neogene cooling might be useful in understanding latitudinal provinciality. Thunell and Belyea (1982) have shown that Neogene Atlantic planktonic foraminiferal provinces shifted dramatically in the Middle Miocene and Late Pliocene during the development of the East Antarctic Ice Sheet and the initiation of the northern hemisphere ice sheets. At these times there were equatorward migrations of cool, high-latitude provinces and accompanying contraction of low-latitude provinces. Berggren and Hollister (1974) and McIntyre et al. (1972) noted that the polar front has swept back and forth during the last 250 ky, alternately compressing and expanding the tropics at least six times. The exponential nature of rediversification during each recovery would tend to enhance the diversity gradient even if fractional (per-taxon) rates of speciation were latitudinally invariant. This is because (all other things being equal) a biota with larger initial diversity will have a faster rate of arithmetic growth, since diversification starts on a steeper part of the exponential growth curve (Stanley, 1979).

Stanley (1979) also emphasized that global cooling events might be expected to cause higher extinction rates among tropical species, a prediction that is consistent with many observed extinction patterns, and a prediction later verified in the Foraminifera (Stanley et al., 1988). This model carries the corollary that the distributions of surviving low-latitude species should be compressed equatorward during cooling events (e.g. Thunell and Belyea, 1982), which in turn implies that subsequent recovery should be characterized by rediversification from the tropics, a process that could, in itself, maintain a latitudinal diversity gradient even if the number of niches were not latitude dependent. This is consistent with Jenkins' (1992) observation of equatorward biogeographic contraction prior to extinction.

Lipps (1970) emphasized the effect of sea surface temperatures at high latitudes on vertical and horizontal thermal gradients. Lipps proposed a model suggesting that during times of polar warming the absence of steep thermal gradients eliminates barriers that otherwise maintain species diversity through genetic isolation and allopatry; conversely, the potential for speciation would be greatest when the effectiveness of thermal barriers to gene flow is enhanced by strong localized thermal gradients caused by high-latitude cooling. Lipps' hypothesis implies that Stanley's (1979) 'crucible of speciation' may be the polar front or temperate region (where gradients would be steepest) rather than the tropics. Detailed information on the geographic distribution of stratigraphic first appearances might provide a means to test this hypothesis. Lohmann and Schweitzer (1990) have pre-

Large-scale distribution patterns

sented evidence suggesting that the position of a different gradient, the thermocline, may play a key role in determining the differential reproductive success of subpopulations of *Globorotalia truncatulinoides*. Hemleben et al. (1989) have pointed out that the pycnocline and the chlorophyll maximum can play a similar role, and may act as barriers to gene flow during the speciation process. This raises the possibility that the lack of a well-developed thermocline characteristic of polar regions may be a key factor in suppressing speciation in those areas. It would then follow that equatorward movement of the polar front should suppress speciation over a broader area. Additionally, Wei and Kennett (1986) suggest that increased provinciality during the development of polar ice may drive the diversification process, especially in the globorotaliids; it is also established that latitudinal provincialization became more developed during times of polar cooling (Thunell, 1981).

7.3.3 Antitropicality and bipolarity

Most cool-water planktonic foraminiferal species, including *Neogloboquadrina pachyderma*, *Globigerina bulloides*, and *Globorotalia inflata*, occur in latitudinally delineated biogeographic provinces separated by equatorial water masses (Figs. 7.3, 7.4). This can also be true of morphotypes – specifically coiling direction – of some species (e.g. *Neogloboquadrina pachyderma*, *Globorotalia truncatulinoides*). Bipolarity has been the subject of investigation since the mid 19th century (Hooker, 1847), and in extant groups is usually considered to be the result of relatively recent Plio-Pleistocene cooling. The fact that the phenomenon can be detected as far back as the Early Jurassic does not require that present bipolarity is of ancient origin. However, the subfamilial level of differentiation in some living bipolar mollusca suggests the phenomenon may be the result of considerable evolutionary history (Crame, 1993). The question of whether bipolarity should be interpreted in a framework of vicariant evolution or dispersal history is deserving of closer scrutiny by foraminiferologists, for it is in this group that we have the stratigraphic and phylogenetic control to resolve the issue.

Hedgpeth (1957b) and Lipps (1979) have discussed several hypotheses to explain bipolarity, including submergence, a phenomenon in which extra-tropical cool-water species stay within their preferred thermal conditions by living in deeper waters at lower latitudes. The general form of this explanation appears to be valid in the analogous context of some antitropical plant species that are found in high altitude tropical settings (Thorne, 1972). Although submergence has been observed in *Globorotalia menardii* (Hemleben et al., 1989), *Globigerina bulloides*, *Globorotalia inflata*, and a few other cold-temperate and cold water species (Boltovskoy, 1971b), the phenomenon is unlikely to explain bipolarity, because other limiting habitat requirements (such as photic and nutrient levels) are not satisfied in the tropics where ideal thermal conditions may only be found in deeper water.

Bipolarity might also be the result of migration from more equatorial provinces into contiguous higher-latitude water masses, or the result of dumbbell allopatry during warming trends (McGowan, 1971; Lazarus, 1983). An additional hypothesis explaining bipolarity suggests it is a historical vestige of dissection of a previously continuous distribution by post-glacial warming in the tropics, with sufficiently frequent mixing between latitudinally disjunct populations to maintain genetic continuity (Bé, 1977; Bé and Tolderlund, 1971).

7.3.4 Continental positions

High latitude foraminiferal provinces tend to have lateral continuity. At lower latitudes, however, continuity is interrupted by land masses, particularly the Americas. The Pliocene closure of the Isthmus of Panama isolated Atlantic and Pacific tropical faunas and led to their independent faunal development. Today, *Globigerinella adamsi*, *Globoquadrina conglomerata*, *Globorotaloides hexagonus*, *Globorotalia menardii neoflexuosa*, and *Globorotalia theyeri* are confined to the Indo-Pacific (see Vincent and Berger, 1981; Bolli and Krasheninnikov, 1977; Bé, 1977; Thompson et al., 1979), and pink *Globigerinoides ruber* has disappeared from the Indian and Pacific Oceans (Thompson et al., 1979). Additionally, coiling directions in *Pulleniatina obliquiloculata* cease to correlate between the Atlantic and Pacific basins after the development of the Isthmus of Panama (Saito, 1976).

In general, low-latitude species that evolved before the development of the Isthmus tend to show a more continuous circumglobal distribution than late-evolving species. For example, several descendants of *Globorotalia cultrata* that evolved after the Pliocene are restricted to the Atlantic basin (Vincent and Berger, 1981; Schott, 1935). *Globorotalia cultrata* itself disappears from the tropical Atlantic during glacial times (Schott, 1935; Vincent and Berger, 1981; Morin et al., 1970), and populations only become reestablished in the Atlantic basin when the 18°C isotherm moves poleward of southernmost South Africa, thus allowing the species to circumvent the continental barrier at high southern latitudes. These repopulation events are discussed by Thompson et al. (1979), Ericson and Wollin (1968), and Schweitzer and Lohmann (1991).

7.4 MESO-SCALE DISTRIBUTION

7.4.1

Although large-scale foraminiferal biogeographic provinces are relatively simple and monotonous by comparison with similar-sized terrestrial provinces (McGowan, 1971), they are not devoid of small-scale structure. Research on regional and local-scale variation in distribution patterns has revealed them to be more than mere high-resolution details of the known large-scale patterns; instead, they arise from distinct smaller-scale oceanographic phenomena and have different implications for evolution, diversity, and biogeography. Thus, the key to understanding large-scale distribution patterns may not be found in comparably large-scaled phenomena, but in the cumulative effect of smaller-scale phenomena which themselves may show systematic latitudinal variation.

7.4.2 Genetic isolation

For example, Stanley et al. (1988) suggest that higher taxonomic turnover in globorotalids is probably related to their generally discontinuous distribution, possibly because many are found in areas of (low to mid-latitude) upwelling and are symbiont-barren. Since smaller, more localized populations will have a greater likelihood of genetic isolation and greater vulnerability to localized change, sub-provincial ecological discontinuities are of particular interest for their potential influence on speciation, extinction, and turnover rates, and, a temperature-mediated latitudinal gradient in environmental patchiness might be a more immediate cause of low-latitude speciation rates than temperature itself.

Boltovskoy (1976) also presented an analysis of planktonic distribution patterns that contrasts sharply with the first-order global-scale latitudinal zonations. He focused on localized phenomena such as upwelling, peculiar hydrographic conditions, and complicated current gyres, belts, fronts, and tongues of converging water masses for his explanation of planktonic foraminiferal distribution patterns in the waters surrounding South America. While he does not deny the existence of larger scale global patterns, Boltovskoy contends that they are not, in themselves, an adequate framework for understanding the biogeography of planktonic Foraminifera. This perspective is reinforced by Wang et al. (1985), Ottens (1991), Ottens and Nederbragt (1992), and Hilbrecht (1996), among others; their work provides clear evidence that it is at this scale that faunal discontinuities are most readily related to hydrographic boundaries.

There are indications that Boltovskoy's focus on hydrographic detail may have critical explanatory value as our understanding of speciation in the plankton develops. One of the most problematic aspects of foraminiferal evolution is the mechanism of genetic isolation in the pelagic realm. Lipps (1970, 1979), McGowan (1971), Lazarus (1983), and others have noted the limited potential for allopatric speciation in large, panmictic populations of planktonic Foraminifera. In this regard it may be relevant that a significant number of species that Boltovskoy describes in his South American biogeographic studies are not among the widely recognized Recent species (e.g. *Globigerina diplostoma*, *G. juvenilis*, *G. radians*, *G. rosacea*, *G. subretacea*, *G. trilocularis*, *Globigerinoides cyclostomus*, *G. suleki*, *Globorotalia canariensis*, *G. punctulata*, *G. seiglei*, and *Hastigerina involuta*, among others; Boltovskoy, 1976; see also Rögl, 1985). Boltovskoy mentions that many of these species are found only in restricted areas as isolated specimens, which raises the possibility that these areas may be the genetically isolated 'crucibles' of speciation' discussed by Stanley (1979). Such areas might be expected to produce many short-lived species, most of which never become established on a global scale. Generally speaking, past micropaleontological awareness of species has been biased by a focus on their utility as tools for stratigraphic correlation; consequently, rare, restricted, and short-lived species have been frequently overlooked as isolated oddities. A closer examination of the biogeographic distribution of these 'oddities' may provide valuable clues in understanding mechanisms of speciation in the plankton, and the geographic distribution of these 'crucibles' may have biogeographic implications. Suggested avenues of research might include a comparative study of morphologic variability in these hydrographically distinct areas versus other areas in the open ocean, or a study of the stratigraphic continuity of these unusual forms in relation to the history of their restricted habitats.

However, even at this scale, it is not clear that hydrographic discontinuities are effective geographic barriers to gene flow. Ottens' (1991) study of various Atlantic fronts and currents found that the faunal boundaries between clearly-defined water masses coincided with intervening hydrographic frontal zones. These frontal boundaries were characterized by a high-diversity, low-equitability ecotonal fauna that shared species of both adjoining water masses. The highly gradational nature of these ecotones was supported by multivariate analyses suggesting that foraminiferal populations were more intergradational than the water masses they inhabited.

7.4.3 Directional currents

One question that arises in the context of meso-scale circulation patterns is the effect of directional advection/diffusion on the distribution of the species that inhabit transition zones. Olson (1986) draws attention to the question of how *Globorotalia inflata* maintains itself in the face of a net eastward flow in the south Atlantic – specifically, how individuals are recruited upstream to maintain the population against advection. Olson describes three smaller-scale mechanisms: westward transport by upstream movement of eddy fields, recirculation cells associated with western boundary currents, and the maintenance of a region of prolonged residence at the upstream extremity of the eastward advection.

7.4.4 The biogeography of foraminiferal genotypes

This field is just beginning to influence our understanding of the planktonic Foraminifera. It appears that intraspecific genotypic variation may be seen on roughly the same spatial scale as mesoscale hydrographic features; however, beyond drawing attention to the potential relationship with genetic isolation and speciation, it would be premature to speculate on the significance of this observation. Darling et al. (1998a) have examined various water masses for intra-specific variation in genotype; their preliminary results indicate significant patterns of genotype distribution within and between water masses. The implications of this finding for biogeographic studies has not been fully assessed, but Huber et al. (1997), Darling et al. (1998b), and de Vargas et al. (1998) have discussed cryptic genotypic species within morphotypes previously believed to be monospecific. This implies that the traditional morphospecies concept may not be a fully adequate basis for understanding biogeographic patterns.

7.5 SMALL-SCALE PATCHINESS

Boltovskoy (1971a) provided an early quantification of the geographic scale of abundance variation; useful discussions can be found in Wiebe and Holland (1968), Boltovskoy (1971a) and Boltovskoy and Wright (1976). The phenomenon is probably too ephemeral to play a direct role in genetic isolation during the speciation process; however, Hemleben et al. (1989) suggest that a significant portion of measured lateral patchiness may be due to diurnal vertical migration during sampling. Based on plankton tows, Boltovskoy reported abundance variation by a factor of 90 over distances as small as one nautical mile in the South Atlantic Ocean.

Recent work on patchiness in the plankton has been directed at the more general question of its underlying causes (Powell and Okubo, 1994; Abraham, 1998; Levin and Segel, 1976). Abraham (1998) has pointed out that turbulent stirring of plankton by nondiffusive advection is a likely explanation for patchiness. The concentration spectra of plankton tend to follow a power law over scales ranging from one to 100 km. Phytoplankton distributions are similar to the distribution of the physical quantities (especially, nutrient) that the phytoplankton are presumably tracking. Zooplankton concentrations however, are more variable over short distances– nearly as variable as they are at larger spatial scales. The difference, according to Abraham, can be accounted for by differing response times, i.e. longer-lived zooplankton may not reproduce quickly enough to closely track their nutritional resources. This might explain the closer correlation seen between productivity and foraminiferal abundances in small-mesh plankton tows noted by Berger (1969). Over their shorter lifetimes, juvenile specimens are likely to have experienced less advective transport, and therefore are more likely to reflect recent reproduction in resource-rich waters. Concentration spectra in the planktonic Foraminifera have not been examined quantitatively in the context of Abraham's model; nevertheless, there may be sufficient lifespan-dependent variation in response times between the long-lived genus *Globorotalia* and the shorter-lived *Globigerinoides* to test for consistency with Abraham's prediction.

On an extremely fine scale, Silver et al. (1978) have presented evidence suggesting that the abundance and diversity of microplankton correlate with small-scale variation in the density of marine snow aggregates (fecal pellets, organic detritus, various exoskeletons, etc.). Some may even treat this snow as a substrate (Hilbrecht and Thierstein, 1996; see also Banerji, 1974).

7.6 TEMPORAL CONSIDERATIONS

7.6.1 Temporal patchiness

It is becoming clear that one means of achieving sympatric speciation in plankton may involve genetic isolation through intraspecific variation in the timing of the reproductive cycle. In species that time their reproduction to coincide with specific (but different) parts of the lunar cycle (e.g. Bijma et al., 1990, 1994; Bijma and Hemleben, 1994; Erez et al., 1991), or with seasonal overturn of the mixed layer (e.g. Lohmann and Schweitzer, 1990; Lohmann, 1992), we may find that their speciation rates, and hence their provincial diversity and distribution, may be influenced by geographic variation in the intensity of seasonal upwelling, or temporal variation in such factors as the depth of the thermocline, pycnocline, or chlorophyll maximum (see Wefer and Fischer, 1993; Williams et al., 1981; Sautter et al., 1991; Curry et al., 1983, 1992).

7.6.2 Time scale and biogeographic patterns

7.6.2.1 The effect of recovery time

It may be fruitful to consider the time scale over which historical events might influence biogeographic patterns. It is likely that ecological restabilization after climatic change would appear to be virtually instantaneous when perceived on a geological time scale, however, it does not follow that biogeographic stabilization is beyond the resolving power of biostratigraphers. This is because ecological response time of the biota is not the only determinant of biogeographic patterns. For example, evolutionary recovery plays a significant role, especially when extinction and speciation are latitude-dependent.

What is the time scale for evolutionary recovery in the plankton? The average censorship-corrected species duration is about 9.17 my for the Cenozoic planktonic Foraminifera and the expected and realized time to recover a stable species age distribution after the Cretaceous/Tertiary extinction is about 15 my (Arnold, et al., 1995b; Parker and Arnold, 1997; also cf. Stanley, 1990) After the post-Cretaceous recovery of a stable age distribution in Cenozoic planktonic Foraminifera, the mean species age fluctuates about an average of 5 my. With evolutionary recovery times of this magnitude, we should expect that the effects of late Cenozoic cooling are likely to exert a lingering influence over that component of biogeographic patterns that is influenced by speciation and extinction rate.

On a somewhat shorter climatic time scale, poleward retreat of Quaternary climatic belts and water masses in relation to southernmost South America has mediated the repopulation of the Atlantic basin by *Globorotalia cultrata* (Vincent and Berger, 1981; see discussion under 'continental positions' above). In this case the limiting factor in these repopulation events has been interaction between climatic belts and continental positions rather than ecological responsiveness of *Globorotalia cultrata*.

If recovery times can be constrained by factors with evolutionary or Milankovich time scales, it follows that the historical components of biogeographic equilibration deserve attention at time scales longer than those normally seen in plankton ecology studies. Endler (1982) provides a useful perspective on the relative importance of ecological and historical influences on diversity gradients.

7.6.2.2 Iterative evolution and the global diversity gradient

The repeated appearance of keeled morphotypes (Cifelli, 1969) is the most conspicuous manifestation of iterative evolution in the planktonic Foraminifera. Even though keeled globorotaliids tend to live at relatively low latitudes, their distribution may not be attributable to an ecological-adaptive (*sensu* Seilacher, 1970) relationship between keels and low-latitude habitats. There are two lines of evidence supporting this view. First, the ecological adaptive relevance of the keeled morphology is challenged by the fact that during the Cenozoic iterations similar morphologies developed in different environmental settings (Boersma and Premoli Silva, 1991). Second, other low-latitude morphotypes have similar speciation rates, so it is likely that the relationship between morphology and turnover rates is indirect.

These observations suggest the possibility of a constructional interpretation for the iterative evolution of keels, and for their nonpolar distribution; the larger number of steps required to reach a keeled morphology from globose ancestry virtually guarantees that keeled forms will tend to be evolutionary latecomers relative to their globose ancestors. Consequently, we should expect the buildup of diversity in keeled forms, *even when it occurs at random with respect to adaptation*, to be (a) late relative to that of globose forms, and (b) greatest and earliest where speciation rates are highest, namely in lower latitudes. Thus, iterative evolution in the planktonic Foraminifera may derive from directed selection (see Gould, 1996, for a general discussion of variance-driven trends), and suggests that the key to understanding iterative evolution might be to learn why small globigerine forms survive mass extinction (Arnold et al., 1995a).

7.7 CONCLUSIONS

There are several important unresolved issues in the area of modern planktonic foraminiferal biogeography. The large-scale latitudinally symmetrical faunal provinces do not appear to show a consistent relationship to comparably-scaled hydrographic features. The origins of these provinces are therefore likely to be understood by reference to other causal factors. The first of these is the degree to which smaller-scale hydrographic features such as current, gyre, and frontal systems combine to play a role in determining larger-scale latitudinal distribution patterns. The second is the role historical processes – particularly, latitude-dependent rates of speciation and extinction, and the development of tectonic barriers – have played in establishing faunal provinces and the global diversity gradient. A number of additional factors, including depth habitats, bipolarity, pore size, coiling direction, and iterative evolution, are indirectly related to physicochemical characteristics of the foraminiferal habitat.

As our understanding of the basic governing principles of modern foraminiferal biogeography develops, it becomes easier to interpret the fossil record in the light of those principles. By the same token, modern distribution patterns, since they are partly the result of historical processes, cannot be fully explained without reference to their past development. We are so accustomed to hearing that the present is the key to the past that we sometimes forget that the past can also be the key to understanding the present. It follows that biogeographic studies of modern and fossil Foraminifera must necessarily proceed hand-in-hand.

7.8 ACKNOWLEDGMENTS

The authors gratefully acknowledge the generous assistance and advice of Richard Norris, Barun Sen Gupta, Andrew Feldman, and an anonymous reviewer. Rosemarie Raymond and Tami Karl provided invaluable help in the preparation of the manuscript.

8

Symbiont-bearing Foraminifera

Pamela Hallock

8.1 WHAT ARE SYMBIONT-BEARING FORAMINIFERA?

Of approximately 150 extant families of Foraminifera, less than 10% harbor algal endosymbionts (Lee and Anderson, 1991a). Nevertheless, these families are responsible for much of the carbonate produced by the Foraminifera, because symbiosis is prevalent in tropical larger foraminifers and planktonic foraminifers, the two groups that are the most prolific carbonate producers. Globally, Milliman and Droxler (1995) estimated carbonate production at 5.7 billion tons per year, of which larger foraminifers produce about 0.5% and planktonic foraminifers produce about 20% (Langer, 1997).

Lee and Anderson (1991a), in their review of the biology of symbiosis in Foraminifera, listed four miliolid, three rotaliid, and five globigerinid families as hosts of algal symbionts belonging to three divisions and five classes of the algae. A few members of several families of smaller rotaliid foraminifers (e.g. Asterigerinidae) appear to host endosymbionts, but those relationships await study. In addition, members of several families are able to sequester chloroplasts, which are harvested from algal food, for days to weeks after ingestion (Lopez, 1979; Cedhagen, 1991; Lee and Anderson, 1991a). While this is not a true symbiosis, chloroplast sequestering does enable these protists to benefit directly from photosynthesis.

Algal symbiosis appears to have arisen independently in most of these lineages of Foraminifera, as well as in several now extinct lineages. Evidence for independent origins is strongest for the miliolid families and subfamilies. The ornamented Peneroplidae (Fig. 8.1.A) host symbionts belonging to the red algae (Division Rhodophyta) (Fig. 8.2.A), while the unornamented Peneroplidae (Fig. 8.1.B) and the Archaiasinae (Family Soritidae) (Fig. 8.1.C) host symbionts belonging to the green algae (Division Chlorophyta) (Fig. 8.2B). The Soritinae (Family Soritidae) (Fig. 8.1.D) host dinoflagellate symbionts (Division Chromophyta, Class Pyrrophyceae) (Fig. 8.2.C), and the Alveolinidae (Fig. 8.1.E) host diatom symbionts (Division Chromophyta, Class Bacillariophyceae). Among the planktonic Foraminifera (Fig. 8.3), both dinoflagellate (Fig. 8.2.D) and chrysophyte (Division Chromophyta, Class Chrysophyceae) (Fig. 8.2.E) symbionts are common. Recent isotopic studies (Norris, 1996a) indicate that within globigerinid generic lineages, symbiosis may be independently acquired. The three rotaliid families, Amphisteginidae (Fig. 8.1.F), Calcarinidae (Fig. 8.1.G) and Nummulitidae (Fig. 8.1.H), all primarily host diatom symbionts (Fig. 8.2.F). Current phylogenies indicate that these families arose independently from smaller ancestors, but proof must await molecular-genetics studies. Nevertheless, evidence is strong that foraminifers are physiologically adapted to establishing symbioses (Lee, 1998), and that symbiosis can be highly advantageous under certain environmental conditions (e.g. Hallock, 1981a; Hottinger, 1982).

8.2 ADVANTAGES OF ALGAL SYMBIOSIS

The potential advantages of algal symbiosis to foraminifers lie in at least three major areas: a) energy from photosynthesis; b) enhancement of calcification; and c) uptake of host metabolites by symbiotic algae. None of these areas has been exhaustively studied, nor are they mutually exclusive. For example, both energy from photosynthesis and uptake of CO_2 or phosphatic waste products would presumably aid calcification.

8.2.1 Energy from photosynthesis

Hallock (1981a) mathematically explored the hypothesis that algal symbiosis provides host-symbiont units with substantial energetic advantages over similar organisms that lack endosymbionts. Organisms with the potential to both feed and photosynthesize have access not only to solar energy, but also to dissolved inorganic nutrients (nitrogen and phosphorus in forms

useable by organisms, i.e. NH_4^+, NO_2^-, NO_3^-, PO_4^{-3}) and to organic matter. In severely nutrient-deficient environments within the euphotic zone of the oceans (i.e. where there is sufficient light for net photosynthesis), the most significant concentrations of essential nutrients are in organic matter. Therefore, algal symbiosis enables the foraminifer to function as a primary producer that obtains nutrients by feeding. Hallock's (1981a) model indicated that algal symbiosis provides the host-symbiont system with several orders of magnitude energetic advantage over non-symbiotic competitors in nutrient-deficient environments. Thus, once acquired, algal symbiosis appears to give significant energetic advantage for specialization of the host to symbiosis, providing considerable insight into repeated episodes of evolution of probable symbiont-bearing foraminifers, as judged by the fossil record (Hallock, 1982, 1985, 1987; Lee and Hallock, 1987; Hallock et al., 1991a).

More recent research by Falkowski et al. (1993), Lee (1998), and others, indicates that the host must maintain control of fixed nitrogen supply to the symbiont, which reinforces recognition of the relationship between nutrient-deficient environments and algal symbioses. Because the photosynthetic process is limited by the availability of solar energy and CO_2, symbionts that are severely nitrogen limited but have plenty of sunlight can produce copious amounts of simple sugars and glycerol, which they release to the host. With its metabolic energy requirements met by this photosynthate, the host can use most of the proteins ingested in captured food for its own growth and reproduction. However, if the symbionts have access to abundant fixed nitrogen, they keep their photosynthate for growth and reproduction, causing physiological stress for the host.

Figure 8.1 Scanning electron micrographs of symbiont-bearing benthic foraminifers.
(A) *Peneroplis elegans* d'Orbigny from Conch Reef, Florida Keys, scale bar = 0.1 mm.
(B) *Laevipeneroplis proteus* (d'Orbigny) from Conch Reef, Florida Keys, scale bar = 0.2 mm.
(C) *Archaias angulatus* (Fichtel and Moll) from Conch Reef, Florida Keys, scale bar = 0.1 mm.
(D) *Sorites orbiculus* (Forskal) from Makapuu, Oahu, Hawaii, scale bar = 0.25 mm.
(E) *Alveolinella quoyi* (d'Orbigny) from Lizard Island, Great Barrier Reef, Australia, scale bar = 0.2 mm.
(F) *Amphistegina lessonii* d'Orbigny from the west Australian shelf, scale bar = 0.2 mm.
(G) *Calcarina gaudichaudii* d'Orbigny from Belau, Western Caroline Islands, scale bar = 0.25 mm.
(H) *Heterostegina depressa* d'Orbigny from the west Australian shelf, scale bar = 0.25 mm.

Advantages of algal symbiosis

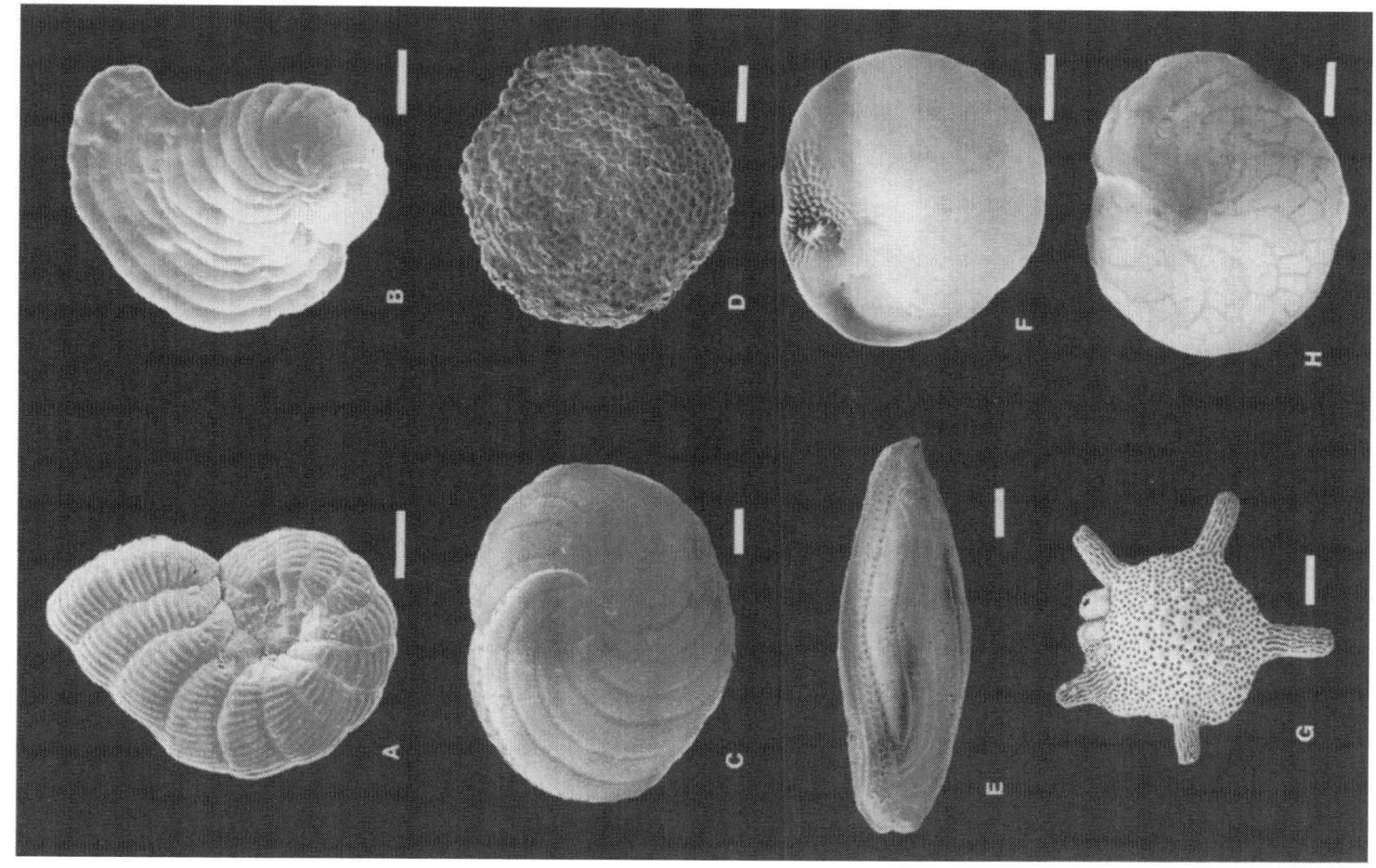

The actual roles of feeding and photosynthesis can differ substantially from theoretical predictions, and vary among the major taxa studied. *Amphistegina* spp. appear to behave most closely to model predictions; physiological studies indicate that ingested food primarily provides nutrients, while respiratory energy comes primarily from photosynthesis (ter Kuile et al., 1987). In contrast, imperforate taxa such as *Archaias*, *Peneroplis*, and *Sorites* appear to be far more energetically dependent upon feeding and, in fact, the role of their symbionts is somewhat enigmatic (Lee and Anderson, 1991a). At the other extreme are some of the Nummulitidae and Calcarinidae, which lack primary and secondary apertures and have not been observed to feed on anything except their endosymbionts (Röttger et al., 1984; Röttger and Krüger, 1990). Clearly this provides a mechanism for receiving proteins and phosphatic acids as well as carbohydrates from endosymbiosis, but does not explain how the host-symbiont unit uptakes essential nutrients. In culture, the foraminifer may be exposed to sufficient nutrients to sustain such a relationship, but in the natural environment, free-living algae should be far superior competitors for dissolved inorganic nutrients than are symbionts that are enclosed within a host organism. In theory, living on the host's nutrient wastes works only if the host is feeding.

One possible explanation for this apparent enigma is that the nummulitids and calcarinids feed upon bacteria, as Lee et al. (1980) experimentally showed for *Heterostegina depressa*. Bacterial feeding can be easily overlooked. Members of both families produce organic attachment mechanisms (Röttger and Krüger, 1990) that Röttger (1973) originally described as rigid hyaline elastic sheaths. The composition of these sheaths should be investigated, for they may provide additional clues to how these foraminifers get required nutrients. When provided with a carbohydrate-rich substrate, certain bacteria are much more efficient at extracting low concentrations of essential nutrients from the water column than are phytoplankton (Azam and Smith, 1991). If the sheaths are carbohydrate-rich, they may provide a substrate for 'farming' bacteria. The foraminifers could then either feed on the bacteria (e.g. Bernhard and Bowser, 1992), or uptake the nutrient wastes of the bacteria and the microplankton that come to feed on the bacteria. Observations of possible bacterial farming by foraminifers are relatively common (e.g. Langer and Gehring, 1993). Hallock et al. (1991b) also postulated that sediment-dwelling, flat-planispiral or discoid foraminifers may take up nutrients that are diffusing out of sediment pore waters, while utilizing sunlight from above.

8.2.2 Algal symbiosis and calcification

Because larger foraminifers with algal symbionts are such prolific calcifiers, conventional wisdom has long held that photosynthesis by the symbionts promotes calcification by splitting of bicarbonate (ter Kuile, 1991) and removal of CO_2 (Equation 8.1):

$$Ca^{2+} + 2HCO_3^- \Rightarrow CO_2 \text{ (to photosynthesis)} + CaCO_3 \text{ (calcification)} + H_2O \quad (8.1)$$

McConnaughey (1989c) and McConnaughey and Whelan (1997) have proposed the reverse interpretation. They postulate that lack of CO_2 limits photosynthesis in warm, shallow, alkaline aquatic environments and that calcification pro-

Figure 8.2 Algal symbionts in or isolated from foraminiferal hosts: (A) micrograph of a section through *Porphyridium purpureum* Hawkins and Lee isolated from *Peneroplis pertusus*, taken with a transmission electron microscope (TEM), P = chloroplast, scale bar = 1 μm; (B) TEM micrograph of *Chlamydomonas hedleyi* Lee et al. freshly extracted from *Archaias angulatus*, P = chloroplast, scale bar = 2 μm; (C) micrograph of '*Symbiodinium*'-like dinoflagellate symbiont isolated from *Amphisorus hemprichii*, taken with a scanning electron microscope (SEM), S = sulcus, F = hypocone flange, scale bar = 2 μm; (D) SEM micrograph of *Gymnodinium béii* Spero isolated from *Orbulina universa*, C = cingulum, S = sulcus, F = hypocone flange, scale bar = 2 μm; (E) TEM micrograph of unidentified chrysophyte algal cells in *Globoquadrina dutertrei*, P = chloroplast, scale bar = 1 μm; (F) SEM micrograph of *Nitzschia panduriformis* Grun isolated from *Calcarina hispida*, scale bar = 2 μm. Illustrations A, B, C, and F by J.J. Lee, D by H.J. Spero, E by Mary Downes Gastrich. D reprinted from Journal of Phycology (v. 23, p. 312) by permission.

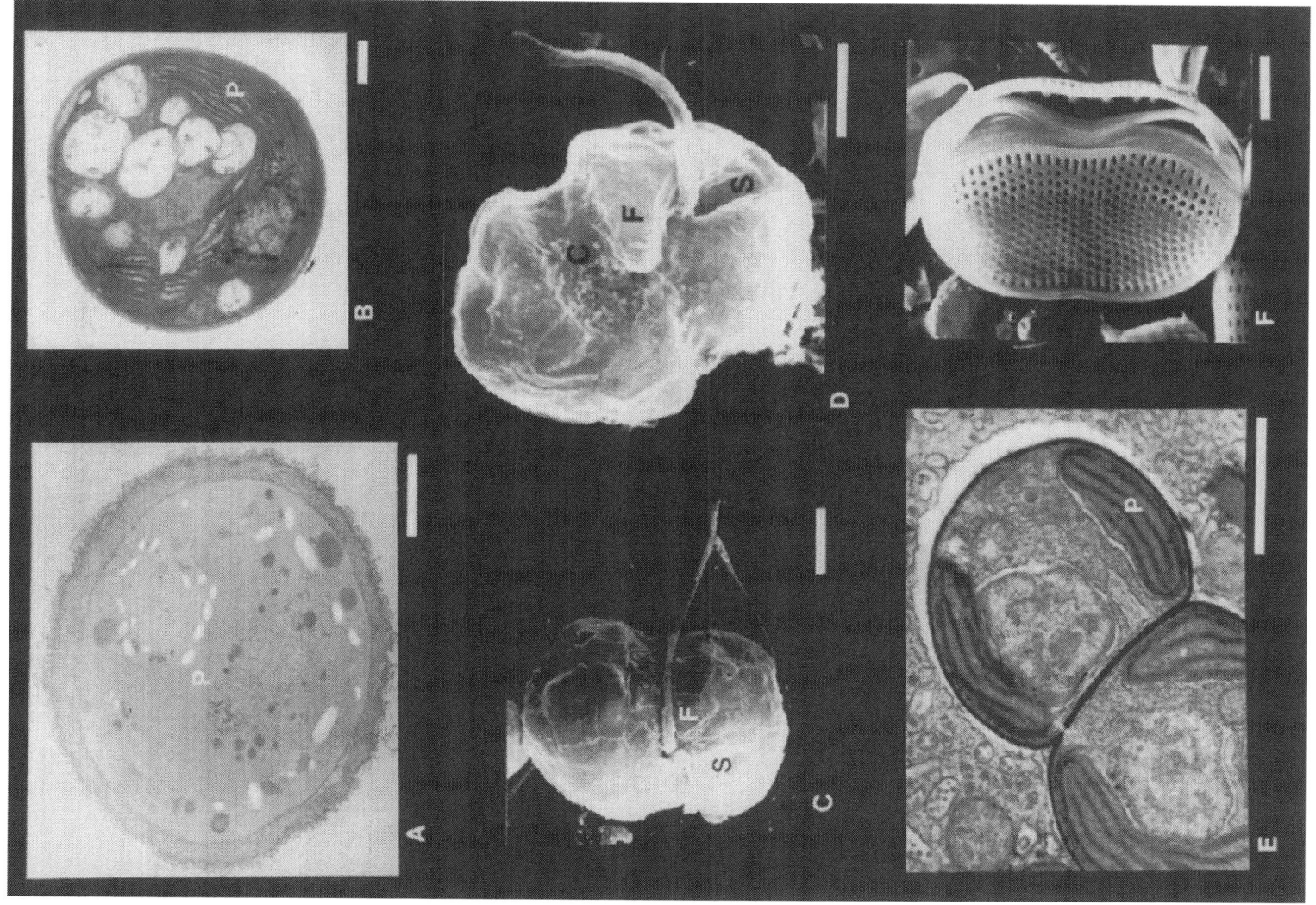

Symbiont-bearing Foraminifera

the organic-carbon synthesis phase of photosynthesis.

Another link between photosynthesis and calcification may simply be the production of ATP, which can be used as an energy source for active transport within the cell. Erez (1983) found essentially normal calcification rates in perforate, symbiont-bearing foraminifers that had been treated with a herbicide that blocks the carbon fixation step in photosynthesis, but not the initial production of ATP. ATP provides the energy source for concentration of the inorganic carbon into internal reservoirs in the larger perforate taxa, and into vesicles in the imperforate species (ter Kuile, 1991). ATP may also provide the energy for removal of ions that can inhibit calcification, including NH_4^+, PO_4^{3-}, and Mg^{2+} (ter Kuile, 1991). Foraminifers with algal endosymbionts may use sunlight rather than food resources as the source of energy for ATP, thereby accounting for the significant enhancement of calcification by light (e.g. Duguay and Taylor, 1978; Duguay 1983; Erez 1983; ter Kuile 1991).

The organic matrix of the test is critical in initiating and directing calcification, particularly in perforate foraminifers (e.g. Hemleben et al., 1977; Angell, 1979, 1980; Weiner, 1986; ter Kuile, 1991). The organic matrix also provides strength and flexibility to the test (Weiner, 1986). Lee (1998) discovered that the large, heavy tests of imperforate taxa such as Marginopora include substantial quantities of organic matter. Similarly, Toler and Hallock (1998) found that normal Amphistegina tests have substantial organic matter, but that the tests of individuals suffering from anomalous symbiont loss may be grossly deficient in organic matter, resulting in weakened and anomalously calcified tests. The organic chamber lining of the shell matrix of many foraminifers, which provides structural integrity to the test, is composed of glycosaminoglycans that are 99.5% polysaccharide and 0.5% protein (Weiner and Erez, 1984). Carbohydrate from photosynthate may be contributing to the organic matrix of the shell. This and other hypotheses concerning the role of the organic matrix in biomineralization are fertile topics for further research.

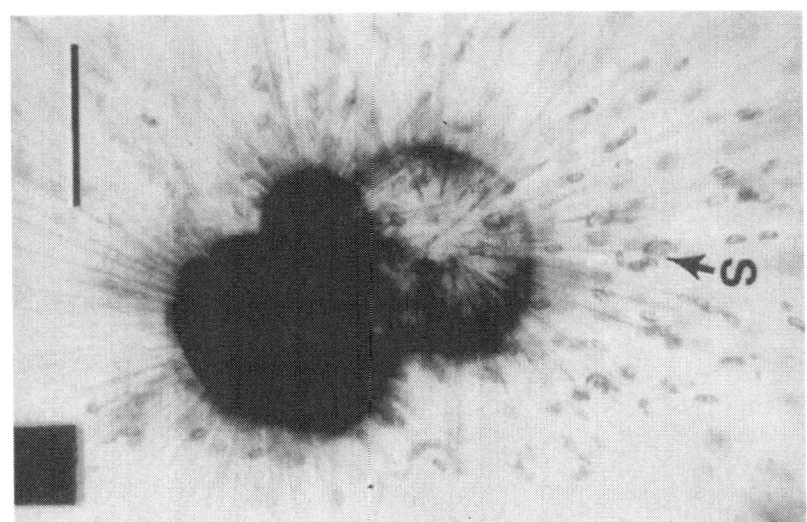

Figure 8.3 Light micrograph of a live *Orbulina universa* illustrating deployment of the dinoflagellate symbionts (S), on the spines of the host. Photo by H.J. Spero, reprinted from Journal of Phycology (v. 23, p. 310) by permission.

vides protons (equation 8.2) that make CO_2 readily available from the much more abundant bicarbonate ions (equation 8.3). That is, calcification:

$$Ca^{2+} + HCO_3^- \rightleftharpoons CaCO_3 + H^+ \quad (8.2)$$

promotes photosynthesis:

$$HCO_3^- + H^+ \rightleftharpoons CH_2O + O_2 \quad (8.3)$$

(CH_2O is a simplified expression for organic matter produced during photosynthesis, i.e. photosynthate). According to this hypothesis, the electron capture phase of photosynthesis provides ATP for active transport of Ca^{2+} and H^+ ions, promoting calcification and making bicarbonate ion a viable source of CO_2 for

8.2.3 Uptake of host metabolites

Another postulated advantage of algal symbiosis, particularly for very large species, is the possible role of the symbionts in removal of host metabolites. Protists are dependent upon processes such as diffusion, active transport, and cytoplasmic streaming for transport of materials into, out of, and within the cell. The assumption behind the hypothesis of metabolic removal is that the larger the foraminifer, the greater the transport problem. Presumably, having intracellular symbionts could partially alleviate this problem. While there is very little evidence either to support or refute this hypothesis, a logical argument against it is that, while the symbionts might remove metabolites during the day, at night they produce their own metabolites, particularly CO_2, which would presumably exacerbate the need for water motion to supply oxygen and to remove carbon dioxide and other metabolites. However, the calcification process could benefit from metabolite removal, because NH_4^+ or PO_4^{-3} can interfere with crystal formation (e.g. ter Kuile, 1991).

8.2.4 Significance of algal symbiosis to ecosystems

Whatever the benefit to individual organisms, the advantage of such symbioses to ecosystems in nutrient-deficient environments is tremendous. Algal symbiosis is one of the major mechanisms that allows mixotrophic nutrition, that is, the ability to both feed and photosynthesize (Hallock, 1981a), in contrast to autotrophic and heterotrophic nutrition which allows one or the other. In ecosystems dominated by purely autotrophic and heterotrophic nutrition, food webs are based on autotrophic primary producers. There is typically a 90% or greater loss of energy and biomass to respiration with each heterotrophic link in the food web. Mixotrophic nutrition, in contrast, provides essentially 'free links' in the food web. That is, when a mixotrophic organism such as a larger foraminifer or zooxanthellate coral captures a unit of prey, the majority of the digestible organic matter in the prey can be used by the host for growth and reproduction. Photosynthesis by the symbionts provides energy for the host's respiratory needs (Falkowski et al., 1993). Thus, the biomass transfer from the prey to the mixotroph can potentially be far greater than the typical 10%. Prolific calcification, regardless of whether it promotes photosynthesis or is a byproduct thereof, provides substratum for whole ecosystems to develop and flourish. Furthermore, although the significance of mixotrophic nutrition in plankton communities is just beginning to be recognized (e.g. Stoecker, 1998), its contribution to recycled production in open-ocean communities appears to be significant. Perhaps most importantly, planktonic Foraminifera, many with algal symbionts, account for about 20% of global carbonate production (Langer, 1997), and thereby play a key role in marine geochemical cycles, whether the foraminiferal tests are dissolved in corrosive deep-sea waters or accumulate as foraminiferal ooze on the seafloor.

8.3 DISTRIBUTIONS OF BENTHIC FORAMINIFERS WITH ALGAL SYMBIONTS

Like most groups of organisms, the larger foraminifers exhibit higher diversities in the Indo-Pacific region than in the central Pacific, Gulf of Aqaba, and western Atlantic/Caribbean regions (Table 8.1). This is particularly true within the three larger rotaliid families (Hallock, 1988a,b). The Indo-Pacific Amphisteginidae (Fig. 8.1.F) and Nummulitidae (Fig. 8.1.H) each include five or six relatively well known and easily distinguishable species, as compared to one or two variable species in the Caribbean. The third rotaliid family, the Calcarinidae (Fig. 8.1.G), is restricted to the Indo-Pacific. Among the imperforate taxa, the Alveolinidae (Fig. 8.1.E), rhodophyte-bearing Peneroplidae (Fig. 8.1.A) and Soritinae (Fig. 8.1.D) are also more diverse in the Indo-Pacific than in the Caribbean. However, for taxa that have chlorophyte symbionts (Table 8.1), i.e. the unornamented Peneroplidae (Fig. 8.1.B) and the

Symbiont-bearing Foraminifera

Table 8.1 Comparison of selected symbiont-bearing benthic Foraminifera from Caribbean and western Pacific regions. The number in parenthesis is the number of species recognized for the genus in the particular area (adapted from Hallock 1988a).

Family (subfamily)	Symbiont Class	Western Pacific	Caribbean
Alveolinidae	Bacillariophyceae	*Alveolinella quoyi*	
Peneroplidae	Rhodophyceae	*Borelis* sp. (1–2)	*Borelis pulchra*
		Dendritina spp. (2)	*Dendritina* spp. (4?)
		Monalysidium sollasi	
		Peneroplis spp. (2)	*Peneroplis* spp. (2)
		Spirolina spp. (2)	*Spirolina* spp. (2)
Soritidae (Archaiasinae)	Chlorophyceae	*Laevipeneroplis malayensis*	*Laevipeneroplis* spp. (3?)
			Androsina lucasi
			Archaias angulatus
			Cyclorbiculina spp. (3)
(Soritinae)	Pyrrophyceae	*Parasorites orbitolitoides*	*Parasorites* spp. (2)
		Amphisorus hemprichii	*Amphisorus hemprichii*
		Marginopora spp. (2)	
		Sorites spp. (2?)	*Sorites* spp. (2?)
Amphisteginidae	Bacillariophyceae	*Amphistegina* spp. (5–6)	*Amphistegina* sp. (1–2?)
Calcarinidae	Bacillariophyceae	*Baculogypsinoides spinosus*	
		Calcarina spp. (3)	
		Neorotalia calcar	
		Schlumbergerella floresiana	
		Assilina ammonoides	
Nummulitidae	Bacillariophyceae	*Cycloclypeus carpenteri*	
		Heterostegina spp. (2)	*Heterostegina antillarum*
		Nummulites venosus	

Archaiasinae (Fig. 8.1.C), the trend is the opposite (Table 8.1). In the Caribbean, this group is represented by five genera and ten or more species, as compared to the western Pacific, where there seems to be only two monospecific genera. Deciphering this anomaly may, in the future, provide insight into the paleoceanographic history of the Caribbean.

Depth trends of larger foraminiferal distributions are a key tool for paleoenvironmental interpretation (e.g. Hottinger, 1983, 1997; Hallock and Glenn, 1985, 1986). The most thorough studies to date on depth distributions of Indo-Pacific living larger foraminifers are those of Reiss and Hottinger (1984), Hallock (1984), and Hohenegger (1994), carried out in the Gulf of Aqaba, Belau (Palau, Western Caroline Islands), and Okinawa, respectively. Hottinger (1983) noted that the maximum depth for symbiont-bearing organisms in the Gulf of Aqaba is 130 m, corresponding to 0.5% of surface light intensity. Figure 8.4 summarizes distributions of four modern larger foraminiferal families, illustrating trends in test shape with depth.

8.3.1 Larger rotaliid foraminifers

Larger foraminifers belonging to the Order Rotaliida share several important characteristics that enable them to effectively exploit an extensive depth range of euphotic habitats in warm, clear, nutrient-deficient seas (Hallock, 1988a,b). One characteristic is the ability to establish endosymbioses with several diatom species. This allows one species of foraminifer to exploit a substantial range of light intensities, which are contingent upon the photic requirements and limitations of several different diatom species (e.g. Lee and Anderson, 1991a). The flexibility of the endosymbiosis is complemented by the

Distributions of benthic foraminifers with algal symbionts

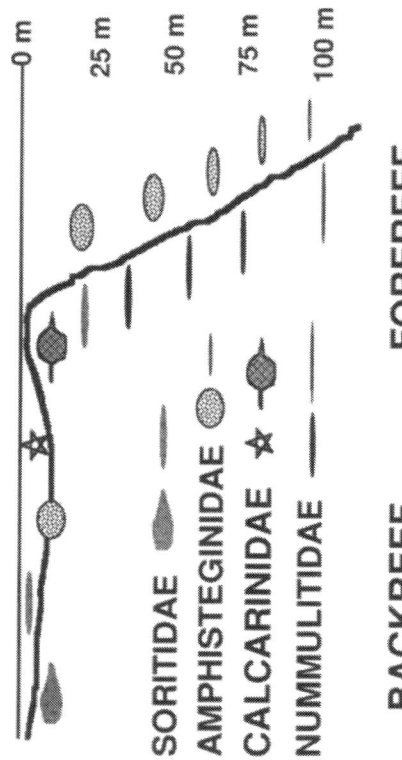

Figure 8.4 Cartoon representation of shape trends with depth in four families of symbiont-bearing benthic foraminifers.

structural characteristics of the perforate, hyaline, lamellar, low-magnesium calcite tests (Hallock, 1988a,b). Calcite secretion with the crystallographic c-axes perpendicular to the test surface, as observed by Towe and Cifelli (1967), provides the potential for the development of very transparent, hyaline tests which can transmit most available light energy. The lamellar structure permits thickening of the test wall through the life of the protist, which may be advantageous in shallow, high-light environments. In the Calcarinidae and Nummulitidae, the lamellar wall structure is modified into a canal system providing a variety of advantages that complement symbiosis (Röttger et al., 1984; Röttger and Krüger, 1990). In the Calcarinidae, in particular, the canal system permits the thickening and translucency of the shell, reducing light penetration and allowing individuals to live in the upper meter of brightly-lit tropical waters. The lamellar structure and canal system also allow for the complex spine systems in the calcarinids, thus providing anchoring and stability in high energy reef-flat and reef-margin environments (Röttger and Krüger, 1990).

Efficient precipitation and maintenance of low-Mg calcite tests do not require greatly elevated carbonate saturation states. Most of the larger rotaliid families arose during the early Paleogene, when atmospheric CO_2 concentrations were two or more times higher than present levels (e.g. Berner, 1994) and so sea-surface carbonate saturation levels were significantly lower. On the other hand, these foraminifers do not thrive under elevated salinities, with concomitant elevated alkalinity. The potential for crystal poisoning by Mg^{2+} should be investigated as the mechanism involved, since Mg^{2+} increasingly interferes with calcite precipitation as carbonate saturation state increases (Morse and Mackenzie, 1990).

(a) Amphisteginidae. The Amphisteginidae are the most studied of the symbiont-bearing families. The best known species are *Amphistegina lobifera* Larsen and *A. lessonii* d'Orbigny (Fig. 8.1.F) in the Indo-Pacific, and *A. gibbosa* d'Orbigny, the sibling species of *A. lessonii*, in the Caribbean. All three occur abundantly at depths less than 30 m, and are amenable to culture. Around some Pacific islands, *A. lobifera* and *A. lessonii* may be so abundant that they are major contributors to coastal sediments (McKee et al., 1959; Hallock 1981b). They live on firm substrates, both reefal and phytal, and may also occur in sandy substrates (Hoheneg-ger, 1994). Generation times appear to be 3–6 months at depths <30 m (Hallock, 1981c; Hallock et al., 1986b), but are probably longer in deeper habitats where there is less light energy. Generation times in *A. lobifera* are 6–12 months (Hallock, 1981c). Harney et al. (1998) and Dettmering et al. (1998) documented trimorphic life cycles in *A. gibbosa*. That is, besides typical alternation of sexual and asexual generations, one or more schizont generations may occur between the agamont and gamont generations.

In the Indo-Pacific region, *Amphistegina* spp. exhibit a fairly straightforward depth zonation (Fig. 8.4) that is accompanied by shape trends from the shallow subtidal down to depths of 100 m if water transparency is sufficient. They apparently do this by cryptic behavior at the shallow end of their depth range, thereby avoiding damaging light intensities, and possibly by utilizing symbiont species that are adapted to lower light intensities at greater depths (Lee et al., 1980). *Amphistegina radiata* (Fichtel and Moll) is common at 20–50 m, and ranges to nearly 100 m in depth (Hallock, 1984; Hohenegger, 1994). *A. radiata* has a limited geographic distribution and does not occur in the central Pacific (e.g. Hawaii). Hottinger et al. (1993) reported a very small *A. radiata*-like form in the Gulf of Aqaba, living at somewhat deeper habitats than those found in the western Pacific. *A. bicirculata* Larsen is similar to *A. lessonii*, but has consistently lower *t/d* ratios of about 0.2–0.35 (Larsen, 1976; Hallock, 1979). Specimens are seldom found at depths <30 m, and can be recovered live to depths >100 m. *Amphistegina papillosa* Said is the deepest dwelling member of the genus, capable of surviving on the minimal light available at depths >100 m (Larsen, 1976). Their tests are typically very flat, appearing almost paper thin, and have tiny papillae on test surfaces, the characteristic for which the species was named. The geographic distribution of *A. papillosa* appears to be similar to that of *A. radiata*.

In the western Atlantic and Caribbean, *Amphistegina gibbosa* is the predominant species of this genus. Whether it is the only species is controversial. Test morphologies are highly variable, and range between a form essentially indistinguishable from *A. lessonii* and the robustly plano-convex 'gibbose' forms for which the species was named. *A. gibbosa* has a wide depth distribution similar to, though generally slightly deeper than, that of *A. lessonii*. Live individuals can often be found at depths <5 m on patch reefs and to 100 m on open carbonate-shelf environments, though their preferred depths appear to be ~15–40 m. Test shape is not as predictable with depth as it is in *A. lessonii* (Martin and Liddell, 1988).

(b) Nummulitidae. Habitats and geographic ranges of most species of Nummulitidae are incompletely known, because their occurrence in deep-euphotic areas (generally >30 m) is beyond prudent SCUBA sampling depth (Fig. 8.4). These protists live on both firm and sandy substrates (Hohenegger, 1994). Some nummulitids lack true primary and secondary apertures; instead, they have canal systems that serve similar fundamental roles in locomotion, growth, excretion, reproduction and protection (Röttger et al., 1984). The canal system permits the extrusion of pseudopodia from any point of the marginal cord. Trimorphic life cycles appear to be the norm in this group (e.g. Leutenegger, 1977a; Röttger et al., 1990), and may partly account for the dearth of sexually-produced agamonts in most populations (Drooger, 1993). Agamonts are often distinctive, even without sectioning to confirm microspheric embryos, because these individuals typically grow to sizes substantially larger than schizonts and gamonts.

Heterostegina depressa d'Orbigny (Fig. 8.1.H) is the most widespread of all larger foraminiferal species, present in the Gulf of Aqaba and throughout the tropical and subtropical Indian and Pacific Oceans. It is the only larger rotaliid species that survived the oceanographic changes in the eastern tropical Pacific associated with the closure of the Central American Seaway

(Crouch and Poag, 1987). The Caribbean sibling species, *Heterostegina antillarum* d'Orbigny, appears to have diverged following the uplift of the Isthmus of Panama. *H. depressa* is the only nummulitid commonly found at depths less than 20 m, though its optimum depths are 20–60 m (Hallock, 1984; Hohenegger, 1994). Shallower-dwelling populations may be sustained primarily by successive asexual generations, while deeper dwelling populations appear to utilize sexual reproduction more commonly in their life cycles (Röttger et al., 1990). Their very low light tolerances (Röttger and Berger, 1972) indicate that cryptic behavior may be necessary for them to survive at shallow depths. Individuals are amenable to culture, as demonstrated by the pioneering laboratory observations of Röttger (1972, 1973, 1974, 1976). Schizont reproduction occurs at about 6 months of age (Röttger and Spindler, 1976). Diameters at reproduction of *H. depressa* in culture range from about 2 mm for schizonts to 4 mm for gamonts to 7–14 mm for agamonts (Röttger et al., 1986, 1990).

Assilina ammonoides (Gronovius) is superficially similar in appearance to *H. depressa*, but chambers of *Assilina* are not subdivided into chamberlets. This species is widely distributed throughout the Indo-Pacific, ranging from the Gulf of Aqaba (Hottinger, 1977; Hottinger et al., 1993) to Hawaii in the central Pacific (Hallock, 1984). *Assilina* is common from 20–100 m, with an optimum depth of around 60 m. Though it can be found on firm substrate, it appears to prefer sand and muddy sand habitats (Hohenegger, 1994).

Nummulites venosus (Fichtel and Moll) is the only extant species of the name genus of the family. Individuals may be relatively lenticular and involute as juvenile and subadult agamonts, or even as adult schizonts and gamonts. Agamonts typically grow to much larger sizes than gamonts and schizonts. Hohenegger (1994) reported their depth range as 20–80 m, peaking in abundance at 40 m.

The two deepest-dwelling nummulitids, *Heterostegina operculinoides* Hofker and *Cycloclypeus carpenteri* Brady, have classic flat, thin, 'deep-euphotic' morphologies (Fig. 8.4). The latter species also differs from the other nummulitids in that the planispiral growth form develops into an orbitoid morphology early in life, so that adult individuals are large, thin disks with slightly elevated (thicker) central regions (Song et al., 1994). Agamont generations of *Cycloclypeus* are apparently quite long lived, with test diameters exceeding 120 mm (Koba, 1978). Gamonts and schizonts reproduce at considerably smaller sizes (Krüger et al., 1996). Although the geographic distribution of *Cycloclypeus* is not well known, it appears to have a relatively restricted distribution in the Indo-Malay and far western Pacific. Another deep-euphotic species, *Heterocyclina tuberculata* (Möbius), has been reported from the Gulf of Aqaba and from the Indian Ocean (e.g. Hottinger et al., 1993).

(c) Calcarinidae. The Calcarinidae, which live predominantly in shallow, high energy reef-flat and reef-margin environments (Fig. 8.4), include five genera: *Baculogypsina*, *Baculogypsinoides*, *Calcarina*, *Neorotalia*, and *Schlumbergerella* (Hohenegger, 1994; and personal communication). With the exception of *Neorotalia calcar* (d'Orbigny), which occurs in the western Indian Ocean region, the Calcarinidae are restricted to the Indo-Malay archipelago and western Pacific (Table 8.1), and are very important carbonate sediment producers in this region. Sediment production estimates, projected from known rates of production by *C. gaudichaudii* d'Orbigny (Fig. 8.1.G) from Belau, can approach those of reef-flat corals at 3–5 kg $CaCO_3$ m^{-2} yr^{-1} (Hallock, 1981b). In the Ryukyu Islands, the famous star-sand beaches are composed primarily of the shells of *Baculogypsina* (Hohenegger, 1994).

The elaborate calcarinid canal systems and spiny morphologies provide numerous points of contact with the external environment. Röttger and Krüger (1990) described an attachment mechanism in *Baculogypsina sphaerulata* (Parker and Jones) that consists of a durable, elastic organic cement, which enables individuals to adhere by a single spine to the algal substratum. This attachment mechanism allows calcarinids to thrive in high energy environments.

The very limited geographic distributions of the Calcarinidae indicate that their dispersal potential must be quite limited. However, factors contributing to the very widespread distributions of *Amphistegina lessonii* and *Heterostegina depressa* are no better understood. A study of biological and ecological factors associated with distributional patterns of larger foraminifers is long overdue.

8.3.2 Larger miliolid taxa

The imperforate foraminifers of the Order Miliolida construct porcelaneous-appearing tests of high-magnesium calcite. Distributions of imperforate taxa characterized by algal endosymbionts are not as well known as those of similar perforate taxa. In large part, this is because of taxonomic difficulties with miliolids, which are morphologically more plastic, and include many species that are superficially similar. From an ecological perspective, the larger miliolids can be discussed by the kind of symbionts they host.

Hallock (1988a,b) noted that the larger miliolids are most common in shallower habitats, and tend to have a more restricted depth range than the larger rotaliids (Fig. 8.4). The miliolid test structure includes a layer of randomly-oriented crystals, covered by a brick-like layer of crystals oriented with the c-axis parallel to the outer wall, resulting in a naturally opaque structure. To efficiently host algal endosymbionts, the shell wall over the chambers must be thinned (Hallock and Peebles, 1993). Thus, test structure may account for some of the distributional limitations on these foraminifers.

Test mineralogy may also provide other advantages and disadvantages, depending upon the environment. High-Mg calcite becomes increasingly easy to precipitate as the carbonate saturation state of the seawater increases (Morse and Mackenzie, 1990). This may partly explain the predominance of Archaiasinae in the western Atlantic and Caribbean (Hallock, 1988a,b). Oceanic salinities are 1–3‰ higher in the tropical Atlantic than in the tropical Pacific, contributing to higher alkalinity and degree of $CaCO_3$ saturation in the Atlantic (Broecker and Peng,

1987). The divergence of tropical ocean chemistries occurred during the Miocene and Pliocene with the emergence of the Isthmus of Panama. During this time, the porcelaneous, high-Mg-calcitic Archaiasinae became the predominant larger foraminifers in western Atlantic and Caribbean (Frost, 1977). In the Indo-Pacific region, localities with elevated salinities, such as the Persian Gulf (Murray, 1973) and Shark Bay, Australia (Davies, 1970; Logan and Cebulski 1970), are dominated by ornamented Peneroplidae. ter Kuile (1991) observed that external sources of bicarbonate are more important than enzymatic processes for calcification in imperforate Foraminifera, providing a clue to the success of these foraminifers in high alkalinity environments. Because high-Mg calcite is relatively weak, and the miliolid shell structure is not bilamellar, organic matter in the shell may provide necessary strength to the test.

The Alveolinidae are the only imperforate taxa known to harbor diatom symbionts (Lee et al., 1989). In modern seas, this family is represented by two genera and a few species. *Alveolinella quoyi* (d'Orbigny) (Fig. 8.1.E) appears to be geographically limited to the Indo-Malay and western Pacific regions. Its habitat includes fore-reef rubble and sands at depths from 5 to 50 m (Lipps and Severin, 1985; Severin and Lipps, 1989; Hohenegger, 1994). The much smaller *Borelis* spp. are circumtropical in distribution and can be found on reef rubble at depths to at least 30 m. *Borelis pulchra* (d'Orbigny) is one of only four symbiont-bearing foraminifers documented in the eastern tropical Pacific by Crouch and Poag (1987).

Two chlorophyte-bearing species have been reported from the Indo-Pacific (Table 8.1). *Parasorites orbitolitoides* (Hofker), a medium depth (10–60 m), sediment-dwelling species, occurs in New Caledonia (Debenay, 1986), off Okinawa (Hohenegger, 1994), on the Great Barrier Reef, and on the west Australian shelf (Hallock, unpublished observation). Cheng and Zheng (1978) described an unornamented peneroplid, which they called *Puteolina malayensis*, occurring abundantly around the Xisha Islands, Guangdong Province, China. Hallock (1984 found a similar unornamented peneroplid on reef flats in Belau, Western Caroline Islands. Live specimens of both species exhibit the grass-green symbiont color characteristic of chlorophyte-bearing foraminiferal taxa. Loeblich and Tappan (1987) considered *Puteolina* to be a junior synonym for *Laevipeneroplis*.

Western Atlantic/Caribbean miliolid species with chlorophyte symbionts have been studied in detail by Lévy (1977, 1991) and by Hallock and Peebles (1993). The larger, internally-complex archaiasines include the *Androsina*-*Archaias*-*Cyclorbiculina* group distinguished by Levy (1977, 1991). *Androsina lucasi* Lévy was described from hypersaline reef flats in the Bahamas (Levy 1977), and is found very abundantly on dwarf-mangrove flats in the Florida Keys (Levy, 1991; Hallock and Peebles, 1993). *Archaias angulatus* (Fichtel and Moll) (Fig. 8.1.C) is abundant on shallow reef (Fig. 8.4) and open shelf sites (Hallock and Peebles, 1993). *Cyclorbiculina compressa* (d'Orbigny) can be found in shallow seagrass beds on the open shelf, but is more common on the reef margin at depths of 10–30 m (Fig. 8.4). Hallock and Peebles (1993) observed that chamberlet outer-wall thickness was distinctive in this group, with *Androsina* characterized by a relatively thick (up to 20 μm) wall, *A. angulatus* by an intermediate wall thickness (∼6–8 μm), and the deeper-dwelling *Cyclorbiculina* by the thinnest (3–4 μm) wall. Hallock and Peebles (1993) postulated that wall thickness was an adaptation to regulate light reaching the endosymbionts.

Lee *et al.* (1974) identified the chlorophyte symbionts of *A. angulatus* as *Chlamydomonas hedleyi*. Live specimens of *Laevipeneroplis proteus* (Fig. 8.1.B) appear to have the same symbionts (Leutenegger, 1984). Lee *et al.* (1979) described the symbionts of *Cyclorbiculina compressa* as *Chlamydomonas provasoli*. Lee and Bock (1976) reported that carbon gain by feeding was more than ten times greater than carbon fixation by photosynthesis in *A. angulatus*. Thus, the principal role that symbiosis appears to play is in enchanced calcification. Duguay (1983) reported that calcification rates varied with light intensity and were 2–3 times faster in the light than in the dark.

Parasorites is also common throughout the Caribbean, and occurs regularly in both soft sediment and reef-rubble samples taken at 10–30 m depth. Lévy (1977) called this genus *Broeckina*, and distinguished two species in the Bahamas: *B. discoidea* (Flint) and *B. orbitolitoides* (Hofker). A comparative study of the Indo-Pacific and Caribbean *Parasorites* and *Laevipeneroplis* is needed to clarify relationships within these genera. Several species of unornamented peneroplines (*Laevipeneroplis* spp., see Fig. 8.1.B). occur throughout the Caribbean in reef and open shelf environments.

Foraminifers that host red algae (Division Rhodophyta) as symbionts include extant members of the Peneroplidae with test-surface ornamentation, i.e. *Peneroplis, Dendritina, Spirolina,* and *Monalysidium* (Loeblich and Tappan, 1987). These foraminifers provide excellent opportunities for further study, particularly with reference to morphologic variability, habitat preferences, and physiology of their symbiotic relationships.

Hawkins and Lee (1990) and Lee (1990b) have studied the unique relationship between the rhodophyte symbiont, *Porphyridium purpureum* (Fig. 8.2.A), and its foraminiferal host. Unlike other symbionts, the rhodophyte cell is not membrane bound within the host cytoplasm, and in that respect could be considered an organelle rather than a symbiont. In culture, *Porphyridium* cells are surrounded by a heavy fibrous polysaccharide sheath, but when the symbionts are located in a host, the sheath is reduced or absent. Lee and Anderson (1991a) suggested that sheath-fiber digestion by the host may be a mechanism of energy transfer from symbiont to host.

Hypersaline environments in Shark Bay, Western Australia, and the Persian Gulf are dominated by peneroplids. In Shark Bay, Davies (1970) and Logan and Cebulski (1970) reported low foraminiferal diversities with assemblages dominated by *P. planatus*, with a few other miliolid species, at salinities up to 70‰. Similarly, *Peneroplis planatus* (Fichtel and Moll), *P. pertusus* (Forskal) and a variety of miliolids dominate shallow-water, hypersaline habitats in the Persian Gulf (Murray, 1973).

Extant members of the subfamily Soritinae host dinoflagellate symbionts. Physiological studies by Lee and co-workers (Lee and Bock, 1976; Faber and Lee, 1991a) indicate that these foraminifers derive most of their carbon needs from their food rather than from their symbionts. So the benefit of the symbiotic relationship remains an open question. More recent observations by Lee et al. (1995, 1997) and Lee (1998) indicate that the soritine foraminifers, like the amphisteginids, do not require a particular species of symbiont, but rather one of a suite of acceptable symbionts. The physiology of the alga, which makes it capable of being a symbiont and recognizable as such by the host, appears to be more important than taxonomic identity. This relative flexibility of the symbiotic relationship is of obvious advantage to the host organism, which is dependent upon symbiosis but can accept any of several possible algal species rather than being dependent upon a single species of algae. Since the foraminiferal zygote must acquire symbionts following zygosis, the possibility of incorporating any of several potential symbiont species may increase the survival rates of sexually-produced individuals (Lee, 1998).

Taxonomic ambiguities hinder interpretation of literature reports of geographic ranges, depth distributions, and habitats of the Soritinae. *Marginopora* has been used in reference to both *Marginopora* and *Amphisorus* species, *Amphisorus* for both *Amphisorus* and *Sorites* species, and *Sorites* for both *Sorites* and *Parasorites*. The large, robust *Marginopora vertebralis* Quoy and Gaimard probably has a geographic and depth distribution similar to that of *Calcarina* spp. *Marginopora* can live on either firm or soft substrate (Hohenegger, 1994), attaching to algal thalli with an organic cement (Ross, 1972).

Amphisorus hemprichii Ehrenberg is intermediate in robustness, and has wide depth and geographic ranges. This species has been reported circumtropically, from the Gulf of Aqaba (e.g. Hottinger et al., 1993) through the Indian Ocean and across the Pacific to Hawaii (Phillips, 1977), the eastern tropical Pacific (Crouch and Poag, 1987), and the Caribbean (Lévy, 1977). It prefers firm substrates and can partially adhere to phytal substrates. *Amphisorus* (identified by Davies, 1970, as *Marginopora*) occurs in Shark Bay, Western Australia, at salinities up to 56‰ and temperature range of 14–38°C.

Several species of *Sorites* live on phytal substrates or in algal-bacterial mats that stabilize sandy substrates. These foraminifers can behave as vagile protists or as attached forms, as they can semipermanently attach to firm substrates by an organic cement (Röttger and Krüger, 1990). The type of surface and its shape may influence the growth and morphology of the foraminifer. Kloos (1980) noted that, in the Netherlands Antilles, living *S. orbiculus* (Forskal) appeared to prefer the seagrass *Thalassia* as substratum.

8.4 PLANKTONIC FORAMINIFERA WITH ALGAL SYMBIONTS

Compared with benthic Foraminifera, there are relatively few extant species of planktonic foraminifers (e.g. Kennett and Srinivasan, 1983). Yet these protists approach global distribution (e.g. Murray, 1991a) and, as previously noted, produce roughly 20% of the calcium carbonate fixed in the world's oceans each year (Langer, 1997).

Hemleben et al. (1989), in their comprehensive compendium on modern species, noted that 'The presence of algal associations with spinose planktonic Foraminifera is one of the most obvious features of living individuals' (p. 86). Algal symbionts include dinoflagellates, which occur in the Globigerinidae and the Hasterigerinidae, and chrysophytes, which are found in representatives of the Globigerinidae, Candeinidae, Pulleniatinidae, Hastigerinidae, and Globorotaliidae (Lee and Anderson, 1991a). As a general rule, symbioses with dinoflagellates appear to be obligative (Hemleben et al., 1989); the exception may be the variety of dinoflagellates that can be associated with the bubble capsule of *Hastigerina pelagica* (d'Orbigny) (Spindler and Hemleben, 1980). On the other hand, symbioses with chrysophytes (Fig. 8.2.E) appear to be facultative, since both Gastrich (1988) and Hemleben et al. (1989) reported that individuals of some species reported to host chrysophyte symbionts commonly lack symbionts during winter months.

Spero (1987) isolated and described the dinoflagellate symbiont in *Orbulina universa* d'Orbigny as *Gymnodinium béii* (Figs. 8.2.D, 8.3). This symbiont occurs in several other species (Lee and Anderson, 1991a), and may be the only dinoflagellate species to establish symbioses with planktonic foraminifers (Gast and Caron, 1996). In their hosts, *G. béii* individuals are small (5–10 µm) and coccoid; 10^3 to 10^4 symbionts may occur in a single host cell (Spero and Parker, 1985). When isolated from the host and incubated in culture, these dinoflagellates develop flagellated gymnodinoid morphologies (Fig. 8.2.D; Spero, 1987). When the planktonic foraminifers reproduce, releasing flagellated swarmers, algal symbionts are either lysed, digested, or released into the environment (Hemleben et al., 1989). Early in their life, the juvenile foraminifers must encounter and incorporate symbionts (Hemleben et al., 1989), indicating that suitable dinoflagellate populations are free-living in the water column.

As discussed earlier, the potential advantages of algal symbiosis include energy from photosynthesis, enhancement of calcification, and uptake of host metabolites by symbiotic algae. This certainly applies to planktonic as well as to benthic foraminiferal symbioses (Hemleben et al., 1989; Caron and Swanberg, 1990). The host deploys its symbionts outside the test along the spines within the rhizopodial network during the day (Fig. 8.3), and withdraws them into the cytoplasm within the shell at night; light reception by the symbionts triggers deployment (Caron et al., 1981; Bé, 1982). This diel cycle appears to allow maximum exposure of the symbionts to light during the day. By bringing the symbionts inside the test at night, they are made less vulnerable to micrograzers and are given enhanced exposure to host metabolites. This behavior may also provide the opportunity to harvest symbionts according to the host's nutritional needs (Hemleben et al., 1989). Symbiosis appears to aid calcification in these foraminifers (Bé et al., 1982).

Algal symbiosis has possibly provided an important energetic advantage in the adaptation of planktonic symbiont-bearing foraminiferal lineages to low nutrient environments, especially in subtropical and tropical oceanic environments (Hallock et al., 1991a; Norris, 1996b).

8.5 LARGER FORAMINIFERS AND GLOBAL CHANGE

Rapidly increasing human populations are altering the Earth's environments in unprecedented ways, or at least at unprecedented rates. Major categories of anthropogenic change include increasing concentrations of greenhouse gases, which influence climate and ocean chemistry; increasing input of anthropogenic nutrients to aquatic systems; and ozone depletion, which increases the intensities of biologically damaging ultraviolet radiation penetrating the surface waters of the oceans. How will these changes affect foraminifers with algal symbionts? Can the histories of symbiont-bearing foraminifers aid scientists in predicting consequences of global change (Fig. 8.5)?

Greenhouse gas-induced global warming may actually be advantageous to many foraminifers with algal symbionts. Warm episodes in the geologic past expanded habitats for both symbiont-bearing planktonic and larger benthic foraminifers, as subtropical belts expanded into higher latitudes, and as sea level rose and flooded continental shelves.

Increasing atmospheric CO_2 also strongly affects ocean chemistry, with predictable effects on photosynthesis and calcification. It is a paradox of carbonate geochemistry that higher concentrations of atmospheric CO_2 actually promote dissolution of $CaCO_3$. At the same time, higher CO_2 concentrations means that calcification is less important as a source of CO_2 for photosynthesis in aquatic systems (McConnaughey 1989c). Doubling to tripling of current CO_2 levels, as are predicted for the 21st century (e.g. Watson et al., 1990), will lower carbonate saturation levels in surface waters of the oceans. The last time atmospheric CO_2 levels were so high was in the Eocene (Berner 1994), when larger rotaliid foraminifers, coralline algae and bryozoans were the dominant producers of shallow-water carbonates. Will these taxa again replace the aragonitic corals and calcareous green algae as the predominant shallow-water carbonate producers?

Human activities have doubled the rates at which fixed nitrogen is entering terrestrial ecosystems, and a substantial proportion of that nitrogen is washing into aquatic systems (e.g. Vitousek, 1997). The consequences for coastal systems are a spectrum of effects, from 'nutrification' which promotes change in benthic community structure (e.g. Birkeland, 1988; Hallock et al., 1993a; Cockey et al., 1996) to 'eutrophication' which can create or expand 'dead zones' in bays, estuaries and deltas, as has been observed in the Mississippi River delta (e.g. Turner and Rabalais, 1994; Rabalais et al., 1996; Sen Gupta et al., 1996).

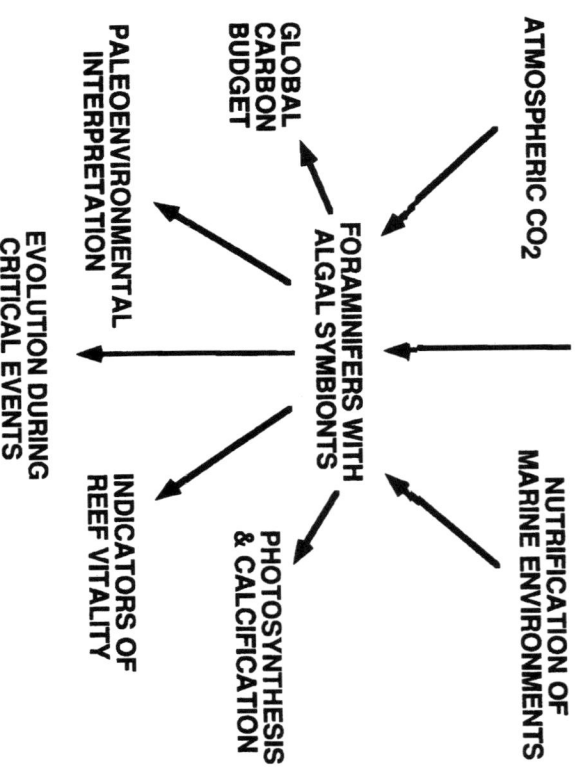

Figure 8.5 Some of the fields that may benefit from research on the response of symbiont-bearing foraminifers to anthropogenically-induced global change.

Influx of nutrients is a serious threat to benthic communities dominated by algal symbiont-bearing organisms. Cockey et al. (1996) compared foraminiferal assemblages from sediment samples collected along transects off Key Largo, Florida, in 1991–92 with assemblages in samples collected in the same area in 1961 (Rose and Lidz, 1977). Assemblages had changed from 60–80% dominance by symbiont-bearing taxa in 1961 to dominance by smaller rotaliid and miliolid taxa by 1992. These changes are consistent with reported declines in populations of reef-building corals on Florida Keys reefs (Dustan and Halas, 1987; Porter and Meier, 1992), and with nearshore nutrient loading reported by Szmant and Forrester (1996). What Cockey et al. (1996) found appeared to be classic community shift in response to nutrification (e.g. Alve 1995a).

Many researchers and scientific agencies do not consider ozone depletion to be a problem for tropical marine communities, because intensities of biologically damaging ultraviolet (UVB) radiation are high and seasonally variable at lower latitudes (Frederick et al., 1989), and because there is the misconception that UVB only penetrates a few meters into seawater. Unfortunately, at least subtropical shallow-water communities may be vulnerable. Stratospheric ozone depletion has increased biologically damaging ultraviolet radiation to the degree that pre-1960s summer solstice intensities are now experienced throughout summer months at subtropical latitudes (Shick et al., 1996). Furthermore, major volcanic events such as the El Chichon eruption in Mexico in 1982 and the Mt. Pinatubo eruption in the Philippines in 1991 inject SO_2 molecules into the stratosphere that provide additional substrate for chlorofluorocarbons to attack ozone molecules. The Mt. Pinatubo eruption resulted in an approximately 4% increase in ozone depletion (Randel et al., 1995), so that UVB intensities in the early 1990s were as much as 15% higher than intensities in the 1960s. The idea that UVB does not penetrate to any significant depths in marine waters is only partly correct. Indeed, UVB is rapidly absorbed by waters with significant amounts of plant pigments or refractory organic compounds ('tannins') of terrestrial origin (Bricaud et al., 1984). However, clear, nutrient-deficient oceanic waters generally do not contain significant concentrations of either phytoplankton or tannins, and as a result, significant doses of UVB can penetrate tens of meters (Smith and Baker, 1979; Gleason and Wellington, 1993).

There is substantial evidence that *Amphistegina* populations are suffering damage from increasing UVB. Beginning in summer 1991, following the Mt. Pinatubo eruption, *Amphistegina* populations in the Florida Keys began to exhibit visible loss of algal endosymbionts (Hallock et al., 1993b). Subsequent sampling along both the east and west coasts of Australia, as well as at several Pacific and western Atlantic localities, revealed that this previously unknown malady was widespread in *Amphistegina* populations in the 1990s (Talge et al., 1997). Monitoring of populations in the Florida Keys between 1992 and 1996 revealed that symbiont loss began to increase each March to summer maxima in June or early July, with partial population recovery by late summer each year. This pattern indicates a relationship to the solar light cycle, which peaks with the summer solstice in the Florida Keys, and not to the seasonal temperature cycle which peaks in August or September (Hallock et al., 1995; Talge et al., 1997; Williams et al., 1997). The kinds of damage exhibited by the afflicted foraminifers are also consistent with UVB damage, which typically influences photosynthesis, protein synthesis, DNA, and behavior in protists (e.g. Hadar and Worrest, 1991). Talge and Hallock (1995) reported progressive cytoplasmic damage that begins with deterioration of symbiont chloroplasts, then digestion of the symbionts by the host, and finally autolysis of the host cytoplasm. Afflicted populations exhibited incidences of shell breakage of 15–40%, compared to 5% observed in populations prior to the event (Toler and Hallock, 1998). Reproduction was profoundly affected (Hallock et al., 1995; Harney et al., 1998), with schizont broods exhibiting a variety of new morphologies, including encrusting forms. Experimental research is needed to substantiate or refute the hypothesis that biologically damaging UV radiation is causing symbiont loss and associated symptoms in *Amphistegina* (Hallock et al., 1995). A parallel concern is whether planktonic foraminifers are also being affected.

8.6 REMARKS

Research on the biology and ecology of modern foraminifers with algal endosymbionts has an exciting future. Anthropogenically-induced changes in the atmosphere and ocean chemistry will most certainly influence these foraminifers. Both field studies and laboratory experiments hold great promise for providing insights into mechanisms ranging from the role of photosynthesis in calcification to coral-reef decline to the global carbon budget (Fig. 8.5).

9

Foraminifera in marginal marine environments

Barun K. Sen Gupta

9.1 INTRODUCTION

Marginal marine habitats, ranging from coastal marshes to inner parts of continental shelves, are usually areas of high organic productivity and relatively high environmental variability. Numerous species of benthic Foraminifera, both eurytopic and stenotopic, have adapted to these environments. Many of these taxa are so characteristic of marginal marine habitats that their abundance in sediment samples immediately brings to the mind of the specialist words such as brackish, coastal, littoral, shallow-water, marsh, estuarine, and reefal. This chapter looks into the common features of distribution of such foraminiferal species and assemblages, and into the limits of their restriction to particular marginal marine habitats. For convenience of description, the foraminiferal distribution is considered mainly under three major environmental headings – coastal marshes and mangrove stands, estuaries and lagoons, and open inner shelves, although they may not be easily separable from each other. The treatment is unequal; more attention is given to brackish-water environments than to those of normal marine salinity.

9.2 COASTAL MARSHES AND MANGROVE SWAMPS

Two groups of vegetation are common in intertidal zones of wet coastal areas (Fig. 9.1). The first, a group of grasses, mainly prevalent in temperate zones, forms salt marshes; the other, a group of trees, at places intermingled with marsh vegetation, is characteristic of mangrove swamps (mangals) of the tropics or the subtropics (Chapman, 1977). Some of the plant genera in either group, e.g. the marsh grasses *Salicornia, Spartina, Juncus, Arthrocnemum,* and *Plantango,* and the mangrove trees *Rhizophora, Avicennia,* and *Acrostichum,* are widespread in both the northern and the southern hemispheres. These remarkable distributions of the plants are probably related to ancient biogeography, but the main areas of salt marshes and mangrove swamps are on coasts protected from strong wave action, or at major river mouths (Chapman, 1977).

9.2.1 Salt marshes

The macro-environment of a given salt marsh may seem uniform, but a variety of habitats is available to smaller organisms (Teal, 1996).

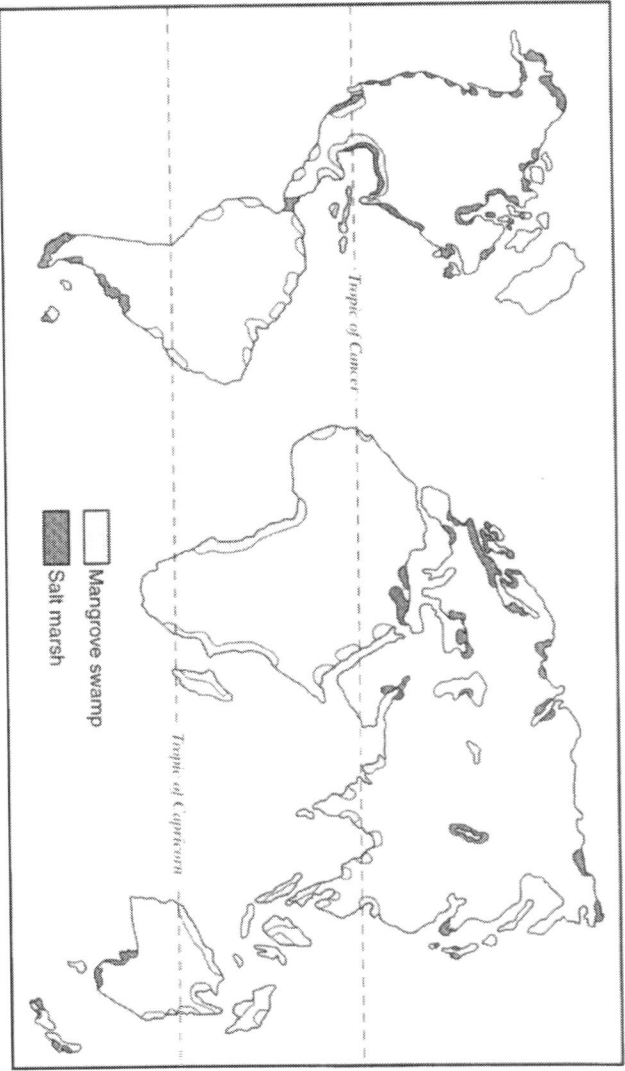

Figure 9.1 Principal areas of salt marshes and mangrove swamps. Modified from Chapman (1977).

Bradshaw (1968) suggested that the following factors are beneficial to Foraminifera living in marsh habitats: (a) lowering of temperature in shade provided by larger and smaller marsh vegetation such as grass, algal mats, and algal clumps; (b) protection from desiccation provided by algal cover; and (c) availability of diatoms and other algae as food. There is no reliable evidence that a particular kind of marsh grass would support a particular kind of foraminiferal assemblage (see Hayward and Hollis, 1994).

There are problems with measurement of total productivity in salt marshes (Long and Mason, 1983), but a consensus exists that the productivity is very high (e.g. Chapman, 1977; Valiela, 1995). This ecosystem is marked by abundant dissolved nutrients, energy-rich reduced compounds, and particulate matter; in some situations, it may be the source of over 40% of the dissolved nitrogen in the less eutrophic, nearshore sea water (Valiela, 1995). The bulk of the primary production is provided by marsh grasses, but a substantial proportion is con-

nected to intertidal algae (Odum, 1971; Long and Mason, 1983).

The inorganic sediment of coastal salt marshes is derived from both terrestrial and marine sources, whose relative importances depend on factors such as the amount of river transport, strength of tidal flow, and wind effects. In addition, accumulating organic debris may eventually be preserved as peat and calcareous shell material. The organic-matter content of the sediment is highly variable even in the near-surface part, e.g. 50% in a Delaware or Massachusetts *Spartina* marsh and 9% in a Morecamb Bay (England) *Puccinellia* marsh (Howes *et al.*, 1981; Long and Mason, 1983). The substrate is anoxic a few centimeters below the surface, except where extensively burrowed (Bertness, 1985).

The grain size of most surficial marsh sediment is fine, because of low current velocities that are further diminished by the baffle of abundant vegetation. The finest sediments are deposited at the landward limit of the tidal excursion, or at the shallow edge of the estuary (Phleger,

1977; Chapman, 1977). The baffle effect of marsh grass on the settling rate of suspended sediment is reflected in the fact that the highest sedimentation rates are frequently at the lowest level of continuous vegetation, and not at the lowest level of the marsh (Adam, 1990). A pure sand substrate is usually too mobile for marsh grasses to take hold, but salt marshes are common on sandy silt substrates (Chapman, 1977). Drainage is poor in salt marsh substrates, except near tidal channels and where animal burrows are abundant (Phleger, 1977). The salinity of substrate pore waters is dependent on several factors, one of which is the ground elevation. In the often-submerged lower salt marsh, salinity is relatively constant and close to that of the flooding water. In the upper marsh, however, the pore-water salinity can be highly variable. Episodes of tidal flooding are infrequent, and in the interim, rainfall may cause a reduction of pore-water salinity. On the other hand, during periods of desiccation, this salinity may increase significantly through evapotranspiration, which may lead to the formation of a saline crust at the surface. In marsh substrates, pore-water salinity higher than that of sea water is not uncommon (Adam, 1990).

Foraminiferal zonation. A suite of widespread agglutinated taxa is generally regarded as typical of coastal salt marshes (Phleger, 1970; Murray, 1971; Phleger, 1977). It includes *Ammotium salsum, Arenoparrella mexicana, Jadammina macrescens, Miliammina fusca, Tipotrocha comprimata,* and *Trochammina inflata* (Fig. 9.2). In addition, a few well-known euryhaline calcareous species, such as *Ammonia beccarii* and *A. parkinsoniana,* are commonly present. Careful examinations of the distributions of these and other marsh species of Foraminifera reveal that low-marsh assemblages can be distinguished from high-marsh ones on the basis of species dominance. For example, along the Atlantic coast of North America, where marshes are extensive and the Foraminifera well recorded, the following species are usually dominant in the three parts of a typical salt marsh that are recognized by their elevations above the low-tide mark: (1) high marsh: *Jadammina macrescens, Tipotrocha comprimata;* (2) middle marsh: *Trochammina inflata;* and (3) low marsh: *Elphidium williamsoni, Miliammina fusca, Ammonia beccarii* (or *A. parkinsoniana), Haynesina germanica* (Murray, 1991b). In a particular marsh, however, the distribution may be much more complex than suggested by the above scheme, because of the complex interplay of biotic and abiotic factors.

The common features and the inherent variability of marsh foraminiferal assemblages are both illustrated by data from three marsh areas along the U.S. Atlantic coast, the first two (Maine and Massachusetts) from between 41° and 45°N latitudes, the third (Georgia) at 31°25N. In these zonal schemes, absence or paucity of some species may be as important as the presence or abundance of some other.

(a) The relationship between surface elevation and the composition of the foraminiferal assemblage in the extensive salt marshes of the Maine coast was studied by Gehrels (1994) along six transects, two of which are shown in Fig. 9.3. The foraminiferal zonation was found to be similar to that reported from the Canadian maritime provinces by Scott and Medioli (1978, 1980a). Using Scott and Medioli's numerical designations of zones, the diagnostic features of the zonal assemblages in Maine are as follows: (1) Zone 1A: 'almost pure' *Jadammina macrescens* forma *macrescens* assemblage; (2) Zone 1B: additional high-marsh species, e.g. *Tipotrocha comprimata, Trochammina inflata,* and *Haplophragmoides manilaensis;* (3) Zone 2A: *Miliammina fusca* replacing *Tipotrocha comprimata* and *Haplophragmoides manilaensis;* (4) Zone 2B: strong dominance of *Miliammina fusca* and appearance of *Ammotium salsum* and calcareous species (Gehrels, 1994).

(b) In the Great Sippewissett Salt Marsh, Massachusetts, *Trochammina inflata* and *Jadammina macrescens* are abundant in all marsh habitats and at all elevations, with *J. macrescens* forma *polystoma* becoming more abundant in high-salinity areas of outer marshes (Scott and Leckie, 1990). A vertical zonation of surface-sediment Foraminifera (related to salinity and ground elevation) in the inner marshes is seen

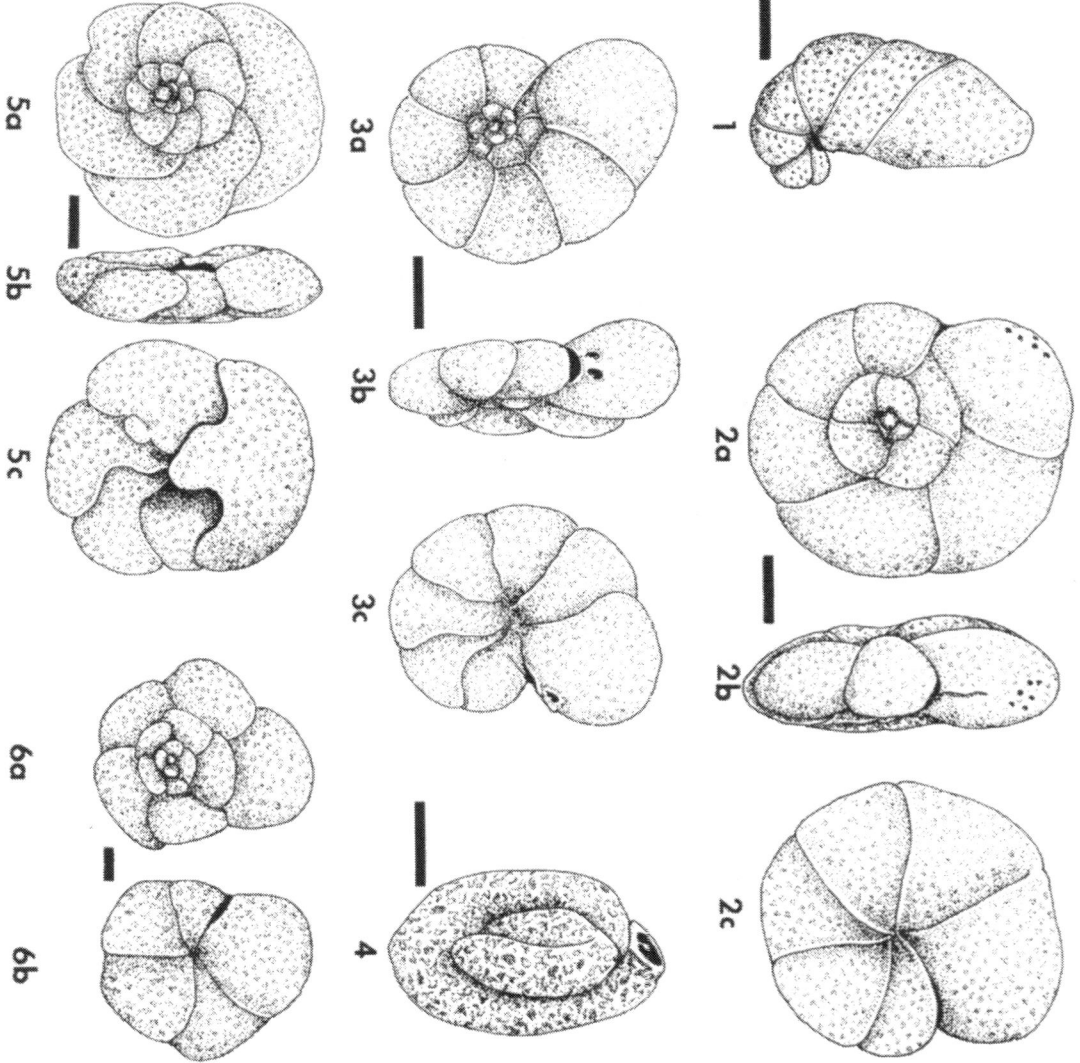

Figure 9.2 Widespread agglutinated Foraminifera of salt marshes: 1, *Ammotium salsum* (Cushman and Brönnimann); 2a,b,c, *Arenoparrella mexicana* (Kornfeld), dorsal, edge, and ventral views; 3a,b,c, *Jadammina macrescens* (Brady), dorsal, edge, and ventral views; 4, *Miliammina fusca* (Brady); 5a,b,c, *Tiphotrocha comprimata* (Cushman and Brönnimann), dorsal, edge, and ventral views; 6a,b, *Trochammina inflata* (Montagu). Scale bars = 0.1 mm. Redrawn from Brady, 1884 (6); Cushman and Brönnimann, 1948 (1); Saunders, 1958 (2, 4, 5); and Haynes, 1973 (3).

in the distribution of a number of less common species. The high-marsh zone (mean high water to landward limit of tides), about 22 cm in vertical extent, is characterized simply by the paucity of such species, and a great abundance of *Trochammina inflata* and *Jadammina macrescens*. The transitional high-marsh zone, just below the mean high water, and about 30 cm in vertical extent, is marked by the abundance of *Tipotrocha comprimata*. The low-marsh zone, with the lowermost stands of tall *Spartina alterniflora*, extends from about 25 cm below mean sea level to about 20 cm above it. The typical foraminiferal assemblage of this zone is varied, with

Coastal marshes and mangrove swamps

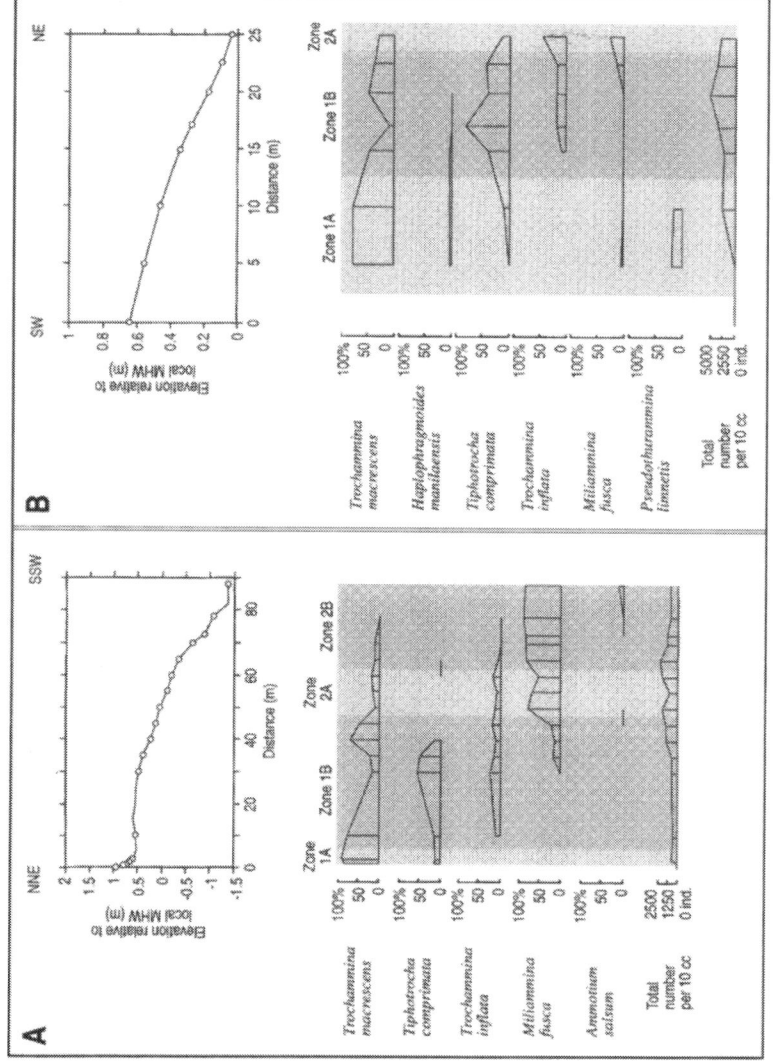

Figure 9.3 Distribution of dominant Foraminifera in Maine marshes. A, Machiasport transect, 44°41′N, 67°24′W; B, Wells Upper Marsh-Edge transect, 43°21′N, 70°33′W. Circles on profiles indicate sampling stations. Redrawn from Gehrels (1994).

abundant *Miliammina fusca*, *Ammotium salsum*, *Polysaccammina hyperhalina*, *Arenoparrella mexicana*, and subtidal estuarine species.

(c) Patterns of foraminiferal species abundance in Sapelo Island (Georgia) salt marshes were reported by Goldstein and Frey (1986). When considered against a simple three-zone scheme of elevation, the dominance of *Miliammina fusca* and *Ammonia parkinsoniana* (*A. tepida* in subsequent publications of Goldstein) here would indeed be typical of the low marsh. The numerical abundance data, however, show that *A. parkinsoniana* is a dominant member of all three foraminiferal associations recognized in Sapelo Island marshes (Goldstein and Frey, 1986). The marsh habitats (within a >2 m tidal range) that support the associations are as follows: (1) tidal-creek banks and streamside-levee marshes (association I); (2) ponded-water marshes (association II); and (3) marshes on major tidal inlets (association III). *Miliammina fusca* also dominates associations I and II. *Arenoparrella mexicana* and *Triloculina oblonga* are two additional dominants of association I. *Jadammina macrescens* and *Trochammina inflata* are not dominant species anywhere, but they are recognized as 'accessory species,' the former in association I, the latter in both associations I and II. *Tiphotrocha comprimata* is extremely rare; *Haynesina germanica* is not reported. Overall, the epibenthic or shallow endobenthic *Miliammina fusca* is the dominant foraminifer in Georgia coastal marshes (Goldstein *et al.*, 1995), whereas in Connecticut and Massachusetts marshes, species whose microhabitats are less restricted (e.g. the epibenthic to deep endobenthic *Trochammina inflata* or *Jadammina macrescens*) are the dominant taxa (Saffert and

Thomas, 1998); apparently, this difference is related to the extensive development of low marshes in Georgia and high marshes in New England (Saffert and Thomas, 1998).

The separation between a high marsh and a low marsh fauna becomes less clear in the microtidal setting of the Gulf of Mexico, with a <0.5 m tidal range along the Louisiana and Texas coasts (Murray, 1991b). For the marsh environment as a whole, all of the species from the Atlantic seaboard mentioned above occur widely in Gulf Coast marshes (see, e.g., Phleger, 1955, 1960b; Scott et al., 1991).

A comparison of marsh Foraminifera from eastern South America (35° to >50°S latitudes) with their counterparts from North America (35° to >50°N) shows a very close similarity, and *Jadammina macrescens* and *Trochammina inflata* are common constituents of all or most assemblages (Scott et al., 1990). The same association is characteristic of high marshes in northern Europe, from microtidal to macrotidal regimes (Murray, 1991b).

Biogeography, local ecology, and the patchiness of species distributions introduce a strong element of variability in the vertical zonation of marsh Foraminifera, but a high-marsh and a low-marsh fauna are marked by the same or similar groups of species in discontinuous geographic locations. An example of such remarkable faunal similarities is provided by a summation of Pacific Rim marsh faunas (Scott et al., 1996; see Table 9.1); the most noticeable features are the overwhelming dominance of *Jadammina macrescens* and *Trochammina inflata* in the high-marsh assemblages, and the consistent occurrence of *Miliammina fusca* in the low-marsh ones.

9.2.2 Marsh Foraminifera as sea-level or tide-level indicators

Locally, the vertical limits of marsh foraminiferal zones may seem to be fixed with relation to mean tide levels. On this basis, the sedimentary record of marsh assemblages has been used to identify past tide levels. For example, the foraminiferal zone boundaries and the abundance peaks of *Tipotrocha comprimata* in Quaternary coastal sediments of Maine may indicate tide levels with a precision of about 15 cm, and thus may be better clues to ancient tide levels than marsh plants (Gehrels, 1994). Even on a much wider regional scale, the presence and varying abundances of typical marsh Foraminifera have convinced some researchers that such data can help determine sea level or tide level with a precision of 5–10 cm (Scott and Medioli, 1980a, 1986). In this kind of paleoecological analysis, the choice of the modern baseline for the comparison of the fossil assemblage attains a special significance. For example, a well-known model of foraminiferal habitat elevation above sea level (Scott and Medioli, 1986) does not fully apply to the marsh assemblage of coastal Georgia, because (a) species considered as typical of the high marsh (*Jadammina macrescens*, *Tipotrocha comprimata*), if present, range from high to low marsh, and (b) the model does not include species (*Reophax nana*, *Textularia palustris*, *Siphotrochammina lobata*) that are regionally common in habitats less than 1.5 above the mean low water (Goldstein and Watkins, 1999).

Environmental factors other than the ebb and flow of tides, especially unrelated salinity variations in substrate pore water may have a critical influence on the distribution of marsh Foraminifera. For example, in the Great Marshes of Barnstable, Massachusetts, the foraminiferal zonation ('marsh fringe,' 'middle marsh,' and 'marsh edge') is related to (a) the salinity gradient, which is strongly affected by precipitation and groundwater seepage, (b) the frequency of flooding, and (c) sediment characteristics, but it does not show a connection with elevation above mean sea level (de Rijk, 1995, de Rijk and Troelstra, 1997). Thus, a global scheme of deciphering minor sea-level changes based on frequency variations of salt-marsh Foraminifera would be unreliable. Furthermore, in the context of the small elevation differences reported for marsh foraminiferal zones, the depths of subsurface microhabitats may become extremely significant. Common infaunal species of Nanaimo, British Columbia, Canada, show the following depth preferences in the substrate: *Jadammina*

Coastal marshes and mangrove swamps

Table 9.1 Marsh faunas of the Pacific Rim. After Scott et al., 1996 (original data sources: Scott, 1976a,b; Patterson, 1990; Jennings and Nelson, 1992; Hayward and Hollis, 1994; Jennings et al., 1995; Scott et al., 1996). Areas: 1, Hokkaido, Japan; 2, British Columbia, Canada; 3, Washington State, U.S.A.; 4, Oregon, U.S.A.; 5, northern California, U.S.A.; 6, central California, U.S.A.; 7, southern California, U.S.A.; 8, Chile; 9, New Zealand. L = Low-marsh assemblage; H = high-marsh assemblage. Asterisks indicate calcareous species; all others are agglutinated.

Species/Area	1	2	3	4	5	6	7	8	9
Jadammina macrescens forma macrescens	H, L	H	H	H					H
Jadammina macrescens forma polystoma			H		H	H, H	H		
Trchammina inflata		H	H	H	H	H, H	H		H
Trochamminita salsa								H	H
Haplophragmoides manilaensis	H								
Haplophragmoides wilberti			H						H
Haplophragmoides spp.				H				H	
Pseudothurammina limnetis								H	
Miliammina fusca	H, L	L	L	L	H, L	L	L	L	
Ammotium salsum		L	L	L					
Ammobaculites exiguus		L		L					
Reophax nana				L					
Polysaccammina hyperhalina							L		
*Ammonia beccarii		L							
*Elphidium spp.		L							L
*Hayensina depressula									L

macrescens, 2–8 cm; Trochammina inflata, 0–20 cm (high marsh) or 0–25 cm (low marsh); Haplophragmoides wilberti, 3–7 cm; and Miliammina fusca, 0–3 cm (Ozarko et al., 1997). Similar documentation is available from other areas. A considerable part of the agglutinated assemblage is found below a sediment depth of 2.5 cm in Massachusetts and Connecticut salt marshes, with Trochammina inflata commonly present at levels as deep as 20–25 cm (Saffert and Thomas, 1998). In the salt marshes of St. Catherines Island, Georgia, various agglutinated species are found within the upper 10 cm of the substrate, but in deeper levels, the common species are Arenoparrella mexicana and Haplophragmoides wilberti (Goldstein et al., 1995). Clearly, a sampling of the uppermost one or two centimeters of the substrate would produce a misleading model for the interpretation of small shifts in past sea level (Ozarko et al., 1997). Finally, taphonomic effects must be factored in, even when calcareous species (very poorly preserved, because of the acidity of marsh sediments) are not taken into consideration. Goldstein and Watkins (1998) estimate that, in salt marshes of the southeastern U.S., as much as 90% of the foraminiferal assemblage in the upper 10 cm of sediment may be removed by taphonomic processes, and that some deep endobenthic species (e.g. *Arenoparrella mexicana*) may be much better preserved than shallow endobenthic species (e.g. *Miliammina fusca*), thus introducing a significant bias in the data. Furthermore, typical high-marsh species are better preserved than low-marsh species (see chapter 16 for a discussion). Thus, although modern distributions of salt-marsh Foraminifera may permit the recognition of microhabitats separated by a few centimeters, especially in temperate latitudes, foraminiferal paleoecological analysis is unlikely to yield past elevation levels that are nearly as precise.

9.2.3 Mangrove swamps

Mangrove swamps cover about 70% of the coasts of the world, and many well-known foraminiferal species of salt marshes also occur in these swamps (Boltovskoy, 1984). In particular, two such marsh species, *Ammotium salsum* and *Arenoparrella mexicana*, also dominate mangrove assemblages in diverse areas, e.g. Trinidad, Florida, Ecuador, Brazil, and Colombia (various reports, summarized in Boltovskoy, 1984). There may be a remarkable similarity between mangrove foraminiferal assemblages from very different longitudes. For example, species of *Ammotium*, *Arenoparrella*, *Haplophragmoides*, *Miliammina*, and *Trochammina* are common to mangrove-stand assemblages in Sumatra (Biswas, 1976) and Trinidad (Todd and Brönnimann, 1957; Saunders, 1958). An exception is seen in the mangrove Foraminifera of northern New Zealand; *Miliammina fusca* and two wide-spread calcareous species of marginal marine waters (*Ammonia beccarii* and *Elphidium excavatum*) are the dominant species (Hayward and Hollis, 1994). The transition from a characteristic mangrove-swamp foraminiferal assemblage to a lagoonal assemblage may take place rather abruptly. On the southern coast of Puerto Rico, such a change takes place within a horizontal distance of a few meters, the true mangrove fauna being entirely agglutinated (except for *Ammonia tepida*), and the lagoonal fauna being largely calcareous (Culver, 1990). Horizontal and vertical zonations of foraminiferal species within mangrove swamps are unclear, but some have been reported from the Brazilian coast (e.g. Zaninetti et al., 1979; Scott et al., 1990). It has been suggested that these foraminiferal zonations may not be directly associated with mangroves, but are controlled by salinity, temperature, substrate organic content, and exposure to the atmosphere (Scott et al., 1990). A parallel argument may be made for many marsh assemblages.

9.3 ESTUARIES AND LAGOONS

An estuary, according to a definition commonly accepted in marine ecology, is a 'semi-enclosed coastal body of water having a free connection with the open sea and within which the seawater is measurably diluted with fresh water deriving from land drainage' (Cameron and Pritchard, 1963). Coastal lagoons, unlike typical estuaries, do not have a wide-open (i.e. free) connection to the open sea (McLusky, 1981). Within any particular latitudinal zone or biogeographic province, similar foraminiferal assemblages exist within true estuaries and coastal lagoons. The broad features of these assemblages and their distributions are summarized below. The common environmental feature is the brackish salinity, between 35‰ and 0.5‰. In addition, estuarine waters may range from well-mixed to highly stratified, and the salinity may vary more than 3‰ from surface to bottom (Officer, 1983).

Foraminiferal communities of estuaries and

lagoons may have conspicuous common elements with both the local marsh or mangrove fauna and the local, inner-shelf, normal-marine fauna; large-scale distribution patterns are generally related to a salinity gradient. Such a pattern is well-illustrated by a comprehensive distribution study of New Zealand marginal marine species (Hayward and Hollis, 1994). Several foraminiferal facies (or species associations) related to salinity and tide levels can be identified here on a regional scale; some of these are typical of intertidal vegetative habitats, but the exact nature of vegetation has little effect on the foraminiferal associations. Eight species, reported from many areas outside New Zealand, are obligate brackish in all of the studied New Zealand estuaries, harbors, inlets, and lagoons. Some are well-adapted to a considerable salinity range, and the foraminiferal facies intergrade (Fig. 9.4). Using their overall distributions, however, the species can be arranged in groups on a scale of preference for increasing salinity: (1) *Trochamminita salsa* (least saline); (2) *Haplophragmoides wilberti*, *Miliammina fusca*; (3) *Trochammina inflata*, *Jadammina macrescens*, *Ammotium fragile*, *Pseudothurammina limnetis*; (4) *Helenina anderseni* (most saline). Several facultative brackish-water species are also present in New Zealand coastal habitats (Fig. 9.4). In the absence of adjacent marsh or mangrove swamps, and the presence of very high seasonal fresh-water discharge, estuarine foraminiferal zonations may be poorly developed. For example, in the Russian River estuary, northern California, the only agglutinated species of significance is *Miliammina fusca*. In the main channel of this estuary, the assemblage is generally dominated by species that are typical of shallow marine habitats of this area, but excludes species of *Ammonia* and *Ammobaculites* that are abundant in nearby estuaries. Furthermore, the marine species invade the estuary only in summer when fresh-water discharge is low, and disappear in winter when discharge is high and the salt-water wedge is removed or reduced in size (Erskian and Lipps, 1977).

Foraminiferal differences among nearby estuaries may relate to tide levels. On the Atlantic seaboard of eastern Canada (Nova Scotia and New Brunswick), such differences are seen in the assemblages of three estuaries: Miramichi, Restigouche, and Chezzetcook, the first mainly shallow subtidal, the second mainly deep subtidal, and the third mainly intertidal (Scott *et al.*, 1980). The sharpest contrast between the intertidal and subtidal estuaries is in the absence of agglutinated species *Ammotium cassis* in the former, which may be due to the speculated preference of *A. cassis* for bottom water with copious suspended particulate matter (Olsson, 1976; Scott *et al.*, 1980), or to the large salinity and temperature fluctuations in this intertidal zone. Furthermore, calcareous species such as *Ammonia beccarii* and *Elphidium williamsoni* are characteristic of intertidal, rather than subtidal, communities. Inter-estuary faunal differences are much less pronounced in the upper estuaries (dominated by the agglutinated *Miliammina fusca*) than in the lower, where the marine influence is strong. In general, however, significant abundances of agglutinated species such as *Saccammina atlantica*, *Reophax arctica*, and *Cribrostomoides crassimargo* are typical of deeper-water eastern Canadian estuaries. Other agglutinated species may show very high local dominance in the deeper parts of an estuary. For example, in the western part of the Restigouche estuary, *Eggerella advena* and *Ammotium cassis* may constitute more than 90% of the assemblage in areas deeper than 10 m, whereas in shallower waters, diverse species, including the calcareous *Elphidium excavatum*, *Haynesina orbiculare*, and *Buccella frigida*, together with the agglutinated *Miliammina fusca*, may be common (Schafer and Cole, 1978).

Extreme dominance of agglutinated species has been reported also from several estuaries far from Restigouche. A striking example is the dominance of *Ammobaculites crassus* in Chesapeake Bay estuaries (Virginia) in 1–15‰ salinity (Ellison and Nichols, 1970; Ellison, 1972). A very high abundance of *A. crassus* is supported by estuarine vegetation (eelgrass) and organic-rich sediment, and this may be the only foraminiferal species in some of these areas. In surrounding habitats, the *Ammobaculites* facies is

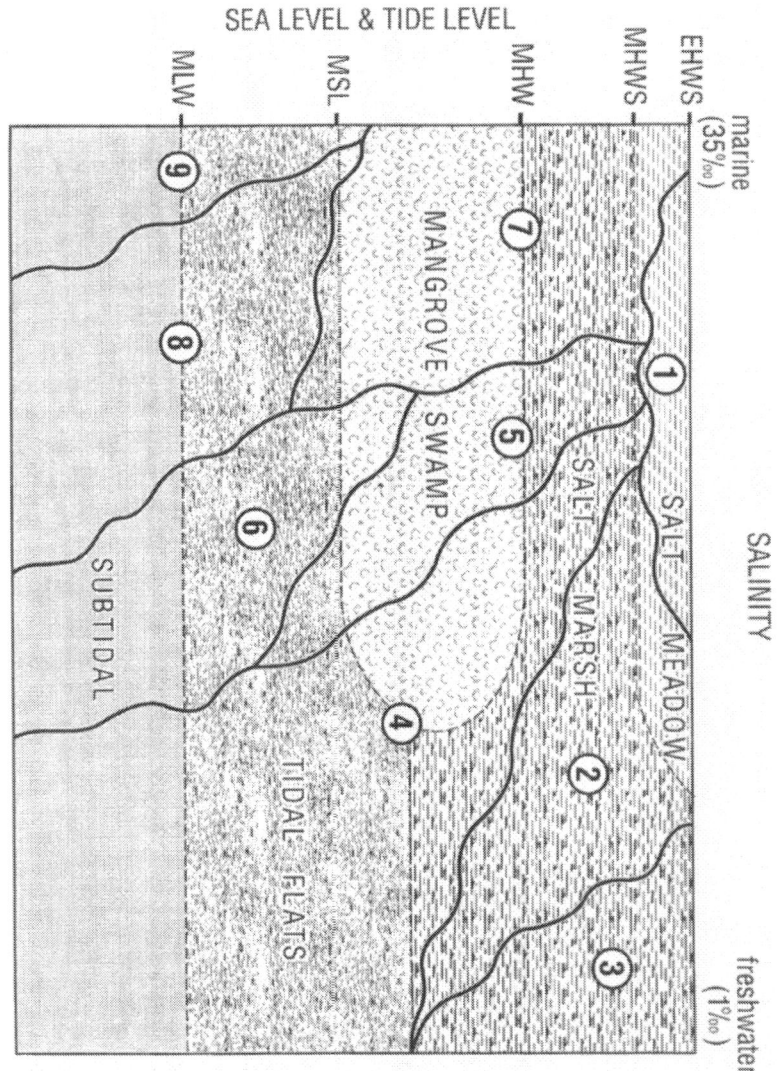

Figure 9.4 New Zealand brackish-water foraminiferal associations (circled numbers), named after dominant species: 1, *Trochammina inflata* association (subdominant *Jadammina macrescens*, *Miliammina fusca*, *Haplophragmoides wilberti*); 2, *Haplophragmoides wilberti* association (subdominant or codominant *Miliammina fusca*, *Trochammina inflata*, *Miliammina salsa*); 3, *Trochamminita salsa* association (subdominant *Haplophragmoides wilberti*); 4, *Miliammina fusca*, *Trochamminita* association (subdominant *Haplophragmoides wilberti*, *Trochammina salsa*, *Trochammina inflata*, *Ammotium fragile*); 5, *Elphidium excavatum* association (subdominant *Miliammina fusca*, *Ammonia beccarii*); 6, *Ammonia beccarii* – *Miliammina fusca* association (subdominant *Reophax moniliforme*, *Textularia earlandi*); 7, *Ammonia beccarii* – *Elphidium excavatum* association (also common: *Haynesina depressula*, *Buccella frigida*, *Helenina anderseni*); 8, *Ammonia beccarii* association (subdominant *Haynesina depressula*, *Elphidium advenum*) A ninth, high-diversity assemblage includes typical brackish-water species (e.g. *Ammonia beccarii*, *Patelliinella inconspicua*, *Quinqueloculina* spp. *Bolivina* spp.) Abbreviations: EHWS, extreme high water, spring level; MHWS, mean high water, spring level; MHW, mean high water, MSL, mean sea level; MLW, mean low water. Modified from Hayward and Hollis (1994).

replaced by an *Elphidium* facies (seaward), a *Miliammina-Ammoastuta* facies (in marshes), and a thecamoebian facies (upstream). Comparable relative abundances of *Ammobaculites* or *Ammotium* have also been reported from the U.S. Gulf coast, e.g. in Sabine Lake of Texas and Louisiana (salinity < 10‰), where *Ammobaculites* or *Ammotium* (taxonomy uncertain) may constitute 40–80% of the assemblage (Kane, 1967). Other areas where a species of *Ammotium* (*A. cassis*) dominates a brackish-water assem-

blage include southern Brazil (Closs, 1963), Baltic Sea (Lutze, 1965; Olsson, 1976), and Sweden (Olsson, 1976). Locally, the effect of salinity change on the relative abundance of *Ammotium* is shown by the data of Phleger (1954) and Anderson (1968) from the same area of the eastern Mississippi Sound, Alabama. The foraminiferal assemblage showed a strong dominance (>90%) of *Ammotium* (reported as *Ammobaculites* sp.) when Phleger sampled the area. Following an increase in salinity (<10‰)

between 1954 and 1967, probably due to the construction of a bridge system that diverted fresh-water drainage away from the Mississippi Sound, *Elphidium gunteri* and *Ammonia parkinsoniana* became the dominant species (Lamb, 1972).

As in the case of Foraminifera of marshes and mangrove swamps, the species thriving at very low estuarine salinities are usually agglutinated taxa. For example, *Miliammina fusca* and *Ammomarginulina fluvialis* can construct their agglutinated tests at about 5‰ salinity in the Hudson River estuary, New York, but *Ammonia tepida* can secrete only the organic lining, and not the hyaline layers (McCrone and Schafer, 1966). In this context, the survival of a few isolated populations of calcareous species in fresh water (section 9.4) demonstrates an extraordinary adaptation related to the geological history of their habitats.

Some agglutinated species can thrive in both brackish and hypersaline waters. The tolerance of such species to unusually high salinities is seen in the distribution of estuarine and lagoonal foraminiferal assemblages along the west African coast (5°–20°N). Near the mouth of the Casamance estuary, the mixohaline calcareous assemblage is dominated by species of *Ammonia* and *Elphidium*, but those of *Bolivina* and *Lagena* are also present. In the upper reaches of the estuary, as the salinity increases (because of the arid climate), the relative abundances of calcareous species progressively decrease, and those of agglutinated species progressively increase, with *Ammotium salsum* dominating. In the Casamance River, specimens of *A. salsum* have been found even in waters with 100‰ salinity. Farther south, in the nearly landlocked Ebrie Lagoon with a much higher rainfall, salinity remains below normal marine (hypohaline), but *A. salsum* is still the dominant species (Debenay, 1990).

Among calcareous taxa, *Ammonia* and some species of *Elphidium* are well-known for their tolerance to salinity fluctuations. These are present in estuarine faunas of many latitudinal zones. In the Pennar estuary, Bay of Bengal, where monsoonal river discharges cause severe seasonal reduction of salinity, living populations of *Ammonia beccarii* and *Elphidium* spp. are found in a salinity range of about 0.5 to 35‰ (Reddy and Jagadishwara Rao, 1984). On the Arabian Sea coast of the Indian peninsula, Nigam et al. (1995) found that the relative abundance of *Rotalidium annectens* covaries with estuarine salinity, and used the stratigraphic variation in this abundance (in an inner shelf core) as a tracer of past monsoonal intensities.

Lagoonal salinities may range from brackish to hypersaline, depending on local climate and tidal flushing. Foraminiferal assemblages of lagoons show great variability, but many are similar to the assemblages of local estuary mouths. On the other hand, different hydrographic characters of adjacent brackish-water lagoons may lead to different foraminiferal assemblages. An illustration is provided by the biotas of Alvarado and Camaronera lagoons on the southern coast of the Gulf of Mexico (Phleger and Lankford, 1978). Alvarado Lagoon is directly connected to the Gulf by an inlet; Camaronera, with no direct link with the Gulf, is connected to Alvarado by a narrow channel, but is more influenced by runoffs from surrounding mangrove swamps. The faunas of both lagoons have a strong mangrove swamp component (e.g. *Ammotium salsum* and *Miliammina fusca*). A marine component (e.g. *Ammonia parkinsoniana* and *Elphidium* spp.) is present in Alvarado, but not in Camaronera, where *Ammotium salsum* usually constitutes about 90% of both living and dead assemblages. In lagoons with significant tidal inflow, the dominance of *Ammonia beccarii* or *A. parkinsoniana* is common. For example, in the lagoon of Venice, Italy, where the degree of marine- and brackish-water mixing and the seasonal variability of hydrographic properties are reflected in the presence of several foraminiferal biotopes, the dominant species is invariably *Ammonia beccarii*, constituting about 50–75% of the assemblage (Albani and Serandrei Barbero, 1982; Albani et al., 1998).

In brackish waters, the general trend of foraminiferal species diversity, as measured by richness (species count), is one of decrease with decreasing salinity. This pattern is well illustrated by data from continental shelves, estuaries, and lagoons of the Black Sea, which is entirely brackish. Foraminifera are present in the oxic (and H₂S-free) upper depths of the Black Sea margin, but there is a persistent diversity gradient among the sampled areas (Yanko and Troitskaja, 1987; Yanko, 1990b, 1998), with the highest number (79) near Bosporus, where the salinity is relatively high (26‰), because of the influx of Sea of Marmara waters. The lowest numbers (<10) are in lagoonal or deltaic areas, where the salinity is depressed to <2‰ by freshwater discharge. A parallel decline is seen also in the number of Mediterranean immigrants that form the main component of the Black Sea foraminiferal assemblages (Fig. 9.5).

The geographic distribution of some brackish-water foraminiferal species covers spectacularly wide latitudinal and longitudinal ranges. These species have a high tolerance to the variability of marginal-marine environments, but why is their distribution not blocked by major oceans? Examining this question in the context of marsh, mangrove-swamp, and tidal-flat Foraminifera of New Zealand, Hayward and Hollis (1994) conclude that these species travel great distances aerially, by accidental transport (and occasional survival) on the muddy feet or feathers of migratory seabirds, because 'for the majority of these birds the first and last landfalls on their journeys are intertidal mud and sand flats.' Such intercontinental sweepstakes dispersal (see Simpson, 1953) by seabirds has been suggested also for small plants, such as the common sundew (*Drosera anglica*), a tiny, carnivorous, bog plant that is widely distributed in the northern hemisphere. The dispersal of this plant to the Hawaiian islands was apparently by means of seeds transported on muddy feet of birds (Carlquist, 1980). The most likely carrier is the Pacific golden plover, which breeds in Alaska, and winters in large numbers in Hawaii, in the habitat favored by the sundew (H.D. Pratt, personal communication).

Transport by birds is also a plausible mechanism for many shorter-distance migrations of foraminiferal species, including that from a

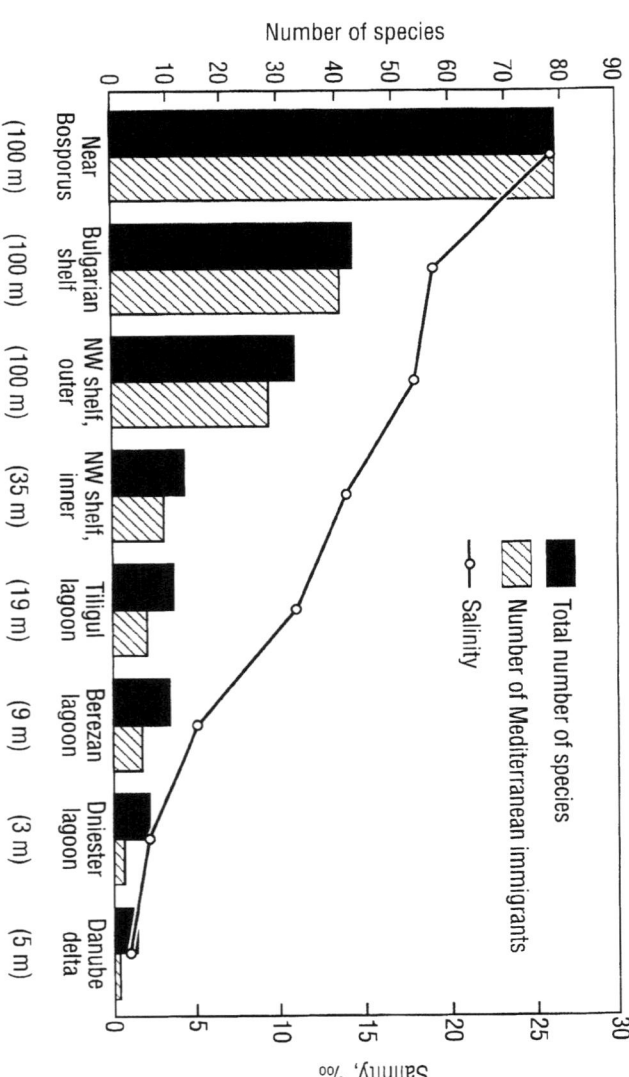

Figure 9.5 Variations in salinity and benthic foraminiferal diversity (richness) at the western margin of Black Sea; depths of sampling areas shown in parentheses. Source: V. Yanko (personal communication).

marine environment to a landlocked saline lake or well (see examples in Resig, 1974). The activity of other animals may also play a role in foraminiferal transport. The introduction of *Ammonia*, *Elphidium*, and miliolids in the landlocked, brackish Salton Sea of California has been ascribed to 'birds, naval seaplanes, transplantation of marine fishes, and speed-boating' (Arnal, 1954). *Trochammina hadai*, a common species of Japanese estuaries, was introduced in the 1980s into San Francisco Bay, California, where it is now abundant; the species was probably released into this habitat with ballast seawater (McGann and Sloan, 1996).

9.4 FRESH-WATER FORAMINIFERA

Typically, the crossing of the threshold from brackish to fresh-water environments is marked by the disappearance of foraminifers other than the organic-walled Allogromiida. There are, however, a few localities where both agglutinated and calcareous species are known to thrive in fresh water, and are interpreted to be the 'survivors of a prehistoric brackish fauna' (Brady et al., 1870). The best documentation of such fresh-water foraminiferal taxa is from northern Argentina and southern Brazil in water depths of a few meters and salinities as low as 0.1‰ (Boltovskoy and Lena, 1971; Boltovskoy and Wright, 1976). A calcareous species, *Nonion tisburyensis*, is the most persistent member of this assemblage, but agglutinated species, belonging to *Miliammina*, *Psammosphaera*, and *Trochammina*, are also known; all of these species occur also in nearby brackish areas. *Miliammina fusca* is known to occur in Lake Maracaibo, Venezuela, in waters of about 1‰ salinity (Hedberg, 1934).

9.5 OPEN INNER SHELVES

9.5.1 Clastic shelves

For the purposes of this discussion, the shallowest part of a continental shelf, from the low tide to a depth of about 30 m, is regarded as the inner shelf, although the foraminiferal biotope in many areas may not be significantly different at somewhat greater depths (e.g. at 50 m). A wide range of species is present among inner-shelf foraminiferal assemblages, and there is a large body of literature on their distributions (see Botovskoy and Wright, 1976; Murray, 1991b). A few examples of assemblages from clastic substrates are given here; those from carbonate substrates are discussed in section 9.5.2. The bottom-water salinity in these habitats is within the normal marine range, i.e. about 34–35‰. Unless indicated otherwise, the data refer to total (living and dead) populations of species.

Compared to inshore brackish areas, open inner shelves, including those of large bays, generally support much higher numbers of foraminiferal species, usually with the dominance of the calcareous group. The large-scale distribution of foraminiferal taxa on inner shelves reflects a biogeographic zonation in which temperature (especially its seasonal variation) is frequently the critical factor that promotes or hinders the proliferation of certain species or assemblages. Precise latitudinal comparisons of inner-shelf foraminiferal communities are difficult to make, because of uneven area and sample coverages, patchiness of small-scale distributions, and non-uniform laboratory procedure. Judging simply by numbers of species reported from entire (inner, middle, and outer) continental shelves, it is probable that for open inner shelves, there is a general diversity increase from higher to lower latitudes, in keeping with the general diversity trend of shallow marine biotas (e.g. Briggs, 1974). Locally, a significant change in species diversity from one shallow-marine biogeographic province to the next is seen in an exceptionally well documented record of foraminiferal distribution in equal-volume samples taken from the Cape Hatteras region, North Carolina (Schnitker, 1971). Cape Hatteras (35°14′N, 75°32′W), where the Gulf Stream leaves the continental margin, is the location of the most pronounced marine faunal boundary on the eastern North American continental shelf, between the Atlantic Northern Inner Shelf and the Atlantic Southern Shelf foraminiferal provinces (Culver and Buzas, 1981b; or the Virginian and Carolinian molluscan provinces, see chapter 6). The mean numbers of species (living and dead) found in two sample groups from 20–25 m water depths (each with 10 samples) are 13 for the northern area and 33 for the southern (and somewhat warmer) area. There is also a pronounced increase in total species richness (s) from inshore waters to those near the shelf edge (at about 80 m). In Schnitker's samples, the mean value of s in the 50–80 m depth range is 35 in the northern area (5 samples), and 47 in the southern area (9 samples). In a large suite of samples taken from the Georgia continental shelf (between 30°41'N and 32°00'N latitudes), the values of s and the Shannon-Wiener function of diversity (see Gibson and Buzas, 1973) are distinctly lower in nearshore waters (where they rise steadily) than in waters deeper than 15 m (Fig. 9.6; Sen Gupta and Kilbourne, 1974).

Several regional studies on Arctic Foraminifera have been published, but the coverage of the inner shelf is poor. On the whole, agglutinated species such as *Spiroplectammina biformis*, *Textularia torquata*, and *Eggerella advena* are dominant or common (Arctic Canada;

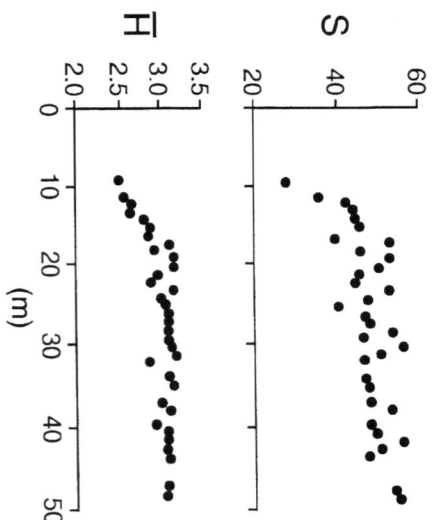

Figure 9.6. Benthic foraminiferal species diversity on part of Georgia shelf, mean values plotted against depth; top, species richness (number of species); bottom, Shannon-Wiener function. Modified from Sen Gupta and Kilbourne (1974).

Vilks, 1989). The calcareous component of the fauna may include several species of *Elphidium* (including *E. excavatum*), *Buccella inusitata*, *Astrononion gallowayi*, *Islandiella islandica*, and various miliolids (Alaska; Loeblich and Tappan, 1953). Many of these have been reported to continue in water depths >100 m (e.g. Schafer and Cole, 1986), but habitat determinations on the basis of distributions of total populations is difficult on high-energy Arctic shelves, because sediment reworking is extensive (Vilks, 1989). In the eastern Arctic, in shallow depths (<30 m) of Freemansundet Strait (Barents Sea), *Cassidulina reniforme* (restricted to cold, northern waters), *Elphidium excavatum*, and *Cibicides lobatulus* (epibenthic on coarse sediment) dominate the assemblage (Hansen and Knudsen, 1992).

The effect of substrates and factors related to water depth on a cold-water nearshore fauna is reported for a 58-species assemblage from McMurdo Sound, Antarctica, where seven biotopes (sediment with boulders, open deeper water, sponge mat, sediment under sponge mat, seasonally anoxic basin, shallower water, and anchor ice) are recognized in waters <27 m deep (Bernhard, 1987). Several species that are relatively rare are restricted to particular biotopes, e.g. *Notodendrodes antarctikos* and *Chilostomella* sp. to the open deeper-water biotope. The more abundant species are present in multiple biotopes, but among them, *Globocassidulina* sp. cf. *G. biora* and *Reophax dentaliniformis* are more common in sediments with boulders; *Epistominella exigua*, *Cribrostomoides jeffreysii*, and *Trochammina ochracea* in shallow areas; *Uvigerina bassensis* in open deeper water; and *Tolypammina vagans* and *Polymorphina* sp. in seasonally anoxic basins.

As in the case of estuaries, species of *Elphidium* and *Ammonia* frequently dominate inner shelf assemblages in many latitudinal zones. In a total assemblage of 22 species from an inner shelf of the English Channel (Lyme Bay, maximum depth about 50 m), the dominant species are *Ammonia beccarii*, *Elphidium excavatum*, *Quinqueloculina lata*, and *Brizalina pseudopunctata* in muddy sands, and *Textularia torquata* in shelly sands. The major difference between the dominance patterns of living and dead assemblages is in the proportion of *Stainforthia fusiformis*, extremely high in the former, but mostly insignificant in the latter, because of postmortem destruction of its delicate tests (Murray, 1986). In the southern North Sea, *Elphidium excavatum* is the dominant foraminifer in about 25–30 m water depth in the living assemblage (Murray, 1992). The foraminiferal community in the intertidal zone of Puerto Deseado, Patagonia (salinity about 32–34‰) consists of about 130 species (Boltovskoy and Lena, 1970), but sizeable living populations were recognized in only four species: *Buliminella elegantissima*, *Elphidium articulatum*, *Epistominella exigua*, and *Elphidium gunteri* (ranked according to relative abundance; Boltovskoy and Lena, 1969).

On the Georgia continental shelf, U.S.A., *Ammonia beccarii* dominates the assemblages in the shallowest waters, but at about 15 m water depth, where there is a shift in the diversity gradient (see above), *Elphidium excavatum* becomes dominant. An inshore thanatotope, whose outer limit is close to the 25-m isobath, has been recognized in this area on the basis of cluster analysis of relative-abundance data. Species common in this thanatotope, besides *A. beccarii* and *E. excavatum*, are *Planulina exorna*, *Planorbulina mediterranensis*, *Asterigerina carinata*, and *Quinqueloculina lamarckiana* (Sen Gupta and Kilbourne, 1976). *Ammonia beccarii*, *Elphidium gunteri*, *Nonionella atlantica*, and *Hanzawaia concentrica* (among others) are dominant on the inner continental shelf of Nigeria (0–35 m; Adegoke et al., 1976). The same or sibling species are dominant on clastic inner shelves of the Caribbean Sea (e.g. Seiglie, 1966) and the northwestern Gulf of Mexico (personal observation). On the inner shelf of Senegal (depths <25 m), the typical species are *Cribroelphidium poeyanum*, *Elphidium gunteri*, *Haynesina depressula*, *Nouria polymorphinoides*, *Pileolina tabernacularis*, *Ptychomiliola separans*, and *Spiroplectinella wrighti* (Debenay and Redois, 1997).

Numerous workers, including Alcide d'Orbigny (Heron-Allen, 1917), have studied continental shelf foraminifers from the Mediterranean Sea (see Murray, 1991b). The species diversity of some inner-shelf assemblages is high, as illustrated by the data on replicate samples of living populations collected from 16 points (spaced one meter apart on a sampling grid) at one locality in the Gulf of Trieste, northern Adriatic Sea (Hohenegger et al., 1993). The water depth here is about 15 m; winter and summer salinities and temperatures are about 36‰ and 42‰, and 9°C and 23°C, respectively. Forty species were found living, using the Rose Bengal staining test. These included eight agglutinated species (*Reophax nana*, *Spiroplectinella sagittula*, *Cribrostomoides jeffreysii*, and *Eggerelloides scabra* dominating), 10 porcelaneous species (*Miliolinella subrotunda* and *Triloculina affinis* dominating), and 22 hyaline species (*Brizalina striatula*, *Nonionella turgida*, *Ammonia tepida*, *Elphidium advenum*, *E. granosum*, *Bulimina* sp., and *Epistominella vitrea* dominating).

As shown by this spotty survey, a largely calcareous assemblage dominated by *Elphidium*, with or without co-dominance of *Ammonia*, is typical of cold-temperate to tropical, inner continental shelves with clastic substrates and normal marine salinity (Sen Gupta, 1977). This nearshore *Elphidium-Ammonia* association was noticed by Natland (1933) in a pioneering study of foraminiferal depth zonation off California, and was later recognized as the characteristic element of a biota present along the eastern Pacific shoreline (in depths of 0–30 m) from Central America to northern California (Smith, 1964). Reports from many other continental shelves indicate that one species of *Elphidium*, *E. excavatum*, may be nearly as widespread as *Ammonia beccarii*. This question is not fully resolved, because taxonomic distinctions among some *Elphidium* species are confusing and highly controversial, due to the intraspecific variability of retral processes. Current practice places at least four previously recognized 'species' (now labeled 'formas') within *E. excavatum* (Feyling-Hanssen, 1972). Further taxonomic investigation may result in a bigger lumping. One of the variants, *E. excavatum* forma *clavatum*, is apparently restricted to a high northern latitude belt on both sides of the Pacific and Atlantic Oceans

(Smith, 1970). This is also the common form of *E. excavatum* in marginal marine environments, including brackish water, in New Zealand (Hayward and Hollis, 1994). In contrast, *Elphidium discoidale* is known be a 'typical warm-water foraminifer' (Boltovskoy, 1970); its presence at 41°S latitude on the northern Argentine inner shelf has been taken as indicative of the influence of a Brazilian coastal water mass (Boltovskoy, 1970).

Species of *Elphidium* are generally known or assumed to be inhabitants of the continental shelf (although not necessarily the inner shelf), and their presence in bathyal or abyssal sediment is regarded as evidence of sediment reworking (e.g. Phleger, 1951b). There are exceptions, however. Populations of *E. excavatum* have been recovered from waters as deep as 2000 m off eastern Canada and northeastern U.S., and recognized as living by staining with Sudan Black B or Rose Bengal (Schafer and Cole, 1982; Corliss and Emerson, 1990). Another species, *E. batialis*, is apparently restricted to deep waters; living populations have been reported from depths of 1000 m off northeastern Japan (Matoba, 1976).

Extraordinarily high turbidity and voluminous sediment influx can prevent the establishment of foraminiferal communities on inner continental shelves. On the Amazon shelf of northern Brazil, no foraminifers were found in samples collected near the river mouth in water depths of 8–20 m (Vilela, 1995).

9.5.2 Coral reefs

Modern larger foraminifers (adult test size > 1 mm) produce the bulk of the global foraminiferal reef carbonate (Langer *et al*., 1997). In the Pacific and Indian Oceans (for which data have been compiled), their distribution and that of reef-building corals have comparable latitudinal limits, 42°N–40°S for the former, and 39°N–36°S for the latter (Belasky, 1996). The worldwide distribution of symbiont-bearing larger Foraminifera has been summarized and discussed in chapter 8. Many of these species and numerous smaller species are well adapted to the shallow, well-lit, but nutrient-poor waters of coral reefs and reef slopes in all tropical seas.

Characteristic reef-flat foraminiferal assemblages are particularly diverse in the Pacific and Indian Oceans, and include large, free or attached, calcareous species with distinctive morphologies, e.g. *Calcarina spengleri*, *Amphistegina lessonii*, *Marginopora vertebralis*, *Homotrema rubra*, *Miniacina miniacea*, and *Carpenteria proteiformis* (Marshall Islands; Cushman *et al*., 1954). A comprehensive list of foraminiferal species constituting a typical Pacific reef-flat community would be much larger, as shown by Baccaert's census (1986) on a small part of the northern Great Barrier Reef, Australia. From three reef flats off Lizard Island, 104 species were identified; eight of these were agglutinated, 43 porcelaneous, and 53 hyaline. The dominant species were as follows: (a) porcelaneous: *Peneroplis planatus*, *Sorites orbiculus*, and *Marginopora vertebralis*, and (b) hyaline: *Amphistegina lobifera*, *Calcarina spengleri*, *Baculogypsina sphaerulata*, and *Elphidium crispum*. The foraminiferal community was found to live mainly on or in the spongy algal cover of the reef, which provides nourishment and protection from desiccation at low tide. Some robust hyaline foraminifers (*Amphistegina*, *Calcarina*, *Baculogypsina*, and *Marginopora*) were found attached by their pseudopodia to the thalli of the calcareous alga *Halimeda*.

The most widespread foraminifer genus of coral reefs and other shallow, tropical carbonate banks or hard ground is *Amphistegina*. Five species are known from the Indo-Pacific region, and four from the Gulf of Aqaba (Reiss and Hottinger, 1984); two of these, *A. lessonii* and *A. lobifera*, are abundant in waters < 30 m deep. A single, indigenous, shallow-water species, *A. gibbosa*, is present in reefal areas of the Caribbean Sea and Gulf of Mexico. Nummulitid genera, except for *Heterostegina*, are mostly present in deeper waters (see chapter 8). *Alveolinella* and *Borelis*, two porcelaneous genera of uncommon morphology (planispirally coiled along an elongate axis, with numerous chamberlets; reminiscent of late Paleozoic fusulinids), are frequently found in Indo-Pacific reef sediment

(Hohenegger, 1994); *Borelis* is also present in other tropical areas (see chapter 8).

In coral reef substrates off Fernando de Noronha, northern Brazil, Lévy *et al.* (1995) observed a depth separation of porcelaneous genera within a water depth of 30 m – a soritid-*Quinqueloculina-Triloculina* group dominating in depths less than 10 m, and a *Pyrgo-Borelis* group in greater depths, the ubiquitous hyaline reef genus *Amphistegina* being associated with the second group. Faunal differences between reef patches and muddy sediment are strikingly visible in two adjacent bays, both shallower than 25 m, on the leeward side of St. Lucia, West Indies (Sen Gupta and Schafer, 1973). The species count is comparable, 138 in Choc Bay (with coral reefs) and 112 in Castries Bay, but the dominance pattern is very different. *Amphistegina gibbosa*, *Rotorbinella rosea*, *Sorites marginalis*, and *Textularia conica* dominate the Choc Bay assemblage, whereas *Ammonia tepida* and *Elphidium poeyanum* dominate the Castries Bay assemblage. *Quinqueloculina lamarckiana* is the only species that occurs abundantly in both bays. As shown by observations in the Gulf of Aqaba, algal covers on hard substrates may be the preferred habitat of many larger or smaller foraminifer species associated with coral reefs. Seasonal transport of 'algal clouds' lead to dispersal of these species (Reiss and Hottinger, 1984).

9.5.3 Seagrass habitats

About fifty species of marine angiosperms, commonly known as seagrasses, inhabit today's inner continental shelves (den Hartog, 1977). They stabilize the seafloor sediment, and provide shelter, including anchor, to a most diverse biota. Thus, the presence of seagrass in subtidal and intertidal habitats may lead to significant modifications of these habitats, causing pronounced changes in benthic communities, including an increase of epifauna and shallow infauna (e.g. Posey, 1988). The trophic resources of seagrass meadows are large and varied, and considerable nutrient recycling takes place in these environments (den Hartog, 1977; Zieman and Zieman, 1989). Seagrass ecosystems are recognized to be among the richest and most productive coastal ecosystems, a considerable part of the primary production being carried out by a variety of epiphytic algae, which directly provide food and shelter to a spectrum of meiofauna and microfauna. The adaptation of benthic Foraminifera to particular species of seagrass is poorly understood, and their possible co-evolution remains an enigma. However, associations of foraminifers and seagrass meadows are widely reported in the literature. The best-known associations are those of the Soritidae, a porcelaneous foraminiferal family (whose member species have dinoflagellate or chlorophyte endosymbionts; see chapter 8), with seagrass meadows, especially those of the tropical and subtropical Thalassia (Bock, 1969; Murray, 1991b; Martin, 1986; Hallock *et al.*, 1986a; Lévy, 1991; Hallock and Peebles, 1993). In fact, several soritid species (e.g. *Archaias angulatus*, *Cyclorbiculina compressa*, *Sorites marginalis*, *S. orbiculus*, *Parasorites orbitoloides*) are regarded as useful tracers of ancient seagrass habitats, and hence as useful paleoenvironmental markers (Brasier, 1975; Eva, 1980; Anderson *et al.*, 1997).

Various porcelaneous and hyaline Foraminifera are known to be attached to the Mediterranean seagrass *Posidonia*. Examples of the first group are species of *Vertebralina*, *Sorites*, *Nubecularia*, and *Cornuspiramia*; those of the second are *Planorbulina*, *Miniacina*, *Cyclocibicides*, and *Webbinella* (Kikuchi and Pérès, 1977; Murray, 1991b; Langer, 1993). In addition, motile grazers and temporarily attached taxa such as species of *Peneroplis* and *Rosalina* are common. Langer (1993) estimates that over 95% of foraminiferal species living in seagrass or macroalgal substrates are permanently or temporarily motile. Furthermore, some of the attached seagrass Foraminifera may be attached to roots or stems, and not to blades of seagrasses (Langer, 1993). For example, in the Gulf of Aqaba, large populations of the hyaline species *Acervulina inhaerens* and *Miniacina* sp. are attached to the stems, and not to the blades, of *Cymodocea*; the tests of soritids (*Amphisorus hemprichii* and *Sorites orbiculus*) attached to *Cymodocea* and *Zostera* are modified for a good fit on the stems (Reiss and Hottinger, 1984). In the same area, the porcelaneous species *Peneroplis planatus* prefers the horizontal rhizomes and stems of *Halophila*, and the sediment underneath, over the erect blades (Faber, 1991).

The dependence of sorites on seagrass or algal turf can be inferred from the composition of the foraminiferal community of West Flower Garden Bank, the northernmost modern coral reef in the Gulf of Mexico. Because of the water depth of the reef (>20 m), extensive vegetative covers are missing, and so are the sorites, although living *Amphistegina* and *Peneroplis* are present (Poag and Tresslar, 1981). It must be emphasized, however, that the soritid-seagrass association is complex, because soritid species may be epiphytic on seagrass in one place, but not in another. *Archaias angulatus* is the dominant shallow-water larger foraminifer in the Florida-Bahamas carbonate province (Hallock et al., 1986a), and is often associated with *Sorites marginalis* in seagrass habitats. However, studies in the Florida Keys show that the first soritid, being also present in reef rubble, is more euryotopic than the second, although its preference for *Thalassia* substrates is well-documented (e.g. Martin, 1986; Hallock et al., 1986a; Hallock and Peebles, 1993). In this province, the euryhaline soritid *Androsina lucasi* is reported from both mangrove and seagrass habitats (Lévy, 1991).

Seagrass habitats are known to support foraminiferal communities even when the water is brackish or hypersaline. The abundance of *Ammobaculites* in Chesapeake Bay, Virginia, provides an example of the first case (see section 9.3), whereas the foraminiferal biota of Shark Bay, a semi-isolated embayment of the Australian Indian Ocean, illustrates the second case (Logan and Cebulski, 1970; Davies, 1970). In salinities ranging between 40‰ and 56‰, seagrass stands support a large foraminiferal community, including the agglutinated *Textularia*, the porcelaneous *Peneroplis*, *Marginopora*, *Quinqueloculina*, and *Triloculina*, and the hyaline *Elphidium*, *Amphistegina* and *Cibicides*. In salinities as high as 70‰, a few porcelaneous taxa survive on substrates with algal cover; the dominant species are *Miliolinella circularis*, *Peneroplis planatus*, and *Spirolina hamelini*. The tolerance of *Peneroplis planatus* to hypersaline conditions is also demonstrated by a study in the Abu Dhabi Lagoon, Persian Gulf. Here the species is epiphytic on seagrass in about 42‰ salinity, and on seaweed in salinities as high as 70‰ (Murray, 1970).

Foraminiferal species richness in tropical or near-tropical seagrass meadows is high; 66 species were found living in a small area of *Thalassia* in the Florida Keys, but the number was adversely affected by turbulence (Bock, 1969). The relationship between population densities of foraminiferal epiphytes and those of host seagrasses is unknown, but in one field test in Papua New Guinea, where a soritid (*Marginopora vertebralis*) is attached to blades of various seagrasses, no correlation was found between the two parameters (Severin, 1987a). As discussed earlier, large populations of the same species flourish in sediments of Pacific reefs (see also Ross, 1972). The dispersal of foraminiferal epiphytes on uprooted or torn seagrass blades has been reported (Bock, 1969; Davaud and Septfontaine, 1995). In addition, gas bubbles trapped in decaying seagrass may help transport foraminiferal tests, as in the case of *Sorites* and *Peneroplis* in Tunisian intertidal areas (Davaud and Septfontaine, 1995).

9.6 SUMMARY

Hundreds of known benthic foraminifer species live in coastal marine environments. Most of them are rare. The dominant species are widely distributed, many across major biogeographic barriers. The transoceanic distribution of some abundant marsh and estuarine species is hard to explain, except by accidental transport and high tolerance to environmental variables. The transition from a brackish to a normal-marine nearshore fauna is generally marked by increases in species diversity and the proportion of calcareous species in the community. A few calcareous genera are represented by the same or sibling species on the soft, clastic substrates of many inner continental shelves, spanning large latitudinal and longitudinal ranges. Hard substrates and marine vegetation in the tropics support a large variety of taxa, including nearly all living species of larger Foraminifera. With a few exceptions, the biogeographic imprint on nearshore, open-marine faunas is best seen in the composition of the entire assemblage, rather than in the presence or absence of a few dominant species.

9.7 ACKNOWLEDGMENTS

I thank Charles Schafer, Susan Goldstein, and Pamela Hallock for reviewing the manuscript, and Mary Lee Eggart for drawing the figures.

10

Benthic foraminiferal microhabitats below the sediment-water interface

Frans J. Jorissen

10.1 INTRODUCTION

Benthic Foraminifera do not live exclusively at the sediment-water interface, and can be found alive at considerable depths in marine sediments, in many cases down to 10 cm (Fig. 10.1). Within this depth interval, large changes take place in the natural environment, especially in the case of fine-grained sediments, the surface layer and the deep sediment layers forming two very different worlds. At the sediment-water interface, the sea water may be rich (even saturated) in oxygen, high-quality organic matter is often available, and in the photic zone, there is light. Deep in the sediment, conditions are drastically different: often there is no oxygen, except in halos around metazoan burrows, but there may be toxic substances (e.g. H_2S) instead. Furthermore, the remaining organic matter may be mostly refractory, with a low nutritional value (see chapter 11). Apparently, the deeper sediment layers, with their poverty of resources and lack of oxygen, form an inhospitable or even hostile environment for many organisms, and as a consequence, animal life is generally scarce (Fenchel and Finlay, 1995). Nevertheless, a relatively important stock of infaunal organisms, including benthic Foraminifera, may be present.

There must be significant differences in the mode of life between the Foraminifera living at the resource-rich, oxygenated, sediment-water interface, and their counterparts living deeper in the sediment. Understanding such differences in the functioning of these two groups of Foraminifera is essential for our comprehension of the ecology of this important group of meiofauna, and its role in marine ecosystems. The facts that benthic Foraminifera fossilize well, and may constitute the only tracers of ancient benthic environments, provide an additional reason to investigate the ecology of both epifaunal and infaunal components of the assemblage.

10.2 ECOLOGICAL CONSTRAINTS AT AND BELOW THE SEDIMENT-WATER INTERFACE

In most oceanic environments, only the top centimeters or millimeters of the sediment contain

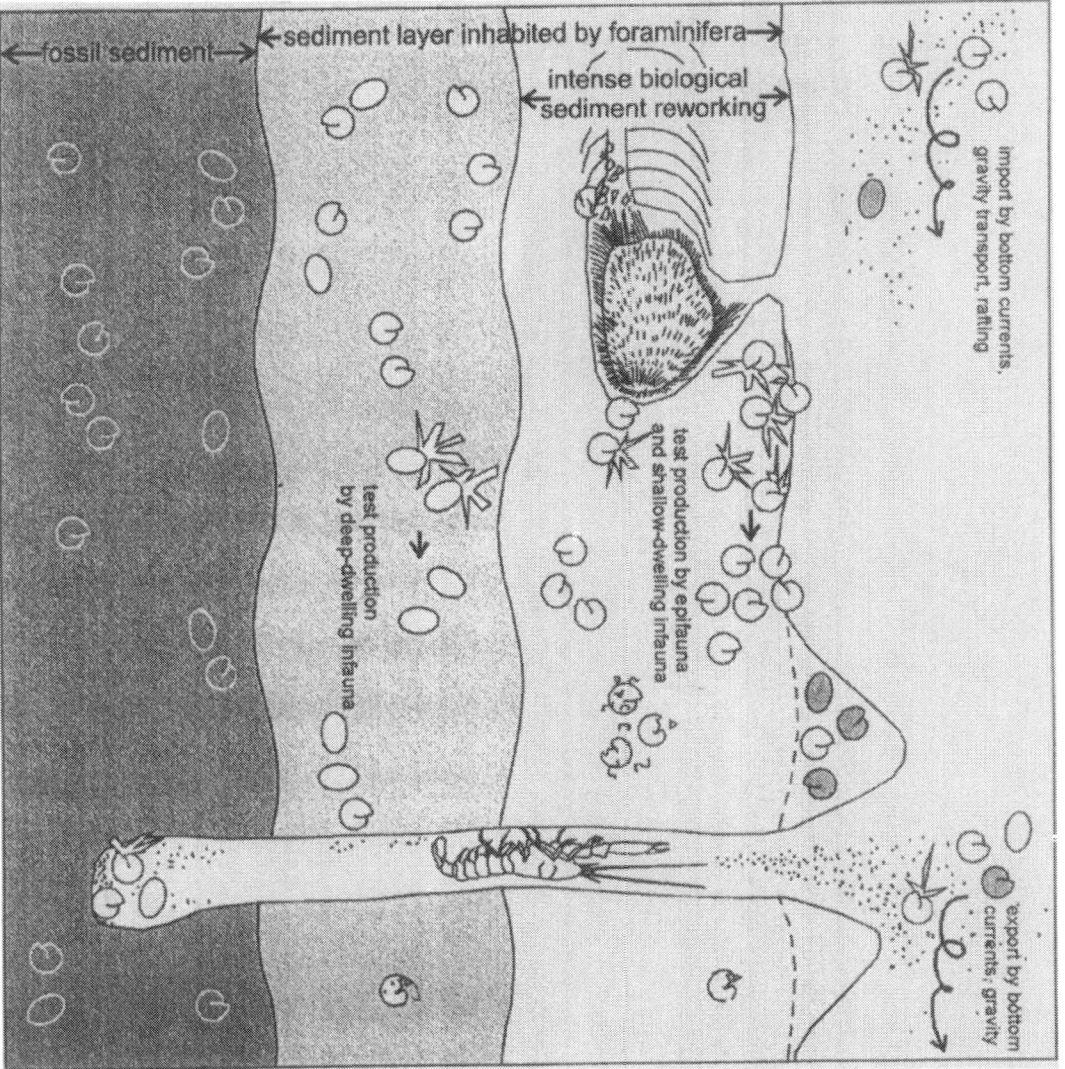

Figure 10.1 Sketch showing the various microhabitats occupied by live foraminifera (in white) in a marine benthic environment. Figure reproduced by courtesy of Henko De Stigter.

oxygen (e.g. Jørgensen and Revsbech, 1989). The oxygen content, which usually shows an exponential downward decrease, is the result of the equilibrium between downward diffusion and the depletion caused by the aerobic degradation of organic matter in the sediment. Macrofaunal burrows, however, may locally create oxic environments deeper in the sediment (Aller and Aller, 1986; Meyers et al., 1987, 1988). A much deeper than usual oxygen penetration may be found in coarse-grained, high-energy, shallow-water environments, or in very oligotrophic deep-sea areas (e.g. Rutgers van der Loeff, 1990).

Below the oxic zone, other oxidants are used as electron acceptors by bacteria responsible for the anaerobic degradation of organic matter. In the microxic zone (see chapter 12), where oxygen drops to minimal values, nitrate, Fe^{4+} and Mn^{3+} are reduced. Below this zone, in completely anoxic sediments, sulfate reduction and methanogenesis take place (Froelich et al., 1979). The precise depth at which each of the oxidants of this succession is used depends again on the downward diffusion of oxygen, and on the amount of reactive organic matter introduced into the sediment. In case of an increasing flux of organic matter, a larger part tends to be mineralized under anaerobic conditions (Fenchel and Finlay, 1995). In such situations, the lower part of the oxic zone may overlap with the upper part of the zone of sulfate reduction (Fenchel, 1969).

The majority of all marine macro- and meiofauna are aerobes, and occur only in the oxic surface layer of the sediment. Some species, however, seem to be present exclusively in the microxic zone, where nitrate reduction takes place, and only a few taxa occur in the zone of sulfate reduction. All three groups are present among protozoans (Fenchel and Finlay, 1995), but most infaunal organisms living in apparent anoxia may actually be microaerophiles that depend on oxygen concentrations below the actual detection limits, or may survive periods of anoxia.

The flux of organic particles from surface waters to the seafloor is the main food source for most deep-oceanic ecosystems. Only a small fraction of the organic matter arriving at the seafloor is directly consumable by the macro- and meiofauna. Most of these labile particles are immediately consumed at the sediment-water interface and in the first millimeters of the sediment (Reimers et al., 1986; Carney, 1989). As a consequence, the organic matter rapidly becomes more refractory with increasing sediment depth. Deeper in the sediment, the remaining (refractory) organic matter has first to be converted into bacterial biomass (Hargrave, 1970; Carney, 1989), or at least be partially degraded by anaerobic microbial activity, before it can be consumed by meio- or macrofauna. The anaerobic bacterial biomass is highest in the sediment layer immediately below the oxic zone (Fenchel and Finlay, 1995). Because of the scarcity of predators and competitors there, this zone will be very favorable for organisms tolerant to the low oxygen levels.

In response to this vertical trend in food availability, two main types of deposit feeders can be distinguished in oceanic ecosystems: one living at the sediment surface, and feeding on labile particulate organic matter, the other living in the sediment, and feeding on bacterially mediated labile organic matter (Levinton, 1989). In general, the often intermittent flux of labile organic matter to the ocean floor favors consumers with an opportunistic life strategy, whereas the deeper sediment layers, with a food source that is much more stable in time, will be inhabited especially by K-strategists (Levinton, 1972, 1989; Rice and Rhoads, 1989).

10.3 BACKGROUND: BENTHIC FORAMINIFERAL MICROHABITAT RESEARCH

A 'microhabitat' is a microenvironment characterized by a combination of physical, chemical and biological conditions (oxygen, food, toxic substances, biological interactions, etc.). These characteristics separate adjacent (and often closely spaced) microhabitats, and make a particular microhabitat attractive or at least tolerable for some taxa, but uninhabitable for others. In any given seafloor habitat, specific microhabitats are present at the sediment-water interface, in the lower part of the water column, and in the top layer of the sediment. In this chapter I will focus on the microhabitats below the sediment-water interface.

The notion of benthic foraminiferal life deep in the sediment is relatively recent. Until the 1960s, the general opinion was that benthic Foraminifera live at the sediment-water interface (e.g. Myers and Cole, 1957), and as a consequence, it was common practice to sample only the top one or two centimeters of the sediment for foraminiferal studies. Early papers that describe Foraminifera deeper in the sediment (e.g. Myers, 1943b; Richter, 1961, 1964; Buzas,

1965, 1974, 1977; Boltovskoy, 1966a; Brooks, 1967; Lee et al., 1969; Schafer, 1971b; Ellison, 1972; Frankel, 1972, 1975a,b; Matera and Lee, 1972) all concern shallow water environments, where living Foraminifera are found in considerable sediment depths, but without noticeable compositional changes with depth. Since the publications of Thiel (1975), Coull et al. (1977), and Basov and Khusid (1983), we know that in deep-sea environments too, Foraminifera can live deep in the sediment. Corliss (1985) was the first to show a vertical succession of deep-sea taxa in the sediment, with some species ('epifaunal') living in the upper centimeters, and other species ('infaunal') having clear subsurface maxima in their populations. A number of later papers (e.g. Gooday, 1986; Mackensen and Douglas, 1989; Corliss and Emerson, 1990; Corliss, 1991; Rathburn et al., 1996; McCorkle et al., 1997; De Stigter et al., 1998; Jorissen et al., 1998) have confirmed the presence of such a vertical distribution in deep-sea environments. On the basis of the presence of living Foraminifera in sediments without measurable oxygen, Bernhard (1989, 1992, 1993, 1996), Bernhard and Reimers (1991), Moodley and Hess (1992), and Bernhard and Alve (1996) have suggested that some benthic Foraminifera may be facultative anaerobes.

Several authors (e.g. Corliss and Chen, 1988; Murray, 1991b; Barmawidjaja et al., 1992; Rathburn et al., 1996) have tried to highlight differences in vertical distribution by defining various microhabitat adaptations, such as 'epifaunal,' 'epibenthic,' 'elevated epibenthic,' 'shallow,' 'intermediate,' 'deep,' and 'predominantly' or 'preferentially infaunal' taxa. On the other hand, several arguments have been raised to indicate that such separations constitute an oversimplification (e.g. Linke and Lutze, 1993).

First, the two equally important parameters that define foraminiferal distribution, i.e. sediment penetration depth and vertical abundance pattern of species, do not necessarily covary. The maximum depth at which a species occurs is defined by the tolerance of the species (modified by accidental transport) to a variable limiting factor (see Jorissen et al., 1995). The abundance pattern, on the contrary, is related mainly to microhabitat preferences of the species. In the literature, however, species are often attributed to microhabitat categories on the basis of both parameters.

Second, there is significant variability in the exact sediment depth at which a particular species can be found; it may live deep in the sediment at one site, but much closer to the sediment-water interface at a different site (Fig. 10.2). Several papers (e.g. Mackensen and Douglas, 1989; Corliss, 1991; Kitazato, 1994) show this phenomenon for the genus *Globobulimina* (Fig. 10.3). Furthermore, even at a single site, the vertical distribution may vary through time (Barmawidjaja et al., 1992; Kitazato and Ohga, 1995). In view of this large spatial and temporal variability, Linke and Lutze (1993) conclude that the species' microhabitat should be considered as the reflection of a dynamic adaptation to optimize food acquisition.

Finally, it is evident that the concept of a strictly vertical stratification of taxa does not altogether correspond to the reality. On the one hand, burrowing macrofauna, which create deep oxic environments and introduce nutritious material into the sediment may cause a large spatial (vertical as well as horizontal) heterogeneity (e.g. Aller and Aller, 1986; Meyers et al., 1987, 1988). On the other hand, in the oxic zone, anoxic micro-environments may be present in the center of organic aggregates or fecal pellets (Fenchel and Finlay, 1995).

A simplified concept with several microhabitat categories, however, may be very useful in paleoceanography, provided that the penetration depth, or the abundance patterns of the various taxa and/or microhabitat categories can be linked to some of the environmental parameters. Adequate knowledge of the microhabitat characteristics of extant taxa is also important for stable isotope studies, in which the $\delta^{13}C$ of

Evaluation of existing microhabitat data

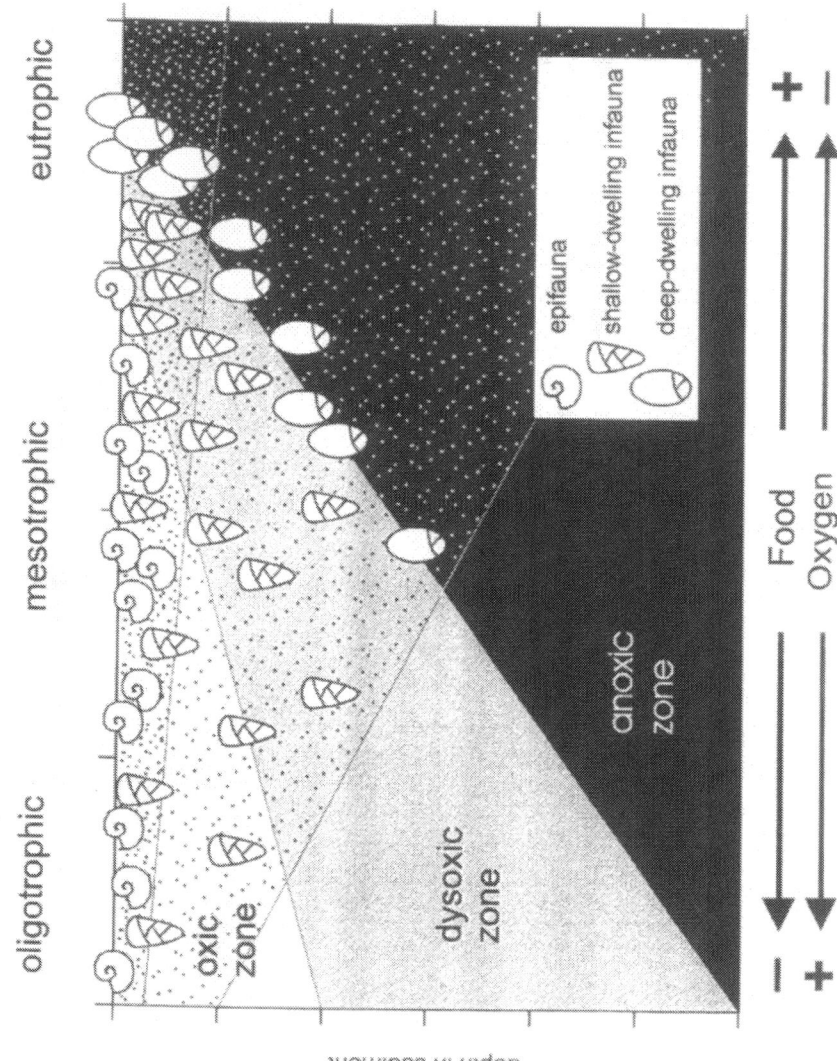

Figure 10.2 Hypothetical scheme showing variation of microhabitat depth of infaunal taxa as a function of the depth of a critical oxygen level in the sediment. Figure reproduced by courtesy of Henko De Stigter.

the benthic foraminiferal shell is used as a proxy of bottom water ventilation and export productivity. Since a significant $\delta^{13}C$ gradient exists in the top centimeters of the sediment, it is of prime importance to know whether the benthic foraminiferal species selected for analysis secrete their tests in isotopic equilibrium, and if so, where in the sediment column this secretion takes place.

The aim of this chapter is to describe benthic foraminiferal microhabitats within the sediment, and to summarize the ideas which have been proposed to explain differences in vertical distribution in the sediment among taxa, among sites, and in time. In addition, it looks into the application of foraminiferal microhabitat information in paleoceanographic studies. It does not include a list of microhabitat preferences of species. Existing lists of such preferences (e.g. Corliss and Chen, 1988; Murray, 1991b; Van der Zwaan and Jorissen, 1991; Barmawidjaja et al., 1992; Rathburn et al., 1996) may be useful as ready references, but their reliability suffers from the fact that they are often based on a mix of real observations and assumptions about relationships between microhabitat and species morphology. Furthermore, these lists generally do not take into account the dynamic nature of the foraminiferal microhabitat; a particular genus or species is not necessarily 'fixed' in a particular microhabitat. These problems are more fully discussed in a later section.

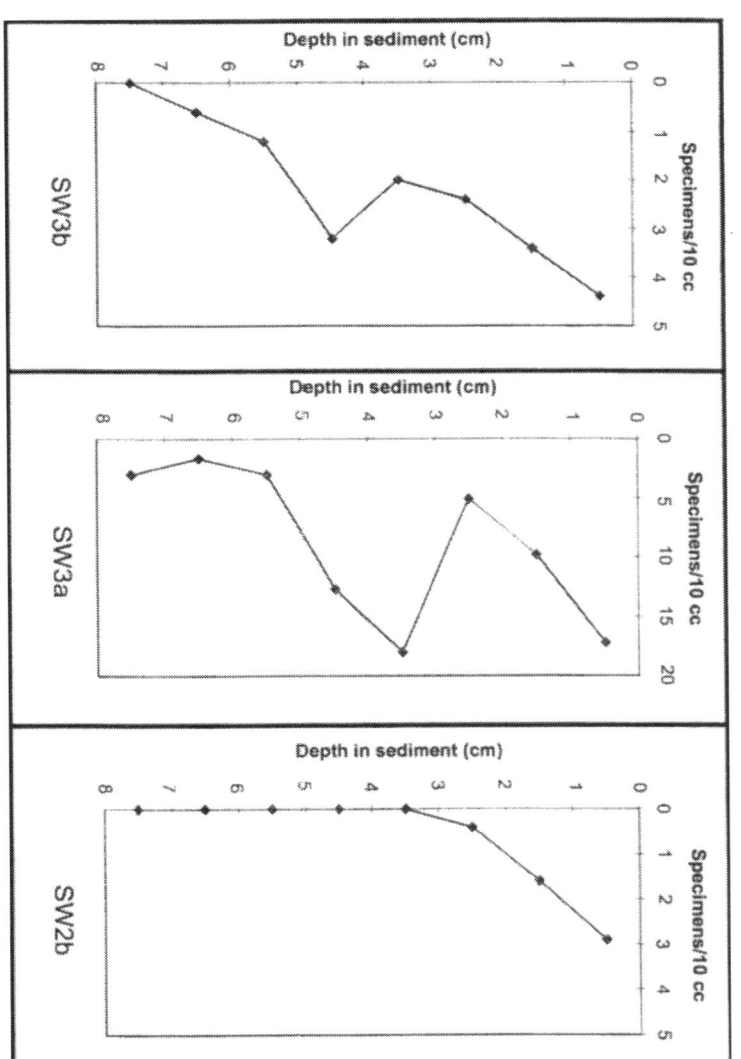

Figure 10.3 Vertical distribution profiles showing variation in the microhabitat depth of *Globobulimina* (fraction > 125 μm) at three sites in the California borderland (after Mackensen and Douglas, 1989). Stations W3a and W3b: central part of the Santa Catalina Basin, water depth 893 m and 897 m, respectively. Station SW2b: western rim of the Santa Monica Basin, water depth 529 m. According to Mackensen and Douglas (1989), bottom waters in Santa Monica Basin below 300–400 m are almost microxic ($O_2 < 0.2$ ml/l), whereas those in Santa Catalina Basin are better oxygenated (0.2–0.5 ml/l). The microhabitat of *Globobulimina* is considerably deeper in Santa Catalina Basin than in Santa Monica Basin.

10.4 EVALUATION OF EXISTING MICROHABITAT DATA

Most published data on foraminiferal microhabitats are based on tests stained by Rose Bengal (Lutze and Altenbach, 1991). It is generally agreed that this procedure is the only one that allows a rapid gathering of numerical data from a large number of samples, but several authors (e.g. Douglas *et al.*, 1978, 1980; Bernhard 1988, 1989; Corliss and Emerson, 1990; Jorissen *et al.*, 1995; McCorkle *et al.*, 1997) have warned that foraminiferal tests may stain for a considerable time after the death of the individuals, especially under low temperatures, or in anaerobic ecosystems deep in the sediment. Generally, however, the time needed for protoplasm degradation appears to be very short in oxic environments. In many cases, the surficial sediment layers contain specimens that are either brightly stained or completely unstained. In the deeper, anoxic sediment layers, on the contrary, I have often observed a wide spectrum of staining, from complete to minimal, and from bright to very dull. Thus, recognizing a foraminiferal test as Rose-Bengal stained is based on subjective criteria. If less perfectly stained tests correspond to individuals that have been dead for some time, then loosely applied staining criteria will lead to an overestimation of the infaunal standing stock.

If we consider the vertical distribution of the entire benthic foraminiferal assemblage, several types of distribution can be distinguished. A

Evaluation of existing microhabitat data

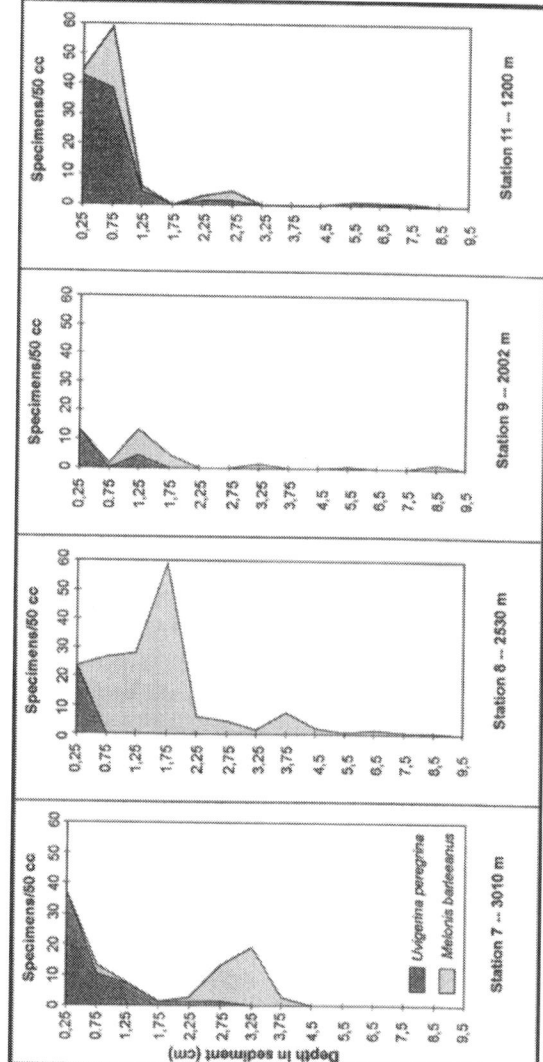

Figure 10.4 Vertical distribution of *Uvigerina peregrina* and *Melonis barleeanus* in a four-station bathymetrical transect from the Cape Blanc upwelling area (fraction > 150 μm; after Jorissen et al., 1998). *U. peregrina* and *M. barleeanus* have very different microhabitat depths at 3010 m water depth (bottom-water O_2 content 4.88 ml/l). With decrease in water depth, *M. barleeanus* is found at progressively shallower depths in the sediment. At 1200 m (bottom-water O_2 3.67 ml/l), the two species are found together in the 0.5–1 cm sediment-depth interval.

number of studies report only minor variations in the number of living Foraminifera from one depth interval to another for a considerable depth in the sediment (e.g. Buzas, 1974, 1977; Collison, 1980; Hohenegger et al., 1993; Murosky and Snyder, 1994; Lueck and Snyder, 1997). This situation is typical for the majority of shallow-water (0–50 m) and/or coarse-grained environments. Sites at greater depths, usually with fine-grained sediments, tend to show a clear maximum in the topmost interval, with an exponential downward decrease. At some sites however, secondary downcore maxima have been described (e.g. Corliss, 1985; Hunt and Corliss, 1993; Rathburn and Corliss, 1994; McCorkle et al., 1997).

Many terms have been proposed to describe the vertical distribution of species. Those introduced by Corliss (1991) are the following: (a) epifauna (taxa found living only in the uppermost centimeter of the substrate), (b) shallow infauna (taxa confined to the 0–2 cm interval), (c) intermediate infauna (1–4 cm), and (d) deep infauna (a subsurface population maximum below 4 cm, usually in the anoxic zone). These terms, widely used in the literature, offer the advantage of a rapid characterization of the vertical distribution patterns. Unfortunately, the separation of these four categories is based on a combination of distributional data and test morphology. The terms epifaunal and shallow infaunal may suggest a fundamentally different life strategy (living on top of the sediment versus within the sediment), but the distinction between the two groups is completely arbitrary, since it is based on an assumed connection between microhabitat and test morphology, and not on observed patterns of vertical distribution (Corliss, 1991). Another drawback of such a rigid classification is the fact that infaunal taxa may show significant variations in their precise living depth (e.g. Corliss, 1985; Corliss and Emerson, 1990). Several authors (e.g. Barmawidjaja et al., 1992; Linke and Lutze, 1993; Alve and Bernhard, 1995; Kitazato and Ohga, 1995) have suggested that even at a single site, there may be short-time variations in this living depth (Fig. 10.5). Although the succession of shallow

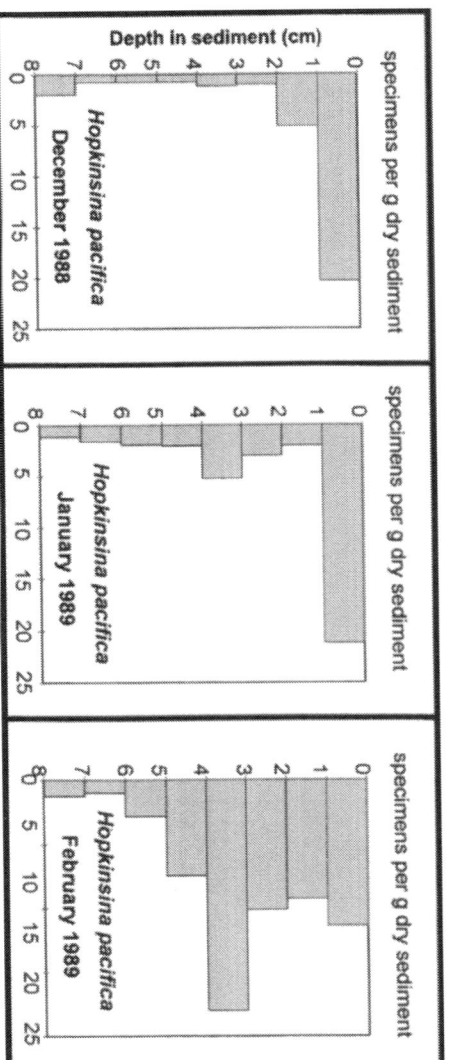

Figure 10.5 Vertical distribution of *Hopkinsina pacifica* at the same station (water depth 32 m) in three different sampling periods (after Barmawidjaja et al., 1992). The succession of samples shows a significant temporal variability in microhabitat. The species lived close to the sediment surface in December 1988. In January 1989, slightly increased numbers were found deeper in the sediment, whereas in February 1989, about equal numbers were found in the five uppermost 1-cm intervals.

infaunal, intermediate infaunal, and deep infaunal taxa remains intact, the precise depth at which each of these groups is found may fluctuate considerably. For example, the genus *Globobulimina* is generally considered as a deep infaunal taxon, because its preferred microhabitat is deep in the sediment where there is a well developed vertical stratification of foraminiferal taxa. With a very thin top layer of oxygenated sediment, however, *Globobulimina* may very well be found much closer to the surface (Figs. 10.2, 10.3). Although microhabitat labels may provide a very useful characterization of species behavior, the attribution of these labels should be based exclusively on distributional data, and not on pre-conceived ideas about the functional morphology of their test. Furthermore, it should not be based on the (highly variable) exact depth in the sediment at which a species lives, but rather on the relative position of the species compared to that of other species, and on the shape of its vertical distribution profile.

10.5 VERTICAL DISTRIBUTION PATTERNS

The existing data on vertical distributions of individual taxa reveal four main patterns

(Fig. 10.6). I will illustrate these patterns by typical examples, but the reader should keep in mind that they are highly variable in space and time, and that even for a single species, different patterns exist. It is important, however, to define these different distribution patterns, because they are a reflection of the response of the organisms to a set of controlling parameters.

The first type of profile (Fig. 10.6, type A) shows a very clear population maximum in the topmost interval, which in most studies is 1 or 0.5 cm thick. Few individuals are found deeper in the sediment. Taxa usually showing this vertical distribution pattern are common in deep oceanic environments. They have been termed epifaunal (e.g. *Hoeglundina elegans* described by Corliss and Emerson, 1990, and Corliss, 1991; see Fig. 10.7a) or shallow infaunal (e.g. *Uvigerina peregrina*, described by the same authors; see Fig. 10.7b). In reality, abundant species are never completely limited to the topmost interval, and are always found in small numbers at the levels below. Buzas (1974) and Buzas et al. (1993) argue that in soft bottomed environments, even taxa living exclusively at the topmost level are most probably infauna. They suggest that the term epifaunal be used only for species living on hard substrates, such as rocks, molluscs, or corals, or perhaps on bacterial films

Factors controlling vertical distribution patterns

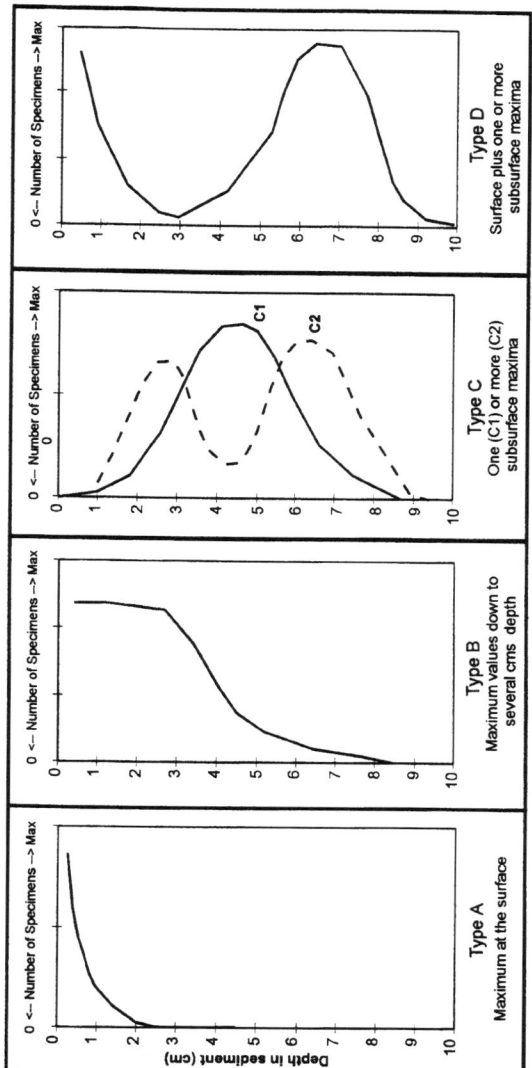

Figure 10.6 Main types of quantitative vertical distribution patterns of benthic Foraminifera; see text for further explanation.

at the sediment-water interface. For such life positions, Lutze and Thiel (1989) proposed the term 'elevated epifauna.' For all taxa that usually show type-A distribution patterns, it may be concluded that they have a marked preference for the conditions found in the top part of the sediment, or do not tolerate the conditions in deeper sediment layers.

The second type of profile (Fig. 10.6, type B) shows similar densities in several successive intervals, without a clear maximum at the topmost level, or deeper in the sediment. *Hopkinsina pacifica* (Fig. 10.7c) in the February sample of Barmawidjaja et al. (1992) is a typical example. Species that repeatedly show such a pattern have been considered as shallow infaunal (if the maximum values occur in the top 2 cm), or, in cases where the high densities continue to much deeper levels, as 'transitional' (Rathburn et al., 1996). This type of distribution is relatively common in coarse grained, shallow-water environments, perhaps because the sediment is intensely burrowed to a considerable depth. The profile is very rare in deep-sea environments, where pore-water characteristics change rapidly within a short depth interval. This type-B distribution profile should be typical for taxa which do not have a clear preference for the topmost sediment layer (or which do not successfully compete there with other taxa), and which tolerate the conditions found deeper in the sediment.

The third type of profile (Fig. 10.6, types C_1 and C_2) shows relatively low values in the first interval(s), and one (C_1) or more (C_2) downcore maxima. *Melonis barleeanus* (Fig. 10.7d; Corliss and Emerson, 1990; Corliss, 1991) and *Globobulimina affinis* (Fig. 10.7e; same authors) provide typical examples. Judging by the precise depth at which the downcore maxima are found, species with such distribution patterns have been termed intermediate (*M. barleeanus*) or deep infaunal (*G. affinis*). Taxa with type-C distribution have provoked a spirited discussion in the literature. The essential questions are how and why these taxa flourish in the poorly oxygenated environment of the deeper levels of the substrate.

The fourth type of profile (Fig. 10.6, type D) shows a combination of a surface maximum with one or several maxima deeper in the sediment. *Bulimina marginata* (Fig. 10.7f; Jorissen et al., in press) or *B. aculeata* of Kitazato (1989) are typical examples. Taxa with such a distribution profile apparently find suitable environments at the sediment surface as well as deeper in the sediment.

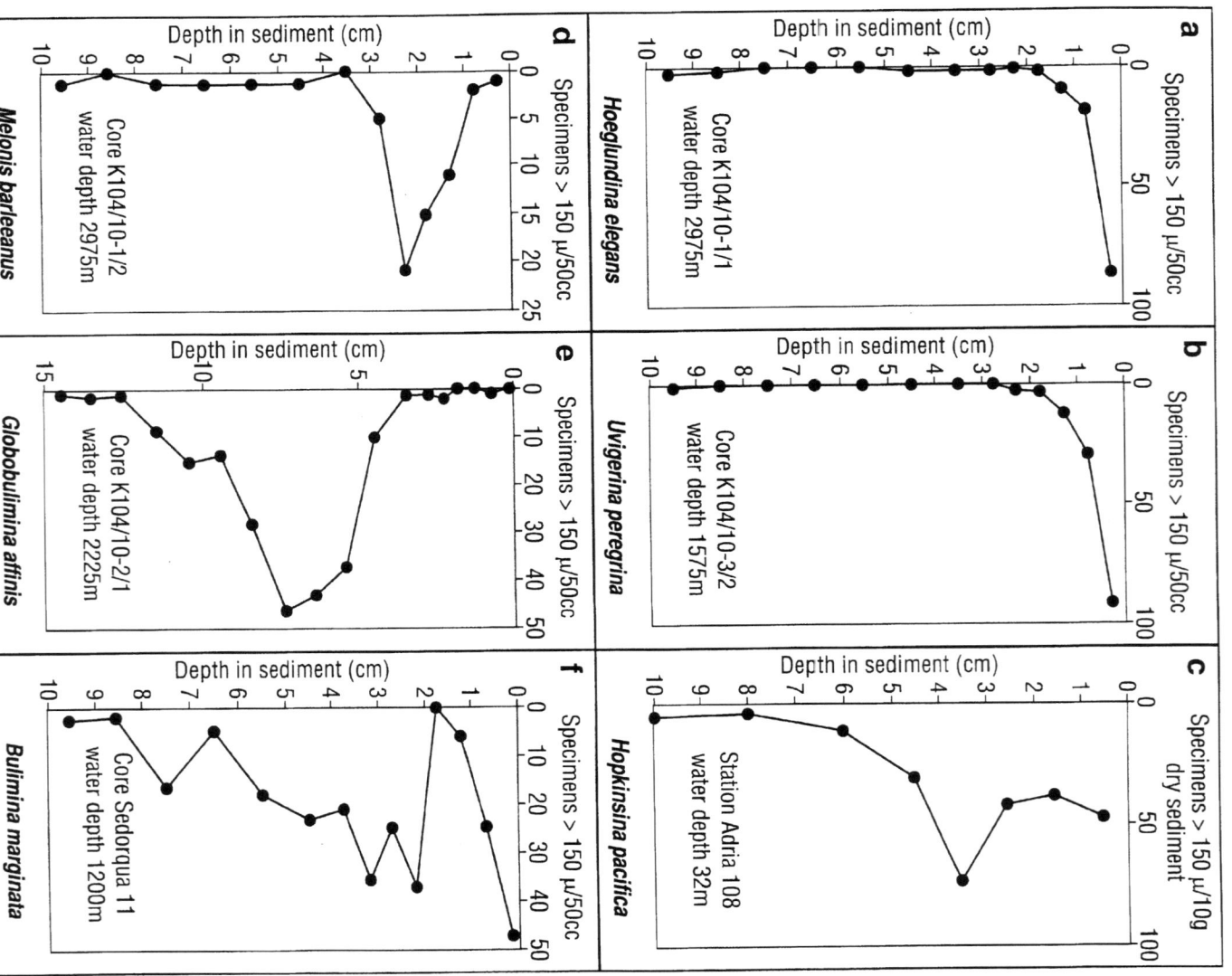

Figure 10.7 Typical examples of vertical distribution patterns of benthic foraminiferal species: a, *Hoeglundina elegans*, core K104/10-1/1, after Corliss (1991); b, *Uvigerina peregrina*, core K104/10-3/2, after Corliss (1991); c, *Hopkinsina pacifica*, station 108, February 1989, after Barmawidjaja et al. (1992); d, *Melonis barleeanus*, core K104/10-1/2, after Corliss (1991); e, *Globobulimina affinis*, core K104/10-2/1, after Corliss (1991); f, *Bulimina marginata*, station 11, after Jorissen et al. (1998).

10.6 FACTORS CONTROLLING VERTICAL DISTRIBUTION PATTERNS

It is evident that these four types of vertical distribution are reflections of the tolerance and/or preference levels of taxa with respect to one or more controlling parameters. Until now, a rather limited array of parameters has been evoked to explain differences in the vertical distribution of benthic Foraminifera. Early papers, dealing with foraminiferal occupation of deeper sediment layers without a conspicuous vertical succession, mainly suggest sediment mixing by wave action, porosity, and bioturbation as the cause of microhabitat depth differences among sites. Following the discovery of a rather invariant vertical succession of species in deep-water sediments, four other factors have been proposed to explain the differences among taxa and among sites.

(1) **Bottom-water oxygenation** may play a role in determining the lower vertical limit of taxa with type-A or type-B distribution. A number of recent field and laboratory studies, however, show significant foraminiferal standing stocks (of taxa with type-C or type-D distribution) in apparently anoxic sediments, suggesting that oxygen concentration is not a critical factor for all taxa (e.g. Bernhard, 1989, 1992, 1993; Corliss and Emerson, 1990; Bernhard and Reimers, 1991; Alve, 1994; Rathburn and Corliss, 1994; Moodley et al., 1997; Jorissen et al., 1998; see also chapter 12). However, even if several taxa can survive prolonged anoxia in laboratory studies (e.g. Alve and Bernhard, 1995; Moodley et al., 1997), oxygen concentration can not be dismissed as an important ecological factor for benthic Foraminifera. It is very well possible that anoxic conditions may inhibit reproduction in many taxa, and thus ultimately cause their disappearance. The total absence of benthic Foraminifera after prolonged anoxia (Bernhard and Reimers, 1991), and in Mediterranean deep-sea sapropels strongly suggests a controlling role for oxygen concentration. Furthermore, the upward movement of several taxa in response to decreasing oxygen in bottom water, and probably also pore water (Alve and Bernhard, 1995), and the very clear succession of species along a bottom-water dissolved oxygen gradient (0.02–0.5 ml/l) described by Bernhard et al. (1997) in Santa Barbara Basin, suggest the existence of a lower tolerance limit for many species in the microxic/dysoxic range (see chapter 12). However, several other parameters of the sedimentary environment, such as porosity, water content, alkalinity, or sulfide content covary with pore-water oxygen concentration, and it is possible that it is not oxygen concentration itself, but one of the critical covarying factors, such as the concentration of toxic substances (sulfides), that restricts the foraminiferal living depth. Furthermore, oxygen concentration (or a related parameter) may limit the maximum penetration depth, but it can hardly explain species abundance profiles.

(2) **Food availability** is the other parameter that may control the foraminiferal microhabitat depth. In oligotrophic parts of the ocean, where oxygen penetration can be very deep (Rutgers van der Loeff, 1990), but where the small quantity of labile organic matter is rapidly consumed at the sediment-water interface (Reimers et al., 1986; Carney, 1989), benthic Foraminifera are (like all macro- and meiofauna) limited to the topmost centimeters of the sediment. Here, food limitation best explains the absence of fauna deeper in the sediment (e.g. Shirayama, 1984; Corliss and Emerson, 1990; Jorissen et al., 1995). Foraminifera feed on a wide range of food particles, but an increasing body of evidence indicates food selectivity in various species (e.g. Caralp, 1989b; Goldstein and Corliss, 1994; Kitazato, 1994; Rathburn and Corliss, 1994; Hemleben and Kitazato, 1995; Kitazato and Ohga, 1995). For instance, Goldstein and Corliss (1994) report that planktonic diatom frustules are common in sediment parcels ingested by Uvigerina peregrina, but are never found in Globobulimina. Kitazato (1994) even suggested that the latter genus has a preference to feed on older organic detritus.

For taxa with type-A distribution, their surface maximum could very well be caused by the presence of labile, easily metabolizable, organic matter at the sediment surface. Although part of the fresh organic matter arriving in the benthic ecosystem is mixed into the sediment by bioturbation, the bulk is consumed at the sediment-water interface (Reimers et al., 1986; Carney, 1989). A specific case of taxa with a type-A distribution, for which the density seems to be controlled by food availability, is found in species that feed on bulk deposits of fresh phytodetritus (so-called 'phytodetritus feeders;' see Gooday and Lambshead, 1989; Gooday, 1993).

Taxa with type-B distribution do not live exclusively at the sediment surface, and must therefore tolerate the paucity of high-quality food items, or a lower food quality. This is even more true for taxa with subsurface maxima (types C and D), which must feed on material with a low nutritional value (Caralp, 1989b), or on labile particles made available by nitrate-, iron-, or sulfate-reducing bacteria that cause anaerobic degradation of organic matter (Alve, 1990; Bernhard, 1992). Jorissen et al. (1998) suggest that intermediate infaunal taxa have their largest populations in the zone of nitrate reduction, whereas deep infaunal species are the only remaining taxa in the zone of sulfate reduction (Fig. 10.8). They suggest that these successive taxa feed either on the decay products of low quality sedimentary organic matter, made available by bacterial anaerobic degradation, or on the bacterial stocks themselves. The exact depth in the sediment of the various oxidants and their accompanying microbial stocks depends on the interplay between the organic flux, bottom-water oxygen concentration, bio-irrigation, and sediment porosity.

(3) **Competition and predation** have rarely been evoked to explain foraminiferal microhabitat depths. Obviously, the reduced predational pressure in the infaunal microhabitat is an advantage for benthic Foraminifera. Theoretically, density peaks of infaunal Foraminifera may be created by a much lower macrofaunal grazing pressure. At present, we do not know whether Foraminifera actively choose infaunal microhabitats to avoid predation. At the sediment surface, habitat space is limited, and competition for space may occur. In food-rich environments, however, competition for resources is minimal, and the environment will be inhabited by opportunistic taxa with large reproductive potentials. Because of their high turnover rate, these taxa will rapidly dominate the assemblages. Many epifaunal and shallow infaunal taxa with type-A distributions (with clear maxima in the resource-rich surface sediments and an exponential decrease below) most probably have such an opportunistic life strategy. Such taxa can rapidly adjust to intermittent food supply, and will often dominate the fossil assemblage, even if they attain high densities only during the most eutrophic periods (Jorissen and Witting, 1999). In this context, species feeding on phytodetritus deposits probably represent an extreme.

Since the anaerobic bacterial conversion of refractory organic matter into labile components is a slow process (Fenchel and Finlay, 1995), taxa living deep in the sediment are adapted to an environment with a relatively constant supply of low-quality food. Logically, such taxa will have a life strategy aimed at very efficient food utilization, in combination with a maximum resistance to ecological stress. Under normal conditions, their densities will be relatively low, but constant in time. However, such normally deep infaunal taxa are known to have amazingly high densities in some cases where bottom-water oxygen concentrations are very low (e.g. Phleger and Soutar, 1973; Sen Gupta and Machain-Castillo, 1993). Under such circumstances, the opportunistic epifaunal or shallow infaunal taxa will probably no longer tolerate the low oxygen concentration, and will disappear. The result of this partial extinction or disappearance is that the normally deep infaunal taxa may find the sediment-surface microhabitat open, and may be able to colonize

Figure 10.8 Comparison of the vertical distributions of *Melonis barleeanus*, *Globobulimina affinis*, and *Bulimina marginata* with profiles of oxygen and nitrate in a five-station bathymetrical transect from the Cape Blanc upwelling area (northwestern Africa). The profiles show that *M. barleeanus* tends to have a maximum in the zone of nitrate reduction, whereas the other two species have significant standing stocks in completely anoxic sediments (after Jorissen et al., 1998).

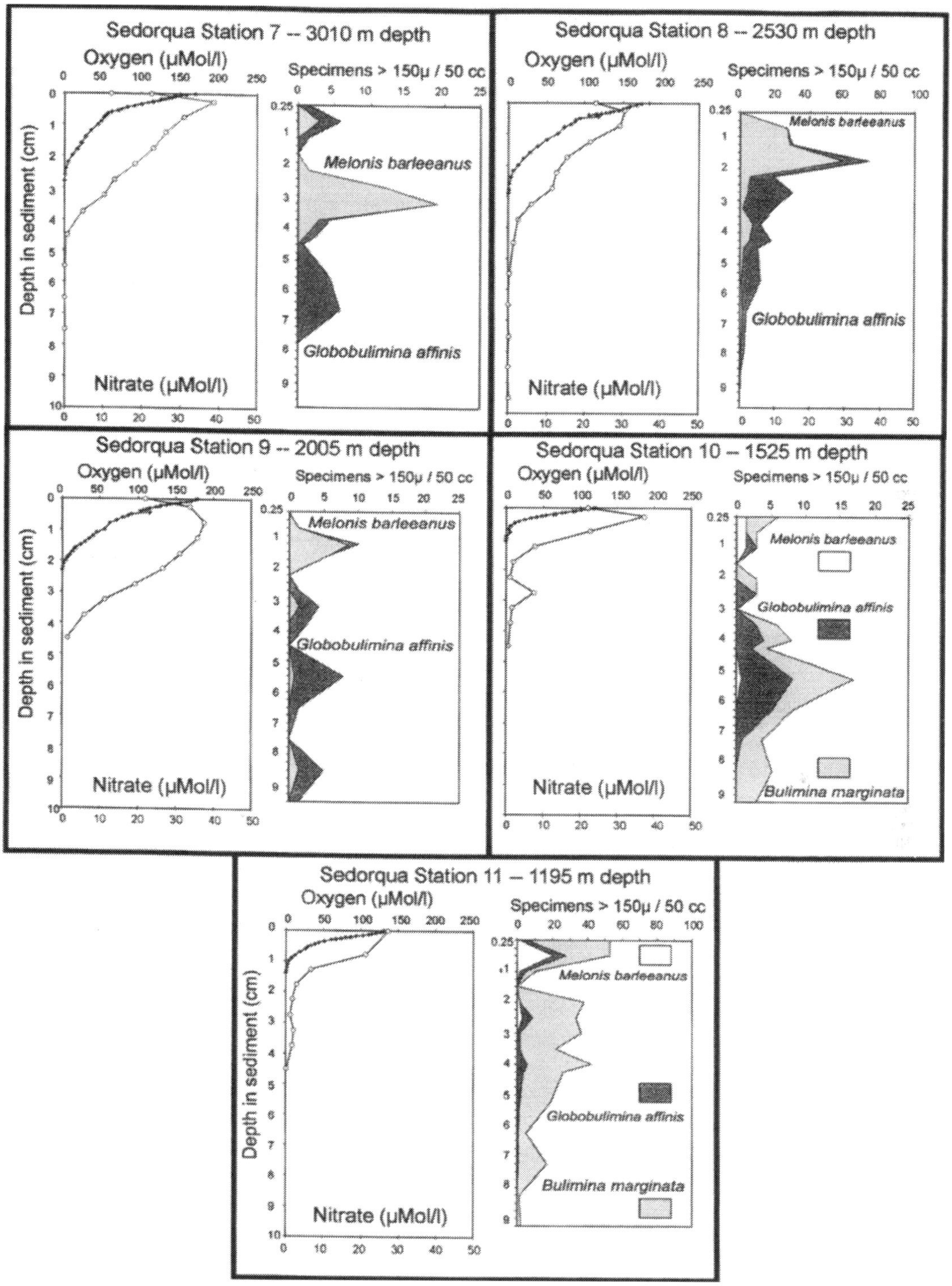

Factors controlling vertical distribution patterns

173

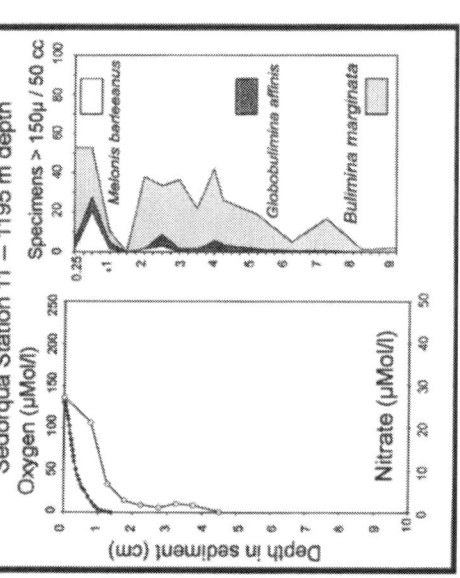

this extremely food-rich environment, where they can reach very high standing stocks.

(4) **Bioturbation** may influence benthic foraminiferal microhabitats in several ways: by creating oxic microenvironments at depth in the sediment (Aller and Aller, 1986; Meyers et al., 1987, 1988), or by trapping food-rich particles, and partially introducing them into the sediment. Thomsen and Altenbach (1993) show a significant increase in bacterial biomass and foraminiferal densities in haloed sediments around artificial burrows. Bioturbation can also actively transport Foraminifera to deeper sediment layers, and cause accidental infaunal occurrence of taxa that are usually found at the sediment surface.

The four factors explained in this section will each have their individual influence on the foraminiferal microhabitat, but they will also interact strongly. Jorissen et al. (1995), following the suggestions of Shirayama (1984) and Corliss and Emerson (1990), developed a conceptual model that shows the interplay between oxygen concentration and food availability (Fig. 10.9). They argue that in oligotrophic settings, a critical food level determines the penetration depth of most species, whereas in eutrophic settings, a critical oxygen level would determine this depth. The tolerance limits to these two factors will strongly vary among species, explaining the differences in the lower depth limits described in the literature.

10.7 RELATIONS BETWEEN TEST MORPHOLOGY AND MICROHABITATS

Several workers have suggested a close relationship between test morphology and microhabitat (e.g. Corliss, 1985; Jones and Charnock, 1985; Corliss and Chen, 1988; Corliss, 1991; Corliss and Fois, 1990). The existence of such a relationship would be very significant, since it would enable us to infer the microhabitats of extinct taxa, and thus extract essential information about ancient ecosystems. According to Corliss and Chen (1988) and Corliss (1991), epifaunal taxa are (a) plano-convex, biconvex or rounded trochospiral, with large pores absent or only found on one side, or (b) milioline. In contrast, infaunal taxa can be rounded planispiral, flattened ovoid, tapered and cylindrical triserial, spherical, or flattened tapered biserial, and tend to have pores all over the test. The main shortcoming of this classification is that the primary separation between epifaunal and infaunal taxa is linked to an arbitrary boundary drawn on the basis of pore patterns (Corliss, 1991), and is only to a minor degree based on actual observations. The plano-convex, rounded, or biconvex trochospiral taxa, listed as epifaunal (Corliss and Chen, 1988; Corliss, 1991; Murray, 1991b; Rathburn et al., 1996), are indeed morphologically distinct from the planispiral, biserial, or triserial taxa listed as shallow infauna, but in the majority of field observations, their vertical distribution patterns do not segregate along such morphological lines.

Furthermore, it appears that even in cases where test form, coiling type, and pore pattern are very similar, important differences in microhabitat may exist. Loubere et al. (1995) show that shallow and deep infaunal populations of *Uvigerina peregrina* have a slightly different morphology, but belong to the same species. Differences in microhabitat selection between morphologically close species of the same genus have been reported for *Bolivina* (Barmawidjaja et al., 1992), *Bulimina* (Jorissen et al., 1998), *Cibicidoides* (Rathburn et al., 1996), and *Melonis* (Jorissen et al., 1998). Barmawidjaja et al. (1992) showed that within a group of closely related *Bolivina*, the ornamented *striatula*-types are always limited to the sediment surface, whereas unornamented, but otherwise morphologically similar, *B. dilatata* and *B. spathulata* have a clear infaunal tendency. This corroborates an earlier observation by Corliss (1991) that only shallow infaunal taxa (in his data set) possess a surface ornamentation. In the genus *Bulimina*, *B. inflata* is limited to the sediment surface, and in view of its overall coarse perforation, should be considered as shallow infaunal, according to the criteria defined by Corliss (1991). In contrast, *B. marginata*, which has a similar test, but a spinose, instead of a costate, ornamentation,

Relations between test morphology and microhabitats

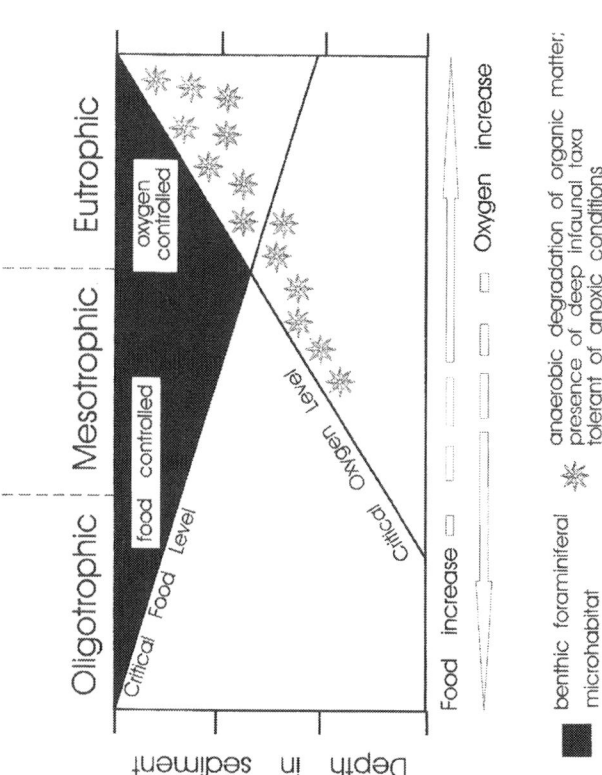

Figure 10.9 Hypothetical model showing the depth of the benthic foraminiferal microhabitat as a function of food availability in the sediment (oligotrophic and mesotrophic ecosystems) and/or oxygen concentration (eutrophic ecosystems). Note that many deep infaunal taxa may be found in completely anoxic conditions (represented by the star symbols). After Jorissen et al., 1995.

often has a type D-distribution (Fig. 10.6), and sometimes shows prominent maxima deep in the sediment (Jorissen et al., 1998).

An examination of the published data on foraminiferal microhabitats shows that the observed microhabitat patterns for most species are very consistent. Although the exact depth at which a specific taxon is found is variable, its position with respect to those of other taxa is very stable in most cases (Fig. 10.4). The genus *Nonionella* provides a striking exception to this rule. *N. turgida* is found with deep infaunal maxima in the western Atlantic Ocean (Corliss and Emerson, 1990) and in the Santa Monica Basin (species identified as *N. stella*, Mackensen and Douglas, 1989), but is the taxon with the most evident epifaunal tendency at shallow sites in the Adriatic Sea (Barmawidjaja et al., 1992).

In view of the large spatial and temporal variability of foraminiferal microhabitats, and the large depth intervals over which living individuals of some taxa are found, a statement about the microhabitat of a species or genus may just be a generalization. For instance, from observations on hard substrates (Lutze and Thiel, 1989), *Cibicides wuellerstorfi* is generally considered as an epifaunal (elevated) taxon. However, non-negligible populations of the species have been described also within soft sediments (e.g. Corliss, 1991; McCorkle et al., 1997; Jorissen et al., 1998), which suggests that not all *C. wuellerstorfi* secrete their tests at the sediment-water interface.

In summary, the relationship between test morphology and microhabitat is complex, and all generalizations have significant exceptions. On the basis of a statistical analysis, Buzas et al. (1993) concluded that for the taxa they considered, microhabitat assignments on the basis of morphology were about 75% accurate. Although it can not be denied that there is a correspondence between test morphology and microhabitat, the afore-mentioned examples show that some taxonomically close species (with only subtle morphological differences) may have significant differences in their microhabitats. It is possible that a thorough study of minor morphological characteristics (ornamentation, pore density, pore diameter, length/width ratio, presence of a basal spine, etc.) may lead to a considerable improvement in our comprehension of the various links between test morphology and microhabitat.

10.8 MICROHABITATS AND CARBON ISOTOPIC COMPOSITIONS

The stable isotopic composition of foraminiferal shells is extensively used in paleoceanography (see chapter 14). In particular, the $\delta^{13}C$ of benthic Foraminifera has been used as a proxy of export productivity and deep water circulation. The $\delta^{13}C$ of the oceanic bottom water depends on two main factors: the downward organic flux, which introduces ^{13}C-depleted organic matter produced in the surface waters, and the ventilation by bottom currents, which tends to supply waters with a high $\delta^{13}C$. Within the sediment, the organic matter is remineralized, releasing ^{13}C-depleted CO_2 to the pore waters. The result is a strong $\delta^{13}C$ gradient in the first few centimeters of the sediment. After the discovery of significant interspecific differences in the $\delta^{13}C$ of benthic Foraminifera, it was suggested that most species form their test in isotopic equilibrium with the composition of the surrounding water, and that the interspecific differences could be the result of microhabitat differences (e.g. Woodruff et al., 1980; Belanger et al., 1981; Grossman, 1984a,b). Several studies have confirmed this hypothesis, showing that generally, epifaunal taxa have a high $\delta^{13}C$ value, whereas infaunal taxa have a lower $\delta^{13}C$ (e.g. Grossman, 1987; McCorkle et al., 1990; Rathburn et al., 1996). The isotopic composition of infaunal taxa appears to be strongly influenced by that of the pore water.

An excellent overview of the relations between foraminiferal microhabitats and stable isotopic compositions is given by McCorkle et al. (1997). Although the interspecific differences are clear, and apparently consistent, the almost total absence of a difference among specimens of deep infaunal taxa sampled at various sediment depths is striking (McCorkle et al., 1990, 1997). According to McCorkle et al. (1997), this may imply that calcification takes place in a relative narrow subzone of the foraminiferal microhabitat range. Loubere et al. (1995), on the contrary, present data suggesting that the calcification of infaunal Uvigerina takes place in a microenvironment associated with macrofaunal activity, with a geochemistry very different from that of the average pore water. The comparison between the $\delta^{13}C$ profiles in pore waters and those of deep infaunal taxa (e.g., Globobulimina in McCorkle et al., 1990, 1997) shows that the offset between the two profiles in a pair increases towards greater depth in the sediment. This suggests that calcification takes place preferentially close to the redox front, an idea which is matched by the suggestion of Bernhard (1992) that Globobulimina lowers its metabolism under completely anoxic conditions. An alternative explanation could be that an individual foraminifer forms its test over a prolonged time interval in a relatively wide depth zone in the sediment, and that the ultimate isotopic composition of its test is a reflection of the mean level within this depth interval.

The species Cibicides wuellerstorfi (also placed under Fontbotia, Planulina or Cibicidoides; see Sen Gupta, 1989), which has been observed on elevated substrates, is supposed to secrete its test in equilibrium with the ambient bottom water, without being influenced by the substrate pore-water chemistry. This species has been used widely as an indicator of bottom-water characteristics (e.g. Duplessy et al., 1984; Sarnthein et al., 1988). However, as stated previously, observations of live C. wuellerstorfi within the sediment suggest that not all individuals of this species secrete their test in isotopic equilibrium with the bottom water. Furthermore, Sarnthein et al. (1988) speculate that regional organic-flux maxima could modify the isotopic composition of the water immediately above the sediment

10.9 PALEOCEANOGRAPHIC IMPLICATIONS OF BENTHIC FORAMINIFERAL MICROHABITATS

The knowledge of microhabitats is essential for a proper utilization of benthic foraminiferal species as paleoceanographic tools. Several authors have noted that the relative proportion of infaunal taxa becomes more significant as the organic flux increases (e.g. Corliss and Chen, 1988; Corliss and Fois, 1990; Rosoff and Corliss, 1992; Jorissen et al., 1995). This suggests the possibility of developing a microhabitat based proxy for the organic flux. Furthermore, several taxa with a morphology indicative of an infaunal microhabitat show a systematic population increase under strongly dysoxic or microxic conditions (e.g. Bernhard, 1986; Kaiho, 1991; Sen Gupta and Machain-Castillo, 1993; Bernhard et al., 1997). The proxy for bottom-water oxygenation developed by Kaiho (1991, 1994) is based on this principle. Kaiho (1994) shows a good correlation between the percentage of a number of 'oxic' indicators (in an assemblage of 'oxic' and 'dysoxic' species) and bottom-water oxygen concentration in the range of 1.5–3.0 ml/l O_2. The 'oxic' taxa, which are considered epifaunal, appear to have a tolerance threshold at about 1.0 ml/l O_2. For the range of 0–1.5 ml/l O_2, Kaiho (1994) proposes a bottom-water oxygenation proxy that utilizes the relative dominance of a category of 'dysoxic' Foraminifera; this group contains taxa that have been described as shallow, intermediate, or deep infaunal. Rathburn and Corliss (1994), however, show that 'low oxygen taxa,' such as *Bolivina*, *Bulimina*, *Globobulimina*, *Uvigerina* and *Chilostomella*, are rare at a number of sites in the Sulu Sea, where bottom-water oxygen concentration is 1.76 ml/l or less. They conclude that the dominance of these taxa is typical of environments with a high organic flux, rather than of environments with low oxygen concentrations.

The parameters of bottom-water oxygenation and organic flux (food availability) are closely interrelated, and it is often extremely difficult to distinguish their separate influences. Further- water interface. In areas with significant phytodetritus deposits, a strong $\delta^{13}C$ gradient, resulting from the liberation of $\delta^{13}C$-depleted CO_2, may develop even above the sediment-water interface. Mackensen et al. (1993c) indicate that such a phenomenon can influence the isotopic composition of epifaunal Foraminifera; the larger food availability could trigger reproduction and/or chamber formation, and calcification could thus take place during times of strong $\delta^{13}C$ gradients close to the sediment-water interface. This 'Mackensen effect' is supported by the suggestion of Jorissen and Wittling (1999) that test production of *C. wuellerstorfi* is limited to a very short period of the year in the distal zones of the Cape Blanc upwelling area, when the organic flux is locally maximal. As a consequence, the isotopic composition of the tests of epifaunal taxa such as *C. wuellerstorfi* may represent conditions present during relatively short periods of time, and will not always reflect the average, long-term, isotopic composition of the bottom water mass.

A comparison of isotopic compositions of epifaunal and infaunal taxa could give important clues about the $\delta^{13}C$ gradient within the sediment, and thus, about the amount of organic matter remineralized in the benthic ecosystem (e.g. McCorkle and Emerson, 1988). Zahn et al. (1986) show an increasing difference in $\delta^{13}C$ between *Cibicides wuellerstorfi* and *Uvigerina peregrina* with an increase in organic flux. McCorkle et al. (1997), however, argue that if Foraminifera position themselves according to a geochemical cue (such as an oxygen gradient, or an organic-rich patch) or a food-related cue (such as bacterial decomposition), then species from a wide range of sediment depths may inhabit geochemically similar microenvironments. As an extreme example, in case of strongly dysoxic or microxic bottom waters, deep infaunal taxa may occupy the sediment surface, and may reflect the isotopic composition of the bottom water, but not of the pore water (Fig. 10.2). Proxies such as the $\Delta\delta^{13}C$ (epifaunal-infaunal difference) should, therefore, be used only after a clear understanding of the benthic environment in which the analyzed foraminiferal species actually lived.

more, bottom-water oxygenation does not necessarily covary with the penetration depth of oxygen in the sediment, and thus, with the extent of the oxygenated infaunal microhabitat. The sediment depth at which the oxygen concentration becomes zero may be very different at sites with very similar bottom-water oxygen concentrations (e.g. Rathburn and Corliss, 1994; Relexans et al., 1996; Jorissen et al., 1998). Within the sediment, the slope of the pore-water oxygen profile is determined by the balance between oxygen diffusion from the sediment surface and oxygen consumption by degrading organic matter. In areas with high organic flux, oxygen values in the substrate will rapidly drop to zero, and the depth of the oxygenated sediment layer will be minimal. Of course, bottom-water oxygen content is not necessarily low in such cases, because bottom currents may cause a strong dominance of infaunal taxa in the sediment is not always indicative of a dysoxic or microxic sediment-water interface.

Our best hope to find foraminiferal markers of benthic ecosystem oxygen content (species that are not primarily dependent on the organic flux) lies in the deep infaunal taxa, because they combine a high tolerance for low oxygen concentrations with that for low-quality food. Logically, the percentage of deep infaunal taxa in a benthic foraminiferal community should covary with the importance of anaerobic degradation of organic matter. As explained below, three different processes are relevant.

(1) Oligotrophic-mesotrophic ecosystems: an increase of the organic flux or export productivity. When the organic flux is very low, the bulk of organic matter is consumed at the oxic sediment-water interface. Thus, very small amounts of organic matter are mixed into the sediment by bioturbation and will be degraded in the anoxic zone. Much of the scarce organic matter brought into the sediment will be completely refractory, and will ultimately be fossilized. As a consequence, deep in the sediment, there is a near absence of anaerobic bacterial degradation, and thus also of deep infaunal taxa. A higher export productivity will increase both the amount of organic matter introduced into the sediment, and the importance of anaerobic degradation processes.

(2) More eutrophic ecosystems: a decrease in the quality of the introduced organic matter. The decrease in labile components may be the result of downslope transport or advection of old, terrestrial, refractory, organic matter from shelf environments, a more efficient recycling of organic matter in the surface waters, or the changing composition of the phytoplankton/zooplankton community. If the labile component of the organic matter, which is directly usable by the epifauna and shallow infauna, decreases, the densities of these two groups will diminish. Also, if the organic matter input remains the same, more organic matter will be degraded under anaerobic conditions deep in the sediment. As a consequence of the reduction of the epifauna and shallow infauna, and the increase in organic matter degradation within the sediment, the proportion of deep infaunal taxa will go up.

(3) Lowered oxygen concentration in bottom water. If bottom-water oxygenation falls below the critical value for a particular species, the species will disappear, probably as a result of failure to reproduce. As a consequence, other taxa that are more tolerant will show an increase in their proportions in the community. If a significant number of epifaunal and/or shallow infaunal taxa disappear, much more trophic resources will become available to deep infaunal taxa; these may eventually move to the sediment surface, and replace taxa less tolerant to dysoxic or microxic conditions (Fig. 10.2). Under such circumstances, deep infaunal taxa can completely dominate benthic foraminiferal faunas; this phenomenon is known to precede sapropel formation in the Mediterranean Sea (e.g. Rohling et al., 1997; Jorissen, 1999).

It appears that in most cases the percentage of deep infaunal taxa can be used as a proxy for the depth of the zero-oxygen sediment layer. Only under extreme conditions, however, when bottom-water oxygenation falls below a critical threshold for most surface-dwelling taxa, can the percentage of deep infaunal taxa be used as a proxy of bottom-water oxygen values. Although Kaiho (1994) remarks that many 'oxic' indicators are systematically absent when oxygen values are below 1 ml/l, this putative multi-species low tolerance limit needs confirmation, and the exact values have to be determined for important species.

A second foraminiferal group which is of promise in paleoceanography consists of the so-called 'phytodetritus feeders' (Gooday, 1988; Gooday and Lambshead, 1989; Lambshead and Gooday, 1990; Gooday et al., 1992a; Gooday, 1993). Smart et al. (1994) and Thomas and Gooday (1996) suggest that the relative abundance of *Epistominella exigua*, *Alabaminella weddellensis*, and other phytodetritus exploiting species may be used as a proxy of pulsed organic matter inputs. An opportunistic lifestyle, shared by all phytodetritus species, enables them to profit from short periods of abundant food availability. However, these periods of feast are not necessarily connected with seasonal influx of phytodetritus; they may be related to other processes that cause an intermittent organic flux. Gooday and Turley (1990) give the example of upwelling areas, in which most of the organic matter is delivered to the sea bottom as phytodetritus. Although upwelling in many areas is labeled as 'permanent', in reality the upwelling process is periodically interrupted (from a few days to several weeks) when the flow of deeper, nutrient-rich waters ceases (e.g. Jones and Halpern, 1981). A different context in which opportunistic 'phytodetritus' species may be successful is that of a very eutrophic ecosystem with very low seasonal bottom-water oxygen content. In such an environment, opportunistic, surface dwelling species will profit from short periods of bottom-water re-oxygenation that would make abundant trophic resources accessible to the benthic fauna.

The so-called 'elevated epifaunal' taxa (Lutze and Thiel, 1989; Altenbach and Sarnthein, 1989; Linke and Lutze, 1993), such as *Cibicides wuellerstorfi* and *Planulina ariminensis*, have tentatively been proposed as indicators of bottom current activity. Putatively, these taxa feed on particles transported by bottom currents, and would therefore be independent of any vertical flux of organic matter. However, observations of live *C. wuellerstorfi* at some depth in the sediment suggest that these taxa are not necessarily confined to elevated positions, and that their use as a proxy for bottom-water current activity may not be realistic.

Of necessity, the foregoing discussion is qualitative. Although our understanding of foraminiferal microhabitats has advanced significantly in the last decade, quantification of the foraminifer-microhabitat relationships is still rudimentary. This quantification remains one of the main challenges of foraminiferal ecology.

10.10 ACKNOWLEDGMENTS

My thinking on microhabitats has been greatly influenced by a number of publications. In particular, the work of Bruce Corliss, Andrew Gooday, and Hiroshi Kitazato, and papers of Y. Shirayama (1984) and Robert Carney (1989) have been eye openers. I also benefited greatly from many discussions with Bert Van der Zwaan, Martin Buzas, Henko De Stigter, Thomas Gibson, Sophie Guichard, Hélène Howa, Thomas Pedersen, Jean-Pierre Peypouquet, Barun Sen Gupta, and Peter Verhallen.

11

Benthic Foraminifera and the flux of organic carbon to the seabed

Paul Loubere and Mohammad Fariduddin

11.1 INTRODUCTION

Organic carbon supply is a fundamental aspect of all biological communities, and the organic carbon flux is generally limited for marine benthic organisms. Benthic organisms shrouded in darkness, at water depths greater than a few tens of meters, are entirely dependent on imported organic carbon for their energy requirements. As we will show in this review, areal variations in the flux of organic carbon to the seafloor have a pervasive effect on the benthic community, including the Foraminifera.

Because the processes and ecology are so different, we will examine separately the marine environments within and below the euphotic zone. Our review will be presented in four sections. The first will examine the production of organic matter in the marine realm and its delivery to the ocean floor. The second will summarize observations concerning Foraminifera and food supply. The third will review our basic understanding of the benthic response to organic carbon flux, and present ideas on and models of the response of benthic Foraminifera to that flux. These models will be examined using data concerning foraminiferal microecology, spatial distributions, morphology and abundances. The last section will survey the state of our knowledge and raise important questions which limit our understanding of benthic Foraminifera and their geologic record.

11.2 ORGANIC CARBON SUPPLY

11.2.1

Organic carbon compounds are initially supplied to the marine biologic community from three dominant sources. These are: nearshore production of benthic plants, production of the open ocean phytoplankton and fluvial supply of particulate organic matter (Newman et al., 1973; Hedges and Parker, 1976; Westerhausen et al., 1993; Rice and Rhoads, 1989). Each of these sources also supplies dissolved organic matter which will feed bacteria and thus enter the particulate food chain. The organic matter from the three sources can be roughly divided into three categories based on its energy content and appeal to the biota. These are: labile, resistant and refractory (Middleburg et al., 1993). The labile material is of the greatest importance to biological productivity in the ocean, and is used up most rapidly. The resistant material is used by a specialized population of organisms and can survive in the marine environment for longer periods of time. Refractory organic carbon is nearly biologically inert. It is important to draw these distinctions of type because benthic organisms, including Foraminifera, will respond mostly to the flux of labile material. These carbon compounds are not generally preserved in marine sediments, which by and large accumulate only the refractory material that is no longer, and perhaps never was, of interest to the biota. In the past it has been the practice to examine the relationship of benthic Foraminifera to organic carbon by comparing taxon abundances to sediment organic carbon content. However, the sediment organic material is a residue from a variety of processes not always directly linked to biological productivity. Recent work on sediment organic carbon has shown that a good deal of the preserved material is adhered to clays, and that sediment organic carbon content is mostly a function of clay content and surface area (Keil et al., 1994; Mayer, 1994; Hedges and Keil, 1995). Also, research on the northwestern and northeastern Atlantic continental margins indicates that much carbon transported from the shelf onto the slope (mid-slope carbon high) and deeper water is degraded, refractory material (Rowe et al., 1986; Duineveld et al., 1997).

A global view of biological productivity and the supply of labile organic matter to the seabed is difficult to create. This view must incorporate three factors: euphotic zone production, the fraction of that production that sinks into the deepsea, and the local flux of material transported along the seafloor (e.g. Reimers et al., 1992; Smith, 1987). Surface-ocean production is seasonally variable and can be episodic or subject to longer term trends. Transport processes along the seafloor are, by their nature, localized and quite variable in time. Nevertheless, a general picture of organic matter generation is available from syntheses of measured euphotic zone productivity (e.g. Berger et al., 1987; Berger, 1989), satellite images of phytopigment concentrations in oceanic surface waters (Feldman, 1994), model estimates of productivity based on the pigment concentrations (Longhurst et al., 1995; Antoine et al., 1996; Behrenfeld and Falkowski, 1997), and the extrapolation and mapping of benthic respiration (Jahnke, 1996).

11.2.2 Flux to the seabed

The supply of organic matter generated in the upper layers of the open ocean can be generally divided into two fractions: the recycled and the new production. New production is traditionally the part of total production which is sustained by new nitrate introduced into the euphotic zone (Eppley and Peterson, 1979; Jumars, 1993). The ratio of new production to total production is referred to as the f-ratio. In any steady state consideration of phytoplankton production, the new production is that part of the total which will escape to the deeper ocean and be oxidized there by the benthos. Therefore, variations in the f-ratio are of considerable significance to the benthic organic carbon supply. The range of values for the ratio is from about 0.4 to 0.05, with some of the lowest values observed in the central equatorial Pacific (McCarthy et al., 1996; Head et al., 1996). Lampitt and Antia (1997) show that for the open ocean there is, nevertheless, a systematic relationship between surface-ocean biological productivity and organic carbon flux to the seafloor.

Besides depending on the f-ratio, the flux of phytoplankton production reaching the seafloor depends on water depth. This relationship is most acute in the upper 1000 m of the water column (Martin et al., 1987; Berger et al., 1987). The relationship between the nature of the flux and the water depth has been examined empirically using sediment trap data, and several different equations have been fitted to the curve. In all cases, the flux of material reaching the seabed at depths greater than 1000 m is only a few percent of the euphotic zone production, indicating that efficient recycling of production occurs in the upper few hundred meters of the water column. The result of this is a slim diet for the deep-sea fauna in most areas of the world ocean.

In certain regions, most notably the northwest Indian Ocean and the northeast Atlantic, surface-ocean biological productivity is highly seasonal and organic matter reaches the seabed in pulses, sometimes of fresh phytodetritus (e.g. Smith et al., 1996). Biological response to these pulses is reviewed below. In other areas of the world ocean, such as the eastern equatorial Pacific, seasonality is muted and longer term cycles (El Niño) influence the flux of organic matter to the seafloor. Where the flux is relatively low, it appears that labile organic matter is oxidized at the sediment-water interface. Labile matter has a life span of less than a year (Cole et al., 1987).

different environment from that found at depth. Because of this difference, we will treat the shallow ocean separately from the deep sea (water depth greater than about 200 meters).

11.3.2 The shallow ocean

Although it is recognized that organic carbon availability is important to benthic Foraminifera in the shallow ocean, it has been difficult to assess its exact effect. This is because organic carbon flux is not usually directly measured in foraminiferal studies (organic carbon content of sediments is only an indirect proxy for labile organic carbon flux), and because availability of food is often covariant with many other ecologic factors that are important to the Foraminifera. Further, it is probably also true that in many nearshore settings food availability is not a primary limiting factor for the benthos. Other variables such as substrate, current and wave regime, temperature, salinity, pore-water oxygen content, and biotic interactions could often be more significant.

In the nearshore region, the effect of labile organic carbon availability has been best documented in areas affected by sewage effluent and eutrophication in estuaries or fjords. For the latter settings, the overconsumption of oxygen and the development of anoxia probably constitute the most important factors impacting the Foraminifera. This subject is examined in chapter 12, and a review of pollution effects on estuarine Foraminifera will be found in chapter 13 and Alve (1995a). Case studies of sewage outfall areas over several decades show definite foraminiferal response to these. Early studies such as those of Watkins (1961) and Bandy et al. (1964b) recorded changes in nearshore, colder-water foraminiferal communities and assemblages that related to closeness of a sewage outfall. Most marked were areas devoid of living Foraminifera and the concentration of a limited number of taxa near outfalls. For example, Bandy et al. (1964b) found that *Buliminella elegantissima* and *Bulimina marginata denudata* were overwhelmingly dominant in the living population of the outfall region for the Los

11.3 BENTHIC FORAMINIFERAL RESPONSES

11.3.1

Since the earliest regional surveys (e.g. Phleger, 1951a; Pujos-Lamy, 1972; Ingle et al., 1980), it has been evident that benthic foraminiferal taxa show water depth zonation. Modern statistical analysis (e.g. Culver, 1988) uses this zonation to determine water depths to within 50-250 meters for selected continental margins. The reason for the zonation of the Foraminifera has not been clearly established since many environmental variables covary with water depth. One school of thought, developed first in the 1970s, holds that characteristics of oceanic water masses control foraminiferal distributions (see chapter 1). To a degree this must be true, since waters in the upper mixed layer of the ocean, except at higher latitudes, are much warmer than those below the thermocline. Also, these upper waters are subject to strong variations in their properties in response to seasonal changes and the weather. The sunlit portion of the oceans above the seasonal thermocline is in many ways a very

Angeles County sewage system in Southern California. Further, in the nearshore, *Discorbis columbiensis* showed a positive distributional response to sewage outfall while *Nonionella* could not tolerate the polluted environment. These observations were corroborated and extended in the follow-up study of Stott et al. (1996) who examined this setting after controls had brought significant environmental improvement. In this case, foraminiferal responses are driven by a very large input of organic matter which will alter not only the availability of food but also the character of the sediments and, perhaps most importantly, the distribution of oxygen in the environment. Strongly anaerobic sediments were not uncommon in the area examined by Bandy and colleagues. Also, studies of sewage outfalls include chemical and metal pollution as potential factors, so the extent to which they can be used to interpret natural settings is open to question. Finally, taphonomic processes may be enhanced in sediments with high organic content so that assemblages preserved in the sediments may be quite different from those found in the living community. Bandy et al. (1964b) found the abundance of agglutinated Foraminifera much increased in their assemblages for this reason. Nevertheless, similarities between foraminiferal communities of polluted environments and those found in the stratigraphic record of sediments with high organic content were noticed early on (e.g. Seiglie, 1968). Furthermore, Schafer et al. (1995) found a general inverse relationship of species diversity to organic carbon loading in the vicinity of aquaculture operations in eastern Canada, and an increase in non-calcareous Foraminifera as organic content of the sediments increased. At very high organic content (>20%), no Foraminifera were observed. The mechanisms responsible for these changes probably are not linked directly to increased food supply, and are likely the product of changing sediment properties, sedimentation rate, and oxygen concentrations. One case where increased food supply may be important is that found along the southern coast of Israel where sewage outfall enhances the productivity of the adjacent continental shelf (Yanko et al., 1994c). This agrees with the results of Watkins (1961), Setty (1976), and Clark (1971). In the Yanko et al. study the foraminiferal abundances were elevated above background, and assemblages contained many large, robust specimens. The composition of assemblages was not much different from that on the adjacent unpolluted shelf. There was no documentation of the organic carbon flux to the seabed in this study, and presumably, it was less dramatic than described in the reports mentioned above. So, it may be that in the shallow-water environment, there is a gradient in foraminiferal response to increasing organic carbon flux. At the low end this response may simply be an increase in the standing stock. At higher fluxes, taxa may be progressively excluded or encouraged by environmental changes driven by organic carbon accumulation and oxidation within the sediments (sediment properties, oxygen availability). At the extreme, Foraminifera are excluded from the environment and a 'dead zone' is produced. Quantification of these steps is not possible with the data at hand.

In shallow marine settings free of anthropogenic influence, the role of labile organic carbon availability is ambiguous. Nevertheless, a number of studies show that biomass of Foraminifera responds to seasonal and regional variability in marine plant production. For example, Murray (1985) has shown a relationship between fertility and foraminiferal abundance in the North Sea. Alve and Murray (1994) have traced the impact of the spring phytoplankton bloom on foraminiferal abundance in a mesotidal inlet in England, Schroder-Adams et al. (1990) document a likely control of foraminiferal abundances in the high Arctic by sea-ice limited biological productivity, and Bernhard (1987) shows a similar productivity control on abundances in the Antarctic. Lueck and Snyder (1997) compared two regions on the continental shelf of North Carolina (U.S.A.), and found differences in foraminiferal abundances linked to benthic community productivity, in this case possibly driven by nutrient enriched groundwater fluxing through the sediments. Earlier, Lee et al. (1966) suggested that many littoral Foraminifera are bloom feeders.

The exact impact of the availability of labile organic carbon on shallow-water foraminiferal communities and assemblages is difficult to assess, because of the correlations that organic carbon flux has to other important environmental variables. For example, Hayward et al. (1996) collected data for both Foraminifera and environmental variables for an ecological analysis of a tidal inlet in New Zealand. They found assemblage changes that could possibly be related to food supply. However, the effects of the environmental factors are obscured by correlations among organic carbon, mud content of the sediments, salt marsh index, total oxidized nitrogen, and dissolved reactive phosphate. Defining taxon ecologic responses to the different environmental variables under these conditions is not possible.

Finally, it is important that labile organic carbon in the shallow-water setting comes in many different forms, from pretreated sewage and bacteria (e.g. Goldstein and Corliss, 1994) to algal mats, algal coatings on sediment grains, and stands of macroalgae. Additionally, shallow-water Foraminifera may bear endosymbionts (see chapter 8), and perhaps even farm bacteria (Langer and Gehring, 1993). This means that foraminiferal taxa will vary not only in response to the quantity of organic matter but also its form. The taxa present and their abundance for a given setting will depend on feeding type adaptations (e.g. Lipps, 1983).

11.3.3 The deep sea

The supply of labile organic carbon is much reduced in the deeper ocean (depth > about 200 m) and is much more likely to be a primary limiting factor in benthic ecology. Altenbach and Sarnthein (1989) and Gooday et al. (1992a) provide a summary of the abundance and possible importance of benthic Foraminifera to deep ocean communities. In many instances, benthic Foraminifera may be a dominant component of the fauna. For example, off Cape Hatteras on the U.S. east coast, *Bathysiphon filiformis* occurs in great abundance and its tubes are a prominent feature of the ocean floor (Gooday et al.,1992b). It is interesting to note that much of the information on foraminiferal biomass and community importance in the deep sea centers on non-calcareous taxa, while the abundance, productivity, and community relations of the calcareous taxa remain obscure. In contrast, the calcareous taxa are usually better preserved in marine sediments, and receive most of the attention in geological and paleoceanographic studies. Gooday et al. (1997) provide an interesting examination of non-calcareous deep-sea Foraminifera and their relationship to organic carbon flux. A review of both agglutinated and calcareous deep-sea Foraminifera with an emphasis on organic carbon flux may be found in Gooday (1994). The review below will concentrate on the calcareous taxa.

Causes for the depth zonation of benthic foraminiferal communities below the thermocline have been the subject of debate for decades. In many ways the foraminiferal zonation parallels that seen for other benthic organisms (reviewed in Loubere, 1996), and is thus a part of the general biotic response to the deep-sea environment. The depth zonation of species and species groups, however, is not consistent from one continental margin to another (Pujos-Lamy, 1972; Miller and Lohmann, 1982; Lutze and Coulbourn, 1983/84). Early attempts to analyze this variation focused on relating foraminiferal taxa to deep-ocean water masses whose physical and chemical properties were supposed to control species distributions (e.g. Schnitker, 1980). More recent water mass based studies show statistical relationships on a regional level (e.g. Denne and Sen Gupta, 1991), but these have not been consistent for inter-regional comparisons (Miller and Lohmann, 1982; Lutze and Coulbourn, 1983/84; Corliss et al., 1986; Mackensen et al., 1993). This is particularly true for the taxon *Uvigerina peregrina*, which at different times was associated with warmer bottom waters and deep waters with low oxygen content. A major shortcoming of the water mass control hypothesis has been the lack of a model based on ecological principles or theory that would explain why relatively small physical and chemical differences in ambient water would control species distributions.

Regional surveys of benthic foraminiferal distributions show that there are horizontal as well as vertical gradients in taxon abundances. This is clearly seen in Poag's (1981) atlas of Foraminifera in the Gulf of Mexico, which illustrates strong distributional changes in the vicinity of the Mississippi River Delta. Similarly, Lutze and Coulbourn (1983/84) recognized lateral changes in benthic foraminiferal communities on the continental margin of northwestern Africa. Some of their findings are shown in Fig. 11.1 which presents regional patterns of abundance for the living taxa. These community or assemblage distribution patterns were associated with changing sedimentary regime, and with organic carbon content of the sediment. A similar interpretation of faunal distributions was made for the northeastern U.S. continental margin by Miller and Lohmann (1982). In the case of the Gulf of Mexico, Loubere et al. (1993a) demonstrated that the flux of organic matter to the seabed was higher on the Mississippi River delta slope than elsewhere in the northwestern Gulf, so that lateral changes in foraminiferal communities could be associated with this flux. Osterman and Kellogg (1979) recognized the impact of surface-ocean productivity on benthic foraminiferal assemblages in a study of surface sediments from the Ross Sea, Antarctica. Sen Gupta et al. (1981) observed unusual foraminiferal assemblages on the Florida continental slope associated with upwelling. Van der Zwaan (1982) argued on the basis of geologic interpretation of Miocene sections in the Mediterranean region that food supply must be a dominant controlling factor of benthic foraminiferal taxon distributions. Boersma (1985) and Woodruff (1985), in their geological investigations, also concluded that food supply was important. Mackensen et al. (1985) examined foraminiferal assemblages on the continental margin of southwestern Norway, and found that some taxon distributions correlated to organic carbon content of the sediments. A larger scale analysis of Rose-Bengal stained (presumed living) benthic Foraminifera from the top centimeter of the sediments and dead assemblages for the South Atlantic by Mackensen et al. (1993a) also found distributions that varied laterally. Part of their data is shown in Fig. 11.2, which presents assemblage distributions the authors associate with increased carbon flux to the seafloor in the vicinity of the Polar Front. Two higher productivity assemblages/communities are vertically separated under what Mackensen et al. (1993a) interpret as a water mass effect (perhaps chiefly a temperature effect). However, the region examined is strongly affected by carbonate dissolution and a shoaling CCD (calcite compensation depth, their Fig. 4). So, changing preservation cannot be discounted as a factor contributing to vertical assemblage gradients in the South Atlantic. In this case, preservation will correlate with changing water masses (Antarctic Bottom Water vs. North Atlantic Deep Water). Schmiedl et al. (1997) conducted a study on the Southwest African margin similar to that of Mackensen et al. (1993a). They found that stained and dead foraminiferal taxon distributions were most strongly associated with interpreted food supply and pore-water oxygen content (neither directly measured). They examined taxon principal component correlations with water depth, porosity, carbonate content, total organic carbon, temperature, salinity, bottom-water oxygen content, phosphate content, and calculated TOC flux. Complete analysis of faunal responses is complicated by the correlations among the environmental variables (not given) which make distinguishing their separate effects difficult.

The benthic foraminiferal assemblage relationship to surface-ocean biological productivity and its related organic carbon flux to the seabed were first unambiguously tested by Loubere (1991) in a study where productivity was statistically uncorrelated with any other significant environmental variable. This work showed a quantitative relationship between productivity and the benthic foraminiferal assemblages, and recognized assemblages with particular ranges of surface-ocean biological productivity. The Loubere (1991) analysis was later expanded to cover the eastern Pacific (Loubere, 1994, 1997), the Atlantic Ocean (Fariduddin and Loubere, 1997), and finally the Indian Ocean (Loubere, 1998), and finally

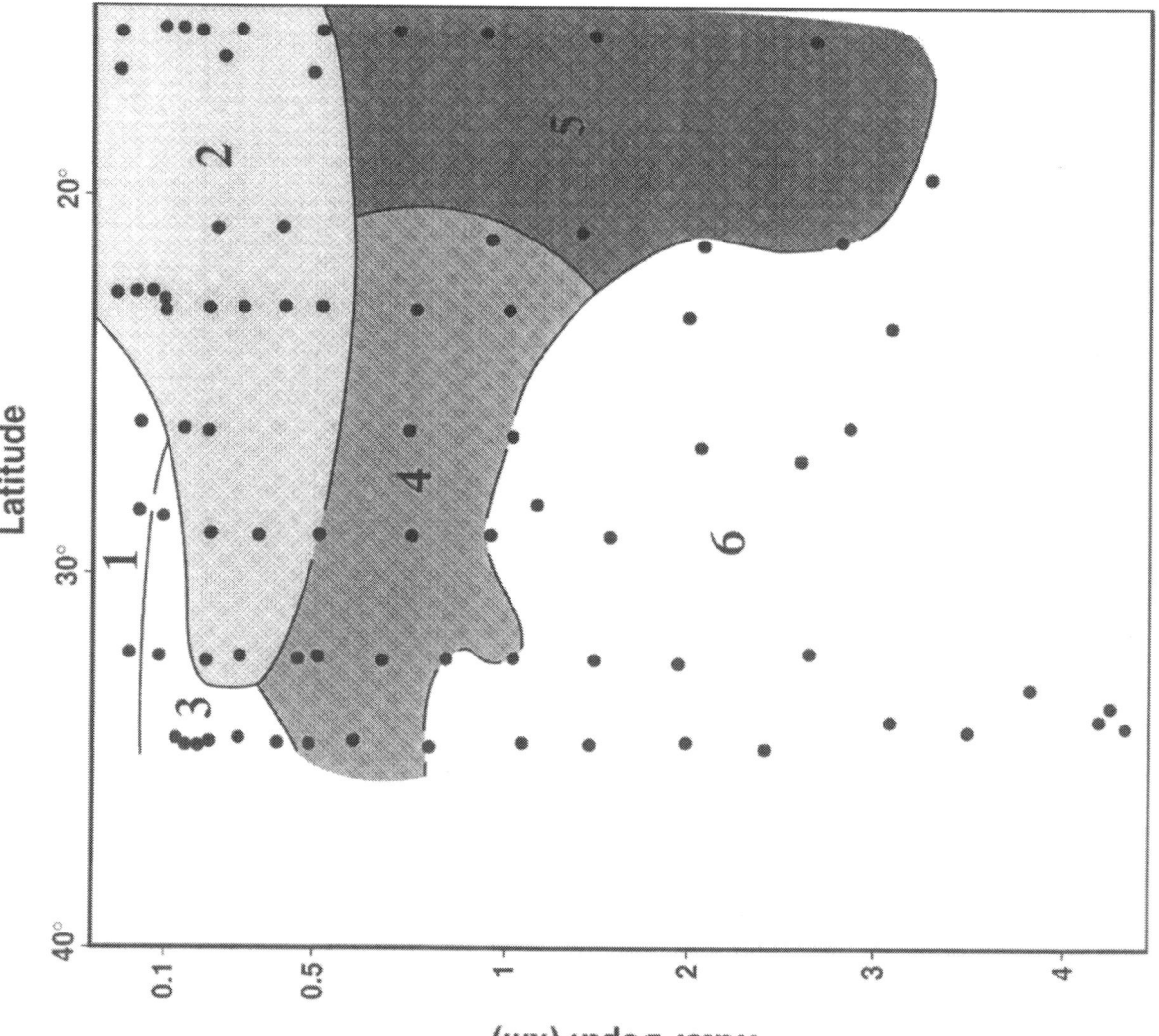

Figure 11.1 Living benthic foraminiferal community groupings on the continental margin of N.W. Africa after Lutze and Coulbourn (1983/84). View as from the ocean looking towards Africa. Groupings are based on correlations among surface sediment benthic foraminiferal abundances and show both depth and latitude related boundaries. 1 = *Cibicides lobatulus* biofacies, 2 = *Cancris auriculus* biofacies, 3 = *Globobulimina* biofacies, 4 = *Uvigerina peregrina finisterrensis* biofacies, 5 = *Uvigerina peregrina/Globobulimina* biofacies, 6 = *Cibicides wuellerstorfi* biofacies.

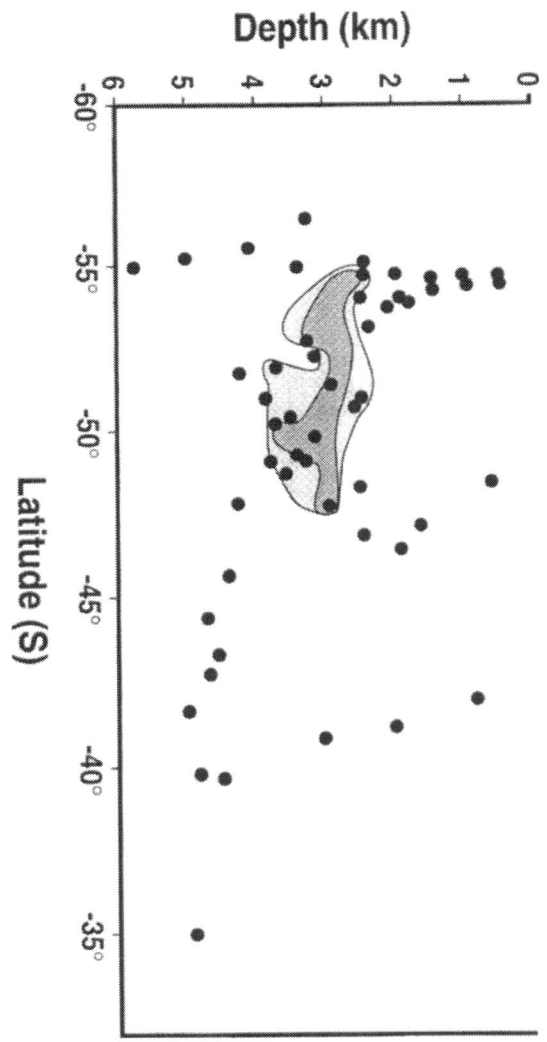

Figure 11.2 Distribution of deep sea benthic foraminiferal communities/assemblages projected onto a latitudinal transect in the South Atlantic, after Mackensen et al. (1993a). Dead assemblage distribution for the Southern High-Productivity Fauna (*Pullenia bulloides* assemblage).

the global ocean (Loubere and Fariduddin, 1999).

These works used geographically selected samples taken within a limited range of water depths so that the biological productivity signal would be uncorrelated to other factors that could influence benthic foraminiferal assemblage composition; this approach avoids misinterpretation of environmental effects through spurious correlations among controlling ecologic factors (e.g. Loubere and Qian, 1997). Figure 11.3 shows the regional patterns of benthic foraminiferal assemblages (factor patterns) found in the above studies for the eastern Pacific and the Atlantic. The higher-productivity upwelling areas of the two oceans are clearly mapped out on the ocean floor by the Foraminifera.

There is a global uniformity in the taxa found associated with different ranges of productivity. Higher- and lower-productivity taxon groupings of Loubere and co-workers (see Figs. 11.4, 11.5) are consistent with the results of other regional surveys in the higher latitude South Atlantic (Mackensen et al., 1993a) and the South African Atlantic continental margin (Schmiedl et al.,

1997). The global data base of taxon abundances for the deep open ocean has also been used to quantify the foraminiferal assemblage to surface-ocean productivity relationship via multiple regression. Assemblages have been used to estimate productivity with an $r^2 = 0.97$ (eastern Pacific, Loubere, 1994) and 0.89 (global ocean, Loubere and Fariduddin, 1999).

In addition to the influence on assemblages, surface-ocean productivity also seems to affect planktonic to benthic (P/B) foraminiferal ratios (Berger and Diester-Haas, 1988) and benthic foraminiferal accumulation rates (Herguera and Berger, 1991). Both of these relationships would result from a correlation between benthic foraminiferal production and flux of organic carbon to the deep-sea floor. Little information is available about benthic foraminiferal productivity (shells generated per unit time), but standing stocks are related to food supply, as seen in the surveys of Lutze and Coulbourn (1983/84) and Schmiedl et al. (1997). Also, examination of P/B ratios and foraminiferal shell accumulation rates must take into account taphonomic processing within the sediments. This is not constant across all oceanic environments, and is still

Benthic foraminiferal responses

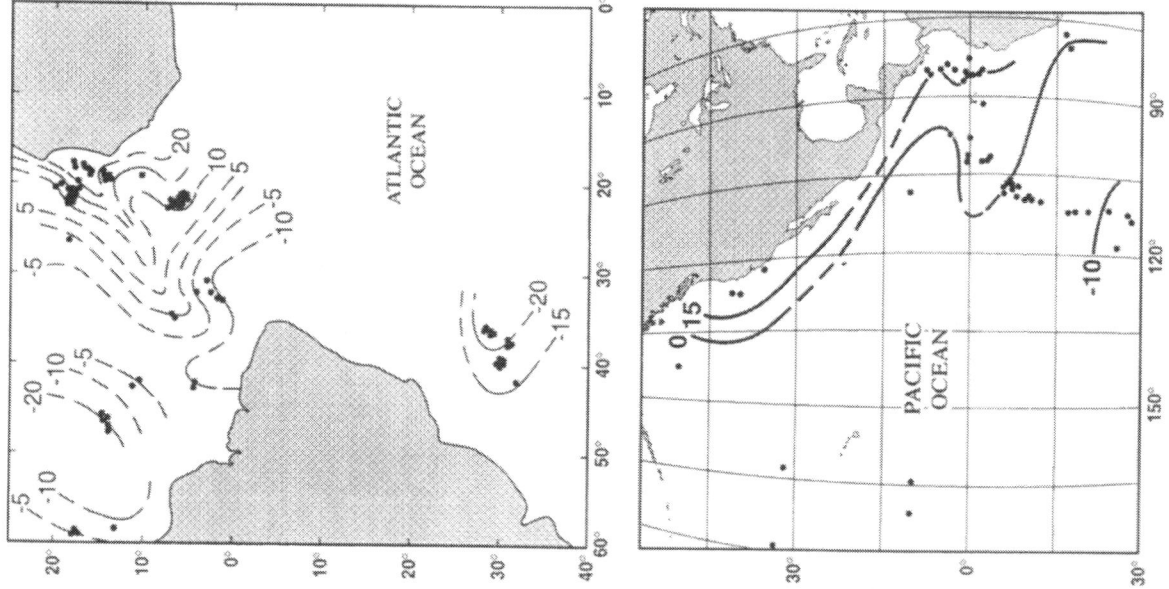

Figure 11.3 Maps of first Principal Component scores for surface sediment assemblages in the Atlantic and Pacific Oceans. In each case the scores account for a large part of the assemblage variance, and their patterns follow average surface ocean productivity gradients. Data from Loubere (1996) and Fariduddin and Loubere (1997). Higher productivity areas have positive scores.

poorly defined. The P/B ratio has been traditionally used to estimate water depth on continental margins, but also includes a productivity signal. Analysis by van der Zwaan et al. (1990) suggests that this signal is largely incorporated in taxa deemed to be infaunal. The relationship between accumulation rate and productivity has been quantitatively calibrated at a relatively lim-

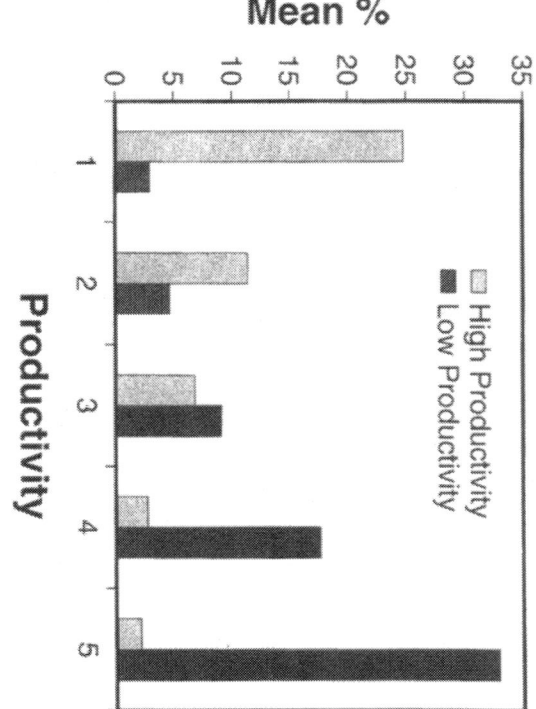

Figure 11.4 Mean abundance of the 'high productivity' and 'low productivity' benthic foraminiferal groups along the global productivity gradient for 207 samples in the Atlantic, Pacific and Indian Oceans (Loubere and Fariduddin, 1999). On the productivity axis: 1 = >200 gC/m²/yr, 2 = 200–150 gC/m²/yr, 3 = 150–90 gC/m²/yr, 4 = 90–50 gC/m²/yr and 5 = <50 gC/m²/yr. The high productivity group includes: *Uvigerina* sp., *M. barleeanus*, *M. pompilioides*, *B. alazanensis*, *Globobulimina* sp. and *S. bulloides*. The low productivity group includes: *G. subglobosa*, *N. umbonifera* and *F. seminuda*.

ited number of locations in the Pacific Ocean. The use of the accumulation rate as a productivity signal depends on the assumption that each foraminiferal test, regardless of species, is equivalent to a set quantity of organic carbon reaching the seafloor. It must also be assumed that taphonomic processes are linked to organic carbon flux to the seafloor so that a consistent productivity signal can be maintained through the transition from living community to fossil assemblage. Naidu and Malmgren (1995) tested both the P/B and benthic foraminiferal accumulation rate tracers for paleoproductivity at a site in the oxygen minimum zone of the Oman margin in the Arabian Sea. They found that neither appeared to properly reflect changes in surface-ocean productivity (hence organic carbon flux to the seabed) through the past 18,000 years. The favored explanation for this was that the low oxygen content of bottom water placed constraints on the benthic foraminiferal community, and that their abundances mainly reflected changes in oxygen supply. The link between organic carbon flux and the P/B ratio and benthic foraminiferal accumulation rates needs further exploration over a broader range of environments. In particular, justification is needed for accepting the assumption that all foraminiferal shells, regardless of species, represent the same quantity of labile organic carbon reaching the seafloor.

Finally, associations have been found between organic carbon flux to the seabed and individual taxon abundances and taxon morphology. Corliss (1985, 1991), Corliss and Chen (1988), and Corliss and Fois (1990) have observed variations in benthic foraminiferal morphotypes which they ascribe to changing organic carbon flux to the seabed and associated microenvironments. Corliss put morphologies into three habitat-groups: epifaunal, shallow infaunal (just below the sediment-water interface), and deeper infaunal. Corliss and Chen divided their morphotypes into nine groups: rounded trochospiral, plano-convex trochospiral, miliolinc, biconvex trochospiral, rounded planispiral, flattened ovoid, tapered and cylindrical, spherical, and flattened tapered. They found regular changes in the abundances of the morphotype groups in transects down continental margins. Deeper-

Benthic foraminiferal responses 191

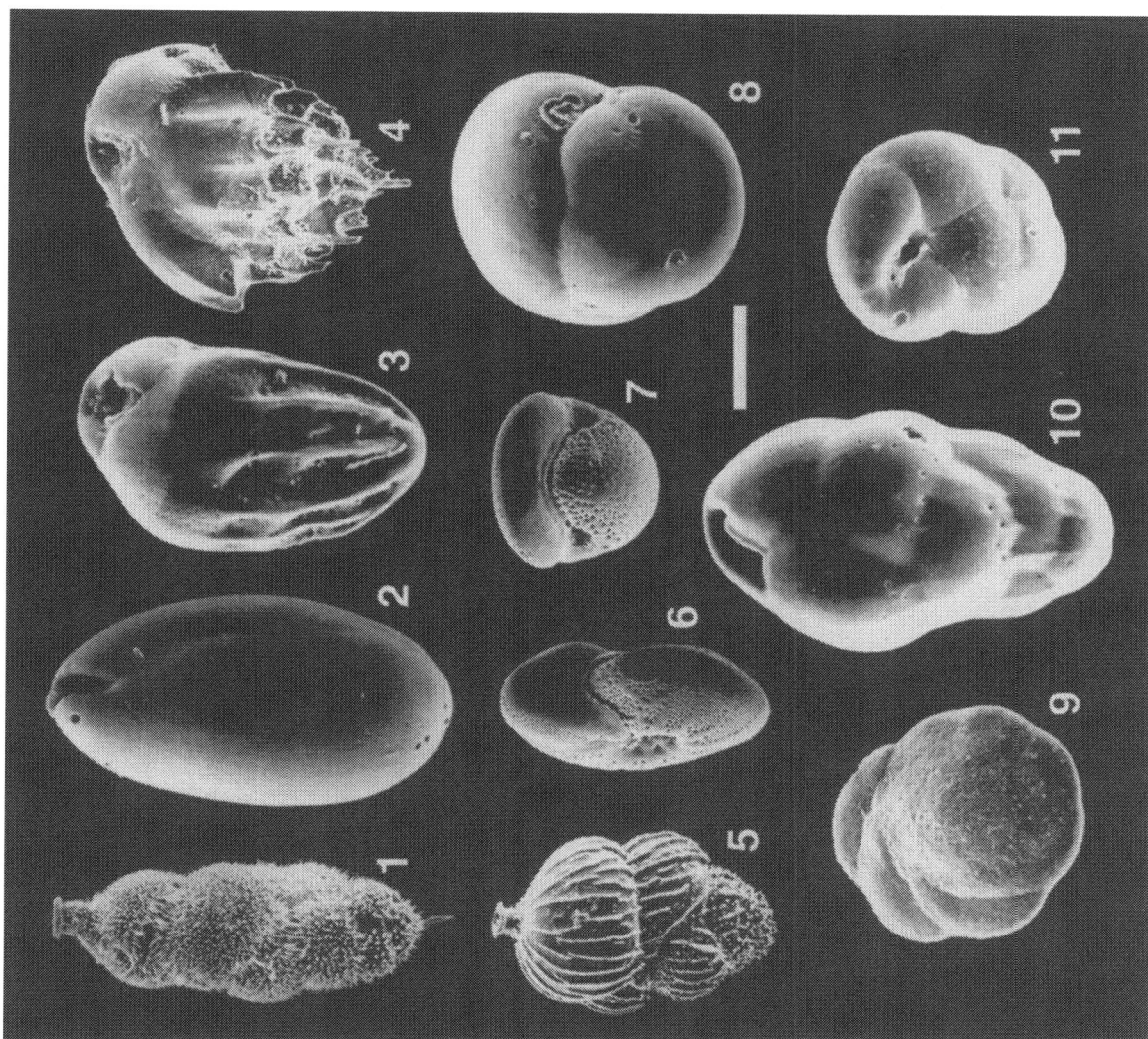

Figure 11.5 High (figures 1–8) and low (figures 9–11) productivity taxa commonly observed in the deep sea. Size of specimen on the longest dimension shown in parentheses in microns, followed by scale bar length for that specimen. **1.** hispid *Uvigerina* sp. (652:167). **2.** *Globobulimina* sp. (835:209). **3.** *Bulimina alazanensis* (371:108). **4.** *Bulimina mexicana* (742:228). **5.** *Uvigerina peregrina* s.l. (719:262). **6.** *Melonis barleeanus* (464:175). **7.** *Melonis pompilioides* (441:268). **8.** *Sphaeroidina bulloides* (255:88). **9.** *Nuttallides umbonifera* (394:158) **10.** *Bulimina transluscens* (267:66) **11.** *Globocassidulina subglobosa* (186:79).

infaunal habitat types (e.g. rounded planispiral, tapered cylindrical) decrease in abundance with increasing water depth.

At the species level, Collins (1989) examined mophometric variation in *Bulimina aculeata* and *B. marginata*, and found shape variations that could be linked to the abundance of organic carbon and mud along the margin of the Gulf of Maine. Boltovskoy et al. (1991) summarized studies showing the effects of food availability on the size of foraminiferal taxa. These appear to be environmentally dependent. Corliss (1979) inferred that in the deep sea, smaller size in *Globocassidulina subglobosa* was associated with limited food supply. Caralp (1989a) associated larger size and higher percentage of abnormal tests in *Melonis barleeanus* at a location on the slope of west Africa with increased supply of little altered organic matter.

11.3.4 Seasonality of the organic carbon flux to the seabed

The discussion so far has treated organic carbon flux to the deeper seabed as a homogeneous ecological factor. However, it is well documented that the flux is often highly variable in time. In many oceanic areas, there are seasonal peaks in surface-ocean biological productivity, and these may produce relatively short bursts of organic carbon rain on the seafloor. For example, Hecker (1990) and Smith et al. (1996) showed that blooms of phytoplankton can be accompanied by accumulation of fresh organic detritus on the seafloor. Pfannkuche (1993) saw a marked increase in the relative abundance of benthic Foraminifera at a North Atlantic sampling station (47°N, 20°W) in response to a benthic flux event. Altenbach (1992) reviewed benthic foraminiferal response to short term events in the deep sea. Linke et al. (1995) presented experimental evidence of a rapid response of benthic Foraminifera to an influx of organic matter. Corliss and Silva (1993) and Silva et al. (1996) showed a rapid seasonal growth response in benthic Foraminifera along the California borderlands, probably in response to increased organic matter flux to the seafloor. Caralp (1984) observed that certain species of deeper-water benthic Foraminifera appear to be more abundant when supplied with fresh organic carbon. Finally, Gooday (1988, 1993, 1996) and Gooday and Lambshead (1989) found that foraminiferal species such as *Alabaminella weddellensis*, *Epistominella exigua*, *E. pusilla*, *Fursenkoina* sp. and *Globocassidulina subglobosa* preferentially use freshly fallen phytoplankton detritus as a microhabitat. The organic carbon flux seasonality signal in benthic foraminiferal assemblages from deep-sea surface sediments was examined by Loubere and Fariduddin (1999). They analyzed a global assemblage data base in relation to average surface-ocean biological productivity and a seasonality index interpreted from Coastal Zone Color Scanner images of oceanic phytoplankton pigment concentrations. Loubere and Fariduddin divided the assemblage data base into groups based on productivity and seasonality, and used Discriminant Function Analysis to test for separation among these groups. Figure 11.6 shows their results. They found a simple patterning of the foraminiferal data with Discriminant Function 1 summarizing the average annual productivity response and Function 2 incorporating the seasonality response. The location of group centroids in Fig. 11.6 shows that the seasonality signal in benthic assemblages is largest at higher average annual productivity (Groups 1 and 2), and decreases as productivity drops (Groups 7, 8, and 9). At low productivities, it is difficult to identify a seasonality driven response in the taxa. This is intuitively satisfying, as one would expect an important ecologic difference between communities experiencing a substantial and continuous flux of organic matter and communities receiving that flux as a large pulse of limited duration, with low food supply in intervening months. For Discriminant Function 2, the seasonality axis, most of the discrimination is based on *E. exigua*, *C. hooperi*, and *C. laevigata* which are more abundant at higher seasonality, and on the hispid *Uvigerina* and *B. alazanensis* which are more abundant at low seasonality. Additionally, comparing mean assemblages shows that *M. barleeanus*, *A. weddellensis*, *C. wuellerstorfi*,

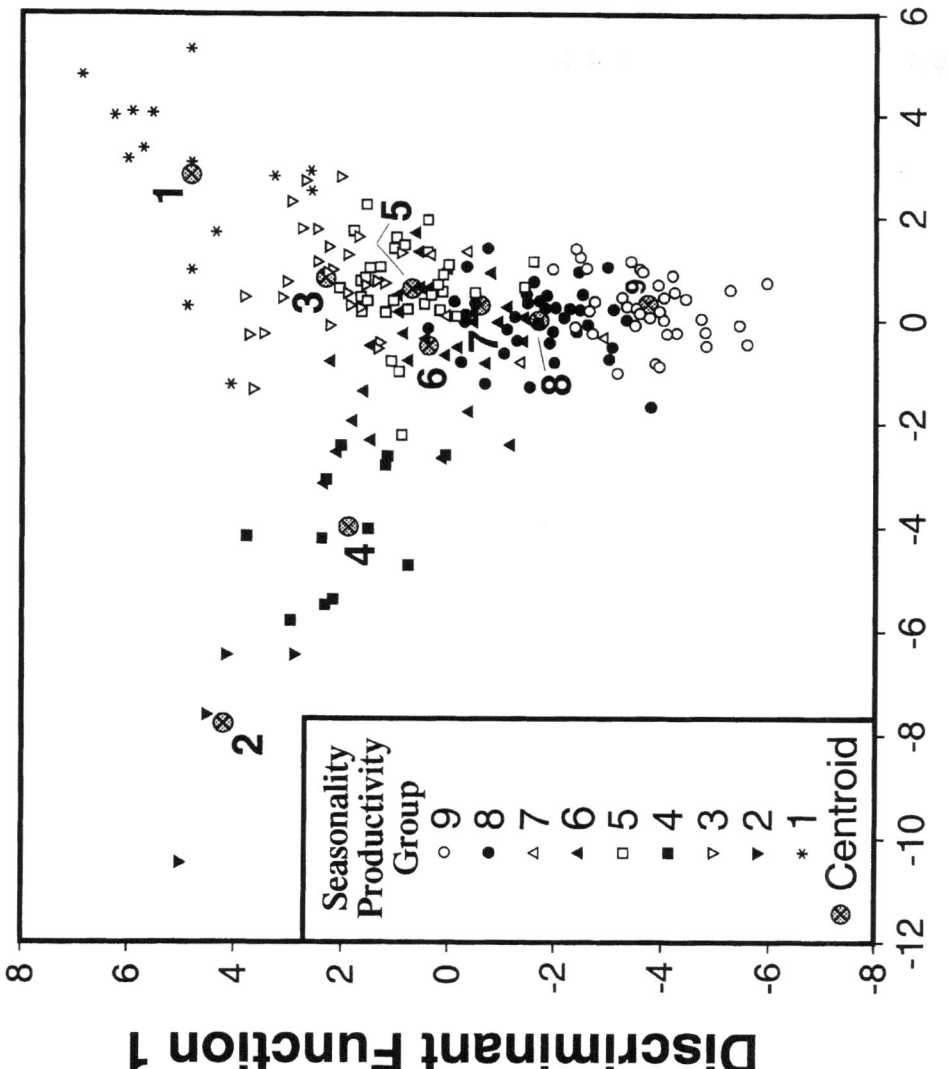

Figure 11.6 Benthic foraminiferal assemblages from the 207 surface sediment samples used in Figures 11.3 and 11.4 plotted in Discriminant Function Axis 1 and 2 space using 9 sample groups based on both productivity and seasonality. Discriminant Function 1 spreads the samples on the basis of mean annual productivity and Discriminant Function 2 on the basis of seasonality. The Groups are (productivity in units of $gC/m^2/yr$): (1) >200, high seasonality, (2) >200, low seasonality, (3) 150–200, high seasonality, (4) 150–200, low seasonality, (5) 90–150, high seasonality, (6) 90–150, low seasonality, (7) 50–90, high seasonality, (8) 50–90, low seasonality, (9) <50, low seasonality. Group centroids are labeled by numbers 1 to 9.

and *M. pompilioides* are more abundant where seasonality is high, whereas *S. bulloides* and *B. mexicana* are more abundant under lower seasonality. Finally, Loubere and Fariduddin (1999) found that distinction could also be made between settings with a single annual pulse of surface-ocean productivity and those with several or intermittent pulses.

11.4 WHY BENTHIC FORAMINIFERA REFLECT FOOD SUPPLY

11.4.1

Any examination of benthic foraminiferal response to organic carbon flux should include a view of the response of benthic organisms as a whole. This is relevant to developing theories concerning foraminiferal ecology and to formulating questions for further research (section 11.5). Our review of the benthos here will be limited to deeper-water environments where availability of food is most clearly a limiting factor.

A broad review of benthic community response to food supply is presented in Pearson and Rosenberg (1987). The environment being considered is muddy, and often seen as relatively unchanging. The dominant organisms are polychaetes, bivalves, peracarid crustaceans (especially tanaids), nematodes, and foraminifers (Pearson and Rosenberg, 1987; Jumars et al., 1990) and the deposit feeders are the dominant feeding guild. An early observation concerning deep-sea organisms was their high diversity (e.g. Sanders, 1968) which seemingly conflicts with the homogeneity of their environment. This diversity is an important, but not yet completely understood, clue about deep-sea ecology.

The broad scale distribution of deep-sea organisms shows several global patterns. The density of deep-sea dwellers decreases with distance from the coastline (Thiel, 1983), with some variation on continental slopes where organic matter depocenters occur (Duineveld et al., 1997; Lampitt et al., 1986). A global map of benthic organism abundance (Belyayev et al., 1973) shows clearly that numbers are highest along continental margins and beneath upwelling areas, and lowest beneath the subtropical gyres.

On a regional scale, a number of studies now show that the flux of organic matter to the seafloor influences the distribution and abundance of benthic organisms. A comprehensive example of this is provided on the continental slope off Cape Hatteras (Diaz et al., 1994). A strong lateral gradient in sediment accumulation rates is accompanied by a large increase in organic carbon deposition in the Cape Hatteras area (DeMaster et al., 1994). This gradient is accompanied by marked changes in benthic community composition and community structure (Hecker, 1994; Blake and Grassle, 1994). Additionally, the abundance of benthic organisms greatly increases in response to an increasing organic carbon flux (Blake and Hilbig, 1994). As the flux goes up, the communities show a decrease in diversity, increased abundance of normally scarce taxa, and the presence of taxa normally limited to shallow (continental shelf) water environments. Analogous variations in benthic abundance and community structure are observed off western Sweden (Rosenberg, 1995), and off Southwest Ireland (Duineveld et al., 1997). In all these settings there are complex mixes of organic matter derived from the continent, which may be degraded, and pulses of labile material from the sea surface. Exactly how the taxa use these different sources of organic matter is unclear. Also important to these environments is benthic disturbance and the action of currents, which may transport considerable sediment and make suspension feeding a viable feeding strategy. Carney (1989) speculates that feeding strategies in the benthos may change depending on the flux of labile material to the seafloor. When rapidly sinking high nutrient pulses of organic matter arrive, detritus feeding metazoans may consume this material directly and rapidly. It is important here that in regions of high seasonality, a substantial portion of the phytoplankton bloom may reach the benthos (Pearson and Rosenberg, 1987; Lampitt, 1985). Between the pulses, bacterial biomass derived from more refractory detritus would be a more important part of the diet.

The average size of organisms diminishes with depth and distance from the continents. Most deep-sea animals are small. Intensive natural selection for particle selection ability is seen as one reason for this (Jumars et al., 1990). Carney (1989) points out that in response to decreased carbon input with depth, we should expect to find in the fauna both a decreased overall abundance and species replacement determined by the efficiency of foraging. Carney also reviews data indicating that the nutritional value of organic matter decreases with depth, further intensifying the pressure on the benthos to search efficiently, hoard resources, and maximize external resources in the processing of food.

Why benthic Foraminifera reflect food supply

Duineveld et al. (1997) review organic carbon accumulation and quality on several continental margins and find in the northeastern Atlantic that much of the material on the slope is degraded and refractory. Wheatcroft and Jumars (1987) show that labile detritus will be rapidly consumed once in the sediments which are subject to selective mixing, so the labile material will not be distributed in the sediment much beyond its point of entry (detritus settling on the seafloor) or generation (bacterially produced labile material).

In concert with these observations, it has been found that abundance and taxon composition in the larger benthos and the meiofauna change progressively down continental margins (Coull, 1972; Coull et al., 1977; Haedrich et al., 1975; Rowe and Menzies, 1969; Rowe et al., 1974, 1982), and that the habitation zone within the sediments thins with distance from the shore line (Shirayama, 1984).

The food resources available to the benthos are subject to the dynamics of the bottom boundary layer (BBL) and the sediment mixed layer (SML), and it is the properties of these to which the benthic organisms will respond. It appears that benthic organisms may follow three feeding strategies (Carney, 1989; Jumars and Gallagher, 1982). They may be opportunistic and rapidly consume newly arrived labile material for use at their leisure. Collection may be accomplished by hydrodynamic trapping of less dense organic material in structures and pits, and by collection into burrows (Jumars et al., 1990; Bett and Rice, 1993). Finally, benthos can also harvest the bacteria which use less desirable, or inaccessible, organic matter. Aller and Aller (1986) showed that burrows and benthic structures could serve as collection points of organic matter, and also as centers of bacterial activity on the deep-sea floor. Thus, structures would offer enhanced feeding opportunities to the benthos. The bacteria would provide not only organic carbon, but also serve to extract nitrogen from surrounding waters and provide it in a usable organic form to the other benthos (Jumars, 1993, p. 41).

Deep-sea diversity remains difficult to understand, but it may be partly explained by a combination of taxon feeding strategy and environmental heterogeneity. Although one might expect most deep-sea benthos to be opportunists feeding on whatever might be present, it appears, counterintuitively, that resource partitioning may be common in abyssal environments. Jumars et al. (1990) consider an optimal foraging theory and conclude that there are advantages in being selective. Evidence for selectivity can be found in holothuroids (Hammond, 1983) and worms (reviews in Fauchald and Jumars, 1979; Lopez and Levinton, 1987).

The idea of environmental heterogeneity also seems initially counterintuitive as the deep sea appears homogeneous on the larger scale. However, Grassle and Morse-Porteous (1987) and Tyler (1995) argue that heterogeneity exists on the deep-sea floor as a result of small scale physical processes, episodic larger events (one might consider benthic storms here, e.g. Hollister and McCave, 1984), and biogenic heterogeneity. Concepts here are reviewed in Smith (1994). Heterogeneity would lead to a succession process with a mosaic of stages developed over the ocean floor. Jumars and Gallagher (1982) suggest a theory for this, using Markovian succession models. Different taxa would flourish in sequence after a disturbance (which might be a phytodetritus pulse) as their ecological specializations match the temporary conditions created by the succession process and the probabilities governing community membership. A key element in this idea would be that disturbances are rare enough to allow succession to develop often, but common enough to prevent climax and competitive exclusion. The influence of disturbance on benthic communities is examined in Thiery (1982), Probert (1984), and Thistle (1981). Thistle and Eckman (1990) present some evidence that benthic organisms associate preferentially with each other, indicating that heterogeneity, in response to biotic factors, does exist on the deep-sea floor.

To summarize, the response of the benthos to organic carbon flux will be mediated by a number of ecologic behaviors. These include:

particle size selection, efficiency in foraging, feeding strategies, flexibility in resource use, resource partitioning and community succession, benthic organism associations, and changing distribution within and upon the sediments.

11.4.2 Theoretical considerations

It is clear that patterns in benthic foraminiferal assemblages and abundances are related to the flux of organic carbon to the seafloor. So far, theoretical ideas about this have been mostly limited to considering adaptations to microenvironments in the sediments and, to a lesser degree, resource selection. The other factors listed in the previous section have not received much attention. Hence, a complete theoretical explanation of foraminiferal response to organic carbon flux has yet to be developed, although Sjoerdsma and van der Zwaan (1992) have presented a general empirical model. Corliss (1985) observed that deep-sea benthic Foraminifera could be classed into broad morphologic groups and that these groups could be associated with particular microenvironments within the sediments. Support for this is presented for material off the northeastern U.S.A. in Corliss and Emerson (1990). An examination of shifting morphotype abundances on the margins of Norway (Corliss and Chen, 1988) and the northern Gulf of Mexico (Corliss and Fois, 1990) show patterns that can be tied to flux of organic carbon to the seafloor, with epifaunal morphotypes becoming most abundant at greater depth where the flux is lowest. Loubere et al. (1993b) examined assemblage changes with water depth in the northern Gulf of Mexico in light of pore-water chemical measurements which could be used to constrain biogeochemical zonation in the surficial sediments (upper 15 cm) and the flux of organic matter to the seafloor. Ideas similar to those above are also presented in chapter 10 and Jorissen et al. (1995). The results of these various studies, when combined with observations on meiofaunal sediment concentration profiles, suggest that foraminiferal species are adapted to different microhabitats that are vertically stratified in the sediments.

This stratification increases and deepens in the sediment column as flux of organic carbon to the seabed increases. Thus, certain taxa are adapted to epifaunal or surface-sediment habitats, others inhabit suboxic settings, while still others exist near the pore-water anoxic boundary within the sediments. Demands of the microenvironment influence test architecture, and this produces the morphotype gradients observed above. Since the existence of the microenvironments is tied to flux of labile organic carbon to the seabed, we see changes in benthic assemblage composition as the importance of different microhabitat groups changes with changing microhabitat development. Note, for example, that most of the high-productivity group taxa shown in Fig. 11.5 are 'infaunal' morphotypes by Corliss' classification, and would inhabit suboxic microhabitats. These ideas are developed in a quantitative framework in Loubere (1997). In this book, chapters 10 and 12 contain more information on microhabitats.

The review so far has emphasized a static, two-dimensional view of foraminiferal taxa that are vertically stratified in the sediments. However, areal and time dimensions must also be added to the picture. Linke and Lutze (1993) examined the concept of habitats in dynamic terms, suggesting that simple vertical stratification within the sediment column in response to general pore-water chemical gradients is an oversimplified view of benthic foraminiferal ecology. These authors find that taxa are distributed in a variety of microenvironments within and on the sediments, which can include such unusual settings as the appendages of benthic invertebrates. Staining and seasonal sampling by Gooday (1986, 1996) and Barmawidjaja et al. (1992) show that many benthic foraminiferal species do not have fixed vertical zonation within deep-sea sediments, and that such zonation as they have can change from month to month. In the subtidal environment, Hohenegger et al. (1993) and Thomsen and Altenbach (1993) observed patchy distributions of Foraminifera, and noted their association with the sediment structures of larger organisms. A number of taxa appeared to live in the oxic halo of burrows. Similar observations for the deep sea (Gulf of Mexico) were made by Loubere et al. (1995), who noted that foraminiferal distributions were patchy and apparently concentrated near burrow structures.

In the context of foraminiferal response to productivity and organic carbon flux to the seabed, the critical factors controlling distribution should be the availability of labile organic matter in different microenvironments within the sediments, the distribution of those microenvironments in time and space, the availability of oxidants for respiration (oxygen being the most chemically efficient one), and competition from other organisms for the resources. Foraminiferal taxa will have adapted to these factors, and taxa present within the sediments will change as the factors change, in response to varying flux of organic matter to the seafloor.

Finally, moving away from the living population and considering assemblages preserved in the sediments, taphonomy (chemical and biotic processes that destroy foraminiferal tests during their incorporation into the sedimentary deposits) is also an important factor. This topic is examined in chapter 16. Also, Loubere et al. (1993b) and Loubere (1997) review taphonomic processes for the deep ocean as these relate to organic carbon flux. Taphonomy apparently enhances the organic carbon flux signal preserved in fossil assemblages.

dominant component of life on the seabed (Altenbach and Sarnthein, 1989; Gooday et al., 1992a), but it remains unclear how they relate to the biological theories of community ecology developed for the metazoa.

Key issues from the biological perspective are those raised for other benthos: (a) how are populations maintained in the deep-sea settings where food supply is severely limited? and (b) how is diversity maintained in the deep-sea environment? For other organisms, as reviewed above, the answers to these questions rest with resource partitioning and environmental heterogeneity, most of which is seasonal (arrival and use of food falls), physical (benthic storms), or biologically generated (seabed environmental alteration by the activities of organisms, e.g. pits and burrows). For many deeper ocean settings, one can imagine each foraminiferal species as a bit player in a show that is running continuously but at ever changing locations, so the taxa do their brief routines at the appropriate time at each spot, flourish for a moment, and then vanish only to pop up at the next venue to repeat their act. A Markovian process was pictured by Jumars and Gallagher (1982) in which environmental change at the seabed is progressive in between disruptions (perhaps a pulse of phytodetritus from the euphotic zone), and taxa replace one another as their fitness allows them to exploit the conditions of the moment in their local setting. The authors imagined a stochastic succession (deterministic only if allowed to run to termination), perhaps with smaller organisms at the beginning and larger ones towards the end. We have some hint of this from Gooday's records of taxa which respond quickly to phytodetritus falls (early stage opportunists in the succession series), and in the evidence for a rapid physiological response of deep-sea Foraminifera to newly available organic matter (Linke et al., 1995). Mostly, however, we have no idea what exactly the different benthic foraminiferal taxa do for a living on and in the seafloor. We do not know what microenvironments they most exploit, and we are ignorant of what stages they occupy in the succession series that develop within their deep-sea environments.

11.5 CONCLUSIONS AND QUESTIONS

The mechanisms that control the benthic foraminiferal response to organic flux are not well understood, and the roles of the Foraminifera in the benthic community have not been clearly determined. While attention to a few large agglutinated foraminiferal taxa under special circumstances has shown their importance to the benthos (e.g. Bathysiphon, Gooday et al., 1992b), little is known about the community position of the many small calcareous Foraminifera that make up the bulk of the geologic record of the benthos in deep-sea sediments. It has been claimed that benthic Foraminifera can be a

It is worth noting here that these series will no doubt vary, depending on both the average quantity and the variability (seasonality) of the flux of labile organic matter from the sea surface. Thus, environmental heterogeneity and disruption in the eastern equatorial Pacific, for instance, will be different from those observed in the highly seasonal northwestern Indian Ocean.

As for food acquisition, it is apparent that benthic metazoa are size selective in the material they ingest and that they have strategies for concentrating organic matter (density sorting). Additionally, they have search strategies to maximize their chances of finding new material. Finally, it also appears that larger benthic organisms can enhance local bacterial production for their own benefit. The resources the different foraminiferal taxa use, however, are presently unknown.

As noted by Carney (1989), there are fundamental ecologic differences among organisms that use freshly arrived detritus, those that feed on the bacteria and other small organisms that rapidly colonize the detritus, and those that feed on bacteria which slowly and steadily degrade the more refractory organic matter within the sediment-mixed zone. These organisms range from those that must use an often highly intermittent food supply as quickly as possible, to those that use a much less productive food source which is nevertheless fairly homogenous and continuously available. In between would be those taxa that take advantage of enhanced bacterial production, perhaps within a burrow structure or lining. The question is, what do the various taxa of the benthic Foraminifera do? There is evidence that living individuals of *Uvigerina peregrina* are unevenly distributed in the sediments and associated with the structures of other benthic organisms (Loubere *et al.*, 1995). For *Cibicides wuellerstorfi*, there is evidence for raised habitat selection (Lutze and Thiel, 1987) and attachment to larger metazoa (Linke and Lutze, 1993), which might be an adaptation for feeding strategy (suspension feeding) or for location in the environment created by the larger host. For most benthic foraminiferal taxa, however, we have no information about living distribution in relation to other benthos or food resources. These resources also include oxidizing agents (e.g. oxygen) in settings where the anoxic boundary occurs within the habitation zone of the sediments. For example, Corliss (1985) and Corliss and Emerson (1990) show that *Globobulimina affinis* lives along the anoxic boundary within the sediments, indicating survival in low oxygen conditions other taxa may not tolerate. However Loubere *et al.* (1995) present evidence that *U. peregrina*, while living within the sediments, may select burrows as a habitat, perhaps because these are better ventilated.

This review shows that a number of broad trends have been described, relating benthic foraminiferal assemblages to surface-ocean biological productivity and the flux of organic carbon to the seafloor. Taxon abundances within benthic foraminiferal assemblages change in predictable ways with shifting organic carbon flux. Benthic foraminiferal accumulation rates too may change predictably. Patterns of taxon abundance can also be associated with seasonality and variability in the organic carbon flux. The assemblage response to increasing surface-ocean biological productivity and organic carbon flux includes the appearance in the deep sea of taxa normally limited to middle and upper portions of the continental margin. The habitation zone of Foraminifera within the sediments thickens as organic carbon flux increases (within the limits normally observed in the deeper ocean). Some taxa have shown selection for depth related microhabitats under higher organic carbon flux conditions. Finally, some taxa appear to be rapid-response opportunists in colonizing newly arrived phytodetritus at the seafloor.

The conclusion of this review must therefore be that we have now reached a stage in our understanding in which we have identified patterns in benthic foraminiferal data that can be consistently linked with organic carbon flux to the seabed. The link has been quantified statistically so that reconstruction of past surface-ocean biological productivity using fossil benthic foraminiferal data is possible. However, our ability to explain benthic foraminiferal taxon occurrence, production, or pattern needs improvement. Confident assessments of paleoproductivity will require a better understanding of which portion of the organic carbon signal different benthic foraminiferal taxa respond to.

11.6 ACKNOWLEDGMENTS

We are grateful to Drs. Andrew Gooday, Frans Jorissen, and Robert Douglas for their reviews of the manuscript. Omissions and errors remain our own. Thanks, finally, to Figen Mekik for help with the S.E.M.

12
Foraminifera of oxygen-depleted environments

Joan M. Bernhard and Barun K. Sen Gupta

12.1 INTRODUCTION

The study of foraminiferal tests from oxygen-depleted environments is of interest in a variety of disciplines, most notably economic geology, environmental geology, ecology, and cell biology. Fossilized Foraminifera from ancient oxygen-poor environments may help identify petroleum source rocks. From an ecological and environmental-impact perspective, foraminiferal tests can be used to deduce historical, baseline conditions prior to environmental changes, including eutrophication connected to anthropogenic activities. Lastly, the physiology of Foraminifera capable of surviving anoxia is of interest to cell biologists because these protists are traditionally considered to be obligate aerobes.

Before discussing aspects of foraminiferal distribution and adaptation in oxygen-depleted environments, it is necessary to define the various terms used to describe oxygen depletion (Table 12.1). The majority of these terms originated from the seemingly disparate disciplines of geology and physiology. In general, the adjectives 'anoxic' and 'anaerobic' both indicate an absence of oxygen. Whereas either term can be used to describe an environment, an organism, or a chemical reaction, 'anoxic' is typically used for environmental descriptions while 'anaerobic' is generally used as a biological descriptor. In some instances, the use of either term is somewhat problematic because analytical detection limits prohibit confident measurement of trace concentrations of oxygen. Some authors have used the term 'anoxic' to refer to conditions where $O_2 = 0-0.1$ ml/l, but associating a term that means 'no oxygen' with values above zero, however small, is confusing. Thus, we use 'microxic' for environments in which oxygen is measurable but less than 0.1 ml O_2/l,

Table 12.1. *Oxygen range limits for some environmental terms used in this chapter.*

Term	O_2 range limits (ml/l)	Comments
oxic	>1.0	
dysoxic	0.1–1.0	
microxic	present to 0.1	with or without reducing conditions
anoxic	0	with or without reducing conditions
postoxic	0	subclass of anoxic, without reducing conditions

Foraminifera of oxygen-depleted environments

and restrict 'anoxic' to environments without detectable O_2. The term is a variant of 'microoxic,' coined by Jørgensen and Revsbech (1983), for 'environments of very low oxygen concentrations.' We employ 'postoxic' (Berner, 1981) as a subclass of 'anoxic' for situations where there is a lack of both oxygen and reducing conditions ('suboxic' of Fenchel and Finlay, 1995, but not of Tyson and Pearson, 1991). For environments with 0.1–1.0 ml O_2/l (~5–45 μM), we employ 'dysoxic,' which is equivalent to the 'dysaerobic' regime of Rhoads and Morse (1971). This definition of dysoxic (Fenchel and Finlay, 1995; Bernhard, 1996) does not agree with that of Tyson and Pearson (1991), who use the 0.2–2.0 ml O_2/l range. Environments with more than 1 ml O_2/l are placed under the single term 'oxic.' Generally, 'hypoxic' is used as a physiological term that refers to any depletion in oxygen that inhibits the normal respiration rate of a particular organism. The term 'microaerophile' is used for an aerobe that requires very little oxygen, but is adversely affected by higher oxygen concentration ($[O_2]$). Oxygen-depleted environments are extensive in the marine realm. Over 1% of the water samples from the world ocean recorded in the U.S. National Oceanographic Data Center database (for the 1905–1982 period) were severely dysoxic or microxic (i.e. <0.2 ml/l; Fig. 12.1; see also Kamykowski and Zentara, 1990). Because oxygen concentrations in sediments are generally lower than $[O_2]$ of the overlying seawater, we expect oxygen depletion in most of the benthic environments corresponding to the shaded regions of Fig. 12.1.

The most widespread dysoxic and microxic marine environment is the subsurface sediment. Since most aerobic, benthic organisms live near the sediment-water interface, oxygen consumption is high in this habitat. At a particular sedimentary depth, depending primarily on respiration rates and abundances of organisms, oxygen demand will exceed supply and sediments will become anoxic. The top of the anoxic zone is typically within the top few decimeters of sediment, even where overlying waters are well-aerated.

The second most laterally extensive oxygen-depleted marine environment is termed the Oxygen Minimum Zone (OMZ). The formation

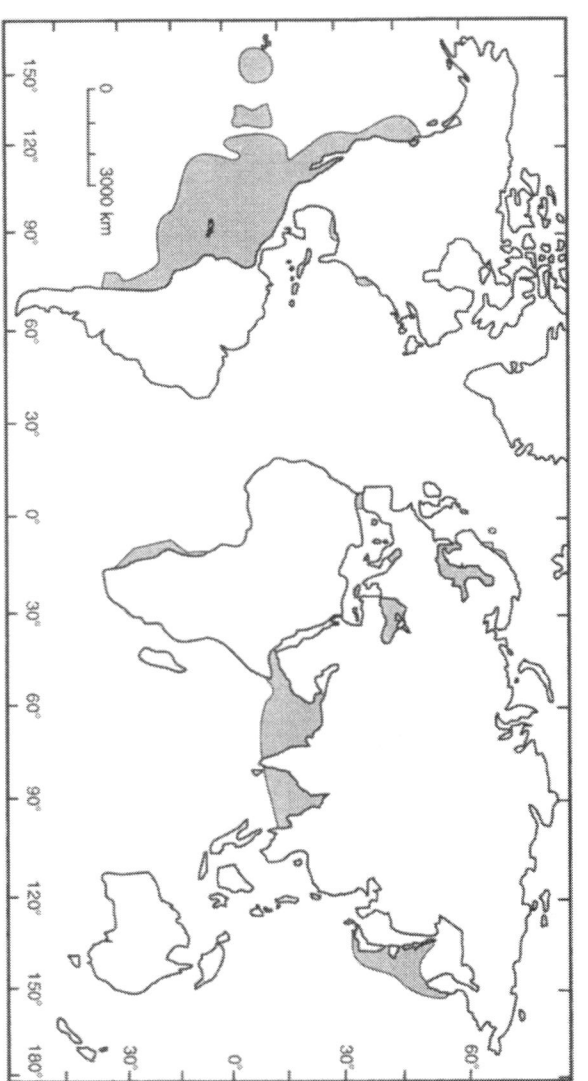

Figure 12.1 Global map (excluding high latitudes) showing areas of water with <0.2 ml O_2/l (redrawn from Kamykowski and Zentara, 1990); data from U.S. National Oceanographic Data Center.

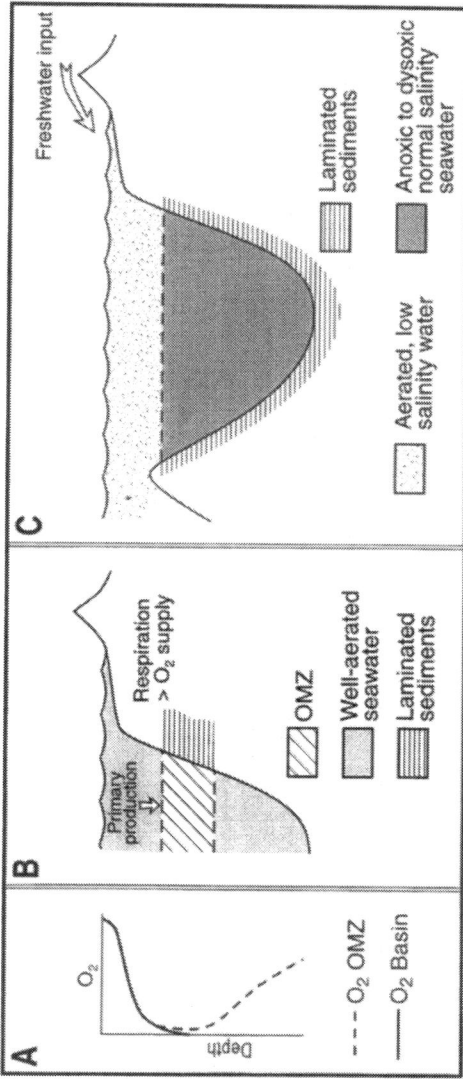

Figure 12.2 Schematic profile of dissolved oxygen (A) in two types of oxygen-depleted water column: Oxygen Minimum Zone (B) and silled basin or fjord (C). See text for explanations (see also Demaison and Moore, 1980, for more detailed descriptions).

of an OMZ depends mainly upon large-scale oceanic circulation, geography, and primary productivity (Figs. 12.2A, B). The intermediate-depth water masses of eastern oceanic margins typically consist of 'aged' water that has not been recently aerated at the sea surface. Thus, the $[O_2]$ in these water masses is depressed compared to surface concentrations. The intermediate-water $[O_2]$ will become even more depleted if the water is situated under a region of high primary productivity, due to the oxidation of the large amounts of organic debris settling through the water column. Because the water column of an OMZ is depleted in oxygen, the $[O_2]$ in surface sediments where the OMZ impinges upon the seafloor will also be depauperate in oxygen.

Some silled basins and fjords also constitute laterally extensive, dysoxic marine environments that may have anoxic surface sediments. In these types of basins, stagnation leading to oxygen depletion can be caused via two major pathways: (1) from the presence of a sill that inhibits recharge of aerated waters, and (2) from freshwater input that will produce a strong halocline, inhibit mixing, and lead to stratification in the bottom waters (Figs. 12.2A, C). If enough carbon loading occurs in either of these situations, bottom waters will become dysoxic, microxic, or anoxic.

Spatially restricted oxygen-depleted environments occur at marine hydrocarbon seeps. Such seeps have fluxes of H_2S emanating from the sediments and commonly support populations of *Beggiatoa*, a large, motile, filamentous, chemolithotrophic, sulfide-oxidizing bacterium. Growth of *Beggiatoa* requires the presence of O_2 in the overlying water and H_2S in the underlying sediment (Jørgensen, 1977; Spies and Davis, 1979; Larkin and Strohl, 1983; but see also Fossing et al., 1995; McHatton et al., 1996). Thus, an oxic-anoxic interface exists within these mats, even if they are very thin (Fig. 12.3). The longevity of *Beggiatoa* mats at hydrocarbon seeps is unknown, but they are necessarily ephemeral, 'being controlled by the shifting point sources of sea-floor hydrocarbon emission' (Sen Gupta et al., 1997). *Beggiatoa* mats are also known from many environments other than hydrocarbon seeps (e.g. silled basins, sewage outfalls).

Another example of spatially and temporally restricted marine dysoxic environments is an area of large food falls. Such areas are organically enriched due to settling of dead organisms such as whales or other vertebrates. The lateral

Diaz and Rosenberg (1995) note that 'there is no other environmental variable of such ecological importance to coastal marine ecosystems that has changed so drastically in such a short period as dissolved oxygen.' Aquaculture facilities have also produced localized anoxic areas occurring under fish cages (Schafer et al., 1995). Other areas that were previously only moderately depleted in O_2 have become severely dysoxic or anoxic (e.g. sediments in Norwegian fjords adjacent to paper mills; Nagy and Alve, 1987; Alve, 1991b).

The following narrative is based mainly on published studies regarding Foraminifera from these diverse types of dysoxic to anoxic environments.

12.2 DISTRIBUTIONAL OBSERVATIONS

In a number of studies, benthic Foraminifera recovered from oxygen-depleted sediments were treated with the 'non-vital stain' Rose Bengal (Table 12.2). The interpretations of these data varied. Reliance on the concept that Foraminifera could not be anaerobes led to the conclusion that the occurrence of stained tests in material processed from anoxic deposits simply reflected transport from a favorable into an unfavorable environment (e.g. Douglas, 1981). A contrary interpretation was that the Foraminifera found in these sediments actually inhabited such oxygen-depleted environments. However, given that Rose Bengal is known to stain dead foraminiferal cytoplasm for weeks to months (Bernhard 1988; Hannah and Rogerson, 1997) and, theoretically, for years (Corliss and Emerson, 1990), it was possible that the Rose Bengal stained Foraminifera recovered from oxygen-depleted sediments were dead specimens whose cytoplasm had not yet degraded. Therefore, in order to determine if Foraminifera actually inhabited dysoxic, microxic, and anoxic environments, a more reliable method to distinguish live from dead specimens was required in conjunction with a precise method to determine pore-water oxygen concentrations. The biochemical assay to determine the nucleotide

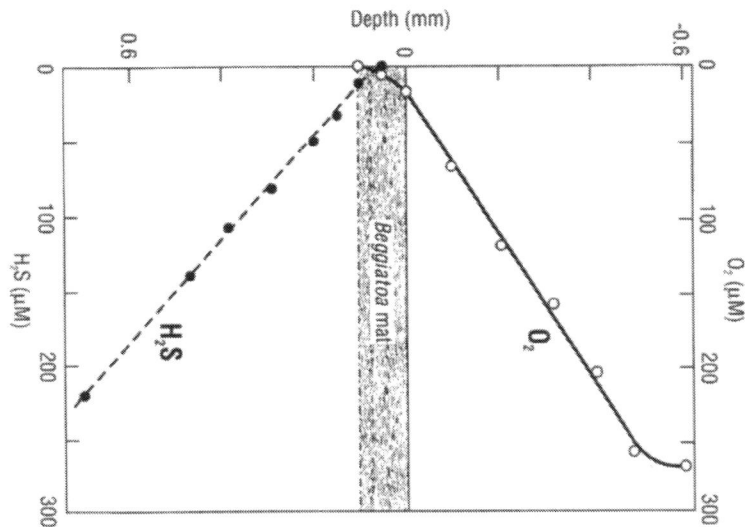

Figure 12.3 Schematic cross section through a *Beggiatoa* mat, showing oxygen (O_2) and hydrogen sulfide (H_2S) profiles which were measured with microelectrodes. Modified from Jørgensen (1982).

extent of these enriched environments obviously depends on the original size of the carcass. The temporal persistence of such patches is on the order of years to decades (Smith and Baco, 1997; Deming et al., 1997).

Seasonal or periodic anoxia, microxia, or dysoxia is also known from coastal areas, including open continental shelves. This is related to eutrophication and oxygen consumption linked with natural environmental factors (e.g. freshwater input, seasonal stratification) or to anthropogenic effects (e.g. nutrient input through fertilizers, sewage outfalls). New York Bight, Chesapeake Bay, Gulf of Mexico, Adriatic Sea, and Orinoco-Paria Shelf are examples of such areas (Boesch and Rabalais, 1991; Malone, 1991; van der Zwaan and Jorissen, 1991). Regarding the effects of anthropogenic activities,

Distributional observations

Table 12.2. Examples of foraminiferal species reported from severely oxygen-depleted samples, and recognized as living by Rose Bengal stain. The species listed were found to be relatively common in their communities. The generic designations of some species are different from those in the cited publications. Oxygen levels: A = anoxic (no detectable O_2); PA = putatively anoxic (from sedimentary or geochemical evidence, O_2 not measured); M = microxic (<0.1 ml/l O_2); D = dysoxic (0.1–1.0 ml/l O_2).

Area (and reference)	Environment	Water depth (m)	O_2 index	Dominant or characteristic species
California borderland, outer basins (Santa Cruz, Santa Catalina, San Nicolas, and Tanner Basins; Douglas and Heitman, 1979)	OMZ, basin floor	1200–1900	D	*Fursenkoina apertura, F. cornuta, Loxostomum pseudobeyrichi, Buliminella tenuata, Chilostomella ovoidea, Bolivina pacifica*
California borderland, inner basins (San Diego Trough, San Pedro and Santa Monica Basins; Douglas and Heitman, 1979)	OMZ, lower slope	400–550	D	*Bolivina argentea, B. spissa, Loxostomum pseudobeyrichi, Epistominella smithi, Uvigerina curticosta*
	OMZ, basin floor	550–950	M/D	*Fursenkoina apertura, F. bramlettei, F. seminuda, F. cornuta, Spiroplectammina earlandi, Buliminella tenuata*
Santa Monica Basin, California (Mackensen and Douglas, 1989)	OMZ, basin floor	529	D	*Cancris inaequalis, Globobulimina pacifica, Rosalina columbiensis, Planulina ariminensis, Trochammina globigeriniformis, T. pacifica*
Santa Catalina Basin, California (Mackensen and Douglas, 1989)	OMZ, basin	893–897	D	*Bolivina spissa, Globobulimina pacifica*
Santa Catalina Basin, California (Kaminski et al., 1995)	OMZ, basin floor	1202, 1309	D	*Saccorhiza sp., Verneuilinulla sp., Reophax dentaliniformis, R. excentricus, Rhizammina irregularis, Bathysiphon filiformis*
San Pedro Basin, California (Kaminski et al., 1995)	OMZ, basin floor	672–874	D	*Textularia sp., Rhizammina irregularis, Trochammina sp., Cribrostomoides wiesneri, Reophax bilocularis*
Santa Barbara Basin, California (Phleger and Soutar, 1973)	OMZ	575–590	D	*Globobulimina hoeglundi, Suggrunda eckisi, Bolivina seminuda, Nonionella stella*
Santa Barbara Basin, California (Bernhard et al., 1997)	OMZ, lower slope	339, 431	D	*Suggrunda eckisi, Uvigerina juncea, Bolivina argentea, B. seminuda* (Each > 10% of assemblage)
	OMZ, basin floor	522–591	M/PA	*Nonionella stella* (> 30%), *Bolivina seminuda, Chilostomella ovoidea, Buliminella tenuata, Spiroplectammina earlandi* (Last 4 species, each 5–10% of assemblage)
Gulf of California (Streeter, 1972; Phleger, 1964b)	OMZ	440–980	D	*Bolivina subadvena, B.* spp.
Baja California (Phleger and Soutar, 1973)	Upwelling	75–100	D	*Bolivina* spp., *Uvigerina* spp., *Bulimina* spp.
Baja California (Phleger and Soutar, 1973)	OMZ	530	D	*Bolivina seminuda, Reophax gracilis*

Foraminifera of oxygen-depleted environments

Table 12.2. (Continued.)

Area (and reference)	Environment	Water depth (m)	O_2 index	Dominant or characteristic species
El Salvador (Smith, 1964)	OMZ	435–900	D	*Reophax dentaliniformis*, *Saccammina* sp. cf. *S. comprima*, *Globobulimina pacifica*, *Uvigerina peregrina*, *Buliminella tenuata*
Peru-Chile Trench (Ingle et al., 1980)	OMZ	135	D	*Bolivina rankini*, *B. interjuncta*, *Bulimina elongata*, *Epistominella exigua*
Sagami Bay, Japan (Ohga and Kitazato, 1997)	OMZ	1450	D	*Textularia kattegatensis*, *Bolivina pacifica*, *B. spissa*, *Bulimina aculeata*, *Fursenkoina* sp., *Chilostomella ovoidea*, *Globobulimina* spp., *Uvigerina peregrina*, *Uvigerina akitaensis*
Northern Arabian Sea (Jannink et al., 1998)	OMZ	495–1000	D	*Bolivina dilatata*, *B. seminuda*, *Bulimina exilis*, *Cassidulina laevigata*, *Ammonia* sp., *Globobulimina affinis*, *Osangularia culter*, *Uvigerina peregrina*, *Recurvoides* sp., *Eggerella* sp.
Green Canyon, Gulf of Mexico (Sen Gupta et al., 1997)	Hydrocarbon seeps, under bacterial mats	543–583	PA	*Bolivina albatrossi*, *B. ordinaria*, *Cassidulina neocarinata*, *Osangularia rugosa*, *Trifarina bradyi*, *Gavelinopsis translucens*
Green Canyon, Gulf of Mexico (Sen Gupta and Aharon, 1994)	Hydrocarbon seep bacterial mats	216	M/D	*Bolivina subaenariensis*, *B. ordinaria*, *Cassidulina neocarinata*, *Uvigerina laevis*
Drammensfjord, Norway (Alve, 1990, 1995b)	Silled basin with high anthropogenic organic load	40–60	PA/D	*Stainforthia fusiformis*, *Bulimina marginata*, *Spiroplectammina biformis*, *Ammodiscus? gullmarensis*
Drammensfjord, Norway (Bernhard and Alve, 1996)	Silled basin with high anthropogenic organic load	45	D	*Stainforthia fusiformis*, *Bulimina marginata*, *Adercotryma glomerata*, *Psammosphaera bowmanni*
Northern Adriatic Sea continental shelf (Jorissen et al., 1992)	Seasonal eutrophication and stratification	36	D	*Hopkinsina pacifica*, *Nonionella turgida*, *Epistominella vitrea*, *Stainforthia fusiformis*, *Bolivina spathulata*, *B. dilatata*
Louisiana continental shelf (Sen Gupta et al., 1996)	Seasonal dysoxia	9–21	M	*Buliminella morgani*, *Ammonia parkinsoniana*
Explorers Cove, McMurdo Sound, Antarctica (Bernhard, 1987)	Seasonal dysoxia in small basins	18	PA	*Tolypammina vagans*, *Polymorphina* sp.
Winter Quarter's Bay, McMurdo Sound, Antarctica (Bernhard, 1989)	Subsurface pore water (1–2 cm below surface)	12	A	*Cassidulinoides porrectus*, *Globocassidulina* sp. cf. *G. biora*, *Cribrostomoides jeffreysii*, *Paratrochammina antarctica*, *Psammosphaera parva*
Frierfjord, Norway (Alve, 1994)	Subsurface pore water (1–5 cm below surface)	90	PA	*Stainforthia fusiformis*
	OMZ, sediment surface	786, 998	D	*Eggerella* cf. *E. scabra*, *Brizalina* sp., *Technitella* sp.
California continental slope (Bernhard, 1992)	Subsurface (2–4 cm below dysoxic surface)	786, 998	A	*Globobulimina pacifica*, *Chilostomella oolina*, *Uvigerina peregrina*, *Bolivina* sp.

Table 12.2. (Continued.)

Area (and reference)	Environment	Water depth (m)	O_2 index	Dominant or characteristic species
South China Sea (Rathburn et al., 1996)	Subsurface (below detected anoxic/oxic interface)	1095, 2150	A	*Astrononion* sp., *Chilostomella oolina*, *Bolivinopsis cubensis*
	Subsurface (below detected anoxic/oxic interface)	4515	A	
Sulu Sea (Rathburn et al., 1996)				*Valvulineria mexicana*, *Globobulimina* sp.
Nova Scotia continental margin (Corliss and Emerson, 1990)	Subsurface pore water (7 cm below surface)	1575	PA	*Globobulimina affinis*, *Nonion grateloupi*, *Elphidium excavatum*

adenosine triphosphate (ATP) concentration developed by DeLaca (1986b) was judged as one such method (Bernhard, 1989, 1992). In these studies, polarographic microelectrodes originally developed by Revsbech et al. (1980) were employed to determine dissolved-oxygen profiles in sediment pore waters from which the Foraminifera were recovered. The caveat in these studies was that the live Foraminifera could have been inhabiting oxygenated microhabitats around such biogenic structures as macrofaunal burrows and tubes, as suggested by Langer et al. (1989) for infaunal tide-flat foraminiferal assemblages and by Moodley (1990) for deep-infaunal Foraminifera from the North Sea.

The core-embedding method of Frankel (1970) and Watling (1988; see also Grimm, 1992; Pike and Kemp, 1996) was recently refined to preserve Foraminifera in their life position within sediments (Bernhard and Bowser, 1996). This technique approaches the issue of foraminiferal associations with aerated microhabitats by preserving foraminiferal life position in sediments where burrowing and tubicolous fauna are absent. The method combines epifluorescence microscopy and enzymatic activity to distinguish hydrolytically active (i.e. live) Foraminifera with epoxy-resin embedded coring to preserve sedimentary and organism *in situ* positions. The use of this technique shows that Foraminifera inhabit the microxic and anoxic sediments of the silled Santa Barbara Basin (Fig. 12.4; Bernhard, 1996; Bernhard et al., 1997). These sediments are sulfidic, as evidenced by abundant sulfide-oxidizing bacteria *Beggiatoa*. However, even though such distributional data strongly suggest that Foraminifera can inhabit anoxic environments, only experimental data can provide compelling evidence for this conclusion.

12.3 EXPERIMENTAL OBSERVATIONS

12.3.1 Foraminiferal responses to oxygen depletion

Some experimental studies have been conducted to assess the response of Foraminifera to anoxia. It is important to reiterate here that when working with such low $[O_2]$, it is difficult to ascertain if a supposedly anoxic system is devoid of even trace amounts of oxygen. Furthermore, it is also important to remember that all species of Foraminifera cannot be expected to respond similarly to oxygen depletion; some species may have different physiological abilities than others.

In a behavioral response experiment, infaunal Foraminifera from a periodically dysoxic fjord started migrating upward in the sediment when oxygen in bottom waters decreased below 2 ml O_2/l (Alve and Bernhard, 1995); however, the timing of species responses varied. For example, *Bulimina marginata* migrated toward aerated habitats more quickly than *Stainforthia fusi-*

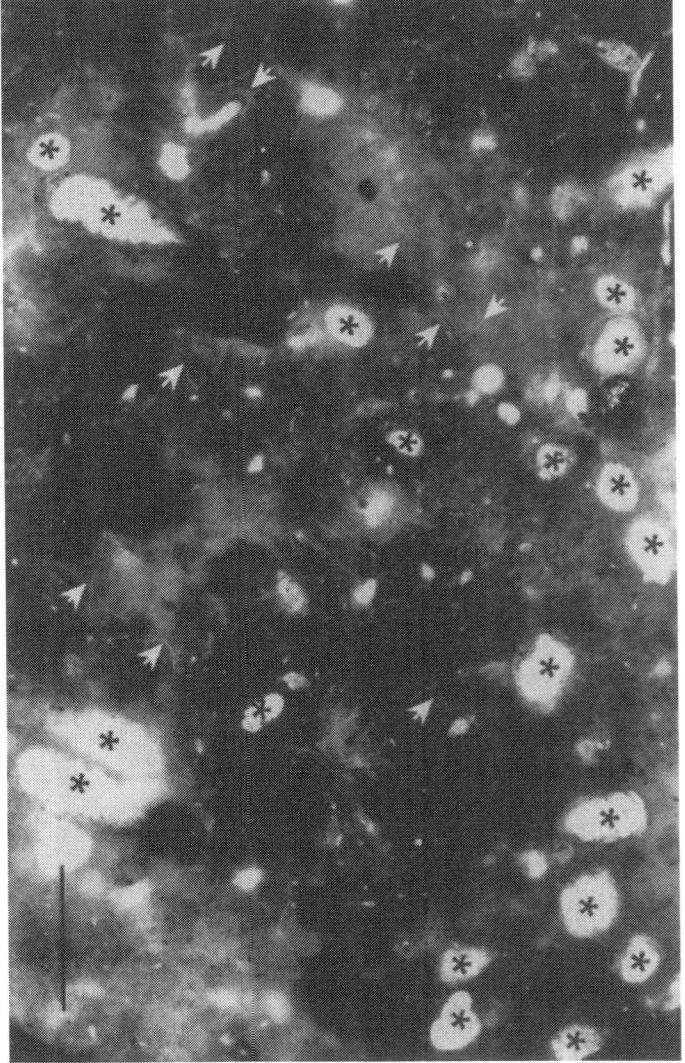

Figure 12.4 Photomicrograph of section through a fluorescently-labeled, embedded core. The light-colored objects are Foraminifera (*) and *Beggiatoa* filaments (white arrows) in their life positions. Light-colored objects without designation are indeterminate organisms such as ciliates, flagellates, or juvenile Foraminifera. Dark objects are sediments (e.g. fecal pellets, clastics). The sample was prepared using the technique of Bernhard and Bowser (1996). Scale bar = 0.5 mm.

formis. Also, *B. marginata* reproduced during the most oxygen-depleted conditions. When bottom waters were re-aerated, some species (e.g. *S. fusiformis*) migrated back into the sediments, presumably tracking a particular geochemical horizon.

Responses of some other species to oxygen depletion have been studied on shorter time scales. In a 7-day experiment, Moodley et al. (1998b) observed that while some buried individuals of *Quinqueloculina seminulum* migrated toward aerated sediments, 40–50% remained in presumably anoxic sediments. In the same study, but after a 56-day experiment, the majority (57%) of *Nonionella turgida* remained in sediments that had undetectable O$_2$, yet the majority of 'soft-shelled' Foraminifera (i.e. allogromiids and saccamminids) migrated into aerated sediments. Considerable numbers (17%) of the soft-shelled Foraminifera,

however, remained in sediments that had undetectable O$_2$.

12.3.2 Survival of Foraminifera exposed to oxygen depletion

The survival of Foraminifera exposed to anoxia has also been studied. Using the concentration of sedimentary particles (food source) around the apertural region as indication of activity, Moodley and Hess (1992) determined that individuals of three infaunal species (*Ammonia beccarii*, *Elphidium excavatum*, *Quinqueloculina seminulum*) survived anoxic incubation for at least one day. In the same study, *E. excavatum*, *Eggerella scabra*, and *Q. seminulum* survived a six-day incubation in dysoxic chambers during a six-day incubation in dysoxic or microxic seawater (i.e. <12.5 μM O$_2$). Two larger agglutinated Foraminifera, *Pelosina arborescens* and *Astrorhiza limicola*, are known to survive putative anoxia for ten days (Cedhagen, 1993). The survival period of *Ammonia beccarii* in such an environment may be as long as 1–2 months (Koshio, 1992, in Kitazato, 1994). Incubations in nitrogen-purged seawater for 30 days showed that some Antarctic Foraminifera (e.g. *Cassidulinoides porrectus*, *Globocassidulina* sp. cf. *G. biora*, *Reophax subdentaliniformis*, *Uvigerina bassensis*) are able to survive microxia and possibly anoxia for considerable periods of time (Bernhard, 1993). The results of that study include the observation that ATP concentrations in specimens recovered after an extended exposure to dysoxia were statistically indistinguishable from those of control specimens incubated in aerated seawater.

Since it is possible that Foraminifera become dormant during exposure to adverse conditions such as oxygen depletion, it is of interest to determine ATP concentration ([ATP]) in specimens during their exposure to microxia or anoxia. Bernhard and Alve (1996) incubated Foraminifera for 24 days in a nitrogen-flushed experimental chamber and then extracted their ATP without aeration. Results showed that the [ATP] for specimens of *Psammosphaera bowmanni* were statistically similar between controls (i.e. aeration) and treatments (i.e. microxia). However, the [ATP] of nitrogen-flushed specimens of other species (*i.e.*, *Bulimina marginata*, *Stainforthia fusiformis*, *Adercotryma glomerata*) were significantly lower than those of specimens extracted under aerated conditions. Considering all available data from this experiment (i.e. survival rates, [ATP] and ultrastructural observations), Bernhard and Alve (1996) concluded that foraminiferal species respond differently to oxygen depletion. Some species are apparently unaffected, while others may become dormant. If encystment is considered to be a type of dormancy, then independent evidence for such dormancy has been provided by Linke and Lutze (1993), who reported cysts of *Elphidium incertum* from an environment of putative anoxia. Also, Hannah and Rogerson (1997) concluded that Foraminifera buried in an anoxic layer become dormant and would require transport via bioturbation for their return to aerated conditions. In yet another long-term anoxic-incubation experiment, certain foraminiferal species survived putative anoxia for 78 days (Moodley et al., 1997). It should be noted that at some time between 33 and 53 days, the experimental incubations became sulfidic. Thus, the observations concerning survival response to anoxia are somewhat compounded by this change in redox chemistry for approximately the last half to two-thirds of the experiment.

Sulfidic conditions commonly co-occur with anoxia. As noted in the introduction, the term 'postoxic' in this chapter implies anoxia without reducing conditions. The experiments described above addressed postoxic conditions. The few experiments that have been conducted to assess the survival of Foraminifera in anoxic, sulfidic conditions (Bernhard, 1993; Moodley et al., 1998a) show that some Foraminifera tolerate such environments. After 30 days, ATP concentrations in specimens from 500 nM H_2S/anoxic treatments did not differ significantly from those of aerated controls (Bernhard, 1993). Under higher concentrations (5 μM H_2S), cytoplasmic movement was observed in Foraminifera after an incubation period of 21 days, but all specimens were dead by the next time point (42 days; Moodley et al., 1998a).

Although experimental results indicate that Foraminifera survive anoxia with or without sulfidic conditions for considerable periods of time, no physiological mechanism responsible for such survival is presently known. It is established, however, that two allogromiid species have an alternative oxidative pathway that may be responsible for their survival in anoxia. Travis and Bowser (1986b) found that the electron-transport inhibitor cyanide did not halt intracellular motility, suggesting that at least some Foraminifera can survive without oxidative phosphorylation. Ultrastructural studies suggest additional possible adaptations and mechanisms to allow foraminiferal survival of anoxia.

12.4 ULTRASTRUCTURAL OBSERVATIONS

A variety of unusual ultrastructural characteristics has been observed in foraminiferal species that are dominant in oxygen-depleted environments. It is possible that these characteristics reflect adaptations to extreme oxygen depletion, and possibly to sulfidic habitats, but no consistent ultrastructural modification has been observed in species from such environments. Furthermore, the published literature does not include quantitative, comparative studies on the ultrastructure of individuals from anoxic sediments and conspecific individuals from aerated sediments. Such comparisons in the future may elucidate the importance of the various ultrastructural modifications.

Three cases of possible bacterial symbioses have been observed in Foraminifera from oxygen-depleted sediments. Two species from the Santa Barbara Basin have putative endosymbionts. *Buliminella tenuata* has numerous rod-shaped bacteria within its cytoplasm (Fig. 12.5A; Bernhard, 1996). These bacteria do not appear to be a food source, since they are intact in all chambers of this multilocular foraminifer. *Nonionella stella* has bacteria within its test, but these prokaryotes are not intracellular (Bernhard and Reimers, 1991). Lastly, infaunal *Globocassidulina* cf. *G. biora* from shallow Antarctic waters is known to have intracellular rod-shaped bacteria that appear to be associated with pore plugs (Bernhard, 1993). One possible role of these putative symbionts is to oxidize H_2S, thereby detoxifying this pore-water constituent. Given the variance in the morphologic attributes of these three types of bacteria, however, it is likely that they have different metabolic capabilities.

Another ultrastructural feature of some Foraminifera from oxygen-depleted environments (*Stainforthia fusiformis*, *Nonionella stella*, *Nonionellina labradorica*) is that they sequester chloro-

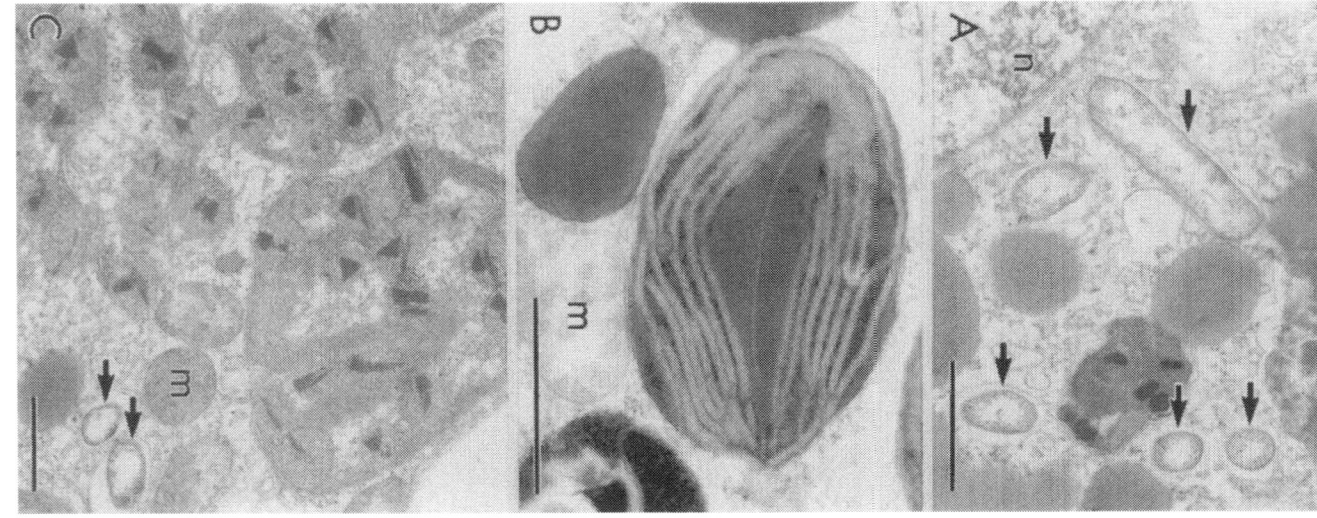

Figure 12.5 Transmission electron micrographs. A. Putative endosymbiotic, rod-shaped bacteria (arrows) in cytoplasm of *Buliminella tenuata*; n = nucleus. B. Sequestered chloroplast in cytoplasm of *Nonionella stella*; m = mitochondria. C. Complex of peroxisome-endoplasmic reticulum in *B. tenuata*; dark polygonal structures are catalase crystals in the core of the membrane bound peroxisomes; stacked membranes linking peroxisomes are the endoplasmic reticulum; m = mitochondria, arrows = putative bacterial symbionts. Scale bars = 1 µm.

plasts (Fig. 12.5B; Leutenegger, 1984; Cedhagen, 1991; Bernhard and Alve, 1996). Such chloroplast husbandry is thought to benefit other protists inhabiting anoxic environments, possibly by providing oxygen to the host (Johnson et al., 1995). A particular complication in interpreting the role of chloroplasts in the cases listed above is that the oxygen-depleted habitats are not in the euphotic zone.

A third ultrastructural feature common to many species from oxygen-depleted environments involves proliferation and aggregation of two typical cellular organelles: endoplasmic reticulum and peroxisomes (P-ER; Fig. 12.5C). Such P-ER complexes have been observed in *Nemogullmia longevariabilis, Gloiogullmia eurystoma, Nonionella stella, Stainforthia fusiformis, Buliminella tenuata,* and *Fursenkoina cornuta* (Nyholm and Nyholm, 1975; Bernhard and Alve, 1996; Bernhard, 1996). The role of these complexes may merely be to break down hydrogen peroxide, which is a byproduct in the anaerobic metabolic pathway of glycolysis. This biochemical avenue has been proposed by Nyholm and Nyholm (1975), although it is not established that Foraminifera rely heavily on glycolysis.

Ultrastructural investigations indicate that organelles which appear to be mitochondria are present in all Foraminifera observed to date, strongly suggesting that these species are aerobes or microaerophiles. In addition, it has been reported that mitochondria of Foraminifera from oxygen-depleted environments are concentrated beneath test pore plugs (Leutenegger and Hansen, 1979). High concentrations of mitochondria, however, have also been observed in apertural cytoplasm (Bernhard and Alve, 1996), which is assumed to form the pseudopodia during network deployment. Optical microscopic examinations (Doyle, 1935; J.M. Bernhard and S.S. Bowser, unpublished data) have shown mitochondrial movements within pseudopods, which can extend to at least ten times the test diameter of a foraminifer (Travis and Bowser, 1991). Thus, it is possible that Foraminifera inhabiting an environment with a steep redox gradient use mitochondrial activity in extended pseudopods to maintain oxidative phosphorylation, even though their tests and cell bodies are located in anoxic sediments.

It is likely that benthic Foraminifera inhabiting anoxic, sulfidic environments use many adaptations in concert to allow survival in such seemingly hostile conditions. The two major chemical barriers are detoxifying H_2S and surviving without or with very little oxygen. As stated earlier, because all Foraminifera examined to date possess organelles that appear to be mitochondria, apparently they are aerobes. We must note, however, that organelles resembling mitochondria in some anaerobic protists are in fact hydrogenosomes (Finlay and Fenchel, 1989). Hydrogenosomes are organelles that perform a variety of functions, most notably (in the context of this chapter) to ferment pyruvate, which is a byproduct of the anaerobic pathway glycolysis. Further enzymatic studies of foraminiferal 'mitochondria' will establish their true identity and functions. Furthermore, it has been shown that mitochondria of certain microaerophilic protists grown under anoxia increase in volume and number, suggesting that these organelles play a role in anaerobic energy metabolism (Bernhard and Fenchel, 1996). Additional biochemical studies are required before we can gain a full understanding of foraminiferal physiology during exposure to microxia or anoxia. For further discussion on possible physiological adaptations used by Foraminifera inhabiting oxygen-depleted environments, see Bernhard (1996).

12.5 GENERALIZATIONS ON LOW-OXYGEN FORAMINIFERAL ASSEMBLAGES (LOFAS)

12.5.1 Systematic trends

While the Foraminifera of a number of oxygen-poor environments remain to be investigated, it is useful to make some generalizations about 'typical' assemblages of such habitats. In general, calcareous perforate species dominate LOFAs, but agglutinated species can also occur in considerable abundance. Very few miliolaceans have been found in natural dysoxic, microxic, or anoxic samples. A species of *Pseudotriloculina* was observed in samples from Jellyfish Lake, Palau, where conditions were mildly dysoxic (i.e. O$_2$ = 35–40 μM; M. Langer and J.H. Lipps, unpublished data). *Spiroloculina attenuata* and *Edentostomata cultrata* were observed in considerable numbers in black, and therefore presumably microxic or anoxic, sediments of harbor inlets of the Madang Lagoon, Papua New Guinea (M. Langer and J.H. Lipps, unpublished data). Also, a variety of small miliolaceans were common in black sediment samples from mangrove sites of Moorea (M. Langer, pers. comm.). Specimens of *Quinqueloculina stalkeri*, which stained with Rose Bengal, were observed in dysoxic fjord sediments (E. Alve, unpublished data). As noted above, *Q. seminulum* can survive anoxia, but appears to prefer aerated conditions (Moodley et al., 1998). There are few documented cases of tectinous Foraminifera in oxygen-depleted sediments. Nyholm and Nyholm (1975) noted the occurrence of *Nemogullmia longevariabilis* and *Gloiogullmia eurystoma* in 'low oxygen concentrations' of the Gullmar fjord, but specific [O$_2$] were not reported. Bernhard (1996) showed an undescribed allogromiid living among *Beggiatoa* filaments (see Bernhard, 1996, Fig. 1). A new species of the closely related testate protist *Gromia* is known to be very abundant at the sediment-water interface in the Arabian Sea OMZ (A.J. Gooday, pers. comm.). Pending a dedicated study, it is highly likely that tectinous Foraminifera and gromids have been overlooked and that they occur in greater abundances in low-oxygen environments than presently thought.

A survey of genus and species distributions, using the data presented in Table 12.2, and some additional information (referenced below), indicates some common features in LOFAs. A brief summary is given here, in terms of major taxonomic groups (see chapter 2 for classification). Among the Order Rotaliida, the Nonionidae and Chilostomellidae (Figs. 12.6A, B, C) are typically common, being represented by seven species of five genera (*Nonion grateloupi*, *Nonionella stella*, *N. turgida*, *Nonionellina labradorica*, *Chilostomella ovoidea*, *C. oolina*, *Astrononion* sp.). The occurrence of *Nonionellina labradorica* in a putatively dysoxic basin was noted by Cedhagen (1991). Other genera from the Order Rotaliida are: *Gavelinopsis* (Figs. 12.6K, N), *Rosalina*, *Valvulineria*, *Epistominella*, *Osangularia*, *Polymorphina*, *Planulina*, *Ammonia*, and *Elphidium*. The last two genera are represented in dysoxic or microxic habitats by the widely distributed species *Ammonia parkinsoniana* (Figs. 12.6H, L), *A. beccarii* (Kitazato, 1994), and *Elphidium excavatum*.

Members of the Order Buliminida are also conspicuous constituents of LOFAs (Figs. 12.6D, E, F, G, J). The genera include *Bolivina*, *Fursenkoina*, *Uvigerina*, *Bulimina*, *Globobulimina*, *Buliminella*, *Cassidulina*, *Cassidulinoides*, *Globocassidulina*, *Stainforthia*, *Hopkinsina*, *Trifarina*, *Brizalina*, *Suggrunda*, and *Loxostomum*.

Uniolocular agglutinated genera known to be common in dysoxic environments include *Ammodiscus*, *Bathysiphon*, *Psammosphaera*, *Rhizammina*, *Saccammina*, *Saccorhiza*, *Technitella*, and *Tolypammina*. In addition, *Pelosina arborescens* and *Astrorhiza limicola* have been observed in putatively dysoxic environments (Cedhagen, 1993). Multilocular agglutinated genera of LOFAs include *Reophax*, *Spiroplectam-*

Figure 12.6 Scanning electron micrographs of Foraminifera common in oxygen-depleted environments. A, *Nonionellina labradorica* (Oslo Fjord, Norway); B, *Nonionella stella* (Santa Barbara Basin, U.S.A.); C, *Chilostomella ovidea* (Santa Barbara Basin, U.S.A.); D, *Buliminella tenuata* (Santa Barbara Basin, U.S.A.); E, *Bulimina marginata* (Oslo Fjord, Norway); F, *Stainforthia fusiformis* (Oslo Fjord, Norway); G, *Globobulimina pacifica* (OMZ off Pt. Sur, California, U.S.A.); H, *Ammonia parkinsoniana* (Gulf of Mexico, off Louisiana, U.S.A.), dorsal view; I, *Spiroplectammina earlandi* (Santa Barbara Basin, U.S.A.); J, *Bolivina albatrossi* (hydrocarbon seep, Gulf of Mexico, off Louisiana, U.S.A.); K, *Gavelinopsis translucens* (hydrocarbon seep, Gulf of Mexico, off Louisiana, U.S.A.), dorsal view; L, *Ammonia parkinsoniana* (Gulf of Mexico, off Louisiana, U.S.A.), ventral view; M, *Trochammina pacifica* (Santa Barbara Basin, U.S.A.); N, *Gavelinopsis translucens* (hydrocarbon seep, Gulf of Mexico, off Louisiana, U.S.A.), ventral view. [H and L from Sen Gupta et al., 1996; J, K, and N from Sen Gupta et al., 1997; M from Bernhard et al., 1997; reprinted with publishers' permission.] Scale bars = 100 μm.

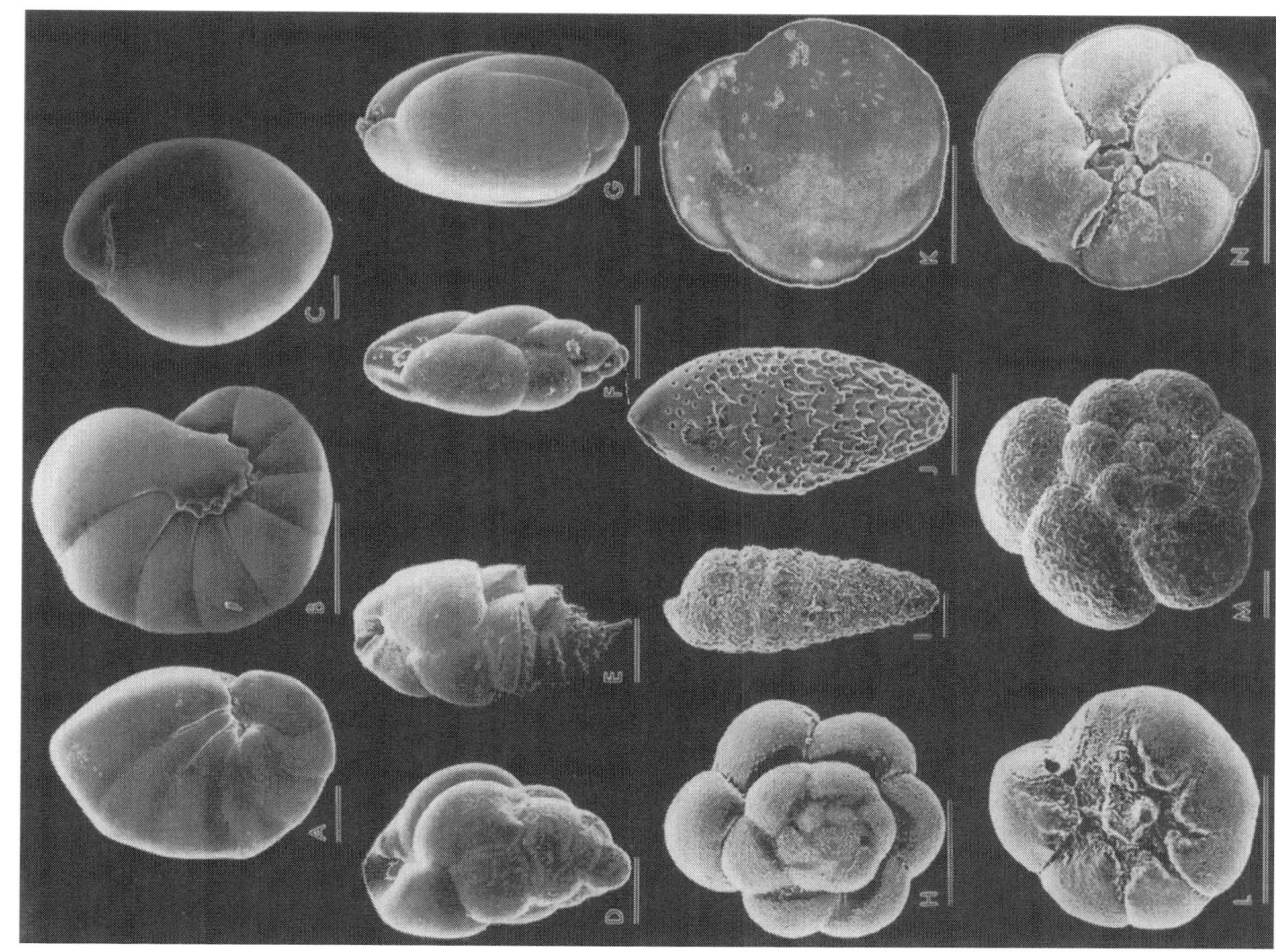

mina (Fig. 12.6I), *Trochammina* (Fig. 12.6M), *Eggerella*, *Adercotryma*, *Bolivinopsis*, *Cribrostomoides*, *Portatrochammina*, *Textularia*, *Cribrostomoides* and *Verneuilinulla*. Also, *Ammotium cassis* was observed to inhabit the redox boundary (Linke and Lutz, 1993).

It is crucial to realize that congeneric species also occur in well-aerated environments; not all species of *Bolivina*, for example, are indicative of oxygen depletion. Interestingly, none of the foraminiferal species observed to date in LOFAs is known to live exclusively in anoxic environments. It is possible that certain species are microaerophiles but fine-scale spatial distributional analyses and biochemical studies have not yet been done to confirm this possibility.

12.5.2 Test attributes

It has been suggested that small-sized Foraminifera might survive episodes of oxygen depletion better than larger species, because of less oxygen requirement (Phleger and Soutar, 1973). Indeed, a number of assemblages in microxic environments are dominated by small foraminiferal species. For example, *Nonionella stella* dominates the Santa Barbara Basin (Bernhard et al., 1997), *Stainforthia fusiformis* is common in many dysoxic areas (Alve, 1990, 1994, 1995b; Jorissen et al., 1992), *Epistominella* spp. are common constituents of LOFAs (Ingle et al., 1980; Jorissen et al., 1992) and *Ammonia parkinsoniana* dominates dysoxic inner-shelf areas of the Gulf of Mexico (Sen Gupta et al., 1996). However, a number of taxa comprising LOFAs are not particularly small (e.g. *Globobulimina*, *Chilostomella*, certain species of *Bolivina*). Because a standard-mesh screen (e.g. 63 μm) has not been used to obtain the sample residue in all studies of LOFAs, it is still uncertain if small species have a competitive advantage over larger species in oxygen-depleted settings. Relatively large-sized (>1 mm) foraminiferal species are not commonly documented from dysoxic, microxic, or anoxic environments (exceptions being *Astrorhiza limicola* and *Pelosina arborescens*; Cedhagen, 1993). In a recent study, Moodley et al. (1997) observed that conclusions regarding the survival of Foraminifera in anoxia would be significantly different if one considered the >63-μm fraction rather than the >38-μm fraction that they used. Thus, they suggest that 38–45 μm should be used as the lower size limit when assessing foraminiferal response to oxygen depletion.

A number of authors (e.g. Harman, 1964; Phleger and Soutar, 1973; Bernhard, 1986) have observed that many calcareous species of LOFAs have thin shells. Miliolaceans of oxygen-depleted environments in the Madang Lagoon also have thin shells (M. Langer and J.H. Lipps, unpublished data). As noted by Sen Gupta and Machain-Castillo (1993), however, not all species from LOFAs are thin-shelled. Given that thin-shelled Foraminifera are more likely to be destroyed during standard laboratory preparation of dry samples, it is possible that the importance of some species has been underestimated. Thus, we suggest that samples to be analyzed for LOFAs should be sieved and picked wet, without prior drying, to prevent excessive damage to thin-shelled forms.

Another trend suggested for LOFA species is that pore size and density are higher in tests from oxygen-depleted environments, compared to those from well-oxygenated environments (Perez-Cruz and Machain-Castillo, 1990; Moodley and Hess, 1992). The proposed explanation for this observation is the widely accepted idea that foraminiferal pores are conduits for oxygen supply to the intracellular milieu (e.g. Berthold, 1976b; Leutenegger and Hansen, 1979), and that larger, more numerous pores could presumably provide more oxygen. As noted above, however, mitochondrial activity in pseudopods may be more important than that associated with pore plugs. In addition, a number of LOFA species (e.g. *Chilostomella ovoidea*, *Nonionella stella*) have very small pores (J.M. Bernhard, pers. obs.), while the occasionally abundant agglutinated species lack pores altogether. Much more detailed study of pore function and pseudopodial activity in Foraminifera are needed to test the significance of pores in the context of microxia.

Lastly, it has been proposed that certain mor-

Generalizations on low-oxygen foraminiferal assemblages (LOFAs)

phologies occur more frequently in Foraminifera from oxygen-depleted environments (Bernhard, 1986), but additional observations do not confirm this trend. The planoconvex morphogroup is rare in most LOFAs observed to date, but some other shapes that were considered indicative of aerated environments are well represented in LOFAs (e.g. spherical: *Chilostomella, Globobulimina, Psammosphaera*).

12.5.3 Abundances

In a number of cases, the reported abundances of Foraminifera in oxygen-depleted sediments are high. Hundreds of stained Foraminifera per cm^3 are documented in Rose Bengal treated samples from different sites (e.g. Phleger and Soutar, 1973; Douglas and Heitman, 1979; Ohga and Kitazato, 1997; Jannink et al., 1998). Bernhard and Reimers (1991) observed up to 2,176 Rose Bengal stained Foraminifera per cm^3 in the microxic Santa Barbara Basin. One reason for such high densities in these habitats is a decrease in predation pressure, because of the severe effect of oxygen depletion on metazoans (e.g. Josefson and Widbom, 1988). There are, however, other cases where oxygen-depleted environments have extremely low foraminiferal densities. In fact, Bernhard and Reimers (1991) found only three Rose Bengal stained specimens per cm^3 during another sampling in Santa Barbara Basin only eight months after observing the extraordinarily high density mentioned above. The reason for this decimation of the assemblage was inferred to be the possible continuation of anoxia for weeks or months. Although it is likely that extended anoxia, in combination with H$_2$S, prohibits the sustenance of large foraminiferal populations, some previously reported low densities are tied to sample processing methods. We reiterate that a proper census of Foraminifera surviving under dysoxia, microxia, or anoxia has to be preceded by sample washing on appropriately fine-mesh sieves (without sample desiccation) and has to include the enumeration of allogromiids.

Taphonomic changes in foraminiferal assemblages are the focus of chapter 16, but it would be worthwhile to make some general comments here on the preservation of Foraminifera in sediments with little or no oxygen. Because calcite dissolution is negligible in some OMZ sediments (Berelson et al., 1996), the calcareous components of the fossil foraminiferal assemblages and the original living assemblages are unlikely to be significantly different in these sediments. On the other hand, calcite dissolution rates are considerable in the mildly dysoxic or oxic sedimentary environments just above and below the OMZ (Berelson et al., 1996). Seasonally dysoxic to anoxic sediments are likely to have substantial rates of calcite dissolution when re-aeration occurs (e.g. Green et al., 1993b). Thus, the calcareous component of these foraminiferal assemblages might be altered greatly from original assemblages.

12.5.4 Application to historical and paleontological records

Understanding the ecology of Foraminifera in oxygen-depleted environments allows interpretations of past environmental conditions from subsurface data. Questions regarding climate change and anthropogenic influence on the environment can be answered using such approaches. For example, using the succession of foraminiferal species observed with respect to bottom-water oxygen concentrations in the Santa Barbara Basin, subsurface data can be analyzed to infer distinctions between [O$_2$] within a range of dysoxia to microxia (Bernhard et al., 1997). Using this proxy model, data from Ocean Drilling Program station 893, which is located in the Santa Barbara Basin, can be reinterpreted, taking into account that *Nonionella stella* represents the most anoxia-tolerant species.

Analyses of foraminiferal data from subsurface samples have already led to interpretations of oxygen-related environmental changes. For example, faunal changes in a Norwegian fjord foraminiferal assemblage over the last ~1,000 years indicate pollution effects superimposed over climatic changes (Alve, 1991b). More specifically, assemblages show a marked decrease in species diversity and increase in abundance over time, with *Spiroplectammina biformis* dominating just prior to the onset of anoxia about 1970. Another study shows that the foraminiferal record of the Po Delta reflects the environmental history of that area for the last 160 years (Barmawidjaja et al., 1995). Strong eutrophication started in 1930, as indicated by the appearance of 'stress-tolerant' species (*Bolivina seminuda, Hopkinsina pacifica,* and *Quinqueloculina stalkeri*), and seasonal anoxia began in 1960, as indicated by the stratigraphic trends of the first two species.

The stratigraphic record of several inner-shelf foraminiferal species of the northwestern Gulf of Mexico demonstrates an overall increase of oxygen stress in the past 100 years. The clues include a decrease in the abundance of *Quinqueloculina* spp. (Rabalais et al., 1996), an increase of *Buliminella morgani* (Blackwelder et al., 1996), and a positive trend in the relative dominance of the more tolerant *Ammonia parkinsoniana* over the less tolerant *Elphidium excavatum* (Sen Gupta et al., 1996). In this area of strong seasonal oxygen depletion at present, the foraminiferal trends match the overall increasing trend of fertilizer use in the United States in the 20th century, and the consequent higher nutrient input into the Gulf of Mexico by rivers, especially the Mississippi.

even anoxic environments. It is established that at least some foraminiferal species survive anoxia and even sulfidic conditions for periods up to a few weeks, but the tolerance of most species to oxygen depletion is unknown. Furthermore, the physiological mechanisms enabling foraminiferal species to survive exposure to anoxia and/or sulfidic conditions are not yet identified. The available data suggest, however, that all Foraminifera are aerobic for at least part of their life, and, in all likelihood, some species are facultative anaerobes. Obligate anaerobes have not been identified among foraminiferal species. The information necessary to understand the diverse aspects of foraminiferal adaptation to oxygen-depleted environments must come from experimental studies. Only with such biological information, it will be possible to construct more accurate databases for use in other disciplines such as paleoecology and paleoceanography.

12.6 CONCLUSIONS

In summary, certain benthic Foraminifera from various water depths inhabit oxygen-poor and

12.7 ACKNOWLEDGMENTS

We thank Elisabeth Alve, Martin Langer, and Nancy Rabalais for their constructive reviews. Supported in part by NSF Grants OCE-9417097 and OCE-9711812 to JMB.

13

Effects of marine pollution on benthic Foraminifera

Valentina Yanko, Anthony J. Arnold, and William C. Parker

13.1 INTRODUCTION

13.1.1

Population growth and the resultant acceleration of domestic, municipal, industrial, agricultural, and recreational activity are the primary causes of anthropogenic pollution of the marine realm (Norse, 1993). Such pollution produces numerous obvious biological effects, including diseases in plant and animal species (e.g. Lamb et al., 1991), local or complete extinction of some species (Vermeij, 1993), changes in community structure (Bresler and Fishelson, 1994; Suchanek, 1993), loss or modification of habitat (Nee and May, 1992), and human health complications. The marine environment, as the ultimate destination of virtually all terrestrial runoff, is especially affected by pollution, and the shallow nearshore marine environment is particularly subject to frequent and extensive industrial and municipal pollution.

With increasing worldwide awareness of environmental problems, ways to detect and monitor marine pollution over time are the subject of active research. Numerous studies have demonstrated the value of various animal species in detecting dangerous ecosystem contamination (James, and Evison, 1979; Organization for Economic Cooperation and Development, 1987). Species which occupy key positions in ecosystems are especially useful biomonitors. Thus, the continual global biogeochemical cycles of inorganic and organic compounds are regulated mainly by biological activity of benthic communities, especially bacteria and protozoa (Meyer-Reil, 1986; Santschi, 1988).

Marine protozoa, especially Foraminifera, play a significant role in global biogeochemical cycles of inorganic and organic compounds, making them one of the most important animal groups on earth (Anderson, 1988; Haynes, 1981; Lee and Anderson, 1991b). They are ubiquitous in marine environments. Their tremendous taxonomic diversity gives them the potential for diverse biological responses to various pollutants, which in turn adds to their potential as index species for monitoring pollution from diverse sources. Their tests are readily preserved, and can record evidence of environmental stresses through time, thus providing historical baseline data even in the absence of background studies. They are small and abundant compared to other hard-shelled taxa (such as mollusks which are often used for pollution monitoring), which makes them particularly easy to recover in statistically significant numbers. They have short reproductive cycles (six months to one year; Boltovskoy, 1964), and rapid growth responses to ecological conditions (Fursenko, 1978). They have biological defense mechanisms (Yanko et al., 1994a) which protect them against unfavorable environmental factors, thus providing detectable biological evidence of the effects of pollution. These characteristics make them powerful tools for continuous in situ biological monitoring of marine environments.

Barely forty years have passed since Zalesny (1959) discovered the effects of pollution on foraminiferal distribution in Santa Monica Bay, California. Resig (1958) and Watkins (1961) subsequently suggested the use of benthic Foraminifera as proxy indicators of marine pollution. Since that time, the foraminiferal literature has seen an exponentially rising tide of papers on the behavior of Foraminifera in polluted areas. Brief reviews have been presented by Boltovskoy and Wright (1976), Alve (1991a,b), Culver and Buzas (1995), Yanko et al. (1994c) and Alve (1995a).

13.1.2 General locations of studies

The geographic locations of studies on marine pollution and Foraminifera are dictated by two main factors: the distribution of human activities that generate pollution, and the distribution of foraminiferologists with support and interest in the study of pollution. As can be seen from Fig. 13.1, the geographic localities of studies in this field are concentrated primarily in industrialized countries. Studies of the effects of coastal pollution on the Foraminifera are concentrated mainly in the northern Pacific Ocean, with additional studies in the south Pacific and Indian Oceans, and the eastern Mediterranean Sea, northwestern Black Sea and Caspian Sea. Only one study has been undertaken on the Atlantic coast of the Americas. Pollution in these areas tends to be dominated by municipal sewage, but also heavy metals, hydrocarbons, fertilizers, coal and fuel ash, and various other chemical pollutants are also represented.

The study of pollution in bays and harbors (again, mainly by municipal sewage but also by aquaculture, paper mills, heavy metals, fertilizers and chemical pollution) have been undertaken in the North Pacific Ocean, North and South Atlantic Oceans, the Caribbean Sea, the Indian coast, and the Gulf of Mexico. The influence of pollution on Foraminifera in estuaries and lagoons has been studied mainly in the North Atlantic Ocean (Canadian), North Sea, South Atlantic Ocean, and along the Indian coast. Most of these studies focused on pollution from aquaculture, paper mills, fertilizers, heavy metals, domestic sewage, and various chemicals.

13.1.3 Research strategies

The use of Foraminifera as indicators of marine pollution may involve quantitative analysis of: (1) foraminiferal diversity, (2) population density/abundance, (3) assemblage structure, (4) test morphology, including size and prolocular morphology, (5) test ultrastructure, (6) test pyritization, (7) test chemistry, and (8) cytoplasmic/biological response.

These eight approaches can be complicated by two general factors:

(1) The first complication relates to *covariation* within and among natural and anthropogenic environmental factors. Most toxins enter the marine system from terrestrial sources, primarily through coastal or estuarine ecosystems where steep natural environmental gradients would exert control over foraminiferal distribution patterns even in the absence of anthropogenic effluents. Separating the effects of these two coincident influences can be problematic (e.g. Collins et al., 1995). Moreover, environmental factors (e.g. dissolved organic carbon, especially humic acids, pH, temperature, salinity, ionic strength, rates of biotic pollutant metabolism, and degradation) can modify the toxicity of pollutants (Forstner and Wittmann, 1979; James,

Introduction

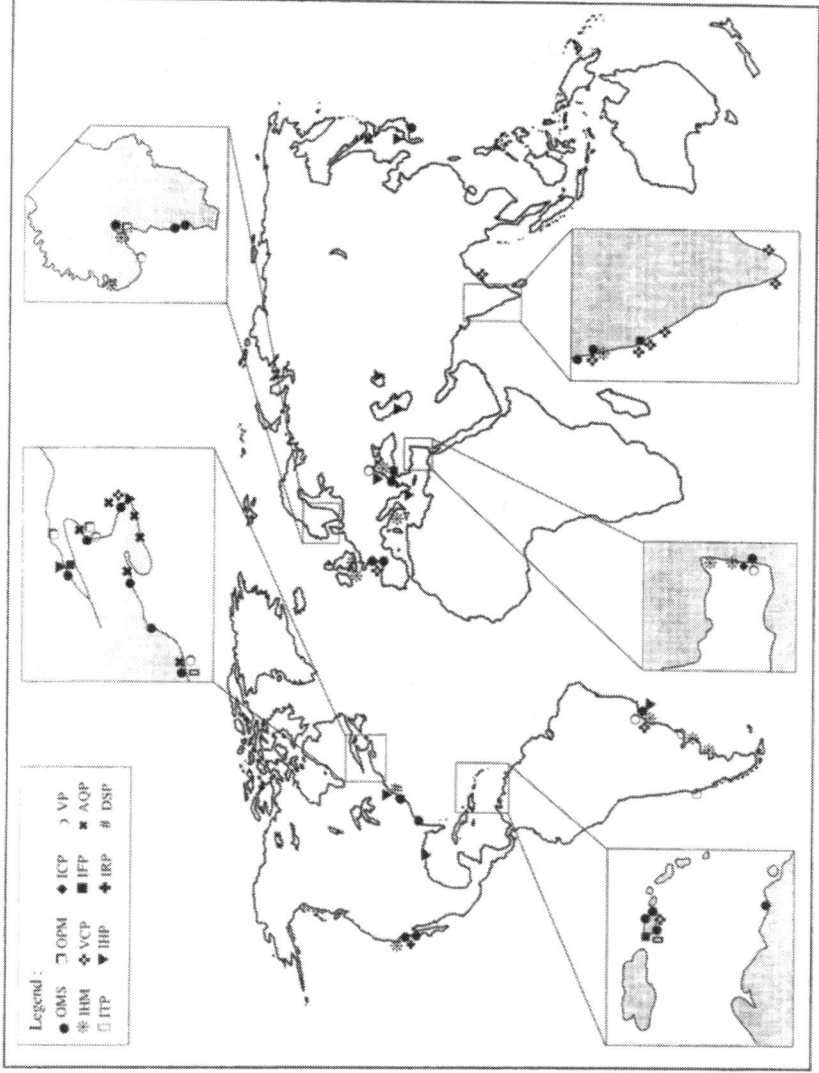

Figure 13.1 Global distribution of studies involving foraminiferal response to pollution. Symbols are as follows: OMS organic pollution by municipal sewage; OPM organic pollution by pulp and paper mills; ICP industrial pollution by coal and fuel ash; IHM industrial pollution by heavy metals; VP various unspecified pollutants; VCP various chemical pollutants, including pesticides; IFP industrial fertilizer pollutants; AQP aquaculture pollution; ITP industrial thermal pollution; IHP industrial pollution by hydrocarbons; IRP industrial pollution by radioactive wastes; DSP dredging and stream discharge pollution.

1989; Paasivarta, 1991; Belfroid *et al.*, 1994; Bresler and Yanko, 1995a,b).

Contaminated estuarine and coastal ecosystems, especially benthic ecosystems, may also contain a broad variety of pollutants. For example, the active components of oil pollution include, as a minimum, numerous polycyclic aromatic hydrocarbons (PAHs), linear hydrocarbons, phenolic compounds, and heavy metals. Active components of fuel ash include various PAHs and heavy metals (Jenner and Bowmer, 1990, 1992; Hamilton *et al.*, 1993). These pollutants may interact to influence toxicity in complex and nonlinear ways (e.g. Green *et al.*, 1993a). Additionally, some natural constituents in sea water and sediments (e.g. acidvolatile sulfide, dissolved organic carbon, or other organic matter) may also interact with pollutants to modify their toxicity (Versteeg and Shorter, 1992; Bresler and Yanko, 1995b). Sediment-dwelling benthic organisms can also affect the behavior of pollutants as well as the chemical properties of bottom sediments and water (e.g. Huttel, 1990). The biological effects of such complex mixtures can be more (or less) toxic than would be expected from simple additive effects of a single pollutant or several pollutants (Malins and Ostrander, 1993; Newmand and

Jagoe, 1996; Howard, 1997). Moreover, effluent sources – particularly from chemical processing plants – rarely produce only a single toxin, which tends to result in covariation among toxin concentrations; this in turn makes it difficult to determine which toxins are producing the observed effects on foraminiferal populations (e.g. Yanko et al., 1994c). The solution to these covariation problems takes three forms: (i) statistical analysis of faunal distribution patterns and toxin/pollutant concentrations, (ii) laboratory experimentation, and (iii) historical analysis.

The statistical analysis is easier where strong point sources of effluent interrupt natural environmental gradients, but can be complicated by nonlinear causal relationships. For example, intermediate levels of some urban and agricultural organic wastes can cause a 'hypertrophic' zone (Alve, 1995a) of increased foraminiferal productivity, while very high concentrations can result in an 'azoic' (Schafer, 1970a) or 'abiotic' zone (Alve, 1995a). As a general rule, the statistical analysis of complex interactions between numerous species and a large number of environmental factors will require a multivariate approach such as factor analysis (see chapter 5). A particular application of factor analysis, the transfer function discussed in chapters 5 and 7, is a technique that would be particularly well suited to such situations; surprisingly, it has seen little use in the field of foraminiferal ecotoxicology.

Laboratory experimentation may identify interactions between species and toxins by growing them under controlled conditions; this allows the researcher to experimentally resolve the problems presented by covariation, if attention is paid to the possibility of interaction among toxins as well as with varying natural conditions.

Historical analysis may be undertaken when there is sufficient stratigraphic accumulation of a pre-industrial foraminiferal record; in that situation it becomes possible to compare modern conditions with preceding unpolluted conditions even without a background study. This approach is complicated by taphonomic effects that themselves may covary with (or indeed be caused by) pollution induced changes in bottom-water chemistry.

(2) A second broad problematic area relates to the *measurement of pollutants*. Effluent concentrations can be measured by extraction from sediments, or by sampling at the sediment-water interface or in the overlying water column, but the biological relevance of such measurements is not well understood. Effluent concentrations can also show considerable temporal variation, depending on the schedules of human activity that produce and release effluents; thus, sampling dates and frequency may have a major effect on results. Additionally, it is not uncommon for effluent concentrations to be taken from published literature rather than measured at the time of sampling for Foraminifera. Further, when toxin concentrations are measured in sediments, the differing properties of sediments must be taken into account. For example, clean sands will interact with toxins in different ways than muds and clays. Toxin concentrations can thus covary with sediment type (e.g. Yanko et al., 1998), which, in turn may also influence foraminiferal distributions.

13.2 FORAMINIFERAL RESPONSES TO DIFFERING SOURCES OF POLLUTION

13.2.1

Given the recent emergence of foraminiferal ecotoxicology as a discipline, it is possible to provide a relatively complete account of work on the subject to date. The discussion below is divided into twelve broad categories: municipal sewage, fertilizers, aquacultures, pulp/paper mills, hydrocarbons, heavy metals, fuel ash, chemical pollutants including pesticides, thermal, radioactive, dredging, and stream discharge. References in these areas are grouped accordingly, and are virtually complete through 1997.

13.2.2 Municipal sewage, fertilizers, and aquacultures

Marine ecosystems are sensitive to suspended or dissolved organic matter from municipal sewage, agricultural fertilizers, and aquacultures. These pollutants can affect marine ecosystems chemically (by depletion of oxygen through oxidation and bacterial decay), biologically (by the introduction of disease-bearing organisms such as viruses, bacteria, and parasitic worms), and physically (warming due to fermentation and reduced photic levels due to turbidity). Dissolved organic material as well as other compounds of phosphorus, silicon, and nitrogen, are usually abundant in such areas, creating artificially high nutrient levels. This organic material is readily metabolized by marine organisms, and can cause an increased foraminiferal abundance (e.g. Watkins, 1961; Bandy et al., 1964a; Seiglie, 1971; Setty, 1976; Yanko et al., 1994c) and diversity (e.g. Resig, 1958, 1960; Yanko et al., 1994c; De Casamajor and Debenay, 1995). Bandy et al. (1964a) discussed a typical example of anomalously high living and dead foraminiferal abundances near a sewage outfall (see chapter 11). Additionally, planktonic Foraminifera were fifty times as abundant in sediment near the outfall as elsewhere at similar depths. Bandy et al. (1964a) also noted that agglutinated species were most abundant among dead tests in the outfall area, which is probably a taphonomic effect related to dissolution in sulfide-rich (Fe$_2$S) black sediments. Other workers have noted that in some areas polluted by domestic sewage, Foraminifera can have unusually large, well ornamented tests and relatively few deformed tests (e.g. Watkins, 1961; Yanko et al., 1994c). These observations suggest that artificially high levels of nutrients may enhance the general viability of foraminiferal populations.

However, this is not always the case. Clark (1971) found a strong inverse relationship between the density of Foraminifera in the sediment and the production level of nearby aquaculture operations. No live Foraminifera were found by Schafer (1970a) in an 'azoic zone' ('abiotic zone' of Alve, 1995a). Similar observations have been made by others (Bandy et al., 1964b; Schafer and Sen Gupta, 1969; LeFurgey and St Jean, 1975). The azoic zone is usually located in the immediate vicinity of the outfall where bacterial breakdown of extreme concentrations of organic material causes oxygen depletion, eutrophication, and high mortality of Foraminifera (e.g. Bandy et al., 1965b; Schafer et al., 1991).

The existence and spatial distribution of the azoic zone is influenced by the sewage type (activated or treated vs. non-activated or untreated), its geographic location (estuary, bay, or open shelf), hydrodynamic regime (current strength, direction), salinity, temperature, and effluent outfall rates (Bates and Spencer, 1979; Alve, 1995a). For example, in the eastern Mediterranean approximately three miles off Palmahim, Israel, a pipe fitted with a diffuser at its end disposes of 1,400 m^3/day of domestic sewage in a water depth of 38 m. The activated sludge (after secondary treatment) is composed of 95% water and 5% solids. In addition to the stable biomass, it may contain pathogenic bacteria, inorganic nutrients, and synthetic organic compounds. The lowest foraminiferal abundances were found at the mouth of the distal end of the pipeline, but there was no azoic zone. The highest diversity and abundance were found at stations located to the north and northwest of the sewage outfall, in an open coastal area downcurrent of the outfall with salinities of 39‰ (Yanko et al., 1994c). By contrast, an azoic zone was noted near the Beledune Fertilizer factory in Restigouche estuary, Atlantic Canada, where salinity varied between 21 and 28‰, and currents spread pollutants throughout the entire estuary (Schafer, 1970a). In this situation, the combined effects of water temperature and salinity caused a density-stratified water column that led to reduced overturn and local enhancement of oxygen deficiency (Schafer et al., 1995). This may be an example of the kind of nonlinear interaction that complicates our understanding of the relationship between pollutants and natural environmental factors.

Additional work on organic pollution by municipal sewage includes Alve, 1991a,b; Alve and Nagy, 1986; Bandy et al., 1965a,b; Bonetti et al., 1996; Cato et al., 1980; Collins et al., 1995; Debenay et al., 1997; Eichler et al., 1995; Govindan et al., 1983; Hirshfield, 1979; LeFurgey and St. Jean, 1973, 1976; Latimer et al., 1997; Lidz, 1965, 1966; Matoba, 1970; McCrone and

Schafer, 1966; Nyholm and Olsson, 1973; Nyholm et al., 1977; Resig, 1960; Schafer, 1970b, 1971a, 1973, 1982; Seiglie, 1964, 1968, 1975; Setty, 1982; Setty et al., 1983; Setty and Nigam, 1982, 1984; Setty et al., 1993, 1997; Yanko, 1993, 1994, 1995, 1996a,b; Zalesny, 1959. Additional work on pollution by fertilizers includes Schafer, 1970a, 1992; Seiglie, 1975; Setty, 1976; Yanko and Flexer, 1991. Work on pollution by aquaculture includes Grant et al., 1995; Schafer, 1970b, 1973; Schafer et al., 1993, 1995; Scott et al., 1997; and Preobrazhenskaya et al., 1991.

13.2.3 Pulp and paper mills

Effluent from pulp and paper mills consists mainly of resistant organic material such as cellulose and lignin, major constituents of wood fibers. The most toxic compounds associated with this effluent are those used to break down wood fibers, rather than the wood fibers themselves. Compounds of mercury are particularly toxic; additionally, sulfides will, under well-oxygenated conditions (usually found downcurrent from the point of discharge), oxidize to sulfates. The presence of sulfides (recognizable by the smell of rotten eggs) normally indicates oxygen-poor conditions, and Foraminifera tend to have low abundances in these areas. Where sulfate levels are high, the environment is usually oxygenated and nutrient-rich, and Foraminifera grow quickly with rapid generational turnover, high productivity, and high abundances. Under these conditions, adult specimens tend to be smaller, probably because of the rapid growth and high reproductive rates characteristic of opportunistic ecological response. However, where sulfate concentrations reach their maximum, foraminiferal abundance is often lower, probably due to coincident high sedimentation rates (Tapley, 1969). In areas surrounded by pulp mills, extreme concentrations of sulfides can create an azoic, reducing environment where coal tar accumulates and Foraminifera are excluded. This variable response to pulp and paper mill effluent is another example of nonlinear faunal response to pollutant concentration. Additional work on organic pollution by pulp and paper mills includes Alve, 1994; Alve and Nagy, 1986, 1988; Bartlett, 1966; Buckley et al., 1974; Latimer et al., 1997; Nagy and Alve, 1987; Schafer, 1970a,b, 1971a, 1973, 1982; Schafer and Cole, 1974, 1995; and Schafer et al., 1975, 1991.

13.2.4 Hydrocarbons

In addition to 5–15% alkanes, typical petroleum products contain aromatic hydrocarbons, including monoaromatic hydrocarbons such as benzene and toluene (the most frequently used light petroleum products). Some of these are proven to be carcinogenic (Kennish, 1992). Lethal doses of aromatic hydrocarbons for marine organisms are in the range of 0.00001 to 0.01% for adults, and at the low end of that range for juveniles; doses as low as 10^{-6}% can inhibit physiological activity, and 10^{-7}% can cause pathological reactions (Bokris, 1982; Rubinin, 1983). Depending on the fraction and molecular weight, the hydrocarbons may form a film on the surface of the water, or heavier oil suspensions and tar may sink to blanket the seafloor.

The small amount of work that has been done on the effect of hydrocarbons on Foraminifera has produced conflicting results. Lockin and Maddocks (1982) reported that petroleum operation at Louisiana offshore petroleum platforms had only a minor negative effect on benthic Foraminifera. Similar results were noted around Ekofisk and Forties petroleum platforms in the North Sea (Murray, 1985). Dermitzakis and Alafousou (1987) suggested that meteoric rainfall intensified the effect of terrestrial oil seeps on the offshore marine environment near Zakynthos Island (Greece), possibly due to changes in pH. Vénec-Peyré (1981, 1984) studied the consequences of the Amoco Cadiz incident (March 16–17, 1978) on benthic Foraminifera in Cale du Dourduff, south of Roscoff, northwestern France, and concluded that it did not affect relative abundances or diversity; however, the accident did cause morphological abnormalities in foraminiferal tests. In contrast, a pronounced negative effect of oil on benthic Foraminifera was noted by Mayer (1980) in the northern Caspian Sea and by Yanko and Flexer (1991) in Odessa Bay where foraminiferal abundance and diversity decreased dramatically in oil-polluted areas. Similar negative effects were noted by Witcomb (1977, 1978) in experimental work on calcareous (*Ammonia beccarii*) and agglutinated species (*Allogromia laticollaris*). He found that crude oil inhibited growth and reproduction in both species, and that petroleum products produced narcosis and death of Foraminifera, and speculated that petroleum products might also cause a decrease in nutrient supply (primarily diatoms). A full understanding of the biological causes of this result awaits further research. V. Yanko (unpublished data) noted that respiratory functions of Foraminifera were inhibited in Black Sea sediments with high concentrations of petroleum products. The breakdown of petroleum was accompanied by the release of H_2S, ammonia, and methane, and by pH as low as 6. (Note that Bradshaw, 1961, found *Ammonia tepida*, a common indicator species, to be very sensitive to pH.)

Work on hydrocarbons also includes papers by Akimoto et al., 1997; Bonetti et al., 1996; Buckley et al., 1974; Casey et al., 1980; Latimer et al., 1997; Schafer, 1992; Schafer et al., 1975; Vénec-Peyré, 1981, 1984; and Yanko and Flexer, 1992.

13.2.5 Heavy metals

The biological relevance of temporal variation of heavy metal toxin concentrations, and of heavy metal concentrations in sediments versus in the water column is not fully understood and, although these factors are undoubtedly important, sampling programs have generally not been designed to assess their relative impact on the Foraminifera. Thus, it is prudent to discuss this research by separating three categories based on sampling methods. The first category includes papers concerning the distribution of living/fossil Foraminifera in sediment samples where the concentration of heavy metals was not measured directly but taken from literature reports. The second group includes information about Foraminifera based on correlation between their distribution and heavy metal concentrations measured in the same sediment samples. The third set of papers concerns ecotoxicological laboratory experiments on Foraminifera and heavy metals.

Studies based on literature reports of heavy metals. This body of research accounts for much of the early pioneering work in the area of foraminiferal ecotoxicology. Boltovskoy (1956) described a stunted fauna (small in size, lacking ornamentation, with a tendency to asymmetry and monstrosity) in some lead-polluted areas of the northern Argentinean shelf. McCrone and Schafer (1966) noted that trace elements may affect morphology of benthic Foraminifera in the Hudson estuary. Schafer (1973) found that foraminiferal diversity decreased in an area adjacent to a Pb–Zn smelter outfall. Setty and Nigam (1984) found depauperate (in both abundance and diversity) populations of benthic Foraminifera, with high percentages of abnormal individuals, in the area adjacent to a titanium processing plant (near Trivandrum, west coast of India) where a mixture of sulfuric acid, soluble iron, and other metallic salts were discharged. A similar pattern was discovered by Naidu et al. (1985) in the Visakhapatnam harbor area (east coast of India) where marine waters were polluted by domestic sewage and a variety of heavy metals (e.g. Cu, Fe, Pb, Zn, Ni, Cr, As). These papers served to draw attention to the fact that foraminiferal morphology – in addition to abundance and diversity – is affected by heavy metal pollution.

Studies based on heavy metal and foraminiferal analyses of the same samples. This body of research is generally more recent and planned with specific ecotoxicological analysis as the primary goal. Ellison et al. (1986) investigated foraminiferal response to trace metal (Zn, Cr, and V) contamination in the Patapsco River and Baltimore Harbor, Maryland. They discovered a very depauperate foraminiferal assemblage (fewer than 10 individuals per g^{-1} of sediment), composed of six species, and dominated by *Ammobaculites crassus*. Alve (1991a) analyzed fossil benthic Foraminifera in two short (170–190 cm length) sediment cores taken in

Sorfjo (Norway) at depths of 15–53 m, and found a historical record of foraminiferal populations that were characterized by reduced abundances, dominance of agglutinated species, frequent occurrence of abnormal tests (with seven different modes of deformation), and high concentrations of pyritized specimens in areas polluted by heavy metals. A comprehensive study of Foraminifera as indicators of heavy metal pollution was undertaken by Sharifi (1991) and Sharifi et al. (1991) in Southampton Water, southern England. Of the 67 species found in 250 grab samples, some were able to tolerate pollution, and their relative abundance increased at the discharge point, whereas other species developed test deformities. Banerji (1992) compared distributions of heavy metals (Cd, Co, Cr, Cu, Fe, Mn, Ni, Pb, Zn) in sediments and in foraminiferal tests. His results show that species diversity corresponds positively with Fe, Mn, and Zn concentrations in the sediments and negatively with Co, Ni, and Pb concentrations. He found that although *Ammonia* and *Elphidium* species occur together, the former prefers environments enriched with Fe, Mn and Zn, and that an increase in concentrations of Cd, Co, and Pb was accompanied by a decrease in the abundances of *Ammonia* and *Lagena* spp. Such elements as Cu, Zn, and Cr were more readily absorbed into foraminiferal tests than Ni and Pb. At present, comparative observation suggests that it may be possible to develop a scale of gradational species response to heavy metal contamination by using the heavy minifera from areas with high concentrations of heavy metals develop stunted tests with numerous deformities. Coccioni et al. (1997) studied living and non-living benthic foraminiferal distributions at fifteen sites throughout the Goro Lagoon, Italy. The concentrations of eleven elements (V, Cr, Co, Ni, Cu, Zn, Ga, As, Pb, Th, and Cd) and total organic carbon (TOC) in the sediments were measured, and a total of 77

species from 43 genera were identified. Some sites displayed marked enrichment in Cr, Ni, Zn, Pb, and As, with Al-normalized values higher than the average values of nearby unpolluted alluvial plain pelites. These sites also exhibited an increase in TOC, a general reduction in foraminiferal test size, and a decrease of benthic foraminiferal species richness, with a concurrent increased abundance of tolerant and opportunistic species such as *Cribroelphidium translucens*. A similar trend was found by Stubbles (1993) and Stubbles et al. (1996a,b) who studied living and dead benthic Foraminifera in Restronguet Creek, Erme and Fowey estuaries, Cornwall, UK. Using semiquantitative microprobe analysis, they found higher concentrations of several heavy metals, including Cd, in the cytoplasm of deformed Foraminifera than in the cytoplasm of non-deformed individuals. The authors suggest that if heavy metals are responsible for deformation of foraminiferal tests, these metals should be dissolved in the water rather than stored in the sediments. This has opened a potentially important avenue of research that may increase our understanding of the biological relevance of heavy metals that are sequestered in sediments versus those dissolved in the water column. However, due to the semiquantitative nature of the instrumentation, further analysis is required.

Research reported in Yanko (1994, 1995, 1996a,b), Yanko et al. (1992, 1994a,b,c, 1995, 1998), and Yanko, ed. (1995, 1996) was directed at the study of benthic Foraminifera as indicators of heavy metal pollution along the eastern Mediterranean coast. Eighty-seven stations were sampled at one mile intervals on a rectangular grid covering the polluted Haifa Bay coastal area, with the relatively clean coast of nearby Atlit Bay as a control. The responses of benthic Foraminifera to ten heavy metals (Cd, Cr, Cu, Pb, Zn, As, Co, Ni, Ti, V) showed that reduced diversity and abundance, stunting of the tests, pyritization, and the presence of anomalous morphologies are closely related to trace metal contamination (Yanko et al., 1998). According to the experimental results of Bresler and Yanko (1995b), there is significant biological influence

Foraminiferal responses to differing sources of pollution

of heavy metals on foraminiferal cytoplasm. Mercury ions that penetrate the cytoplasm readily interact with the sulfhydril groups of proteins by blocking them and inhibiting their function. Intracytoplasmic Cd especially interferes with sites that normally interact with calcium; particularly, Cd can penetrate mitochondria and interfere with respiratory functions. However, the Cd-sensitivity of different species, individuals, and even tissues, varies widely.

In general, it can be concluded that there is a negative correlation between concentrations of heavy metals in sediments and foraminiferal abundance and diversity, and a positive correlation between the abundance of deformed tests and heavy metals.

Work on heavy metal pollution also includes publications by Alve and Olsgard, 1997; Banerji, 1989; Bonetti et al., 1996; Kravchuk et al., 1997; Latimer et al., 1997; Schafer and Cole, 1995; Van Geen et al., 1993; Yanko and Flexer, 1991; Yanko and Kronfeld, 1992; and Yanko and Kravchuk, 1996.

13.2.6 Fuel ash

The influence of coal and fuel ash pollution on benthic Foraminifera has been studied along the coast of Hadera, Israel, near a coal-fired power station (Yanko, 1993, 1994, 1995; Yanko et al., 1994c). Fuel ash particles, derived from the combustion of hydrocarbon fuels, dramatically decreases species richness and reproductive rate in Foraminifera, but does not seem to affect the test size. Agglutinated species are less affected by this kind of pollution than calcareous species. It has been speculated that coal and fuel ash particles decrease the food supply (bacteria and diatoms), and also affect foraminiferal metabolism directly (Yanko, 1994). Furthermore, some trace metals and PAHs, contained in fuel and coal ash in very low concentrations, interfere with defense systems and affect nutrient metabolism in Foraminifera (Yanko, 1994).

Additional papers on pollution by coal and fuel ash include work by Yanko, 1993, 1995, 1996b; and Yanko et al., 1994b,c.

13.2.7 Miscellaneous chemical pollutants including pesticides

There are a number of chemical pollutants, including pesticides, that affect foraminiferal abundance and diversity in much the same ways as heavy metals. Some also may be responsible for erosion and corrosion of foraminiferal tests (e.g. in Thana Creek, Bombay Area, India; Setty, 1982). Following exposure to pesticides, foraminiferal biotas can exhibit biochemical and histological alteration in some specimens. Such exposure can also degrade immune systems and cause mutagenic changes (Komarovskiy et al., 1993).

Additional research in this area includes work by Alzugaray et al., 1979; Banerji, 1977; Bartlett, 1972; Bergsten et al., 1992; Bhalla and Nigam, 1986; Boltovskoy and Boltovskoy, 1968; Bonetti et al., 1997a,b; Bresler et al., 1996a,b; Buckley et al., 1974; Geslin et al., 1997a,b, 1998; Jayaraju and Reddeppa Reddi, 1996b; Kameswara and Satyanarayana, 1979; Naidu et al., 1985; Olsson et al., 1973; Seiglie, 1973, 1975; Setty and Nigam, 1980, 1984; Schafer, 1968, 1970a; Schafer et al., 1975; Varshney et al., 1988; Wright, 1968; and Yanko and Kravchuk, 1992.

13.2.8 Thermal and radioactive waste

Research on thermal and radioactive waste is not extensive. An increase in foraminiferal abundance and a decrease of diversity in the Long Island Sound have been related to a power-plant-induced increase of water temperature (Hechtel et al., 1970). Attempts to relate ^{137}Cs contamination from the Chernobyl reactor accident to foraminiferal indices in Iskenderun Bay (Turkey) yielded inconclusive results (Yanko, ed., 1996).

Other works on industrial thermal pollution include Hechtel et al., 1970, and Seiglie, 1975. Work on pollution by radioactive waste includes Reish, 1983.

13.2.9 Dredging and stream discharge

Although the ecological effects of dredging and stream discharge have not been extensively investigated, it is likely that they will affect turbidity (and therefore photic levels), and mobilize nutrients and pollutants that would otherwise remain sequestered in sediments. It has been suggested that these activities change the habitat and community structure of foraminiferal assemblages (Belanger, 1976), although the mechanisms are not well understood.

Additional work on pollution and Foraminifera that do not fall in the preceding categories include Alzugaray et al., 1979; Banerji, 1977; Bartlett, 1972; Bergsten et al., 1992; Boltovskoy and Boltovskoy, 1968; Boltovskoy et al., 1991; Boltovskoy and Wright, 1976; Bonetti et al., 1997a,b; Bresler et al., 1996a,b; Culver and Buzas, 1995; Olsson et al., 1973; Schafer, 1968, 1971a, 1973, 1975; Wright, 1968; Yanko, 1997; Geslin and Devenay, 1998; Geslin et al., 1997a,b; and Yanko and Kravchuk, 1992.

13.3 SPECIAL PROBLEMS IN FORAMINIFERAL ECOTOXICOLOGY

13.3.1 Opportunistic (resistant) species

Species that are abundant in polluted areas are likely to be tolerant (resistant) to the pollutants found there. However, even in these species toxins may produce detectable effects in their cytoplasm and test (Bresler and Yanko, 1995b; Yanko et al., 1998). Species that are sensitive to pollution often express that sensitivity through their absence.

Species identified as resistant in coastal zones, bays, harbors, estuaries and lagoons include approximately 11 agglutinated and 47 calcareous species (Table 13.1). The highest number of agglutinated species (6) was found in estuaries while the highest number of calcareous species (33) was noted in coastal zones (Table 13.1). This may be an example of covariation between a natural gradient (salinity) and foraminiferal distribution patterns in an area affected by pollution.

Most eurytopic species are geographically widespread, living within a broad range of latitudes, and many can tolerate a wide range of salinity and depth. For example, *Ammonia tepida* is distributed in the Black Sea from the Danube delta (depth 3–5 m, salinity 1–3‰) to the Bosphorus area (102 m, 26‰) (Yanko and Troitskaja, 1987; Yanko, 1990a,b). In the eastern Mediterranean, this species is widely distributed on the shelf at salinities in the range of 39‰ (Yanko et al., 1994a). There are also several taxa (e.g. buliminids, bolivinids, uvigerinids) which can tolerate the oxygen-deficient conditions that often accompany pollution. The dominance of agglutinated Foraminifera in areas close to domestic outfalls (e.g. Bandy et al., 1964a) may be more closely related to fresh-water input than to discharge of pollutants or dissolution of calcareous forms (Alve, 1995a).

Alve (1995a) concluded that, in general, those species that are most abundant and geographically widespread are most tolerant of environmental pollution. If Alve's conclusion is generally valid, then these eurytopic species offer the possibility of comparative studies in widely separated geographic areas – an aspect of foraminiferal ecotoxicology that has not yet been explored.

13.3.2 Morphological deformity of foraminiferal tests

13.3.2.1 Distribution and correlation

Morphological deformities in fossil foraminiferal tests have been noted by researchers since the last century (e.g. Carpenter, 1856; Rhumbler, 1911). In recent years, reports of deformities in modern Foraminifera have become increasingly common, and further documentation of deformed fossils has been made (e.g. Bogdanowich, 1952, 1960; Pflum and Frerichs, 1976). Most of the available data on deformities were summarized by Boltovskoy and Wright (1976), Haynes (1981), and Boltovskoy et al. (1991), who noted that deformities may be attributed to mechanical damage or environmental stress, but concluded that there is no consensus as to the underlying causes of most deformities. Deformed tests of Foraminifera have been reported from areas contaminated by heavy

Special problems in foraminiferal ecotoxicology

Table 13.1 Pollution tolerant species and the environments in which they have been studied.

Species	Coastal zone	Bay and harbor	Estuary	Lagoon
Ammobaculites crassus	+			
A. salsus				+
Ammomarginulina fluvialis		+		
Eggerella advena	+	+	+	
Eggerelloides scabrus		+	+	
Miliammina earlandi?				+
M. fusca	+	+		
Reophax arctica	+			
Spiroplectammina biformis			+	
Trochammina inflata			+	
T. pacifica	+	+		
Ammonia annectens	+			
A. beccarii	+	+		
A. caspica	+			
A. dentata	+			
A. sobrina	+			
A. tepida	+	+		+
Ammonia sp.	+			
Amphistegina lobifera	+		+	
Bolivina vaughani	+			
Buccella frigida	+	+		
Bulimina marginata denudata	+			
B. striata	+			
B. subornata	+			
Buliminella elegantissima	+	+		
Cibicides akneriana	+			
C. adenum	+			
Cribroelphidium translucens	+			+
Discorbis columbiensis	+			
Elphidium articulatum	+			
E. barletti	+			
E. caspicum (=gunteri)	+			
E. clavatum/incertum group	+	++	+	
Elphidium excavatum	+	+	+	
E. lidoense	+			
E. margaritaceum	+			
E. norrangi	+			
E. orbiculare		+		
E. poeyanum	+			
E. translucens	+	++		
Florilus boueanum (=Nonion boueanum)	+			
F. grateloupi (=Nonion grateloupi)			+	
F. scaphus	+			
Fursenkoina pontoni	+			
Haynesina depressula	+			
Martinottiella communis	+			
Miliolinella subrotunda	+			
Protelphidium paralium (=Haynesina germanica)	+			
Pseudotriloculina subgranulata	+			
Quinqueloculina rhodiensis		+		+
Q. seminulum	+	+		
Rutherfordoides cornuta	+			
Spiroloculina excavata	+			
Stainforthia fusiformis			+	
Triloculina brevidentata		+		
T. marioni	+			
Uvigerina dirupta	+			
U. peregrina	+			

metals, domestic sewage, and various chemicals, including liquid hydrocarbons. See Boltovskoy et al. (1991), Alve (1995a), Yanko et al. (1998) for detailed reviews of deformities and their probable reasons. Examples of deformed tests from polluted environments can be seen in Fig. 13.2.

Measures of deformity rely on the kind, degree, frequency, and species-specificity of deformity, but the frequency is the easiest measure to quantify. The percentage of deformed Foraminifera can increase dramatically in polluted areas (e.g. Lidz, 1965) where Foraminifera display a wide variety of deformities, including extreme compression, double apertures, twisted coiling, aberrant chamber shape, and protuberances. Various other workers have catalogued similar lists of deformities, but the genesis of specific deformities is often an unresolved matter. Some deformities undoubtedly result from weak calcification or subsequent damage to areas that are weakly calcified. Other deformities (e.g. twisted keels, distortion of equatorial plane) may result from repair and overgrowth by subsequent whorls that cover such damage, resulting in distortion of the normal shell geometry (Röttger and Hallock, 1982; Wetmore, 1998). Thus, deformities that have quite different appearances may have the same underlying physiological cause. Other deformities (e.g. multiple apertures or twinning) are clearly different in nature and may be attributable to differing responses to different toxins. Yanko et al. (1995), using sulfaflavine fluorescence and chlortetracycline fluorescence, were able to distinguish morphological deformities caused by mechanical damage from those caused by pathological morphogenesis.

Compared with other pollutants, it appears that trace metals have the most conspicuous deleterious effect upon Foraminifera. Like many other kinds of pollutants, heavy metals often cause reduced population density and diversity, and stunting of tests, but increased frequency of deformed tests is a common aspect of virtually all studies of heavy metal toxicity. Yanko et al. (1998) report that at least 30% (65 species from 20 calcareous families and one agglutinated family) of all foraminiferal specimens living on the northern Israeli continental shelf exhibited one of 11 distinct types of morphological deformity in their tests. High proportions of deformed tests in living Foraminifera (up to 10% of the entire assemblage) were also found at all sites showing high metal concentrations in the Goro Lagoon, Italy. This contrasts with observations of 1% or fewer deformed specimens in natural populations. The types of deformity include: abnormal coiling, aberrant chamber shape and size, poor development of the last whorl, twisted chamber arrangement, supernumerary chambers, protuberances, multiple apertures, irregular keel, twinning, lateral asymmetry, and lack of ornamentation (Coccioni et al., 1997). A similar pattern was found in Sorfjord, Western Norway (Alve, 1991a), and in Southampton Water, southern England (Sharifi et al., 1991). Deformed Foraminifera are represented among the porcelaneous, hyaline, and agglutinated suborders, among various modes of life (epifaunal, infaunal, attached, epiphytic, symbiotic, muddwelling, sand-dwelling), and among different morphotypes (milioline, trochospiral, planispiral, flattened, etc) (Setty and Nigam, 1980; Banerji, 1989; Vénec-Peyré, 1981). Thus, morphological deformities do not show differential

Figure 13.2 Examples of test deformities in live Foraminifera found in Haifa Bay region, Israeli shelf, eastern Mediterranean. 1, *Eggerella advena* (Cushman), specimen with twisted chamber arrangement; 2, *Adelosina pulchella* d'Orbigny, specimen with twisted chamber arrangement of the first whorl and aberrant chamber shape; 3, *Nonionella atlantica* Cushman, specimen with aberrant chamber shape and size; 4–6, *Ammonia compacta* Hofker, specimens with aberrant shape of the last three chambers (4), twisting of the test (5), and non-development of test (6); 7–9, *Ammonia tepida* (Cushman), anomalous protuberance on dorsal side (7), twisting of the entire side (8), and twinning of two specimens by ventral side (9); 10, *Adelosina intricata* (Terquem), specimen with wrong coiling, twisted chamber arrangement, aberrant chamber shape, and double aperture; 11, *Vertebralina striata* d'Orbigny, specimen with additional chamber, and aberrant shape of chambers and aperture; 12, *Peneroplis planatus* (Fichtel and Moll), twinning of two specimens; 13, *Triloculina marioni* Schlumberger, severely deformed specimen; 14, *Cycloforina villafranca* (J. and Y. Le Calvez), severely deformed specimen; 15, *Pararotalia spinigera* (Le Calvez), twinning of two specimens by dorsal side.

Special problems in foraminiferal ecotoxicology

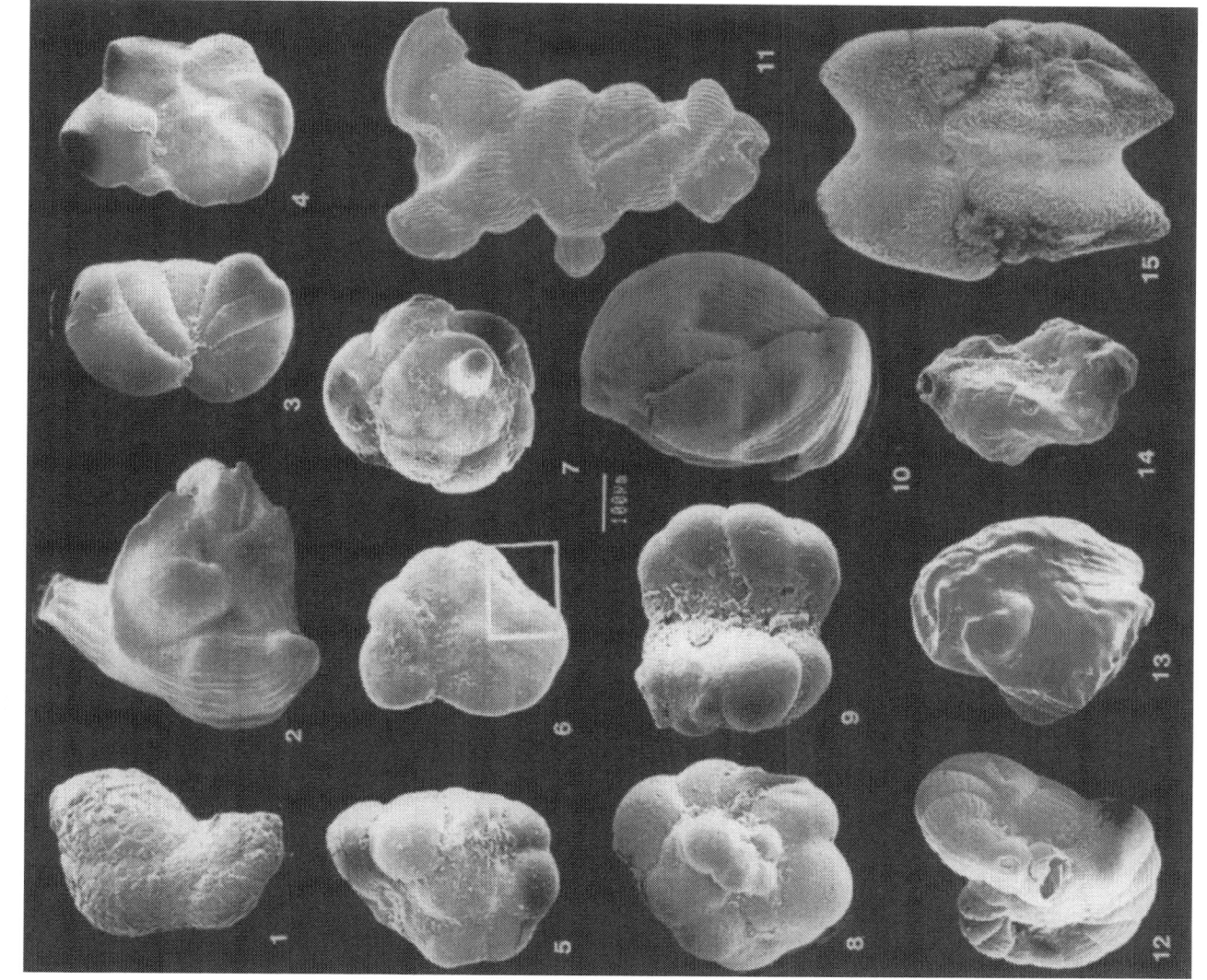

representation based on taxonomic affinity, feeding strategy, or test morphology.

There are indications, however, that some types of environmental stress may cause species-specific deformity. For example, *Adelosina cliarensis* exhibits increased frequency of deformation in response to low salinity, while *Amphistegina lobifera* appears to show an increased incidence of deformity in response to increased Cd concentrations, *Cibicides advenum* seems responsive to Cr, and *Pseudotriloculina subgranulata* to Ti.

High frequencies of test deformity of living benthic Foraminifera are generally regarded to be sensitive *in situ* indicators of marine pollution by heavy metals. However, the biochemical and crystallographic mechanisms of the development of such deformities remain to be studied by culture experiments under controlled conditions and known heavy metal concentrations.

13.3.2.2 Wall texture of deformed tests

The study of the wall texture of abnormal tests, as a possible explanation of deformation related to biomineralization processes, is a new research domain. Geslin *et al.* (1998) have studied ultrastructural deformation in the genus *Ammonia* using scanning electron micrographs. Abnormalities consistently observed in the walls of these deformed tests involve either disorganization of the wall texture due to changes in crystallite arrangement and orientation (Debenay *et al.*, 1996), or the presence of interlamellar cavities.

Normal tests of *Ammonia tepida* are made of crystallites arranged in elongate calcitic elements normal to the wall. These elements are roughly continuous from one lamella to the other. In places, large cleaved crystals may form, with cleavages regularly oblique to the test surface. In deformed tests, calcitic elements may be oriented irregularly. This 'crystalline disorganization' may result from introduction of alien elements in the crystalline framework during calcification. Sharifi *et al.* (1991) showed that the deformed tests contain a high proportion of metals such as Cu and Zn, and Yanko and Kronfeld (1993) found that the deformed tests exhibit an increased Mg/Ca ratio. Interlamellar empty cavities were also observed in some deformed specimens, even when crystalline organization was normal. Such cavities were reported by Vénec-Peyré (1981). On a different scale, these cavities may be compared with the interlamellar cavities formed in the abnormal shells of some bivalves, particularly of the oyster *Crassostrea gigas* by the hypersecretion of a jelly (Héral *et al.*, 1981, *in* Alzieu, 1991). The organic process leading to these secretions may result from a metabolic perturbation.

Early exploratory research has led to several hypotheses regarding anthropogenic causes of morphological deformity in Foraminifera. Four general explanations are suggested. Test deformity may be caused by (1) direct physiological or metabolic interference of heavy metal pollutants; (2) pollution-induced changes in physical and chemical environmental parameters indirectly resulting in pathological morphogenesis; (3) poor nutritional state in Foraminifera, perhaps due to the effect of habitat damage on other organisms in the food web; and (4) anthropogenic intensification of the normal (low-level) background causes of test deformity seen in natural populations. It is clear that in the near future, controlled laboratory experimentation will play a central role in assessing these hypotheses before a full understanding of the relationship between foraminiferal test deformity and pollution is developed.

13.3.2.3 Morphometry and cytology

Morphometric and cytological studies of normal and abnormal *Amphistegina lobifera* tests from the north Israeli coast have been undertaken to distinguish and describe tests with varying morphologies and to understand the pathogenesis of abnormalities (Yanko, ed., 1995; Yanko *et al.*, 1995). Although only a single index of deformity was used, the deformed and undeformed populations of specimens were statistically distinct. A normal test of *A. lobifera* may be described as a bi-convex lens. Several categories of shell deformation were identified that

Special problems in foraminiferal ecotoxicology

rier-mediated transport system for elimination of anionic xenobiotics from the cytoplasm; (3) active intralysosomal accumulation and isolation of some cationic xenobiotics; and (4) haloperoxidases that transform xenobiotics to their haloderivatives (Bresler and Yanko, 1995a).

13.3.3 Pyritization

Pyritization has been found in living Foraminifera as well as in fossils, though the percentage of pyritized tests is significantly higher in empty tests than in tests with protoplasm. Two taxa, *Ammonia tepida* and *Porosononion martkobi ponticus*, are regularly pyritized in the Black Sea (Yanko and Kravchuk, 1992). The degree of pyritization of living individual tests ranged from 2% to 50%, and sometimes higher. The reasons for pyritization in marine sediments and foraminiferal tests are not completely clear. Some have suggested that it is connected to chemical processes that result in metabolization of organic matter under anaerobic conditions by sulfate-reducing bacteria, diffusion of sulfide into sediments, or concentration and reactivity of the iron minerals. The process is clearly connected to the redox conditions and the concentration of H_2S. High percentages of pyritized foraminiferal tests have also been found in oxygen-deficient polluted areas. The frequency of pyritized foraminiferal tests may therefore show promise as a parameter to indicate certain types of polluted environments.

13.3.4 Asexual reproduction

Foraminifera can reproduce by both sexual and asexual modes (see chapter 3). Fursenko (1978) has suggested that under stressful conditions Foraminifera preferentially revert to the asexual part of their life cycle. The causes of stress can include, for example, hyposalinity (Yanko, 1989, 1990a) and decreased nutrient levels (Fursenko, 1978). Trace metal pollution may also stress the Foraminifera by causing cellular injury and subsequently lead to a decrease in the efficiency of metabolism and protein synthesis (Ganote and Vander Heide, 1987). Life-supporting metabolic

caused distortion of that natural shape. These deformities include dorso-ventral asymmetry, loss of a segment of the peripheral margin, lateral asymmetry, irregular keel, abnormal aperture, and various other miscellaneous deformations.

Of these types of deformation, only one (loss of a segment of the periphery) was associated with an increase of sulfaflavine fluorescence (which measures protein content in the shell), and only in the immediate area of the defect. These data indicate that segment loss may have a different pathogenesis than other abnormalities; namely, segment loss is likely to be a result of shell damage and regeneration. During regeneration, especially in the early stages of this process, the protein/Ca ratio increases in the new part of the shell, probably due to intensification of protein synthesis. This suggests that the other remaining test deformities may be the result of pathological morphogenesis rather than of damage and subsequent repair. While the cytoskeleton may play an important role in normal and pathological morphogenesis in metazoan and protozoan cells (Albrecht-Buchler, 1977; Anderheide et al., 1977; Brandle and Gabbiani, 1983), the synthesis of shell-building proteins and their calcification is not apparently involved in pathological morphogenesis of the shell.

It has been proposed that trace metal pollutants weaken the Foraminifera and enable bacteria to attack their cytoplasm (Alve, 1991a). This is readily apparent from stunting of the test and morphological deformities (Alve, 1991a; Yanko et al., 1994c), and is probably related to the fact that heavy metals (e.g. Cd) dramatically increase membrane permeability and mortality of Foraminifera (Bresler and Yanko, 1995b).

The extent to which Foraminifera are protected from pollutants is also a factor deserving some attention, since it will increase our understanding of the factors controlling distribution patterns. Research in this area suggests several potential biological defense systems; they include (1) a mucopolysaccharide coat that forms an additional diffusion barrier and binds some cationic xenobiotics; (2) a membrane car-

systems then function at a reduced level (Bas-erga, 1985) and the energetic cost of meiosis may be too great compared to mitosis (Effrussi and Farber, 1975). This hypothesis is supported by the observation that megalospheric forms of *Ammonia tepida* are strongly dominant where toxic trace metal pollution is prevalent (Yanko et al., 1994c). If a high percentage of megalospheric forms is characteristic of stressed environments, then this characteristic, in conjunction with other indices, may prove a useful tool in monitoring marine pollution.

13.3.5 Chemistry of deformed tests

Several studies have been undertaken to determine whether elevated concentrations of heavy metals in sediments affect test chemistry and morphology (Sharifi, 1991; Sharifi et al., 1991; Yanko and Kronfeld, 1993). The primary result of these studies is that deformed Foraminifera show elevated Mg/Ca ratios when compared to non-deformed Foraminifera, especially in severely polluted areas. Deformed tests of all studied species are characterized by increased Mg concentration in their tests, so it is unlikely that this is a species-specific effect. Several hypotheses might be suggested to explain this observation: One is that heavy metals directly affect the crystal structure of the calcite shell, or foraminiferal cytoskeleton, or both. Another is that heavy-metal toxicity affects foraminiferal metabolism in ways that influence Mg/Ca ratios indirectly during calcification. A third is that other pollution-associated environmental effects mediate Mg/Ca ratios. The process of shell calcification includes the development of a glycoprotein organic matrix, *anlagen*, followed by mineralization by Ca^{++} and bicarbonate in the glycoprotein centers (Fursenko, 1978; Hemleben et al., 1977). Other cations (e.g. Ba and Cd) can also be included in the crystal structure of the test (Fritz et al., 1992; Lea and Boyle, 1989). It is likely that the biochemical transport systems and sites for the Ca^{++} binding cannot easily distinguish between these ions. Trace metals may also affect the ratio of the major element (Ca and Mg) uptake (Yanko and Kronfeld,

1992, 1993). Any of these factors may affect the crystal structure and cause strong morphological deformities in foraminiferal tests. The cytoskeleton, which defines the shape of the organism, may also be affected by heavy metals as has already been shown for the ciliates (Anderheide et al., 1977).

13.3.6 Cytology

Organisms have numerous adaptive biological defense mechanisms that protect them against foreign chemicals in their environment (xenobiotics). If these anti-xenobiotic defense mechanisms fail to protect the organisms, the results will be expressed as a pathological disruption of biological structures on various molecular to ecosystemic levels of hierarchical organization. Even if the biological effect of a single toxic compound is simple and well-understood in isolation, the behavior of the same pollutant in complex natural ecosystems inevitably becomes complicated and nonlinear. Understanding this complexity will require the application of cross-disciplinary new methodologies. An example is the use of fluorescent microscopy and fluorometry to study the cytoplasmic response of Foraminifera to pollution (Bresler and Yanko 1994b, 1995a,b; Bresler et al., 1995, 1996a, 1997). If the 'health' of foraminiferal species can be objectively characterized by biological parameters (e.g. biophysical, morphophysiological, histopathological, cytogenetic, physiological, and biochemical bioindicators) and measured using vital/supravital microfluorometry, then changes in these parameters can be used as early response indicators of exposure to environmental pollutants. Fluorescent probes allow the scientist to visualize and examine quantitatively the structural and chemical organization of cells and their organelles, including specific functions, such as genetic activity or carrier-mediated transport and metabolism, with great precision and sensitivity. Such techniques would enable us to: (1) assess the interaction of pollutant and antixenobiotic biological defense mechanisms; (2) determine the effect of pollutants on structures and metabolic reactions; and (3) predict the future behavior of a given species under polluted conditions. Accordingly, the following objectives can be set: (1) to examine the health of pollution-tolerant species (e.g. *Ammonia tepida*) under natural conditions; (2) to examine the response of the these species to a spectrum of natural conditions (varying temperature, salinity, concentrations of natural xenobiotics, and dissolved organic matter); and (3) then to examine how varying levels of a contaminant can modify these natural responses to yield pathological and pre-pathological changes that could serve as indicators of the degree of pollution. As with other organisms, Foraminifera have a number of defense mechanisms that can protect them against xenobiotics (Bresler and Yanko, 1995a; Yanko et al., 1994a). For example, carrier-mediated System of Active Transport of Organic Anionic xenobiotics (SATOA) eliminates many endo- and xenobiotics from the cytoplasm. Therefore, the quantitative study of SATOA in Foraminifera can be used for early ecological monitoring and prediction of the impact of anthropogenic pollution on ecosystems, as well as for retrospective analysis of paleoecosystems.

All these parameters can be examined by the use of biophysical, cytophysiological, biochemical, and morphological vital microfluorometrical techniques, including fluorescent analysis at the microscopic level (Bresler and Nikifirov, 1981). New devices for vital biophysical studies, especially contact fluorescent microscopes and microspectrofluorometers, can be used to examine, *in situ*, various biological parameters at the molecular and cellular levels and their distribution at higher levels of biological organization. The main parameters (and methods) of interest are the following:

(1) Monitoring of respiration and metabolic state of mitochondria by measurement of inherent blue fluorescence of reduced nicotinamide adenine dinucleotide (NAD) and green fluorescence of oxidized flavine adenine dinucleotide (FAD) in living cells and tissues.

(2) Detection of conformation changes of tryptophan-containing proteins by inherent ultraviolet (UV) fluorescence. For example, inherent UV fluorescence of some tryptophan-containing proteins has been used to study their binding with copper ions (Engel and Breawer, 1987; Bresler and Yanko, 1995b).

(3) Determination of enzyme activity *in situ* by using corresponding fluorogenic substrates and microfluorometry. The activity of some intracellular enzymes also may be sensitive indicators of cell viability (Bresler and Yanko, 1994).

(4) The study of activity and kinetics of transport systems used for the elimination of xenobiotics, such as the system of active transport of organic anions (SATOA) and multixenobiotic resistance (MXR) transporter, by using marker fluorescent substrates of SATOA or MXR, specific inhibitors, and microfluorometry (Bresler et al., 1975, 1979, 1983, 1985, 1990; Bresler and Fishelson, 1994; Bresler and Yanko, 1995a,b; Fishelson et al., 1996).

(5) The examination of cell cycle phases, functional state of nuclear chromatin, DNA concentration and aneuploidy (DNA variability in individual nuclei), and DNA damage by using versatile probe acridine orange (AO) and two-wavelength microfluorometry (Darzynkiewicz 1990; Fishelson et al., 1996).

(6) Cell chemistry, i.e. content of DNA, RNA, proteins, mucopolysaccharides and carbohydrates, lipids, thiol groups, and intra- and extracellular ions (especially calcium), can be studied with special fluorescent probes and microfluorometry.

(7) Permeability of plasma membranes, epithelial layers, or histohematic barriers can be examined by using various fluorescent markers, especially fluorescein, and microfluorometry (Bresler and Fishelson, 1994; Bresler and Yanko 1995).

(8) Cell viability can be studied by using vital staining with AO or neutral red, fluorescent microscopy of their intralysomal, and microfluorometry (Bresler and Fishelson 1994; Bresler and Yanko, 1995b). This approach is often used in ecotoxicology to distinguish living and dead cells and tissues.

(9) Cell and tissue morphology and pathomorphology can be examined by using contact fluorescent microscopy and epi-microscopy to detect early signs of pathology, to identify the

type of pathology, and to identify specific target organelles, cells, and organs. In the field of ecology and ecotoxicology of aquatic animals, especially invertebrates, environmental pathology is clearly underdeveloped as compared with mammalian ecology and ecotoxicology (Hinton et al., 1992; Cotran et al., 1989; Wester and Vos, 1994). The field of foraminiferal pathology lags even farther behind. Contact epi-microscopy in incident light and contact fluorescent microscopy are promising tools for aqueous ecotoxicology (Bresler and Fishelson, 1994; Bresler and Yanko, 1994a,b, 1995a,b; Fishelson et al., 1996).

(10) Cytological indications of genotoxicity and clastogenicity, especially micronucleus tests employing contact fluorescent microscopy, contact epi-microscopy, or conventional microscopy are the most universally useful and sensitive methods for detecting environmental genotoxicity produced by chemical or physical factors (Fishelson et al., 1996).

13.4 CONCLUSIONS

An environmental event could be characteristically transient, resulting in varying rates of foraminiferal recovery that may range from rapid species-specific ecological opportunism to more delayed recovery and even to permanent local extinction. Even when an environmental insult is continuous rather than transient, some species may respond by showing a positive preference for the new conditions, others by showing varying levels of tolerance or intolerance. These kinds of behavior are reflected in shifting patterns of foraminiferal dominance and abundance that are not well understood – partly because the time scale of environmental insult is rarely well documented, partly because foraminiferal responses are often complex and nonlinear, and partly because biotic patterns often covary with natural and anthropogenic environmental gradients that can be difficult to distinguish. Although these questions are posed here in the specific context of foraminiferal response to pollutants, it is unavoidable that they will touch on more fundamental issues relating to the nature of opportunism, and the meaning of ecological specialization or generalization in other taxa. This is one area in which basic scientific research on Foraminifera is inseparable from the otherwise pragmatic issues of detection, monitoring, and remediation of pollution.

At the organismal level of analysis, we find that ecophenotypic responses among Foraminifera can range from test deformity to subtle changes in size and age distribution. Some of these responses are almost certainly pathological and species-specific, and some may be toxin specific as well. Some biological causes of morphological test deformity may be fundamentally genetic, or due to disruption of normal metabolic processes such as calcification, leading to weak, damage-prone test walls. Controlled laboratory experimentation and detailed cytological studies will certainly play a major role in resolving some of these questions.

Coal miners once used canaries to warn them of toxic atmospheric conditions; they did so without any understanding of the cellular biology of canaries. One might suppose that, as a purely practical expedient, we could take similar advantage of the Foraminifera as environmental indicators without understanding the underlying reasons for their ecological responses, but this is not the case. Foraminifera not only behave differently in different circumstances, but indicator species are rarely so obliging as to conveniently and consistently manifest themselves wherever they are needed to assist in our efforts at monitoring and detection of pollution. Thus, not only are species unique, but virtually every locality is unique as well, and generalization becomes difficult under the best of circumstances. For this reason, we are unlikely to identify species that have the simple, straightforward utility of the canary; instead, we will have to rely on a deeper understanding of biological and ecological processes if the Foraminifera are to achieve their full potential as environmental indicators.

13.5 ACKNOWLEDGMENTS

We thank the staff of the Laboratoire de Géologie and Laboratoire d'Etude des Bio-Indicat-

Acknowledgments

teurs Marins, University of Angers, France, for the use of their facilities during the preparation of the manuscript. We also thank Sophie Sanchez and Emmanuelle Geslin for preparing figures, and Emmanuelle Geslin for providing pictures of deformed Foraminifera. We sincerely thank Dr. J.-P. Debenay, University of Angers, France, and Dr. David Scott, Dalhousie University, Canada, for their constructive suggestions and comments during preparation of the manuscript. We thank especially Dr. V. Bresler, Tel Aviv University, Israel, for his many helpful contributions and insights. Dr. Pamela Hallock of the University of South Florida and an anonymous reviewer contributed very useful reviews. The University of Angers was very generous in providing V. Yanko with a one-month visiting professorship during the completion of the manuscript.

PART III: GEOCHEMISTRY OF SHELLS

14
Stable oxygen and carbon isotopes in foraminiferal carbonate shells

Eelco J. Rohling and Steve Cooke

14.1 INTRODUCTION

Analyses of stable oxygen and carbon isotopes from foraminiferal shells have played a pivotal role in paleoceanography since the pioneering efforts of Emiliani (1955) who, building on work of Urey (1947), McCrea (1950) and Epstein et al. (1953), interpreted the isotopic record from deep-sea cores as a proxy for a series of Pleistocene climate/temperature cycles. Cores from various locations in the Atlantic, Pacific and Indian Oceans provided isotopic records showing similar trends. Shackleton and Opdyke (1973) correlated the isotope stratigraphy with magnetic stratigraphy, dating 22 recognizable isotopic stages. Analyzing not only records for planktonic Foraminifera, but also for deep-sea benthic Foraminifera – which avoid the 'noise' imposed by short-term temperature and salinity fluctuations – Shackleton and Opdyke (1973) demonstrated that the $\delta^{18}O$ signal predominantly reflects fluctuations in global ice volume, while temperature plays a secondary role. This discovery started widespread use of $\delta^{18}O$ records in global stratigraphic correlations (e.g. Imbrie et al., 1984b, 1992). Turning attention to downcore $\delta^{13}C$ variations, Shackleton (1977a) showed their potential significance in studying water mass movement and paleoproductivity, and postulated a connection between climatically induced changes in the terrestrial biosphere with observed carbonate dissolution cycles and the flux of dissolved CO_2 in the oceans.

Detailed age control for $\delta^{18}O$ records around the world has been established by 'stacking' a great number of records in various ways to form a global curve for comparison with models of astronomically forced ice volume fluctuations (Imbrie et al., 1984b; Pisias et al., 1984; Prell et al., 1986; Martinson et al., 1987; Imbrie et al., 1992). Consequently, oxygen isotope stratigraphy has become not only a global correlation tool, but also an established dating tool (Fig. 14.1). In addition, the primary ice-volume control on (benthic) oxygen isotope records has led to their use in the approximation of past sea level variations after calibration with studies of other sea level indicators (e.g. Chappell and Shackleton, 1986; Shackleton, 1987; Bard et al., 1996; Linsley et al., 1996; Rohling et al., 1998).

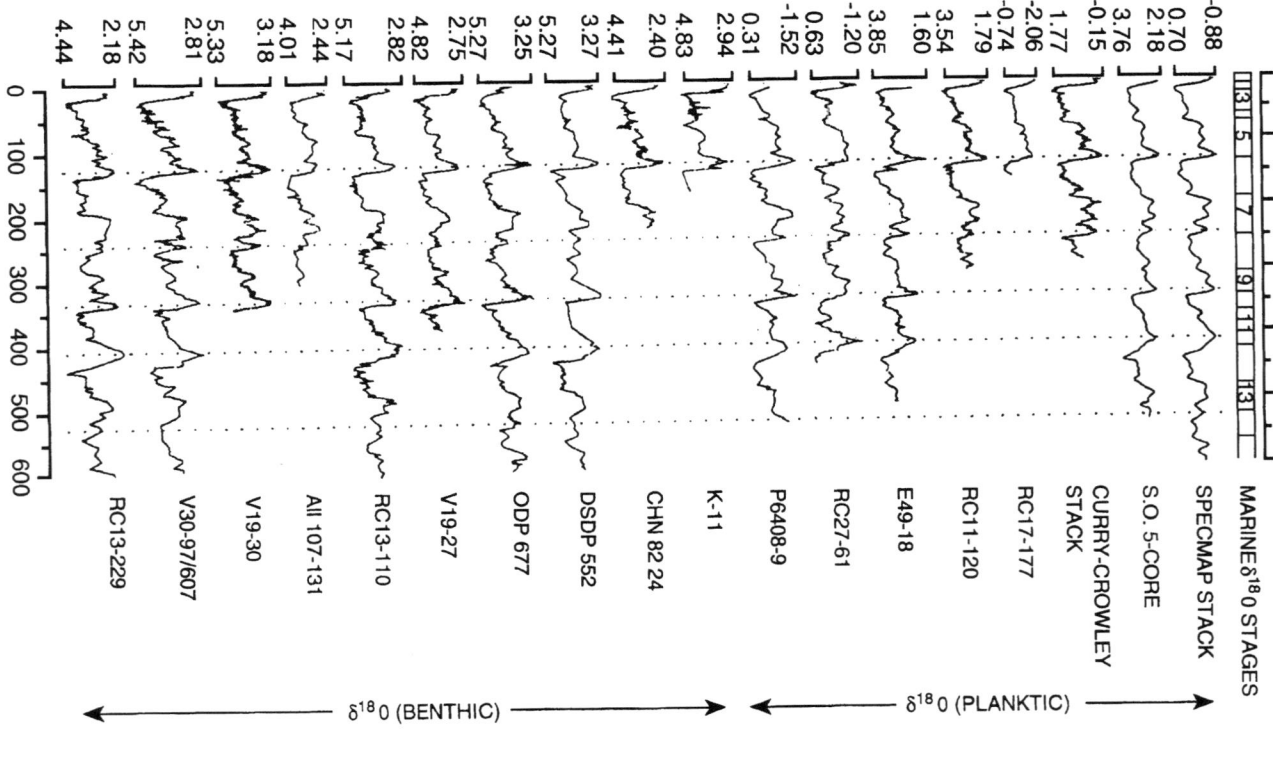

Figure 14.1 Overview of Quaternary oxygen isotope records from various locations, illustrating their potential in global correlation and dating through recognition of Marine Isotope Stages and a standard chronology (after Imbrie et al., 1992). For location map and further details about the cores, see Imbrie et al. (1992).

Introduction

There are three stable isotopes of oxygen: ^{16}O, ^{17}O, and ^{18}O, with relative natural abundances of 99.76%, 0.04%, and 0.20%, respectively. Research on oxygen isotopic ratios normally concerns $^{18}O/^{16}O$ ratios. There are two stable isotopes of carbon: ^{12}C (98.89%) and ^{13}C (1.11%). Basically, molecules consisting of light isotopes react more easily than those consisting of heavy isotopes. Partitioning of isotopes between substances is called fractionation. If R_A and R_B are the heavy/light ratios for any two isotopes (e.g. $^{18}O/^{16}O$) in exchanging chemical compounds A and B, then the fractionation factor is defined as $\alpha_{A-B} = R_A/R_B$. Fractionation mainly results from isotopic exchange reactions and kinetic effects. The former are also known as 'equilibrium isotope fractionation' processes and are essentially temperature dependent. Kinetic effects cause deviations from equilibrium due to different rates of reaction for the various isotopic species. Important kinetic effects are associated with diffusion. Detailed accounts on the physico-chemical behavior of isotopes, and on equilibrium and kinetic fractionation may be obtained from Craig et al. (1963), Craig and Gordon (1965), Ehhalt and Knott (1965), Merlivat (1978), Merlivat and Jouzel (1979), Garlick (1974), Stewart (1975), Gonfiantini (1986), Knox et al. (1992), Hoefs (1997), and references therein.

While absolute abundances of minor isotopes (such as ^{18}O and ^{13}C) cannot be determined accurately, it is still possible to get quantitative estimates by comparing results for a known external standard (*std*) with those for the unknown sample (*sam*). These differences in isotope ratios are defined as: $\delta_{sam}\,‰ = 10^3 \times (R_{sam} - R_{std})/R_{std}$. A positive δ value indicates enrichment in the heavy isotope, relative to the standard, and conversely, depletion is shown by a negative δ value.

Stable isotopes of oxygen and carbon in carbonates are analyzed by mass spectrometric determination of the mass ratios of carbon dioxide (CO_2) obtained from the sample by reaction of carbonate with phosphoric acid: $CaCO_3 + H_3PO_4 \rightleftharpoons CaHPO_4 + CO_2 + H_2O$ (see McCrea, 1950), with reference to a standard CO_2 of known isotopic composition. The standard for both oxygen and carbon in carbonates is referred to as PDB (Pee Dee Belemnite), having $\delta^{18}O = 0$ and $\delta^{13}C = 0$, by definition (Epstein et al., 1953). The PDB standard (no longer available) is a guard from *Belemnitella americana*, a Cretaceous belemnite from the Pee Dee Formation in North Carolina, U.S.A.

Various international standards have been run against PDB for comparative purposes. Two are commonly used and distributed by the National Institute of Standards and Technology (NIST) in Gaithersberg, Maryland, U.S.A., and the International Atomic Energy Agency (IAEA) in Vienna, Austria. They are: (a) NBS-18 (carbonatite), for the analysis of carbonates with $\delta^{13}C$ and $\delta^{18}O$ in per mil (‰) difference from Vienna Pee Dee Belemnite (VPDB) or Vienna Standard Mean Ocean Water (VSMOW) and (b) NBS-19 (limestone), for $\delta^{13}C$ and $\delta^{18}O$ analysis of carbonates, used to define the VPDB scale (Coplen, 1988; 1994). The isotopic compositions of these reference materials, as given by NIST (1992) are listed in Table 14.1. To convert VPDB to VSMOW, use $\delta^{18}O_{VSMOW} = 1.03092\, \delta^{18}O_{VPDB} + 30.92$ (NIST, 1992; also Coplen et al., 1983).

Some further corrections are needed. The Isotope Ratio Mass Spectrometer (IRMS) measures two ratios: mass $45/44$ ($=\delta 45$), and mass $46/44$ ($=\delta 46$). The final results required are $\delta^{13}C$ and $\delta^{18}O$ relative to VPDB, and a correction for the ^{17}O contribution is applied. A further complication results from fractionation between $\delta^{18}O$ in carbonate and in the CO_2 produced by reaction with phosphoric acid, which mainly depends on the temperature at which that reaction takes place. The analyzed $\delta^{18}O$ is corrected for this effect. The correction is determined by experiment to suit the technique used to gener-

Table 14.1 Isotopic compositions (in ‰) of reference materials (National Institute of Standards and Technology, 1992).

	$\delta^{13}C_{VPDB}$	$\delta^{18}O_{VPDB}$	$\delta^{18}O_{VSMOW}$
NBS-18	−5.04	−23.05	17.66
NBS-19	1.95	−2.20	28.65

ate CO_2. There is no similar fractionation effect on carbon (Swart et al., 1991).

Major contributions of $\delta^{18}O$ and $\delta^{13}C$ to paleoceanography in the applied sense are captured in Emiliani (1955), Shackleton and Opdyke (1973), Shackleton and Kennett (1975), Savin et al. (1975), Shackleton (1977a,b), Keigwin (1979), Savin et al. (1981), Duplessy et al. (1984), Imbrie et al. (1984b), Vergnaud-Grazzini (1985), Chappell and Shackleton (1986), Kennett (1986), Berger and Labeyrie (1987), Shackleton (1987), Woodruff and Savin (1989), Savin and Woodruff (1990), Imbrie et al. (1992), Zachos et al. (1994), and Sarnthein et al. (1995), and are reviewed in, for example, Haq (1984), Kennett (1982), Crowley and North (1991), Frakes et al. (1992), and Broecker (1995). We, instead, review the fundamental controls on foraminiferal carbonate. Several have only recently been discovered, and we aim to offer an overview, with pointers to the relevant specialist literature. Since isotope ratios in carbonates to a great extent reflect those in the ambient water, the following sections first evaluate the processes governing $\delta^{18}O$ and $\delta^{13}C$ in seawater, and then those causing fractionation during carbonate formation. To facilitate evaluation of the paleoceanographic value of $\delta^{18}O$ and $\delta^{13}C$, section 14.4 summarizes the various controls and highlights analytical strategies to minimize complications.

14.2 OXYGEN ISOTOPES

14.2.1 Oxygen isotope ratios in seawater

Seawater $\delta^{18}O$ is intimately linked with the hydrological cycle, consisting of evaporation, atmospheric vapor transport, and return of freshwater to the ocean via precipitation and runoff, or iceberg melting. Furthermore, long-term freshwater storage in aquifers and (especially) ice sheets significantly affects seawater $\delta^{18}O$ (Fig. 14.2). Seasonal sea ice formation and melting impose strong local variability. Finally, the spatial $\delta^{18}O$ distribution in the oceans depends on advection and mixing of water masses from different source regions.

14.2.1.1 Evaporation

Isotopic exchange at the sea-air interface is given by $H_2^{16}O_{liquid} + H_2^{18}O_{vapor} \rightleftharpoons H_2^{18}O_{liquid} + H_2^{16}O_{vapor}$. Because of higher vapor pressures, the lighter molecular species are preferentially enriched in the vapor phase. The fractionation factor for equilibrium exchange is $\alpha_{l-v} = [^{18}O/^{16}O]_l/[^{18}O/^{16}O]_v$. The most commonly used relationship between α_{l-v} and temperature is $\alpha_{l-v} = \exp\{(1.137T^{-2}) \times 10^3 - (0.4156T^{-1}) - 2.0667 \times 10^{-3}\}$, with T in Kelvin, illustrating a decrease in fractionation with increasing temperature (Majoube, 1971). The $\delta^{18}O$ difference between seawater and vapor then equals $10^3 \ln(\alpha)$‰, which at 20°C amounts to 9.8‰. The equilibrium enrichment factor ε equals $\alpha - 1$, and is reported as a ‰ value.

In addition, there is kinetic fractionation during molecular diffusion within the boundary layer between the water-air interface and the fully turbulent region where no further fractionation occurs (e.g. Craig and Gordon, 1965; Ehhalt and Knott, 1965; Stewart, 1975; Merlivat and Jouzel, 1979; Gonfiantini, 1986). The magnitude of kinetic enrichment depends on relative air humidity in the turbulent region, changing by about 0.7‰ for every 5% change in relative humidity (Gonfiantini, 1986), and to a lesser extent on roughness of the water-atmosphere interface, with a threshold around near-surface mean wind speeds of 7 m s^{-1} (Merlivat and Jouzel, 1979). In exceptional settings, this roughness threshold may have been persistently exceeded in the geological past (e.g. Rohling, 1994). Finally, the $\delta^{18}O$ of newly evaporated water also depends on that of the surface water, and of the vapor already present in the turbulent region of the atmosphere (full set of equations in Gonfiantini, 1986).

Preferential uptake of lighter isotopes during evaporation increases $\delta^{18}O$ values in the remaining surface waters. Because factors such as relative humidity are difficult to assess for the geological past, geological studies best consider

Oxygen isotopes

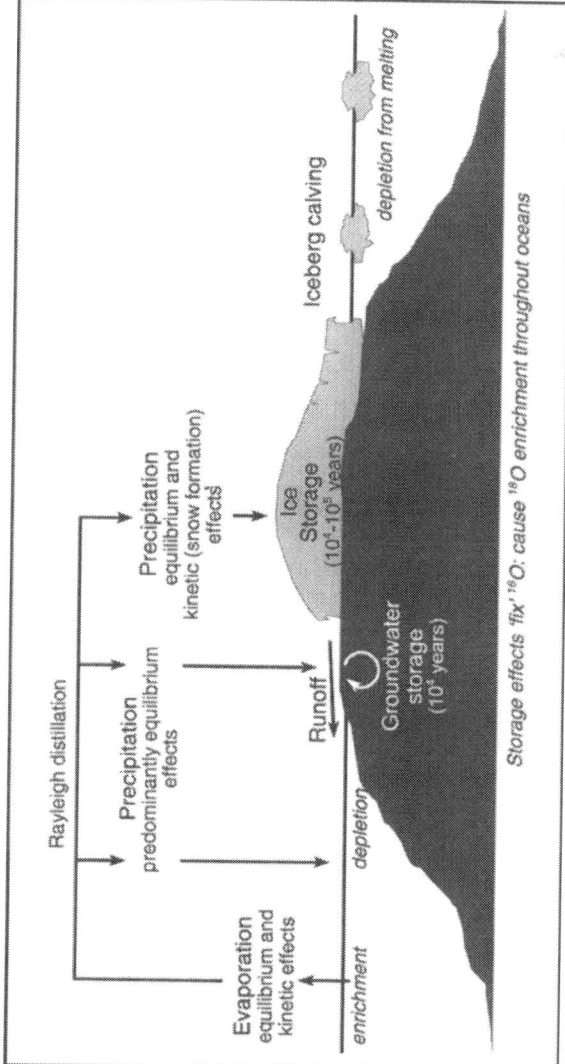

Figure 14.2 Schematic presentation of the influences of the hydrological cycle on oxygen isotope ratios. Effects on seawater are described in italics.

equilibrium fractionation and a constant value for kinetic fractionation, using likely ranges of change in kinetic fractionation to determine confidence intervals.

14.2.1.2 Precipitation and atmospheric vapor transport

Fractionation during condensation is basically the same as during evaporation, but acts in opposite sense. Normally, kinetic effects are negligible, so that droplets are near equilibrium with atmospheric vapor (Ehhalt and Knott, 1965; Stewart, 1975). The isotopic compositions of original vapor, precipitation, and remaining atmospheric vapor are related through basic Rayleigh distillation (Dansgaard, 1964; Garlick, 1974). Consequently, the first precipitation has a similar $\delta^{18}O$ to the original seawater, while longer pathways from the source region, with progressively more rain out, cause increasing depletion in vapor and associated new precipitation (Fig. 14.3). Successive condensations during transport towards colder regions cause a quasi-linear relationship of 0.69‰ °C^{-1} between $\delta^{18}O$ of precipitation and temperature (valid between −40 and +15°C). Consequently, high latitude precipitation is significantly more depleted than that in the tropics (reaching −60‰ or less in Antarctica; Lorius, 1983; Rozanski et al., 1993). Above +15°C, the so-called 'amount effect' dominates, with 1.5‰ depletion in the $\delta^{18}O$ of precipitation for every 100 mm increase in rainfall. For further reading, see Dansgaard (1964), Craig and Gordon (1965), Jouzel et al. (1975), Stewart (1975), Rozanski et al. (1982, 1993), Merlivat and Jouzel (1979), Joussaume and Jouzel (1993), Hoefs (1997), and Hoffmann and Heimann (1997).

Changes in $\delta^{18}O$ of precipitation affect oceanic surface waters through addition of the fresh water, either directly, or via run-off. Whereas arid areas show the evaporative surface water ^{18}O enrichment, regions in reasonable proximity to a river mouth are affected by the volumetrically weighted average isotopic composition of precipitation over the catchment basin. A high-latitude river imports freshwater with generally lower $\delta^{18}O$ values than a low-latitude river, e.g. Arctic McKenzie $\delta^{18}O \approx -20$‰, (pre-Aswan dam) Nile $\delta^{18}O \approx -2$‰, and Parana (Argen-

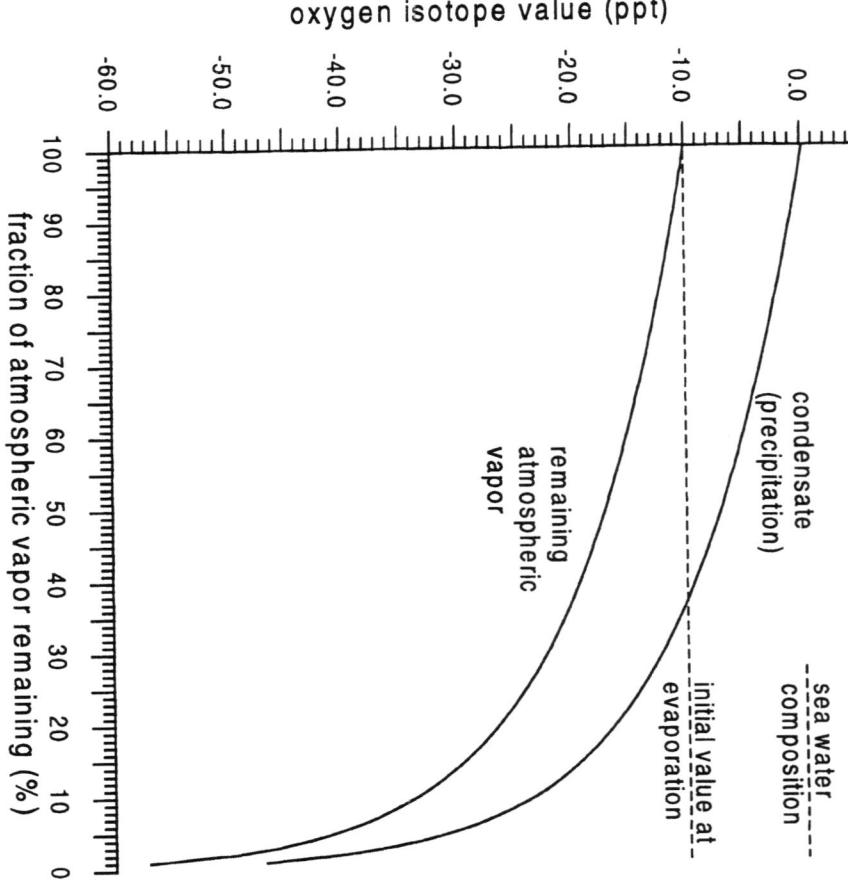

Figure 14.3 The relationships between isotope compositions of atmospheric vapor and precipitation, relative to evaporation, with an original composition of −10‰ and fractionation at constant temperature of 15°C.

tina) $\delta^{18}O \approx -4‰$ (overview in Rohling and Bigg, 1998).

Long-term storage of precipitation causes two main delayed responses. Icebergs calving from continental icesheets import continental freshwater with fossil isotopic signatures. Ice cores in the Greenland and Antarctic ice sheets include ice older than 100,000 years (Lorius et al., 1985; Taylor et al., 1993; Grootes et al., 1993; Jouzel et al., 1993) to even 400,000 years (Petit et al., 1997), so that the isotopic signatures of bergs from those icesheets should not be considered as a result of the modern freshwater cycle. Similarly, but less importantly, aquifers may accumulate waters as old as 35,000 years (e.g. Rozanski, 1985), and at later stages contribute to discharge.

14.2.1.3 Glacial ice-volume

Apart from delayed return of fossil signals to the ocean, long-term storage in glacial icesheets and, to a lesser extent, in major aquifers, also affect the global $\delta^{18}O$ budget. Because storage time-scales in the order of 10^4–10^5 years exceed those of ocean ventilation (in the order of 10^3 years), the storage effects influence $\delta^{18}O$ values equally in surface and deep waters.

The most important fluctuations are related to the volume of glacial ice sheets. These are built up by high latitude precipitation at very low temperatures towards the end of the Rayleigh distillation (Fig. 14.2), and so record extremely low $\delta^{18}O$ values (Fig. 14.3). Preferential sequestration of ^{16}O in ice sheets leaves the

Oxygen isotopes

oceans enriched in ^{18}O. At the same time, build up of ice volume lowers global sea level. Research on δ^{18}O changes in fossil carbonate, with accurate constraint of sea level variations from fossil coral reef studies, illustrates that the relationship between sea level lowering and mean oceanic δ^{18}O increase approximates $0.012 \pm 0.001\textperthousand$ m^{-1} (Aharon, 1983; Labeyrie et al., 1987; Shackleton, 1987; Fairbanks, 1989). Although this relationship provides a sound working model for well matured ice sheets, the processes behind it may invoke a more nonlinear relationship for growing or recently matured icesheets (see Mix and Ruddiman, 1984).

14.2.1.4 Sea ice freezing and melting

Newly formed sea ice is $2.57 \pm 0.10\textperthousand$ enriched relative to seawater δ^{18}O (Macdonald et al., 1995). This difference imposes a distinct seasonal fluctuation associated with ice formation and melting (cf. Strain and Tan, 1993). These seasonal influences do not necessarily cancel out in the long term, since increases in surface-water salinity due to sea ice formation may lead to convection and transport of existing surface waters into the ocean interior; the replacement waters likely were not affected as much by freezing processes (Rohling and Bigg, 1998). Large errors may arise in interpretations of oxygen isotopic change near (present or past) sea-ice margins when freezing/melting effects are overlooked.

14.2.1.5 Advection

Advection and mixing of water masses from different source areas are very important for the basic δ^{18}O composition at any site. Each source area concerns a basin or region, which may be very remote from the study site, where surface waters are imprinted with a certain δ^{18}O composition by the freshwater cycle, freezing/melting of sea ice, etc. This pre-set composition behaves as a virtually conservative property for the newly formed watermass, provided this watermass does not come into contact with further δ^{18}O sinks or sources. In practice, therefore, δ^{18}O is a useful conservative tracer for watermass transport and mixing in the subsurface ocean (e.g. Weiss et al., 1979; Fairbanks, 1982; Paren and Potter, 1984; Kipphut, 1990; Frew et al., 1995).

The δ^{18}O of a mixing endmember is a volumetrically weighted average of the δ^{18}O compositions of its components. Hence, any change in the relative proportions or isotopic compositions of the mixing components affects the basic endmember δ^{18}O. Changes in δ^{18}O at any site must, therefore, be viewed within the broader context of water mass formation and mixing on basin-wide scales, instead of being ascribed purely to local changes in surface forcing (e.g. freshwater budget). Emphasizing the importance of advection, Rohling and Bigg (1998) and Schmidt (1998) called for caution when interpreting past δ^{18}O variations; after the necessary correction for ice volume effect, surface forcing processes of both local (direct) and remote (through advection/mixing) origin need to be considered. This contrasts with the classical paleoceanographic interpretation that deals with local processes only.

14.2.2 Oxygen isotope ratios in foraminiferal carbonate

Equilibrium fractionations between water and the various carbonate species (CaCO$_3$, H$_2$CO$_3$, HCO$_3^-$, CO$_3^{2-}$) determine an important temperature influence on the δ^{18}O of foraminiferal carbonate. In addition, several processes cause deviations from equilibrium, both in planktonic Foraminifera (e.g. Shackleton et al., 1973; Fairbanks and Wiebe, 1980; Duplessy et al., 1981; Bouvier-Soumagnac and Duplessy, 1985) and in benthic Foraminifera (e.g. Duplessy et al., 1970; Woodruff et al., 1980; Vincent et al., 1981; Wefer and Berger, 1991).

14.2.2.1 Equilibrium fractionation.

The overall reaction for precipitation of carbonate is: $Ca^{2+} + 2HCO_3^- \rightleftharpoons CaCO_3 + CO_2 + H_2O$. Between 0 and 500°C, the equilibrium fractionation factor α_{c-w} between calcite and water changes according to $\alpha_{c-w} = \exp\{(2.78T^{-2} \times 10^3 - 3.39 \times 10^{-3}\}$, with T in Kelvin (O'Neil et al., 1969). Recently, Kim and O'Neil (1997) showed a more detailed relationship where the $\delta^{18}O$ change with temperature is more pronounced at low temperatures (up to 0.25‰ °C^{-1}) than at higher temperatures (around 0.2‰ °C^{-1}). The temperature dependence of fractionation fueled initiatives to develop 'isotopic paleothermometers' or 'paleotemperature equations' (e.g. Urey, 1947; McCrea, 1950; Epstein et al., 1953; O'Neil et al., 1969; Shackleton, 1974; Erez and Luz, 1983). A comprehensive summary, including new calibrations using data from cultured Foraminifera, was presented by Bemis et al. (1998).

Since temperature decreases with increasing depth in the surface ocean, vertical migrations influence equilibrium fractionation. Many planktonic foraminiferal species show a $\delta^{18}O$ increase with growth that suggests calcification in progressively deeper, colder, waters (among others, Emiliani, 1954; Berger, 1971; Emiliani, 1971; Berger et al., 1978; Fairbanks et al., 1982; Bouvier-Soumagnac and Duplessy, 1985; Kroon and Darling, 1995). There are, however, also suggestions that a species like *Globigerina bulloides* calcifies at depth as a juvenile and later migrates to shallower waters (Spero and Lea, 1996; Bemis et al., 1998).

14.2.2.2 Deviations from equilibrium $\delta^{18}O$ in foraminiferal calcite

14.2.2.2.1 Research is beginning to link $\delta^{18}O$ disequilibrium in foraminiferal shells to variations in seawater chemistry and depth-specific habitats, but the reports are largely descriptive. Five main causes of disequilibrium have been identified: the ontogenic effect; the symbiont photosynthesis effect; the respiration effect; the gametogenic calcite effect; and the effect of changes in $[CO_3^{2-}]$. The various effects may operate in opposite ways, masking one another. All are important for planktonic Foraminifera, but a great variety of deviations from equilibrium also exists in deep-sea benthic Foraminifera (e.g. Duplessy et al., 1970; Woodruff et al., 1980; Vincent et al., 1981; Wefer and Berger, 1991). Since these benthic species live in an environment with very stable low temperatures and a complete absence of photosynthetic activity, the disequilibria suggest an important role of microhabitat differentiation combined with pore water chemistry and food supply. The various effects are not strictly separate, and there may be considerable overlap between their regulating processes.

14.2.2.2.2 Ontogenic effect In laboratory experiments with constant $\delta^{18}O_{water}$ and temperature, *Globigerina bulloides* shows a progressive $\delta^{18}O$ increase of up to 0.8‰ with shell development; juvenile chambers are strongly depleted (around 1.15‰), while the final chamber is less depleted (around 0.30‰), relative to equilibrium (Spero and Lea, 1996). The mass-balanced average of the individual chambers gives a systematic whole-shell depletion of around 0.7‰. Since a similar trend of increasing values through ontogeny was observed in $\delta^{13}C$, an explanation was offered in terms of incorporation of metabolic (respired) CO_2 during calcification. Higher metabolic rates in juveniles would cause the strongest depletions, while adults gradually trend towards equilibrium.

The $\delta^{18}O$ trend is to some extent corroborated by reports of a size-dependent $\delta^{18}O$ trend in *G. bulloides* (e.g. Kroon and Darling, 1995), although the trend in those real-ocean results is a factor of two smaller than that observed under laboratory conditions. Spero and Lea (1996) found a similar difference when comparing laboratory results with data from fossil *G. bulloides* from Chatham Rise, speculating that the reduced signal was caused by vertical migrations from deeper/cooler waters during early stages to very shallow/warmer water during later stages (see also Bemis et al., 1998).

14.2.2.2.3 Symbiont photosynthesis In the photosynthetic symbiont-bearing planktonic foraminiferal species *Globigerinoides sacculifer*, Spero and Lea (1993) observed no variations in shell $\delta^{18}O$ with ontogeny within the size range 350–850 μm, supporting earlier conclusions that growth alone does not cause disequilibrium in this species (Erez and Luz, 1982, 1983; Wefer and Berger, 1991). However, a distinct chamber $\delta^{18}O$ decrease is seen with increasing irradiance levels (Spero and Lea, 1993). A similar but weaker decrease with increasing irradiance occurs in photosynthetic symbiont-bearing *Orbulina universa* (Spero, 1992; Spero and Lea, 1993; Spero et al., 1997). In addition, increased growth rates were observed with increasing light intensities, corroborating observations of light-enhanced calcification rates under elevated irradiance in photosynthetic symbiont-bearing corals (Chalker and Taylor, 1975) and larger Foraminifera (Ter Kuile and Erez, 1984). McConnaughey (1989a) and Wefer and Berger (1991) reported decreasing skeletal $\delta^{18}O$ values with increasing growth rates. The processes involved center around increasing kinetic discrimination against the heavy isotopes during CO_2 diffusion through the skeletal membrane, with rapid $CO_2 + H_2O \rightleftharpoons H_2CO_3$ reaction cycles (McConnaughey, 1989b; Spero and Lea, 1993).

14.2.2.2.4 Respiration

Studies on photosynthetic symbiont-bearing corals indicate that the process of photosynthesis *per se* invokes no appreciable fractionation effects for $\delta^{18}O$ (Swart, 1983). Respiration, on the contrary, does cause ^{18}O depletion (Lane and Doyle, 1956). Relative to ambient dissolved oxygen, the oxygen used in respiration is depleted by 21‰ in near-shore, shallow waters (Kroopnick, 1975) and 11‰ in the deep ocean (Grossman, 1987). The $\delta^{18}O$ of ambient dissolved oxygen in surface waters commonly ranges around +24 to +26‰ (SMOW) (Kroopnick et al., 1972; Kroopnick, 1975). In North Atlantic station Geosecs II, preferential respiratory ^{16}O utilization causes a marked $\delta^{18}O$ peak in dissolved oxygen (+31‰ SMOW) around 1000 m depth (Kroopnick et al., 1972). Utilization of depleted respiratory products during calcification (Belanger et al., 1981; Grossman, 1987) might cause skeletal ^{18}O depletion.

14.2.2.2.5 Gametogenic calcite

Several planktonic foraminiferal species deposit a veneer of calcite on the surface of their shell at the end of the life-cycle (Bé, 1980; Duplessy et al., 1981; Deuser, 1987; Spero and Lea, 1993; Bemis et al., 1998). *Globigerinoides sacculifer* secretes the additional calcite over a period of up to 16 hours before gamete release (Bé, 1980), and its gametogenic calcite layer comprises 18 to 28% of the shell mass (Bé, 1980; Duplessy et al., 1981) (around 26% in *Orbulina universa*, Bouvier-Soumagnac and Duplessy, 1985). Specimens covered by gametogenic calcite are called thick-walled. Gametogenic calcite is ^{18}O enriched relative to earlier (thin-walled) stages of the shell. These layers are, therefore, very important for whole-shell isotopic analyses.

Duplessy et al. (1981) speculated that the early stages of *G. sacculifer* are deposited at distinct disequilibrium in warm shallow waters, whereas the gametogenic layer is deposited in colder waters at depths of up to several hundreds of meters, possibly in near equilibrium. Bouvier-Soumagnac and Duplessy (1985) presented similar cases for *O. universa*, *Neogloboquadrina dutertrei*, and *Globorotalia menardii*. Kroon and Darling (1995) apply such arguments to reconstruct changes between last glacial maximum and Holocene vertical temperature gradients in the Arabian Sea and Panama Basin. Spero and Lea (1993), on the contrary, considered that vertical distribution studies of living planktonic Foraminifera do not support calcification at great depths, so that another, unidentified, mechanism should cause the ^{18}O enrichments in gametogenic calcite. However, in a subsequent study by these and other workers (Bemis et al., 1998), the calcification-at-depth hypothesis was invoked again, without further discussion. Clearly, the nature of the enrichment in gametogenic calcite is yet to be resolved.

14.2.2.2.6 Carbonate ion concentrations

Spero et al. (1997) subjected specimens of *Orbulina universa* to variations in $[CO_3^{2-}]$ at constant alkalinity, under both high and low irradiance conditions. They observed a constant $\delta^{18}O$ offset between the high and low irradiance experiments, while the ratio of change in shell $\delta^{18}O$ with change in $[CO_3^{2-}]$ remained similar for both groups. A second experiment with manipulation of $[CO_3^{2-}]$ by changes in alkalinity with constant ΣCO_2 corroborated the results of the first experiment. A third experiment concerned *Globigerina bulloides*, which bears no symbionts, and again a change was observed in shell $\delta^{18}O$ with $[CO_3^{2-}]$

variations. Spero et al. (1997), therefore, concluded that foraminiferal $\delta^{18}O$ decreases with increasing [CO_3^{2-}], that the magnitude of this response is species-specific, and that symbiont photosynthesis plays no role. These findings for biological carbonates endorse McCrea's (1950) observations on inorganic precipitates, suggesting a common, abiological, kinetic fractionation effect, which may be related to calcification rates and the pH dependent balance between CO_2 hydration and hydroxylation (McCrea, 1950; McConnaughey, 1989b; Usdowski and Hoefs, 1993; Spero et al., 1997; and references therein).

Bemis et al. (1998) re-evaluated data on the benthic Foraminifera *Uvigerina* and *Cibicidoides* and found that the epifaunal *Cibicidoides* precipitates its shell close to oxygen isotopic equilibrium with ambient seawater, while *Uvigerina* shows mild ^{18}O enrichment. Those authors speculated that this enrichment might result from a more infaunal habitat with low pore-water pH and decreased [CO_3^{2-}].

14.2.2.3 Aragonite versus calcite

Some benthic Foraminifera (e.g. *Hoeglundina elegans*) construct their test of aragonite rather than calcite. *H. elegans* is enriched relative to the equilibrium value for calcite by $0.78 \pm 0.19\%$ (Grossmann, 1984a). This agrees well with experimental observations that, at room temperature, inorganically precipitated aragonite is about 0.6‰ enriched relative to inorganically precipitated calcite, while theory suggests an enrichment of 0.79‰ (Tarutani et al., 1969). The temperature dependence of the aragonite-water fractionation is similar to that of the calcite-water fractionation (Grossman and Ku, 1986).

14.3 CARBON ISOTOPES

14.3.1 Carbon isotopes and the global carbon cycle

There are two main carbon reservoirs: organic matter and sedimentary carbonates. For comprehensive schematics of fluxes within the global carbon cycle, see Compton and Mallinson (1996), Mackenzie (1998), and references therein.

The organic carbon cycle revolves around CO_2 fixation into organic biomass through photosynthesis, in both the marine and the terrestrial biospheres: $CO_2 + H_2O + \text{energy (sunlight)} \rightarrow CH_2O + O_2$. Respiration under the presence of oxygen follows the reverse reaction. The organic carbon cycle acts on a wide range of time scales, from alteration between daytime photosynthesis and night-time respiration within plants to cycles in the order of 10^8 years, where organic carbon is stored in sediments, only to become exposed and oxidized much later.

Weathering of most ordinary types of exposed or uplifted rocks also draws down CO_2 from the atmosphere. Schematically representing the rocks as calcsilicates ($CaSiO_3$), the weathering reaction follows: $CaSiO_3 + CO_2 \rightarrow CaCO_3 + SiO_2$. The $CaCO_3$ dissociates in water, utilizing more CO_2 (see below). Long-term cycles of orogeny and weathering (of order 10^8 years), therefore, cause fluctuations of atmospheric CO_2 concentrations, which also equilibrate with total dissolved inorganic carbon in the oceans.

The inorganic carbon pool in the oceans is governed by the carbonate reactions. Most of the CO_2 in water is contained in HCO_3^- (the bicarbonate ion), due to $H_2O + CO_2 \rightleftharpoons H^+ + HCO_3^-$, while a further (weak) reaction may dissociate HCO_3^- according to $HCO_3^- \rightleftharpoons H^+ + CO_3^{2-}$. At normal seawater pH of 7.8–8.3, HCO_3^- dominates and there are only small amounts of CO_3^{2-}. Total dissolved inorganic carbon (DIC) consists of HCO_3^-, CO_3^{2-}, and dissolved CO_2. Calcium carbonate, biogenic and abiogenic, interacts with the inorganic carbon pool via the precipitation/dissolution equation $2HCO_3^- + Ca^{2+} \rightleftharpoons CaCO_3 + CO_2 + H_2O$.

The average $\delta^{13}C$ of the carbonate reservoir is around 0‰, while the organic carbon reservoir averages around −25‰ (Fig. 14.4; also Hoefs, 1997). Extremely depleted values are known from methane in the form of gas-hydrates within the continental slope, with typical values between −35‰ and −80‰. Seepage of gas-hydrates (clathrates) may cause consider-

Carbon isotopes

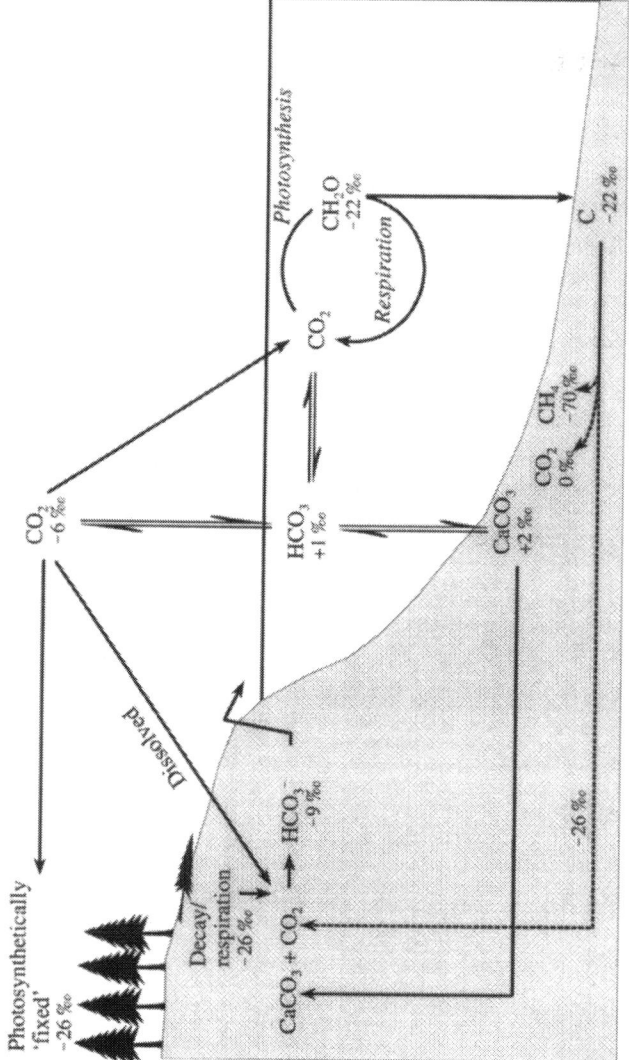

Figure 14.4 Main interactions between the terrestrial and marine organic and inorganic carbon cycles, with general mean carbon isotope values for the main phases (after Garlick, 1974). This diagram depicts these interactions in highly simplified form; no effort has been made to incorporate a correct stoichiometry. Values are only rough approximations. Double arrows indicate isotopic equilibration.

able $\delta^{13}C$ depletions in infaunal benthic Foraminifera (Wefer et al., 1994).

There is a clear distinction between the $\delta^{13}C$ depletions in terrestrial (−26‰) and marine organic matter (−22‰) (Fig. 14.4). Swart (1983) argued that dissolved CO_2 is the main carbon species involved in photosynthesis in the oceans, with HCO_3^- and CO_3^{2-} utilized only at lower efficiencies. Since dissolved CO_2 is strongly ^{13}C depleted relative to HCO_3^-, and not much different from gaseous CO_2 (Fig. 14.5), Swart proposed that the heavier $\delta^{13}C$ signature of marine algae stems from different CO_2 assimilation mechanisms in terrestrial and aquatic plants, and absence of translocation processes in the non-vascular algae. The ability to utilize HCO_3^-, however, was later found to differ between phytoplankton taxa, compromising Swart's arguments (e.g. Morel et al., 1994; Riebesell and Wolf-Gladrow, 1995).

14.3.2 Carbon isotopes in seawater.

14.3.2.1 Photosynthesis, respiration, export productivity, and surface-deep $\delta^{13}C$ gradients

Photosynthesis is strongly discriminative in favor of ^{12}C, and marine phytoplankton forms organic matter with $\delta^{13}C$ values of −20 to −23‰ relative to ambient water. Photosynthesis is restricted to the euphotic layer and due to the preferential uptake of ^{12}C during photosynthesis, the dissolved carbon in surface waters is relatively enriched in ^{13}C. Through equilibrations, this enrichment affects surface water HCO_3^- and the carbonates formed thereof (Fig. 14.6).

As organic matter is remineralized, its low $\delta^{13}C$ values are released into the water column, again equilibrating with HCO_3^- and so affecting carbonates. Where remineralization occurs within the mixed layer, this effect to some extent offsets the enrichment due to photosynthesis.

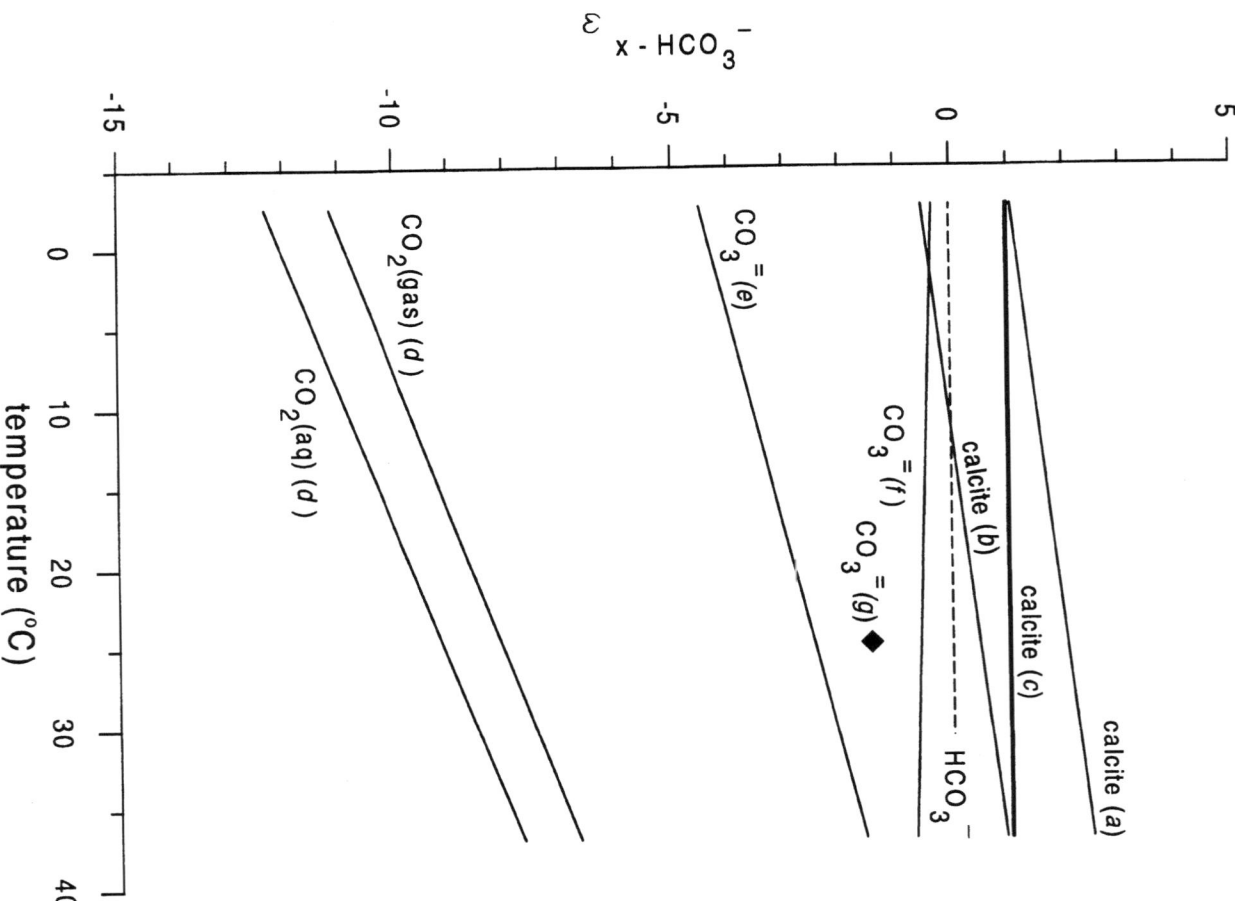

Figure 14.5 Temperature dependence of the carbon isotope enrichment factor ϵ (‰) relative to HCO_3^-. Sources: (a) Emrich et al. (1970); (b) Grossman (1984b); (c) Romanek et al. (1992); (d) Mook et al. (1974); (e) Swart (1983); (f) Freeman and Hayes (1992); (g) Turner (1982; at pH >9).

However, export production from the mixed layer constitutes a loss of ^{13}C depleted marine organic matter to deeper waters. Upon remineralization at depth, an effective transfer of ^{12}C has occurred from surface to deep water. Hence, increases in export productivity will enhance gradients between increased $\delta^{13}C$ in surface waters and decreased values in deep waters,

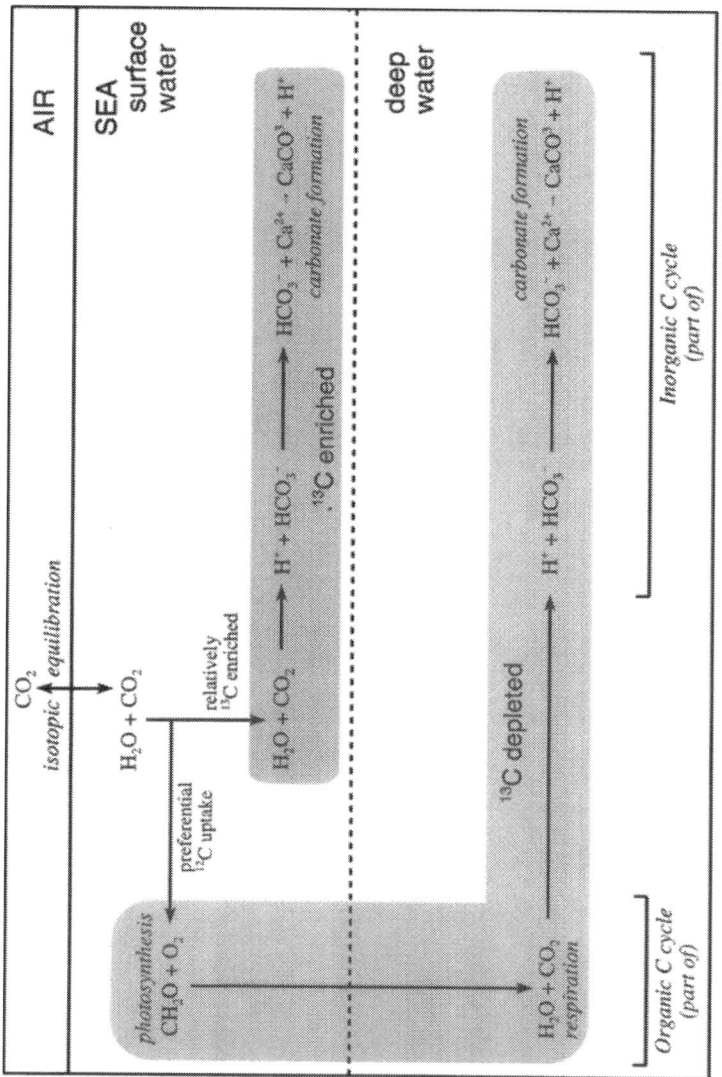

Figure 14.6 Schematic presentation of the generation of a carbon isotope gradient between the sea surface and deep water due to export production and interactions between the marine organic and inorganic carbon cycles. There was no effort to incorporate a correct stoichiometry.

which will be recorded in calcareous fossils (Figure 14.6).

Remineralization at depth releases not only ^{13}C depleted CO_2, but also nutrients, into deep water. Consequently, enhanced ^{13}C depletion in the present-day oceans correlates well with enhanced nutrient concentrations, where the expected relationship between $\delta^{13}C$ (in ‰) and phosphate concentrations (in µmol kg^{-1}) is -0.93‰ per µmol kg^{-1} (see Broeker, 1982; Broecker and Peng, 1982, pp. 308 and 309). There are similar relationships between $\delta^{13}C$ and nitrate concentrations (Ortiz et al., 1996). If sufficient validation is possible from independent evidence, this $\delta^{13}C$:nutrient correlation has great potential in paleoceanographic applications, as demonstrated by the applications of paired $\delta^{13}C$ and Cd/Ca analyses pioneered by Boyle and Keigwin (1982; 1985/86; 1987) and Boyle (1986).

Lateral gradients in deep water $\delta^{13}C$ may be used to trace the history of deep water from its source area. The deep water $\delta^{13}C$ reflects: (1) time of exposure to organic matter decay (true age); (2) the amount of organic matter decayed within the deep water (i.e. export production along its pathway); and (3) the rapidity of organic matter decay, which is temperature dependent (respiration rates roughly double for each 10°C temperature increase; Swart, 1983). This technique of deep water tracing is often called 'ageing' of deep water, where age obviously is just a relative concept. The age of deep water provides a powerful tool for reconstruction of ocean circulation. For example, the relatively high $\delta^{13}C$ values in the present-day deep North Atlantic ($+1.0$‰, with average surface waters at $+1.6$‰; Kroopnick et al., 1972) correctly identify it as a basin with active deep water formation and consequently young deep waters. Low North Pacific deep water $\delta^{13}C$ values ($-0.2‰$, with average surface waters at $+1.5$ to $+2.0‰$; Broecker and Peng, 1982; p. 308) successfully identify these waters as old, derived from remote source-regions. Lynch-Steiglitz and Fairbanks (1994) used Cd/Ca ratios to deconvolve $\delta^{13}C$ signals into a part related to the age of deep water (associated with nutrient enrichment) and a part related to the air-sea exchange defined in the deep water formation area (see Broecker and Maier-Reimer, 1992). Thus, likely glacial deep water source areas were identified that are very different from those of today.

Geographic shifts of deep water sources greatly affect the world ocean's surface-deep $\delta^{13}C$ gradients, which are low in actively overturning basins and high in non-overturning basins with old deep waters. Such ocean-wide patterns should, therefore, be established before past local/regional variability in surface-deep $\delta^{13}C$ gradients can be used to quantify export production.

14.3.2.2 Interactions with $\delta^{13}C$ of atmospheric CO_2

Interactions between $\delta^{13}C$ of atmospheric CO_2 and the marine reservoir (Fig. 14.6) depend on: (1) spatial variability in the equilibration between atmospheric CO_2 and dissolved inorganic carbon, and (2) geographically widespread temporal variability in the $\delta^{13}C$ of atmospheric CO_2. For atmospheric signals to be recorded in the marine reservoir, a signal of sufficient magnitude and duration is needed. Because the atmospheric CO_2 reservoir is orders of magnitude smaller than the marine reservoir, a recordable signal transmitted by the atmosphere should involve the terrestrial biosphere and/or lithosphere.

Differences in photosynthetic pathways cause C_3 plants to become much more $\delta^{13}C$ depleted than C_4 plants (Kelly et al., 1993). Cerling et al. (1993) argued that the late Miocene saw an increase in dominance of C_4 plants, which include many grasses, relative to C_3 plants, of which most trees are a subset (Leavitt, 1993).

This would have reduced the mean relative atmospheric ^{13}C enrichment caused by terrestrial plants. This signal, anchored in the terrestrial biosphere, was sufficiently strong and long-lived to help explain the late Miocene shift to lower $\delta^{13}C$ values in marine carbonates (Derry and France-Lanord, 1996). Because of its long-term characteristic, the signal affected surface and deep waters equally, in contrast with export production or deep water age fluctuations that influence gradients between surface and deep waters.

14.3.2.3 Carbon burial and global isotope shifts

14.3.2.3.1 Organic carbon
On the long term, the water column is in steady state, so that the particulate transport of ^{13}C depleted organic matter is matched by upwelling of nutrient-rich, ^{13}C depleted waters. However, some periods in geological history were characterized by higher than average organic matter preservation and removal from the system by inclusion in sediments. Such a situation not only constitutes a sink of carbon, so that eventually the atmospheric CO_2 concentration should drop, but simultaneously causes a residual ^{13}C enrichment throughout the oceans and atmosphere. This line of reasoning was developed to explain the 'carbon shift' associated with the widely documented Middle Miocene cooling (Vincent and Berger, 1985), where the appointed organic carbon sink was the deposition of the Monterey Formation of California.

14.3.2.3.2 Inorganic carbon
Weathering of the total sedimentary carbonate reservoir reflects its mean $\delta^{13}C$, which during the Neogene was very stable around $1.8 \pm 0.2‰$ (Derry and France-Lanord, 1996). The stability of this value allowed these authors to develop relatively straightforward isotopic balance equations to estimate the fractions of organic carbon in the total eroded carbon and in the total carbon burial flux. These relationships center around Δ_E, the mean isotopic difference between the sedimentary carbonate and organic carbon being eroded, and Δ_B, the mean isotopic differ-

ence between carbonates and organic carbon deposited at time t. If we use a rough approximation that $\Delta_E \approx \Delta_B$, the relationships indicate that the ratio between mean carbonate $\delta^{13}C$ and $\delta^{13}C$ of carbonate formed at time t depends mainly on the difference between the fractions of organic carbon eroded and buried at time t. This would imply that variations in the organic carbon pool drive global $\delta^{13}C$ fluctuations, while the inorganic carbon pool instead monitors or records the changes.

14.3.3 Carbon isotope ratios in foraminiferal carbonate

14.3.3.1 Equilibrium fractionation

14.3.3.1.1 Equilibrium between carbonate and dissolved inorganic carbon

Grossman (1984b) analyzed $\delta^{13}C$ for both calcitic and aragonitic (*Hoeglundina elegans*) benthic Foraminifera, evaluated the results against inorganic precipitates, and presented new equilibrium equations for aragonite and calcite. The isotopic enrichment factor for calcite (c) versus bicarbonate (b) was $\varepsilon_{c-b}(‰) = 10.51 - 2980T^{-1}$, with T in Kelvin. Grossman's (1984b) equation for calcite returns values about 1.5‰ lower than that of Emrich et al. (1970), which concerned a mixture of aragonite and calcite (see also Fig. 14.5). Romanek et al. (1992) reported a different, temperature independent, relationship between the $\delta^{13}C$ values of equilibrium carbonate and bicarbonate: $\delta^{13}C_{eqcarb} = \delta^{13}C_{HCO_3^-} + 1.0$. Aragonite shows a weak inverse relationship with temperature (Grossman, 1984b; Grossman and Ku, 1986; Wefer and Berger, 1991).

Often, carbonate $\delta^{13}C$ equilibrium is reported relative to the $\delta^{13}C$ of total dissolved inorganic carbon (i.e. the $\delta^{13}C$ of $\Sigma CO_2 = \delta^{13}C_{DIC}$), rather than relative to the $\delta^{13}C$ of bicarbonate. This is because the value for $\delta^{13}C_{DIC}$ can be either analytically determined (Kroopnick, 1974), or estimated from apparent oxygen utilization rates (Kroopnick, 1985), whereas the $\delta^{13}C$ of bicarbonate can only be obtained indirectly from calculations using $\delta^{13}C_{DIC} = (f\delta^{13}C)_{HCO_3^-} + (f\delta^{13}C)_{CO_3^{2-}} + (f\delta^{13}C)_{CO_2^{aq}}$, where f indicates the mole fraction per dissolved inorganic species. The mole fraction for CO_2^{aq} is very small at normal seawater pH of 7.8–8.3, so that $\delta^{13}C_{DIC}$ is only slightly (0.2 to 0.4‰) lower than $\delta^{13}C_{HCO_3^-}$ due to dominance of HCO_3^- over CO_3^{2-}. Information on pH and the concentrations of the various inorganic carbon species is essential for accurate evaluation of the equilibrium state of carbonate precipitation, which is not a trivial problem when sampling natural environments.

14.3.3.1.2 Apparent disequilibria: differential depth habitats or microhabitat effect

Changes in depth of calcification during growth and differences among preferred depths of different planktonic foraminiferal species may cause apparent $\delta^{13}C$ deviations from surface water equilibrium, because the gradient in $\delta^{13}C$ is steep between the surface and the thermocline (Kroopnick et al., 1972; Garlick, 1974; Kroopnick 1985; Tan, 1989). Hence, these calcification depth preferences must be taken into account before decisions are made on the degree of disequilibrium and its potential causes (e.g. Bouvier-Soumagnac and Duplessy, 1985; Wefer and Berger, 1991; Ravelo and Fairbanks, 1995; Ortiz et al., 1996). Since temperature drops in the oceans with increasing depth, there is also a strong $\delta^{18}O$ relationship with calcification depth (see section 14.2.2.1). Covariations between increasing $\delta^{18}O$ and decreasing $\delta^{13}C$ with growth in several planktonic Foraminifera suggest that calcification at later growth stages occurs well below the mixed layer (Bouvier-Soumagnac and Duplessy, 1985). Ravelo and Fairbanks (1995) assessed the potential of these covariations for reconstructions of past surface water hydrography, concluding that non-spinose species offer the greatest potential because they are less affected by biological fractionation effects.

Concerning benthic Foraminifera, the question of equilibrium should be viewed within the context of ambient pore water $\delta^{13}C$ at the species' preferred living depth or microhabitat (Woodruff et al., 1980; Belanger et al., 1981; Grossman, 1984a,b; 1987; McCorkle et al., 1985;

1990; Zahn et al., 1986; Wefer and Berger, 1991; Loubere et al., 1995). McCorkle et al. (1990) consistently found lower $\delta^{13}C$ values in deep dwelling taxa than in shallow dwelling taxa. Pore-water $\delta^{13}C$ gradients may reach 1‰ depletion per cm depth within sediment due to decomposition of sedimentary organic matter (Grossman, 1984a,b; McCorkle et al., 1985; Grossman, 1987). There are additional intraspecific controls on the depletions by the amount (Zahn et al., 1986; Loubere, 1987) and mechanisms (Loubere, 1987) of food supply within the sediment. The epibenthic species *Cibicides wuellerstorfi* (also described under *Cibicidoides*, *Planulina*, and *Fontbotia*) forms its test nearest to equilibrium and so provides the best measure for bottom water $\delta^{13}C_{DIC}$ variations through time (e.g. Woodruff et al., 1980; Graham et al., 1981; Zahn et al., 1986; Grossman, 1987; Wefer and Berger, 1991; Mackensen et al., 1993), but see Chapter 10 for possible complications.

14.3.3.2 Deviations from equilibrium $\delta^{13}C$ in foraminiferal carbonate

14.3.3.2.1
Foraminiferal $\delta^{13}C$ disequilibrium may be caused by: (1) utilization of metabolic CO_2 during shell formation, (2) photosynthetic activity of symbionts, (3) growth rate, and (4) variation in carbonate ion concentrations in ambient waters. The effects are not strictly separate; there may be strong overlaps between regulating processes. For detailed overviews, see Grossman (1987), Ravelo and Fairbanks (1995), Spero et al. (1991; 1997), and references therein.

14.3.3.2.2 Respiratory CO_2: 'vital' effects
Vital effects are reflected in the incorporation of isotopically light metabolic CO_2 into the carbonate skeleton (among others Keith and Weber, 1965; Weber and Woodhead, 1970; Vinot-Bertouille and Duplessy, 1973). The vital effect magnitude is proportional to the amount of metabolic CO_2 within the organism's internal CO_2 pool (Erez, 1978), which, in turn, reflects the organism's ability for gas-exchange with ambient water. Organisms from oxygen minimum zones around the world show the least influence of vital effects, suggesting that they are specially adapted for efficient gas-exchange (Leutenegger and Hansen, 1979; Grossman, 1984a, 1987).

Respired products are ^{18}O depleted relative to unused oxygen (section 14.2.2.4) while the food source (sedimentary organic matter) would cause likely ^{13}C depletions in metabolic CO_2 (see Lane and Doyle, 1956; Degens et al., 1968; Kroopnick, 1975; De Niro and Epstein, 1978). Hence, the incorporation of metabolic carbon-oxygen compounds should cause reductions of both skeletal $\delta^{18}O$ and $\delta^{13}C$. However, this expected relationship holds only to a limited extent (Grossman, 1987), and laboratory cultures show that large variations in $\delta^{13}C$ of food used by *Orbulina universa* and *Globigerina bulloides* cause only negligible shifts in shell $\delta^{13}C$ (Spero and Lea, 1993, 1996; see also Ortiz et al., 1996). Ortiz et al. (1996) concluded that the major cause for shell $\delta^{13}C$ fluctuations is not food $\delta^{13}C$, but metabolic rates controlled by temperature. This is supported by reduced $\delta^{13}C$ values in gastropod shells and corals due to enhanced metabolic activity associated with spawning (Wefer and Berger, 1991; Gagan et al., 1994). Photosynthetic symbiont-bearing larger Foraminifera also shift to very low $\delta^{13}C$ values in the reproductive period (Wefer and Berger, 1991).

14.3.3.2.3 Symbiont photosynthesis
A wide range of photosynthetic (symbiont bearing) organisms that precipitate calcium carbonate display increasing skeletal ^{13}C enrichment with increasing light intensity (McConnaughey, 1989a). Spero and Lea (1993) noted such a relationship in *Globigerinoides sacculifer*, ascribing it to elevated utilization of $^{12}CO_2$ by photosynthetic symbionts, which increases the calcifying microenvironment in $H^{13}CO_3^-$ and so produces ^{13}C enriched chambers. A similar relationship is known for *Orbulina universa*, although the relationship disappears when photosynthetic activity is prevented (Spero and Williams, 1988). At very low light

levels, δ^{13}C values of *G. sacculifer* shift slightly below equilibrium, suggesting that photosynthetic effects become suppressed and that some respired CO_2 gets incorporated into the shell (to a proportion of 0–3% of shell carbon; Spero and Lea, 1993). Similar values were observed for *O. universa* (Spero, 1992). Influences of light intensity or photosynthetic activity cannot be easily accounted for in data from Foraminifera grown in natural dark-light alternations, unless the proportions are known of the shell fractions deposited during dark and light periods (40 and 60%, respectively, for *O. universa*; Spero et al., 1991).

14.3.3.2.4 Changes with growth Romanek et al. (1992) found no significant δ^{13}C fractionations due to differences in calcification rates alone. However, most Foraminifera experience major physiological changes during growth. In *Globigerinella aequilateralis* and *Orbulina universa*, symbiont density increases with test size (Faber et al., 1985; Spero and Parker, 1985), which in turn increases total gross photosynthesis so that each new chamber shows increasing ^{13}C enrichment. An analysis of whole-shell δ^{13}C gives an integrated value of the masses and different δ^{13}C compositions of all individual chambers (Spero et al., 1991), and will therefore be different for the same species in different size-classes. However, progressive increases in δ^{18}O in *Orbulina universa* in the natural environment suggest migration to progressively deeper habitats with lower light intensity during growth, causing progressive ^{13}C depletion which may (partially) offset the enrichment due to increased symbiont density (Ravelo and Fairbanks, 1995).

In non-symbiont-bearing species, a change with size is expected in the depletion caused by contamination of shell δ^{13}C with metabolic or respiratory CO_2. Depletions should be strongest in small specimens from early life stages with high metabolic rates, decreasing towards equilibrium in adult stages (cf. Berger et al., 1978; Wefer and Berger, 1991). Bouvier-Soumagnac and Duplessy (1985) reported such trends for *Globorotalia menardii* and *Neogloboquadrina dutertrei*. Ravelo and Fairbanks (1995) confirmed the trend in *N. dutertrei*, but observed little to no size-dependent fractionation in *G. menardii*, *Globorotalia tumida*, *Globorotalia inflata*, *Globorotalia crassaformis*, *Globorotalia truncatulinoides*, or *Pulleniatina obliquiloculata*.

Deep-sea benthic Foraminifera show no significant change in skeletal δ^{13}C with size (Vincent et al., 1981; Dunbar and Wefer, 1984; Grossman, 1984; 1987; Wefer and Berger, 1991).

14.3.3.2.5 Carbonate ion concentration Similar to δ^{18}O, foraminiferal δ^{13}C decreases with increasing $[CO_3^{2-}]$. The signal magnitude is species-specific, and symbiont photosynthesis plays no role (Spero et al., 1997). These results combined with abiogenic data (McCrea, 1950) suggest a common, abiological, kinetic fractionation effect (cf. section 14.2.2.6).

14.3.3.3 Aragonite versus calcite

The aragonitic benthic foraminifer *Hoeglundina elegans* shows constant δ^{13}C values with depth in the California borderland study area, whereas $\delta^{13}C_{DIC}$ increases with depth (Grossman, 1984a). This may suggest a negative temperature dependence of bicarbonate-aragonite fractionation (also Grossman, 1984b; Grossman and Ku, 1986). To date, fractionations associated with aragonite formation remain poorly understood.

14.4 SUMMARY

Table 14.2 summarizes the main processes determining seawater δ^{18}O at any study site, and those determining fractionations between δ^{18}O of foraminiferal carbonate and of seawater, including typical magnitudes of the isotopic changes due to each effect. Table 14.3 is similar, but for δ^{13}C.

To investigate the main controlling processes and eliminate the noise introduced by minor ones, specific analytical strategies have been

Stable oxygen and carbon isotopes in foraminiferal carbonate shells

Table 14.2 Summary of the main processes determining seawater $\delta^{18}O$ at any study site (white) and those determining fractionations between $\delta^{18}O$ of carbonate and of seawater (shaded). Ticks indicate predominant influences on surface and/or deep waters, and planktonic and/or benthic Foraminifera. Last column lists typical magnitudes of isotopic change due to given effects.

Oxygen isotopes Process	Deep/Benthic	Surface/Planktonic	Impact and typical magnitude
evaporation: ice-volume effect	✓	✓	global; up to 2‰ (0.012‰ m^{-1} sea level change)
evaporation: 'normal' effect	✓(!)	✓	local; surface 1‰, (!) may affect deeper waters through mode water formation
precipitation		✓	local; 1‰
runoff		✓	local; >1‰ near river mouth or melting ice
sea ice freezing	✓(!)	✓	local; surface 1‰, (!) may affect deeper waters through mode water formation
sea ice melting		✓	local; 1‰
watermass transport and mixing	✓	✓	everywhere; magnitudes under investigation
equilibrium fractionation	✓	✓	everywhere, temperature dependent, 0.2‰ °C^{-1}
depth habitat/vertical migrations	✓	✓	1‰ depending on local temperature gradient
microhabitat effect	✓		1‰ depending on local gradient in pore-water
ontogenetic effects	?	✓	species specific <1‰
photosynthetic symbiont effect		✓	species (or specimen) specific <1‰
vital effect	✓	✓	(?) <1‰, not well known for Foraminifera
gametogenic calcite	✓	✓	species (?) specific (?) <1‰
changing carbonate ion concentration	✓	✓	<1‰, poorly known for natural conditions

adopted in paleoceanographic research. The vital effect is commonly considered to be species-specific, and avoided by study of monospecific records. The effects of symbiont density, gametogenic calcite formation, and changes in calcification depth during growth are avoided by analysing either thin-walled, or thick-walled, specimens of the selected species from similar ontogenic stages, using narrowly constrained size-fractions. No studies have yet established in sufficient detail the temporal changes in oceanic $[CO_3^{2-}]$ to allow assessment of their impact on foraminiferal isotope records.

The ice volume effect exerts by far the most important control on $\delta^{18}O$ records, allowing both global correlations and absolute dating (Figure 14.1). Also very important is the influence of ambient temperature during calcification. In a 'glacial world,' this influence is less relevant for deep-sea benthos, since oceanic deep-sea temperature fluctuations are unlikely to exceed 1 to 2°C. However, larger deep-sea temperature fluctuations may have prevailed in previous geological periods when the deep-sea was filled with so-called warm saline deep water, such as is found today in isolated basins like the Red Sea and the Mediterranean. For planktonic foraminiferal $\delta^{18}O$ records, temperature influences are always very important. Temperature effects may be constrained through the use of other paleotemperature indicators, such as transfer functions or geochemical proxies (e.g. alkenone records).

Secondary influences on benthic foraminiferal $\delta^{18}O$ records originate from the microhabitat and $[CO_3^{2-}]$ effects, which likely are related, but

Summary

Table 14.3 Summary of the main processes determining seawater $\delta^{13}C$ at any study site (white) and those determining fractionations between $\delta^{13}C$ of carbonate and of seawater (shaded). Ticks indicate predominant influences on surface and/or deep waters, and planktonic and/or benthic Foraminifera. Last column lists typical magnitudes of isotopic change due to given effects.

Carbon isotopes Process	Deep/Benthic	Surface/Planktonic	Impact and typical magnitude
photosynthesis		✓	global, but locally variable; < 1‰
respiration	✓	✓	local; < 1‰
export production	— causes gradients —		function of photosynthesis, respiration, 'age' of deep water
'age' of deep water	✓		along deep water path; up to > 1‰
shifts in terrestrial vegetation	✓	✓	global; > 1‰
burial/oxidation sedimentary organic matter	✓	✓	global; > 1‰
equilibrium fractionation	✓	✓	everywhere; < 1‰ to negligible (uncertain!)
depth habitat/vertical migrations	✓	✓	up to 1‰ depending on local temperature gradient
microhabitat effect	✓		1‰ or more depending on local gradient in pore-water (very strong near gas-hydrate seepage)
growth-related effects	✓ (some)	✓	species (or specimen?) specific <1‰
photosynthetic symbiont effect		✓	specimen specific <1‰
vital effect	✓	✓	species specific <1‰, not well known for Foraminifera
changing carbonate ion concentration	✓	✓	<1‰, poorly known for natural conditions

still are not fully understood or quantified. Away from sea-ice margins, secondary controls on planktonic $\delta^{18}O$ records are exerted by local freshwater cycle effects and $[CO_3^{2-}]$ variations. Temporal variations due to the $[CO_3^{2-}]$ effect are not yet sufficiently known. The assumption that, through time, a systematic relationship should exist between salinity and $\delta^{18}O$ due to action of the freshwater cycle has given rise to the term 'salinity effect.' Recent work is casting doubt on this assumption, and thus on the potential of oxygen isotopes in the determination of paleosalinity. Temporal changes in sub-surface water sources, advective pathways, and mixing of water masses appear to complicate interpretation of $\delta^{18}O$ records, especially for planktonic species.

For $\delta^{13}C$, the major controls are: global shifts related to changes in terrestrial vegetation and/or large-scale burial/oxidation of sedimentary organic matter, and the interrelated influences of export production, respiration at depth, and age of deep water. The global effects are established by inter-comparison of a large number of records from various worldwide locations. The effect of export production, etc., may be estimated from comparison of planktonic records with records for epiphytic benthic species known to calcify near equilibrium. This approach is most successful when paired with analyses of other nutrient proxies, such as Cd/Ca ratios. The age of deep water is assessed similarly, but in a wider geographical context.

Other influences on benthic foraminiferal $\delta^{13}C$ are due to the microhabitat effect, and the $[CO_3^{2-}]$ effect, which likely are related to one another. Seepage of clathrates may cause very strong anomalies in the $\delta^{13}C$ values of infaunal benthic species. Additional control on planktonic foraminiferal $\delta^{13}C$ records is exerted by $[CO_3^{2-}]$ fluctuations through time. This effect may be important, but is not yet well quantified.

14.5 ACKNOWLEDGMENTS

We thank David Lea, Paul Aharon, and Barun Sen Gupta for constructive reviews, comments, and suggestions, and Kate Davis for drawing services.

15

Trace elements in foraminiferal calcite

David W. Lea

15.1 INTRODUCTION

The trace element composition of calcitic foraminifer shells has become an important means by which paleoceanographers deduce past oceanic conditions. Pelagic foraminifer shells are composed of extremely pure calcite, typically about 99% by weight $CaCO_3$. Trace elements such as Mg, Sr, Ba and Cd comprise the remaining 1% and occur in calcite foraminifer shells at individual abundances of 0.25% or less. Trace elements are incorporated directly from seawater during shell precipitation. For this reason, shell composition reflects both seawater composition and the physical and biological conditions present during precipitation.

The idea that chemical signals encoded into skeletal carbonates could be used to assess past environmental and climatic information dates back to at least the early part of the twentieth century (Clarke and Wheeler, 1922). This idea did not come to fruition until decades later, however, when Harold Urey and his group at the University of Chicago were able to demonstrate the potential of oxygen isotope variations for paleothermometry (Epstein et al., 1953; Emiliani, 1955). The trace element component of climate proxy research has always lagged behind that of isotopic research. This might be due to the attitude prevalent in the Chicago school that trace element incorporation was not likely to be as systematic (S. Epstein, pers. comm., 1992).

The direct investigation of trace elements in foraminifer shells was hindered by the difficulty of trace element determination in the small samples typical of these shells. The first studies to show real potential were those of Michael Bender and his students at the University of Rhode Island, which focused on using shell Sr, Mg, and Na to establish Cenozoic ocean chemical histories (Bender et al., 1975; Graham et al., 1982). Arguably though, trace elements did not become an important paleoceanographic tool until Edward Boyle's pioneering studies at the Massachusetts Institute of Technology, in which he demonstrated that foraminiferal Cd could be used to assess past nutrient phosphate concentrations (Boyle, 1981; Boyle and Keigwin, 1982; Hester and Boyle, 1982). Boyle's research pushed foraminiferal trace element research into a new realm because Cd is a unique nutrient proxy that is integral to defining past ocean circulation changes (Boyle and Keigwin, 1982, 1985/1986, 1987). In addition, Boyle's findings set new standards of analysis for the extremely low levels of metals present and the care with which such determinations had to be made (Boyle, 1981). Trace elements in Foraminifera are no longer just a curiosity needed for chemical bookkeeping but have become a unique tool to understand the past. This paradigm shift drives trace element research today as we endeavor to refine our toolbox of elemental proxies while continuously pursuing new leads for proxy development.

We are currently in the midst of a revolution in the investigation of trace elements in Foraminifera, and our knowledge in this area is increasing rapidly. This is especially true for minor elements like Mg, which appears to have potential as a paleotemperature proxy. This flurry of activity is largely driven by improvements in analytical capabilities and an expansion in the number of laboratories undertaking such investigations. Culturing of live individuals has also played an important role in this proxy development, because the potential usefulness of trace elements can be verified directly by experimentation.

In this review, I focus on the abundance and application of four broad groups of trace elements incorporated in foraminifer shells:

(1) 'nutrient' proxies such as Cd and Ba, which provide information on seawater nutrient, carbon and carbonate levels;
(2) 'physical' proxies such as Mg, Sr, F, and B isotopes, which dominantly reflect physical parameters such as temperature and pressure;
(3) 'chemical' proxies such as Li, U, V, Sr, and Nd isotopes, which provide diverse information on the history of ocean chemistry; and
(4) 'diagenetic' proxies such as Mn, which reflect secondary post-depositional processes.

Naturally, there is some overlap among these broad groups, but the divisions are a helpful way to view the toolbox of elemental proxies available to the paleoceanographer.

15.2 TRACE ELEMENTS IN THE OCEAN

The diverse oceanic behavior and distribution of the trace elements are the key to utilizing elemental variation in foraminifer shells. Chemical oceanographers broadly group elemental behavior in the ocean according to the biogeochemical cycling of the elements in the ocean (Broecker and Peng, 1982; Bruland, 1983). These groups include: (1) nutrient-like elements, those that act as biological nutrients or mimic such behavior; (2) conservative elements, those that occur in fixed proportion to the major salts in seawater and are nearly unaffected by biological cycling, and (3) particle-reactive elements, those that are dominated by solid particle-seawater interactions.

Nutrient-like elements (Cd, Ba, Zn) show large and systematic variations in their seawater chemistry which result from involvement in biological cycling (Bruland, 1983). Minimum nutrient concentrations are found in oligotrophic surface waters due to algal removal of nutrients, whereas maximum concentrations are found in Pacific deep waters due to decomposition of nutrient-rich particulate matter. Deep water masses have unique trace element imprints due to variations in source waters and patterns of deep-water nutrient concentrations are found in North Atlantic bottom waters and maximum concentrations in Pacific bottom waters. Cd, which follows phosphate, has almost a thousand-fold concentration range in the oceans. Ba and Zn, which follow alkalinity and silicic acid respectively, vary by five to ten fold. The large modern ocean variation in these elements is expected to be reflected in the shell chemistry of Foraminifera calcifying in different hydrographic settings. The impact of physical and/or biological processes on calcification can also influence the presence of these elements in the foraminifer shells (Elderfield et al., 1996).

The ratio of conservative elements (Mg, Sr, B, Li, F, V, U) to Ca is nearly fixed in seawater, and among the three groups, conservative elements have the longest oceanic residence times. Only V and U are present in seawater at truly trace concentrations ($<10^{-6}$ mol/kg). Any variations in these elements in foraminifer shells found in modern samples must reflect the impact of physical and/or biological processes on calcification.

In shells from older sediments, variations in the abundance of a conservative element relative to Ca might also reflect changes in seawater chemistry, which responds to shifting oceanic source and sink patterns. Both Sr and B have important isotope systems which can be monitored using foraminifer shells (see below).

Particle reactive elements (Mn, Nd) are rapidly cycled and have typically short oceanic residence times They are less regularly distributed in the oceans, and can be enriched in the surface ocean by the dissolution of aeolian particles. Solid phase Mn is released in suboxic (little or no O_2 present) pore-waters by reduction to soluble Mn^{2+}, and this behavior leads to the deposition of Mn in or on foraminifer shells. Nd displays a strong isotopic variation in seawater because the isotopic composition of its sources varies between ocean basins.

15.3 INCORPORATION OF TRACE ELEMENTS IN FORAMINIFERAL CALCITE

15.3.1

The ideal situation from a geochemical point of view is that trace elements are incorporated homogeneously into calcite and regulated by strict physical (thermodynamic) laws. This ideal of pure thermodynamic control is an important concept, because it predicts regular, reproducible behavior for the incorporation of trace elements. There is abundant evidence, however, that the incorporation of trace elements in foraminiferal calcite does not take place in such an ideal, thermodynamic manner. Foraminifera, as living organisms, actively precipitate their shells, affecting both the structure and chemistry of shell calcite. Active precipitation argues for significant biological or kinetic (processes affected by the rate of reactions) controls on trace element substitution.

15.3.2 Thermodynamics of trace element incorporation

A primary goal in interpreting trace element compositions in precipitated minerals is to relate those concentrations to the composition and physical conditions at the time of precipitation. This is most commonly accomplished by the use of a constant that relates mineral composition to fluid composition. The relationship between shell calcite composition and seawater is best expressed by an *empirical partition coefficient D*, which is defined for the specific case of Foraminifera in seawater by the relationship:

$$[TE]/[Ca]_{foraminifer\ shell}$$
$$= D \times [TE]/[Ca^{2+}]_{seawater} \quad (1)$$

where the bracketed concentrations indicate the actual concentration ratios of trace element (TE) to Ca in calcite and seawater (Morse and Bender, 1990; Mucci and Morse, 1990). If D is greater than 1, the trace element is preferentially concentrated in the shell. If D is less than 1, the trace element is preferentially excluded from the shell. It is important to realize that the partition coefficient is not a thermodynamic property of the system, but rather represents an empirical measure of the trace element to calcium ratio in the shell relative to the same ratio in seawater for a specific set of physical and biological conditions.

The partition coefficient is distinct from the thermodynamic equilibrium or *distribution constant* (occasionally termed distribution coefficient) K, which can be derived from an exchange reaction:

$$CaCO_3 + TE^{2+} \Leftrightarrow TECO_3 + Ca^{2+} \quad (2)$$

The equilibrium constant for reaction (2) is defined by:

$$(a_{TECO_3}/a_{CaCO_3})_{calcite} = K \times (a_{TE^{2+}}/a_{Ca^{2+}})_{seawater} \quad (3)$$

where a is the activity of solid and solution phases. Activities, which represent thermodynamic or effective concentrations, are not easily measurable and do not relate in any necessarily simple way to bulk measured concentrations. Because the distribution constant K is an intrinsic thermodynamic property of the system, it can be calculated from the thermodynamic properties of the products and reactants. Given that there is no simple way to determine solid phase activities and that the empirical partition coefficient generally does not reflect thermodynamic equilibrium, the best practice is to determine the partition coefficient D by empirical means, and use the thermodynamic constant K as a point of comparison only.

The thermodynamic constant K will change with properties such as temperature if the solubility of the pure trace metal phase changes differentially relative to pure calcite. A documented example of this is the solid solution of $SrCO_3$ in aragonite, for which the solubility of $SrCO_3$ increases to a greater extent with rising temperature than for aragonite, leading to progressively lower Sr/Ca (less solid $SrCO_3$) at higher temperatures. This thermodynamic relationship is exploited as a paleotemperature tool in corals (Beck et al., 1992). The extent to which D will change with environmental parameters is dependent on both thermodynamic and kinetic (biological) factors. Any parameter that changes the rate of calcification also has the potential to change D (Lorens, 1981), although it is not easy to predict the potential magnitude of such changes in biological systems. For example, calcification rate increases with rising pH, which increases the incorporation of Sr in calcite (Morse and Bender, 1990). One of the challenges faced by researchers is sorting out the extent to which thermodynamic and kinetic influences determine the dependence of trace elements such as Mg on temperature. True thermodynamic dependence, such as is observed for oxygen isotopes, is most likely to lead to robust proxies that will not be undermined by unpredictable kinetic influences.

There are two general mechanisms for trace element incorporation in foraminiferal calcite: direct solid solution, in which the trace element substitutes directly for Ca^{2+} in the calcite structure, and trapping, in which the trace element occurs as a discrete phase or absorbed ion (Pingitore, 1986). Substitution by isomorphous solid solution undoubtedly provides the more robust mechanism for trace element incorporation, because it is most likely to be primarily regulated by thermodynamics. Trace elements with ionic radii compatible with the Ca^{2+} site and chemical structures isomorphous with calcite are most likely to exhibit regular ionic substitution into foraminifer shells (Reeder, 1983) (Table 15.1). Trace element occurrence by trapping is far less likely to lead to homogeneous mineral composition, and trapping is more likely to be affected by kinetic factors such as precipitation rate. It must also be recognized that some trace elements might be incorporated by a combination of factors, in which case the element might be uniformly distributed by solid solution but also concentrated preferentially in some parts of the crystal by trapping.

15.3.3 Biology of trace element incorporation and role of live culturing

Foraminifera are living organisms, and, therefore their biology influences the precipitation of shell calcite. Geochemists have termed this the 'vital effect,' a term that generally encompasses the sum of biological influences without attempting to unravel their causes. Comparison of empirical partition coefficients (D) with predicted thermodynamic distribution constants (K) indicates that the biology of calcification offsets foraminifer shells from equilibrium values (Elderfield et al., 1996). Shell calcification is relatively rapid, variable in time, and influenced by external factors, all of which contribute to non-equilibrium precipitation (Lea et al., 1995).

Empirical partition coefficients are most commonly determined by calibrating foraminiferal shell chemistry from core-top sediments with estimates of seawater chemistry and physical conditions (Hester and Boyle, 1982; Lea and Boyle, 1989; Boyle, 1992; Rosenthal et al., 1997b). These calibrations implicitly include all vital effects, as well as any possible post-depositional factors. Core-top calibrations, however, cannot be used to separate and attribute individual biological influences or determine how vital effects might vary spatially, especially through the secondary influence of oceanographic parameters.

Live culturing is an important means by

263

Incorporation of trace elements in foraminiferal calcite

Table 15.1 Trace element abundance in foraminiferal calcite. The values quoted for planktonic and benthic Foraminifera are the normal observed ranges of shell abundances. The values quoted for seawater concentration are the normal observed ranges of total element concentration in the pelagic surface and deep ocean. The partition coefficient is the ratio of metal/Ca in the foraminifer shell to metal/Ca in seawater. Proxy indicates the mostly closely allied seawater property for each trace element. Ionic radii from Shannon (1976), crystal structures from Speer (1983). Calcite is rhombohedral, aragonite is orthorhombic. Foraminiferal data and partition coefficients from sources cited in text. Seawater data from Bruland (1983).

Element	Ion in calcite	Ionic radius (Å)	Crystal structure	Planktonic (mol/mol Ca)	Benthic (mol/mol Ca)	Seawater concentration (mol/kg)	Partition coefficient D	Proxy
Calcium	Ca^{2+}	1.00	rhombohedral	—	—	10.3×10^{-3}		
Carbon	CO_3^{2-}	2.50	rhombohedral	—	—	$2-2.5 \times 10^{-3}$		
Magnesium	Mg^{2+}	0.72	rhombohedral	$0.5-5 \times 10^{-3}$	$0.5-10 \times 10^{-3}$	53.2×10^{-3}	$0.1-1 \times 10^{-3}$	temperature
Sodium	Na^+	1.02		$4-7 \times 10^{-3}$ (neritic = 0.13–0.15)		468×10^{-3}	10×10^{-6}	?
Strontium	Sr^{2+}	1.31	orthorhombic	$1.2-1.6 \times 10^{-3}$	$0.9-1.6 \times 10^{-3}$ (neritic = $2-2.4 \times 10^{-3}$)	90×10^{-6}	$0.11-0.19$	seawater chemistry, pressure?
Fluorine	F^-	1.33		$0.5-3 \times 10^{-3}$	$0.3-4 \times 10^{-3}$	68×10^{-6}		
Boron	$B(OH)_4^-$			60×10^{-6}	60×10^{-6}	0.416×10^{-3}		pH
Lithium	Li^+	0.76		$10-30 \times 10^{-6}$	$10-75 \times 10^{-6}$	25×10^{-6}	0.01	seawater chemistry
Manganese	Mn^{2+}	0.83	rhombohedral	$1-500 \times 10^{-6}$	$1-100 \times 10^{-6}$	$0.2-3 \times 10^{-9}$	2?	diagenesis
Zinc	Zn^{2+}	0.74	rhombohedral	$1.5-6 \times 10^{-6}$		$0.05-9.0 \times 10^{-9}$		silicic acid
Barium	Ba^{2+}	1.47	orthorhombic	$0.5-2(10) \times 10^{-6}$	$1.5-5 \times 10^{-6}$	$32-150 \times 10^{-9}$	$0.15-0.4$	alkalinity
Iron	$Fe^{2+}+?$	0.78	rhombohedral	$<0.1 \times 10^{-6}$	$<0.1 \times 10^{-6}$	$0-2.5 \times 10^{-9}$		diagenesis?
Copper	Cu^{2+}	0.73	rhombohedral	$<0.1 \times 10^{-6}$	$<0.2 \times 10^{-6}$	$0.5-6 \times 10^{-9}$		nutrient
Neodymium	Nd^{3+}	0.98	orthorhombic	$<0.1 \times 10^{-6}$		$5-35 \times 10^{-12}$	<100	seawater chemistry
Cadmium	Cd^{2+}	0.95	rhombohedral	$0.002-0.1 \times 10^{-6}$	$0.02-0.25 \times 10^{-6}$	$0.001-1.1 \times 10^{-9}$	$1.3-3.0$	phosphate
Vanadium	HVO_4^{2-}			$20-40 \times 10^{-9}$	112×10^{-9}	$20-35 \times 10^{-9}$	$2-32 \times 10^{-3}$	seawater chemistry
Uranium	UO_2^{2+}	3.46	orthorhombic?	$5-10 \times 10^{-9}$		13.6×10^{-9}	$7-8 \times 10^{-3}$	seawater chemistry

which such biological effects can be unraveled. For example, factors that are known to influence Foraminifera, such as light (via its influence on symbiotic dinoflagellates), temperature, salinity, and pH, can be varied systematically by experimentation. Since the early 1980s, live culturing of Foraminifera has become an important tool to assess trace element incorporation in shells. Culturing offers the advantage of direct experimentation, which removes much of the ambiguity associated with calibration by indirect means. To date most culturing studies have focused on spinose planktonic Foraminifera, but some activity has been directed towards culturing benthic species and non-spinose planktonic species (Bé et al., 1977a; Hemleben et al., 1989; Chandler et al., 1996).

Pioneering studies conducted by Peggy Delaney and Allan Bé assessed Cd, Mg, Sr, Na, and Li incorporation in tropical spinose Foraminifera (Delaney et al., 1985; Delaney, 1989). Subsequently, different research groups have investigated Ba, Cd, B, and Ca uptake (Lea and Spero, 1992; Lea and Spero, 1994; Lea et al., 1995; Sanyal et al., 1996; Mashiotta et al., 1997), U and V uptake (Russell et al., 1994; Hastings et al., 1996b), and Mg uptake (Nürnberg et al., 1996; Mashiotta et al., in press). Culturing studies are beginning to reveal the detailed biological influences on trace element uptake. One example of such an influence is the observation that symbiotic dinoflagellates sequester Cd, thus reducing the Cd content of shell calcite (Mashiotta et al., 1997).

15.4 SAMPLE PREPARATION AND ANALYTICAL TECHNIQUES

Many of the trace elements determined in foraminifer shells are in very low abundances, and the presence of extraneous phases which contain high trace element levels can obscure the determination of the primary material. It is therefore necessary to purify the foraminifer shells by both physical and chemical steps. Rigorous purification procedures were developed by Edward Boyle to determine the very low levels of Cd in shells (Boyle, 1981; Boyle and Keigwin, 1985/1986). These consist of alternate steps of physical agitation to remove detrital grains and chemical treatment, including oxidation of organic matter, reduction of Fe and Mn oxides, and acid leaching of adsorbed ions. Boyle's purification techniques, with various degrees of modification depending on individual circumstances for each element, are the accepted standard for preparing foraminifer shells for trace element determination. Modifications of this purification cleaning method have been made for foraminiferal Ba (Lea and Boyle, 1993) and improved Cd determination (Rosenthal et al., 1997a).

Given the range of trace elements determined in foraminifer shells, it is not surprising that there are a number of methods used to make measurements. Because trace elements have been routinely determined in foraminifer shells only since about 1980, the analytical techniques are less standardized than for stable isotope determinations. Among the predominant analytical techniques are:

Atomic Absorption Spectrophotometry (AAS): AAS has been used to determine Ca, Mg, Na, Sr, Li, Mn, Cd, and Zn in foraminifer shells (Boyle, 1981; Delaney et al., 1985). AAS relies on the unique atomic absorption spectra of each element; trace element abundances are quantified by comparing the absorption of a sample to that of a known standard. Graphite furnace AAS (GFAAS) is an extremely sensitive technique which is used to determine the very low levels of Cd and Zn in foraminifer shells.

Inductively Coupled Plasma Mass Spectrometry (ICP-MS): ICP-MS has been used to determine Ca, Mg, Sr, Mn, Ba, Cd, U, and V in foraminifer shells (Lea and Boyle, 1993; Russell et al., 1994; Hastings et al., 1996b; Lea and Martin, 1996; Rosenthal et al., 1997b). ICP-MS uses a quadrupole or magnet to directly differentiate the masses of individual isotopes ionized in a plasma. Trace element abundances are quantified by either isotope dilution, internal standardization, and/or reference to gravimetric standards. ICP-MS is comparable in sensitivity to GFAAS but offers the advantage of simultaneous determination of elements.

Nutrient proxies: Cd and Ba

Thermal Ionization Mass Spectrometry (TIMS): TIMS has been used to determine Sr, Sr isotopes, B, B isotopes, Ba, U, and V (DePaolo and Ingram, 1985; Russell et al., 1994; Hastings et al., 1996b; Sanyal et al., 1996). TIMS uses a magnet to differentiate the masses of individual isotopes ionized from a solid filament. Trace element abundances are quantified by isotope dilution; isotope ratios are quantified by reference to standards with known ratios. TIMS is a relatively slow technique but offers superior precision by a factor of 10–1000 over ICP-MS and AAS.

A technique likely to become important in the near future is *High Resolution Multi-Collector ICP-MS*. This technique combines the precision of TIMS with the rapid throughput of ICP-MS (Halliday et al., 1998). It is likely that in the future, geochemists will be able to determine both low level trace elements such as Cd and high precision isotope ratios such as $^{87/86}$Sr by this technique.

15.5 ABUNDANCE OF TRACE ELEMENTS IN FORAMINIFERAL CALCITE

Abundances of trace elements in Foraminifera are commonly presented in molar units (mol element per mol Ca) or sometimes in weight units (usually ppm, which denotes μg of the trace element per g of calcite). Molar units are preferable because they can be directly related to elemental ratios in seawater. To convert between units, use the following equation:

ppm = mol element/mol Ca
 × atomic weight/100 g

example:

0.1 μmol Cd/mol × 112.411 g Cd/mol/100 g

= 0.112 ppm = 112 ppb

Fifteen trace elements have been sufficiently documented so that their actual presence in shell calcite (as opposed to in extraneous phases such as organic compounds, oxides, or clays) is rea-

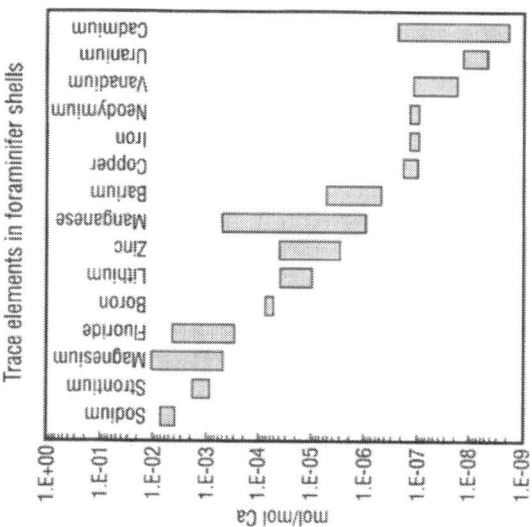

Figure 15.1 Trace element abundances in foraminifer shells in moles of element per mole Ca. The ranges are the minimum and maximum observed concentrations (Table 15.1). Data sources are listed in the text.

sonably certain (Table 15.1; Fig. 15.1). Four elements, Mg, Na, Sr, and F, are present at abundances of greater than 10^{-3} mol/mol Ca. Because these elements occur at levels of up to 0.25% by weight, they are often termed *minor elements*. Five of the trace elements, B, Li, Mn, Zn, and Ba are present at abundances between 10^{-3} and 10^{-6} mol/mol. The remaining six trace elements, Fe, Cu, Nd, Cd, V, and U are present at abundances between 10^{-6} and 10^{-9} mol/mol. The metals Mg, Sr, Mn, Zn, Ba, Fe, Nd, and Cd are known to form solid solutions isomorphous with either calcite or aragonite (Table 15.1) (Speer, 1983). Therefore these metals are most likely to be directly interpretable in terms of their chemical behavior in shells.

15.6 NUTRIENT PROXIES: Cd AND Ba

15.6.1

The most developed and well understood trace element proxies are those used to assess past nutrient concentrations, mainly Cd and Ba. Understanding the concentration and distribution of nutrients and carbon in ancient oceans is a prime problem in paleoceanography (Boyle, 1990). Using planktonic and benthic Foraminifera, nutrient proxies can be used to reconstruct nutrient and carbon chemistry in surface and deep waters. Levels of surface water nutrients are directly linked to the cycle of carbon dioxide and oceanic productivity by Redfield ratios (Broecker and Peng, 1993). Because the distribution of nutrients in the deep ocean is a direct reflection of the thermohaline flow of abyssal waters, deep-water nutrient distributions can in turn be used to deconvolute water mass mixing or to fingerprint source waters.

15.6.2 Cadmium

The oceanic behavior of Cd closely mimics that of phosphate in the water column, and Cd is the most direct nutrient analog available (Fig. 15.2a) (Boyle, 1976, 1988a). Cd also forms a solid solution with calcite, and therefore, Cd is expected to exhibit systematic behavior when incorporated into shells. Cd occurs at very low concentrations in the oceans, ranging from

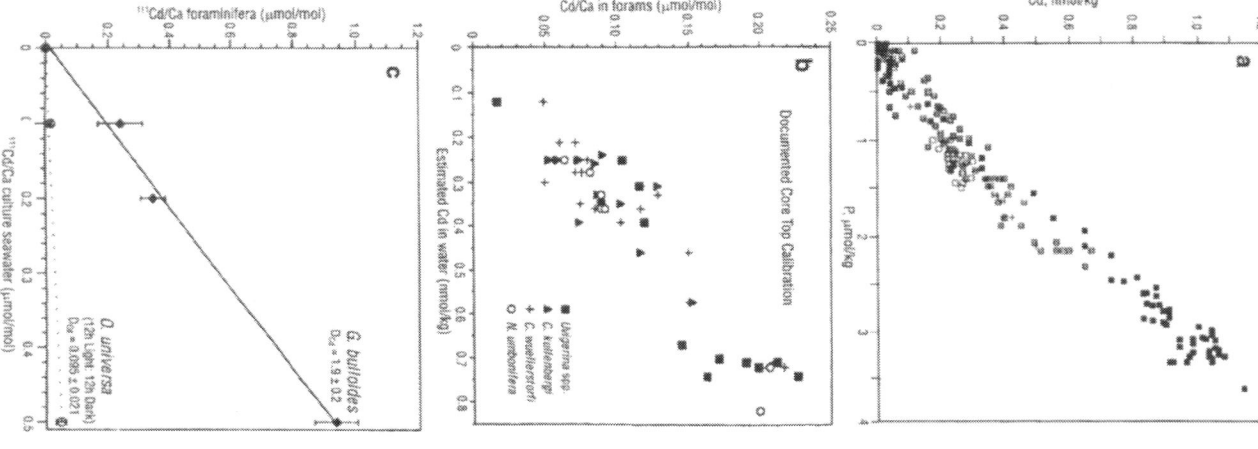

Figure 15.2 Foraminiferal Cd as a paleoceanographic proxy. (a) The correlation between Cd and phosphate, a primary limiting nutrient, in present-day seawater (Boyle, 1988a). The most nutrient-depleted oceanic surface waters are similarly low in Cd and P; the most nutrient-rich Pacific deep waters are similarly enriched in Cd and P. Reprinted from Boyle, 1988a. (b) Core-top calibration of Cd in benthic Foraminifera versus estimated bottom water Cd concentrations (from Boyle, 1988a). Species plotted include *Uvigerina* spp., *Cibicidoides kullenbergi*, *Nuttallides umbonifera*, and *Cibicides wuellerstorfi*. The data demonstrate that the benthic foraminifer shells take up Cd with a partition coefficient of 2.9 ± 0.6, and that there are no significant differences in Cd uptake among species. (c) Culturing calibration of Cd uptake in the planktonic species *Globigerina bulloides* and *Orbulina universa* (Mashiotta et al., 1997). Foraminifera were cultured in seawater enriched with the rare stable isotope ^{111}Cd. The results demonstrate that the shells of symbiont-barren *G. bulloides* take up Cd with a partition coefficient of 1.9 ± 0.2, similar to benthic species. In contrast, symbiont-bearing *O. universa* incorporates very little Cd in shells ($D = 0.095 ± 0.021$), presumably because the symbiotic algae deplete the calcifying environment of Cd. Reprinted from *Geochimica et Cosmochimica Acta*, 61, Mashiotta, T.A. et al., Experimental determination of Cd uptake in shells of the planktonic foraminifers *Orbulina universa* and *Globigerina bulloides*: Implications for surface water paleoreconstructions, 4053–4065, Copyright 1997, with permission from Elsevier Science.

10^{-12} mol/kg in the most nutrient depleted surface waters to 10^{-9} mol/kg in the most nutrient-enriched deep waters (Bruland, 1983). It follows that the abundance of Cd in foraminifer shells is also very low, ranging from 0.001 µmol/mol in tropical spinose planktonic species such as *Globigerinoides sacculifer* and *G. ruber* to 0.250 µmol/mol in benthic genera *Cibicidoides* and *Uvigerina* from the Pacific. The low levels of shell Cd make shell purification particularly critical and Cd analysis challenging.

Regular uptake of Cd into foraminifer shells has been demonstrated by comparing the Cd/Ca of core-top benthic Foraminifera to bottom water Cd concentrations (Fig. 15.2b) (Hester and Boyle, 1982; Boyle, 1988a, 1992). These studies demonstrate that the partition coefficient D for Cd in benthic foraminifer shells is between 1 and 3. Research indicates a depth (pressure?) effect on Cd incorporation, and Boyle has proposed that this effect can be corrected by interpolating between D values of 1.3 (at depths <1150 m) and 2.9 (at depths >3000 m) (Boyle, 1992). There are insignificant differences in D among calcitic species. Potential complications in using benthic Cd include: (1) the diagenetic addition of sedimentary Cd trapped or added by Mn-carbonate overgrowths (see below) (Boyle, 1983); (2) influence of pore water Cd on benthic Foraminifera, particularly those with infaunal modes of life (McCorkle and Klinkhammer, 1991; Martin *et al.*, 1996); and (3) a possible dissolution effect on shells deposited below the lysocline (McCorkle *et al.*, 1995).

The vast majority of effort in studying shell Cd has been directed at determining bottom water concentrations of Cd, mainly with the objective of assessing shifts in abyssal circulation. Cd records were instrumental in establishing that the flux of North Atlantic Deep Water (NADW) was weaker during cold glacial climate periods (Figs. 15.3a,b) (Boyle and Keigwin, 1982, 1985/1986, 1987; Boyle, 1990, 1995; Boyle and Rosener, 1990; Boyle and Rosenthal, 1996; Rosenthal *et al.*, 1997a). Boyle used Cd to establish the 'deepening' of nutrients during glacial episodes, which might have contributed to the atmospheric pCO_2 drawdown (Boyle, 1988b,c), and to assess changing mean ocean nutrients (Boyle, 1986, 1992). Boyle's findings have been verified and extended by other workers (Lynch-Steiglitz and Fairbanks, 1994; Ohkouchi *et al.*, 1994; Oppo and Rosenthal, 1994; Bertram *et al.*, 1995; Lea, 1995; Martin and Lea, 1998; Lynch-Steiglitz *et al.*, 1996; van Geen *et al.*, 1996). The use of Cd has been extended to the aragonitic genus *Hoeglundina* for studies of intermediate waters (Boyle *et al.*, 1995; Marchitto *et al.*, 1998), and to neritic benthic species to reconstruct paleo-upwelling in the California Current (van Geen *et al.*, 1992; van Geen and Husby, 1996). Some attempts have been made to investigate Cd in pre-Pleistocene sediments, but the potential for diagenetic influence is recognized as considerable (Delaney and Boyle, 1987; Delaney, 1990).

There has been less progress in utilizing Cd signals in planktonic Foraminifera. Boyle's early work showed that Cd could be measured in planktonic species and that differences in Cd/Ca between species tracked known depth preferences (Boyle, 1981). Because the limited surface water Cd range makes it difficult to do core-top calibrations, Cd uptake in planktonic species is best assessed by culturing studies (Fig. 15.2c) (Delaney, 1989; Mashiotta *et al.*, 1997). These studies demonstrate uptake of Cd with a partition coefficient of about 2. Mashiotta *et al.* (1997) further demonstrated that certain symbiont-bearing species have much lower uptake coefficients (0.1 to 0.4), most probably due to sequestration of Cd by symbiotic dinoflagellate algae. Published down-core work has mostly been confined to the polar species *Neogloboquadrina pachyderma* (Boyle, 1988b; Keigwin and Boyle, 1989), with recent work demonstrating significant sub-Antarctic nutrient shifts in *N. pachyderma* and *Globigerina bulloides* records (Mashiotta and Lea, 1997; Rosenthal *et al.*, 1997a).

15.6.3 Barium

Barium behaves like a nutrient in the oceans. In contrast to Cd, Ba is less readily regenerated

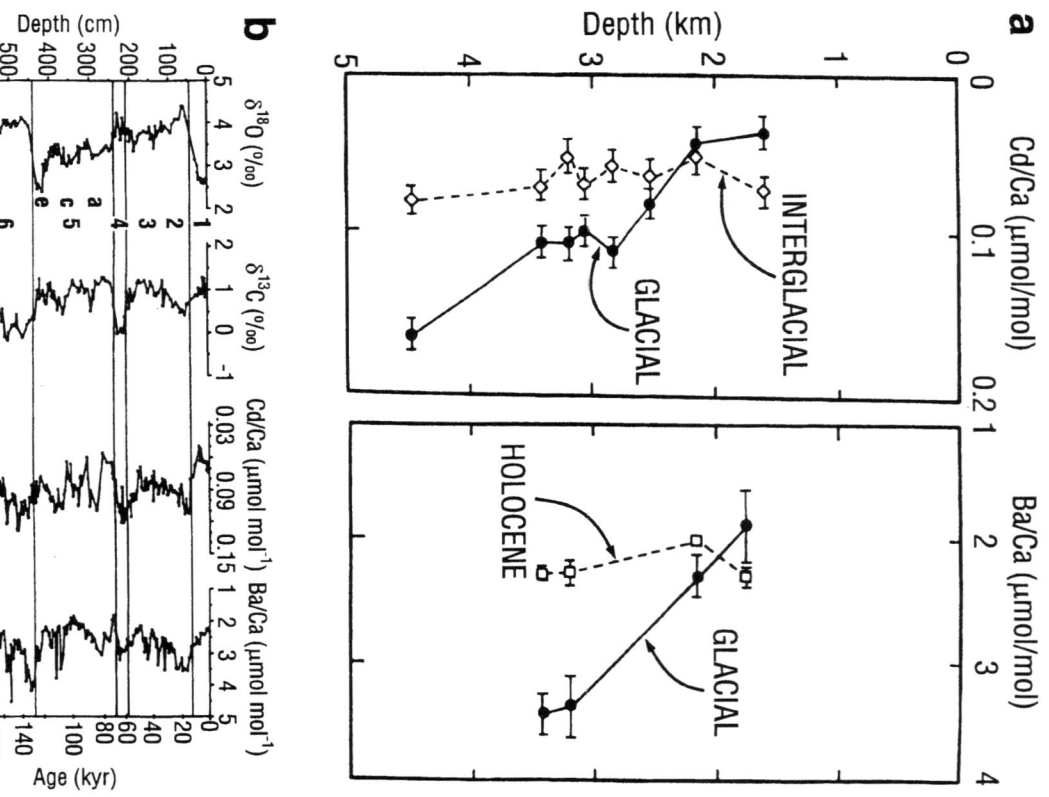

Figure 15.3 Paleoceanographic time series and hydrographic reconstruction using the paleo-nutrient proxies Cd and Ba. (a) Comparison of Holocene and glacial (20 kyr BP) depth profiles for Cd and Ba in the North Atlantic, as reconstructed from the composition of benthic foraminifer shells (Boyle and Keigwin, 1987; Lea and Boyle, 1990b). The data demonstrate that during the last glacial maximum, the Cd and Ba (and hence nutrient) content of abyssal Atlantic waters rose appreciably in response to a decline in the production rate of North Atlantic Deep Water. In contrast, the nutrient content of intermediate waters (<2 km water depth) was lower. Reprinted from *The Glacial World According to Wally*, Eldigio Press, Palisades, NY, Copyright 1993. (b) Time series of oxygen and carbon isotopes, Cd/Ca, and Ba/Ca in benthic Foraminifera from core CHN82-24-4PC in the North Atlantic at 42°N, 33°W, 3427 m water depth (Boyle and Keigwin, 1985/1986; Lea and Boyle, 1990a). The data demonstrate synchronous changes in the nutrient proxies (δ^{13}C, Cd/Ca, and Ba/Ca) that are clearly correlated to the waxing and waning of the continental ice sheets, as indicated by δ^{18}O. Differences between the proxies reflect their unique geochemistry. Reprinted by permission from *Nature* (Lea and Boyle, 1990a), Copyright 1990 Macmillan Magazines Ltd.

from sinking particles and therefore is most similar to the refractory properties alkalinity, sum of excess base, and silicic acid (Lea and Boyle, 1989, 1990b; Lea, 1993). Ba is depleted in surface waters through the precipitation of barite, $BaSO_4$ (Bishop, 1988). Deep waters are enriched by the dissolution of this barite, which predominantly dissolves on the seafloor (Chan et al., 1977). The oceanic distribution of Ba reflects a combination of biogeochemical cycling and abyssal circulation, with concentrations ranging from 30×10^{-9} mol/kg in the nutrient depleted Pacific surface waters to 150×10^{-9} mol/kg in the most nutrient-rich waters of the north Pacific (Ostlund et al., 1987).

Benthic Foraminifera reflect the distribution of bottom water Ba concentrations, ranging from about 2 µmol/mol in the North Atlantic to about 5 µmol/mol in the North Pacific (Lea and Boyle, 1989). They take up Ba with a partition coefficient of about 0.35, with small differences among species. A partition coefficient less than 1 indicates that Ba is discriminated against during precipitation, probably because it has an ionic radius sufficiently large to favor incorporation in the more open orthorhombic structure (Table 15.1). Foraminiferal Ba concentrations are about 20 times higher than Cd, but shell purification requirements are still considerable, because of the potential for barite contamination (Lea and Boyle, 1991, 1993). Ba incorporation in shells might also be affected by dissolution in sites below the lysocline, or alternatively by pressure affects (McCorkle et al., 1995).

The paleoceanographic application of Ba has focused on reconstructing circulation changes and alkalinity shifts. Downcore records from the Atlantic ocean indicate that Ba increased in bottom waters by about 50% during glacial episodes (Figs. 15.3a,b) (Lea and Boyle, 1990a,b). In contrast, Ba was only 10–20% higher in glacial Circumpolar Deep Water (CPDW) and about 20% lower in glacial Pacific deep waters (Lea and Boyle, 1990b; Lea, 1993, 1995). The implication of these changes is that reduced production of NADW during glacial episodes essentially eliminated the large gradient in bottom water Ba that exists today between the Atlantic and Pacific. The picture of glacial abyssal circulation derived from benthic Ba is somewhat different than that from Cd and $\delta^{13}C$, and current research focuses on understanding these differences and how they provide clues to shifts in physical, chemical and biological factors between glacial and interglacial episodes (Martin and Lea, 1998). Ba has also been used to estimate alkalinity changes in Antarctic waters. Results from the glacial sections of Southern Ocean cores suggest that alkalinity shifts due to circulation changes are too small to account for the glacial drawdown in atmospheric pCO_2 (Lea, 1993, 1995).

Culturing results and core-top determinations demonstrate that Ba is incorporated into spinose planktonic shells with a partition coefficient of 0.15, less than half of D for benthic shells (Lea and Boyle, 1991; Lea and Spero, 1992, 1994). This difference presumably relates to calcification rate differences between planktonic and benthic Foraminifera. There is evidence that non-spinose species incorporate considerably more Ba, although an explanation is wanting. Downcore Ba records from planktonic Foraminifera have not revealed climatically significant shifts (Lea and Boyle, 1990a, 1991)

15.7 PHYSICAL PROXIES: Mg, Sr, F, AND $^{10}B/^{11}B$

15.7.1

Physical proxies are those elements for which shell variability is primarily mediated by physical factors such as temperature, salinity, pressure, or pH. The best candidates are those elements that behave conservatively in the oceans, and therefore occur in nearly constant proportion to calcium in seawater. (Boron isotopes are unique among the physical proxies; see below.) The controls on shell chemistry might occur through the direct influence of physical factors on the trace element partition coefficient, or alternatively, occur indirectly through the effect of physical parameters on biological factors such as calcification rate. The influence of calcification rate on trace element incorporation is probably related to shifts in mass transport and surface reaction kinetics (Morse and Bender, 1990). Paleoceanographers are inclined to establish relationships between shell trace elements and physical parameters by empirical means, and leave the details of the chemical and biological controls to future studies. But if Mg, Sr, and F incorporation is mediated by a complex indirect pathway involving calcification rate, it is less likely that these elements will be robust proxies of physical changes in the past. One area of particular concern is that there is a general relationship between Mg and Sr in shells, suggesting that their incorporation might be linked (Carpenter and Lohmann, 1992).

15.7.2 Magnesium

The study of Mg in carbonate fossils (including Foraminifera) has been an area of geological interest for almost a century (Clarke and Wheeler, 1922). At that time it was already recognized that carbonate shells precipitating in warm water tended to contain higher levels of Mg than their counterparts in cold waters. Two down-core records from the subantarctic Indian Ocean first indicated that planktonic shell Mg variations correlate with climate change in the late Quaternary, with higher levels of Mg associated with warm climate periods (Cronblad and Malmgren, 1981). However, early systematic attempts to isolate temperature as a controlling factor on planktonic foraminiferal Mg, using core-top, sediment trap, sediment, and cultured samples, failed to yield an unambiguous relationship between Mg and inferred growth temperature (Savin and Douglas, 1973; Bender et al., 1975; Delaney et al., 1985).

Mg/Ca in planktonic Foraminifera varies from about 0.5 to 5 mmol/mol, with a increase in Mg from cold to warm waters. Surface-dwelling spinose species contain more Mg than their deeper-dwelling non-spinose counterparts, presumably because of temperature control (Savin and Douglas, 1973; Bender et al., 1975; Delaney et al., 1985; Rosenthal and Boyle, 1993). Benthic foraminifer Mg/Ca ranges from 0.5 to 10 mmol/mol, with the highest values in shells from the shallowest (warmest) sites (Izuka, 1988; Rathburn and Deckker, 1997; Rosenthal et al., 1997b). Given that seawater Mg/Ca is 5.17 mol/mol (Bruland, 1983), the partition coefficient for foraminifer shells is of order 0.001, indicating that shell precipitation strongly discriminates against Mg.

Interest in using shell Mg as a proxy of sea surface temperature (SST) has intensified in the 1990s. Culturing and surface sediment studies have demonstrated a strong dependence of both planktonic and benthic shell Mg/Ca on growth temperature (Figs. 15.4a,c), while down-core studies suggest that systematic oscillations in shell Mg with climate change do exist in the deep-sea record (Nürnberg, 1995; Nürnberg et al., 1996; Mashiotta et al., in press; Rathburn and Deckker, 1997; Rosenthal et al., 1997b). Parallel studies, however, have suggested that

Figure 15.4 Magnesium and Sr in foraminifer shells. (**a**) Compilation of Mg/Ca in core-top and cultured planktonic Foraminifera versus actual or inferred growth temperature (Nürnberg et al., 1996). The closed circles indicate results from cultured specimens of *Globigerinoides sacculifer*. Most of the data describe an exponential relationship between shell Mg/Ca and seawater temperature. Shell Mg/Ca doubles for every 8°C increase in temperature. Reprinted from *Geochimica et Cosmochimica Acta*, 60, Nürnberg, D. et al., Assessing the reliability of magnesium in foraminiferal calcite as a proxy for water mass temperatures, 803–814, Copyright 1996, with permission from Elsevier Science. (**b**) Magnesium/Ca and Sr/Ca in core-top specimens of *Globorotalia tumida* from the Ontong Java Plateau plotted versus water depth (Brown and Elderfield, 1996). The calcite saturation horizon is at about 3200 m; the foraminiferal lysocline is at about 3400 m. The data indicate that post-depositional dissolution of the shells leads to decreases in Mg/Ca and Sr/Ca. Apparently, the portion of the *G. tumida* shells enriched in Mg and Sr is the most likely fraction to be removed by dissolution. Reprinted from Brown and Elderfield, 1996. (**c**) Magnesium/Ca and Sr/Ca in core-top specimens of *Cibicidoides* and *Cibicides* from broad oceanic regions plotted versus water depth (Rosenthal et al., 1997b). The data demonstrate that Mg/Ca in benthic foraminifers follows water temperature. In contrast, Sr/Ca shows a linear decrease with depth, which might reflect the influence of pressure. Reprinted from *Geochimica et Cosmochimica Acta*, 61, Rosenthal, Y. et al., Temperature control on the incorporation of Mg, Sr, F and Cd into benthic foraminiferal shells from Little Bahama Bank: prospects for thermocline paleoceanography, 3633–3643, Copyright 1997, with permission from Elsevier Science.

Physical proxies: Mg, Sr, F, and $^{13}B/^{11}B$

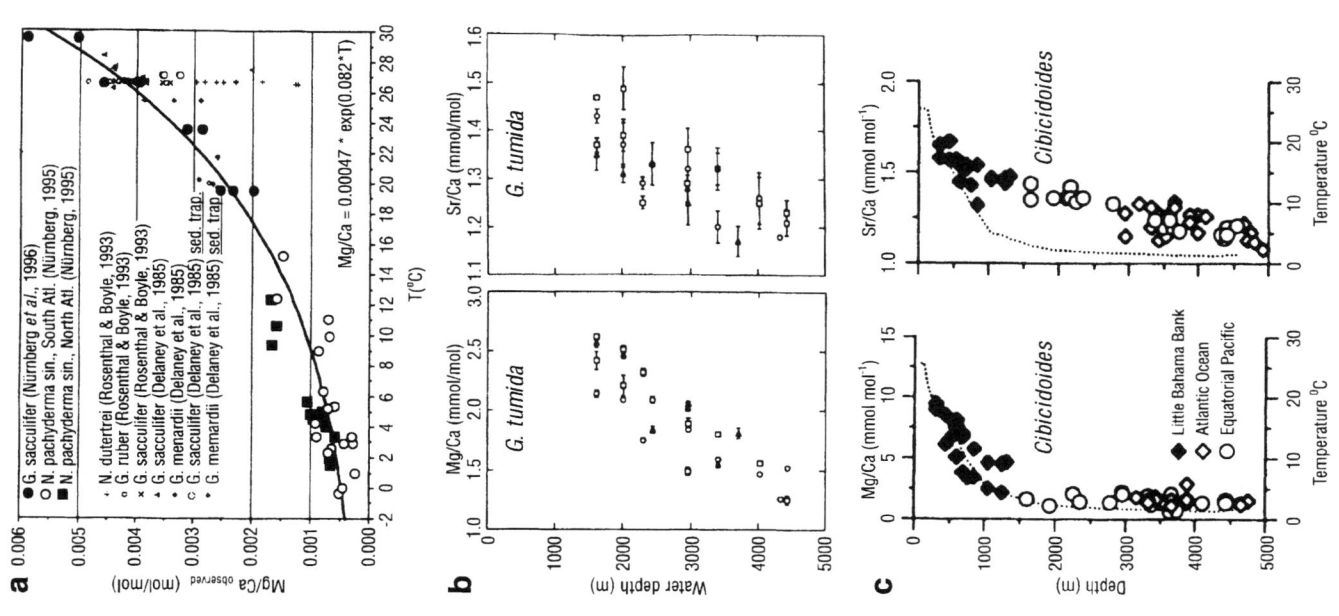

there are strong post-depositional effects on shell Mg in some species, most likely due to preferential dissolution of Mg-enriched portions of the shells (Fig. 15.4b) (Savin and Douglas, 1973; Hecht et al., 1975; Lorens et al., 1977; Rosenthal and Boyle, 1993; Russell et al., 1994; Brown and Elderfield, 1996).

Sorting out the controls and potential usefulness of Mg is a most important contemporary problem in foraminiferal trace element research. If shell Mg can be used for paleothermometry, it would become a critical tool in paleoceanographic and paleoenvironmental research. Because shell Mg and $\delta^{18}O$ can be measured in the same phase, it is possible to calculate the $\delta^{18}O$ composition of the water from which the shell precipitated, if Mg can be converted to temperature (Mashiotta et al., in press). Benthic Mg/Ca might be the best information on the history of deep-water temperatures. Research will be required on many fronts, including: (1) establishing why shell Mg varies with temperature (i.e. thermodynamic control versus kinetic or biological factors); (2) why different species have different shell Mg/Ca, and how that relates to foraminiferal habitat; and (3) what secondary factors might influence Mg, including post-depositional dissolution, and how these effects vary from species to species.

15.7.3 Strontium

Strontium is a conservative element in seawater with a long residence time of about 5 My. In similar fashion to Mg studies, systematic attempts to isolate the factors controlling foraminiferal Sr, using core-top, sediment trap, sediment and cultured samples, have failed to yield unambiguous relationships (Bender et al., 1975; Delaney et al., 1985). These studies, however, demonstrate that Sr/Ca is much more uniform than Mg/Ca in planktonic Foraminifera, varying from about 1.2 to 1.6 mmol/mol, and that Sr is incorporated with a partition coefficient of about 0.16. An 80 My record of shell Sr suggests that oceanic Sr concentrations have changed significantly (Graham et al., 1982; Delaney and Boyle, 1986), and a published late Quaternary record (Cronblad and Malmgren, 1981) suggests that shell Sr variations correlate with climate change.

Recent studies, focused on benthic Foraminifera (Fig. 15.4c) (McCorkle et al., 1995; Elderfield et al., 1996; Rathburn and Deckker, 1997; Rosenthal et al., 1997b), have demonstrated that there is a systematic decrease in benthic shell Sr with water depth throughout the oceans. Temperature, pressure and calcite saturation have all been suggested as potential controls. However, the linearity of the Sr decrease with depth and the uniformity of this relationship in the oceans suggest that pressure is the most likely cause of the change.

Foraminifer shells record small but systematic shifts of about 5% in Sr/Ca over the last 250 kyrs (Martin et al., 1997). These shifts are clearly correlated with climate episodes, and provide tantalizing evidence that oceanic Sr concentrations might have oscillated in response to changes in the partitioning of shelf carbonates (high in Sr) and pelagic carbonates (depleted in Sr) (Stoll and Schrag, 1998). However, confidently ascribing secular shifts in shell Sr to corresponding shifts in seawater Sr/Ca requires eliminating all other potential influences, including physical properties such as temperature, and secondary influences such as dissolution, which also change synchronously with climate.

15.7.4 Fluorine

Fluorine is a conservative element in seawater with a residence time of 0.5 My. Fluoride is one of the few anions that has been studied in carbonates (others include borate and sulphate), partly because anion incorporation is much less understood than cation incorporation. Theoretical considerations suggest that the proportion of F to Ca might reflect salinity variations (Rosenthal and Boyle, 1993). Recent studies do not demonstrate consistent relationships between shell F/Ca and temperature and salinity (Opdyke et al., 1993; Rosenthal and Boyle, 1993; Rosenthal et al., 1997b). A decrease in F/Ca of planktonic shells with increasing water depth demonstrates that post-depositional dissolution modifies the fluorine of deposited shells (Rosenthal and Boyle, 1993).

15.7.5 Boron isotopes

The ratio of ^{10}B to ^{11}B (denoted $\delta^{11}B$) does not vary within the ocean. There is, however, a large isotopic fractionation between the two aqueous species – 'boric acid, $B(OH)_3$, and borate, $B(OH)_4^-$ (Spivack et al., 1993). The ratio between boric acid and borate is a strong function of pH. If the charged borate species is the only one that is incorporated into foraminifer shells, the $\delta^{11}B$ composition of shells serves as a proxy of pH, a relationship demonstrated by both core-top and culturing studies (Spivack et al., 1993; Sanyal et al., 1995, 1996). Studies of ancient sediments suggest that shell $\delta^{11}B$ records substantial oceanic shifts in pH between glacial and interglacial episodes. However, the implied pH shifts are less homogeneous than might be expected, suggesting that oceanic pH changes in complex ways, or alternatively, there are other undocumented influences on shell $\delta^{11}B$.

15.8 CHEMICAL PROXIES: Li, U, V, $^{87}Sr/^{86}Sr$, AND $^{143}Nd/^{144}Nd$

15.8.1

Chemical proxies record secular changes in ocean chemistry. Like the physical proxies, chemical proxies are generally conservative in seawater. They differ from the physical proxies because variability in shell content over time is thought to be primarily mediated by changes in seawater composition. Seawater composition of these elements is controlled by inputs and outputs that are sensitive to climate change or tectonic reorganization. The chemical proxies include the isotope systems of Sr and Nd. Secular variations in the Sr isotopic composition of seawater are well established over geological time and have proven to be an important stratigraphic and geochemical tool.

15.8.2 Lithium

Li is a conservative element in seawater with a long residence time (>1 My). Therefore, on long time scales, seawater Li might vary with shifts in the extent of seafloor spreading (Delaney and Boyle, 1986). One of its major oceanic sources is the hydrothermal interaction of seafloor basalt and seawater (von Damm et al., 1985). Delaney attempted to document such shifts, and concluded that the limited variation in shell Li/Ca over the last 100 My constrains potential long term changes in hydrothermal venting of Li (and by implication production of seafloor basalt) to $\pm 30\%$.

15.8.3 Uranium and Vanadium

Both U and V, nearly conservative in seawater, have major oceanic sinks in suboxic (little or no oxygen) sediments, where reduction of U and V leads to their incorporation into insoluble phases. Thus, it is hypothesized that shifts in the areal extent of suboxic sediments would decrease the seawater concentrations of U and V, and this change would be recorded in foraminifer shells (Russell et al., 1994, 1996; Hastings et al., 1996a,b). Uranium and V occur as oxyanions in seawater and therefore would not be expected to substitute into shell calcite in any simple way. Russell et al. (1996) and Hastings et al. (1996a,b) used planktonic culturing to demonstrate the U and V are incorporated into shell calcite in proportion to their seawater concentration, both with partition coefficients of about 0.01. Down-core records of these elements are somewhat equivocal as to the extent of seawater shifts in U and V, partly because foraminifer U/Ca and V/Ca are subject to post-depositional change.

15.8.4 Strontium isotopes

The $^{87}Sr/^{86}Sr$ ratio of seawater is constant throughout the ocean because of the 5 My residence time of Sr (Faure, 1986). But on long time scales, seawater $^{87}Sr/^{86}Sr$ changes, because it reflects shifting balances between the various source and sinks of dissolved Sr. Over the last 24 My (since the late Oligocene), the $^{87}Sr/^{86}Sr$ ratio of the oceans, as recorded in foraminifer shells and bulk deep-sea carbonates, has risen quite dramatically from about 0.7082 to the present value of over 0.7091 (Fig. 15.5). The nearly monotonic rise over the period serves as a useful stratigraphic tool (DePaolo and Ingram, 1985; Hodell et al., 1991). The cause of this increase is hypothesized to be changes in the isotopic composition and flux of Sr from rivers draining uplifted continental areas such as the Himalayas, which include rocks enriched in radiogenic Sr (high $^{87}Sr/^{86}Sr$) (Raymo et al., 1988; Edmond, 1992; Raymo and Ruddiman, 1992).

Foraminifer shells contain about 1.4 mmol/mol Sr/Ca (Fig. 15.1). Some researchers have used them exclusively for Sr isotopic work, and others argue that the same results can be achieved using bulk carbonate (Richter and DePaolo, 1988). Because all of the Sr in foraminifer shells is precipitated from seawater, and because these shells are likely to be less prone to diagenesis than the finer carbonate fraction,

it seems prudent to use foraminifer shells for Sr isotopic work.

15.8.5 Neodymium isotopes

In contrast to Sr, Nd is particle reactive and has a low seawater concentration ($<25 \times 10^{-12}$ mol/kg) and a relatively short residence time (Bruland, 1983). The $^{143}Nd/^{144}Nd$ ratio of seawater varies from about 0.5120 in the Atlantic Ocean to 0.5125 in the Pacific Ocean (Faure, 1986). This difference arises because average continental rocks are depleted, whereas oceanic basalts are enriched, in $^{143}Nd/^{144}Nd$. The Atlantic Ocean derives its Nd from the many rivers draining a dominantly continental terrain (for example the Amazon, Congo, and Mississippi). The Pacific derives its Nd from far fewer major rivers, which drain a dominantly basalt terrain, and from interaction with the great ridges of young basalt that characterize the Pacific basin.

Nd might be incorporated into Foraminifera via solid solution, although $NdCO_3$ is isomorphous with aragonite rather than calcite (Speer,

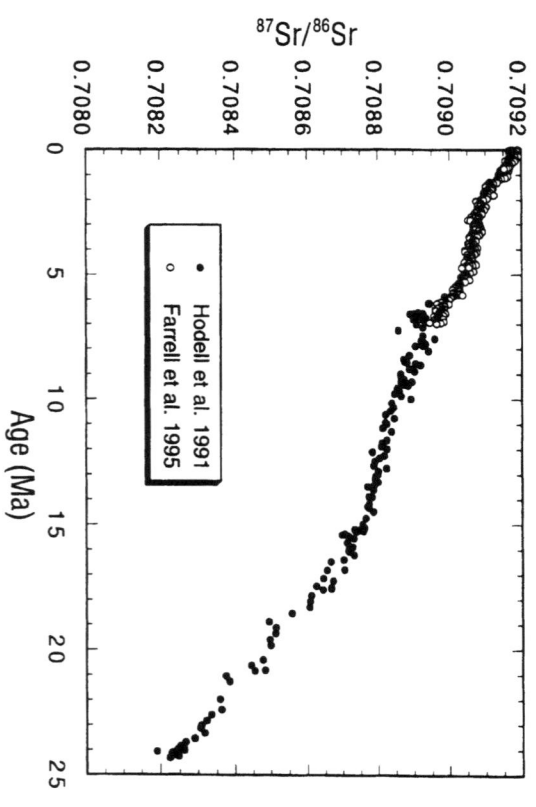

Figure 15.5 High resolution strontium isotope stratigraphy for the last 24 My, based on analyses of planktonic foraminifer shells; data from DSDP Hole 588 (Hodell et al., 1991) and ODP Site 758 (Farrell et al., 1995). The data indicate a rapid rise in seawater $^{87}Sr/^{86}Sr$ over this time period, presumably in response to an increase in the weathering of uplifted radiogenic rocks. The rise is sufficiently systematic that it can be used as a stratigraphic and chronological tool. Modified from Hodell et al., 1991.

1983). There have been a number of efforts to use the isotopic composition of foraminiferal Nd as a recorder of shifts in weathering patterns (Palmer and Elderfield, 1986). Because Nd has a strong affinity for the Mn and Fe oxide phases that coat shells, it is very difficult to be certain that the measured Nd actually comes from shell calcite (Palmer, 1985; Palmer and Elderfield, 1986).

15.9 DIAGENETIC PROXIES

15.9.1

These are proxies that reveal information about the post-depositional history of foraminifer shells. Although diagenetic proxies do not provide primary information about past environments, they are a critical source of information about the long-term integrity of the primary chemical signal encoded in shells. Mn is the most important of the diagenetic proxies, because in most environments its presence above background levels indicates that Mn has been added to the shells by secondary precipitation. The physical proxies Mg, Sr, and F also appear to reflect aspects of the diagenetic history of foraminifer shells. In the context of using these elements as recorders of physical parameters, it is imperative that researchers separate the influence of primary and secondary factors on shell composition.

15.9.2 Manganese

A major issue in the study of any chemical proxy in marine sediments is the extent to which the primary chemical signature might be altered by post-depositional processes. One way in which this might happen is the precipitation of secondary coatings on shells. An example of such coatings is Mn-carbonate, a mineral that forms in the reducing conditions typical of ocean-floor sediments. Under the suboxic conditions that typically underlie productive oceanic regions, solid phase Mn is mobilized and released into pore waters by reduction to Mn^{2+}, which is followed by precipitation of $MnCO_3$ (Boyle, 1983). Mn-carbonate is less soluble than calcite, and therefore the coatings cannot be easily separated from primary shell material. Mn-carbonate coatings are distinct from the Mn-oxide coatings which are far more common but can be removed by chemical reduction during sample preparation (Boyle, 1981). Mn-carbonate coatings either contain or trap high levels of certain trace elements such as Cd and Ba. An additional complication is that infaunal benthic Foraminifera incorporate pore water Mn into their shells, and pore water levels can vary by two orders of magnitude (Martin et al., 1996).

$MnCO_3$ precipitates appear to be ubiquitous in deep-sea cores, and in some oceanic regions it is difficult to find a site in which shells are not coated by precipitates. Researchers disagree in their definition of what is considered an acceptable level of shell Mn/Ca, from as low as 50 μmol/mol to as high as >150 μmol/mol (Boyle, 1983; Boyle and Keigwin, 1985/1986; Delaney, 1990; Ohkouchi et al., 1994). With the exception of infaunal benthic Foraminifera, primary shell material has <1 μmol/mol Mn/Ca. Because Mn-carbonate shell coatings are a critical limiting factor for foraminiferal trace element proxies like Cd, investigations of how Mn-carbonate forms, why it appears to be precipitated heterogeneously between various foraminifer species, and how coatings might be removed from primary shell material will all further foraminiferal trace element research.

15.10 NEW FRONTIERS IN TRACE ELEMENT PALEOCEANOGRAPHY

Geochemists undoubtedly will continue to search for new foraminiferal trace element proxies. Most of the trace elements that would be expected to substitute in foraminifer shells at measurable concentrations have already been studied (Table 15.1). The prime remaining candidate is the transition metal Zn. Seawater Zn is a nutrient proxy somewhat intermediate between Cd and Ba, and it shows a strong oceanic association with silicic acid (Bruland, 1983).

This association suggests that Zn might be a unique candidate for the reconstruction of silicic acid concentrations in past surface waters. Zn also forms a solid solution in the calcite series (Reeder, 1983). The biggest potential drawback to utilizing foraminiferal Zn is that it is highly contamination prone (Boyle, 1981). Other trace elements that might be worthy of investigation in Foraminifera include:

(1) Na and K, and possibly Rb and Cs, which are conservative alkali metals that could possibly serve as physical proxies. Levels of Na in foraminifer shells are about 5 mmol/mol, but a specific control has not been demonstrated (Bender et al., 1975; Delaney et al., 1985).

(2) Fe, Co, Ni, Cu, and Ag are all transition metals which are possible nutrient and/or particle-reactivity proxies (Bruland, 1983; Martin et al., 1983; Martin and Gordon, 1988). Shell-bound Fe will be extremely difficult to determine, because of contamination from Fe bearing oxides and clays (Boyle, 1981). Both Co and Ag are present at $<50 \times 10^{-12}$ mol/kg in seawater and will be consequently very low in foraminifer shells.

(3) REE, the rare earth elements including La, Ce, Nd, Sm, Eu, and Yb, might be useful as seawater chemistry and particle-reactivity proxies (Elderfield and Greaves, 1982; de Baar et al., 1985). Preliminary research suggests that it is difficult to separate shell bound REE from oxide-bound REE (Palmer, 1985).

Much of the research on nutrient proxies like Ba and Cd has focused on deep-water benthic Foraminifera, because of the interest in establishing changes in abyssal flow. The application of trace elements to the study of thermocline and upper intermediate waters is a relatively new, uncharted area (Rosenthal et al., 1997b; Marchitto et al., 1998). There are other important questions that might be answered using nutrient proxies in planktonic Foraminifera. Cd, in particular, appears to be a promising tool to characterize changes in nutrient supply and utilization in surface waters. Ba might be a sensitive tracer of riverine and melt water discharge.

Another frontier is the application of trace elements to studies of anthropogenic perturbation. It has already been demonstrated that Holocene shallow-water benthic Foraminifera record changing seawater Cd due to upwelling and pollution (van Geen et al., 1992; van Geen and Husby, 1996). It should be possible to use this technique to demonstrate changes in coastal waters in response to pollution.

Finally, the application of foraminiferal trace elements to longer, million year time scales has so far been limited to only a handful of records (Graham et al., 1982; Delaney and Boyle, 1986, 1987; Delaney, 1990). Elements present at truly trace concentrations, such as Cd, will be necessarily more difficult to study on these time scales, because the potential for diagenetic addition is high. But minor elements such as Mg and Sr, which might be less prone to diagenetic alteration, offer the potential to investigate some important problems, including the evolution of seawater temperatures and chemistry in the Tertiary.

15.11 SUMMARY AND CONCLUSIONS

Trace elements in foraminifer shells are controlled by seawater composition and the physical and biological conditions during calcification. Because it is possible to calibrate shell composition against the controlling factors, foraminiferal trace elements provide researchers with a toolbox of powerful proxies to investigate the chemical, physical, and biological evolution of the oceans. Some of the most important challenges faced by trace element researchers are to (1) establish precise relationships among shell chemistry, seawater composition, and physical and biological factors; (2) to apply elemental tracers to the past and take into account the range of potential complications that affect proxy interpretation; and (3) to establish which secondary factors such as diagenesis may affect post-depositional shell chemistry. With a precise knowledge of the factors that control shell composition, and in conjunction with stable isotopes, foraminiferal trace elements should provide a very powerful tool to study ocean and climate evolution.

15.12 ACKNOWLEDGMENTS

I thank Ed Boyle, MIT, for introducing me to the foraminiferal trace element field. Thanks go to Pam Martin, Lui Chan, and Jeff Hanor for comments and suggestions on the manuscript, to Tamara Garcia for organizing references, and to Mary Lee Eggart for improving the figures. The work and ideas of collaborators and students, especially Howie Spero, Glen Shen, Yair Rosenthal, Harry Elderfield, Pamela Martin, and Tracy Mashiotta have greatly contributed to my understanding of trace elements in Foraminifera. NSF and NOAA support has been critical in providing the resources for my research in this field.

PART IV: PRESERVATION OF RECORD

16

Taphonomy and temporal resolution of foraminiferal assemblages

Ronald E. Martin

16.1 INTRODUCTION

The surface mixed layer of sediment, which ranges in thickness from a few centimeters to as much as a meter, acts as a low-pass filter that damps high frequency signals before their incorporation into the historical record. This damping mechanism is referred to as time-averaging, which is the process by which fossils of different ages are mixed into a single assemblage. Because of time-averaging, a fossil assemblage represents a *minimal* duration of (at best) a few decades, and more likely hundreds to thousands of years, unless the assemblage is rapidly preserved by unusual conditions (Lagerstätten). Time-averaging occurs because the generation times of organisms are inherently much shorter than net rates of sediment accumulation and burial (Kidwell, 1993). The mixed layer is also a taphonomically active zone (Davies et al., 1989) in which stratigraphic signals are damped by biological mixing (bioturbation) and dissolution.

This chapter reviews what little is really known about the taphonomy and temporal resolution of foraminiferal assemblages in major depositional settings. Although post-mortem transportation of tests has been demonstrated to vary with respect to such factors as test size, shape, and density (e.g. Kontrovitz et al., 1978, 1979; Zhang et al., 1993), studies of assemblages suggest that little post-mortem transport of Foraminifera normally occurs (e.g. Snyder et al., 1990a,b). Therefore, the effects of bioturbation and dissolution on the formation of foraminiferal assemblages are emphasized.

16.2 BIOTURBATION: TEMPORAL RESOLUTION AND PORE WATER CHEMISTRY

The most popular bioturbation models are based on the concept of diffusion (see Matisoff, 1982; Cutler, 1993; Martin, 1993, for reviews). Diffusion-based models assume that mixing is a random redistribution of sediment particles by large numbers of organisms over many individual transport events, and that, taken collectively, small transport events move particles over large distances (Martin, 1998, derives the relevant equations using a random walk model). The Guinasso-Schink (1975) model, in particular, may be reduced to a dimensionless parameter (G) that represents the ratio of bioturbation ('biodiffusion') rate (D), sedimentation rate (v), and mixed layer thickness (m):

$$G = D/mv \quad (1)$$

Reported biodiffusion coefficients vary by about six orders of magnitude and decrease from shallow water ($D \cong 10^{-6}$ cm^2 sec^{-1}) to the deep sea ($D \cong 10^{-8}$ cm^2 sec^{-1}; Matisoff, 1982; biodiffusion coefficients are also often stated in terms of thousands of years). Biodiffusion coefficients also typically decrease with depth, even within the same environment (Fig. 16.1; Aller and Cochran, 1976; Benninger et al., 1979; Benoit et al., 1979; Cochran and Aller, 1979). Equation (1) has been criticized on a number of grounds. For example, according to the equation, a thick mixed layer should result in a better-preserved signal than a smeared one (Wheatcroft, 1990; Wheatcroft et al., 1990; see Martin, 1998, for review of other criticisms). Nevertheless, G is heuristically useful in understanding the interplay of bioturbation and sedimentation rates and mixed layer thickness in generating a stratigraphic signal. When G is small ($\leqslant 0.1$; rapid v or slow mixing), an impulse tracer (such as a microtektite or volcanic ash layer) is transferred through the mixed layer before it can be extensively re-worked, and its concentration profile is bell-shaped or 'Gaussian' (Fig. 16.2). When G is large ($\geqslant 1$; slow v or rapid mixing), the tracer exhibits an exponential decrease upward and a nearly uniform distribution in the mixed layer (Fig. 16.2).

Under conditions of a thin mixed layer ($m \cong 5$–10 cm) and rapid bioturbation, equation (1) reduces to a box model, in which tracers are assumed to be rapidly and homogeneously distributed in the mixed layer (Figures 16.1, 16.2), an assumption that is often unjustified (Berger et al., 1979). The most frequently cited box model is that of Berger and Heath (1968):

$$\frac{-dP}{P} = \frac{-dL}{m} \quad (2)$$

where P = probability of finding a particle in the mixed layer, L = thickness of sediment deposited on the layer, and m = mixed layer thickness.

Integrating (2) results in a decay formula:

$$P = P_0 e^{(-S/m)} \quad (3)$$

Thus, if species z becomes extinct, the distribution of the species is given by:

$$P_z = P_{sz} e^{l-(S_e + m)/m} \quad (4)$$

where P_{sz} = original concentration of z at a distance of m below the level of extinction, and S_e = sediment thickness above (after) extinction.

According to (4), the concentration of an

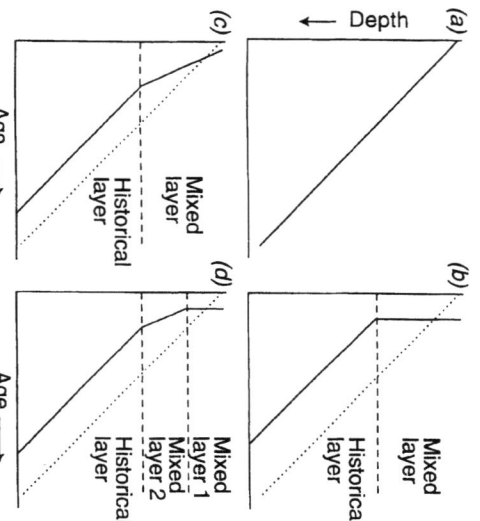

Figure 16.1 Hypothetical plots of mean tracer age versus depth in sediment. (A) No bioturbation. Slope of line is constant and determined by sediment accumulation rate only. (B) Completely bioturbated mixed layer. Within mixed layer, mean tracer age (solid line) is the same at all depths because of homogeneous mixing, and tracer age profile is shifted toward somewhat older ages because of upward reworking of older remains from historical layer. By contrast, age profile of tracer in *historical* layer is displaced toward younger mean age relative to unmixed profile (dotted line) because of downward reworking of younger material from mixed layer. (C) Gradual decrease of bioturbation rate with depth in mixed layer. Slope of age profile within mixed layer is proportional to D. Case C is intermediate between cases A and B. (D) Mixed layer consists of two layers. Mixed layers 1 and 2 have values like those for cases B and C, respectively; thus, mixed layer 1 is homogeneously mixed, whereas mixed layer 2 is not. (Modified from Cutler, 1993).

Bioturbation: temporal resolution and pore water chemistry

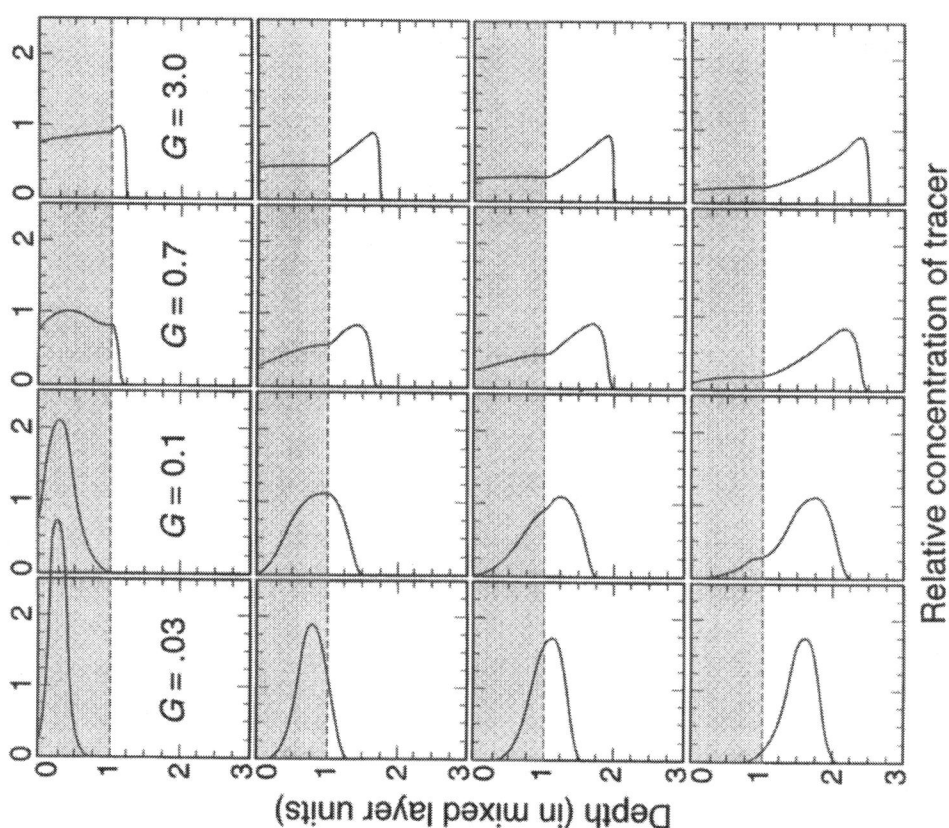

Figure 16.2 Time series showing the downward transmission of an impulse signal in relation to the mixing parameter G (equation (1)). Mixed layer indicated by stippling. Depth in mixed layer units; time normalized to time required for one mixed layer thickness to accumulate. When G is small (rapid sedimentation, slow mixing), an impulse tracer is buried below the mixed layer before it can be extensively reworked (bell-shaped profile). If G is large (slow sedimentation, rapid reworking), the concentration of tracer decreases upward exponentially, and its concentration in the mixed layer is relatively uniform. Modified from Guinasso and Schink (1975) after Martin (1993).

extinct species above its true level of extinction decreases upward exponentially according to the thickness of sediment deposited after its extinction. Based on equation (4), Berger and Heath (1968) calculated the proportion of the original concentration of a species z at a distance S_e above its disappearance. By specifying acceptable levels of reworking (contamination), the level of stratigraphic resolution was calculated. In their example, if $m = 4$ cm and contaminant level (due to reworking) is 10% of the original concentration of the species, then the original extinction level may be as much as 9 cm deeper in the section (Fig. 16.3; see also Fig. 16.4). For a sedimentation rate of $1 \, \text{cm} \, \text{kyr}^{-1}$, this means a resolution of 9000 years; for a rate of $4 \, \text{cm} \, \text{kyr}^{-1}$, a resolution of 2250 years is obtained. According to the model, the exact level of extinction is indicated when the concentration of the species is $1/e$ or 0.37 times its maximum

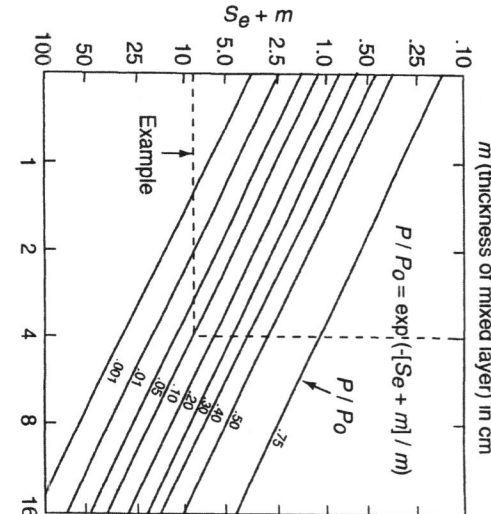

Figure 16.3 Proportion of the original concentration of a species (P/P_0) found in sediment at a distance S_e above its level of disappearance. See text for further discussion (modified from Berger and Heath, 1968).

concentration below, and is independent of the mixed layer thickness (Berger and Heath, 1968). Similar models were developed by these authors for species appearances: first appearance datums (FADs) tend to be smeared downward much less than last appearance datums (LADs) are smeared upward, because bioturbators are largely confined to the mixed layer, and tend to remain near the sediment-water interface (SWI) as sediment is deposited at the SWI from the water column (see also Glass, 1969).

Reworking of substantially older (ca. hundreds-of-thousands to millions-of-years) or younger microfossils into younger (or older) sediments by 'leaking' or 'piping' (remanié) is not usually a serious problem, and is all but ignored by biostratigraphers. In most cases, microfossil-based biostratigraphic zonations are sufficiently precise at such time scales that reworked specimens are typically recognized by their anomalous stratigraphic occurrence and qualitative state of preservation (surface degradation, breakage, infilling with foreign sediment). Berger and Heath (1968) concluded that bioturbation would not normally be responsible for such reworking, as the concentration of the reworked marker would probably be on the order of 10^{-6} of its original concentration when, in their example, the thickness of sediment separating Recent from older material was as little as 1 m. They suggested that erosion is the dominant process mixing older assemblages into younger pelagic sediments. Cutler and Flessa (1990) came to a similar conclusion for shallow-water assemblages: bioturbation is a relatively inefficient means of producing stratigraphic disorder, but physical reworking disorders sequences rapidly.

In the case of ecostratigraphic studies, Berger and Heath (1968) concluded that serious stratigraphic errors may occur if the stratigraphic range of a species is similar in thickness to the mixed layer; this is likely to occur in the deep-sea during times of climatic fluctuations, when species may alternately appear and disappear relatively rapidly, leaving sufficient time for substantial biological reworking (cf. Fig.16.4d). Such signals are more easily deciphered under regimes of higher sediment accumulation rates (e.g. Martin et al., 1993; Martin and Fletcher, 1995, for shallow continental slope of the northeast Gulf of Mexico). On even shorter time scales, size-selective transport of sediment particles (e.g. Foraminifera versus coccolithophorids, microtektites) back to the SWI by bioturbators may produce artifactual peaks (McIntyre et al., 1967; Glass, 1969; Robbins, 1986; Wheatcroft and Jumars, 1987; Wheatcroft, 1992; cf. Ruddiman and Glover, 1972; Ruddiman et al., 1980).

Besides smearing stratigraphic signals, bioturbation also affects pore water chemistry and hardpart preservation. Typically, beneath a surficial oxidized zone, bioturbation oxidizes organic matter and sulfides to produce carbonic and sulfuric acids, respectively (Walter and Burton, 1990):

$$CH_2O + O_2 \rightarrow H_2CO_3 \quad (5)$$

$$2O_2 + HS^- \rightarrow SO_4^= + H^+ \quad (6)$$

Conversely, bacterial sulfate reduction increases pore water alkalinity (total dissolved bicarbonate and carbonate ion, and smaller contributions of other ions such as borate), thereby enhancing shell ($CaCO_3$) preservation (Walter and Burton,

Preservation and temporal resolution in marine settings

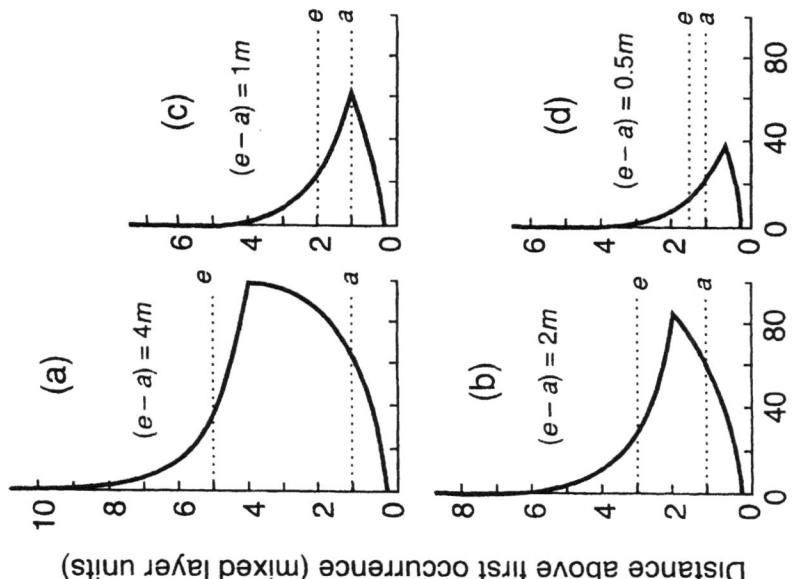

Figure 16.4 Biostratigraphic distribution of a taxon after vertical mixing. a and e denote levels of appearance and extinction, respectively, in each of four examples (a–d) of decreasing stratigraphic duration; thicknesses are measured in multiples of mixed layer thickness (m). Thin (short) intervals are more likely to be obscured by bioturbation (see text for further discussion). Modified from Berger and Heath (1968).

$$2CH_2O + SO_4^=$$
$$\rightarrow HS^- + HCO_3^- + H_2CO_3 \qquad (7)$$

Alkalinity may also increase deeper in the sediment column as a result of other oxidation-reduction reactions involving organic carbon that use different electron acceptors (see Canfield and Raiswell, 1991, for review).

16.3 PRESERVATION AND TEMPORAL RESOLUTION IN MARINE SETTINGS

16.3.1 Carbonate shelves

Large reef-dwelling Foraminifera, such as *Amphistegina gibbosa* and *Archaias angulatus*, often form highly-abraded, current-winnowed lags in shallow-water carbonate environments (Martin, 1986; Martin and Wright, 1988) that may dominate assemblages to the point of obscuring reef zonations (Martin and Liddell, 1988, 1989, 1991). These and other species would therefore be expected to persist in sediment for relatively long periods of time and to be mixed extensively both upward and downward in the mixed layer, which may be up to ~1 m thick in carbonate sediments (Walter and Burton, 1990).

Kotler et al. (1991, 1992) and Martin and Liddell (1991) conducted laboratory and field experiments that simulated abrasion, dissolution, and bioerosion of common reef foraminiferal species based on energy conditions and depositional setting ('taphofacies') under which assemblages form (Liddell et al., 1987; Liddell and Martin, 1989). With the exception of fragile species such as *Planorbulina acervalis*, the Foraminifera examined were resistant to abrasion. Abrasion-resistant forms varied substantially in susceptibility to dissolution, however: *Archaias angulatus*, which is prevalent in back-reef environments, dissolved rapidly, whereas *Amphistegina gibbosa*, which characterizes the reef crest and shallow fore reef, dissolved much more slowly. Differences in dissolution rate probably resulted from differences in both test architecture and mineralogy: tests of *Amphistegina gibbosa* and *Archaias angulatus* are, for example, characterized by 4–5% and 14–16% Mg-calcite, respectively.

Although Kotler et al. (1991, 1992) experimentally reproduced some natural abrasion and dissolution-related test surface features, surface features obtained in bioerosion experiments did not resemble natural features. This is not to say that bioerosion does not occur in carbonate sediments, as the process has been documented in a number of cases. Biological destruction of foraminiferal tests is caused by microbes (e.g. fungi), especially in quiet-water environments, and from selective or indiscriminate ingestion of tests by invertebrates and vertebrates, although the intensity of destruction varies considerably (see Martin and Liddell, 1991, for discussion and references). Nevertheless, in studies to date, shells of large taxa, such as bivalves, appear to be destroyed primarily by bioerosion (Aller, 1995; Cutler, 1995), whereas foraminiferal tests are lost primarily to dissolution (Buzas, 1965; Green et al., 1992, 1993b; Martin et al., 1995, 1996; Powell et al., 1984 noted similar behavior for juvenile molluscs).

Based on the slow rates of experimental test degradation versus the highly degraded nature of many natural tests, Kotler et al. (1991, 1992) and Martin and Liddell (1991) concluded that test degradation is inhibited in carbonate sediments. Indeed, subsequent radiocarbon dating demonstrated that pristine to highly degraded tests of *Amphistegina* and *Archaias* from natural

assemblages range from modern to >2,000 calendar yrs (ages corrected for reservoir and vital effects; Martin et al., 1995, 1996). Mixing of older material with younger sediment appears to be extensive in carbonate-rich environments because high sedimentary $CaCO_3$ levels buffer dissolution and promote time-averaging. Indeed, based on amino acid racemization techniques, Murray-Wallace and Belperio (1995) found that the large reef-dwelling foraminifer *Marginopora vertebralis* was reworked from late Pleistocene (ca. 125,000 ka) into modern carbonate tidal flat sediments, and that reworked specimens (remanié) were indistinguishable from modern ones.

Kotler et al.'s (1992) results are in marked contrast to the results of Walter and Burton (1990), who found that red algal (18 mol% Mg-calcite), echinoid (12 mol% Mg), and coral (aragonite) substrates dissolved relatively rapidly in field experiments. The carbonate substrates utilized by Walter and Burton (1990) would appear to be far more reactive, however, than Foraminifera (Kotler et al., 1992). Thus, differential solubility of carbonate particles in carbonate environments probably results not only from differences in mineralogy, but also from differences in (1) substrate size, shape, and surface area (surface/volume ratio; relatively high in red algae, low in Foraminifera), (2) organic matter content, and (3) microstructure ('Sorby Principle'; Folk and Robles, 1964).

16.3.2 Siliciclastic tidal flats

It is almost axiomatic in taphonomy that, in general, the bigger the shell, the longer it lasts (depending on mineralogy, microstructure, etc.). One deduction from this tenet is that big shells should be older, and should appear older, than small shells from the same horizon. Macrofossil assemblages should therefore exhibit much greater variation in the durations of time-averaging than microfossil assemblages from the same deposit (Martin and Liddell, 1991; Martin, 1993; Kowalewski, 1997). Comparison of time-averaging of hardparts belonging to different taxa bears on such crucial topics as distinguishing reworking from survivorship across extinction horizons (Signor-Lipps effect; Signor and Lipps, 1982; Flessa, 1990; Meldahl, 1990; MacLeod and Huber, 1996), and biostratigraphic zonations based on different taxa that are used to assess the rates and mechanisms of extinction.

Martin et al. (1995, 1996) tested the above hypotheses by comparing the state of preservation (taphonomic grade) and age of *Chione* (bivalve) and foraminiferal tests from Holocene tidal flats of Bahia la Choya, Mexico (northern Gulf of California). They found that hardpart size and taphonomic grade are not infallible indicators of shell age, preservability, or temporal resolution of fossil assemblages, as did Flessa et al. (1993; contrary to Brett and Baird, 1986; Brandt, 1989). Disarticulated *Chione* collected from the SWI exhibited an age range of several hundred years to ~80–125 Ka based on Accelerator Mass Spectrometer (AMS) ^{14}C dates and amino acid racemization (D-Alloisoleucine/L-Isoleucine) values, and old (or young) valves ranged from highly altered to virtually pristine. Their age range is much greater than that reported by Flessa et al. (1993) from the same area (see also Wehmiller et al., 1995; Flessa and Kowalewski, 1994).

Foraminiferal tests at Choya Bay were surprisingly old (up to ~2,000 calendar years), despite their pristine appearance, which suggested a young age (Martin et al., 1995, 1996; dated tests consisted of *Buccella mansfieldi* and *Elphidium* cf. *E. crispum*). The substantial age differences between bivalves and Foraminifera hinted that the means of test preservation differed from that of bivalves. Foraminifera reproduced in discrete (~a few weeks) seasonal pulses, which were followed by periods of intense dissolution of several months duration related to low sediment accumulation rates (~0.038 cm yr^{-1}; Flessa et al., 1993) and intensive bioturbation (oxidation of organic matter and sulfides to produce carbonic and sulfuric acids, respectively; equations 5 and 6). After each seasonal reproductive pulse of $CaCO_3$, some tests are apparently rapidly incorporated into a subsurface shell layer (up to ~1 m below the SWI) by Conveyor Belt Deposit Feeders (CDFs; van Straaten, 1952; Rhoads and Stanley, 1965; Meldahl, 1987) and preserved there, as the rest of the pulse quickly dissolves. Ultimately, some of these older tests, as well as bivalves, are exhumed by CDFs and storms, which biases assemblages toward ages older than those predicted (cf. Shroba, 1993). Indeed, Meldahl et al. (1997) found that durations of time-averaging of bivalve assemblages decreased to a few hundred years in settings of apparently higher sediment accumulation rates elsewhere in the Gulf of California.

At Choya Bay, however, foraminiferal abundance tends to increase to the north across the flat, indicating that conditions suitable for test preservation can vary dramatically over relatively short distances. The depth to the subsurface shell layer shallows northward from >60 cm on the southern flat to ~10 cm in some places over a Pleistocene outcrop. Burrow densities (estimated visually) also tend to decrease to the north, especially when sediment thickness is ≤20–25 cm. The shallowness of the Pleistocene platform on the northern margin of the bay apparently inhibits the intensity of bioturbation (i.e. bioturbators cannot burrow to their preferred habitat depth), and this allows alkalinity to build-up via sulfate reduction, especially in the summer (see seasonal geochemical data in Martin et al., 1995).

16.3.3 Marshes

Not surprisingly, marshes and other coastal environments have received considerable scrutiny from sedimentologists, stratigraphers, and geomorphologists because of their accessibility, their ecological and economic importance, and their sensitivity to sea-level change, especially in light of natural Holocene sea-level rise that is confounded with apparent anthropogenic global warming. Foraminifera have been used to reconstruct high-frequency (decadal to millenial), low amplitude (<10 m) changes of Holocene sea level to ±5–10 cm (Scott, 1976a; Scott and Medioli, 1978, 1980a, 1986; Williams, 1989, 1994; Thomas and Varekamp, 1991; Varekamp et al., 1992; Gehrels, 1994; Nydick et al., 1995;

Varekamp and Thomas, 1998; see also chapter 9). This resolution surpasses that of (1) marsh plants (e.g. *Spartina alterniflora*; Goldstein, 1988b; Gehrels, 1994), which exhibit coarser zonations and may decay beyond recognition; (2) the Holocene portion of the marine oxygen isotope curve; and (3) coral reef terraces (e.g. Wheeler and Aharon, 1991).

Marshes would appear to exhibit intrinsically high temporal resolution. Bioturbation in salt marshes 'does not constantly churn sediments as is commonly the case in shallow subtidal settings' (Goldstein et al., 1996, p. 11) because, although dense halophyte roots pump oxygen into surficial sediment (which would ordinarily promote bioturbation), they also impede bioturbation by crabs, insects, and polychaetes (Basan and Frey, 1977; Frey and Basan, 1981; Howard and Frey, 1985; Sharma et al., 1987; Nydick et al., 1995). Bioturbation in marshes is also counteracted by high rates of sedimentation (e.g. Sharma et al., 1987; Fletcher et al., 1992; Nydick et al., 1995), which should decrease attenuation of stratigraphic signals by rapidly transmitting signals through the mixed layer (Fig. 16.2). For example, assuming $v \cong 0.3$–0.5 cm yr^{-1} (cf. equation (1); e.g. Church et al., 1981, 1987; Krishnaswami et al., 1980; Sharma et al., 1987; Luther et al., 1991), the transit time through the mixed layer (T_m) is only ~40–60 years, which surpasses the T_m of ~2,000–5,000 years for many deep-sea cores ($m \cong 5$–10 cm; $v \cong 2$–5 cm kyr^{-1}) used in 'high-resolution' paleoclimate studies (Schiffelbein, 1985, 1986). Rates of bioturbation in marshes and mixed layer thickness tend to increase into the lower marsh, however, as subtidal settings are approached.

Hippensteel and Martin (1999) conducted a study of temporal resolution in South Carolina (Folly Beach) marshes and back-barrier overwash fans based on the Guinasso-Schink (1975) model (equation (1)). Using deep-sea microtektite (tracer) concentration profiles, Officer and Lynch (1983) solved for G:

$$G = \frac{\beta_2 + \sqrt{\beta_2^2 + \pi^2 \beta_1(\beta_2 - \beta_1)}}{2\pi^2 \beta_1} \quad (8)$$

where β_1 and β_2 are the slopes (fitted by least squares) of the base and upwardly-smeared portions of the tracer layer, respectively (cf. Figures 16.2, 16.4); i.e. the vertical concentration gradient. Hippensteel and Martin (1999) calculated β_1 and β_2 from the slopes of the base and upwardly bioturbated portions of washovers fans (~25 cm in thickness); these fans were enriched in Oligo-Miocene Foraminifera (tracers) that had been eroded from subtidal offshore outcrops by storms and redeposited in back-barrier marshes. Using equation (1), and assuming $m = 20$ cm and $v = 0.2$ cm yr^{-1} (Sharma et al., 1987), Hippensteel (1995) calculated an average D of 1.0×10^{-7} cm^2 sec^{-1} ($\pm 0.14 \times 10^{-7}$ cm^2 sec^{-1}, 95% Confidence Interval) for a high marsh site ($n = 2$ washovers). At two sites located at the high marsh-low marsh boundary, average D was 3.45×10^{-7} cm^2 sec^{-1} and 5.94×10^{-7} cm^2 sec^{-1} (± 0.39 and 0.79×10^{-7} cm^2 sec^{-1}, respectively; $n = 3$ for each site). For a streamside site, D was 7.88×10^{-7} cm^2 sec^{-1} $\pm 0.863 \times 10^{-7}$ cm^2 sec^{-1} ($n = 3$). These rates correspond to observed burrow densities in the marsh. Low and intermediate marsh bioturbation rates fall at the low end of the range for intertidal-shallow subtidal environments such as Long Island Sound (~10^{-7}–10^{-4} cm^2 sec^{-1}; Matisoff, 1982), whereas high marsh values approach low deep-sea rates (10^{-8}–10^{-9} cm^2 sec^{-1}; Matisoff, 1982), which argues for excellent temporal resolution (low signal attenuation) in marsh sediments.

Hippensteel (1995) also restored washover events to their presumed original levels. The original datum (x_0) can be restored from the observed tracer (Oligo-Miocene Foraminifera) peak x_m by

$$x_0 = x_m - \left[1 - \frac{\ln\frac{8\pi^2 G^2 + 2}{4G + 1}}{\pi^2 G - 1}\right] m \quad (9)$$

(Officer and Lynch, 1983; see also Officer, 1982; Officer and Lynch, 1982). Using equations (8) and (9), Hippensteel (1995) calculated displacements and corresponding temporal offsets of washovers that generally agree with the trend of increasing bioturbation from high to low marsh. For a high marsh site, he calculated a displacement of 5–13 cm and a temporal offset of 28–65 years for $n = 2$ washovers. For two sites at the high–low marsh boundary, displacements and temporal offsets were 7–34 cm and ~40–170 years, respectively (total $n = 6$), but for a stream-side site only 0.4–14 cm and 2–68 years ($n = 3$). These values again indicate resolution that potentially surpasses that of deep-sea cores.

Much of the dynamics of formation of marsh foraminiferal assemblages has been overlooked, however (Jonasson and Patterson, 1992; Goldstein and Harben, 1993; Hoge, 1994, 1995; Goldstein et al., 1996). Differential preservation of foraminiferal assemblages can, for example, mimic the magnitude and frequency of sea-level change determined from foraminiferal assemblages (Fig. 16.5). As van de Plassche (1991,

p. 176) warns, 'until ... higher age and depth resolution is obtained, the precise relation between the nature and magnitude of ... low-amplitude sea-level movements ... and causes and effects of climate change ... remains unknown.' Alteration of surface assemblages is critical because marsh zonations, and corresponding inferences about sea level, are recognized downcore primarily using either relative (%) or absolute (number of tests gram^{-1} sediment) abundances of key species. In low marshes, fragile agglutinated (e.g. *Ammotium salsum, Miliammina fusca*) and calcareous (e.g. *Ammonia beccarii*) Foraminifera are often lost via oxidation of organic test cements and dissolution, respectively, so that the fossil assemblage may be dominated by typical high marsh, robust agglutinated species (such as *Jadammina macrescens* and *Trochammina inflata*) that comprised much smaller proportions of the original

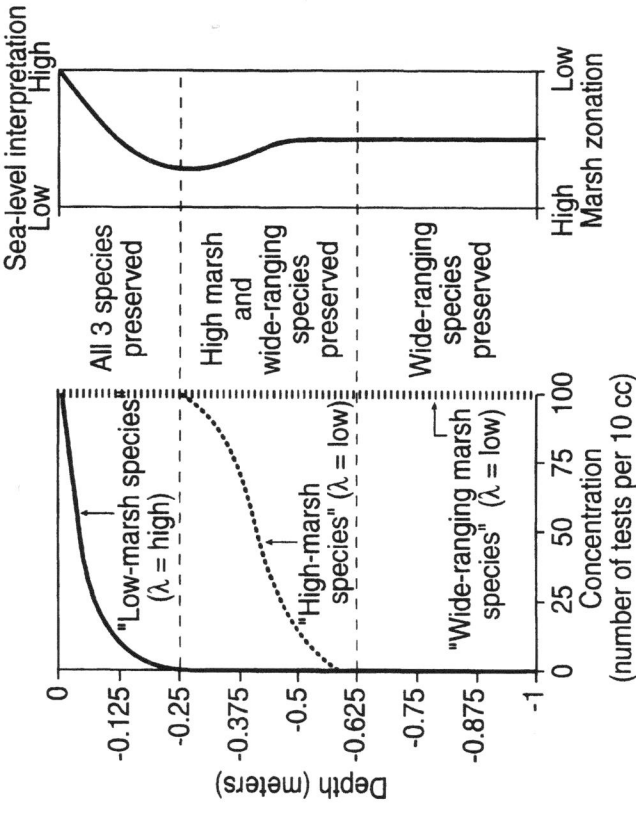

Figure 16.5 Hypothetical effects of differential preservation of marsh foraminiferal assemblages on sea-level interpretation. Left column shows hypothetical assemblages: solid curved line = *Ammotium salsum* (epifaunal-shallow infaunal, mainly inhabiting low marsh, and exhibiting high rate of decay or high 'λ'); dotted line = *Jadammina macrescens* (epifaunal-infaunal, mainly higher marsh, low λ); dashed vertical line = *Arenoparrella mexicana* (wide-ranging epifaunal to deep infaunal, low λ). Biodiffusion coefficient (*D*) and sedimentation rate (*v*) held constant. Concentrations are absolute, not relative. Right column: sea-level interpretation. Differential preservation of robust species mimics sea-level rise and fall when none has occurred.

living assemblage at the SWI (Jonasson and Patterson, 1992; Goldstein and Harben, 1993; Patterson et al., 1994; Goldstein et al., 1996; Fig. 16.5; cf. Scott and Medioli, 1980b). A number of sea-level curves are in fact based on abundance changes of *J. macrescens* and other robust species. The lack of Foraminifera in highest high marsh and non-marine sediments has also been widely employed as a sea level indicator, but this condition does not necessarily imply a non-marine origin. Test loss in the high marsh no doubt also occurs during early diagenesis, just as in the low marsh. Although not yet investigated for Foraminifera, differential preservation of marsh assemblages may also vary according to latitude because of differences in metabolizability of organic matter (Reaves, 1986).

Differential preservation of infaunal species may also affect the formation of marsh assemblages and, potentially, sea-level interpretations. Goldstein and Harben (1993; see also Goldstein, 1988b; Goldstein et al., 1996) found that the abundance of the common marsh species *Arenoparrella mexicana* changed from ~5% at the surface to ~50% within the top 3–5 cm of sediment because of large infaunal populations. This species, which may live to depths of ~30 cm and 'bypass' the mixed layer, is resistant to degradation and may dominate high marsh death assemblages despite small living populations.

16.3.4 Offshore shelf and slope environments

Gradients in water energy and surface productivity ($CaCO_3$ and organic carbon) and oxygen availability occur across the shelf and into slope environments (Fig. 16.6; Berger and Killingley, 1982; Ekdale et al., 1984). Nevertheless, just as in shallow-water settings, sedimentation rate, which decreases with water depth, may be the overriding factor in the formation and time-averaging of microfossil assemblages in shelf and slope settings. Lin and Morse (1991) concluded that off the Mississippi Delta and Texas–Louisiana shelf, for example, rates of sulfate reduction (and alkalinity generation; cf. equation (7)) and pyrite concentration generally decrease exponentially with increasing water depth, all of which reflect decreasing sedimentation rates (Lin and Morse, 1991; Loubere et al., 1993a,b; Middleburg et al., 1997). Sulfate reduction rates in this region are intermediate between those of shallow nearshore organic carbon-rich sediments and carbon-poor deep-sea sediments (Canfield, 1991; euxinic basins are an exception; e.g. Berger and Soutar, 1970; see also Canfield and Raiswell, 1991). At high sedimentation rates, labile organic matter undergoes a shorter period of oxic and suboxic degradation before it is incorporated into subsurface layers where it can support sulfate reduction (Canfield, 1991; Lin and Morse, 1991). The decline in sulfate reduction rates across the shelf and slope, and especially beyond the shelf-slope break, may be related not only to a decline in sedimentation rates in deeper settings (Nozaki et al., 1977; Carpenter et al., 1982; Smith and Schafer, 1984) but also to decreased surface water productivity, as a commonly-observed peak in foraminiferal (benthic and planktonic) abundance occurs near the continental shelf edge (e.g. Bandy, 1953). As rates of sulfate reduction decline across the shelf and slope (Lin and Morse, 1991), rates of bioturbation must either decline or be counteracted by increased input of $CaCO_3$ or sediment for good preservation to occur.

In the case of microfossils, the exact relationships between sedimentation, shell input, sulfate reduction, etc., and the formation of foraminiferal assemblages on the deeper shelf have only recently begun to be explored in detail. Douglas et al. (1980) concluded that life and death assemblages of the upper slope (100–400 m) of the southern California borderland are strongly similar (based on surface samples), but Loubere and Gary (1990; see also Loubere et al., 1993a,b) concluded that there was substantial specimen loss in the upper 10 cm of boxcores from off the Mississippi Delta and the western Gulf of Mexico continental slope. Denne and Sen Gupta (1989) came to similar conclusions for Texas–Louisiana slope assemblages: they found that bathyal calcareous species could be grouped into those that are well-preserved (increasing

Preservation and temporal resolution in marine settings

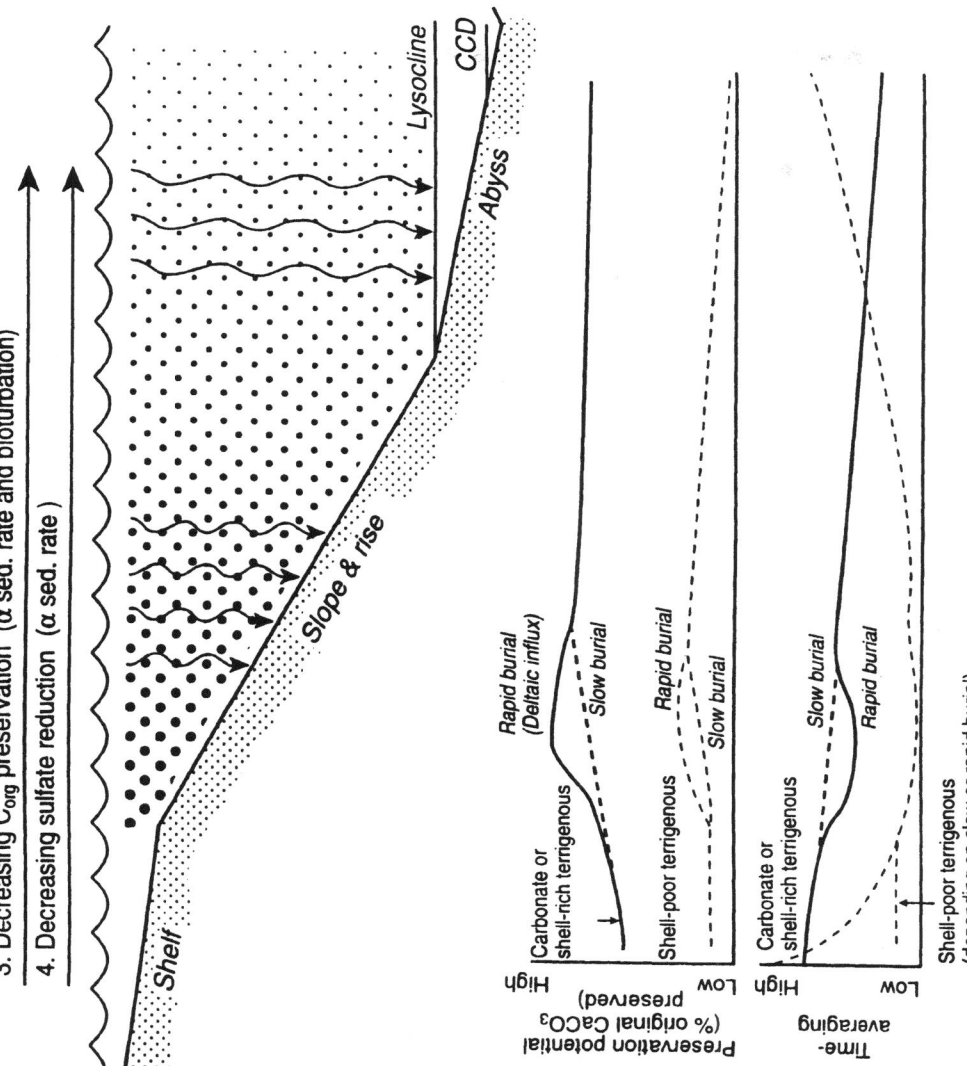

Figure 16.6 Speculative gradients in preservation and time-averaging across a passive continental margin. Gradients are based primarily on decreasing rates of bioturbation with water depth (decreasing values of D), and, in descending order, on decreasing rates of sedimentation, organic matter burial, and sulfate reduction. 'Preservation potential' is defined as the percent original shell (CaCO$_3$) material preserved. In carbonate environments, high rates of bioturbation are probably counteracted by high shell concentrations and sulfate reduction, thereby promoting preservation and time-averaging. In shell-poor shallow-water terrigenous sediments, assemblages may be either more or less time-averaged than carbonate-rich assemblages, depending on sedimentation and bioturbation rates. In deltaic environments (shelf and slope), rapid burial should inhibit time-averaging, but sediment starvation (via delta lobe-switching) probably promotes it. Time-averaging is expected to increase on the continental rise, but low rates of bioturbation keep time-averaging at a minimum above the lysocline. Below the lysocline, and especially the CCD, extensive dissolution and reworking may accentuate time-averaging depending upon corrosiveness of bottom waters. See text for further discussion. (Modified from Martin, 1993).

downcore), moderately preserved (no trend), and poorly preserved (decreasing downcore). Agglutinated species were either resistant to disaggregation (no trend) or disaggregation-prone (decreasing downcore; see also Smith, 1987; Murray, 1989).

Benthic Foraminifera in slope and deep-sea environments also frequently exhibit depth stratification and microhabitat preferences that reflect changes in surface productivity, organic carbon influx, and pore water oxygen content (Corliss, 1985; Loubere et al., 1993a,b; Rathburn and Miao, 1995). Depth stratification may represent a situation analogous to infaunal macroinvertebrates mixing with long dead epifaunal species (K. Flessa, 1993, personal communication); changes in pore water chemistry with depth in sediment may also affect stable isotope ratios of tests of foraminifers living infaunally (McCorkle et al., 1990). Corliss and Emerson (1990) concluded that habitat depth in sediment is related to organic carbon input (which decreases with water depth) and dissolved oxygen in the pore waters (based on dissolved Mn^{2+} profiles). Shelf species tend to be epifaunal (shallow oxic layer), whereas on the continental slope and rise, the oxidized surface layer is relatively thick and Foraminifera are primarily deep infaunal species (see also Loubere et al., 1993a).

Unfortunately, because of a paucity of dates, durations of time-averaging of shelf and slope foraminiferal assemblages must for the present be based on the accumulation of macroinvertebrate hardparts (cf. results for Choya Bay). Flessa and Kowalewski (1994; see also Flessa, 1993) compiled 734 published radiocarbon dates (many conventional and uncalibrated) from modern nearshore (<10m) and shelf (>10m) habitats, assuming that the maximum age of a shell serves as an estimate of time-averaging. Deep shelf shells ($n = 126$ localities total) exhibited a bimodal distribution: slightly more than 25% (33 localities) fell into the 0–3,000 year class, whereas ~25% (31 localities) fell into the 9,000–12,000 age class, with a median of 9,435 years. Nearly 70% (42 localities) of nearshore shells (66 localities total) fell into the 0–500 year class. The median age of all shells was ~1,255 years. For both deep and shallow shelves, the number of shells in greater age classes declined rapidly toward the maximum age class of 36,000–39,000 years, which is near the upper limit of radiocarbon dating.

Flessa (1993) suggested a number of explanations for the general increase in duration of time-averaging away from shore (see also Flessa and Kowalewski, 1994). Shells may tend to be younger in nearshore settings because of faster rates of destruction (especially via bioerosion but also because of abrasion and fragmentation, and predation); greater sediment accumulation rates, which ought to leave younger shells nearer the SWI barring other processes; higher rates of shell production, which would bias assemblages toward younger ages; the possible counteraction of increased sedimentation on bioturbation; and the Holocene rise in sea level: very old shells may not have been able to accumulate in many nearshore settings because sea level reached within ~10 m of its present position only ~7,000 years ago. Thus, the relatively recent rise in sea level may have restricted the potential duration of time-averaging in nearshore sediments, while shells continued to accumulate further offshore.

16.3.5 Deep sea

The onset of $CaCO_3$ dissolution in the deep-sea begins ~0.5–1 km above the lysocline (Emerson and Bender, 1981); the lysocline tends to shallow toward the continental margins because of oxidation of greater amounts of organic matter of both marine and terrigenous origin (Bé, 1977; Berger, 1977). In the sediment itself, dissolution is concentrated in the mixed layer (Archer et al., 1989), which is normally on the order of 5–10 cm thick.

Much of the work on dissolution of calcareous hardparts has been on planktonic Foraminifera because of their use in biostratigraphic and paleoceanographic interpretation. Douglas (1971) developed a dissolution-susceptible scale for planktonic Foraminifera (later modified by Malmgren, 1987). Planktonic species that have somewhat higher Mg test concentrations are more susceptible to dissolution (Savin and Douglas, 1973; Bender et al., 1975); also, species that are most susceptible to test dissolution tend to settle the most slowly (e.g. Berger, 1967, 1968, 1970a, 1971; Parker and Berger, 1971; see Bé, 1977, for review). This is because most shallow-dwelling species harbor symbiotic dinoflagellates and typically have small thin-walled porous tests in order to remain afloat in the photic zone (e.g. *Globigerinoides ruber*), whereas deeper-dwelling species often have dissolution-resistant features such as thick test walls and rope-like keels that decrease their buoyancy (e.g. *Globorotalia menardii*). Preferential settling of certain species may also affect their dissolution behavior: in the case of *Globorotalia truncatulinoides*, for example, the exposed cone of the test was more severely affected by dissolution than the flat (spiral surface) in experiments (Bé et al., 1977b). Morphological features may also differ in their mineralogy and dissolution susceptibility (Brown and Elderfield, 1996), and sediment infilling tends to confine dissolution to the outer surfaces of tests (Hecht et al., 1975; Keir and Hurd, 1983).

Although planktonic tests are typically not transported far as they settle through the water column, they begin to dissolve, especially after they have reached the ocean bottom, as a result of the oxidation of organic matter and sulfides (equations (5) and (6); Adelseck and Berger, 1977). Consequently, the number of 'assemblages' present in the plankton may be reduced in number in sediment: Bé and Hutson (1977) found that in the tropical and subtropical Indian Ocean six 'life assemblages' were reduced to two thanatocoenoses in sediment and that the number of species in the sediment assemblages was greater than in the planktonic assemblages. The apparent sea surface temperature (SST) reflected by the thanatocoenosis may therefore be inaccurate (e.g. Bé and Hutson, 1977). Le and Thunell (1996) developed a method which filters out the effect of differential dissolution on the calculation of SSTs.

Broecker et al. (1991) developed a radiocarbon-based age (mixing) model for deep-sea assemblages based on the Berger-Heath (1968) approach. This model is based on the assumption that dissolution within the mixed layer is proportional to the residence (replacement) time of biogenic grains within the mixed layer, and that the age and thickness of the mixed layer reflect the extent of dissolution. Broecker et al. (1991) hypothesized that there are three basic forms of dissolution in the deep sea: (1) homogeneous dissolution, in which each grain loses a constant fraction of its mass per unit time (irrespective of grain type): homogeneous dissolution should shift the mass distribution of assemblages toward younger grains because the replacement time of grains in the mixed layer by new grains from the pelagic rain will be reduced; therefore, the greater the extent of homogeneous dissolution, the younger the age (based on ^{14}C dates) of core top assemblages; (2) sequential dissolution, in which grain type A dissolves completely before grain type B begins to dissolve, and so on: in this case, core top ages should increase with the extent of dissolution; and (3) interface dissolution of all sediment grains at the SWI before burial: like sequential dissolution, interface dissolution increases the replacement time of grains in the mixed layer and thus increases the radiocarbon age of the core top.

To determine where in the spectrum dissolution actually occurs, Broecker et al. (1991) employed two approaches. One was to compare mixed layer depths calculated from downcore radiocarbon dates on bulk $CaCO_3$ with those calculated from (a) actual core-top ages and (b) Holocene accumulation rates, assuming a steady-state system (based on the Berger-Heath model) with no dissolution. In this model, calculated mixed layer thicknesses are proportional to radiocarbon age. Therefore, to the extent that homogeneous dissolution has occurred, the calculated mixed layer thickness will be smaller than the measured thickness. The second approach was to compare radiocarbon dates on core tops from a range of water depths (and therefore range of dissolution), but all collected within a relatively small area so as to minimize variation in pelagic rain rates of biogenic particles (planktonic Foraminifera, etc.). In the first test, measured mixed layer thicknesses were less than thicknesses calculated from the model (i.e. homogeneous dissolution does not occur). In the second test, ages approximate those for sequential or interface dissolution (i.e. ages are older than those predicted by the model).

Broecker et al. (1991) concluded, however, that neither interface or sequential dissolution could be occurring. They ruled out interface dissolution because dissolution appears to occur within the sediment (Archer et al., 1989), and not exclusively at the SWI. Sequential dissolution was also ruled out because in the deepest cores (near or below CCD), planktonics are absent and benthics nearly so (Broecker et al., 1991, table 3); i.e. microfossil components appear to be degraded at nearly equal rates. Since homogeneous dissolution also does not appear to occur, these authors sought an explanation for core top assemblage ages based on changes in deep-water $CO_3^=$ ion concentration through time. They suggested that Pacific waters became more corrosive, and Atlantic waters less so, during the last glacial-interglacial transition. Under such conditions, Holocene accumulation rates would have been reduced by chemical erosion in the Pacific, thereby increasing the likelihood of reworking older (glacial) sediments into the mixing zone (cf. Berger and Heath model; see also Murray-Wallace and Belperio, 1995). Broecker et al. (1991) determined that radiocarbon ages for Pacific deep-sea core tops were 8,000-10,000 years greater than those for Atlantic core tops from comparable depths below the lysocline.

Differential preservation in deep-sea sediments may be more complicated than Broecker et al. (1991) concluded, however. Dissolution is neither purely homogeneous or sequential: benthic Foraminifera tend to be more resistant than planktonics (Berger, 1968; Corliss and Honjo, 1981; Bé, 1977). The benthic/planktonic ratio, for example, has often been used as an index of post-mortem alteration of deep-sea assemblages (Thunell, 1976) and even planktonic tests may show differential resistance (Berger, 1968). Benthic Foraminifera also differ in their resistance to dissolution, but the relationship between foraminiferal ecology, microstructure, habitat, and preservation is unclear. Corliss and Honjo (1981), for example, found that the reef-dwelling *Amphistegina* was much less resistant to dissolution than characteristic bathyal and abyssal species, such as *Nuttallides umbonifera*, which prefers waters beneath the CCD (Bremer and Lohmann, 1982).

Thus, like differential preservation of Foraminifera on shallow shelves, dissolution-resistant benthic (or planktonic) Foraminifera may erroneously increase deep-sea core-top age estimates (cf. Rathburn and Miao, 1995). Indeed, all forms that co-occurred in sediment of Broecker et al.'s (1991) study showed evidence of partial dissolution. Moreover, DuBois and Prell (1988) found that in the tropical Atlantic, mixed layer ages of sublysocline (>4400 m) cores decreased (by ca. 500-1,000 years) relative to core tops from above the lysocline. They found that increased weight percent fragmentation and percent resistant planktonics coincided with changes in age at this depth. Therefore, in sediments below the lysocline, the radiocarbon age structure of the mixed layer in the Atlantic is opposite to that of the Pacific (see also Broecker et al., 1991). Decreased corrosiveness (relative to the Pacific) of overlying waters and higher carbonate content of sediments have apparently allowed a type of sequential dissolution to proceed in Atlantic sublysocline environments that produces younger (not older) core top ages; i.e. old skeletons are removed faster than young ones so that mixed layer ages decrease (DuBois and Prell, 1988). In terms of mixed layer age, this is just the opposite of sequential dissolution as defined by Broecker et al. (1991). DuBois and Prell (1988) concluded that in the case of dissolution, the steady-state model is inappropriate for calculating temporal resolution and that ^{14}C stratigraphies from *different preservational settings cannot be strictly compared*: although sediment may have the same radiocarbon age, the proportions of the components producing that age may not be the same if the particles have different preservational histories.

To complicate matters further, Loubere

(1989) found that, based on the Berger-Heath (1968) model, significant variation in species abundances occur in the mixed layer as a result of taxon depth stratification. Infaunal taxa increase non-linearly in abundance with depth to the level of their true habitat, below which taxon abundance remains constant, whereas epifaunal assemblages may be significantly modified. He concluded that the best representation of total taxon abundance occurs at the base of the bioturbated zone (see also Denne and Sen Gupta, 1989; cf. Rathburn and Miao, 1995).

Loubere (1991; see also Loubere, 1997) also found that certain deep-sea (East Pacific Rise) Foraminifera respond to surface productivity (organic carbon) gradients. Significantly, some species appear to be highly adaptable (in terms of microhabitat preference and depth stratification) to changes in food availability and environmental conditions (Linke and Lutze, 1993). At great depths, deep-water epifaunal species predominate because organic carbon (food) becomes limiting.

16.4 DECONVOLUTION: THE RECONSTRUCTION OF SIGNAL INPUTS

In theory it is possible to reconstruct any input to the stratigraphic record. Unfortunately, such approaches have so far met with only limited success. A number of attempts have been made at direct deconvolution (unmixing or 'unfiltering') of sedimentary signals (e.g. $^{18}\delta O$) based on the Berger-Heath and Guinasso-Schink mixing models (Berger et al., 1977; Schiffelbein, 1985, 1986), but the deconvolution overestimated mixing intensity and produced artificial overshoots and offsets (Jones and Ruddiman, 1982). Christensen (1986) and co-workers (Christensen and Bhunia, 1986; Christensen and Goetz, 1987; Christensen and Osuna, 1989; Christensen and Klein, 1991; see also Robbins, 1982) were more successful in reconstructing fluxes of pollutants and radiotracers in lake sediments using both the Guinasso-Schink (1975) and Berger-Heath (1968) mixing models; they assumed that bioturbation and sedimentation rates are constant and they treated sediment compaction effects by assuming particular porosity profiles. Although these assumptions appear valid for the thin mixed layer of lacustrine environments (~5–10 cm) where Christensen et al. worked, they do not appear to hold for most marine environments, with the exception of the deep-sea, which is also typified by a thin mixed layer.

In response to these difficulties, Bard et al. (1987) developed a technique based on a discretized version of the Laplace transform. They first deconvolved abundance curves of species of planktonic Foraminifera and then the isotopic signals stored in their shells. Other workers have noted that even at an abrupt lithologic or paleoclimatic boundary, abundant species above and below the boundary that are indicative of climate change are worked upward and downward across the boundary (Berger and Heath, 1968; Hutson, 1980; see also Andree et al., 1984; Broecker et al., 1984; Peng and Broecker, 1984; Andree, 1987). In Bard et al.'s (1987) technique, comparison of actual data with unmixed curves enabled recognition of bioturbation. Nevertheless, restored signals may be erroneous when species abundances approach zero; the technique also assumes that bioturbation and sedimentation rates remain constant (box model of Berger and Heath, 1968).

Peng et al. (1977, 1979) developed numerical models of *continuous* inputs (as opposed to impulse signals like those discussed above). In such models, the Guinasso-Schink or Berger-Heath models (or modifications thereof) are solved 'in reverse' by specifying various sedimentary parameters (e.g. m, v, D) and solving for the unknown (e.g. test inputs). Given the spatio-temporal variation in test inputs, however ((Buzas, 1965, 1968, 1969, 1970; Green et al., 1993b; Martin et al., 1995, 1996; see Murray, 1991b, for brief review), it is probably best to use averaged inputs (determined from seasonal studies) in an attempt to smooth data and prevent artificial overshoots. Actual test inputs can then presumably be determined by varying test inputs into the model (while holding other parameters constant) until preserved concentrations predicted by the model are similar to those sampled in cores.

Although numerical models have the advantage of removing amplification of noise, like analytical models, they have the disadvantage of not providing unique solutions. In theory, different equations or values of sedimentary parameters may produce the same result (Boudreau, 1986a,b, 1997; Bard et al., 1987) and small errors in measurement may swamp the system (Simon, 1986). Considering the difficulties of analytical solutions, however, if estimates of sedimentary parameters (D, m, v) can be reasonably constrained, numerical models may provide the greatest promise for reconstructing stratigraphic signals. For example, Pizzuto and Schwendt (1997) modeled six thousand years of sediment accumulation and autocompaction in a Delaware (U.S.A.) marsh using a FORTRAN program (SQUISH3) based on finite-consolidation strain theory:

$$\frac{\partial^2 e}{\partial z^2} - \lambda(\gamma_s - \gamma)\frac{\partial e}{\partial z} = \frac{1}{G}\frac{\partial e}{\partial t}, \quad (10)$$

where $(\gamma_s - \gamma)$ is the submerged unit weight of sediment, G is a finite strain consolidation coefficient, and z is the volume of solids per unit area above an arbitrary datum, and

$$e = (e_i - e_f)e^{-\gamma\sigma} + e_f, \quad (11)$$

in which e_i and e_f are the void ratios at the beginning and end of primary consolidation, respectively, and σ is the effective stress. The model was applied to an accumulating column of sediment consisting of sediment layers of specified void ratios deposited at specified time intervals. Material properties of the sediment were determined initially from laboratory and field studies and rates constrained by radiocarbon dates. The model was then used to reproduce the distribution of void ratios within a vibracore, the actual thicknesses of sedimentary units, and the history of elevation changes of the SWI that was consistent with both a previously-determined sea-level curve for the Delaware coast and the downcore sequence of paleoenvironments. According to the model, horizons have been lowered as much as 2.3 m by autocompaction alone, the rate of which has ranged from one-half to one-third of the rate of sea-level rise!

16.5 THE CIRCUMVENTION OF TIME-AVERAGING

Methods of minimizing time-averaging are of critical importance in the study of paleoclimate signals preserved in deep-sea cores. Schiffelbein (1984; see also Schiffelbein, 1985, 1986) concluded that in deep-sea cores with sedimentation rates of up to 7 cm/ka, high frequency (ca. 3,000 yr) signals show severe attenuation. One way to accentuate signal-to-noise ratios is to 'stack' records from different sites (e.g. Imbrie et al., 1984a).

By contrast, methods of circumventing time-averaging have received much less attention in shallow-shelf settings. McKinney and Frederick (1992; see also McKinney and Allmon, 1995; McKinney, 1996; McKinney et al., 1996) examined patterns of local extinction using the abundances of 25 species of benthic Foraminifera collected at 1 m intervals from a single section of the Eo-Oligocene Ocala Limestone of northern Florida. They analyzed the population abundance fluctuations through time (upsection) using a fractal-based technique called rescaled-range analysis (Sugihara and May, 1990). This method appears to minimize the effects of time-averaging and potential hiatuses (Sadler and Strauss, 1990) because it is fractal-based (independent of scale). Let $n(t)$ equal the abundance of a species during a particular time interval t, and let $x'(t)$ represent the normalized deviations of abundance $[n'(t) = \bar{n}(t) - n(t)]$ for each t between 0 and T or the entire time interval]. The rescaled range is then

$$R(T) = \max n'(t) - \min n'(t) \quad (12)$$

where $0 \leq t \leq T$. Variations in $R(T)$ through time are then analyzed with a fractal model

$$R(T) = cT^H, \quad (13)$$

where c is a proportionality constant $[R(T) \propto T^H]$ and $H = 1/F$, where F = the fractal dimension. $F = 1$ for a straight line and $F = 2$ for a plane; if $F = 2$, then $H = 0.5$, which means that the plane is 'filled' by the curve and represents a random walk (Sugihara and May, 1990). For $H = 0.5$, the time series (the collection of n's over the entire time interval T) of rescaled abundance variations R represents a random walk (Brownian motion) no matter what the scale of Δt (duration of observation); abundance fluctuations show no 'persistent' trend in a particular direction (increase or decrease). As F decreases from 2 to 1, H increases above 0.5, and R becomes less-and-less plane-filling (tending toward a line). In this case, there is a persistent trend of increasing variation in abundance at every scale of Δt. There will be 'higher highs' and 'lower lows' because as Δt increases, variation also increases. If, on the other hand, H decreases to <0.5, variation decreases ('antipersistent'). McKinney and Frederick (1992) found a significant negative correlation ($r = -0.60$; $p < 0.05$) between H of a species and its stratigraphic range, and concluded that populations with greater abundance fluctuations go extinct sooner than those that maintain relatively stable populations.

16.6 CONCLUSIONS

Shells of different taxa may be degraded by different pathways in the same depositional setting because of differences in size, mineralogy, microstructure, sedimentation rate, and pore water chemistry. Thus, intuitively obvious generalizations about taphonomy may be false (e.g. Martin et al., 1996; Martin, 1998). Moreover, most actualistic studies of foraminiferal taphonomy have concentrated on shallow-water environments, no doubt because of their accessibility and perhaps also funding, whereas much of the fossil record formed in deeper shelf and slope environments. Generalizations based on shallow-water settings may prove to be inapplicable to deep-water settings.

Some depositional settings are better-suited for particular types of investigations than others, depending on the desired scale of temporal resolution (Kowalewski, 1997). Realistically, the best temporal resolution that can probably be attained in most cases is in the deep sea, where relatively continuous cores normally provide adequate temporal resolution. But even in this setting, signals may be damped (Schiffelbein, 1984) and the effects of bioturbation and erosion underestimated (Berger et al., 1979; Martin et al., 1993; Martin and Fletcher, 1995). On the other hand, sites of rapid burial, such as deltas, may be suitable for paleobiologic investigations on ecologic scales, although on longer (evolutionary-biostratigraphic) scales, the continuity of section may become an impediment because of delta lobe-switching or sea-level change, and must be evaluated (e.g. Martin et al., 1993; Martin and Fletcher, 1995).

Although it is viewed negatively by most workers, time-averaging is often an advantage, since short-term noise is damped (Behrensmeyer and Kidwell, 1985). For example, modern macroinvertebrate death assemblages from soft-bottom habitats are comparable to repeated (and expensive) biological surveys in assessing the 'long-term' dynamics (hundreds of years) of biological communities (Kidwell and Flessa, 1995). Given the sensitivity of Foraminifera to environmental change (e.g. Alve, 1995a), micropaleontology is well-suited to contribute to the paradigm shift in the earth sciences from resource exploitation to resource conservation. But, micropaleontologists must begin to accentuate what can be regained from the fossil record rather than what is lost (Behrensmeyer and Kidwell, 1985; Martin, 1991, 1995). They must seek more quantitative models of the distribution and preservation of microfossils, the reconstruction of the shell original inputs (signals), and the implications for community homeostasis. This will be no small feat, given the difficulties encountered so far, but we can only learn by trying.

16.7 ACKNOWLEDGMENTS

The author's investigations of foraminiferal taphonomy have been supported by the

National Science Foundation; this support is very gratefully acknowledged. Barbara Broge drafted figures and Cheryl Doherty typed portions of the manuscript. Scott Hippensteel kindly produced Fig. 16.5. The manuscript benefitted substantially from reviews by Laurie Anderson, Sue Kidwell, Scott Snyder, and Barun Sen Gupta.

REFERENCES

Abraham, E.R. (1998) The generation of plankton patchiness by turbulent stirring. *Nature*, **391**, 577–80.

Adam, P. (1990) *Saltmarsh Ecology*, Cambridge University Press, Cambridge.

Adegoke, O.S., Omatsola, N.E. and Salami, N.B. (1976) Benthic foraminiferal biofacies off the Niger Delta, in *First International Symposium on Benthic Foraminifera of Continental Margins, Part A: Ecology and Biology*, (eds C.T. Schafer and B.R. Pelletier), *Maritime Sediments*, Special Publication No. 1, pp. 279–92.

Adelseck, C.G. and Berger, W.H. (1977) On the dissolution of planktonic foraminifera and associated microfossils during settling and on the sea floor, in *Dissolution of Deep-Sea Carbonates*, (eds W.V. Sliter, A.W.H. Bé and W.H. Berger), Cushman Foundation for Foraminiferal Research Special Publication No. 13, pp. 70–81.

Aharon, P. (1983) 140,000-yr isotope climatic record from raised coral reef in New Guinea. *Nature*, **304**, 720–3.

Akimoto, K., Azuma, N., Ohshima, H. et al. (1997) Distribution of living benthic foraminifera in the anomalous physical and chemical conditions under the influence of the cold methane seepage, Sagami Trough, Japan. *First International Conference on Applications of Micropaleontology in Environmental Sciences, June 15–20, 1997, Tel Aviv, Israel, Abstracts*, pp. 26–7.

Albani, A.D., Favero, V.M. and Serandrei Barbero, R. (1998) Distribution of sediment and benthic foraminifera in the Gulf of Venice, Italy. *Estuarine, Coastal and Shelf Science*, **46**, 251–65.

Albani, A.D. and Serandrei Barbero, R. (1982) A foraminiferal fauna from the lagoon of Venice, Italy. *Journal of Foraminiferal Research*, **12**, 234–41.

Albrecht-Buchler, G. (1977) Daughter 3T3 cells. Are they mirror images of each other? *Journal of Cell Biology*, **72**, 595–603.

Alexander, S.P. and DeLaca, T.E. (1987) Feeding adaptations of the Foraminiferan *Cibicides refulgens* living epizoically and parasitically on the Antarctic scallop *Adamussium colbecki*. *Biological Bulletin*, **173**, 136–59.

Allen, R.D. (1964) Cytoplasmic streaming and locomotion in marine Foraminifera, in *Primitive Motile Systems in Cell Biology*, (eds R.D. Allen and N. Kamiya), Academic Press, New York, pp. 407–32.

Aller, J.Y. (1995) Molluscan death assemblages on the Amazon Shelf: Implication for physical and biological controls on benthic populations. *Palaeogeography, Palaeoclimatology, Palaeoecology*, **118**, 181–212.

Aller, J.Y. and Aller, R.C. (1986) Evidence for localized enhancement of biological activity associated with tube and burrow structures in deep-sea sediments at the HEBBLE site, western North Atlantic. *Deep-Sea Research*, **33**, 755–90.

Aller, R.C. and Cochran, J.K. (1976) $^{234}Th/^{238}U$ disequilibrium in near-shore sediment: Particle reworking and diagenetic time scales. *Earth and Planetary Science Letters*, **29**, 37–50.

Altenbach, A. (1992) Short term processes in the foraminiferal response to organic flux rates, in *Approaches to Paleoproductivity Reconstructions*, (eds G. van der Zwaan et al), *Marine Micropaleontology*, **19**, 119–29.

Altenbach, A. and Sarnthein, M. (1989) Productivity record in benthic foraminifera, in *Productivity of the Ocean: Present and Past*, (eds W.H. Berger, V.S. Smetacek and G. Wefer), John Wiley, New York, pp. 255–69.

Altenbach, A.V., Unsöld, G. and Wagler, E. (1988) The hydrodynamic environment of *Saccorhiza ramosa*. *Meyniana*, **40**, 119–32.

Alve, E. (1990) Variations in estuarine foraminiferal biofacies with diminishing oxygen conditions in Drammensfjord, SE Norway, in *Paleoecology, Biostratigraphy, Paleocean-

References

Alve, E. (1991a) Benthic foraminifera in sediment cores reflecting heavy metal pollution in Sorfjord, Western Norway. *Journal of Foraminiferal Research*, **21**, 1–19.

Alve, E. (1991b) Foraminifera, climatic change, and pollution: a study of Late Holocene sediments in Drammensfjord, Southeast Norway. *The Holocene*, **1** (3), 243–61.

Alve, E. (1994) Opportunistic features of the foraminifer *Stainforthia fusiformis* (Williamson): Evidence from Frierfjord, Norway. *Journal of Micropalaeontology*, **13**, 24.

Alve, E. (1995a) Benthic foraminifera response to estuarine pollution: a review. *Journal of Foraminiferal Research*, **25**, 190–203.

Alve, E. (1995b) Benthic foraminiferal distribution and recolonization of formerly anoxic environments in Drammensfjord, southern Norway. *Marine Micropaleontology*, **25**, 169–86.

Alve, E. and Bernhard, J.M. (1995) Vertical migratory response of benthic foraminifera to controlled oxygen concentrations in an experimental mesocosm. *Marine Ecology Progress Series*, **116**, 137–51.

Alve, E. and Nagy, J. (1986) Estuarine foraminiferal distribution in Sandebutka, a branch of the Oslo Fjord. *Journal of Foraminiferal Research*, **16** (4), 261–84.

Alve, E. and Nagy, J. (1988) Pollution-induced changes in estuarine foraminiferal distribution in the Oslo Fjord. *Abhandlungen der Geologischen Bundesanstalt*, **41**, 11–2.

Alve, E. and Olsgard, F. (1997) Benthic foraminiferal colonization in experiments with cu-contaminated sediments, in *First International Conference on Applications of Micropaleontology in Environmental Sciences, June 15–20, 1997, Tel Aviv, Israel, Abstracts*, pp. 28–30.

Alzieu, C. (1991) Environmental Problems Caused by TBT in France: Assessment, Regulations, Prospects. *Marine Environmental Research*, **32**, 7–17.

Alzugaray Henríquez, J.G., Unibe Barichivich, J.C. and Velasquez Mera, J.G. (1979) Foraminíferos bentónicos recientes como indicadores biologicos de contaminación litoral en canal Tenglo (41° 30′S, 72° 59′W), Chile. *Seminario para optar al titulo de Ingeniero de Ejecución en acuicultura*, Universidad de Chile Sede Osorno, p. 113.

Anderheide, K., Frankel, J. and Williams, N. (1977) Formation and positioning of surface-related structures in protozoa. *Microbiol. Rev*, **44**, 252–302.

Anderson, J.B. (1968) Ecology of Foraminifera from Mississippi Sound and surrounding waters. *Alabama Academy of Science Journal*, **39**, 261–9.

Anderson, L.C., Sen Gupta, B.K., McBride, R.A. and Byrnes, M.R. (1997) Reduced seasonality of Holocene climate and pervasive mixing of Holocene marine section: Northeastern Gulf of Mexico shelf. *Geology*, **25**, 127–130.

Anderson, O.R. (1983) *Radiolaria*, Springer-Verlag, Berlin.

Anderson, O.R. (1988) *Comparative Protozoology: Ecology, Physiology, Life History*, Springer-Verlag, Heidelberg.

Anderson, O.R. and Bé, A.W.H. (1976) A cytochemical fine structure study of phagotrophy in a planktonic foraminifer, *Hastigerina pelagica* (d'Orbigny). *Biological Bulletin of the Marine Biological Laboratory, Woods Hole*, **151**, 437–49.

Anderson, O.R., Lee, J.J. and Faber, W.W. (1991) Collection, maintenance and culture methods for the study of living Foraminifera, in *Biology of Foraminifera*, (eds J.J. Lee and O.R. Anderson), Academic Press, London, pp. 225–358.

Andree, M. (1987) The impact of bioturbation on AMS ^{14}C dates on handpicked foraminifera: A statistical model. *Radiocarbon*, **29**, 169–75.

Andree, M., Beer, J., Oeschger, H. *et al*. (1984) ^{14}C measurements on foraminifera of deep sea cores V28–238 and their preliminary interpretation. *Nuclear Instruments and Methods in Physics Research*, **B5**, 340–5.

Angell, R.W. (1967a) The test structure and composition of the foraminifer *Rosalina floridana*. *Journal of Protozoology*, **14**, 299–307.

Angell, R.W. (1967b) The process of chamber formation in the foraminifer *Rosalina floridana*. *Journal of Protozoology*, **14**, 566–74.

Angell, R.W. (1967c) Test recalcification in *Rosalina floridana* (Cushman). *Contributions from the Cushman Foundation for Foraminiferal Research*, **18**, 176–7.

Angell, R.W. (1971) Observations on gametogenesis in the foraminifer *Spiroloculina hyalina* Schulze. *Journal of Foraminiferal Research*, **1**, 39–42.

Angell, R.W. (1979) Calcification during chamber development in *Rosalina floridana*. *Journal of Foraminiferal Research*, **9**, 341–53.

Angell, R.W. (1980) Test morphogenesis (chamber formation) in the foraminifer *Spiroloculina hyalina* Schulze. *Journal of Foraminiferal Research*, **10**, 89–101.

Antoine, D., Jean-Michel, A. and Morel, A. (1996) Oceanic primary production: 2. Estimation at global scale from satellite (coastal zone color scanner) chlorophyll. *Global Biogeochemical Cycles*, **10**, 57–69.

Archer, D., Emerson, S. and Reimers, C. (1989) Dissolution of calcite in deep-sea sediments: pH and O_2 microelectrode results. *Geochimica et Cosmochimica Acta*, **53**, 2831–45.

Arnal, R.E. (1954) Preliminary report on the sediments and Foraminifera of the Salton Sea, southern California. *Bulletin of the Geological Society of America*, **65**, 1227–8.

Arnold, A.J. (1977) *Distribution of Benthic Foraminifera in the Surface Sediments of the Georgia-South Carolina Continental Slope*, Unpublished M.S. thesis, University of Georgia, Athens.

Arnold, A.J. (1982) Species survivorship in the Cenozoic Globigerinida, in *Proceedings of the North American*

References

Paleontological Conference III, Montreal, August 5–7, 1982, (eds B. Mamet and M.J. Copeland), Business and Economic Service Ltd, Toronto, pp. 9–12.

Arnold, A.J. (1983) Foraminiferal thanatocoenoces on the continental slope off Georgia and South Carolina. *Journal of Foraminiferal Research*, **13**, 79–90.

Arnold, A.J., Kelly, D.C. and Parker, W.C. (1995a) Causality and Cope's Rule: evidence from the planktonic foraminifera. *Journal of Paleontology*, **69**, 203–10.

Arnold, A.J., Parker, W.C. and Hansard S.P. (1995b) Aspects of the post-Cretaceous recovery of the Cenozoic planktic foraminifera. *Marine Micropaleontology*, **26**, 319–27.

Arnold, A.J. and Sen Gupta, B.K. (1981) Diversity changes in the foraminiferal thanatocoenoces of the Georgia-South Carolina continental slope. *Journal of Foraminiferal Research*, **11**, 268–76.

Arnold, Z.M. (1954) Variation and isomorphism in *Allogromia laticollaris*: A clue to Foraminiferal evolution. *Contributions from the Cushman Foundation for Foraminiferal Research*, **5**, 78–87.

Arnold, Z.M. (1955) Life history and cytology of the Foraminiferan *Allogromia laticollaris*. *University of California Publications in Zoology*, **61**, 167–252.

Arnold, Z.M. (1964) Biological observations on the foraminifer *Spiroloculina hyalina* Schulze. *University of California Publications in Zoology*, **72**, 1–93.

Arnold, Z.M. (1967) Biological observations on the foraminifer/*Calcituba polymorpha* Roboz. *Archiv für Protistenkunde*, **110**, 280–304.

Arnold, Z.M. (1972) Observations on the biology of the protozoan *Gromia oviformis* Dujardin. *University of California Publications in Zoology*, **100**, 1–168.

Arnold, Z.M. (1974) Field and laboratory techniques for the study of living foraminifera, in *Foraminifera, v. I*, (eds R.H. Hedley and C.G. Adams), Academic Press, London, pp. 153–206.

Arnold, Z.M. (1984) The gamontic karyology of the saccamminid *Psammophaga simplora* Arnold. *Journal of Foraminiferal Research*, **14**, 171–86.

Azam, F. and Smith, D.C. (1991) Bacterial influence on the variability in the oceans biogeochemical state: A mechanistic view, in *Particle Analysis in Oceanography*, (ed S. Demers), Springer-Verlag, Berlin, NATO ASI Series, Vol. G 27, pp. 213–46.

Baccaert, J. (1986) Foraminiferal bio- and thanatocoenoses of reef flats, Lizard Island, Great Barrier Reef, Australia. Nature of substrate. *Annales de la Société Royale Zoologique de Belgique*, **116**, 3–14.

Backus, R.H. (1986) Biogeographic Boundaries in the Open Ocean, in *Pelagic Biogeography. Proceedings of an International Conference: the Netherlands 29 May–5 June 1985*, (eds A.C. Pierrot-Bults, S. van der Spoel, B.J. Zahuranec and R.K. Johnson), Unesco, pp. 9–24.

Bandy, O.L. (1953) Ecology and paleoecology of some California foraminifera. Part 1. The frequency distribution of Recent foraminifera off California. *Journal of Paleontology*, **27**, 161–82.

Bandy, O.L. (1956) Ecology of Foraminifera of the Northeastern Gulf of Mexico. *U.S. Geological Survey Professional Paper*, **274**, 179–204.

Bandy, O.L. (1959) Geologic significance of coiling ratios in the foraminifer *Globigerina pachyderma* (Ehrenberg). *Bulletin of the Geological Society of America*, **70**, 1708.

Bandy, O.L. (1960) Geologic significance of coiling ratios in the foraminifer *Globigerina pachyderma* (Ehrenberg). *Journal of Paleontology*, **34**, 671–81.

Bandy, O.L. (1964) Cenozoic planktonic foraminiferal zonation. *Micropaleontology*, **10** (1), 1–17.

Bandy, O.L., Ingle, J.C. and Resig, J.M. (1964a) Foraminiferal trends, Laguna Beach outfall area, California. *Limnology and Oceanography*, **9**, 112–23.

Bandy, O.L., Ingle, J.C. and Resig, J.M. (1964b) Foraminifera: Los Angeles County outfall area, California. *Limnology and Oceanography*, **9**, 124–37.

Bandy, O.L., Ingle, J.C. and Resig, J.M. (1965a) Foraminiferal trends, Hyperion outfall, California. *Limnology and Oceanography*, **10**, 314–32.

Bandy, O.L., Ingle, J.C. and Resig, J.M. (1965b) Modifications of foraminiferal distributions by the Orange County outfall, California. *Marine Technology Society Transactions*, pp. 54–76.

Banerji, R.K. (1974) Patchiness in the distribution of planktonic foraminifera in oceanic waters and its probable cause. *Geophytology*, **4** (1), 83–94.

Banerji, R.K. (1977) Benthic foraminifera as an aid to recognize polluted environment: *Proceedings of the Indian-Colloquium in Micropalaeontology and Stratigraphy, Dehra Dun, India, Dec. 1974–Jan. 1975*, pt. 4, pp. 1–6.

Banerji, R.K. (1989) Foraminifera and discrimination of polluted environment along the Bombay Coast, Kalia, Prabha. Micropaleontology of the Shelf Sequences of India, *Indian Colloquium on Micropaleontology and Stratigraphy, University of Delhi, Delhi – India*, pt. 12, pp. 98–117.

Banerji, R.K. (1992) Heavy metals and benthic foraminiferal distribution along Bombay coast, India. *Benthos '90, Sendai, Studies in Benthic Foraminifera*, Tokai University Press, pp. 151–8

Banner, F.T. (1982) A classification and introduction to the Globigerinacea, in *Aspects of Micropaleontology*, (eds F.T. Banner and A.R. Lord), George Allen and Unwin, London, pp. 142–239.

Bard, E., Arnold, M., Duprat, J. *et al.* (1987) Reconstruction of the last deglaciation: deconvolved records of ^{18}O profiles, micropaleontological variations and accelerator mass spectrometric ^{14}C dating. *Climate Dynamics*, **1**, 101–12.

Bard, E., Jouannic, C., Hamelin, B. *et al.* (1996) Pleistocene sea levels and tectonic uplift based on dating of corals from Sumba Island, Indonesia. *Geophysical Research Letters*, **23**, 1473–6.

Barker, R.W. (1960) Taxonomic notes on the species figured by H.B. Brady in his report on the foraminifera dredged by H.M.S. Challenger during the years 1873–1876. *Soci-

References

Barmawidjaja, D.M., Jorissen, F.J., Puskaric, S. and Van der Zwaan, G.J. (1992) Microhabitat selection by benthic foraminifera in the northern Adriatic Sea. *Journal of Foraminiferal Research*, **22**, 297–317.

Barmawidjaja, D.M., Van der Zwaan, G.J., Jorissen, F.J. and Puskaric, S. (1995) 150 Years of eutrophication in the northern Adriatic Sea: evidence from a benthic foraminiferal record. *Marine Geology*, **122**, 367–84.

Bartlett, G.A. (1966) Distribution and abundance of foraminifera and Thecamoebina in Miramichi River and Bay (unpublished manuscript), *Reports of Atlantic Oceanographic Laboratory*, **66** (2), 104 pp.

Bartlett, G.A. (1972) Ecology and the concentration and effect of pollutants in nearshore marine environments, *International Symposium on Identification and Measurement of Environmental Pollutants, National Research Council, Canada, Abstracts*, p. 277.

Basan, P.B. and Frey, R.W. (1977) Actual-palaeontology and neoichnology of salt marshes near Sapelo Island, Georgia, in *Trace Fossils 2*, (eds T.P. Crimes and J.C. Harper), Geological Journal Special Issue, **9**, 41–70.

Baserga, R. (1985) *The Biology of Cell Reproduction*, Harvard University Press, Cambridge.

Basov, I.A. and Khusid, T.A. (1983) Biomass of benthic foraminifera in sediments of the Sea of Okhotsk. *Oceanology*, **33**, 489–95.

Bates, J.M. and Spencer, R.S. (1979) Modification of miniferal trends by the Chesapeake-Elisabeth sewage outfall, Virginia. *Journal of Foraminiferal Research*, **9**, 125–40.

Bé, A.W.H. (1968) Shell porosity of Recent planktonic foraminifera as a climatic index. *Science*, **161**, 881–4.

Bé, A.W.H. (1977) An ecological, zoogeographic and taxonomic review of recent planktonic foraminifera, in *Oceanic Micropalaeontology*, (ed A.T.S. Ramsay), Academic Press, London, pp. 1–100.

Bé, A.W.H. (1980) Gametogenic calcification in a spinose planktonic foraminifer, *Globigerinoides sacculifer* (Brady). *Marine Micropalaeontology*, **5**, 283–310.

Bé, A.W.H. (1982) Biology of planktonic foraminifera, in *Foraminifera – Notes for a Short Course*, (ed T.W. Broadhead), University of Tennessee Studies in Geology, Knoxville, TN, pp. 51–89.

Bé, A.W.H., Hemleben, C., Anderson, O.R. et al. (1977a) Laboratory and field observations of living planktonic Foraminifera. *Micropaleontology*, **23**, 155–79.

Bé, A.W.H., Hemleben, C., Anderson, O.R. and Spindler, M. (1979) Chamber formation in planktonic Foraminifera. *Micropaleontology*, **25**, 294–307.

Bé, A.W.H. and Hutson, W.H. (1977) Ecology of planktonic foraminifera and biogeographic patterns of life and fossil assemblages in the Indian Ocean. *Micropaleontology*, **23**, 369–414.

Bé, A.W.H., Morse, J.W. and Harrison, S.M. (1977b) Progressive dissolution and ultrastructural breakdown of planktonic foraminifera, in *Dissolution of Deep-Sea Carbonates*, (eds W.V. Sliter, A.W.H. Bé and W.H. Berger), Cushman Foundation for Foraminiferal Research Special Publication No. 13, pp. 27–55.

Bé, A.W.H. and Spero, H.J. (1981) Shell regeneration and biological recovery of planktonic Foraminifera after physical injury induced in laboratory culture. *Micropaleontology*, **27**, 305–16.

Bé, A.W.H., Spero, H.J. and Anderson, O.R. (1982) Effects of symbiont elimination and reinfection on the life processes of the planktonic foraminifer *Globigerinoides sacculifer*. *Marine Biology*, **70**, 73–86.

Bé, A.W.H. and Tolderund, D.S. (1971) Distribution and ecology of living planktonic foraminifera in surface waters of the Atlantic and Indian Oceans, in *The Micropaleontology of Oceans*, (eds B.M. Funnell and W.R. Riedel), Cambridge University Press, Cambridge, UK, pp. 105–149.

Beck, J.W., Edwards, R.L., Ito, E. et al. (1992) Sea-surface temperature from coral skeletal strontium/calcium ratios. *Science*, **257**, 644–7.

Behrenfeld, M. and Falkowski, P. (1997) Photosynthetic rates derived from satellite based chlorophyll concentration. *Limnology and Oceanography*, **42**, 1–20.

Behrensmeyer, A.K. and Kidwell, S.M. (1985) Taphonomy's contributions to paleobiology. *Paleobiology*, **11**, 105–19.

Belanger, P.E. (1976) The effect of dredge spoil disposal on the benthonic foraminifera of Rhode Island Sound. *Environmental Protection Agency* intragency publication, 160 pp.

Belanger, P.E., Curry, W.B. and Matthews, R.K. (1981) Core-top evaluation of benthic foraminiferal isotopic ratios for paleo-oceanographic interpretations. *Palaeogeography, Palaeoclimatology, Palaeoecology*, **33**, 205–20.

Belasky, P. (1996) Biogeography of Indo-Pacific larger foraminifera and scleractinian corals: A probabilistic approach to estimating taxonomic diversity, faunal similarity, and sampling bias. *Palaeogeography, Palaeoclimatology, Palaeoecology*, **122**, 119–41.

Belfroid A., Sikkenk M., Seinen W. et al. (1994) The toxicokinetic behavior of chlorbenzenes in earthworm (*Eisenia andrei*) experiments in soil. *Environmental Toxicology and Chemistry*, **13**, 93–9.

Bellemo, S. (1974a) Ultrastructures in recent radial and granular calcareous Foraminifera. *Bulletin of Geological Institutions of University of Uppsala*, **4**, 117–22.

Bellemo, S. (1974b) The compound and intermediate wall structures in Cibicidinae (Foraminifera) with remarks on the radial and granular wall structures. *Bulletin of Geological Institutions of University of Uppsala*, **6**, 1–11.

Bellemo, S. (1976) Wall ultrastructure in the foraminifer *Cibicides floridanus* (Cushman). *Micropaleontology*, **22**, 352–62.

Belyaeva, N.V. (1976) Quantitative distribution of planktonic foraminifera in the sediment of the world ocean, in *Progress in Micropaleontology: Selected papers in*

References

Honor of Prof. Kiyoshi Asano, (eds Y. Takayanagi and T. Saito), Micropaleontology Press, New York, pp. 10–6.

Belyayev, G., Vinogradova, N., Levenshteyn, R. *et al.* (1973) Distribution patterns of deep-water bottom fauna related to the idea of the biological structure of the ocean. *Oceanology*, **13**, 114–21.

Bemis, B.E., Spero, H., Bijma, J. and Lea, D.W. (1998) Reevaluation of the oxygen isotopic composition of planktonic foraminifera: experimental results and revised paleotemperature equations. *Paleoceanography*, **13**, 150–60.

Bender, H. (1992) Chamber formation and biomineralization in *Textularia candeiana* d'Orbigny (Sarcodina: Textulariina). *Journal of Foraminiferal Research*, **22**, 229–41.

Bender, M.L., Lorens, R.B. and Williams, D.F. (1975) Sodium, magnesium, and strontium in the tests of planktonic foraminifera. *Micropaleontology*, **21**, 448–59.

Benninger, L.K., Aller, R.C., Cochran, J.K. and Turekian, K.K. (1979) Effects of biological sediment mixing on the ^{210}Pb chronology and trace metal distribution in a Long Island Sound sediment core. *Earth and Planetary Science Letters*, **43**, 241–59.

Benoit, G.J, Turekian, K.K. and Benninger, L.K. (1979) Radiocarbon dating of a core from Long Island Sound. *Estuarine and Coastal Marine Science*, **9**, 171–80.

Bentaleb, I. and Fontugne, M. (1996) Anthropogenic CO_2 invasion of the surface ocean: its influence on the organic carbon isotope composition of phytoplankton. *Comptes Rendus, Academie des Sciences, Paris*, **322**, ser. IIa, 743–8.

Berelson, W.M, McManus, J., Coale, K.H. *et al.* (1996) Biogenic matter diagenesis on the sea floor: A comparison between two continental margin transects. *Journal of Marine Research*, **54**, 731–62.

Berger, W.H. (1967) Foraminiferal ooze: Solution at depths. *Science*, **156**, 383–5.

Berger, W.H. (1968) Planktonic foraminifera: Selective solution and paleoclimate interpretation. *Deep-Sea Research*, **15**, 31–43.

Berger, W.H. (1969) Ecologic patterns of living planktonic foraminifera. *Deep-Sea Research*, **16**, 1–24.

Berger, W.H. (1970a) Planktonic foraminifera, differential production and expatriation off Baja California. *Limnology and Oceanography*, **15** (2), 183–204.

Berger, W.H. (1970b) Planktonic foraminifera: Selective solution and the lysocline. *Marine Geology*, **8**, 111–38.

Berger, W.H. (1971) Sedimentation of planktonic foraminifera. *Marine Geology*, **11**, 325–58.

Berger, W.H. (1977) Carbon dioxide excursions and the deep-sea record: Aspects of the problem, in *The Fate of Fossil Fuel CO_2 in the Oceans*, (eds N.R. Andersen and A. Malahoff), Plenum Press, New York, pp. 505–42.

Berger, W.H. (1989) Global maps of ocean productivity, in *Productivity of the Oceans: Present and Past*, (eds W. Berger, V. Smetacek and G. Wefer), John Wiley and Sons, New York, pp. 429–55.

Berger, W.H. and Diester-Haas, L. (1988) Paleoproductivity: the benthic/planktonic ratio in foraminifera as a productivity index. *Marine Geology*, **81**, 15–25.

Berger, W.H, Ekdale, A.A. and Bryant, P.P. (1979) Selective preservation of burrows in deep-sea carbonates. *Marine Geology*, **32**, 205–30.

Berger, W.H., Fischer, K., Lai, C. and Wu, G. (1987) Ocean Productivity and Organic Carbon Flux. *Scripps Institution of Oceanography*, Ref. Publication 87–30.

Berger W.H. and Gardner, J.V. (1975) On the determination of Pleistocene temperatures from planktonic foraminifera. *Journal of Foraminiferal Research*, **5**, 102–13.

Berger, W.H. and Heath, G.R. (1968) Vertical mixing in pelagic sediments. *Journal of Marine Research*, **26**, 134–43.

Berger, W.H., Johnson, R.F. and Killingley, J.S. (1977) 'Unmixing' of the deep-sea record and the deglacial meltwater spike. *Nature*, **269**, 661–3.

Berger, W.H. and Killingley, J.S. (1982) Box cores from the equatorial Pacific: ^{14}C sedimentation rates and benthic mixing. *Marine Geology*, **45**, 93–125.

Berger, W.H., Killingley, J.S. and Vincent, E. (1978) Stable isotopes in deep-sea carbonates: box core ERDC–92, West equatorial Pacific. *Oceanologica Acta*, **1**, 203–16.

Berger, W.H. and Labeyrie, L.D. (1987) *Abrupt climatic change, evidence and implications*, NATO ASI Series, C, Mathematical and Physical Sciences, v. 216, D. Reidel, Hingham, Massachusetts.

Berger, W.H., Smetacec, V.S. and Wefer, G. (1989) Ocean productivity and paleoproductivity – an overview, in *Productivity of the Ocean: Present and Past*, (eds W.H. Berger, V.S. Smetacec and G. Wefer), Wiley, Chichester, pp. 1–34.

Berger, W.H. and Soutar, A. (1967) Planktonic Foraminifera: Field experiment on production rate. *Science*, **156** (3781), 1495–7.

Berger, W.H. and Soutar, A. (1970) Preservation of plankton shells in an anaerobic basin off California. *Geological Society of America Bulletin*, **81**, 275–82.

Berggren, W.A. (1965) Review: Alfred R. Loeblich and Helen Tappan (with collaborators): Treatise on Invertebrate Paleontology, (ed R.C. Moore), Part C: Protista 2 – Sarcodina, chiefly 'Thecamoebians' and Foraminiferida. *Micropaleontology*, **11**, 122–4.

Berggren, W.A. and Hollister, C.D. (1974) Paleogeography, Paleobiogeography and the History of Circulation in the Atlantic Ocean, in *Studies in Paleo-Oceanography*, (ed W.W. Hay), Society of Economic Paleontologists and Mineralogists, Tulsa, Oklahoma, pp. 126–86.

Bergsten, H., Malmgren, B. and Nordberg, K. (1992) The benthic foraminifer *Bulimina marginata* d'Orbigny as an indicator of environmental changes in the Recent Skagerrak–Bedrock, Quaternary and modern environments. *Geologiska Foereningen's i Stockholm Foerhandlingar* (Proc. Geol. Soc. Stockh.), **114**, 237–9.

Bernard, C. and Fenchel, T. (1996) Some microaerobic ciliates are facultative anaerobes. *European Journal of Protistology*, **32**, 293–7.

References

Berner, R.A. (1981) A new geochemical classification of sedimentary environments. *Journal of Sedimentary Petrology*, **51**, 359–65.

Berner, R.A. (1994) Geocard II: A revised model for atmospheric CO$_2$ over Phanerozoic time. *American Journal of Science*, **294**, 56–91.

Bernhard, J.M. (1986) Characteristic assemblages and morphologies of benthic foraminifera from anoxic, organic-rich deposits: Jurassic through Holocene. *Journal of Foraminiferal Research*, **16**, 207–15.

Bernhard, J.M. (1987) Foraminiferal biotopes in Explorers Cove, McMurdo Sound, Antarctica. *Journal of Foraminiferal Research*, **17**, 286–97.

Bernhard, J.M. (1988) Postmortem vital staining in benthic foraminifera: Duration and importance in population and distributional studies. *Journal of Foraminiferal Research*, **18**, 143–6.

Bernhard, J.M. (1989) The distribution of benthic Foraminifera with respect to oxygen concentration and organic carbon levels in shallow-water Antarctic sediments. *Limnology and Oceanography*, **34**, 1131–41.

Bernhard, J.M. (1992) Benthic foraminiferal distribution and biomass related to pore-water oxygen content: Central California continental slope and rise. *Deep-Sea Research*, **39**, 585–605.

Bernhard, J.M. (1993) Experimental and field evidence of Antarctic foraminiferal tolerance to anoxia and hydrogen sulfide. *Marine Micropaleontology*, **20**, 203–13.

Bernhard, J.M. (1996) Microaerophilic and facultative anaerobic benthic foraminifera: A review of experimental and ultrastructural evidence. *Revue de Paléobiologie*, **15**, 261–75.

Bernhard, J.M. and Alve, E. (1996) Survival, ATP pool, and ultrastructural characterization of foraminifera from Drammensfjord (Norway): Response to anoxia. *Marine Micropaleontology*, **28**, 5–17.

Bernhard, J.M. and Bowser, S.S. (1992) Bacterial biofilms as a trophic resource for certain benthic foraminifera. *Marine Ecology Progress Series*, **83**, 263–72.

Bernhard, J.M. and Bowser, S.S. (1996) Novel epifluorescence microscopy method to determine life position of foraminifera in sediments. *Journal of Micropalaeontology*, **15**, 68.

Bernhard, J.M. and Reimers, C.E. (1991) Benthic foraminiferal population fluctuations related to anoxia: Santa Barbara Basin. *Biogeochemistry*, **15**, 127–49.

Bernhard, J.M., Sen Gupta, B.K. and Borne, P.F. (1997) Benthic foraminiferal proxy to estimate dysoxic bottom-water oxygen concentrations: Santa Barbara Basin, U.S. Pacific continental margin. *Journal of Foraminiferal Research*, **27**, 301–10.

Berthold, W.-U. (1976a) Biomineralisation bei miliolidien Foraminiferen und die Matrizen-Hypothese. *Naturwissenschaften*, **63**, 196–7.

Berthold, W.-U. (1976b) Ultrastructure and function of wall perforations in *Patellina corrugata* Williamson, Foraminifera. *Journal of Foraminiferal Research*, **6**, 22–9.

Berthold, W.-U. (1976c) Test morphology and morphogenesis in *Patellina corrugata* Williamson. *Journal of Foraminiferal Research*, **6**, 167–85.

Bertness, M.D. (1985) Fiddler crab regulation of *Spartina alterniflora* production on a New England salt marsh. *Ecology*, **66**, 1042–55.

Bertram, C.J., Elderfield, H., Shackleton, N.J. and MacDonald, J.A. (1995) Cadmium/calcium and carbon isotope reconstructions of the glacial northeast Atlantic ocean. *Paleoceanography*, **10**, 563–78.

Bett, B. and Rice, A. (1993) The feeding behavior of an abyssal echiuran revealed by in-situ time-lapse photography. *Deep-Sea Research*, **40**, 1767–79.

Bhalla, S.N. and Nigam, R. (1986) Recent foraminifera from polluted marine environment of Velsao Beach, South Goa, India. *Revue de Paléobiologie*, **5**, 43–6.

Bijma, J., Farber, W.W., and Hemleben, C. (1990) Temperature and salinity limits for growth and survival of some planktonic foraminifers in laboratory cultures. *Journal of Foraminiferal Research*, **20**, 128–48.

Bijma, J. and Hemleben, C. (1994) Population dynamics of the planktonic foraminifer *Globigerinoides sacculifer* (Brady) from the central Red Sea. *Deep-Sea Research*, **41** (3), 485–510.

Bijma, J., Hemleben, C. and Wellmitz, A. (1994) Lunar-influenced carbonate flux of the planktonic foraminifer *Globigerinoides sacculifer* (Brady) from the central Red Sea. *Deep-Sea Research*, **41** (3), 511–30.

Birkeland, C. (1988) Geographic comparisons of coral-reef community processes. *Proceedings, 6th International Coral Reef Symposium, Townsville, Australia*, **1**, 211–20.

Bishop, J.K.B. (1988) The barite-opal-organic carbon association in oceanic particulate matter. *Nature*, **332**, 341–3.

Biswas, B. (1976) Bathymetry of Holocene foraminifera and Quaternary sea-level changes on the Sunda Shelf. *Journal of Foraminiferal Research*, **6**, 107–125.

Blackmon, P.D. and Todd, R. (1959) Mineralogy of some Foraminifera. *Journal of Paleontology*, **33**, 1–15.

Blackwelder, P., Hood, T., Alvarez-Zarikian, C. et al. (1996) Benthic foraminifera from the NECOP study area impacted by the Mississippi River plume and seasonal hypoxia. *Quaternary International*, **31**, 19–36.

Blake, D. and Grassle, J. (1994) Benthic community structure on the U.S. South Atlantic slope off the Carolinas: spatial heterogeneity in a current dominated system. *Deep-Sea Research*, **41**, 835–74.

Blake, D. and Hilbig, B. (1994) Dense infaunal assemblages on the continental slope off Cape Hatteras, North Carolina. *Deep-Sea Research*, **41**, 875–900.

Blow, W.H. (1979) *The Cainozoic Globigerinida*, v. 1–3, E.J. Brill, Leiden.

Bock, W.D. (1969) *Thalassia testudinum*, a habitat and means of dispersal for shallow water benthonic foraminifera. *Gulf Coast Association of Geological Societies Transactions*, **19**, 337–40.

Boersma, A. (1985) Biostratigraphy and biogeography of Tertiary bathyal benthic foraminifera: Tasman Sea,

References

Coral Sea, and on the Chatham Rise (Deep Sea Drilling Project Leg 90). *Initial Reports of the Deep Sea Drilling Project,* **90**, 961–1035.

Boersma, A. and Premoli Silva I. (1983) Paleocene planktonic foraminiferal biogeography and paleoceanography of the Atlantic Ocean. *Micropaleontology,* **29** (4), 355–81.

Boersma, A. and Premoli Silva I. (1991) Distribution of Paleogene planktonic foraminifera – analogies with the recent? *Palaeogeography, Palaeoclimatology, and Palaeoecology,* **83**, 29–48.

Boesch, D.F. and Rabalais, N.N. (1991) Effects of hypoxia on continental shelf benthos: Comparisons between the New York Bight and the northern Gulf of Mexico, in *Modern and Ancient Continental Shelf Anoxia,* (eds R.V. Tyson and T.H. Pearson), *Geological Society of London Special Publication,* No. 58, pp. 27–34.

Bogdanowich, A.K. (1952) Miliolids and peneroplids. *Trudi Vsesouzniy Nauchno-Issledovatelskiy Geologo-Razvedochniy Institute,* Novaja serija, v. 64, 338 pp.

Bogdanowich, A.K. (1960) About systematic significance of meander chamber arrangement of some *Nubecularia. Voprosi Micropaleontologii,* **3**, 3–7.

Bokris, G. (ed) (1982) *Environmental Chemistry,* Pub. Mir, Moscow.

Bolli, H.M. (1950) The direction of coiling in the evolution of some Globorotaliidae. *Contributions to the Cushman Foundation for Foraminiferal Research,* **1**, 82–9.

Bolli, H.M. (1951) Notes on the direction of coiling of rotaliid foraminifera. *Contributions to the Cushman Foundation for Foraminiferal Research,* **2**, 139–43.

Bolli, H.M. (1971) The direction of coiling in planktonic foraminifera, in *The Micropaleontology of the Oceans,* (eds B.M. Funnel and W.R. Riedel), London, pp. 639–48.

Bolli, H.M. and Krasheninnikov, V.A. (1977) Problems in Paleogene and Neogene correlations based on planktonic foraminifera. *Micropaleontology,* **23**, 436–52.

Boltovskoy, E. (1956) Applications of chemical ecology in the study of foraminifera. *Micropaleontology,* **2**, 321–5.

Boltovskoy, E. (1964) Seasonal occurences of some living foraminifera in Puerto Deseado' (Patagonia, Argentina). *Jour. Cons. Perm. Iner. Explor. Mer.,* **29**, 136–45.

Boltovskoy, E. (1966a) Depth at which foraminifera can survive in sediments. *Contributions to the Cushman Foundation of Foraminiferal Research,* **17**, 43–5.

Boltovskoy, E. (1966b) The subtropical/subantarctic zone of convergence (Atlantic Ocean, western part). *Serv. Hydrogr. Nav., Argentina,* **640**, 1 69.

Boltovskoy, E. (1969) Foraminifera as hydrological indicators. *Proceedings of the 1st International Conference on Planktonic Microfossils,* Geneva, **2**, 1–14.

Boltovskoy, E. (1970) Distribution of the marine littoral Foraminifera in Argentina, Uruguay, and southern Brazil. *Marine Biology,* **6**, 335–44.

Boltovskoy, E. (1971a) Patchiness in the distribution of planktonic foraminifera. *Proceedings of the Second Planktonic Conference, Rome, 1970,* (ed A. Farinacci), Edizioni Technoscienza, Roma, pp. 107–16.

Boltovskoy, E. (1971b) Foraminiferal assemblages of the epipelagic zone, in *The Micropaleontology of Oceans,* (eds B.M. Funnell and W.R. Riedel), Cambridge University Press, Cambridge, 277–88.

Boltovskoy, E. (1976) Distribution of Recent foraminifera of the South American region, in *Foraminifera,* v. 2, (eds R.H. Hedley and G.C. Adams), Academic Press, pp. 171–236.

Boltovskoy, E. (1984) Foraminifera of mangrove swamps. *Physis (Buenos Aires),* sec. A, **42** (102), 1–9.

Boltovskoy, E. and Boltovskoy, D. (1968) Foraminiferos y Tecamebas de la parte inferior del Rio Quequen Grande, Prov. De Buenos Aires, Argentina. *Mus. Arg. Cienc. Nat., Rev., Hidrobiol.,* **2**, 127 64.

Boltovskoy, E., Giussani, G., Watanabe, S. and Wright, R. (1980) *Atlas of Benthic Shelf Foraminifera of the Southwest Atlantic,* Dr. W. Junk b.v., The Hague.

Boltovskoy, E. and Lena, H. (1969) Seasonal occurrences, standing crop and production in benthic foraminifera of Puerto Deseado. *Contributions from the Cushman Foundation for Foraminiferal Research,* **20**, 87–95.

Boltovskoy, E. and Lena, H. (1970) Additional note on unrecorded foraminifera from littoral of Puerto Deseado (Patagonia, Argentina). *Contributions from the Cushman Foundation for Foraminiferal Research,* **21**, 148–55.

Boltovskoy, E. and Lena, H. (1971) The foraminifera (except Family Allogromiidae) which dwell in fresh water. *Journal of Foraminiferal Research,* **1**, 71–6.

Boltovskoy, E., Scott, D. and Medioli, F. (1991) Morphological variations of benthic foraminiferal tests in response to changes in ecological parameters: a review. *Journal of Paleontology,* **65**, 175–85.

Boltovskoy, E. and Wright, R. (1976) *Recent Foraminifera,* W. Junk, The Hague.

Bonetti, C., Debenay, J.-P. and Eichler, B.B. (1997a) Deformations in benthic foraminifers tests from a polluted Brazilian coast system. *First International Conference on Applications of Micropaleontology in Environmental Sciences, June 15–20, 1997, Tel Aviv, Israel, Abstracts,* pp. 41–2.

Bonetti, C., Geraque, E. and Schaeffer-Novelli, Y. (1997b) Avaliaçao das consequencias de um aterro sobre manguezal atraves do estudo de foraminiferos. *Resumo expandido submetido a X Semana Nacional de Oceanografia, Itajai (State of Santa Catarina), October 5–10, 1997, Abstracts Volume,* p. 340.

Bonetti, C., Eichler, B.B. and Debenay, J.-P. (1996) Estudo preliminar das condiçoes ecologicas das Baias de Santos e Sao Vicente (SP) com base na distribuiçao de foraminiferos bentonicos. *Bolm. de Resumos do III Simposio sobre Oceanografia – IOUSP, Sao Paulo, Abstracts,* p. 340.

Bornmalm, L., Corliss, B.H. and Tedesco, K. (1997) Laboratory observations of rates and patterns of movement of continental-margin benthic foraminifera. *Marine Micropaleontology,* **29**, 175–84.

References

Boudreau, B.P. (1986a) Mathematics of tracer mixing in sediments: I. Spatially-dependent, diffusive mixing. *American Journal of Science*, **286**, 161–98.

Boudreau, B.P. (1986b) Mathematics of tracer mixing in sediments: II. Nonlocal mixing and biological conveyor-belt phenomena. *American Journal of Science*, **286**, 199–238.

Boudreau, B.P. (1997) *Diagenetic Models and Their Implementation: Modelling Transport and Reactions in Aquatic Sediments*, Springer-Verlag, Berlin.

Bouvier-Soumagnac, Y. and Duplessy, J.C. (1985) Carbon and oxygen isotopic composition of planktonic foraminifera from laboratory culture, plankton tows and recent sediment: implications for the reconstruction of paleoclimatic conditions and of the global carbon cycle. *Journal of Foraminiferal Research*, **15**, 302–20.

Bowser, S.S., Alexander, S.P., Stockton, W.L. and DeLaca, T.E. (1992) Extracellular matrix augments mechanical properties of pseudopodia in the carnivorous foraminiferan *Astrammina rara*: Role in prey capture. *Journal of Protozoology*, **39**, 724–32.

Bowser, S.S. and Bernhard, J.M. (1993) Structure, bioadhesive distribution, and elastic properties of the agglutinated test of *Astrammina rara*, Protozoa, Foraminifera. *Journal of Eukaryotic Microbiology*, **40**, 121–31.

Bowser, S.S., DeLaca, T.E. and Rieder, C.L. (1986) Novel extracellular matrix and microtubule cables associated with pseudopodia of *Astrammina rara*, a carnivorous Antarctic foraminifer. *Journal of Ultrastructure and Molecular Structure Research*, **94**, 149–60.

Bowser, S.S, Gooday, A.J., Alexander, S.P. and Bernhard, J.M. (1995) Larger agglutinated Foraminifera of McMurdo Sound, Antarctica: Are *Astrammina rara* and *Notodendrodes antarctikos* allogromiids incognito? *Marine Micropaleontology*, **26**, 75–88.

Bowser, S.S., McGee-Russell, S.M. and Rieder, C.L. (1985) Digestion of prey in Foraminifera is not anomalous: A correlation of light microscopic, cytochemical, and HVEM technics to study phagotrophy in two allogromiids. *Tissue & Cell*, **17**, 823–39.

Bowser, S.S. and Rieder, C.L. (1985) Evidence that cell surface motility in *Allogromia* is mediated by cytoplasmic microtubules. *Canadian Journal of Biochemistry and Cell Biology*, **63**, 608–20.

Bowser, S.S., Travis, J.L. and Rieder, C.L. (1988) Microtubules associated with actin-containing filaments at discrete sites along the ventral surface of *Allogromia* reticulopods. *Journal of Cell Science*, **89**, 297–307.

Boyle, E.A. (1976) On the marine geochemistry of cadmium. *Nature*, **263**, 42–4.

Boyle, E.A. (1981) Cadmium, zinc, copper, and barium in foraminifera tests. *Earth and Planetary Science Letters*, **53**, 11–35.

Boyle, E.A. (1983) Manganese carbonate overgrowths on foraminifera tests. *Geochimica et Cosmochimica Acta*, **47**, 1815–9.

Boyle, E.A. (1986) Paired carbon isotope and cadmium data from benthic foraminifera: implications for changes in oceanic phosphorous, oceanic circulation and atmospheric carbon dioxide. *Geochimica et Cosmochimica Acta*, **50**, 265–76.

Boyle, E.A. (1988a) Cadmium: Chemical tracer of deepwater paleoceanography. *Paleoceanography*, **3**, 471–89.

Boyle, E.A. (1988b) The role of vertical chemical fractionation in controlling late Quaternary atmospheric carbon dioxide. *Journal of Geophysical Research*, **93**, 15701–15.

Boyle, E.A. (1988c) Vertical oceanic nutrient fractionation and glacial/interglacial CO_2 cycles. *Nature*, **331**, 55–6.

Boyle, E.A. (1990) Quaternary deepwater paleoceanography. *Science*, **249**, 863–70.

Boyle, E.A. (1992) Cadmium and $\delta^{13}C$ paleochemical ocean distributions during the stage 2 glacial maximum. *Annual Review of Earth and Planetary Sciences*, **20**, 245–87.

Boyle, E.A. (1995) Last glacial maximum North Atlantic Deep Water: On, off, or somewhere in between. *Philosophical Transactions of Royal Society of London*, **B 348**, 243–53.

Boyle, E.A. and Keigwin, L.D. (1982) Deep circulation of the North Atlantic over the last 200,000 years: Geochemical evidence. *Science*, **218**, 784–7.

Boyle, E.A. and Keigwin, L.D. (1985/1986) Comparison of Atlantic and Pacific paleochemical records for the last 215,000 years: changes in deep ocean circulation and chemical inventories. *Earth and Planetary Science Letters*, **76**, 135–50.

Boyle, E.A. and Keigwin, L.D. (1987) North Atlantic thermohaline circulation during the past 20,000 years linked to high-latitude surface temperature. *Nature*, **330**, 35–40.

Boyle, E.A., Labeyrie, L. and Duplessy, J.C. (1995) Calcitic foraminiferal data confirmed by cadmium in aragonitic *Hoeglundina* – Application to the last glacial maximum in the northern Indian Ocean. *Paleoceanography*, **10**, 881–900.

Boyle, E.A. and Rosenthal, Y. (1996) Chemical hydrography of the South Atlantic during the Last Glacial Maximum: Contradictions, artifacts and resolutions, in *The South Atlantic: Present and Past Circulation*, (eds G. Wefer, W.H. Berger, G. Siedler and D.J. Webb), Springer-Verlag, Berlin.

Bradshaw, J.S. (1957) Laboratory studies on the rate of growth of the foraminifer, '*Streblus beccarii*' (Linné). *Journal of Paleontology*, **31**, 1138–47.

Bradshaw, J.S. (1959) Ecology of living planktonic foraminifera in the North and Equatorial Pacific Ocean. *Cushman Foundation for Foraminiferal Research Contributions*, **10**, 25–64.

Bradshaw, J.S. (1961) Laboratory experiments on the ecol-

References

ogy of foraminifera. *Contributions from the Cushman Foundation for Foraminiferal Research*, **12**, 87–106.

Bradshaw, J.S. (1968) Environmental parameters and marsh Foraminifera. *Limnology and Oceanography*, **13**, 26–38.

Brady, G.S., Robertson, D. and Brady, H.B. (1870) The Ostracoda and Foraminifera of tidal rivers, Part II. *Annals and Magazine of Natural History*, ser. 4, **6**, 273–308.

Brady, H.B. (1884) Report on the Foraminifera dredged by H.M.S. Challenger, during the years 1873–1876, in *Report on the Scientific Results of the Voyage of H.M.S. Challenger during the years 1873–1876, Zoology*, (ed J. Murray), Neill and Company, Edinburgh, **9**, 1–814.

Brandle, E. and Gabbiani, G. (1983) The role of cytoskeletal and cytocontractile elements in pathologic processes. *Am. J. Pathol*, **110**, 361–72.

Brandt, D.S. (1989) Taphonomic grades as a classification for fossiliferous assemblages and implications for paleoecology. *Palaios*, **4**, 303–9.

Brasier, M.D. (1975) An outline history of seagrass communities. *Palaeontology*, **18**, 678–702.

Bremer, M.L. and Lohmann, G.P. (1982) Evidence for primary control of the distribution of certain Atlantic Ocean benthonic foraminifera by degree of carbonate saturation. *Deep-Sea Research*, **29**, 987–98.

Bresler, V., Belyaeva, E. and Mozhaeva, M. (1990) A comparative study on the system of active transport of organic acids in Malpighian tubules of insects. *Journal of Insect Physiology*, **36**, 259–70.

Bresler, V., Bresler, S., Kazbekov, E. *et al.* (1979) On the active transport of organic acid (fluorescein) in the choroid plexus of the rabbit. *Acta Biochimica et Biophysica*, **550**, 110–9.

Bresler, V., Bresler, S. and Nikiforov, A. (1975) Structure and active transport in the plasma membranes of the tubules of frog kidney. *Biochimica et Biophysica Acta*, **406**, 526–37.

Bresler, V. and Fishelson, L. (1994) Microfluorometrical study of benzo(a)pyrene and marker xenobiotics' bioaccumulation in the bivalve *Donax trunculus* from clean and polluted sites along the Mediterranean shore of Israel. *Disease of Aquatic Animals*, **19**, 193–202.

Bresler, V., Mozhaeva, M. and Belyaeva, E. (1985) A comparative study on the system of active transport of organic acids in Malpighian tubules of the tropical cockroach, *Blaberus giganteus*. *Comparative Biochemistry and Physiology*, **80A**, 393–7.

Bresler, V., Mozhaeva, M. and Nikiforov, A. (1983) Role of Cl$^-$ in organic acid active transport in renal proximal tubules of rat. *General Physiology and Biochemistry*, **2**, 39–52.

Bresler, V. and Nikiforov, A. (1981) *Transport of organic acids through plasma membranes*, Nauka, Leningrad.

Bresler, V. and Yanko, V. (1994a) Study of the eastern Mediterranean coastal environment: 2. Ecotoxicology of benthic foraminifera and methods for determination of toxic action (experimental study). *Sixth Annual Symposium on the Eastern Mediterranean Continental Margin of Israel, Haifa-Israel, Abstracts Volume*, pp. 61–3.

Bresler, V. and Yanko, V. (1994b) Cytophysiological approaches to the detection of xenobiotics action on benthic foraminifera. *Forams 94 International Symposium on Foraminifera, Berkeley, California-USA, Abstracts Volume*.

Bresler, V. and Yanko, V. (1995a) Chemical ecology: A new approach to study living benthic epiphytic foraminifera. *Journal of Foraminiferal Research*, **25**, 267–79.

Bresler, V. and Yanko, V. (1995b) Acute toxicity of heavy metals for benthic epiphytic foraminifera *Pararotalia spinigera* (Le Calvez) and influence of seaweed-derived DOC. *Environmental Toxicology and Chemistry*, **14**, 1687–95.

Bresler, V., Yanko, V. and Fishelson, L. (1995) New methodology to detect primary cellular responses and early signs of environmental Pathology and Clastogenicity in Marine Benthic Communities. *Rapport du XXXIVe Congres de la CIESM, Valletta-Malta*, **34**, p. 98.

Bresler, V., Yanko, V. and Fishelson, L. (1996a) New methodological approach for detection of early responses to environmental pathology and clastogenin marine biota. *The Ecosystem of the Gulf of Aqaba in Relation to the Enhanced Economical Development and the Peace Process~III, Eilat-Israel, Abstracts Volume*, p. 27.

Bresler, V., Yanko, V. and Fishelson, L. (1997) *In situ* visualization and quantitative examination of structural organization, specific functions, metabolism and genetic alterations at molecular and cellular level. *First International Conference on Applications of Micropaleontology in Environmental Sciences, June 15–20, 1997, Tel Aviv, Israel, Abstracts Volume*, p. 44.

Bresler, V., Yanko, V. and Gasith, A. (1996b) Transport systems of xenobiotics in Mediterranean animals and their ecological significance. *Second International Symposium on Eastern Mediterranean Geology, Jerusalem-Israel, Abstracts Volume*, p. 3.

Brett, C.E. and Baird, G.C. (1986) Comparative taphonomy: A key to paleoenvironmental interpretation based on fossil preservation. *Palaios*, **3**, 207–27.

Bricaud, A., Morel, A. and Prieur, L. (1981) Absorption by dissolved organic matter of the sea (yellow substance) in the UV and visible domains. *Limnology and Oceanography*, **26**, 43–53.

Briggs, J.C. (1974) *Marine Zoogeography*, McGraw Hill, New York.

Broecker, W.S. (1982) Glacial to interglacial changes in ocean chemistry. *Progress in Oceanography*, **11**, 151–97.

Broecker, W.S. (1995) *The Glacial World According to Wally*, Eldigio Press, Columbia University, Palisades, NY.

Broecker, W.S., Klas, M., Clark, E. *et al.* (1991) The influence of $CaCO_3$ dissolution on core top radiocarbon ages for deep-sea sediments. *Paleoceanography*, **6**, 593–608.

Broecker, W.S. and Maier-Reimer, E. (1992) The influence of air and sea exchange on the carbon isotope distribution in the sea. *Global Biogeochemical Cycles*, **6**, 315–20.

References

Broecker, W.S., Mix, A., Andree, M. and Oeschger, H. (1984) Radiocarbon measurements on coexisting benthic and planktic foraminifera shells: Potential for reconstructing ocean ventilation times over the past 20,000 years. *Nuclear Instruments and Methods in Physics Research*, **B5**, 331–9.

Broecker, W.S. and Peng, T-H. (1982) *Tracers in the Sea*, Eldigio Press, Palisades, NY.

Broecker, W.S. and Peng, T.-H. (1993) What caused the glacial to interglacial CO_2 change? in *The Global Carbon Cycle*, (ed M. Heimann), Springer-Verlag, Berlin, pp. 95–115.

Brooks, A.L. (1967) Standing crop, vertical distribution and morphometrics of *Ammonia beccarii* (Linné). *Limnology and Oceanography*, **12**, 667–84.

Brown, S. and Elderfield, H. (1996) Variations in Mg/Ca and Sr/Ca ratios of planktonic foraminifera caused by postdepositional dissolution : Evidence of shallow Mg-dependent dissolution. *Paleoceanography*, **11**, 543–51.

Bruland, K.W. (1983) Trace elements in sea-water, in *Chemical Oceanography*, v. 8 (ed J. P. Riley and R. Chester), Academic Press, London, pp. 157–220.

Brusca, R.C. and Wallerstein, B.R. (1979) Zoogeographic patterns of idoteid isopods in the northeast Pacific, with a review of shallow water zoogeography of the area. *Bulletin of the Biological Society of Washington*, **3**, 67–105.

Buchanan, J.B. and Hedley, R.H. (1960) A contribution to the biology of *Astrammina limicola* (Foraminifera). *Journal of the Marine Biological Association, U.K.*, **39**, 549–60.

Buckley, D.E., Owens, E.H., Schafer, C.T. *et al.* (1974) Canso Strait and Chedabucto Bay: A multidisciplinary study of the impact of man on the marine environment. *Geological Survey of Canada, Paper 74-30*, pp. 133–60.

Buzas, M.A. (1965) The distribution and abundance of foraminifera in Long Island Sound. *Smithsonian Miscellaneous Collection*, **149**, No. 1, 94 pp.

Buzas, M.A. (1966) The discrimination of morphological groups of *Elphidium* (foraminifer) in Long Island Sound through canonical analysis and invariant characters. *Journal of Paleontology*, **40**, 585–94.

Buzas, M.A. (1968) On the spatial distribution of foraminifera. *Contributions from the Cushman Foundation for Foraminiferal Research*, **19**, 1–11.

Buzas, M.A. (1969) Foraminiferal species densities and environmental variables in an estuary. *Limnology and Oceanography*, **14**, 411–22.

Buzas, M.A. (1970) Spatial homogeneity: Statistical analyses of unispecies and multispecies populations of foraminifera. *Ecology*, **51**, 874–9.

Buzas, M.A. (1974) Vertical distribution of *Ammobaculites* in the Rhode River, Maryland. *Journal of Foraminiferal Research*, **4**, 144–7.

Buzas, M. A. (1977) Vertical distribution of foraminifera in the Indian River, Florida. *Journal of Foraminiferal Research*, **7**, 234–7.

Buzas, M.A. and Culver, S.J. (1980) Foraminifera: distribution of provinces in the western North Atlantic. *Science*, **209**, 687–9.

Buzas, M.A. and Culver, S.J. (1982) Biogeography of modern benthic Foraminifera, in *Foraminifera. Notes for a Short Course*, (ed T.W. Broadhead), University of Tennessee, Studies in Geology, **6**, 90–106.

Buzas, M.A. and Culver, S.J. (1986) Geographic origin of benthic foraminiferal species. *Science*, **232**, 775–6.

Buzas, M.A. and Culver, S.J. (1989) Biogeographic and evolutionary patterns of continental margin benthic foraminifera. *Paleobiology*, **15**, 11–9.

Buzas, M.A. and Culver, S.J. (1990) Recent benthic foraminifera on the Pacific continental margin of North and Central America. *Journal of Foraminiferal Research*, **20**, 326–35.

Buzas, M.A. and Culver, S.J. (1991) Species diversity and dispersal of benthic Foraminifera. *BioScience*, **41**, 483–9.

Buzas, M.A., Culver, S.J. and Jorissen, F.J. (1993) A statistical evaluation of the microhabitats of living (stained) infaunal benthic foraminifera. *Marine Micropaleontology*, **20**, 311–20.

Cachon, J. and Cachon, M. (1971) Le système axopodial des Radiolaires Nassellaires. *Archiv für Protistenkunde*, **113**, 80–97.

Cachon, J. and Cachon, M. (1972) Le système axopodial des Radiolaires Sphaeroidés I. Centroaxoplastidiés. *Archiv für Protistenkunde*, **114**, 51–64.

Cameron, W.M. and Pritchard, D.W. (1963) Estuaries, in *The Sea*, v. 2, (ed M. N. Hill), John Wiley, New York, pp. 306–24.

Canfield, D.E. (1991) Sulfate reduction in deep-sea sediments. *American Journal of Science*, **291**, 177–88.

Canfield, D.E. and Raiswell, R. (1991) Carbonate precipitation and dissolution: Its relevance to fossil preservation, in *Taphonomy: Releasing the Data Locked in the Fossil Record*, (eds P.A. Allison and D.E.G. Briggs), Plenum Press, New York, pp. 411–53.

Caralp, M.H. (1984) Impact de la matiere organique dans des zones de forte productivite sur certains foraminifères benthiques. *Oceanologica Acta*, **7**, 509–15.

Caralp, M.H. (1989a) Size and morphology of the benthic foraminifer *Melonis barleeanum*: relationships with marine organic matter. *Journal of Foraminiferal Research*, **19**, 235–45.

Caralp, M.H. (1989b) Abundance of *Bulimina exilis* and *Melonis barleeanum*: Relationship to the quality of marine organic matter. *Geo-Marine Letters*, **9**, 37–43.

Carlquist, S. (1980) *Hawaii: A Natural History*, Natural History Press, Garden City, New York.

Carney, R.S. (1989) Examining relationships between organic carbon flux and deep-sea deposit feeding, in *Ecology of Marine Deposit Feeders*, (eds G. Lopez, G. Taghon and J. Levinton), **31**, Springer-Verlag, New York, pp. 24–58.

Caron, D., Bé, A.W.H. and Anderson, O.R. (1981) Effects of variations in light intensity on life processes of the

References

planktonic foraminifer *Globigerina sacculifer* in laboratory culture. *Journal of the Marine Biological Association of the United Kingdom*, **62**, 435–52.

Caron, D. and Swanberg, N. (1990) The ecology of planktonic sarcodines. *Aquatic Sciences*, **3**, 147–80.

Carpenter, R., Peterson, M.L. and Bennett, J.T. (1982) ^{210}Pb-derived sediment accumulation and mixing rates for the Washington continental slope. *Marine Geology*, **48**, 135–64.

Carpenter, S.J. and Lohmann, K.C. (1992) Sr/Mg ratios of modern marine calcite: Empirical indicators of ocean chemistry and precipitation rate. *Geochimica et Cosmochimica Acta*, **56**, 1837–49.

Carpenter, W.B. (1856) Researches in the foraminifera. *Royal Society of London, Philosophical Transactions*, **146**, 547–69.

Carpenter, W.B., Parker, W.K. and Jones, T.R. (1862) *Introduction to the Study of the Foraminifera*, Ray Society, London.

Casey, R., Amos, A., Anderson, J. *et al.* (1980) A preliminary report on the microplankton and microbenthos responses to the 1979 Gulf of Mexico oil spills (Ixtos I and Burmah Agate) with comments on avenues of oil in the water column and on the bottom. *Gulf Coast Association of Geological Societies Transactions*, **30**, 273–81.

Cato, I., Olsson, L. and Rosenberg, R. (1980) Recovery and decontamination of estuaries, in *Chemistry and Biogeochemistry of Estuaries*, (eds E. Ollauson and I. Cato), John Wiley and Sons Ltd, Chichester, pp. 403–40.

Cavalier-Smith, T. (1993) Kingdom Protozoa and its 18 phyla. *Microbiological Reviews*, **57**, 953–94.

Cedhagen, T. (1988) Position in the sediment and feeding of *Astrorhiza limicola* Sandahl, 1857 (Foraminiferida). *Sarsia*, **73**, 43–7.

Cedhagen, T. (1991) Retention of chloroplasts and bathymetric distribution in the sublittoral foraminiferan *Nonionellina labradorica*. *Ophelia*, **33**, 17–30.

Cedhagen, T. (1993) Taxonomy and biology of *Pelosina arborescens* with comparative notes on *Astrorhiza limicola* (Foraminiferida). *Ophelia*, **37**, 143–62.

Cedhagen, T. (1994) Taxonomy and biology of *Hyrrokkin sarcophaga* n. gen. et sp. n., a parasitic Foraminiferan (Rosalinidae). *Sarsia*, **79**, 65–82.

Cerling, T.E., Wang, Y. and Quade, J. (1993) Expansion of C4 ecosystems as an indicator of global ecological change in the late Miocene. *Nature*, **361**, 344–5.

Chalker, C.D. and Taylor, D.L. (1975) Light-enhanced calcification and the role of oxidative phosphorylation in calcification of the coral *Acropora cervicornis*. *Proceedings of the Royal Society of London*, **190**, 323–31.

Chan, L.H., Drummond, D., Edmond, J.M. and Grant, B. (1977) On the barium data from the Atlantic GEOSECS expedition. *Deep-Sea Research*, **24**, 613–49.

Chandler, G.T., Williams, D.F., Spero, H.J. and Gao, X.D. (1996) Sediment microhabitat effects on carbon stable isotopic signatures of microcosm-cultured benthic foraminifera. *Limnology and Oceanography*, **41**, 680–8.

Chang, S-K. and Yoon, H.I. (1995) Foraminiferal assemblages from bottom sediments at Marian Cove, South Shetland Islands, West Antarctica. *Marine Micropaleontology*, **26**, 223–32.

Chapman, F. (1902) *The Foraminifera*, Longmans, Green and Co, London.

Chapman, V.J. (1977) Introduction, in *Wet Coastal Ecosystems*, (ed V.J. Chapman), Elsevier, Amsterdam, pp. 1–29.

Chappell, J. and Shackleton, N.J. (1986) Oxygen isotopes and sea level. *Nature*, **324**, 137–40.

Cheng, T-C. and Zheng, S. (1978) The Recent Foraminifera of the Xisha Islands, Guangdong Province, China. *Studia Marina Sinica*, **12**, 148–310.

Christensen, E.R. (1986) A model for radionuclides in sediments influenced by mixing and compaction. *Journal of Geophysical Research*, **87**, 566–72.

Christensen, E.R. and Bhunia, P.K. (1986) Modeling radiotracers in sediments: Comparison with observations in Lakes Huron and Michigan. *Journal of Geophysical Research*, **91**, 8559–71.

Christensen, E.R. and Goetz, R.H. (1987) Historical fluxes of particle-bound pollutants from deconvolved sedimentary records. *Environmental Science and Technology*, **21**, 1088–96.

Christensen, E.R. and Klein, R.J. (1991) 'Unmixing' of ^{137}Cs, Pb, Zn, and Cd records in Lake sediments. *Environmental Science and Technology*, **35**, 1627–37.

Christensen, E.R. and Osuna, J.L. (1989) Atmospheric fluxes of lead, zinc, and cadmium from frequency domain deconvolution of sedimentary records. *Journal of Geophysical Research*, **94**, 14585–97.

Church, T.M., Biggs, R.B. and Sharma, P. (1987) The birth and death of salt marshes: Geochemical evidence for sediment accumulation and erosion. *EOS, Transactions of American Geophysical Union, (Supplement)*, **68**, 305.

Church, T.M., Lord, C.J. and Somayajulu, B.L.K. (1981) Uranium, thorium and lead nuclides in a Delaware salt marsh sediment. *Estuaries, Coastal and Shelf Science*, **13**, 267–75.

Cifelli, R. (1969) Radiation of Cenozoic planktonic foraminifera. *Systematic Zoology*, **18**, 154–68.

Cifelli, R. (1971) On the temperature relationship of planktonic foraminifera. *Journal of Foraminiferal Research*, **1**, 170–7.

Cifelli, R. (1976) Book review: Foraminifera, v. 1, by R. H. Hedley and C. G. Adams. *Journal of Foraminiferal Research*, **6**, 76–7.

Cifelli, R. (1990) Foraminiferal classification from d'Orbigny to Galloway. *Cushman Foundation for Foraminiferal Research Special Publication*, No. 27, pp. 1–88.

Cifelli, R. and Scott G. (1986) Stratigraphic record of the Neogene globorotalid radiation (planktonic foraminiferida). *Smithsonian Contributions to Paleobiology*, 58pp.

Cifelli, R. and Smith, R.K. (1969) Problems in the distribution of recent planktonic foraminifera and their relationships with water mass boundaries in the North Atlantic.

References

Cifelli, R. and Smith, R.K. (1970) Distribution of planktonic foraminifera in the vicinity of the North Atlantic Current. *Smithsonian Contributions to Paleobiology*, 4, 1–52.

Cisne, J.L. and Rabe, B.D. (1978) Coenocorrelation: Gradient analysis of fossil communities and its application in stratigraphy. *Lethaia*, 11, 341–64.

Clark, D.F. (1971) Effects of aquaculture outfall on benthonic foraminifera in Clam Bay, Nova Scotia. *Maritime Sediments*, 7, 76–84.

Clarke, F.W. and Wheeler, W.C. (1922) The inorganic constituents of marine invertebrates. *USGS Prof. Paper*, **124**, 55.

CLIMAP Project Members (1976) The surface of the ice age earth. *Science*, **191**, 1131–7.

CLIMAP Project Members (1981) Seasonal reconstruction of the earth's surface at the last glacial maximum, in *Geological Society of America Map and Chart Series 36* (Text Map and Microfiche), Leader A. McIntyre, Geological Society of America.

Closs, D. (1963) Foraminiferos e Tecamebas de Lagoa dos Patos (RGS), *Boletim Escola de Geologia, Universidade Federal do Rio Grande do Sul, Porto Alegre*, 11, 1–130.

Coccioni, R., Gabbianelli, G., Gentiloni Silverj, D. et al. (1997) Benthic foraminiferal response to heavy metal pollution in the Goro Lagoon (Italy). *First International Conference on Applications of Micropaleontology in Environmental Sciences, June 15–20, 1997, Tel Aviv, Israel, Abstracts Volume*, pp. 47–8.

Cochran, J.K. and Aller, R.C. (1979) Particle reworking in sediments from the New York Bight Apex: Evidence from $^{234}Th/^{238}U$ disequilibrium. *Estuarine and Coastal Marine Science*, 9, 739–47.

Cockey, E.M., Hallock, P. and Lidz, B.H. (1996) Decadal-scale changes in benthic foraminiferal assemblages off Key Largo, Florida. *Coral Reefs*, 15, 237–48.

Cole, F.J. (1926) *The History of Protozoology*, University of London Press, London, 64.

Cole, J., Honjo, S. and Erez, J. (1987) Benthic decomposition of organic matter at a deep sea site in the Panama Basin. *Nature*, 327, 703–4.

Collen, J.D. (1998) *Metarotaliella tuvaluensis* sp. nov. from Funafuti Atoll, western Pacific Ocean: Relationship to miliolid Foraminifera. *Journal of Foraminiferal Research*, **28**, 66–75.

Collins, E.S., Scott, D.B., Gayes, P.T. and Medioli, F.S. (1995) Foraminifera in Winyah Bay and North Inlet Marshes, South Carolina – relationship to local pollution sources. *Journal of Foraminiferal Research*, 25, 212–23.

Collins, L. (1989) Relationship of environmental gradients to morphologic variation within *Bulimina aculeata* and *Bulimina marginata*, Gulf of Maine area. *Journal of Foraminiferal Research*, 19, 222–34.

Collison, P. (1980) Vertical distribution of foraminifera off the coast of Northumberland, England. *Journal of Foraminiferal Research*, 10, 75–8.

Compton, J.S. and Mallinson, D.J. (1996) Geochemical consequences of increased late Cenozoic weathering rates and the global CO_2 balance since 100 Ma. *Paleoceanography*, 11, 431–46.

Coomans, H.E. (1962) The marine mollusk fauna of the Virginian area as a basis for defining zoogeographical provinces. *Beaufortia*, 9, 83–104.

Coplen, T.B. (1988) Normalisation of oxygen and hydrogen isotope data. *Chemical Geology (Isotope Geoscience Section)*, 72, 293–7.

Coplen, T.B. (1994) Reporting of stable hydrogen, carbon, and oxygen isotopic abundances. *Pure and Applied Chemistry*, 66, 273–6.

Coplen, T.B., Kendall, C. and Hopple, J. (1983) Comparison of stable isotope reference samples. *Nature*, **302**, 236–8.

Corfield, R.M. and Cartlidge, J.E. (1991) Isotopic evidence for the depth stratification of fossil and Recent Globigerinina: a review. *Historical Biology*, **5**, 37–63.

Corliss, B.H. (1979) Size variation in the deep-sea benthic foraminifer *Globocassidulina subglobosa* (Brady) in the southern Indian Ocean. *Journal of Foraminiferal Research*, 9, 50–9.

Corliss, B.H. (1985) Microhabitats of benthic foraminifera within deep-sea sediments. *Nature*, **314**, 435–8.

Corliss, B.H. (1991) Morphology and microhabitat preferences of benthic foraminifera from the northwest Atlantic Ocean. *Marine Micropaleontology*, 17, 195–236.

Corliss, B.H. and Chen, C. (1988) Morphotype patterns of Norwegian Sea deep-sea benthic foraminifera and ecological implications. *Geology*, 16, 716–9.

Corliss, B.H. and Emerson, S. (1990) Distribution of Rose Bengal stained deep-sea benthic foraminifera from the Nova Scotian continental margin and Gulf of Maine. *Deep-Sea Research*, 37, 381–400.

Corliss, B.H. and Fois, E. (1990) Morphotype analysis of deep-sea benthic foraminifera from the Northwest Gulf of Mexico. *Palaios*, 5, 589–605.

Corliss, B.H. and Honjo, S. (1981) Dissolution of deep-sea benthonic Foraminifera. *Micropaleontology*, 27, 356–78.

Corliss, B.H., Martinson, D. and Keffer, T. (1986) Late Quaternary deep ocean circulation. *Geological Society of America Bulletin*, 97, 1106–21.

Corliss, B.H. and Silva, K. (1993) Rapid growth of deep sea benthic foraminifera. *Geology*, 21, 991–4.

Cosijn, A.J. (1938) *Statistical studies on the phylogeny of some Foraminifera*, Techn. Hoogesch. Delft Proefschr., Leiden.

Cotran, R.S., Kumar, V. and Robbins, S.L. (1989) *Robbins Pathologic Basis of Disease*, 4th ed, Saunders Company, Philadelphia.

Coull, B.C. (1972) Species diversity and faunal affinities of meiobenthic Copepoda in the deep sea. *Marine Biology*, **14**, 48–51.

Coull, B.C., Ellison, R.L., Fleeger, J.W. et al. (1977) Quantitative estimates of the meiofauna from the deep sea off North Carolina, USA. *Marine Biology*, **39**, 233–40.

References

Craig, H. and Gordon, L.I. (1965) Isotope oceanography: deuterium and oxygen 18 variations in the ocean and the marine atmosphere. *Univeristy of Rhode Island Occasional Publications*, **3**, 277–374.

Craig, H., Gordon, L.I. and Horibe, Y. (1963) Isotopic exchange effects in the evaporation of water; 1. low-temperature experimental results. *Journal of Geophysical Research*, **68** (17), 5079–87.

Crame, J.A. (1993) Bipolar molluscs and their evolutionary implications. *Journal of Biogeography*, **20**, 145–61.

Cronblad, H.G. and Malmgren, B.A. (1981) Climatically controlled variation of Sr and Mg in Quaternary planktonic foraminifera. *Nature*, **291**, 61–4.

Crouch, R.W. and Poag, C.W. (1987) Benthic foraminifera of the Panamanian Province: distributions and origins. *Journal of Foraminiferal Research*, **17**, 153–76.

Crowley, T.J. and North, G.R. (1991) *Paleoclimatology*, Oxford University Press, Oxford, U.K.

Culver, S.J. (1980) Bibliography of North American Recent benthic Foraminifera. *Journal of Foraminiferal Research*, **10**, 286–302.

Culver, S.J. (1988) New foraminiferal depth zonation of the northwestern Gulf of Mexico. *Palaios*, **3**, 69–85.

Culver, S.J. (1990) Benthic foraminifera of Puerto Rican mangrove-lagoon systems: Potential for paleoenvironmental interpretations. *Palaios*, **5**, 34–51.

Culver, S.J. and Buzas, M.A. (1980) Distribution of Recent benthic foraminifera off the North American Atlantic coast. *Smithsonian Contributions to Marine Science*, No. 6, 1–512.

Culver, S.J. and Buzas, M.A. (1981a) Distribution of Recent benthic foraminifera in the Gulf of Mexico. *Smithsonian Contributions to Marine Science*, No. 8, 1–898.

Culver, S.J. and Buzas, M.A. (1981b) Distribution of Recent benthic foraminifera on the Atlantic continental margin of North America. *Journal of Foraminiferal Research*, **11**, 217–40.

Culver, S.J. and Buzas, M.A. (1981c) Foraminifera: distribution of provinces in the Gulf of Mexico. *Nature*, **290**, 328–9.

Culver, S.J. and Buzas, M.A. (1982a) Distribution of Recent benthic foraminifera in the Caribbean area. *Smithsonian Contributions to Marine Science*, No. 14, 1–382.

Culver, S.J. and Buzas, M.A. (1982b) Recent benthic foraminiferal provinces between Newfoundland and Yucatan. *Geological Society of America Bulletin*, **93**, 269–77.

Culver, S.J. and Buzas, M.A. (1983) Recent benthic foraminiferal provinces in the Gulf of Mexico. *Journal of Foraminiferal Research*, **13**, 21–31.

Culver, S.J. and Buzas, M.A. (1985) Distribution of Recent benthic foraminifera off the North American Pacific coast from Oregon to Alaska. *Smithsonian Contributions to Marine Science*, No. 26, 1–234.

Culver, S.J. and Buzas, M.A. (1986) Distribution of Recent benthic foraminifera off the North American Pacific coast from California to Baja. *Smithsonian Contributions to Marine Science*, No. 28, 1–634.

Culver, S.J. and Buzas, M.A. (1987) Distribution of Recent benthic foraminifera off the Pacific coast of Mexico and Central America. *Smithsonian Contributions to Marine Science*, No. 30, 1–184.

Culver, S.J. and Buzas, M.A. (1995) The effects of anthropogenic habitat disturbance, habitat destruction, and global warming on shallow marine benthic foraminifera. *Journal of Foraminiferal Research*, **25**, 204–11.

Curry, W.B., Ostermann, D.R., Guptha, M.V.S. and Ittekkot, V. (1992) Foraminiferal production and monsoonal upwelling in the Arabian Sea: evidence from sediment traps, in *Upwelling systems: evolution since the Miocene*, (eds C.P. Summerhayes, W.L. Prell and K.C. Emis), Geol Soc. London, London, pp. 93–106.

Curry, W.B., Thunell, R.C. and Honjo, S. (1983) Seasonal changes in the isotopic composition of planktonic foraminifera collected in Panama Basin sediment traps. *Earth and Planetary Science Letters*, **64**, 33–43.

Cushman, J.A. (1925) An introduction to the morphology and classification of the Foraminifera. *Smithsonian Miscellaneous Collections*, **77** (4), 1–77.

Cushman, J.A. (1927) An outline of a reclassification of the Foraminifera. *Contributions from the Cushman Laboratory for Foraminiferal Research*, **3** (1), 1–105.

Cushman, J.A. (1928) Foraminifera: Their Classification and Economic Use. *Cushman Laboratory for Foraminiferal Research Special Publication*, No. 1, pp. 1–401.

Cushman, J.A. (1933) Foraminifera: Their Classification and Economic Use, 2nd Ed. *Cushman Laboratory for Foraminiferal Research Special Publication*, No. 4, pp. 1–349.

Cushman, J.A. (1940) *Foraminifera: Their Classification and Economic Use*, 3rd Ed, Harvard University Press, Cambridge.

Cushman, J.A. (1945) Parallel evolution in the Foraminifera. *American Journal of Science*, **243-A**, 117–21.

Cushman, J.A. (1948) *Foraminifera: Their Classification and Economic Use*, 4th Ed., Harvard University Press, Cambridge.

Cushman, J.A. and Brönnimann, P. (1948) Some new genera and species from brackish water of Trinidad. *Contributions from the Cushman Laboratory for Foraminiferal Research*, **24** (1), 15–21.

Cushman, J.A., Todd, R. and Post, R.J. (1954) Recent Foraminifera of the Marshall Islands. *U.S. Geological Survey Professional Paper*, **260-H**, 319–84.

Cutler, A.H. (1993) Mathematical models of temporal mixing in the fossil record, in *Taphonomic Approaches to Time Resolution in Fossil Assemblages*, (eds S.M. Kidwell and A.K. Behrensmeyer), Paleontological Society Short Courses in Paleontology No. 6, pp. 169–87.

Cutler, A.H. (1995) Taphonomic implications of shell surface textures in Bahia la Choya, northern Gulf of California. *Palaeogeography, Palaeoclimatology, Palaeoecology*, **114**, 219–40.

Cutler, A.H. and Flessa, K.W. (1990) Fossils out of sequence: Computer simulations and strategies for dealing with stratigraphic disorder. *Palaios*, **5**, 227–35.

References

Dahlgren, L. (1962) A new monothalamous foraminifer, *Ovammina opaca* n. gen., n. sp., belonging to the family Saccamminidae. *Zoologiska Bidrag från Uppsala*, **33**, 197–200.

Dahlgren, L. (1964) On the nuclear cytology and reproduction in the monothalamous foraminifer *Ovammina opaca* Dahlgren. *Zoologiska Bidrag från Uppsala*, **36**, 315–34.

Dana, J.D. (1853) On an isothermal oceanic chart illustrating the geographical distribution of marine animals. *American Journal of Science*, **16**, 153–67.

Dansgaard, W (1964) Stable isotopes in precipitation. *Tellus*, **16**, 436–68.

Darling, K.F., Kroon, D., Wade, C.M. *et al.* (1998a) The distribution of planktic foraminiferal genotypes in the modern ocean, in *International Symposium on Foraminifera, Forams '98, Monterrey, Mexico. Proceedings and Abstracts with Programs*, (eds J.F. Longoria and M.A. Gamper), Sociedad Mexicana de Paleontología, A.C., pp. 23.

Darling, K.F., Wade, C.M. and Kroon, D. (1998b) Planktic foraminiferal rDNA molecular phylogeny indicates ancient divergences in some cryptic spinose species, in *International Symposium on Foraminifera, Forams '98, Monterrey, Mexico. Proceedings and Abstracts with Programs*, (eds J.F. Longoria and M.A. Gamper), Sociedad Mexicana de Paleontología, A.C., pp. 23.

Darlington, P.J. (1959) Area, Climate and Evolution. *Evolution*, **13**, 488–510.

Darzynkiewicz, Z. (1990) Probing nuclear chromatin by flow cytometry, in *Flow Cytometry and Sorting*, 2nd ed, (eds M. Melamed, T. Lindmo and M. Mendelsohn), Wiley-Liss Publ., New York, pp. 315–40.

Davaud, E. and Septfontaine, M. (1995) Post-mortem offshore transportation of epiphytic foraminifera: recent example from the Tunisian coastline. *Journal of Sedimentary Research*, **A65**, 136–42.

David, M., Campiglio, C. and Darling, R. (1974) Progresses in R- and Q-mode analysis: correspondence analysis and its application to the study of geological processes. *Canadian Journal of Earth Sciences*, **11**, 131–46.

Davies, D.J., Powell, E.N. and Stanton, R.J. (1989) Relative rates of shell dissolution and net sediment accumulation – a commentary: Can shell beds form by the gradual accumulation of biogenic debris on the sea floor? *Lethaia*, **22**, 207–12.

Davies, G.R. (1970) Carbonate bank sedimentation, eastern Shark Bay, Western Australia, in *Carbonate Sedimentation and Environments, Shark Bay, Western Australia*, (ed B.W. Logan), Memoir 13, American Association of Petroleum Geologists, Tulsa, Oklahoma, pp. 85–168.

Davis, J.C. (1986) *Statistics and Data Analysis in Geology*, John Wiley and Sons, New York.

de Baar, H.J.W., Bacon, M.P. and Brewer, P.G. (1985) Rare earth elements in the Pacific and Atlantic oceans. *Geochimica et Cosmochimica Acta*, **49**, 1943–59.

Debenay, J.-P. (1986) Recherches sur le Sedimentation *Actuelle et les Thanatocoenosis de Foraminifères de Grande Taille Dans le Lagon Sud-oest et sur la Marge Insulaire Sud de Nouvelle-Caledonia*, Ph.D. thesis, University Aix-Marseille, France.

Debenay, J.-P. (1990) Recent foraminiferal assemblages and their distribution relative to environmental stress in the paralic environments of west Africa (Cape Timiris to Ebrie Lagoon). *Journal of Foraminiferal Research*, **20**, 267–82.

Debenay, J.-P., Andre, O., Bezir, S. and Rambaud, S. (1997) Foraminifera used as biomarkers in La Turballe Harbour (Loire Atlantique, France). *Coastal zone monitoring and medium to long term forecasting, French-Japanise International Symposium, Paris, October 6–8, 1997, Abstracts Volume*.

Debenay, J.-P., Guillou, J.-J. and Lesourd, M. (1996) Colloidal calcite in foraminiferal tests: Crystallization and texture of the test. *Journal of Foraminiferal Research*, **26**, 277–88.

Debenay, J.-P. and Redois, F. (1997) Recent foraminifera of the northern continental shelf of Senegal. *Revue de Micropaléontologie*, **40**, 15–38.

De Casamajor, M.N. and Debenay, J.-P. (1995) Les Foraminifères, bio-indicateurs des environnements paraliques: reaction à divers types de pollution dans l'estuaire de l'Adour. *ANPP-Colloque International Marqu Biologiques de Pollution, Abstracts Volume, Chinon-France*, pp. 371–7.

Decrouez, D. (1989) Generic ranges of Foraminiferida. *Revue de Paléobiologie*, **8**, 263–321.

Degens, E.T., Guillard, R.R.L., Sackett, W.M. and Hellebust, J.A. (1968) Metabolic fractionation of carbon isotopes in marine plankton, I. Temperature and respiration experiments. *Deep-Sea Research*, **15**, 1–9.

DeLaca, T.E. (1982) Use of dissolved amino acids by the foraminifer *Notodendrodes antarctikos*. *American Zoologist*, **22**, 683–90.

DeLaca, T.E. (1986a) The morphology and ecology of *Astrammina rara*. *Journal of Foraminiferal Research*, **16**, 216–23.

DeLaca, T.E. (1986b) Determination of benthic rhizopod biomass using ATP analysis. *Journal of Foraminiferal Research*, **16**, 285–92.

DeLaca, T.E., Karl, D.M. and Lipps, J.H (1981) Direct use of dissolved organic carbon by agglutinated Foraminifera. *Nature*, **289**, 287–9.

Delaney, M.L. (1989) Uptake of cadmium into calcite shells by planktonic foraminifera. *Chemical Geology*, **78**, 159–65.

Delaney, M.L. (1990) Miocene benthic foraminiferal Cd/Ca records: South Atlantic and western Equatorial Pacific. *Paleoceanography*, **5**, 743–60.

Delaney, M.L., Bé, A.W.H. and Boyle, E.A. (1985) Li, Sr, Mg, and Na in foraminiferal calcite shells from laboratory culture, sediment traps, and sediment cores. *Geochimica et Cosmochimica Acta*, **49**, 1327–41.

Delaney, M.L. and Boyle, E.A. (1986) Lithium in foraminifera shells: Implications for high-temperature hydrothermal circulation fluxes and oceanic crustal generation rates. *Earth and Planetary Science Letters*, **80**, 91–105.

Delaney, M.L. and Boyle, E.A. (1987) Cd/Ca in late Miocene benthic foraminifera and changes in the global organic carbon budget. *Nature*, **330**, 156–9.

Demaison, G.J. and Moore, G.T. (1980) Anoxic environments and oil source bed genesis. *Organic Geochemistry*, **2**, 9–31.

DeMaster, D., Pope, R., Levin, L. and Blair, N. (1994) Biological mixing intensity and rates of organic carbon accumulation in North Carolina slope sediments. *Deep-Sea Research*, **41**, 735–54.

Deming, J. W., Reysenbach, A.-L., Macko, S.A. and Smith, C.R. (1997) Evidence for the microbial basis of a chemoautotrophic invertebrate community at a whale fall on the deep seafloor: Bone-colonizing bacteria and invertebrate endosymbionts. *Microscopy Research and Technique*, **37**, 162–70.

den Hartog, C. (1977) Structure, function, and classification in seagrass communities, in *Seagrass Ecosystems, A Scientific Perspective*, (eds C.P. McRoy and C. Helfferich), Marcel Dekker, New York, pp. 89–121.

DeNiro, M.J. and Epstein, S. (1978) Influence of diet on the distribution of carbon isotopes in animals. *Geochimica et Cosmochimica Acta*, **42**, 495–506.

Denne, R.A. and Sen Gupta, B.K. (1989) Effects of taphonomy and habitat on the record of benthic foraminifera in modern sediments. *Palaios*, **4**, 414–23.

Denne, R.A. and Sen Gupta, B.K. (1991) Association of bathyal Foraminifera with water masses in the northwestern Gulf of Mexico. *Marine Micropaleontology*, **17**, 173–93.

Denne, R.A and Sen Gupta, B.K. (1993) Matching of benthic foraminiferal depth limits and water-mass boundaries in the northwestern Gulf of Mexico: an investigation of species occurrences. *Journal of Foraminiferal Research*, **23**, 108–17.

DePaolo, D.J. and Ingram, B.L. (1985) High-resolution stratigraphy with strontium isotopes. *Science*, **227**, 938–41.

De Rijk, S. (1995) Salinity control on the distribution of salt marsh foraminifera. *Journal of Foraminiferal Research*, **25**, 156–66.

De Rijk, S. and Troelstra, S.R. (1997) Salt marsh foraminifera from the Great Marshes, Massachusetts: environmental controls. *Palaeogeography, Palaeoclimatology, Palaeoecology*, **130**, 81–112.

Dermitzakis, M.D. and Alafousou, P. (1987) The geological framework and the observed oil seeps of Zakynthos Island: Their possible influence on the pollution of the marine environment. *Thalassographica*, **10**, 7–22.

Derry, L.A. and France-Lanord, C. (1996) Neogene growth of the sedimentary organic carbon reservoir. *Paleoceanography*, **11** (3), 267–75.

De Stigter, H.C., Jorissen, F.J. and Van der Zwaan, G.J. (1998) Bathymetric distribution and microhabitat partitioning of live (Rose Bengal stained) benthic foraminifera along a shelf to deep sea transect in the southern Adriatic Sea. *Journal of Foraminiferal Research*, **28**, 40–65.

Dettmering, C., Röttger, R., Hohenegger, J. and Schmaljohann, R. (1998) The trimorphic life cyle in foraminifera: Observations from culture allow new evaluations. *European Journal of Protistology*, **34**, 363–8.

Deuser, W.G. (1987) Seasonal variations in isotopic composition and deep-water fluxes of the tests of perennially abundant planktonic foraminifera of the Sargasso Sea: results from sediment-trap collections and their paleoceanographic significance. *Journal of Foraminiferal Research*, **17**, 14–27.

Deutsch, S. and Lipps, J.H. (1976) Test structure of the foraminifer *Carterina*. *Journal of Paleontology*, **50**, 312–7.

De Vargas, C., Norris, R., Zaninetti, L. and Pawlowski J. (1998) Cryptic Diversity and Speciation in the Open Ocean. *International Symposium on Foraminifera, Forams '98, Monterrey, Mexico. Proceedings and Abstracts with Programs*, (eds J.F. Longoria and M.A. Gamper), Sociedad Mexicana de Paleontologia, A.C., pp. 25.

D'Hondt, S., Zachos, J.C. and Schultz, G. (1994) Stable isotope signals and photosymbiosis in late Paleocene planktic foraminifera. *Paleobiology*, **20**, 391–406.

Diaz, R., Blake, J. and Cutter, G. (eds) (1994) Input, Accumulation and Cycling of Materials on the Continental Slope off Cape Hatteras, Theme Issue. *Deep-Sea Research*, **41**.

Diaz, R.J. and Rosenberg, R. (1995) Marine benthic hypoxia: A review of its ecological effects and the behavioural responses of benthic macrofauna. *Oceanography and Marine Biology: An Annual Review*, **33**, 245–303.

Dillion, W.R. and Goldstein, M. (1984) *Multivariate Analysis Methods and Applications*, John Wiley and Sons, New York.

Dobell, C. (1932) *Antony van Leeuwenhoek and his 'Little Animals,'* Harcourt, Brace and Company, New York.

Dobzhansky, T. (1973) Nothing in biology makes sense except in the light of evolution. *American Biology Teacher*, **35**, 125–9.

d'Orbigny, A. (1826) Tableau Méthodique de la Classe des Céphalopodes. *Annales des Sciences Naturelles, Paris (Série 1)*, **7**, 245–314.

d'Orbigny, A.D. (1846) *Foraminifères Fossiles du Bassin Tertiare de Vienne (Autriche)*, Gide, Paris.

d'Orbigny, A. (1852) *Cours Élémentaire de Paléontologie et de Géologie Stratigraphique*, Victor Masson, Paris.

Douglas, R.G. (1971) Cretaceous foraminifera from the northwest Pacific Ocean: Leg 6, Deep Sea Drilling Project. *Initial Reports of the Deep Sea Drilling Project*, **6**, 1027–53.

Douglas, R.G. (1981) Paleoecology of continental margin basins: A modern case history from the borderland of southern California, in *Depositional Systems of Active Continental Margin Basins*, (eds. R.G. Douglas, I.P. Colburn and D.S. Gorsline), Short Course Notes, Society of Economic and Petroleum Mineralogists, Pacific Section, San Francisco, pp. 121–56.

References

Douglas, R.G. and Heitman, H.L. (1979) Slope and basin benthic Foraminifera of the California borderland, in *Geology of Continental Slopes*, (eds. L.J. Doyle and O.H. Pilkey), *Special Publication No. 27, Society of Economic Paleontologists and Mineralogists*, pp. 231–46.

Douglas, R.G., Liestman, J., Walch, C. et al. (1980) The transition from live to sediment assemblage in benthic foraminifera from the southern California borderland, in *Quaternary depositional environments from the Pacific coast*, (eds. M.E. Field, A.H. Bouma, I.P. Colburn, et al.), *Society of Economic Paleontologists and Mineralogists, Los Angeles*, pp. 257–280.

Douglas, R.G., Wall, L. and Cotton, M.L. (1978) *The influence of sample quality and methods on the recovery of live benthic foraminifera in the southern California Bight*, Bureau of Land Management, Technical report 20.0, v. 2, Washington D.C., pp. 1–37.

Douglas, R.G. and Woodruff, F. (1981) Deep-sea benthic foraminifera, in *The Sea, v. 7, The Oceanic Lithosphere*, (ed C. Emiliani), John Wiley, New York, pp. 1233–327.

Doyle, W.L. (1935) Distribution of mitochondria in the foraminiferan, *Iridia diaphana*. *Science*, **81**, 387.

Drooger, C.W. (1993) *Radial Foraminifera: Morphometrics and Evolution*, North Holland Press, New York.

Dubois, L.G. and Prell, W.L. (1988) Effects of carbonate dissolution on the radiocarbon age structure of sediment mixed layers. *Deep-Sea Research*, **35**, 1875–85.

Duguay, L.E. (1983) Comparative laboratory and field studies on calcification and carbon fixation in foraminiferal-algal associations. *Journal of Foraminiferal Research*, **13**, 252–61.

Duguay, L.E. and Taylor, D.L. (1978) Primary production and calcification by the soritid foraminifera *Archaias angulatus* (Fichtel and Moll). *Journal of Protozoology*, **25**, 356–61.

Duineveld, G., Lavaleye, M., Berghuis, E. et al (1997) Patterns of benthic fauna and benthic respiration on the Celtic continental margin in relation to the distribution of phytodetritus. *Internationale Revue der Gesamten Hydrobiologie*, **82**, 395–424.

Dujardin, F. (1835a) Observations nouvelles sur les Céphalopodes microscopiques. *Annales des Sciences Naturelles, Paris (Seconde Série, Zoologie)*, **3**, 108–9 (Note: published as 'M. Desjardins').

Dujardin, F. (1835b) Observations nouvelles sur les prétendus Céphalopodes microscopiques. *Annales des Sciences Naturelles, Paris (Seconde Série, Zoologie)*, **3**, 312–6.

Dujardin, F. (1835c) Recherches sur les organismes inférieures. *Annales des Sciences Naturelles, Zoologie*, ser. 2, **4**, 343–77.

Dujardin, F. (1835d) Observations sur les rhizopodes et les infusoires. *L'Académie des Sciences Paris, Comptes Rendus*, **1**, 338–40.

Dunbar, R.B. and Wefer, G. (1984) Stable isotope fractionation in benthic foraminifera from the Peruvian continental margin. *Marine Geology*, **59**, 215–25.

Duplessy, J.C., Blanc, P. and Bé, A.W.H. (1981) Oxygen-18 enrichment of planktonic foraminifera due to gametogenic calcification below the euphotic zone. *Science*, **213**, 1247–50.

Duplessy, J.C., Lalou, C. and Vinot, A.C. (1970) Differential isotopic fractionation in benthic foraminifera and paleotemperatures reassessed. *Science*, **168**, 250–1.

Duplessy, J.C., Shackleton, N.J., Matthews, R.K. et al. (1984) ^{13}C record of benthic foraminifera in the last interglacial ocean: implications for the carbon cycle and the global deep water circulation. *Quaternary Research*, **21**, 225–43.

Durazzi, J.T. and Stehli, F.G. (1972) Average generic age, the planetary temperature gradient, and pole location. *Systematic Zoology*, **21**, 384–9.

Dustan, P. and Halas, J.C. (1987) Changes in the reef-coral community of Carysfort Reef, Key Largo, Florida: 1974–1982. *Coral Reefs*, **6**, 91–106.

Eckman, J.E. (1994) Modelling physical-biological coupling in the ocean in the U.S. GLOBEC program. *Deep-Sea Research*, **41** (1), 1–5.

Edmond, J.M. (1992) Himalayan tectonics, weathering processes, and strontium isotope record in marine limestones. *Science*, **258**, 1594–7.

Elfrussi, B. and Farber, J.L. (1975) *Hybridization of Somatic Cells*, Academic Press, New York.

Ehalt, D. and Knott, K. (1965) Kinetische Isotopentrennung bei der Verdampfung von Wasser. *Tellus*, **XVII**, 389–97.

Ehrenberg, C.G. (1854) *Mikrogeologie*, L. Voss, Leipzig.

Eichler, B.B., Debenay, J.-P., Bonetti, C. and Duleba, W. (1995) Répartition des foraminifères benthiques dans la zone sud-ouest du système estuarien-lagunaire d'Iguape-Cananéia (Brésil). *Boletin do Instituto Oceanográfica USP, São Paulo*, **43** (1), 1–17.

Ekdale, A.A., Bromley, R.G. and Pemberton, S.G. (1984) Ichnology: The use of trace fossils in sedimentology and stratigraphy. *Society of Economic Paleontologists and Mineralogists*, Short Course Number 15, Tulsa, Oklahoma.

Ekman, S. (1953) *Zoogeography of the Sea*, Sidgwick and Jackson, London.

Elderfield, H. Bertram, C. and Erez, J. (1996) Biomineralization model for the incorporation of trace elements into foraminiferal calcium carbonate. *Earth and Planetary Science Letters*, **142**, 409–23.

Elderfield, H. and Greaves, M. (1982) The rare earth elements in seawater. *Nature*, **296**, 214–9.

Ellis, B.F. and Messina, A.R. (1940 and later) *Catalogue of Foraminifera*. American Museum of Natural History, New York.

Ellison, R.L. (1972) *Ammobaculites*, foraminiferal proprietor of Chesapeake Bay estuaries. *Geological Society of America Memoir*, **133**, 247–62.

Ellison, R.L., Broome, R. and Ogilvie, R. (1986) Foraminiferal response to trace metal contamination in the Patapsco river and Baltimore Harbor, Maryland. *Marine Pollution Bulletin*, **17**, 419–23.

Ellison, R.L. and Nichols, M.M. (1970) Estuarine Foramini-

References

fera from the Rappahanock River, Virginia. *Contributions from the Cushman Foundation for Foraminiferal Research*, **21**, 1–17.

Emerson, S. and Bender, M. (1981) Carbon fluxes at the sediment-water interface of the deep-sea: Calcium carbonate preservation. *Journal of Marine Research*, **39**, 139–62.

Emiliani, C. (1954) Depth habitats of some species of pelagic foraminifera as indicated by oxygen isotope ratios. *American Journal of Science*, **252**, 149–58.

Emiliani, C. (1955) Pleistocene temperatures. *Journal of Geology*, **63**, 538–78.

Emiliani, C. (1971) Depth habitats of growth stages of pelagic foraminifera. *Science*, **173**, 1122–4.

Emrich, K., Ehhalt, D.H. and Vogel, J.C. (1970) Carbon isotope fractionation during the precipitation of calcium carbonate. *Earth and Planetary Science Letters*, **8**, 363–71.

Endler, J.A. (1982) Problems in Distinguishing Historical from Ecological Factors in Bigeography. *American Zoologist*, **22**, 441–52.

Engel, D.W. and Broawer, M. (1987) Metal regulation and molting in the blue crab *Callinectes sapidus*: Metallothionein function in metal metabolism. *Biol. Bull.*, **173**, 239–51.

Eppley, R. and Peterson, B. (1979) Particulate organic matter flux and planktonic new production in the deep ocean. *Nature*, **282**, 677–80.

Epstein, S., Buchsbaum, R., Lowenstam, H.A. and Urey, H.C. (1953) Revised carbonate-water isotopic temperature scale. *Geological Society of America Bulletin*, **64**, 1315–25.

Erez, J. (1978) Vital effect on stable-isotope composition seen in foraminifera and coral skeletons. *Nature*, **273**, 199–202.

Erez, J. (1983) Calcification rates, photosynthesis and light in planktonic foraminifera, in *Biomineralization and Biological Metal Accumulation*, (eds P. Westbroek and E.J. de Jong), Reidel, Dordrecht, pp. 307–12.

Erez, J., Almogi-Labin, A. and Avraham, S. (1991) On the life history of planktonic foraminifera: lunar reproduction cycle in *Globiberinoides Sacculifer* (Brady). *Paleoceanography*, **6** (3), 295–306.

Erez, J. and Luz, B. (1982) Temperature control of oxygen isotope fractionation of cultured planktonic foraminifera. *Nature*, **297**, 220–2.

Erez, J. and Luz, B. (1983) Experimental paleotemperature equation for planktonic foraminifera. *Geochimica et Cosmochimica Acta*, **47**, 1025–31.

Ericson, D.B. (1959) Coiling direction of *Globigerina pachyderma* as a climatic index. *Science*, **130**, 219–20.

Ericson, D.B. and Wollin, G. (1968) Pleistocene climates and chronology in deep sea sediments. *Science*, **162**, 1227–34.

Ericson, D.B., Wollin, G. and Wollin, J. (1954) Coiling direction of *Globorotalia truncatulinoides* in deep-sea cores. *Deep-Sea Research*, **2**, 152–8.

Erskian, M.G. and Lipps, J.H. (1977) Distributions of foraminifera in the Russian River estuary, northern California. *Micropaleontology*, **23**, 453–69.

Eva, A.N. (1980) Pre-Miocene seagrass communities in the Caribbean. *Palaeontology*, **23**, 231–6.

Faber, W.W. (1991) Distribution and substrate preference of *Peneroplis planatus* and *P. arietinus* from the *Halophila* meadow near Wadi Taba, Eilat, Israel. *Journal of Foraminiferal Research*, **21**, 218–21.

Faber, W.W., Anderson, O.R., Lindsey, J.L. and Caron, D.A. (1985) Algal-foraminiferal symbiosis in the planktonic foraminifer *Globigerinella aequilateralis*, I, Occurrence and stability of two mutually exclusive chrysophyte endosymbionts and their ultrastructure. *Journal of Foraminiferal Research*, **18**, 334–43.

Faber, W.W. and Lee, J.J. (1991a) Feeding and growth of the foraminifer *Peneroplis planatus* (Fichtel and Moll) Montfort. *Symbiosis*, **10**, 63–82.

Faber, W.W. and Lee, J.J. (1991b) Histochemical evidence for digestion in *Heterostegina depressa* and *Operculina ammonoides* (Foraminifera). *Endocytobiosis and Cell Research*, **8**, 53–9.

Fairbanks, R.G. (1982) The origin of continental shelf and slope water in the New York Bight and Gulf of Maine: evidence from $H_2^{18}O/H_2^{16}O$ ratio measurements. *Journal of Geophysical Research*, **87**, 5796–808.

Fairbanks, R.G. (1989) A 17,000 year glacio-eustatic sea level record: influence of glacial melting rates on the Younger dryas event and deep-ocean circulation. *Nature*, **342**, 637–42.

Fairbanks, R.G., Sverdlove, M., Free, R. *et al.* (1982) Vertical distribution and isotopic fractionation of living planktonic foraminifera in the Panama Basin. *Nature*, **298**, 841–4.

Fairbanks, R.G. and Wiebe, P.H. (1980) Foraminifera and chlorophyll maximum: vertical distribution, seasonal succession, and paleoceanographic significance. *Science*, **209**, 1524–6.

Fairbanks, R.G., Wiebe, P.H. and Bé, A.W.H. (1980) Vertical distribution and isotopic composition of living planktonic foraminifera in the western North Atlantic. *Science*, **207**, 61–3.

Falkowski, P.G., Dubinsky, Z., Muscatine, L. and McCloskey, L. (1993) Population control in symbiotic corals. *BioScience*, **43**, 606–11.

Fariduddin, M. and Loubere, P. (1997) The surface ocean productivity response of deeper water benthic foraminifera in the Atlantic. *Marine Micropaleontology*, **32**, 289–310.

Farrell, J.W., Clemens, S.C. and Gromet, L.P. (1995) Improved chronostratigraphic reference curve of late Neogene seawater $^{87}Sr/^{86}Sr$. *Geology*, **23**, 403–6.

Fauchald, K. and Jumars, P. (1979) The diet of worms: a study of polychaete feeding guilds. *Oceanography and Marine Biology*, **17**, 193–284.

Faure, G. (1986) *Principles of Isotope Geology*, John Wiley & Sons, New York.

References

Feldman, A.H., Parker, W.C. and Arnold, A.J. (1998) Development and maintenance of the global latitudinal diversity gradient: evidence from the planktonic foraminifera, in *International Symposium on Foraminifera, Forams '98, Monterrey, Mexico. Proceedings and Abstracts with Programs*, (eds J.F. Longoria and M.A. Gamper), Sociedad Mexicana de Paleontología, A.C., pp. 35.

Feldman, G. (1994) SeaWiFS Project, Nimbus-7 Coastal Zone Color Scanner Data. Nat. Atmos. Space Adm. (http://seawifs.gsfc.nasa.gov/SEAWIFS/IMAGES/CZCS_DATA.html).

Fenchel, T. (1969) The ecology of marine microbenthos. IV. Structure and function of the benthic ecosystem. *Ophelia*, **6**, 1–182.

Fenchel, T. and Finlay, B.J. (1995) *Ecology and Evolution in Anoxic Worlds*, Oxford University Press, Oxford.

Feyling-Hanssen, R.W. (1972) The foraminifer *Elphidium excavatum* (Terquem) and its variant forms. *Micropaleontology*, **18**, 337–54.

Fichtel, L.v. and Moll, J.P.C.v. (1798) *Testacea Microscopica Aliaque Minuta ex Generibus Argonauta et Nautilus ad Naturam Delineata et Descripta*, Anton Pichler, Vienna.

Finlay, B.J. and Fenchel, T. (1989) Hydrogenosomes in some anaerobic protozoa resemble mitochondria. *FEMS Microbiology Letters*, **65**, 311–4.

Fisher, R.A. (1930) *The Genetical Theory of Natural Selection*, Oxford, Clarendon Press.

Fishelson, L., Bresler, V. and Abelson, A. (1996) The use of marine molluscs and other animals for biomarker-based pollution monitoring in coastal areas, in *MARSI-Biological Indicators of Natural and Man-made Changes in Marine and Coastal Waters. Program and Abstracts of the Second Workshop, October 27–28, Jerusalem-Israel*, pp. 7–11.

Flessa, K.W. (1990) The 'facts' of mass extinctions, in *Global Catastrophes in Earth History: An Interdisciplinary Conference on Impacts, Volcanism, and Mass Mortality*, (eds V.L. Sharpton and P.D. Ward), Geological Society of America Special Paper 247.

Flessa, K.W. (1993) Time-averaging and temporal resolution in recent marine shelly faunas, in *Taphonomic Approaches to Time Resolution in Fossil Assemblages*, (eds S.M. Kidwell and A.K. Behrensmeyer), Paleontological Society Short Courses in Paleontology No. 6, pp. 9–33.

Flessa, K.W., Cutler, A.H. and Meldahl, K.H. (1993) Time and taphonomy: quantitative estimates of time-averaging and stratigraphic disorder in a shallow marine habitat. *Paleobiology*, **19**, 266–86.

Flessa, K.W. and Kowalewski, M. (1994) Shell survival and time-averaging in nearshore and shelf environments: Estimates from the radiocarbon literature. *Lethaia*, **27**, 153–65.

Fletcher, C.H., Knebel, H.J. and Kraft, J.C. (1992) Holocene depocenter migration and sediment accumulation in Delaware Bay: A submerging marginal marine sedimentary basin. *Marine Geology*, **103**, 165–83.

Folk, R.L. and Robles, R. (1964) Carbonate sands of Isla Perez, Alacran reef complex, Yucatan. *Journal of Geology*, **72**, 255–92.

Forstner, U. and Wittmann, G.T.W. (1979) *Metal pollution in the aquatic environment*, Springer-Verlag, Berlin.

Fossing, H., Gallardo, V.A., Jørgensen, B.B. et al. (1995) Concentration and transport of nitrate by the mat-forming sulphur bacterium *Thioploca*. *Nature*, **374**, 713–5.

Føyn, B. (1936) Foraminiferenstudien I. Der Lebenszyklus von *Discorbis vilardeboana* d'Orbigny. *Bergens Museums årbok, Naturvidensk rekke*, **2**, 1–22.

Føyn, B. (1954) The multinucleate generation of the foraminifer *Saccammina sphaerica* M. Sars. *Nytt Magasin for Zoologi*, **2**, 82–4.

Frakes, L.A., Francis, J.E. and Syktus, J.I. (1992) *Climate Modes of the Phanerozoic*, Cambridge University Press, Cambridge, U.K.

Frankel, L. (1970) A technique for investigating microorganism associations. *Journal of Paleontology*, **44**, 575–7.

Frankel, L. (1972) Subsurface reproduction in foraminifera. *Journal of Paleontology*, **46**, 62–5.

Frankel, L. (1975a) Pseudopodia of surface and subsurface dwelling *Miliammina fusca* (Brady). *Journal of Foraminiferal Research*, **5**, 211–7.

Frankel, L. (1975b) Subsurface feeding in foraminifera. *Journal of Paleontology*, **49**, 563–5.

Franz, D.R. and Merrill, A.S. (1980) Molluscan distribution patterns on the continental shelf of the Middle Atlantic Bight (northwestern Atlantic). *Malacologia*, **19**, 209–25.

Frederick, J.E., Snell, H.E. and Haywood, E.K. (1989) Solar ultraviolet radiation at the earth's surface. *Photochemistry and Photobiology*, **50**, 443–50.

Freeman, K.H. and Hayes, J.M. (1992) Fractionation of carbon isotopes by phytoplankton and estimates of ancient CO_2 levels. *Global Biogeochemical Cycles*, **6** (2), 185–98.

French, L.S. (1979) *Wall Structure of Selected Species of Hyaline Foraminifera*, Unpublished M.S. thesis, University of Georgia, Athens.

Frew, R.D., Heywood, K.J. and Dennis, P.F. (1995) Oxygen isotope study of water masses in the Princess Elisabeth Trough, Antarctica. *Marine Chemistry*, **49**, 141–53.

Frey, R.W. and Basan, P.D. (1981) Taphonomy of relict salt marsh deposits, Cabretta Island, Georgia. *Senckenbergiana maritima*, **13**, 111–55.

Fritz, L.W., Ferrence, G. and Jacobsen, T.R. (1992) Induction of barite mineralization in the Asiatic clam, *Corbicula fluminea*. *Limnology and Oceanography*, **37**, 442–8.

Froelich, P.N., Klinkhammer, G.P., Bender, M.L. et al. (1979) Early oxidation of organic matter in pelagic sediments of the eastern equatorial Atlantic: suboxic diagenesis. *Geochimica et Cosmochimica Acta*, **43**, 1075–90.

Frost, S.H. (1977) Cenozoic reef systems of the Caribbean – prospects for paleoecologic synthesis, in *Reefs and Related Carbonates – Ecology and Sedimentology*, (eds S.H. Frost, M.P. Weiss and J.B. Saunders), American Association of Petroleum Geologists, Tulsa, OK, Studies in Geology No. 4, pp. 93–110.

References

Furbish, D.J. and Arnold, A.J. (1997) Hydrodynamical strategies in the morphological evolution of spinose planktonic foraminifera. *Geological Society of America Bulletin*, **109** (8), 1055–72 and data repository item 9732.

Fursenko, A.V. (1958) Osnovnye etapy razvitiya faun foraminifer v geologicheskom proshlom. *Trudy Instituta Geologicheskikh Nauk, Akademiia Nauk Belorusskoi SSR, Minsk*, **1**, 10–29.

Fursenko, A.V. (1978) *Introduction to the study of Foraminifera* (in Russian), Nauka, Novosibirsk.

Gagan, M.K., Chivas, A.R. and Isdale, P.J. (1994) High-resolution isotopic records from corals using ocean temperature and mass-spawning chronometers. *Earth and Planetary Science Letters*, **121**, 549–58.

Galloway, J.J. (1933) *A Manual of Foraminifera*, Principia Press, Bloomington.

Gandolfi, R. (1942) Ricerche micropaleontologiche e stratigrafiche sulla Scaglia e sul Flysch Cretacici del Dintorni di Balerna (Canton Ticino). *Rivista Italiana Paleontologica*, **1**, 35–87.

Ganote, C.E. and Van der Heide, R.S. (1987) Cytoskeletal lesions in anoxic myocardial injury: a conventional and high-voltage electron microscopic and immunofluorescence study. *American Journal of Pathology*, **129**, 327–35.

Garlick, G.D. (1974) The stable isotopes of oxygen, carbon, and hydrogen in the marine environment, in *The Sea*, v. 5, (ed. E.D. Goldberg), John Wiley & Sons, New York, pp. 393–425.

Gast, R.J. and Caron, D.A. (1996) Molecular phylogeny of symbiotic dinoflagellates from planktonic foraminifera and radiolarians. *Molecular Biology and Evolution*, **13**, 1192–7.

Gastrich, M.D. (1988) Ultrastructure of a new intracellular symbiotic alga found within planktonic foraminifera. *Journal of Phycology*, **23**, 623–32.

Gehrels, W.R. (1994) Determining relative sea-level change from salt-marsh Foraminifera and plant zones on the coast of Maine, U.S.A. *Journal of Coastal Research*, **10**, 990–1009.

Geslin, E., Debenay, J.-P. and Lesourd, M. (1997a) Wall texture of deformed tests of foraminifera: implications for environmental monitoring. *VII COLACMAR Congresso Latino-americano sobre Ciências do Mar, 22–26 de septembro de 1997, Santos, São Paulo, Brazil*, pp. 358–9.

Geslin, E., Debenay, J.-P. and Lesourd, M. (1997b) Wall structure of deformed tests of foraminifera in relation with environmental stress. *First International Conference on Applications of Micropaleontology in Environmental Sciences, June 15–20, 1997, Tel Aviv, Israel, Abstracts Volume*, pp. 63–4.

Geslin, E., Debenay, J.-P. and Lesourd, M. (1998) Abnormal texture in the wall of deformed tests of Ammonia (Hialine foraminifer). *Journal of Foraminiferal Research*, **28**, 148–56.

Gibson, T.G. and Buzas, M.A. (1973) Species diversity: Patterns in modern and Miocene foraminifera of the eastern margin of North America. *Geological Society of America Bulletin*, **84**, 217–38.

Giraudeau, J. and Rogers, J. (1994) Phytoplankton biomass and sea surface temperature estimates from sea-bed distribution of nannofossils and planktonic foraminifera in the Benguela upwelling system. *Micropaleontology*, **40**, 275–85.

Glaessner, M.F. (1945) *Principles of Micropalaeontology*, Melbourne University Press, Melbourne.

Glass, B.P. (1969) Reworking of deep-sea sediments as indicated by the vertical dispersion of the Australasian and Ivory Coast microtektite horizons. *Earth and Planetary Science Letters*, **6**, 409–15.

Gleason, D. and Wellington, G. (1993) Ultraviolet radiation and coral bleaching. *Nature*, **365**, 836–8.

Goldstein, S.T. (1988a) On the life cycle of *Saccammina alba* Hedley, 1962. *Journal of Foraminiferal Research*, **18**, 311–25.

Goldstein, S.T. (1988b) Foraminifera of relict salt marsh deposits, St. Catherines Island, Georgia: Taphonomic implications. *Palaios*, **3**, 327–34.

Goldstein, S.T. (1997) Gametogenesis and the antiquity of reproductive pattern in the Foraminiferida. *Journal of Foraminiferal Research*, **27**, 319–28.

Goldstein, S.T. and Barker, W.W. (1988) Test ultrastructure and taphonomy of the monothalamous agglutinated foraminifer *Cribrothalammina* n. gen. *alba* (Heron-Allen and Earland). *Journal of Foraminiferal Research*, **18**, 130–6.

Goldstein, S.T. and Barker, W.W. (1990) Gametogenesis in the monothalamous agglutinated foraminifer *Cribrothalammina alba*. *Journal of Protozoology*, **37**, 20–7.

Goldstein, S.T. and Corliss, B.H. (1994) Deposit feeding in selected deep-sea and shallow-water benthic foraminifera. *Deep-Sea Research*, **41**, 229–41.

Goldstein, S.T. and Frey, R.W. (1986) Salt marsh Foraminifera, Sapelo Island, Georgia. *Senckenbergiana Maritima*, **18**, 97–121.

Goldstein, S.T. and Harben, E.B. (1993) Taphofacies implications of infaunal foraminiferal assemblages in a Georgia salt marsh, Sapelo Island. *Micropaleontology*, **39**, 53–62.

Goldstein, S.T. and Moodley, L. (1993) Gametogenesis and the life cycle of the foraminifer *Ammonia beccarii* (Linné) forma *tepida* (Cushman). *Journal of Foraminiferal Research*, **23**, 213–20.

Goldstein, S.T. and Watkins, G.T. (1998) Elevation and the distribution of salt-marsh foraminifera of St. Catherines Island, Georgia: A taphonomic approach. *Palaios*, **13**, 570–80.

Goldstein, S.T. and Watkins, G.T. (1999) Taphonomy of salt-marsh foraminifera: An example from coastal Georgia. *Palaeogeography, Palaeoclimatology, Palaeoecology*, **149**, 103–14.

Goldstein, S.T., Watkins, G.T. and Kuhn, R.M. (1995) Microhabitats of salt marsh foraminifera: St. Catherines island, Georgia, U.S.A. *Marine Micropaleontology*, **26**, 17–29.

References

Gonfiantini, R. (1986) Environmental isotopes in lake studies, in *Handbook of Environmental Isotope Geochemistry*, v. 2, (eds P. Fritz and J.C. Fontes), Elsevier, Amsterdam, pp. 113–68.

Gooday, A.J. (1986) Meiofaunal foraminiferans from the bathyal Porcupine Seabight (northeast Atlantic): size structure, standing stock, taxonomic composition, species diversity and vertical distribution in the sediment. *Deep-Sea Research*, **33**, 1345–73.

Gooday, A.J. (1988) A response by benthic foraminifera to the deposition of phytodetritus in the deep sea. *Nature*, **332**, 70–3.

Gooday, A.J. (1993) Deep-sea benthic foraminiferal species which exploit phytodetritus: Characteristic features and controls on distribution. *Marine Micropaleontology*, **22**, 187–205.

Gooday, A.J. (1994) The biology of deep-sea Foraminifera: A review of some advances and their applications to paleoceanography. *Palaios*, **9**, 14–31.

Gooday, A.J. (1996) Epifaunal and shallow infaunal foraminiferal communities at three abyssal NE Atlantic sites subject to differing phytodetritus input regimes. *Deep-Sea Research*, **43**, 1395–1421.

Gooday, A.J. and Lambshead, P.J.D. (1989) Influence of seasonally deposited phytodetritus on benthic foraminiferal populations in the bathyal northeast Atlantic: the species response. *Marine Ecology Progress Series*, **58**, 53–67.

Gooday, A.J., Levin, L.A., Linke, P. and Heeger, T. (1992a) The role of benthic foraminifera in deep-sea food webs and carbon cycling, in *Deep Sea Food Chains and the Global Carbon Cycle*, (eds G. Rowe and V. Pariente), Nato ASI series C, **360**, Kluwer Academic Publishers, Dordrecht, Netherlands, pp. 63–92.

Gooday, A.J., Levin, L.A., Thomas, C. and Hecker, B. (1992b) The distribution and ecology of *Bathysiphon filiformis* Sars and *B. major* de Folin (Protista, Foraminiferida) on the continental slope off North Carolina. *Journal of Foraminiferal Research*, **22**, 129–46.

Gooday, A.J., Shires, R. and Jones, A. (1997) Large, deep-sea agglutinated foraminifera: two differing kinds of organization and their possible ecological significance. *Journal of Foraminiferal Research*, **27**, 278–91.

Gooday, A.J. and Turley, C.M. (1990) Responses by benthic organisms to inputs of organic material to the ocean floor. A review. *Philosophical Transactions of the Royal Society of London*, **A331**, 119–38.

Gould, S.J. (1996) *Full House: the spread of excellence from Plato to Darwin*, Harmony Books, New York.

Govindan, K., Varshney, P.K. and Desai, B.N. (1983) Benthic studies in South Gujarat estuaries. *Mahasagar*, **16** (3), 349–56.

Graham, D.W., Bender, M.L., Williams, D.F. and Keigwin, L.D. (1982) Strontium-calcium ratios in Cenozoic planktonic foraminifera. *Geochimica et Cosmochimica Acta*, **46**, 1281–92.

Graham, D.W., Corliss, B.H., Bender, M.L. and Keigwin, L.D. (1981) Carbon and oxygen isotope disequilibria of Recent deep-sea benthic foraminifera. *Marine Micropaleontology*, **6**, 483–97.

Grant, J., Hatcher, A., Scott, D.B. *et al.* (1995) A multidisciplinary approach to evaluating impacts of shellfish aquaculture on benthic communities. *Estuaries*, **18** (1A), 124–44.

Grassle, J. and Morse-Porteous, L. (1987) Macrofaunal colonization of disturbed deep-sea environments and the structure of deep-sea benthic communities. *Deep-Sea Research*, **34**, 1911–50.

Grazzini, C.V. (1976) Non-equilibrium isotopic compositions of shells of planktonic foraminifera in the Mediterranean Sea. *Palaeogeography, Palaeoclimatology, Palaeoecology*, **20**, 263–76.

Green, A.S., Chandler, G.T. and Blood, E.R. (1993a) Aqueous-, pore-water and sediment-phase cadmium: Toxicity relationships for a meiobenthic copepod. *Environmental Toxicology and Chemistry*, **12**, 1497–506.

Green, M.A., Aller, R.C. and Aller, J.Y. (1992) Experimental evaluation of the influences of biogenic reworking on carbonate preservation in nearshore sediments. *Marine Geology*, **107**, 175–81.

Green, M.A., Aller, R.C. and Aller, J.Y. (1993b) Carbonate dissolution and temporal abundances of Foraminifera in Long Island Sound sediments. *Limnology and Oceanography*, **38**, 331–45.

Grell, K.G. (1954) Der Generationswechsel der polythalamen Foraminifere *Rotaliella heterocaryotica*. *Archiv für Protistenkunde*, **100**, 268–86.

Grell, K.G. (1957) Untersuchungen über die Fortpflanzung und Sexualität der Foraminiferen, I. *Rotaliella roscoffensis*. *Archiv für Protistenkunde*, **102**, 147–64.

Grell, K.G. (1958a) Untersuchungen über die Fortpflanzung und Sexualität der Foraminiferen, II. *Rubratella intermedia*. *Archiv für Protistenkunde*, **102**, 291–308.

Grell, K.G. (1958b) Untersuchungen über die Fortpflanzung und Sexualität der Foraminiferen, III. *Glabratella sulcata*. *Archiv für Protistenkunde*, **102**, 449–72.

Grell, K.G. (1958c) Studien zum Differenzierungsproblem an Foraminiferen. *Naturwissenschaften*, **45**, 3–32.

Grell, K.G. (1979) Cytogenetic systems and evolution in Foraminifera. *Journal of Foraminiferal Research*, **9**, 1–14.

Grell, K.G. (1967) Sexual reproduction in protozoa, in *Research in Protozoology*, v. 2, (ed T.T. Chen), Pergamon Press, Oxford, pp. 149–213.

Grell, K.G. (1988) The life cycle of the monothalamous foraminifer *Heterotheca lobata*, n. gen., n. sp. *Journal of Foraminiferal Research*, **18**, 54–74.

Grigelis, A. A. (1978) Higher foraminiferal taxa. *Paleontological Journal*, **12**, 1–9.

Grimm, K. A. (1992) Preparation of weakly consolidated, laminated hemipelagic sediments for high-resolution visual microanalysis: An analytical method, in *Proceedings of the Ocean Drilling Program, Scientific Results*, **127/128**, Pt. 1, (eds K.A. Pisciotto, J.C. Ingle, M.T. von

References

Breymann et al.), Ocean Drilling Program, College Station, TX, USA, pp. 57–62.

Grønlund, H. and Hansen, H.J. (1976) Scanning electron microscopy of some recent and fossil nodosariid Foraminifera. *Bulletin of the Geological Society of Denmark*, **25**, 49–62.

Grootes, P.M., Stuiver, M., White, J.W.C. et al. (1993) Comparison of oxygen isotope records from the GISP2 and GRIP Greenland Ice cores. *Nature*, **366**, 552–4.

Grossman, E.L. (1984a) Stable isotope fractionation in live benthic foraminifera from the Southern California borderland. *Palaeogeography, Palaeoclimatology, Palaeoecology*, **47**, 301–27.

Grossman, E.L. (1984b) Carbon isotopic fractionation in live benthic foraminifera – comparison with inorganic precipitate studies. *Geochimica et Cosmochimica Acta*, **48**, 1505–12.

Grossman, E.L. (1987) Stable isotopes in modern benthic foraminifera: A study of vital effect. *Journal of Foraminiferal Research*, **17**, 48–61.

Grossman, E.L. and Ku, T.L. (1986) Oxygen and carbon isotope fractionation in biogenic aragonite: temperature effects. *Chemical Geology (Isotope Geoscience Section)*, **59**, 59–74.

Guinasso, N.L. and Schink, D.R. (1975) Quantitative estimates of biological mixing rates in abyssal sediments. *Journal of Geophysical Research*, **80**, 3032–43.

Haake, F-W. (1971) Ultrastructures of miliolid walls. *Journal of Foraminiferal Research*, **1**, 187–9.

Hadar, D-P. and Worrest, R.C. (1991) Effects of enhanced solar ultraviolet radiation on aquatic ecosystems. *Photochemistry and Photobiology*, **53**, 717–25.

Haedrich, R., Rowe, G. and Polloni, P. (1975) Zonation and faunal composition of epibenthic populations on the continental slope south of New England. *Journal of Marine Research*, **33**, 191–212.

Hall, C.A. (1964) Shallow-water marine climates and molluscan provinces. *Ecology*, **45**, 226–34.

Halliday, A.N., Lee, D-C., Christensen, J.N. et al. (1998) Applications of multiple collector-ICPMS to cosmochemistry, geochemistry, and paleoceanography. *Geochimica et Cosmochimica Acta*, **62**, 919–40.

Hallock, P. (1979) Trends in test shape with depth in large, symbiont-bearing foraminifera. *Journal of Foraminiferal Research*, **9**, 61–9.

Hallock, P. (1981a) Algal symbiosis: a mathematical analysis. *Marine Biology*, **62**, 249–55.

Hallock, P. (1981b) Production of carbonate sediments by selected foraminifera on two Pacific coral reefs. *Journal of Sedimentary Petrology*, **51**, 467–74.

Hallock, P. (1981c) Light dependence in *Amphistegina*. *Journal of Foraminiferal Research*, **11**, 40–6.

Hallock, P. (1982) Evolution and extinction in larger foraminifera. *Proceedings, Third North American Paleontological Convention*, **1**, 221–5.

Hallock, P. (1984) Distribution of larger foraminiferal assemblages on two Pacific coral reefs. *Journal of Foraminiferal Research*, **14**, 250–61.

Hallock, P. (1985) Why are larger foraminifera large? *Paleobiology*, **11**, 195–208.

Hallock, P. (1987) Fluctuations in the trophic resource continuum: A factor in global diversity cycles? *Paleoceanography*, **2**, 457–71.

Hallock, P. (1988a) Interoceanic differences in Foraminifera with symbiotic algae: A result of nutrient supplies? *Proceedings, 6th International Coral Reef Symposium, Townsville, Australia*, **3**, 251–5.

Hallock, P. (1988b) Diversification in algal symbiont-bearing Foraminifera: A response to oligotrophy? *Revue de Paléobiologie, vol. spéc. Benthos '86*, **2**, 789–97.

Hallock, P., Cottey, T.L., Forward, L.B. and Halas, J. (1986a) Population biology and sediment production of *Archaias angulatus* (Foraminiferida) in Largo Sound, Florida. *Journal of Foraminiferal Research*, **16**, 1–8.

Hallock, P., Forward, L.B. and Hansen, H.J. (1986b) Environmental influence of test shape in *Amphistegina*. *Journal of Foraminiferal Research*, **16**, 224–31.

Hallock, P. and Glenn, E.C. (1985) Numerical analysis of foraminiferal assemblages: A tool for recognizing depositional facies in lower Miocene reef complexes. *Journal of Paleontology*, **59**, 1384–96.

Hallock, P. and Glenn, E.C. (1986) Larger foraminifera: a tool for paleoenvironmental analysis of Cenozoic carbonate depositional facies. *Palaios*, **1**, 55–64.

Hallock, P., Müller-Karger, F.E. and Halas, J.C. (1993a) Coral reef decline. *Research and Exploration*, **9**, 358–78.

Hallock, P. and Peebles, M. W. (1993) Foraminifera with chlorophyte endosymbionts: Habitats of six species in the Florida Keys. *Marine Micropaleontology*, **20**, 277–92.

Hallock, P., Premoli Silva, I. and Boersma, A. (1991a) Similarities between planktonic and larger foraminiferal evolutionary trends through Paleogene paleoceanographic changes. *Palaeogeography, Palaeoclimatology, Palaeoecology*, **83**, 49–64.

Hallock, P., Röttger, R. and Wetmore, K. (1991b) Hypotheses on form and function in foraminifera, in *Biology of Foraminifera*, (eds J.J. Lee and O.R. Anderson), Academic Press, New York, pp. 41–72.

Hallock, P. and Talge, H.K. (1994) A predatory foraminifer, *Floresina amphiphaga*, n. sp., from the Florida Keys. *Journal of Foraminiferal Research*, **24**, 210–3.

Hallock, P., Talge, H.K., Cockey, E.M. and Muller, R.G. (1995) A new disease in reef-dwelling foraminifera: implications for coastal sedimentation. *Journal of Foraminiferal Research*, **25**, 280–6.

Hallock, P., Talge, H.K., Smith, K. and Cockey, E.M. (1993b) Bleaching in a reef-dwelling foraminifera *Amphistegina gibbosa*. *Proceedings, 7th International Coral Reef Symposium, Guam*, **1**, 44–9.

Haman, D. (1971) Morphologic variability of the genus *Technitella* Norman, 1978. *Micropaleontology*, **17**, 471–4.

Haman, D. (1988) Book review: Foraminiferal Genera and Their Classification, by Alfred R. Loeblich and Helen Tappan. *Journal of Foraminiferal Research*, **18**, 271–4.

References

Hamilton K.L., Nelson W.G. and Curley J.L. (1993) Toxicological evaluation of the effects of waste-to-energy ash concrete on two marine species. *Environmental Toxicology and Chemistry*, **12**, 1919–30.

Hammond, L. (1983) Nutrition of deposit feeding holothuroids and echinoids from a shallow reef lagoon, Discovery Bay, Jamaica. *Marine Ecology Progress Series*, **10**, 297–305.

Hammond, P.M., Aguirre-Hudson, B., Dodd, M. et al. (1995) The current magnitude of biodiversity, in *Global Biodiversity Assessment*, (ed. V.H. Heywood), Cambridge University Press, Cambridge, U.K., pp. 113–38.

Hannah, F. and Rogerson, A. (1997) The temporal and spatial distribution of foraminiferans in marine benthic sediments of the Clyde Sea area, Scotland. *Estuarine, Coastal and Shelf Science*, **44**, 377–83.

Hansard, S.P. (1994) Geographic patterns in the evolution of *Orbulina universa*, M.S. thesis, Florida State University.

Hansen, A. and Knudsen, K.L. (1992) Recent foraminifera in Feemansundet, eastern Svalbard. *LUNDQUA Report*, **35**, 177–89.

Hansen, H.J. (1968) X-ray diffraction investigations of a radiate and a granulate foraminifer. *Bulletin of the Geological Society of Denmark*, **18**, 345–8.

Hansen, H.J. (1970) Electron-microscopical studies on the ultrastructures of some perforate calcitic radiate and granulate Foraminifera. *Biol. Skr. Dan. Vid. Selsk.*, **17** (2), 1–16.

Hansen, H.J. (1972a) Two species of the genus *Turrilina* with different wall structure. *Lethaia*, **5**, 39–45.

Hansen, H.J. (1972b) Pore plates and pore pseudopodia in *Amphistegina*. *Micropaleontology*, **18**, 223–30.

Hansen, H.J. and Hanzlikova, E. (1974) Ultrastructures of some siliceous foraminifera. *Revista Española de Micropaleontología*, **6**, 447–66.

Hansen, H.J. and Lykke-Andersen, A.-L. (1976) Wall structure and classification of fossil and recent elphidiid and nonionid Foraminifera. *Fossils and Strata*, **10**, 1–37.

Hansen, H.J. and Reiss, Z. (1971) Electron microscopy of rotaliacean wall structures. *Bulletin of the Geological Society of Denmark*, **20**, 329–46.

Hansen, H.J. and Reiss, Z. (1972) Scanning electron microscopy of some astergerinid Foraminifera. *Journal of Foraminiferal Research*, **2**, 191–9.

Hansen, H.J. and Revets, S.A. (1992) A revision and classification of the Discorbidae, Rosalinidae, and Rotaliidae. *Journal of Foraminiferal Research*, **22**, 166–80.

Haq, B.U. (1984) Paleoceanography: a synoptic overview of 200 million years of ocean history, in *Marine Geology and Oceanography of Arabian Sea and Coastal Pakistan*, (eds B.U. Haq and J.D. Milliman), Van Nostrand Reinhold Company, New York, pp. 201–30.

Hargrave, B.T. (1970) The utilisation of benthic microflora by *Hyalella azteca* (Amphipoda). *Journal of Animal Ecology*, **39**, 427–37.

Harloff, J. and Mackensen, A. (1997) Recent benthic foraminiferal associations and ecology of the Scotia Sea and Argentine Basin. *Marine Micropaleontology*, **31**, 1–29

Harman, R.A. (1964) Distribution of foraminifera in the Santa Barbara Basin, California. *Micropaleontology*, **10**, 81–96.

Harney, J.N., Hallock, P. and Talge, H.K. (1998) Observations of a trimorphic life cycle in *Amphistegina gibbosa* populations from the Florida Keys. *Journal of Foraminiferal Research*, **28**, 141–7.

Hart, M.B. and Williams, C.L. (1993) Protozoa, in *The Fossil Record 2*, (ed M.J. Benton), Chapman & Hall, London, pp. 43–70.

Hastings, D.W., Emerson, S.R. and Mix, A.C. (1996a) Vanadium in foraminiferal calcite as a tracer for changes in the areal extent of reducing sediments. *Paleoceanography*, **11**, 665–78.

Hastings, D.W., Emerson, S.R. and Nelson, B.K. (1996b) Vanadium in foraminifera calcite: Evaluation of a method to determine paleo-seawater concentrations. *Geochimica et Cosmochimica Acta*, **60**, 3701–15.

Hawkins, E.K. and Lee, J.J. (1990) Fine structure of the cell surface of a cultured endosymbiont strain of *Porphyridium* sp. *Transactions of the American Microscopists Society*, **109**, 352–60.

Haynes, J.R. (1973) Cardigan Bay Recent Foraminifera (Cruises of the R.V. Antur, 1962–64). *Bulletin of the British Museum (Natural History), Zoology*, Supplement **4**, 1–245.

Haynes, J.R. (1981) *Foraminifera*, John Wiley, New York.

Haynes, J.R. (1990) The classification of the Foraminifera— A review of historical and philosophical perspectives. *Paleontology*, **33**, 503–28.

Hayward, B.W., Grenfell, H., Cairns, G. and Smith, A. (1996) Environmental controls on benthic foraminiferal and thecamoebian associations in a New Zealand tidal inlet. *Journal of Foraminiferal Research*, **26**, 150–71.

Hayward, B.W. and Hollis, C.J. (1994) Brackish foraminifera in New Zealand: A taxonomic and ecologic review. *Micropaleontology*, **40**, 185–222.

Hazel, J.E. (1977) Use of certain multivariate and other techniques in assemblage zonal biostratigraphy; examples utilizing Cambrian, Cretaceous, and Tertiary benthic invertebrates, in *Concepts and Methods of Biostratigraphy*, (eds. E.G. Kauffman and J.E. Hazel), Dowden, Hutchinson, & Ross, Stroudsburg, Pa, pp. 187–212.

Head, E., Harrison, W., Irwin, B. et al. (1996) Plankton dynamics and carbon flux in an area of upwelling off the coast of Morocco. *Deep-Sea Research*, **43**, 1713–38.

References

Hecht, A.D., Eslinger, E.V. and Garmon, L.B. (1975) Experimental studies on the dissolution of planktonic Foraminifera, in *Dissolution of Deep-Sea Carbonates*, (eds W.V. Sliter, A.W.H. Bé and W.H. Berger), Cushman Foundation for Foraminiferal Research Special Publication, **13**, pp. 59–69.

Hechtel, I.G., Ernst, E.J. and Kalin, R. (1970) Biological effects of thermal pollution, Northport, New York. *State University of New York, Marine Science Research Contribution, Report Series*, **3**, 83–5.

Hecker, B. (1990) Photographic evidence for the rapid flux of particles to the sea floor and their transport down the continental slope. *Deep-Sea Research*, **37**, 1773–82.

Hecker, B. (1994) Unusual megafaunal assemblages on the continental slope of Cape Hatteras. *Deep-Sea Research*, **41**, 809–34.

Hedberg, H.D. (1934) Some Recent and fossil brackish to fresh-water Foraminifera. *Journal of Paleontology*, **8**, 469–76.

Hedges, J. and Keil, R. (1995) Sedimentary organic matter preservation: an assessment and speculative synthesis. *Marine Chemistry*, **49**, 81–115.

Hedges, J. and Parker, P. (1976) Land-derived organic matter in surface sediments from the Gulf of Mexico. *Geochimica et Cosmochimica Acta*, **40**, 1019–29.

Hedgpeth, J.W. (1953) An introduction to zoogeography of the northwestern Gulf of Mexico with reference to the invertebrate fauna. *Institute of Marine Science*, **3**, 107–224.

Hedgpeth, J.W. (1957a) Concepts of Marine Ecology, in *Treatise on marine ecology and paleoecology*, (ed J.W. Hedgpeth), *Geological Society of America Memoir 67*, **1**, 29–52.

Hedgpeth, J.W. (1957b) Marine biogeography, in *Treatise on marine ecology and paleoecology*, (ed J.W. Hedgpeth), *Geological Society of America Memoir 67*, **1**, 359–82.

Hedley, R.H. (1958) A contribution to the biology and cytology of *Haliphysema* (Foraminifera). *Zoological Society of London*, **130**, 569–76.

Heeger, T. (1990) Elektronenmikroskopische Untersuchungen zur Ernährungsbiologie benthischer Foraminiferen. *Berichte aus dem Sonderforschungsbereich*, **313**, 1–139.

Hemleben, C., Anderson, O.R., Berthold, W. and Spindler, M. (1986) Calcification and chamber formation in Foraminifera – a brief overview, in *Biomineralization in Lower Plants and Animals*, (eds B.S.C. Leadbeater and R. Riding), Systematics Association, Special Volume, **30**, 237–49.

Hemleben, C., Bé, A.W.H., Anderson, O.R. and Tuntivate, S. (1977) Test morphology, organic layers and chamber formation of the planktonic foraminifer *Globorotalia menardii* (d'Orbigny). *Journal of Foraminiferal Research*, **7**, 1–25.

Hemleben C. and Bijma, J. (1994) Foraminiferal population dynamics and stable carbon isotopes, in *Carbon cycling in the Glacial Ocean: Constraints on the Ocean's Role in Global Change*, (eds Zahn et al.), NATO ASI Series, I, Springer-Verlag, Berlin, Heidelberg, **17**, 145–66.

Hemleben, C. and Kitazato, H. (1995) Deep-Sea foraminifera under long time observation in the laboratory. *Deep-Sea Research*, **42**, 827–32.

Hemleben, C., Spindler, M. and Anderson, O. R. (1989) *Modern Planktonic Foraminifera*, Springer Verlag, Berlin.

Herguera, J. and Berger, W. (1991) Paleoproductivity from benthic foraminifera abundance: glacial to postglacial change in the west-equatorial Pacific. *Geology*, **19**, 1173–6.

Hermelin, J.O. and Shimmield, G.B. (1990) The importance of the oxygen minimum zone and sediment geochemistry in the distribution of Recent benthic foraminifera in the Northwest Indian Ocean. *Marine Geology*, **91**, 1–29.

Heron-Allen, E. (1917) Alcide d'Orbigny, his life and his work. *Journal of the Royal Microscopic Society*, ser. 2, **37**, 1–105, 433–4.

Hester, K. and Boyle, E. (1982) Water chemistry control of cadmium content in Recent benthic foraminifera. *Nature*, **298**, 260–2.

Hickey, L.J., West, R.M., Dawson, M.R. and Choi, D.K. (1983) Arctic terrestrial biota: paleomagnetic evidence of age disparity with mid-northern latitudes during the Late Cretaceous and Early Tertiary. *Science*, **221**, 1153–4.

Hilbig, B. (1994) Faunistic and zoogeographical characterization of the benthic infauna on the Carolina continental slope. *Deep-Sea Research*, **41**, 929–50.

Hilbrecht, H. (1996) Extant planktic foraminifera and the physical environment in the Atlantic and Indian Oceans. *Mitteilungen aus dem Geologischen Institut der Eidgen. Technischen Hochschule und dem Geologischen Institut der Eidgen. Technischen Hochschule und der Universität Zurich, Neue Folge*, **300**, 93 pp.

Hilbrecht, H. and Thierstein, H.R. (1996) Benthic behavior of planktic foraminifera. *Geology*, **24** (3), 200–2.

Hinton, D.E., Baumann, P.C., Gardner, G.R. *et al.* (1992) Histopathologic biomarkers, in *Biomarkers: Biochemical, Physiological and Histological Biomarkers of Anthropogenic Stress*, (eds R.J. Hugget, R.A. Kimmerle, P.M. Mehrle and H.L. Bergman), Lewis Publ., London, pp. 155–209.

Hippensteel, S.P. (1995) *Foraminifera as an Indicator of Overwash Deposits, Barrier Island Sediment Supply, and Barrier Island Migration: Folly Beach, South Carolina*, M.S. thesis, Department of Geology, University of Delaware.

Hippensteel, S.P. and Martin, R.E. (1999) Foraminifera as an indicator of overwash deposits, barrier island sediment supply, and barrier island evolution: Folly Island, South Carolina. *Palaeogeography, Palaeoclimatology, Palaeoecology*, **149**, 115–25.

Hirshfield, H.I. (1979) Recent benthic Foraminifera in Aegean littoral sediment. *Journal of Protozoology*, **263** (1), 28A.

References

Hodell, D.A., Mueller, P.A. and Garrido, J.R. (1991) Variations in the strontium isotopic composition of seawater during the Neogene. *Geology*, **19**, 24–7.

Hoefs, J. (1997) *Stable Isotope Geochemistry*, 4th ed., Springer-Verlag, Berlin.

Hoffmann, G. and Heimann, M. (1997) Water isotope modeling in the Asian monsoon region. *Quaternary International*, **37**, 115–28.

Hofker, J. (1927) The Foraminifera of the Siboga Expedition. *Siboga Expedition Monographs*, **4**, 78–104.

Hofker, J. (1972) Is the direction of coiling in the early stages of an evolution of planktonic foraminifera at random? (50% right and 50% left). *Revista Española de Micropaleontología*, **4**, 11–7.

Hoge, B.E. (1994) Wetland ecology and paleoecology: Relationships between biogeochemistry and preservable taxa. *Current Topics in Wetland Biogeochemistry*, **1**, 48–67.

Hoge, B.E. (1995) Wetland microfossil taphonomy: A model for the interpretation of fine-scale sea-level fluctuations. *Geological Society of America Annual Meeting Abstracts with Program*, **27**, 28.

Hohenegger, J. (1994) Distribution of living larger foraminifera NW of Sesoko-Jima, Okinawa, Japan. *Marine Ecology*, **15**, 291–334.

Hohenegger, J., Piller, W. and Baal, C. (1993) Horizontal and vertical spatial microdistribution of foraminifers in the shallow subtidal Gulf of Trieste, Northern Adriatic Sea. *Journal of Foraminiferal Research*, **23**, 79–101.

Hollister, C. and McCave, I. (1984) Sedimentation under deep-sea storms. *Nature*, **309**, 220–5.

Holzmann, M. and Pawlowski, J. (1997) Molecular, morphological and ecological evidence for species recognition in *Ammonia* (Foraminifera). *Journal of Foraminiferal Research*, **27**, 311–8.

Hooker, J.D. (1847) *The Botany, the antarctic voyage of H.M. discovery ships Erebus and Terror, in the years 1839–1843*, Reeve Brothers, London.

Hottinger, L. (1977) Distribution of larger Peneroplidae, *Borelis*, and Nummulitidae in the Gulf of Elat, Red Sea. *Utrecht Micropaleontological Bulletin*, **15**, 35–109.

Hottinger, L. (1982) Larger foraminifera, giant cells with a historical background. *Naturwissenschaften*, **69**, 361–71.

Hottinger, L. (1983) Processes determining the distribution of larger foraminifera in space and time. *Utrecht Micropaleontological Bulletin*, **30**, 239–53.

Hottinger, L. (1997) Shallow benthic foraminiferal assemblages as signals for depth of their deposition and their limitations. *Societe Geologique de France, Bulletin*, **168**, 491–505.

Hottinger, L., Halicz, E. and Reiss, Z. (1993) *Recent Foraminiferida from the Gulf of Aqaba, Red Sea*. Slovenska akademija znanosti in umetnosti, Ljubljana.

Howard, J.D. and Frey, R.W. (1985) Physical and biogenic aspects of backbarrier sedimentary sequences, Georgia coast, U.S.A. *Marine Geology*, **63**, 77–127.

Howard, V. (1997) Synergistic effects of chemical mixtures – can we rely on traditional toxicology? *The Ecologist*, **27**, 192–5.

Howes, B.L., Howarth, R.W., Teal, J.M. and Valiela, I. (1981) Oxidation-reduction potentials in a salt marsh: Spatial patterns and interactions with primary production. *Limnology and Oceanography*, **26**, 350–60.

Huber, B.T., Bijma, J. and Darling, K. (1997) Cryptic speciation in the living planktonic foraminifera *Globigerinella siphonifera* (d'Orbigny). *Paleobiology*, **25** (1), 33–62.

Huber, L.J. and Arabie, P. (1985) Comparing Partitions. *Journal of Classification*, **2**, 193–218.

Hunt, A.S. and Corliss, B.H. (1993) Distribution and microhabitats of living (stained) benthic foraminifera from the Canadian Arctic Archipelago. *Marine Micropaleontology*, **20**, 321–45.

Hunter, R.S.T. (1985) *Shape Change in the Evolution of Selected Cenozoic Planktonic Foraminifera: Evolutionary Implications and Utility in High-resolution Stratigraphy*, M.S. thesis, Florida State University.

Hutson, W.H. (1977) Transfer functions under no-analog conditions: experiments with Indian Ocean planktonic Foraminifera. *Quaternary Research*, **8**, 355–67.

Hutson, W.H. (1980) Bioturbation of deep-sea sediments: Oxygen isotopes and stratigraphic uncertainty. *Geology*, **8**, 127–30.

Huttel, M. (1990) Influence of the lugworm *Arenicola marina* on pore-water nutrient profiles of sand flat sediments. *Marine Ecology Progress Series*, **62**, 241–8.

Imbrie, J., Boyle, E.A., Clemens, S.C. *et al.* (1992) On the structure and origin of major glaciation cycles. 1. Linear responses to Milankovitch forcing. *Paleoceanography*, **7**, 701–38.

Imbrie, J., Hays, J.D., Martinson, D.G. *et al.* (1984a) The orbital theory of Pleistocene climate: support from a revised chronology of the marine $\delta^{18}O$ record, in *Milankovitch and Climate, Part 1*, (eds A. Berger *et al.*), D. Reidel, Dordrecht, The Netherlands, pp. 269–305.

Imbrie, J. and Kipp N.G. (1971) A new micropaleontological method for quantitative paleoclimatology: application to a late Pleistocene Caribbean core, in *The Late Cenozoic Glacial Ages*, (ed K.K. Turekian), Yale University Press, New Haven, pp. 71–181.

Imbrie, J., Shackleton, N.J., Pisias, N.G. *et al.* (1984b) The orbital theory of Pleistocene climate: support from a revised chronology of the marine $\delta^{18}O$ record, in *Milankovitch and Climate*, (eds. A. Berger *et al.*), D. Reidel, Hingham, Massachusetts, pp. 269–305.

Ingle, J.C., Keller, G. and Kolpack, R.L. (1980) Benthic foraminiferal biofacies, sediments and water masses of the southern Peru-Chile Trench area, southeastern Pacific Ocean. *Micropaleontology*, **26**, 113–50.

International Commission of Zoological Nomenclature (1985) *International Code of Zoological Nomenclature*, University of California Press, Berkeley.

Isaaks, E.H. and Srivastava, R.M. (1989) *An Introduction to Applied Geostatistics*, Oxford University Press, Oxford.

Ishman, S.E. (1996) A benthic foraminiferal record of middle

References

to late Pliocene (3.15–2.85 Ma) deep water change in the North Atlantic. *Marine Micropaleontology*, **27**, 165–80.

Ishman, S.E. and Domack, E.W. (1994) Oceanographic controls on benthic foraminifers from the Bellingshausen margin of the Antarctic Peninsula. *Marine Micropaleontology*, **24**, 119–55.

Izuka, S.K. (1988) Relationships of Magnesium and other minor elements in tests of *Cassidulina subglobosa* and *C. oriangulata* to physical oceanic properties. *Journal of Foraminiferal Research*, **18**, 151–7.

Jahn, B. (1953) Elektronenmikroskopische Untersuchungen an Foraminiferenschalen. *Zeitschrift für wissenschaftlische Mikroskopie und Mikrotechnik*, **61**, 294–7.

Jahn, T.L. and Rinaldi, R.A. (1959) Protoplasmic movement in the Foraminiferan, *Allogromia laticollaris*, and a theory of its mechanism. *Biological Bulletin*, **117**, 100–18.

Jahnke, R. (1996) The global ocean flux of particulate organic carbon: Areal distribution and magnitude. *Global Biogeochemical Cycles*, **10**, 71–88.

James, A. and Evison, L. (eds) (1979) *Biological Indicators of Water Quality*, John Wiley and Sons, New York.

James, M.O. (1989) Biotransformation and disposition of PAH in aquatic invertebrates, in *Metabolism of Polycyclic Aromatic Hydrocarbons in the Aquatic Environment*, (ed U. Varanasi), CRC Press, Boca Raton, FL, pp. 69–91.

Jannink, N.T., Zachariasse, W.J. and van der Zwaan, G.J. (1998) Living (Rose Bengal stained) benthic foraminifera from the Pakistan continental margin (northern Arabian Sea). *Deep-Sea Research*, **45**, 1483–1513.

Jayaraju, N. and Reddeppa Reddi, K. (1996a) Factor analysis of benthic foraminifera from coastal and estuarine sediments of Kovalam-Tuticorin, South India. *Journal of the Geological Society of India*, **48**, 309–18.

Jayaraju, N. and Reddeppa Reddi, K.R. (1996b) Impact of pollution on coastal zone monitoring with benthic foraminifera of Tuticorin, south east coast of India. *Indian Journal of Marine Sciences*, **25**, 376–8.

Jenkins, D.G. (1992) Predicting extinctions of some extant planktic foraminifera. *Marine Micropaleontology*, **19**, 239–43.

Jenner H.A. and Bowmer T. (1990) The accumulation of metals and their toxicity in the marine intertidal invertebrates *Cerastoderma edule*, *Macoma baltica*, *Arenicola marina* exposed to pulverised fuel ash in mesocosms. *Environmental Pollution*, **66**, 139–56.

Jenner H.A. and Bowmer T. (1992) The accumulation of metals and toxic effects in *Nereis virens* exposed to pulverised fuel ash. *Environmental Monitoring and Assessment*, **21**, 85–98.

Jennings, A.E. and Nelson, A.R. (1992) Foraminiferal assemblage zones in Oregon tidal marshes—relation to marsh floral zones and sea level. *Journal of Foraminiferal Research*, **22**, 13–29.

Jennings, A.E., Nelson, A.R., Scott, D.B. and Aravena, J.C. (1995) Marsh foraminiferal assemblages in the Valdivia Estuary, south-central Chile, relative to vascular plants and sea level. *Journal of Coastal Research*, **11**, 107–23.

Jepps, M.W. (1942) Studies on *Polystomella* Lamarck (Foraminifera). *Journal of the Marine Biological Association of the United Kingdom*, **25**, 607–66.

Jepps, M.W. (1956) *The Protozoa, Sarcodina*, Oliver and Boyd, Edinburgh.

Johnson, P.W., Donaghay, P.L., Small, E.B. and Sieburth, J.McN. (1995) Ultrastructure and ecology of *Perispira ovum* (Ciliophora: Litostomatea): An aerobic planktonic ciliate that sequesters chloroplasts, mitochondria and paramylon of *Euglena proxima* in a micro-oxic habitat. *Journal of Eukaryotic Microbiology*, **42**, 323–35.

Jonasson, K.E. and Patterson, R.T. (1992) Preservation potential of salt marsh foraminifera from the Fraser River delta, British Columbia. *Micropaleontology*, **38**, 289–301.

Jonasson, K.E., Schröder-Adams, C.J. and R.T. Patterson (1995) Benthic foraminiferal distribution at Middle Valley, Juan de Fuca Ridge, a northeast Pacific hydrothermal venting site. *Marine Micropaleontology*, **25**, 151–67.

Jones, B.H. and Halpern, D. (1981) Biological and physical aspects of a coastal upwelling event observed during March-April 1974 off northwest Africa. *Deep-Sea Research*, **28A**, 71–81.

Jones, G.A. and Ruddiman, W.F. (1982) Assessing the global meltwater spike. *Quaternary Research*, **17**, 148–72.

Jones, M.H. (1997) *Late Quaternary Foraminifera from Lower Bathyal and Abyssal Sediments, Gulf of Mexico: A Record of Paleoceanographic Change*, Unpublished Ph.D. thesis, Louisiana State University, Baton Rouge.

Jones, R.W. (1994) *The Challenger Foraminifera*, Oxford University Press, Oxford.

Jones, R.W. and Charnock, M.A. (1985) 'Morphogroups' of agglutinating foraminifera, their life positions and feeding habits and potential applicability in (paleo)-ecological studies. *Revue de Paléobiologie*, **4**, 311–20.

Jones, T.R. (1876) Remarks on the Foraminifera, with special reference to their variability of form, illustrated by the Cristellarians. *Monthly Microscopic Journal*, **15**, 61–2.

Jørgensen, B.B. (1977) Distribution of colorless sulfur bacteria (*Beggiatoa* spp.) in a coastal marine sediment. *Marine Biology*, **41**, 19–28.

Jørgensen, B.B. (1982) Ecology of the bacteria of the sulfur cycle with special reference to the anoxic-oxic interface environments. *Philosophical Transactions, Royal Society of London*, **B298**, 543–61.

Jørgensen, B.B., Erez, J., Revsbech, N.P. and Cohen, Y. (1985) Symbiotic photosynthesis in a planktonic Foraminiferan, *Globigerinoides sacculifer* (Brady), studied with microelectrodes. *Limnology and Oceanography*, **30**, 1253–67.

Jørgensen, B.B. and Revsbech, N.P. (1983) Colorless sulfur bacteria, *Beggiatoa* spp. and *Thiovulum* spp., in O_2 and H_2S microgradients. *Applied and Environmental Microbiology*, **45**, 1261–70.

References

Jørgensen, B.B. and Revsbech, N.P. (1989) Oxygen uptake, bacterial distribution and carbon-nitrogen-sulfur cycling in sediments from the Baltic Sea – North Sea transition. *Ophelia*, **31**, 29–49.

Jorissen, F.J. (1999) Benthic foraminiferal successions across late Quaternary Mediterranean sapropels. *Marine Geology*, **153**, 91–101.

Jorissen, F.J., Barmawidjaja, D.M., Puskaric, S. and van der Zwaan, G.J. (1992) Vertical distribution of benthic Foraminifera in the northern Adriatic Sea: The relation with high organic flux. *Marine Micropaleontology*, **19**, 131–46.

Jorissen, F.J., De Stigter, H.C. and Widmark, J.G.V. (1995) A conceptual model explaining benthic foraminiferal microhabitats. *Marine Micropaleontology*, **26**, 3–15.

Jorissen, F.J. and Wittling, I. (1999) Ecological evidence from live-dead comparisons of benthic foraminiferal faunas off Cape Blanc (NW Africa). *Palaeogeography, Palaeoclimatology and Palaeoecology*, **149**, 151–70.

Jorissen, F.J., Wittling, I., Peypouquet, J.P. et al. (1998) Live benthic foraminiferal faunas off Cape Blanc, NW Africa; Community structure and microhabitats. *Deep-Sea Research*, **45**, 2157–88.

Josefson, A.B. and Widbom, B. (1988) Differential response of benthic macrofauna and meiofauna to hypoxia in the Gullmar Fjord basin. *Marine Biology*, **100**, 31–40.

Joussaume, S. and Jouzel, J. (1993) Paleoclimatic tracers: an investigation using an atmospheric general circulation model under ice age conditions, 2. water isotopes. *Journal of Geophysical Research*, **98** (D2), 2807–30.

Jouzel, J., Barkov, N.I., Barnola, J.M. et al. (1993) Extending the Vostok ice-core record of palaeoclimate to the penultimate glacial period. *Nature*, **364**, 407–12.

Jouzel, J., Merlivat, L. and Roth, E. (1975) Isotopic study of hail. *Journal of Geophysical Research*, **80**, 5015–30.

Jumars, P. (1993) *Concepts in Biological Oceanography*, Oxford University Press, U.K.

Jumars, P. and Gallagher, E. (1982) Deep-sea community structure: three plays on the benthic proscenium, in *The Environment of the Deep Sea*, (eds W. Ernst and G. Morin), Prentice-Hall, Inc, Englewood Cliffs, N.J., pp. 217–55.

Jumars, P., Mayer, L., Deming, J. et al. (1990) Deep-sea deposit-feeding strategies suggested by environmental and feeding constraints. *Philosophical Transactions of the Royal Society of London*, **331**, 85–101.

Kahler, F. (1942) Beiträge zur Kenntnis der Fusuliniden der Ostalpen: Lebensraum und Lebensweise der Fusuliniden. *Palaeontographica*, **94**, 1–29.

Kaiho, K. (1991) Global changes of Paleogene aerobic/anaerobic benthic foraminifera and deep-sea circulation. *Palaeogeography, Palaeoclimatology, Palaeoecology*, **83**, 65–85.

Kaiho, K. (1994) Benthic foraminiferal dissolved-oxygen index and dissolved-oxygen levels in the modern ocean. *Geology*, **22**, 719–22.

Kameswara Rao, K. and Satyanarayana Rao, T.S. (1979) Studies on pollution ecology of foraminifera of the Trivandrum Coast. *Indian Journal of Marine Science*, **8**, 31–5.

Kaminski, M.A., Boersma, A., Tyszka, J. and Holbourn, A.E.L. (1995) Response of deep-water agglutinated foraminifera to dysoxic conditions in the California Borderland basins, in *Proceedings of the Fourth International Workshop on Agglutinated Foraminifera*, (eds. M.A. Kaminski, S. Geroch and M.A. Gasinski), Grzybowski Foundation Special Publication no. 3, pp. 131–40.

Kamykowski, D. and Zentara, S.-J. (1990) Hypoxia in the world ocean as recorded in the historical data set. *Deep-Sea Research*, **37**, 1861–74.

Kane, H.E. (1967) Recent foraminiferal biofacies in Sabine Lake and environs, Texas and Louisiana. *Journal of Paleontology*, **41**, 947–64.

Kauffman, E.G. and Scott R.W. (1976) Basic concepts of community ecology and paleoecology, in *Structure and Classification of Paleocommunities*, (eds R.W. Scott and R.R. West), Dowden, Hutchinson and Ross, Stroudsburg, Pennsylvania, pp. 1–28.

Keigwin, L.D. (1979) Late Cenozoic stable isotope stratigraphy and paleoceanography of DSDP sites from the East equatorial and central North Pacific Ocean. *Earth and Planetary Science Letters*, **45**, 361–82.

Keigwin, L.D. and Boyle, E.A. (1989) Late Quaternary paleochemistry of high-latitude surface waters. *Palaeogeography, Palaeoclimatology, Palaeoecology*, **73**, 85–106.

Keil, R., Montlucon, D., Prahl, F. and Hedges, J. (1994) Sorptive preservation of labile organic matter in marine sediments. *Nature*, **370**, 549–52.

Keir, R.S. and Hurd, D.C. (1983) The effect of encapsulated fine grain sediment and test morphology on the resistance of planktonic foraminifera to dissolution. *Marine Micropaleontology*, **8**, 193–214.

Keith, M.L. and Weber, J.N. (1965) Systematic relationships between modern carbon and oxygen isotopes in carbonates deposited by modern corals and algae. *Science*, **150**, 498–501.

Kelly, D.C., Arnold, A.J. and Parker, W.C. (1996) Paedomorphosis and the origin of the Paleogene planktonic foraminiferal genus *Morozovella*. *Paleobiology*, **22** (2), 266–81.

Kelly, E.F., Yonker, C. and Marino, B. (1993) Stable carbon isotope composition of paleosols: an application to Holocene, in *Climate Change in Continental Isotopic Records*, (eds P.K. Swart, K.C. Lohmann, J. McKenzie and S. Savin), Geophysical Monograph Series, v. 78, American Geophysical Union, Washington D.C., pp. 233–9.

Kennett, J.P. (1976) Phenotypic variation in some Recent and Late Cenozoic planktonic foraminifera, in *Foraminifera*, (eds R.H. Hedley and C.G. Adams), Academic Press, London, **2**, 111–70.

Kennett, J.P. (1982) *Marine Geology*, Prentice Hall, Englewood Cliffs, NJ.

Kennett, J.P. (1986) Miocene to Early Pliocene oxygen and

References

carbon isotope stratigraphy in the southwest Pacific, Deep Sea Drilling Project Leg 90. *Initial Reports of the Deep-Sea Drilling Project*, **90**, 1383–411.

Kennett J.P. and Srinivasan M.S. (1983) *Neogene Planktonic Foraminifera: a Phylogenetic Atlas*, Hutchinson Ross Publishing Co., Stroudsberg, Pennsylvania.

Kennish, M.J. (1992) Polynuclear aromatic hydrocarbons, in *Ecology of Estuaries*, CRC Press, Boca Raton, Florida, pp. 133–81.

Kidwell, S.M. (1993) Time-averaging and temporal resolution in Recent marine shelly faunas, in *Taphonomic Approaches to Time Resolution in Fossil Assemblages*, (eds S.M. Kidwell and A.K. Behrensmeyer), Paleontological Society Short Courses in Paleontology No. 6, pp. 9–33.

Kidwell, S.M. and Flessa, K.W. (1995) The quality of the fossil record: Populations, species, and communities. *Annual Review of Ecology and Systematics*, **26**, 269–99.

Kikuchi, T. and Pérès, J.M. (1977) Consumer ecology of seagrass beds, in *Seagrass Ecosystems, A Scientific Perspective*, (eds C.P. McRoy and C. Helfferich), Marcel Dekker, New York, pp. 147–92.

Kim, S.T. and O'Neil, J.R. (1997) Equilibrium and nonequilibrium oxygen isotope effects in synthetic calcites. *Geochimica et Cosmochimica Acta*, **61**, 3461–75.

Kinoshita, R.K., Bernhard, J.M., Hayden, J.H. and Bowser, S.S. (1996) Shell morphogenesis in the giant Antarctic protist, *Astrammina rara*. *Molecular Biology of the Cell*, **7S**, 63a.

Kipphut, G.W. (1990) Glacial meltwater input to the Alaska coastal current: evidence from oxygen isotope measurements. *Journal of Geophysical Research*, **95**, 5177–81.

Kitazato, H. (1989) Vertical distribution of benthic foraminifera within sediments (Preliminary Report). *Benthos Results (Bulletin Japanese Association of Benthology)*, **35/36**, 41–51.

Kitazato, H. (1994) Foraminiferal microhabitats in four marine environments around Japan. *Marine Micropaleontology*, **24**, 29–41.

Kitazato, H. and Ohga, T. (1995) Seasonal changes in deep-sea benthic foraminiferal populations: Results of long-term observations at Sagami Bay, Japan, in *Biogeochemical Processes and Ocean Flux in the Western Pacific*, (eds H. Sakai and Y. Nozaki), Terra Scientific Publishing Company, Tokyo, pp. 331–42.

Kitching, J.A. (1964) The axopods of the sun animalcule *Actinophrys sol* (Heliozoa), in *Primitive Motile Systems in Cell Biology*, (eds R.D. Allen and N. Kamiya), Academic Press, New York, pp. 445–56.

Kloos, D.P. (1980) Studies on the foraminifer *Sorites orbiculus*. *Geologie En Mijnbouw*, **59**, 375–83.

Klovan, J.E. and Imbrie, J. (1971) An algorithm and Fortran IV Program for large-scale Q-mode analysis. *Mathematical Geology*, **3**, 61–7.

Knox, M., Quay, P.D. and Wilbur, D. (1992) Kinetic isotopic fractionation during air-water gas transfer of O_2, N_2, CH_4, and H_2. *Journal of Geophysical Research*.

Koba, M. (1978) Distribution and environment of Recent *Cycloclypeus*. *Science Reports of the Tohoku University*, series 7, **28**, 283–311.

Komarovskiy, F., Karasina, F. and Chirkina Z. (1993) Bioaccumulation of resistant pesticides in Danube fish. *Vodni Resyrsi*, **20** (4), 520–2.

Kontrovitz, M., Kilmartin, K.C. and Snyder, S.W. (1979) Threshold velocities of tests of planktic foraminifera. *Journal of Foraminiferal Research*, **9**, 228–32.

Kontrovitz, M., Snyder, S.W. and Brown, R.J. (1978) A flume study of the movement of foraminifera tests. *Palaeogeography, Palaeoclimatology, Palaeoecology*, **23**, 141–50.

Kotler, E, Martin, R.E. and Liddell, W.D. (1991) Abrasion-resistance of modern reef-dwelling foraminifera from Discovery Bay, Jamaica – implications for test preservation, in *Fifth Symposium on the Geology of the Bahamas, Proceedings*, (ed R. Bain), pp. 125–38.

Kotler, E., Martin, R.E. and Liddell, W.D. (1992) Experimental analysis of abrasion and dissolution resistance of modern reef-dwelling foraminifera: Implications for the reservation of biogenic carbonate. *Palaios*, **7**, 244–76.

Kowalewski, M. (1997) The reciprocal taphonomic model. *Lethaia*, **30**, 86–8.

Kravchuk, O.P., Motnenko, I., Penciner, J. *et al.* (1997) The geoecological environment of the northern Israeli shelf and its affect on foraminifera. *First International Conference on Applications of Micropaleontology in Environmental Sciences, June 15–20, 1997, Tel Aviv, Israel, Abstracts Volume*, p. 74.

Krishnaswami, S., Benninger, L.K., Aller, R.C. and Vondamm, K.L. (1980) Atmospherically derived radionuclides as tracers of sediment mixing and accumulation in near shore marine and lake sediments: Evidence from ^7Be, ^{210}Pb, and $^{239,240}Pu$. *Earth and Planetary Science Letters*, **47**, 307–18.

Kroon, D. and Darling, K. (1995) Size and upwelling control of the stable isotope composition of *Neogloboquadrina dutertrei* (d'Orbigny), *Globigerinoides ruber* (d'Orbigny) and *Globigerina bulloides* d'Orbigny: examples from the Panama Basin and Arabian Sea. *Journal of Foraminiferal Research*, **25**, 39–52.

Kroopnick, P.M. (1974) Correlations between ^{13}C and ΣCO_2 in surface waters and atmospheric CO_2. *Earth and Planetary Science Letters*, **22**, 397–403.

Kroopnick, P.M. (1975) Respiration, photosynthesis, and oxygen isotope fractionation in oceanic surface water. *Limnology and Oceanography*, **20**, 988–92.

Kroopnick, P.M. (1985) The distribution of ^{13}C of ΣCO_2 in the world oceans. *Deep-Sea Research*, **32**, 57–84.

Kroopnick, P.M., Margolis, S.V. and Wong, C.S. (1977) ^{13}C variations in marine carbonate sediments as indicators of the CO_2 balance between the atmosphere and oceans, in *The Fate of Fossil Fuel in the Oceans*, (eds N.R. Anderson and A. Malahoff), Plenum Press, New York, pp. 295–321.

Kroopnick, P.M., Weiss, R.F. and Craig, H. (1972) Total

References

CO$_2$, ^{13}C, and dissolved oxygen-^{18}O at GEOSECS II in the north Atlantic. *Earth and Planetary Science Letters*, **16**, 103–10.

Krüger, R., Röttger, R., Lietz, R. and Hohenegger, J. (1996) Biology and reproductive processes of the larger foraminiferan *Cycloclypeus carpenteri* (Protozoa, Nummulitidae). *Archiv für Protistenkund*, **147**, 307–21.

Labeyrie, L.D., Duplessy, J.C. and Blanc, P.L. (1987) Variations in the mode of formation and temperature of oceanic deep waters over the past 125,000 years. *Nature*, **327**, 477–82.

Lagoe, M.B. (1979) Recent benthonic foraminiferal biofacies in the Arctic Ocean. *Micropaleontology*, **25**, 214–24.

Lamb, G.M. (1972) Distribution of Holocene Foraminiferida in Mobile Bay and the effect of salinity changes. *Geological Survey of Alabama Circular*, **82**, 1–12.

Lamb, T., Bickham, J.W., Gibbons, J.W. *et al.* (1991) Genetic damage in a population of slider turtles (*Trachemys scripta*) inhabiting a radioactive reservoir. *Archive of Environmental Contamination and Toxicology*, **20**, 138–42.

Lambshead, P.J.D. and Gooday, A.J. (1990) The impact of seasonally deposited phytodetritus on epifaunal and shallow infaunal benthic Foraminiferal populations in the bathyal northeast Atlantic: The assemblage response. *Deep-Sea Research*, **8**, 1263–83.

Lampitt, R. (1985) Evidence for the seasonal deposition of detritus to the deep-sea floor and its subsequent resuspension. *Deep-Sea Research*, **32**, 885–97.

Lampitt, R. and Antia, A. (1997) Particle flux in the deep seas: regional characteristics and temporal variability. *Deep-Sea Research*, **44**, 1377–403.

Lampitt, R., Billett, D. and Rice, A. (1986) Biomass of the invertebrate megabenthos from 500 to 4100 m in the northeast Atlantic Ocean. *Marine Biology*, **93**, 69–81.

Lane, G.A. and Doyle, M. (1956) Fractionation of oxygen isotopes during respiration. *Science*, **123**, 574.

Langer, M.R. (1992) Biosynthesis of glycosaminoglycans in Foraminifera: A review. *Marine Micropaleontology*, **19**, 245–55.

Langer, M.R. (1993) Epiphytic foraminifera. *Marine Micropaleontology*, **20**, 235–65.

Langer, M.R. (1997) *Evolutionary, Environmental and Economical Significance of Foraminifera*. Habilitationsschrift, Geowissenschaftliche Fakultät Tübingen, 40 pp.

Langer, M.R. and Gehring, C.A. (1993) Bacteria farming: a possible feeding strategy of some smaller, motile foraminifera. *Journal of Foraminiferal Research*, **23**, 40–6.

Langer, M.R., Hottinger, L.E. and Huber, B. (1989) Functional morphology in low diverse benthic foraminiferal assemblages from tidal flats of the North Sea. *Senckenbergiana maritima*, **20**, 81–99.

Langer, M.R., Silk, M.J. and Lipps, J.H. (1997) Global ocean carbonate and carbon dioxide production: the role of reef foraminifera. *Journal of Foraminiferal Research*, **27**, 271–7.

Lankford, R.R. and Phleger, F.B (1973) Foraminifera from the nearshore turbulent zone, western North America. *Journal of Foraminiferal Research*, **3**, 101–32.

Larkin, J.M. and Strohl, W.R. (1983) *Beggiatoa, Thiotrix,* and *Thioploca. Annual Review of Microbiology*, **37**, 341–67.

Larsen, A.R. (1976) Studies of Recent *Amphistegina*, taxonomy and some ecological aspects. *Israel Journal of Earth-Sciences*, **25**, 1–26.

Larsen, A.R. and Drooger, C.W. (1977) Relative thickness of the tests in the *Amphistegina* species of the Gulf of Elat. *Utrecht Micropaleontological Bulletin*, **30**, 225–40.

Latimer, J., Boothman, W., Tobin, R. *et al.* (1997) Historical reconstruction of contamination levels and ecological effects in a highly contaminated estuary. *Estuarine Research Federation annual meeting in Providence, Rhode Island*, October 1997, Abstracts Volume, pp. 104–5.

Lazarus, D. (1983) Speciation in pelagic Protista and its study in the planktonic microfossil record: a review. *Paleobiology*, **9** (4), 327–40.

Lazarus, D., Hilbrecht, H., Spencer-Cervato, C. and Thierstein, H. (1995) Sympatric speciation and phyletic change in *Globorotalia truncatulinoides*. *Paleobiology*, **21** (1), 28–51.

Le, J. and Thunell, R.C. (1996) Modelling planktic foraminiferal assemblage changes and application to sea surface temperature estimation in the western equatorial Pacific. *Marine Micropaleontology*, **28**, 211–29.

Le Calvez, J. (1936a) Observations sur le genre *Iridia*. *Archives de Zoologie Expérimentale et Générale*, **78**, 115–31.

Le Calvez, J. (1936b) Modifications du test des Foraminifères pélagiques en rapport avec la reproduction: *Orbulina universa* d'Orb. et *Tretomphalus bulloides* d'Orb. *Annales de Protistologie*, **5**, 125–33.

Le Calvez, J. (1938) Recherches sur les Foraminifères. 1. Développement et reproduction. *Archives de Zoologie Expérimentale et Générale*, **80**, 163–333.

Le Calvez, J. (1946) Place de la réduction chromatique et alternance de phases nucléaires dans le cycle des foraminifères. *L'Académie des Sciences Paris, Comptes Rendus*, **222**, 612–4.

Le Calvez, J. (1947) *Entosolenia marginata*, foraminifère apogamique extoparasite d'un autre foraminifère *Discorbis vilardeboanus*. *L'Académie des Sciences Paris, Comptes Rendus*, **224**, 1448–50.

Le Calvez, J. (1950) Recherches sur les Foraminifères. 2. Place de la méiose et sexualité. *Archives de Zoologie Expérimentale et Générale*, **87**, 211–43.

Lea, D.W. (1993) Constraints on the alkalinity and circulation of glacial Circumpolar Deep Water from benthic foraminiferal barium. *Global Biogeochemical Cycles*, **7**, 695–710.

Lea, D.W. (1995) A trace metal perspective on the evolution of Antarctic Circumpolar Deepwater chemistry. *Paleoceanography*, **10**, 733–47.

Lea, D.W. and Boyle, E.A. (1989) Barium content of benthic foraminifera controlled by bottom water composition. *Nature*, **338**, 751–3.

References

Lea, D.W. and Boyle, E.A. (1990a) A 210,000-year record of barium variability in the deep northwest Atlantic Ocean. *Nature*, **347**, 269–72.

Lea, D.W. and Boyle, E.A. (1990b) Foraminiferal reconstruction of barium distributions in water masses of the glacial oceans. *Paleoceanography*, **5**, 719–42.

Lea, D.W. and Boyle, E.A. (1991) Barium in planktonic foraminifera. *Geochimica et Cosmochimica Acta*, **55**, 3321–31.

Lea, D.W. and Boyle, E.A. (1993) Determination of carbonate-bound barium in corals and foraminifera by isotope dilution plasma mass spectrometry. *Chemical Geology*, **103**, 73–84.

Lea, D.W. and Martin, P.A. (1996) A rapid mass spectrometric method for the simultaneous analysis of barium, cadmium and strontium in foraminifera shells. *Geochimica et Cosmochimica Acta*, **60**, 3143–9.

Lea, D.W., Martin, P.A., Chan, D.A. and Spero, H.J. (1995) Calcium uptake and calcification rate in the planktonic foraminifer *Orbulina universa*. *Journal of Foraminiferal Research*, **25**, 14–23.

Lea, D.W. and Spero, H.J. (1992) Experimental determination of barium uptake in shells of the planktonic foraminifera *Orbulina universa* at 22°C. *Geochimica et Cosmochimica Acta*, **56**, 2673–80.

Lea, D.W. and Spero, H.J. (1994) Assessing the reliability of paleochemical tracers: barium uptake in the shells of planktonic foraminifera. *Paleoceanography*, **9**, 445–52.

Leavitt, S.W. (1993) Environmental information from $^{13}C/^{12}C$ ratios of wood, in *Climate Change in Continental Isotopic Records*, (eds P.K. Swart, K.C. Lohmann, J. McKenzie and S. Savin), *Geophysical monograph series*, **78**, American Geophysical Union, Washington DC, pp. 325–31.

Lee, J.J. (1980) Nutrition and physiology of the foraminifera, in *Biochemistry and Physiology of Protozoa, v. 3*, (eds M. Levandowsky and S.H. Hutner), Academic Press, New York, pp. 43–66.

Lee, J.J. (1990a) Phylum Granuloreticulosa (Foraminifera), in *Handbook of Protoctista*, (eds L. Margulis, J.O. Corliss, M. Melkonian and D.J. Chapman), Jones and Bartlett, Boston, pp. 524–48.

Lee, J.J. (1990b) Fine structure of the rhodophycean *Porphyridium purpureum in situ* in *Peneroplis pertusus* (Forskal) and *P. acicularis* (Batsch) and in axenic culture. *Journal of Foraminiferal Research*, **20**, 162–9.

Lee, J.J. (1998) Living sands: Larger foraminifera and their endosymbiotic algae. *Symbiosis*, **25**, 71–100.

Lee, J.J. and Anderson, O.R. (1991a) Symbiosis in Foraminifera, in *Biology of Foraminifera*, (eds J.J. Lee and O.R. Anderson), Academic Press, London, pp. 157–220.

Lee, J.J. and Anderson O.R. (eds) (1991b) *Biology of Foraminifera*, Academic Press, London.

Lee, J.J. and Bock, W.D. (1976) The importance of feeding in two species of soritid foraminifera with algal symbionts. *Bulletin of Marine Science*, **26**, 530–7.

Lee, J.J., Crockett, L.J., Hagen, J. and Stone, R. (1974) The taxonomic identity and physiological ecology of *Chlamydomonas hedleyi* sp. nov., algal flagellate symbiont from the foraminifer *Archaias angulatus*. *British Journal of Phycology*, **9**, 407–22.

Lee, J.J., Faber, W.W., Anderson, O.R. and Pawlowski, J. (1991a) Life cycles of Foraminifera, in *Biology of the Foraminifera*, (eds J.J. Lee and O.R. Anderson), Academic Press, London, pp. 285–334.

Lee, J.J., Faber, W.W. and Lee, R.E. (1991b) Granular reticular digestion – a possible preadaption to benthic foraminiferal symbiosis? *Symbiosis*, **10**, 47–61.

Lee, J.J., Faber, W.W., Nathanson, B. *et al.* (1992) Endosymbiotic diatoms from larger Foraminifera collected in Pacific habitats. *Symbiosis*, **14**, 265–81.

Lee, J.J. and Hallock, P. (1987) Algal symbiosis as a driving force in the evolution of larger foraminifera. *Annals, New York Academy of Science*, **503**, 330–47.

Lee, J.J., Lanners, E. and ter Kuile, B. (1988) Retention of chloroplasts by the foraminifer *Elphidium crispum*. *Symbiosis*, **5**, 45–60.

Lee, J.J., McEnery, M.E. and Garrison, J.R. (1980) Experimental studies of larger foraminifera and their symbionts from the Gulf of Elat on the Red Sea. *Journal of Foraminiferal Research*, **10**, 31–47.

Lee, J.J., McEnery, M.E., Kahn, E. and Schuster, F. (1979) Symbiosis and the evolution of larger foraminifera. *Micropaleontology*, **25**, 118–40.

Lee, J.J., McEnery, M., Pierce, S. *et al.* (1966) Tracer experiments in feeding littoral foraminifera. *Journal of Protozoology*, **13**, 659–70.

Lee, J.J., McEnery, M., ter Kuile, B. *et al.* (1989) Identification and distribution of endosymbiotic diatoms in larger Foraminifera. *Micropaleontology*, **35**, 353–66.

Lee, J.J., Morales, J., Bacus, S. *et al.* (1997) Progress in characterizing the endosymbiotic dinoflagellates of soritid foraminifera and related studies on some stages in the life cycle of *Marginopora vertebralis*. *Journal of Foraminiferal Research*, **27**, 254–63.

Lee, J.J., Muller, W.A., Stone, R.J. *et al.* (1969) Standing crop of foraminifera in sublittoral epiphytic communities of a Long Island salt marsh. *Marine Biology*, **4**, 44–61.

Lee, J.J., Wray, C.G. and Lawrence, C. (1995) Could foraminiferal zooxanthellae be derived from environmental pools contributed to by different coelenterate hosts? *Acta Protozoologica*, **34**, 75–85.

LeFurgey, A. and St. Jean, J. (1973) Foraminifera in estuarine ponds designed for waste control and aquaculture, in *Structure and Functioning of Estuarine Systems Exposed to Treated Sewage Wastes, III*, (eds E.J. Kuenzler, A.F. Chestnut and S.M. Weiss), University of North Carolina, Sea Grant Program, Chapel Hill, North Carolina, pp. 51–96.

LeFurgey, A. and St. Jean, J. (1975) Foraminifera in estuarine ponds designed for waste control and aquaculture. *Benthonics '75, Dalhousie University, Halifax, Nova Scotia, Abstracts*, p. 26.

References

LeFurgey, A. and St. Jean, J. (1976) Foraminifera in brackish-water ponds designed for waste control and aquaculture studies in north Carolina. *Journal of Foraminiferal Research*, **6**, 274–94.

Leidy, J. (1879) Fresh-water rhizopods of North America. *United States Geological Survey of the Territories*, **12**, 1–324.

Leutenegger, S. (1977a) Reproductive cycles of larger foraminifera and depth distributions of generations. *Utrecht Micropaleontological Bulletin*, **15**, 27–34.

Leutenegger, S. (1977b) Ultrastructure de foraminifères perforés et imperforés ainsi que de leurs symbiotes. *Cahiers de Micropaléontologie*, **3**, 52 pp.

Leutenegger, S. (1984) Symbiosis in benthic Foraminifera: Specificity and host adaptations. *Journal of Foraminiferal Research*, **14**, 16–35.

Leutenegger, S. and Hansen, H.J. (1979) Ultrastructural and radiotracer studies of pore function in Foraminifera. *Marine Biology*, **54**, 11–6.

Levin, S.A. and Segel, L.A. (1976) Hypothesis for the origin of planktonic patchiness. *Nature*, **259**, 659.

Levine, N.D., Corliss, J.O., Cox, F.E.G. *et al.* (1980) A newly revised classification of the Protozoa. *Journal of Protozoology*, **27**, 37–58.

Levinton, J.S. (1989) Deposit feeding and coastal oceanography, in *Ecology of Marine Deposit Feeders*, (eds G. Lopez, G. Taghon and J. Levinton), Springer-Verlag, pp. 1–23.

Levinton, J.S. (1972) Stability and trophic structure in deposit-feeding and suspension-feeding communities. *American Naturalist*, **106**, 472–86.

Lévy, A. (1977) Revision micropaléontologique des Soritidae actuels Bahamiens; un nouveau genre: *Androsina*. *Recherches Exploration-Production Elf-Aquitaine, Bulletin*, **1**, 393–449.

Lévy, A. (1991) Peuplements actuels et thanatocénoses à Soritidae et Peneroplidae des Keys de Floride (USA). *Oceanologica Acta*, **14**, 515–24.

Lévy, A., Mathieu, R., Poignant, A. *et al.* (1995) Benthic foraminifera from the Fernando de Noronha Archipelago (northern Brazil). *Marine Micropaleontology*, **26**, 89–97.

Liddell, W.D., Boss, S.K., Nelson, C.V. and Martin, R.E. (1987) Sedimentological and foraminiferal characterization of shelf and slope environments (1–234 m), north Jamaica, in *Third Symposium on the Geology of the Bahamas, Proceedings*, (ed H.A. Curran), pp. 91–8.

Liddell, W.D. and Martin, R.E. (1989) Taphofacies in modern carbonate environments: implications for formation of foraminiferal sediment assemblages. *International Geological Congress, Abstracts*, **2**, 299.

Lidz, L. (1965) Sedimentary environment and foraminiferal parameters – Nantucket Bay, Massachusetts. *Limnology and Oceanography*, **10**, 392–402.

Lidz, L. (1966) Planktonic Foraminifera in the water column of the mainland shelf off Newport Beach, California. *Limnology and Oceanography*, **11**, 257–63.

Lin, S. and Morse, J.W. (1991) Sulfate reduction and iron sulfide mineral formation in Gulf of Mexico anoxic sediments. *American Journal of Science*, **291**, 55–89.

Linke, P., Altenbach, A., Graf, G. and Heeger, T. (1995) Response of deep-sea benthic foraminifera to a simulated sedimentation event. *Journal of Foraminiferal Research*, **25**, 75–82.

Linke, P. and Lutze, G.F. (1993) Microhabitat preferences of benthic foraminifera – a static concept or a dynamic adaptation to optimize food acquisition? *Marine Micropaleontology*, **20**, 215–34.

Linsley, B.K. (1996) Oxygen-isotope record of sea level and climate variations in the Sulu Sea over the past 150,000 years. *Nature*, **380**, 234–7.

Lipps, J.H. (1970) Plankton Evolution. *Evolution*, **24** (1), 1–22.

Lipps, J.H. (1976) Coiling ratios in planktonic foraminifera: Adaptive strategy and paleoenvironmental interpretation. *American Assoc. Petroleum Geologists Bulletin*, **60**, 2184–5.

Lipps, J.H. (1979) The Ecology and paleoecology of planktic foraminifera in *Foraminiferal Ecology and Paleoecology*, (eds J.H. Lipps, W.H. Berger, M.A. Buzas *et al.*), *SEPM Short Course No. 2*, Houston Texas, pp. 62–104.

Lipps, J.H. (1981) What, if anything, is micropaleontology? *Paleobiology*, **7**, 167–99.

Lipps, J.H. (1983) Biotic interactions in benthic foraminifera, in *Biotic Interactions in Recent and Fossil Benthic Communities*, (eds M.J.J. Tevez and P.L. McCall), Plenum, New York, pp. 331–76.

Lipps, J.H. and Krebs, W.N. (1974) Planktonic foraminifera associated with Antarctic sea ice. *Journal of Foraminiferal Research*, **4**, 80–5.

Lipps, J.H. and Severin, K.P. (1984/1985) *Alveolinella quoyi*, a living fusiform foraminifera, at Motupore Islands, Papua, New Guinea. *Science in New Guinea*, **11**, 126–37.

Lipps, J.H. and Warme, J.E. (1966) Planktonic foraminiferal biofacies in the Okhotsk Sea. *Contributions to the Cushman Foundation for Foraminiferal Research*, **17**, 125–34.

Lister, J.J. (1895) Contributions to the life history of the Foraminifera. *Philosophical Transactions of the Royal Society of London, Series B*, **186**, 401–53.

Lister, J.J. (1903) The Foraminifera, in *A Treatise on Zoology*, (ed E.R. Lankester), Adam and Charles Black, London, pp. 47–149.

Lockin, J.A. and Maddocks, R.F. (1982) Recent foraminifera around petroleum production platforms on the southwest Louisiana Shelf. *Gulf Coast Association of Geological Societies Transactions*, **32**, 377–97.

Loeblich, A.R. and Tappan, H. (1953) Studies of Arctic Foraminifera. *Smithsonian Miscellaneous Collections*, **121** (7), 150 pp.

Loeblich, A.R. and Tappan, H. (1964a) Sarcodina, Chiefly 'Thecamoebians' and Foraminiferida, in *Treatise on Invertebrate Paleontology*, (ed R.C. Moore), Geological Society of America, Boulder, Part C, v. 1–2, 900 pp.

References

Loeblich, A.R. and Tappan, H. (1964b) Foraminiferal classification and evolution. *Journal of the Geological Society of India*, **5**, 5–40.

Loeblich, A.R. and Tappan, H. (1974) Recent advances in the classification of the Foraminiferida, in *Foraminifera*, v. 1, (ed R.H. Hedley and C.G. Adams), Academic Press, London, pp. 1–53.

Loeblich, A.R. and Tappan, H. (1984) Suprageneric classification of the Foraminiferida (Protozoa). *Micropaleontology*, **30**, 1–70.

Loeblich, A.R. and Tappan, H. (1987) *Foraminiferal Genera and Their Classification*, v. 1–2, Van Nostrand Reinhold, New York.

Loeblich, A.R. and Tappan, H. (1989) Publication Date of Foraminiferal Genera and Their Classification. *Journal of Paleontology*, **63**, 253.

Loeblich, A.R. and Tappan, H. (1992) Present status of foraminiferal classification, in *Studies in Benthic Foraminifera*, (eds Y. Takayanagi and T. Saito), *Proceedings of the Fourth International Symposium on Benthic Foraminifera, Sendai, 1990 (Benthos '90)*, Tokai University Press, Tokyo, Japan, pp. 93–102.

Logan, B.W. and Cebulski, D.E. (1970) Sedimentary environments of Shark Bay, Western Australia, in *Carbonate Sedimentation and Environments, Shark Bay, Western Australia*, (ed B.W. Logan), American Association of Petroleum Geologists, Tulsa, Oklahoma, Memoir 13, pp. 1–37.

Lohmann, G.P. (1992) Increasing seasonal upwelling in the tropical South Atlantic over the past 700,000 yrs: Evidence from deep-living planktonic foraminifera. *Marine Micropaleontology*, **19**, 1–12.

Lohmann, G.P. (1995) A model for variation in the chemistry of planktonic foraminifera due to secondary calcification and selective dissolution. *Paleoceanography*, **10** (3), 445–58.

Lohmann, G.P. and Schweitzer, P.N. (1990) Growth and chemistry as probes of the past thermocline. *Paleoceanography*, 5 (1), 55–75.

Long, S.P. and Mason, C.F. (1983) *Saltmarsh Ecology*, Blackie, Glasgow.

Longhurst, A., Sathyendranath, S., Platt, T. and Caverhill, C. (1995) A estimate of global primary production in the ocean from satellite radiometer data. *Journal of Plankton Research*, **17**, 1245–71.

Lopez, G. and Levinton, J. (1987) Ecology of deposit-feeding animals in marine sediments. *Quarterly Reviews of Biology*, **62**, 235–60.

Lopez, R. (1979) Algal chloroplasts in the protoplasm of three species of benthic Foraminifera: Taxonomic affinity, viability and persistence. *Marine Biology*, **53**, 201–11.

Lorens, R.B. (1981) Sr, Cd, Mn and Co distribution coefficients in calcite as a function of calcite precipitation rate. *Geochimica et Cosmochimica Acta*, **45**, 553–61.

Lorens, R.B., Williams, D.F. and Bender, M.L. (1977) The early nonstructural chemical diagenesis of foraminiferal calcite. *Journal of Sedimentary Petrology*, **47**, 1602–9.

Lorius, C. (1983) Antarctica: survey of near-surface mean isotopic values, in *The Climate Record of the Polar Ice Sheet*, (ed G. de Q. Robin), Cambridge University Press, New York, pp. 52–6.

Lorius, C., Jouzel, J., Ritz, S. *et al.* (1985) A 150,000 year climatic record from Antarctic ice. *Nature*, **316**, 591–6.

Loubere, P. (1989) Bioturbation and sedimentation rate control of benthic microfossil taxon abundances in surface sediments: A theoretical approach to the analysis of species microhabitats. *Marine Micropaleontology*, **14**, 317–25.

Loubere, P. (1991) Deep-sea benthic foraminiferal assemblage response to a surface ocean productivity gradient: A test. *Paleoceanography*, **6**, 193–204.

Loubere, P. (1994) Quantitative estimation of surface ocean productivity and bottom water oxygen concentration using benthic foraminifera. *Paleoceanography*, **9**, 723–37.

Loubere, P. (1996) The surface ocean productivity and bottom water oxygen signals in deep water benthic foraminiferal assemblages. *Marine Micropaleontology*, **28**, 247–61.

Loubere, P. (1997) Benthic foraminiferal assemblage formation, organic carbon flux and oxygen concentrations on the outer continental shelf and slope. *Journal of Foraminiferal Research*, **27**, 93–100.

Loubere, P. (1998) The impact of seasonality on the benthos as reflected in the assemblages of deep sea foraminifera. *Deep-Sea Research*, **45**, 409–32.

Loubere, P. and Fariduddin, M. (1999) Quantitative estimation of global patterns of surface ocean biological productivity and its seasonal variation on time scales from centuries to millennia. *Global Biogeochemical Cycles*, **13**, 115–33.

Loubere, P. and Gary, A. (1990) Taphonomic process and species microhabitats in the living to fossil assemblage transition of deeper water benthic foraminifera. *Palaios*, **5**, 375–81.

Loubere, P., Gary, A. and Lagoe, M. (1993a) Sea-bed biogeochemistry and benthic foraminiferal bathymetric zonation on the slope of the northwest Gulf of Mexico. *Palaios*, **8**, 439–49.

Loubere, P., Gary, A. and Lagoe, M. (1993b) Generation of the benthic foraminiferal assemblage: Theory and preliminary data. *Marine Micropaleontology*, **20**, 165–82.

Loubere, P., Meyers, P. and Gary, A. (1995) Benthic foraminiferal microhabitat selection, carbon isotope values, and association with larger animals: A test with *Uvigerina peregrina*. *Journal of Foraminiferal Research*, **25**, 83–95.

Loubere, P. and Qian, H. (1997) Reconstructing paleoecology and paleoenvironmental variables using factor analysis and regression: some limitations. *Marine Micropaleontology*, **31**, 205–17.

Lueck, K.L.O. and Snyder, S.W. (1997) Lateral variations among populations of stained benthic foraminifera in surface sediments of the North Carolina continental shelf (U.S.A.). *Journal of Foraminiferal Research*, **27**, 20–41.

References

Luther, G.W., Ferdelman, T.G., Kostka, J.E., et al. (1991) Temporal and spatial variability of reduced sulfur species (FeS$_2$,S$_2$O$_3^{2-}$) and porewater parameters in salt marsh sediments. *Biogeochemistry*, **14**, 57–88.

Lutze, G.F. (1965) Zur Foraminiferen-Fauna der Ostsee. *Meyniana*, **15**, 75–142.

Lutze, G.F. and Altenbach, A.V. (1988) *Rupertina stabilis* (Wallich), a highly adapted, suspension feeding foraminifer. *Meyniana*, **40**, 55–69.

Lutze, G.F. and Altenbach, A. (1991) Technik und Signifikanz der Lebendfärbung benthischer Foraminiferen mit Bengalrot. *Geologisches Jahrbuch*, **A128**, 251–65.

Lutze, G.F. and Coulbourn, W. (1983/84) Recent benthic foraminifera from the continental margin of northwest Africa: Community structure and distribution. *Marine Micropaleontology*, **8**, 361–401.

Lutze, G.F. and Thiel, H. (1987) *Cibicidoides wuellerstorfi* and *Planulina ariminensis*, elevated epibenthic foraminifera. *Ber. Sonderforschungsbereich*, 313, Nr. 6, S. 17–30, 17–25. University of Kiel, Germany.

Lutze, G.F. and Thiel, H. (1989) Epibenthic foraminifera from elevated microhabitats: *Cibicidoides wuellerstorfi* and *Planulina ariminensis*. *Journal of Foraminiferal Research*, **19**, 153–8.

Lynch-Steiglitz, J. and Fairbanks, R.G. (1994) A conservative tracer for glacial ocean circulation from carbon isotope and paleo-nutrient measurements in benthic foraminifera. *Nature*, **369**, 308–10.

Lynch-Steiglitz, J., Van Geen, A. and Fairbanks, R.G. (1996) Interocean exchange of glacial North Atlantic intermediate water – evidence from subantarctic Cd/Ca and carbon isotope measurements. *Paleoceanography*, **11**, 191–201.

Macdonald, R.W., Paton, D.W., Carmack, E.C. and Omstedt, A. (1995) The freshwater budget and under-ice spreading of Mackenzie River water in the Canadian Beaufort Sea based on salinity and $^{18}O/^{16}O$ measurements in water and ice. *Journal of Geophysical Research*, **100C**, 895–919.

Mackensen, A. and Douglas, R.G. (1989) Down-core distribution of live and dead deep-water benthic Foraminifera in box cores from the Weddell Sea and the California continental borderland. *Deep-Sea Research*, **36**, 879–900.

Mackensen, A., Fütterer, D., Grobe, H and Schmiedl, G. (1993a) Benthic foraminiferal assemblages from the eastern south Atlantic Polar Front region between 35 and 57 S: distribution, ecology and fossilization potential. *Marine Micropaleontology*, **22**, 33–69.

Mackensen, A., Grobe, H., Hubberten, H.W. and Kuhn, G. (1993b) Benthic foraminiferal assemblages and the δ^{13}C-signal in the Atlantic sector of the Southern Ocean, glacial-to-interglacial contrasts, in *Carbon Cycling in the Glacial Ocean, Constraints on the Ocean's Role in Global Change, Quantitative Approaches in Paleoceanography*, (eds R. Zahn, T.F. Pedersen, M.A. Kaminski and L. Labeyrie), NATO ASI Series, Series I: Global Environmental Change, **17**, 105–35.

Mackensen, A., Hubberten, H.W., Bickert, T. et al. (1993c) The δ^{13}C in benthic foraminiferal tests of *Fontbotia wuellerstorfi* (Schwager) relative to the δ^{13}C of dissolved inorganic carbon in southern ocean deep water. Implications for glacial ocean circulation models. *Paleoceanography*, **8**, 587–610.

Mackensen, A., Sejrup, H. and Jansen, E. (1985) The distribution of living and dead benthic foraminifera on the continental slope and rise off southwest Norway. *Marine Micropaleontology*, **9**, 275–306.

Mackenzie, F.T. (1998) *Our Changing Planet: An Introduction to Earth System Science and Global Environmental Change*, 2nd ed, Prentice Hall, Upper Saddle River, New Jersey.

MacLeod, K.G. and Huber, B.T. (1996) Strontium isotopic evidence for extensive reworking in sediments spanning the Cretaceous-Tertiary boundary at ODP site 738. *Geology*, **24**, 463–6.

Majoube, M. (1971) Fractionnement en oxygene 18 et deuterium entre l'eau et sa vapeur. *Journal Chim. Phys*, **10**, 1423–36.

Malins, D.C. and Osttander, G.K. (eds) (1993) *Aquatic Toxicology, Molecular, Biochemical and Cellular Perspectives*, Levis Publ., Boca Raton, Florida.

Malmgren, B.A. (1974) Morphometric studies of planktonic foraminifers from the type Danian of southern Scandinavia. *Stockholm Contributions to Geology*, **24**, 1–126.

Malmgren, B.A. (1987) Differential dissolution of Upper Cretaceous planktonic foraminifera from a temperate region of the South Atlantic Ocean. *Marine Micropaleontology*, **11**, 251–71.

Malone, T.C. (1991) River flow, phytoplankton production and oxygen depletion in Chesapeake Bay, in *Modern and Ancient Continental Shelf Anoxia*, (eds R.V. Tyson and T.H. Pearson), Geological Society of London Special Publication, **58**, pp. 83–93.

Marchitto, T.M., Curry, W.B. and Oppo, D.W. (1998) Millennial-scale changes in North Atlantic circulation since the last glaciation. *Nature*, **393**, 557–61.

Margulis, L. (1990) Introduction, in *Handbook of Protoctista* (eds L. Margulis, J.O. Corliss, M. Melkonian and D.J. Chapman), Jones and Bartlett, Boston, pp. xi–xxiii.

Martin, J.H. and Gordon, R.M. (1988) Northeast Pacific iron distributions in relation to phytoplankton productivity. *Deep-Sea Research*, **35**, 177–96.

Martin, J.H., Knauer, G.A. and Gordon, R.M. (1983) Silver distributions and fluxes in north-east Pacific waters. *Nature*, **305**, 306–9.

Martin, J.H., Knauer, G.A., Karl, D. and Broenkow, W. (1987) VERTEX: carbon cycling in the northeast Pacific. *Deep-Sea Research*, **34**, 267–86.

Martin, P.A. and Lea, D.W. (1998) Comparison of water mass changes derived from Cd/Ca and carbon isotope records: implications for changing Ba composition of Deep Atlantic Water Masses. *Paleoceanography*, **13**, 572–85.

Martin, P.A., Lea, D.W., Mashiotta, T.A. et al (1997) Gla-

References

cial-interglacial variation in mean ocean Sr? *EOS, Transactions of American Geophysical Union*, **78** (46), F388.

Martin, P.A., Lea, D.W., McCorkle, D.C. *et al.* (1996) Trace metal composition of benthic Foraminifera as an indicator of microhabitat preference. *Geological Society of America Abstracts with Programs*, **28** (7), 428.

Martin, R.E. (1986) Habitat and distribution of the foraminifer *Archaias angulatus* (Fichtel and Moll) (Miliolina, Soritidae), northern Florida Keys. *Journal of Foraminiferal Research*, **16**, 201–6.

Martin, R.E. (1991) Beyond biostratigraphy: Micropaleontology in transition? *Palaios*, **6**, 437–8.

Martin, R.E. (1993) Time and taphonomy: Actualistic evidence for time-averaging of benthic foraminiferal assemblages, in *Taphonomic Approaches to Time Resolution in Fossil Assemblages*, (eds S.M. Kidwell and A.K. Behrensmeyer), Paleontological Society Short Courses in Paleontology No. 6, pp. 34–56.

Martin, R.E. (1995) The once and future profession of micropaleontology. *Journal of Foraminiferal Research*, **25**, 372–3.

Martin, R.E. (1998) *One Long Experiment: Scale and Process in Earth History*, Columbia University Press, New York.

Martin, R.E. and Fletcher, R. R. (1995) Graphic correlation of Plio-Pleistocene sequence boundaries, Gulf of Mexico: Oxygen isotopes, ice volume, and sea level, in *Graphic Correlation and the Composite Standard Approach*, (eds K.O. Mann, H.R. Lane and J.A. Stein), SEPM (Society for Sedimentary Geology) Special Publication Number 53, Tulsa, pp. 235–48.

Martin, R.E., Harris, M.S. and Liddell, W.D. (1995) Taphonomy and time-averaging of foraminiferal assemblages in Holocene tidal flat sediments, Bahia la Choya, Sonora, Mexico (northern Gulf of California). *Marine Micropaleontology*, **26**, 187–206.

Martin, R.E. and Liddell, W.D. (1988) Foraminiferal biofacies on a north coast fringing reef (1–75m), Discovery Bay, Jamaica. *Palaios*, **3**, 298–314.

Martin, R.E. and Liddell, W.D. (1989) Relation of counting methods to taphonomic gradients and biofacies zonation of foraminiferal sediment assemblages. *Marine Micropaleontology*, **15**, 67–89.

Martin, R.E. and Liddell, W.D. (1991) Taphonomy of foraminifera in modern carbonate environments: implications for the formation of foraminiferal assemblages, in *Fossilization: The Processes of Taphonomy*, (ed S.K. Donovan), Belhaven Press, London, pp. 170–94.

Martin, R.E., Neff, E.D, Johnson, G.W. and Krantz, D.E. (1993) Biostratigraphic expression of Pleistocene sequence boundaries, Gulf of Mexico. *Palaios*, **8**, 155–71.

Martin, R.E., Wehmiller, J.F., Harris, S.M. and Liddell, W.D. (1996) Comparative taphonomy of bivalves and foraminifera from Holocene tidal flat sediments, Bahia la Choya, Sonora, Mexico (northern Gulf of California): Taphonomic grades and temporal resolution. *Paleobiology*, **22**, 80–90.

Martin, R.E. and Wright, R.C. (1988) Information loss in the transition from life to death assemblages of foraminifera in back reef environments, Key Largo, Florida. *Journal of Paleontology*, **62**, 399–410.

Martinson, D.G., Pisias, N.G, Hayes, J.D. *et al.* (1987) Age dating and the orbital theory of the ice-ages: development of a high-resolution 0 to 300,000 year chronostratigraphy. *Quaternary Research*, **27**, 1–29.

Mashiotta, T.A. and Lea, D.W. (1997) Planktic Cd indicates enhanced nutrient utilization in the glacial Subantarctic. *EOS, Transactions of American Geophysical Union*, **78** (46), F391.

Mashiotta, T.A., Lea, D.W. and Spero, H.J. (1997) Experimental determination of Cd uptake in shells of the planktonic foraminifera *Orbulina universa* and *Globigerina bulloides*: Implications for surface water paleo-reconstructions. *Geochimica et Cosmochimica Acta*, **61**, 4053–65.

Mashiotta, T.A., Lea, D.W. and Spero, H.J. (in press) Glacial-interglacial changes in subantarctic sea surface temperature and δ^{18}O-water using foraminiferal Mg. *Earth and Planetary Science Letters*.

Matera, N.J. and Lee, J.J. (1972) Environmental factors affecting the standing crop of foraminifera in sublittoral and psammolittoral communities of a Long Island salt marsh. *Marine Biology*, **14**, 89–103.

Matisoff, G. (1982) Mathematical models of bioturbation, in *Animal-Sediment Relations*, (eds P.I. McCall and M.J.S. Tevesz), Plenum Press, New York, pp. 289–330.

Matoba, Y. (1970) Distribution of recent shallow water foraminifera in Matsushima Bay, Miyagi Prefecture, northeast Japan. *Sci. Rept., Tohoku Univ.*, **2** Geol., **42** (1), 1–85.

Matoba, Y. (1976) Recent foraminiferal assemblages off Sendai, northeast Japan, in *First International Symposium on Benthic Foraminifera of Continental Margins, Part A: Ecology and Biology*, (eds C.T. Schafer and B.R. Pelletier), Maritime Sediments, Special Publication No. 1, pp. 205–20.

Maturo, F.J.S. (1968) The distributional pattern of the Bryozoa of the east coast of the United States exclusive of New England. *Atti della Soc7Ifeta Italiano di Scienze Naturali e del Museo Civico di Storia Naturali di Milano*, **108**, 261–84.

Mayer, E.M. (1980) *Foraminifera of the Caspian and Aral Seas*, Unpubl. Ph.D. thesis, Moscow University.

Mayer, L. (1994) Surface area control of organic carbon accumulation in continental shelf sediments. *Geochimica et Cosmochimica Acta*, **58**, 1271–84.

McCarthy, J., Garside, C., Nevins, J. and Barber, R. (1996) New production along 140°W in the equatorial Pacific during and following the 1992 El Nino event. *Deep-Sea Research, II*, **43**, 1065–93.

McConnaughey, T. (1989a) ^{13}C and ^{18}O isotopic disequilibrium in biological carbonates: I. Patterns. *Geochimica et Cosmochimica Acta*, **53**, 151–62.

McConnaughey, T. (1989b) ^{13}C and ^{18}O isotopic disequilib-

References

rium in biological carbonates: II. *In vitro* simulation of kinetic isotope effects. *Geochimica et Cosmochimica Acta*, **53**, 163–71.

McConnaughey, T.A. (1989c) Biomineralization mechanisms, in *Origin, Evolution, and Modern Aspects of Biomineralization in Plants and Animals*, (ed R.E. Crick), Plenum, New York, pp. 57–73.

McConnaughey, T.A. and Whelan, J.F. (1997) Calcification generates protons for nutrient and bicarbonate uptake. *Earth-Science Reviews*, **42**, 95–117.

McCorkle, D.C., Corliss, B.H. and Farnham, C.A. (1997) Vertical distributions and stable isotopic compositions of live (stained) benthic foraminifera from the North Carolina and California continental margin. *Deep-Sea Research*, I, **44**, 983–1024.

McCorkle, D.C. and Emerson, S.R. (1988) The relationship between porewater carbon isotopic composition and bottom water oxygen concentration. *Geochimica et Cosmochimica Acta*, **52**, 1169–78.

McCorkle, D.C., Emerson, S.R. and Quay, P.D. (1985) Stable carbon isotopes in marine porewaters. *Earth and Planetary Science Letters*, **74**, 13–26.

McCorkle, D.C., Martin, P.A., Lea, D.W. and Klinkhammer, G.P. (1995) Evidence of a dissolution effect on benthic shell chemistry: $\delta^{13}C$, Cd/Ca, Ba/Ca, and Sr/Ca from the Ontong Java Plateau. *Paleoceanography*, **10**, 699–714.

McCorkle, D.C., Keigwin, L.D., Corliss, B.H. and Emerson, S.R. (1990) The influence of microhabitats on the carbon isotopic composition of deep-sea benthic foraminifera. *Paleoceanography*, **5**, 161–85.

McCorkle, D.C. and Klinkhammer, G.P. (1991) Porewater cadmium geochemistry and the porewater cadmium:$\delta^{13}C$ relationship. *Geochimica et Cosmochimica Acta*, **55**, 161–8.

McCoy, E.D. and Heck, K.L. (1983) Centres of origin revisited. *Paleobiology*, **9**, 17–9.

McCrea, J.M. (1950) On the isotope chemistry of carbonates and a paleotemperature scale. *Journal of Chemical Physics*, **18**, 849–57.

McCrone, A.W. and Schafer, C. (1966) Geochemical and sedimentary environments of foraminifera in the Hudson River estuary, New York. *Micropaleontology*, **12**, 505–9.

McEnery, M.E. and Lee, J.J. (1976) *Allogromia laticollaris*: A Foraminiferan with an unusual apogamic metagenic life cycle. *Journal of Protozoology*, **23**, 94–108.

McGann, M. and Sloan, D. (1996) Recent introduction of the foraminifer *Trochammina hadai* Uchio into San Francisco Bay, California, USA. *Marine Micropaleontology*, **28**, 1–3.

McGowan, J.A. (1971) Oceanic biogeography of the Pacific, in *The Micropaleontology of Oceans*, (eds B.M. Funnell and W.R. Riedel), Cambridge University Press, Cambridge, pp. 3–74.

McGowan, J.A. (1974) The nature of oceanic ecosystems, in *The Biology of the Oceanic Pacific*, (ed C.B. Miller), Corvallis, pp. 9–28.

McGowan, J.A. (1986) The Biogeography of Pelagic Ecosystems, in *Pelagic Biogeography, Proceedings of an International Conference: the Netherlands 29 May–5 June 1985*, (eds A.C. Pierrot-Bults, S. van der Spoel, B.J. Zahuranec and R.K. Johnson), Unesco, pp. 191–200.

McGowran, B., Li, Q., Cann, J. *et al.* (1997) Biogeographic impact of the Leeuwin Current in southern Australia since the late middle Eocene. *Palaeogeography, Palaeoclimatology, Palaeoecology*, **136**, 19–40.

McHatton, S.C., Barry, J.P., Jannasch, H.W. and Nelson, D.C. (1996) High nitrate concentration in vacuolate, autotrophic marine *Beggiatoa* spp. *Applied and Environmental Microbiology*, **62**, 954–8.

McIntyre, A., Bé, A.W.H. and Preikstas, R. (1967) Coccoliths and the Plio-Pleistocene boundary. *Progress in Oceanography*, **4**, 3–25.

McIntyre, A., Ruddimann, W.F. and Jantzen, R. (1972) Southward penetrations of the North Atlantic polar front; faunal and floral evidence of large-scale surface-water mass movements over the past 225,000 years. *Deep-Sea Research*, **19**, 61–77.

McKee, E.D., Chronic, J. and Leopold, E.B. (1959) Sedimentary belts in the lagoon of Kapingimarangi Atoll. *Bulletin of the American Association of Petroleum Geologists*, **43**, 501–62.

McKinney, M.L. (1996) The biology of fossil abundance. *Revista Española de Paleontologia*, **11**, 125–33.

McKinney, M.L. and Allmon, W.D. (1995) Metapopulations and disturbance: From patch dynamics to biodiversity dynamics, in *New Approaches to Speciation in the Fossil Record*, (eds D.H. Erwin and R.L. Anstey), Columbia University Press, New York, pp. 123–83.

McKinney, M.L. and Frederick, D. (1992) Extinction and population dynamics: New methods and evidence from Paleogene foraminifera. *Geology*, **20**, 343–6.

McKinney, M.L., Lockwood, J.L. and Frederick, D.R. (1996) Rare species and scale-dependence in ecosystem stasis, in *New Perspectives on Faunal Stability in the Fossil Record*, (eds L.C. Ivany and K.M. Schopf), *Palaeogeography, Palaeoclimatology, Palaeoecology*, **127**, 191–207.

McLusky, D.S. (1981) *The Estuarine Ecosystem*, John Wiley, New York.

Meldahl, K.H. (1987) Sedimentologic and taphonomic implications of biogenic stratification. *Palaios*, **2**, 350–8.

Meldahl, K.H. (1990) Sampling, species abundance and the stratigraphic signature of mass extinction: A test using Holocene tidal flat molluscs. *Geology*, **18**, 899–3.

Meldahl, K.H., Flessa, K.W. and Cutler, A.H. (1997) Time-averaging and postmortem skeletal survival in benthic fossil assemblages: Quantitative comparisons among Holocene environments. *Paleobiology*, **23**, 207–29.

Merlivat, L. (1978) The dependence of bulk evaporation coefficients on air-water interfacial conditions as determined by the isotopic method. *Journal of Geophysical Research*, **83** (C6), 2977–80.

References

Merlivat, L. and Jouzel, J. (1979) Global climatic interpretation of the Deuterium-Oxygen 18 relationship for precipitation. *Journal of Geophysical Research*, **84** (C8), 5029–33.

Meyer-Reil, L.A. (1986) Measurement of hydrolytic activity and incorporation of dissolved organic substrates by microorganisms in marine sediments. *Marine Ecology Progress Series*, **31**, 143–9.

Meyer-Reil, L.A. and Köster, M. (1991) Fine-scale distribution of hydrolytic activity associated with foraminiferans and bacteria in deep-sea sediments of the Norwegian-Greenland Sea. *Kieler Meeresforschungen, Sonderheft Nr.*, **8**, 121–6.

Meyers, M.B, Fossing, H. and Powell, E.N. (1987) Microdistribution of interstitial meiofauna, oxygen and sulfide gradients, and the tubes of macro-infauna. *Marine Ecology Progress Series*, **35**, 223–41.

Meyers, M.B, Powell, E.N. and Fossing, H. (1988) Movement of oxybiotic and thiobiotic meiofauna in response to changes in pore-water oxygen and sulfide gradients around macro-infaunal tubes. *Marine Biology*, **98**, 395–414.

Middelburg, J.J., Soetaert, K. and Herman, P.M.J. (1997) Empirical relationships for use in global diagenetic models. *Deep-Sea Research*, **44**, 327–44.

Middelburg, J., Vlug, T. and Van der Nat, F. (1993) Organic matter mineralization in marine systems. *Global Planetary Change*, **8**, 47–58.

Millendorf, S.A, Brower, J.C. and Dyman, T.S. (1978) A comparison of methods for the quantification of assemblage zones. *Computers & Geosciences*, **4**, 229–42.

Miller, K. and Lohmann, G. (1982) Environmental distribution of Recent benthic foraminifera on the northeast United States continental slope. *Geological Society of America Bulletin*, **93**, 200–6.

Milligan, G.W. (1996) Clustering validation: results and implications for applied analysis, in *Clustering and Classification*, (eds P. Arabie, L.J. Hubert and G. De Soete), World Scientific, Singapore, pp. 341–75.

Milligan, G.W. and Cooper, M.C. (1986) A study for the comparability of external criteria for hierarchical cluster analysis. *Multivariate Behavior Research*, **21**, 441–58.

Milliman, J.D. and Droxler, A.W. (1995) Calcium carbonate sedimentation in the global ocean: Linkages between the neritic and pelagic environments. *Oceanography*, **8**, 92–5.

Milne-Edwards, H. (1838) Mémoire sur la distribution géographique des Crustacés. *Annales Sciences Naturelles (Zoologie)*, **10**, 139–74.

Mix, A.C. and Ruddiman, W.F. (1984) Oxygen-isotope analyses and Pleistocene ice volumes. *Quaternary Research*, **21**, 1–20.

Moodley, L. (1990) Southern North Sea seafloor and subsurface distribution of living benthic foraminifera. *Netherlands Journal of Sea Research*, **27**, 57–71.

Moodley, L. and Hess, C. (1992) Tolerance of infaunal benthic foraminifera for low and high oxygen concentrations. *Biological Bulletin*, **183**, 94–8.

Moodley, L., van der Zwaan, G.J., Herman, P.M.J. *et al.* (1997) Differential response of benthic meiofauna to long-term anoxia with special reference to Foraminifera (Protista: Sarcodina). *Marine Ecology Progress Series*, **158**, 151–63.

Moodley, L., Schaub, B.E.M., van der Zwaan, G.J. and Herman, P.M.J. (1998a) Tolerance of benthic foraminifera (Protista: Sarcodina) to hydrogen sulphide. *Marine Ecology Progress Series*, **169**, 77–86.

Moodley, L., van der Zwaan, G.J., Rutten, G.M.W. *et al.* (1998b) Subsurface activity of benthic foraminifera in relation to porewater oxygen content: laboratory experiments. *Marine Micropaleontology*, **34**, 91–106.

Mook, W.G., Bommersen, J.C. and Staverman, W.H. (1974) Carbon isotope fractionation between dissolved bicarbonate and gaseous carbon dioxide. *Earth and Planetary Science Letters*, **22**, 169–76.

Morel, F.M.M., Reinfelder, J.R., Roberts, S.B. *et al.* (1994) Zinc and carbon co-limitation of marine phytoplankton. *Nature*, **369**, 740–2.

Morin, R.W., Theyer, F. and Heath, G.R. (1970) Pleistocene climates in the Atlantic and Pacific Oceans: a reevaluated comparison based on deep-sea sediments. *Science*, **169**, 365–6.

Morse, J.W. and Bender, M.L. (1990) Partition coefficients in calcite: Examination of factors influencing the validity of experimental results and their application to natural systems. *Chemical Geology*, **82**, 265–77.

Morse, J.W. and Mackenzie, F.T. (1990) Geochemistry of Sedimentary Carbonates. *Developments in Sedimentology* 48, Elsevier, Amsterdam.

Mucci, A. and Morse, J.W. (1990) Chemistry of low-temperature abiotic calcites: experimental studies on coprecipitation, stability and fractionation. *Aquatic Sciences*, **2**, 217–54.

Murosky, M.W. and Snyder, S.W. (1994) Vertical distribution of stained benthic foraminifera in sediments of Southern Onslow Bay, North Carolina continental shelf. *Journal of Foraminiferal Research*, **24**, 158–70.

Murray, J. (1897) On the distribution of the pelagic Foraminifera at the surface and on the floor of the ocean. *Natural Science (ecology)*, **11**, 17–27.

Murray, J.W. (1970) The foraminifera of the hypersaline Abu Dhabi Lagoon, Persian Gulf. *Lethaia*, **3**, 51–68.

Murray, J.W. (1971) Living foraminiferids of tidal marshes: A review. *Journal of Foraminiferal Research*, **1**, 153–61.

Murray, J.W. (1973) *Distribution and Ecology of Living Benthic Foraminiferids*, Crane Russak, New York.

Murray, J.W. (1985) Recent foraminifera from the North Sea (Forties and Ekofisk areas) and the continental shelf west of Scotland. *Journal of Micropaleontology*, **4**, 117–25.

References

Murray, J.W. (1986) Living and dead Holocene foraminifera of Lyme Bay, southern England. *Journal of Foraminiferal Research*, **16**, 347–52.

Murray, J.W. (1989) Syndepositional dissolution of calcareous foraminifera in modern shallow-water sediments. *Marine Micropaleontology*, **15**, 117–21.

Murray, J.W. (1991a) Ecology and distribution of planktonic foraminifera, in *Biology of Foraminifera*, (eds J.J. Lee and O.R. Anderson), Academic Press, New York, pp. 257–84.

Murray, J.W. (1991b) *Ecology and Palaeoecology of Benthic Foraminifera*, John Wiley, New York and Longman Scientific and Technical, Harlow, U.K.

Murray, J.W. (1992) Distribution and population dynamics of benthic foraminifera from the southern North Sea. *Journal of Foraminiferal Research*, **22**, 114–28.

Murray-Wallace, C.V. and Belperio, A.P. (1995) Identification of remanié fossils using amino acid racemisation. *Alcheringa*, **18**, 219–27.

Myers, E.H. (1935) Morphogenesis of the test and the biological significance of dimorphism in the foraminifer *Patellina corrugata* Williamson. *Bulletin of the Scripps Institution of Oceanography of the University of California, Technical Series*, **3**, 393–404.

Myers, E.H. (1936) The life-cycle of *Spirillina vivipara* Ehrenberg, with notes on morphogenesis, systematics and distribution of the Foraminifera. *Journal of the Royal Microscopical Society*, **56**, 120–46.

Myers, E.H. (1940) Observations on the origin and fate of flagellated gametes in multiple tests of *Discorbis* (Foraminifera). *Journal of the Marine Biological Association, U.K.*, **24**, 201–26.

Myers, E.H. (1943a) Biology, ecology, and morphogenesis of a pelagic foraminifer. *Stanford University Publications in the Biological Sciences*, **9**, 5–30.

Myers, E.H. (1943b) Life activities of foraminifera in relation to marine ecology. *Proceedings of the American Philosophical Society*, **86**, 439–58.

Myers, E.H. and Cole, W.S. (1957) Foraminifera, in *Treatise on Marine Ecology and Paleoecology*, Part 1, (ed J.W. Hedgpeth), Geological Society of America, Memoir, v. 1, pp. 1075–82.

Nagappa, Y. (1957) Direction of coiling in *Globorotalia* as an aid in correlation. *Micropaleontology*, **3**, 393–8.

Nagy, J. and Alve, E. (1987) Temporal changes in foraminiferal faunas and impact of pollution in Sandebucta, Oslo Fjord. *Marine Micropaleontology*, **12**, 109–28.

Naidu, P. and Malmgren, B. (1995) Do benthic foraminifer records represent a productivity index in oxygen minimum zone areas? An evaluation from the Oman margin, Arabian Sea. *Marine Micropaleontology*, **26**, 49–55.

Naidu, T.Y., Rao, D.C. and Rao, M.S. (1985) Foraminifera as pollution indicators in the Vissakhapatnam Harbour Complex, east coast of India. *Bulletin of Geological, Mining and Metallurgical Society of India*, **52**, 88–96.

National Institute of Standards & Technology (1992) *Report of Investigation, Reference Materials*, 8543–46.

Natland, M.L. (1933) The temperature- and depth-distribution of some Recent and fossil Foraminifera in the southern California region. *Scripps Institute of Oceanography Bulletin, Technical Series*, **3**, 225–30.

Nee, S. and May, R.M. (1992) Dynamics of metapopulations: habitat destruction and competitive coexistence. *Journal of Animal Ecology*, **61**, 37–40.

Newman, J., Parker, P. and Behrens, W. (1973) Organic carbon isotope ratios in Quaternary cores from the Gulf of Mexico. *Geochimica et Cosmochimica Acta*, **37**, 225–38.

Newmand M.C. and Jagoe, Ch.H. (1996) *Ecotoxicology. A Heirarchical Treatment*, CRC Levis Publ, New York.

Nigam, R. (1987) Distribution, factor analysis and ecology of benthic foraminifera within inner shelf regime of Venguria-Bhatkal sector, West Coast, India. *Journal of the Geological Society of India*, **29**, 327–34.

Nigam, R., Khare, N. and Nair, R.R. (1995) Foraminiferal evidences for 77-year cycles of droughts in India and its possible modulation by the Gleissberg solar cycle. *Journal of Coastal Research*, **11**, 1099–107.

Norris, R.D. (1991a) Biased extinctions and evolutionary trends. *Paleobiology*, **17** (4), 388–99.

Norris, R.D. (1991b) Parallel evolution in the keel structure of planktonic foraminifera. *Journal of the Geological Society Special Publication*, **8**, 291.

Norris, R.D. (1992) Extinction, selectivity and ecology in planktonic foraminifera. *Palaeogeography, Palaeoclimatology, Palaeoecology*, **95**, 1–17.

Norris, R.D. (1996a) Symbiosis as an evolutionary innovation in the radiation of planktic foraminifera. *Paleontological Society Special Publication*, **8**, 291.

Norris, R.D. (1996b) Symbiosis as an evolutionary innovation in the radiation of Paleocene planktic foraminifera. *Paleobiology*, **22**, 461–80.

Norris, R.D., Corfield R.M. and Cartlidge J. (1996) What is gradualism? Cryptic speciation in globorotaliid foraminifera. *Paleobiology*, **22** (3), 386–405.

Norse, E.A. (1993) *Global Marine Biodiversity*, Island Press, Washington, D.C.

Nowlin, W.D. and Parker C.A. (1974) Effects of a cold-air outbreak on shelf waters of the Gulf of Mexico. *Journal of Physical Oceanography*, **4**, 467–86.

Nozaki, Y., Cochran, J.K. and Turekian, K.K. (1977) Radiocarbon and ^{210}Pb distribution in submersible taken deep sea cores from project Famous. *Earth and Planetary Science Letters*, **34**, 167–73.

Nürnberg, D. (1995) Magnesium in tests of *Neogloboquadrina pachyderma* sinistral from high Northern and Southern latitudes. *Journal of Foraminiferal Research*, **25**, 350–68.

Nürnberg, D., Bijma, J. and Hemleben, C. (1996) Assessing the reliability of magnesium in foraminiferal calcite as a proxy for water mass temperatures. *Geochimica et Cosmochimica Acta*, **60**, 803–14.

Nydick, K.R., Bidwell, A.B., Thomas, E. and Varekamp, J.C. (1995) A sea-level rise curve from Guilford, Connecticut, USA. *Marine Geology*, **124**, 137–59.

References

Nyholm, K.-G. (1956) On the life cycle and cytology of the Foraminiferan *Nemogullmia longivariabilis*. *Zoologiska Bidrag från Uppsala*, **31**, 483–95.

Nyholm, K.-G. (1957) Orientation and binding power of Recent monothalamous Foraminifera in soft sediments. *Micropaleontology*, **3**, 75–6.

Nyholm, K.-G. (1974) New monothalamous Foraminifera. *Zoon*, **2**, 117–22.

Nyholm, K.-G. and Nyholm, P.-G. (1975) Ultrastructure of monothalamous foraminifera. *Zoon*, **3**, 141–50.

Nyholm, K.-G. and Olsson, I. (1973) Seasonal fluctuations of the meiobenthos in an estuary on the Swedish west coast. *Zoon*, **1**, 69–76.

Nyholm, K.-G., Olsson, I. and Andren, L. (1977) Quantitative investigations on the macro- and meiobenthic fauna in the Gota River estuary. *Zoon*, **5**, 15–28.

Oberhänsli, H. (1992) Planktonic foraminifers as tracers of ocean currents in the eastern South Atlantic. *Paleoceanography*, **7**, 607–32.

Oberhänsli, H., Bénier, C., Meinecke, G. *et al.* (1992) Planktonic foraminifers as tracers of oceanic currents in the eastern South Atlantic. *Paleoceanography*, **7** (5), 607–32.

Odum, E.P. (1971) *Fundamentals of Ecology*, W.B. Saunders Co., Philadelphia.

Officer, C.B. (1982) Mixing, sedimentation rates and age dating for sediment cores. *Marine Geology*, **46**, 261–78.

Officer, C.B. (1983) Physics of estuarine circulation, in *Estuaries and Enclosed Seas*, (ed B.H. Ketchum), Elsevier, Amsterdam, p. 15–41.

Officer, C.B. and Lynch, D.R. (1982) Interpretation procedures for the determination of sediment parameters from time-dependent flux inputs. *Earth and Planetary Science Letters*, **61**, 55–62.

Officer, C.B. and Lynch, D.R. (1983) Determination of mixing parameters from tracer distributions in deep-sea sediment cores. *Marine Geology*, **52**, 59–74.

Ohga, T. and Kitazato, H. (1997) Seasonal changes in bathyal foraminiferal populations in response to the flux of organic matter (Sagami Bay, Japan). *Terra Nova*, **9**, 33–7.

Ohkouchi, N., Kawahata, H., Murayama, M. *et al.* (1994) Was deep water formed in the North Pacific during the Late Quaternary? Cadium evidence from the northwest Pacific. *Earth and Planetary Science Letters*, **124**, 185–94.

Olson, D.B. (1986) Transition Zones and Faunal Boundaries in Relationship to Physical Properties of the Ocean, in *Pelagic Biogeography, Proceedings of an International Conference: the Netherlands 29 May–5 June 1985*, (eds A.C. Pierrot-Bults, S. van der Spoel, B.J. Zahuranec and R.K. Johnson), Unesco, pp. 219–25.

Olsson, I. (1976) Distribution and ecology of the foraminiferan *Ammotium cassis* (Parker) in some Swedish estuaries. *Zoon*, **4**, 137–47.

Olsson, J., Rosenberg, R. and Olundh, E. (1973) Benthic fauna and zooplankton in some polluted Swedish estuaries. *Ambio*, **2**, 158–63.

Olsson, R.K. (1970) Paleocene planktonic foraminiferal biostratigraphy and paleozoogeography of New Jersey. *Journal of Paleontology*, **44**, 589–604.

Olsson, R.K. (1982) Cenozoic Planktonic Foraminifera: a Paleobiogeographic Summary, in *Foraminifera: notes for a short course organized by M.A. Buzas and B.K. Sen Gupta*, (ed T.W. Broadhead), University of Tennessee Department of Geological Sciences Studies in Geology, **6**, 127–47.

Olsson, R.K., Hemleben, C., Berggren W.A. and Huber B.T. (eds) (1999) *Atlas of Paleocene Planktonic Foraminifera*, Smithsonian Contributions to Paleobiology no. 85.

O'Neil, J.R., Clayton, R.N. and Mayeda, T.K. (1969) Oxygen isotope fractionation on divalent metal carbonates. *Journal of Chemical Physics*, **51**, 5547–58.

Opdyke, B.N., Walter, L.M. and Huston, T.J. (1993) Fluoride content of foraminiferal calcite – Relations to life habitat, oxygen isotope composition, and minor element chemistry. *Geology*, **21**, 169–72.

Oppo, D.W. and Rosenthal, Y. (1994) Cd/Ca changes in a deep Cape Basin core over the past 730,000 years: Response of circumpolar deepwater variability to northern hemisphere ice sheet melting? *Paleoceanography*, **9**, 661–75.

Organization for Economic Cooperation and Development (1987) *The use of biological tests for water pollution assessment and control*, Environmental Monograph No 11. OECD Water Management Policy Group. Paris, France.

Orloci, L. (1978) *Multivariate Analysis in Vegetation Research*, Junk, The Hague.

Orokos, D.D., Bowser, S.S. and Travis, J.L. (1997) Reactivation of cell surface transport in *Reticulomyxa*. *Cell Motility and the Cytoskeleton*, **37**, 139–48.

Orr, W.N. (1967) Secondary calcification in the foraminiferal genus *Globorotalia*. *Science*, **157**, 1554–5.

Orr, W.N. and Jenkins, G. (1977) Cenozoic Planktonic Foraminiferal Zonation and Selective Test Solution, in *Oceanographic Micropaleontology*, (ed A.T.S. Ramsay), Academic Press, London, pp. 163–203.

Ortiz, J.D., Mix, A.C. and Collier, R.W. (1995) Environmental control of living symbiotic and asymbiotic foraminifera of the California Current. *Paleoceanography*, **10** (6), 987–1009.

Ortiz, J.D., Mix, A.C., Rugh, W. *et al.* (1996) Deep-dwelling planktonic foraminifera of the northeastern Pacific Ocean reveal environmental control of oxygen and carbon isotopic disequilibria. *Geochimica et Cosmochimica Acta*, **60** (22), 4509–23.

Osterman, L. and Kellogg, T. (1979) Recent benthic foraminiferal distributions from the Ross Sea, Antarctica: relation to ecologic and oceanographic conditions. *Journal of Foraminiferal Research*, **9**, 250–69.

Ostlund, H.G., Craig, H., Broecker, W.S. and Spencer, D.W. (1987) *GEOSECS Atlantic, Pacific, and Indian Ocean Expeditions, v. 7, Shorebased Data and Graphics*, National Science Foundation, Washington, D.C.

References

Ottens, J.J. (1991) Planktic foraminifera as North Atlantic water mass indicators. *Oceanologica Acta*, **14** (2), 123–40.

Ottens, J.J. and Nederbragt, A.J. (1992) Planktic foraminiferal diversity as indicator of ocean environments. *Marine Micropaleontology*, **19**, 13–28.

Ozarko, D.L., Patterson, R.T. and Williams, H.F.L. (1997) Marsh foraminifera from Nanaimo, British Columbia (Canada): Implications of infaunal habitats and taphonomic biasing. *Journal of Foraminiferal Research*, **27**, 51–68.

Paasivarta J. (1991) *Chemical Ecotoxicology*, Lewis Publ, Boca Raton, Florida.

Palmer, M.R. (1985) Rare earth elements in foraminifera tests. *Earth and Planetary Science Letters*, **73**, 285–98.

Palmer, M.R. and Elderfield, H. (1986) Rare earth elements and neodymium isotopes in ferromanganese oxide coatings of Cenozoic foraminifera from the Atlantic Ocean. *Geochimica et Cosmochimica Acta*, **50**, 409–17.

Paren, J.G. and Potter, J.R. (1984) Isotopic tracers in polar seas and glacier ice. *Journal of Geophysical Research*, **89**, 749–50.

Parker, F.L. (1948) Foraminifera of the continental shelf from the Gulf of Maine to Maryland. *Bulletin of the Harvard Museum of Comparative Zoology*, **100**, 213–41.

Parker, F.L. (1954) Distribution of the Foraminifera in the north-eastern Gulf of Mexico. *Bulletin of the Harvard Museum of Comparative Zoology*, **111**, 453–588.

Parker, F.L. (1960) Living Planktonic Foraminifera from the equatorial and south east Pacific. *Tohoku University Special Science Reports in Geology*, **4**, 71–82.

Parker, F.L. (1971) Distribution of planktonic foraminifera in Recent deep sea sediments, in *The Micropaleontology of Oceans*, (eds B.M. Funnell and W.R. Riedel), Cambridge University Press, Cambridge, pp. 289–307.

Parker, F.L. and Berger, W.H. (1971) Faunal and solution patterns of planktonic foraminifera in surface sediments of the South Pacific. *Deep-Sea Research* **18**, 73–107.

Parker, W.C. and Arnold, A.J. (1997) Species Survivorship in the Cenozoic Planktonic Foraminifera: A Test of Exponential and Weibull models. *Palaios*, **12**, 3–11.

Parker, W.C., Feldman A. and Arnold, A.J. (in press) Paleobiogeographic patterns in the morphologic diversification of the Neogene planktonic foraminifera. *Palaeogeography, Palaeoclimatology and Palaeoecology*.

Patterson, R.T. (1990) Intertidal benthic foraminiferal biofacies on the Fraser River Delta, British Columbia: Modern distribution and paleoecological importance. *Micropaleontology*, **35**, 229–44.

Patterson, R.T., Ozarko, D., Guilbault, J.-P. and Clague, J.J. (1994) Distribution and preservation potential of marsh foraminiferal biofacies from the lower mainland and Vancouver Island, British Columbia. *Geological Society of America Annual Meeting Abstracts with Programs*, **26**, 530.

Pawlowski, J. (1989) Association of Foraminifera with the alga *Enteromorpha*. *Revue de Paleobiologie*, **8**, 73–5.

Pawlowski, J., Bolivar, I., Fahrni, F. *et al.* (1996) Early origin of foraminifera suggested by SSU rRNA gene sequences. *Molecular Biology and Evolution*, **13**, 445–50.

Pawlowski, J., Bolivar I., Fahrni, F. and Zaninetti, L. (1994a) Taxonomic identification of foraminifera using ribosomal DNA sequences. *Micropaleontology*, **40**, 373–7.

Pawlowski, J., Bolivar, I., Fahrni, J. and Zaninetti, L. (1995) DNA analysis of '*Ammonia beccarii*' morphotypes: one or more species? *Marine Micropaleontology*, **26**, 171–8.

Pawlowski, J., Bolivar I., Guiard-Maffia, J. and Gouy, M. (1994b) Phylogenetic position of foraminifera inferred from LSU rRNA gene sequences. *Molecular Biology and Evolution*, **11**, 929–38.

Pawlowski, J., De Vargas, C., Fahrni, J. and Bowser, S. (1998a) *Reticulomyxa filosa* – an 'athalamid' freshwater foraminifer. *Forams 98, International Symposium on Foraminifera, Sociedad Mexicana de Paleontologia, A. C., Special Publication, July 5, 1998*, 78–9.

Pawlowski, J., De Vargas, C., Fahrni, J. and Zaninetti, L. (1998b) The evolutionary systematics of Foraminifera: a molecular perspective. *Forams 98, International Symposium on Foraminifera, Sociedad Mexicana de Paleontologia, A. C., Special Publication, July 5, 1998*, p. 79.

Pawlowski, J. and Lee, J.J. (1992) The life cycle of *Rotaliella elatiana* n. sp.: A tiny macroalgavorous foraminifer from the Gulf of Elat. *Journal of Protozoology*, **39**, 131–43.

Pearson, T. and Rosenberg, R. (1987) Feast and famine: structuring factors in marine benthic communities, in *Organization of Communities*, (eds J Gee and P. Giller), Blackwell Scientific Publications, Oxford, England, pp. 373–98.

Peng, T.-H., Broecker, W.S. and Berger, W.H. (1979) Rates of benthic mixing in deep-sea sediment as determined by radio-active tracers. *Quaternary Research*, **11**, 141–9.

Peng, T.-H., Broecker, W.S., Kipphut, G. and Shackleton, N. (1977) Benthic mixing in deep sea cores as determined by ^{14}C dating and its implications regarding climate stratigraphy and the fate of fossil fuel CO_2, in *The Fate of Fossil Fuel CO_2 in the Oceans*, (eds N.R. Andersen and A. Malahoff), Plenum Press, New York, pp. 355–73.

Perez-Cruz, L.L. and Machain-Castillo, M.L. (1990) Benthic foraminifera of the oxygen minimum zone, continental shelf of the Gulf of Tehuantepec, Mexico. *Journal of Foraminiferal Research*, **20**, 312–25.

Petit, J.R., Basile, I., Leruyuet, A. *et al.* (1997) Four climate cycles in Vostok ice core. *Nature*, **387**, 359.

Pfannkuche, O. (1993) Benthic response to the sedimentation of particulate organic matter at the BIOTRANS station, 47°N, 20°W. *Deep-Sea Research*, **40**, 135–9.

Pflum, C.E. and Frerichs, W.E. (1976) Gulf of Mexico deepwater foraminifers. *Cushman Foundation for Foraminiferal Research, Special Publication*, **14**, 1–108.

References

Phillips, F.J. (1977) Protozoa, in *Reef and Shore Fauna of Hawaii, Section 1: Protozoa through Ctenophora*, (eds D. Devaney and L.G. Eldridge), Bishop Museum Press, Honolulu, pp. 12–52.

Phleger, F.B (1951a) Ecology of Foraminifera, northwest Gulf of Mexico, Part 1, Foraminifera distribution. *Geological Society of America Memoir*, **46**, 88 pp.

Phleger, F.B. (1951b) Displaced Foraminifera faunas. *Society of Economic Paleontologists and Mineralogists Special Publication*, No. 2, pp. 66–75.

Phleger, F.B (1954) Ecology of Foraminifera and associated micro-organisms from Mississippi Sound and environs. *Bulletin of the American Association of Petroleum Geologists*, **38**, 584–647.

Phleger, F.B (1955) Ecology of Foraminifera in southeastern Mississippi Delta area. *Bulletin of the American Association of Petroleum Geologists*, **39**, 712–52.

Phleger, F.B (1960a) *Ecology and Distribution of Recent Foraminifera*, The Johns Hopkins Press, Baltimore.

Phleger, F.B (1960b) Sedimentary patterns of microfaunas in northern Gulf of Mexico, in *Recent Sediments, Northwest Gulf of Mexico, 1951–58*, (eds F.P. Shepard, F.B Phleger and T.H. van Andel), American Association of Petroleum Geologists, Tulsa, pp. 267–301.

Phleger, F.B (1964a) Foraminiferal ecology and marine geology. *Marine Geology*, **1**, 16–43.

Phleger, F.B (1964b) Patterns of living benthonic Foraminifera, Gulf of California, in *Marine Geology of the Gulf of California*, (eds T.H. van Andel and G.G. Shor), American Association of Petroleum Geologists, Memoir No. 3, pp. 377–94.

Phleger, F.B (1970) Foraminiferal populations and marine marsh processes. *Limnology and Oceanography*, **15**, 522–34.

Phleger, F.B (1977) Soils of marine marshes, in *Wet Coastal Ecosystems*, (ed V.J. Chapman), Elsevier, Amsterdam, pp. 69–77.

Phleger, F.B and Lankford, R.R. (1978) Foraminifera and ecological processes in the Alvarado Lagoon area, Mexico. *Journal of Foraminiferal Research*, **8**, 127–31.

Phleger, F.B and Parker, F.L. (1951) *Ecology of foraminifera, Northwest Gulf of Mexico*. Geological Society of America, Memoir 46, 1–88, 1–64.

Phleger, F.B and Parker, F.L. (1954) Gulf of Mexico Foraminifera, in *Gulf of Mexico, its origins, waters and marine life*. Fishery Bulletin 89, Fish and Wildlife Service, **55**, 235–41.

Phleger, F.B and Soutar, A. (1973) Production of benthic Foraminifera in three east Pacific oxygen minima. *Micropaleontology*, **19**, 110–15.

Pianka E.R. (1966) Latitudinal gradients in species diversity: a review of concepts. *American Naturalist*, **100** (910), 33–46.

Pielou, E.C. (1979) *Biogeography*, Wiley, New York.

Pike, J. and Kemp, A.E.S. (1996) Silt aggregates in laminated marine sediments produced by agglutinated foraminifera. *Journal of Sedimentary Research*, **66**, 625–31.

Piller, W.E. (1983) Remarks on the Suborder Involutinina Hohenegger and Piller, 1977. *Journal of Foraminiferal Research*, **13**, 191–201.

Pingitore, N.E. (1986) Modes of coprecipitation of Ba^{2+} and Sr^{2+} with calcite, in *Geochemical Processes at Mineral Surfaces*, (eds J.F. Davis and K.F. Hayes), American Chemical Society, Washington, D.C., pp. 574–86.

Pisias, N.G., Martinson, D.G., Moore, T.C. et al. (1984) High resolution stratigraphic correlation of benthic oxygen isotope records spanning the last 300,000 years. *Marine Geology*, **56**, 119–36.

Pizzuto, J.E. and Schwendt, A.E. (1997) Mathematical modeling of autocompaction of a Holocene transgressive valley-fill deposit, Wolfe Glade, Delaware. *Geology*, **25**, 57–60.

Poag, C.W. (1981) *Ecologic Atlas of Benthic Foraminifera of the Gulf of Mexico*, Marine Science International, Hutchinson Ross Publishing Company, Woods Hole, Massachusetts.

Poag, C.W. and Tresslar, R.C. (1981) Living foraminifers of West Flower Garden Bank, northernmost coral reef in the Gulf of Mexico. *Micropaleontology*, **27**, 31–70.

Porter, J.W. and Meier, O.W. (1992) Quantification of loss and change in Floridian reef coral populations. *American Zoologist*, **32**, 625–40.

Posey, M.H. (1988) Community changes associated with the spread of an introduced seagrass, *Zostera japonica*. *Ecology*, **69**, 974–83.

Powell, E.N., Cummins, H., Stanton, R.J. and Staff, G. (1984) Estimation of the size of molluscan larval settlement using the death assemblage. *Estuarine and Coastal Shelf Science*, **18**, 367–84.

Powell, T.M. and Okubo, A. (1994) Turbulence, diffusion, and patchiness in the sea. *Philosophical Transactions of the Royal Society, London, Biological Science*, **343** (1303), 11–8.

Prell, W.L., Imbrie, J., Martinson, D.G. et al. (1986) Graphic correlation of oxygen isotope stratigraphy application to the late Quaternary. *Paleoceanography*, **2** (1), 137–162.

Preobrazhenskaya, T.V., Levchuk, L.K., Troitskaya, T.S. and Fursenko, K.B. (1991) Distribution of benthic Foraminifera in the littoral zone of Shikotan Island (Lesser Kuril Ridge) (in Russian). *Biologia Morja*, **2**, 15–21.

Probert, P. (1984) Disturbance, sediment stability and trophic structure of soft-bottom communities. *Journal of Marine Research*, **42**, 893–921.

Pujos-Lamy, A. (1972) Repartition bathymetrique des Foraminifères benthiques profonds du Golfe de Gascogne, comparaison avec d'autres aires oceaniques. *Revista Espan. Micropaleontol*, **5**, 213–34.

Rabalais, N.N., Turner, R.E, Justic, D. et al. (1996) Nutrient changes in the Mississippi River and system responses on the adjacent continental shelf. *Estuaries*, **19**, 386–407.

Randel, W.J., Fei, W., Russell, J.M. III et al. (1995) Ozone and temperature changes following the eruption of Mt. Pinatubo. *Journal of Geophysical Research*, **100**, 16753–64.

References

Rathburn, A.E. and Corliss, B.H. (1994) The ecology of living (stained) deep-sea benthic foraminifera from the Sulu Sea. *Paleoceanography*, **9**, 87–150.

Rathburn, A.E., Corliss, B.H., Tappa, K.D. and Lohmann, K.C. (1996) Comparisons of the ecology and stable isotopic compositions of living (stained) benthic foraminifera from the Sulu and South China Seas. *Deep-Sea Research*, **43**, 1617–46.

Rathburn, A.E. and Deckker, P.D. (1997) Magnesium and strontium compositions of recent benthic foraminifera from the Coral Sea, Australia and Prydz Bay, Antarctica. *Marine Micropaleontology*, **32**, 231–48.

Rathburn, A.E. and Miao, Q. (1995) The taphonomy of deep-sea benthic foraminifera: Comparison of living and dead assemblages from box and gravity cores taken in the Sulu Sea. *Marine Micropaleontology*, **25**, 127–49.

Rauzer-Chernousova, D.M. and Fursenko, A.V. (1959) *Osnovy paleontologii, Obshchaya chast prosteyshie*, Akad. Nauk. SSSR.

Rauzer-Chernousova, D.M. and Fursenko, A.V. (1962) *Fundamentals of Paleontology, General Part, Protozoa* (Translated from Russian), Israel Program for Scientific Translations, Jerusalem.

Ravelo, A.C. and Fairbanks, R.G. (1992) Oxygen isotopic composition of multiple species of planktonic foraminifera: recorders of the modern photic zone temperature gradient. *Paleoceanography*, **7**, 815–31.

Ravelo, A.C. and Fairbanks, R.G. (1995) Carbon isotopic fractionation in multiple species of planktonic foraminifera from core-tops in the tropical Atlantic. *Journal of Foraminiferal Research*, **25** (1), 53–74.

Raymo, M.E. and Ruddiman, W.F. (1992) Tectonic forcing of late Cenozoic climate. *Nature*, **359**, 117–22.

Raymo, M.E., Ruddiman, W.F. and Froelich, P.N. (1988) Influence of late Cenezoic mountain building on ocean geochemical cycles. *Geology*, **16**, 649–53.

Reaves, C.M. (1986) Organic matter metabolizability and calcium carbonate dissolution in nearshore marine muds. *Journal of Sedimentary Petrology*, **56**, 486–94.

Reddy, K.R. and Jagadishwara Rao, R. (1984) Foraminifera-salinity relationship in the Pennar estuary, India. *Journal of Foraminiferal Research*, **14**, 115–9.

Reeder, R.J. (1983) Crystal chemistry of the rhombohedral carbonates, in *Carbonates: Mineralogy and Chemistry*, (ed R.J. Reeder), Mineralogical Society of America, Washington, D.C., pp.1–47.

Rehder, H.A. (1954) Mollusks, in *Gulf of Mexico, its origin, waters and marine life*, Fishery Bulletin 89, Fish and Wildlife Service, **55**, 469–74.

Reimers, C.E. (1987) An in-situ microprofiling instrument for measuring interfacial pore water gradients: methods and oxygen profiles from the North Pacific Ocean. *Deep-Sea Research*, **34**, 2019–35.

Reimers, C.E., Fisher, K.M., Merewether, R. *et al.* (1986) Oxygen microprofiles measured in situ in deep ocean sediments. *Nature*, **320**, 741–4.

Reimers, C.E., Jahnke, R. and McCorkle, D.C. (1992) Carbon fluxes and burial rates over the continental slope and rise off central California with implications for the global carbon cycle. *Global Biogeochemical Cycles*, **6**, 199–224.

Reish, D.J. (1983) *Survey of the marine benthic infauna collected from the United States radioactive waste disposal sites off the Farallon Islands, California*, Report EPA-520/1-83-006 (EPA520183006), 65 pp.

Reiss, Z. (1957) The Bilamellidea, nov. superfam, and remarks on Cretaceous globorotaliids. *Contributions from the Cushman Foundation for Foraminiferal Research*, **8**, 127–45.

Reiss, Z. (1958) Classification of lamellar Foraminifera. *Micropaleontology*, **4**, 51–70.

Reiss, Z. and Hottinger, L. (1984) *The Gulf of Aqaba – Ecological Micropaleontology*, Springer-Verlag, Berlin.

Relexans, J.C., Deming, J., Dinet, A. *et al.* (1996) Sedimentary organic matter and micro-meiobenthos with relation to trophic conditions in the tropical northeast Atlantic. *Deep-Sea Research*, **1**, **8**, 1343–68.

Resig, J.M. (1958) Microbiology of the mainland shelf of southern California, in *Survey of the continental shelf area of southern California*, Unpublished report submitted to the California State Water Pollution Control Board by the Allan Hancock Foundation of the University of Southern California.

Resig, J.M. (1960) Foraminiferal ecology around ocean outfalls off southern California, in *Waste Disposal in the Marine Environment*, (ed E. Person), Pergamon Press, London, pp. 104–21.

Resig, J.M. (1974) Recent foraminifera from a landlocked Hawaiian lake. *Journal of Foraminiferal Research*, **4**, 69–76.

Resig, J.M., Lowenstam, H.A., Echols, R.J. and Weiner, S. (1980) An extant opaline foraminifer: Test ultrastructure, mineralogy, and taxonomy, in *Studies in Marine Micropaleontology and Paleoecology, A Memorial Volume to Orville R. Bandy*, (ed W.V. Sliter), *Cushman Foundation Special Publication*, No. 19, pp. 205–14.

Reuss, A.E. (1861) Entwurf einer Systematischen Zummenstellung der Foraminiferen. *Sitzungsberichte der K. Akademie der Wissenschaften, Wien*, **44**, 354–96.

Revets, S.A. (1993) The foraminiferal toothplate: A review. *Journal of Micropaleontology*, **12**, 155–69.

Revets, S.A. (1996) The generic revision of the Bolivinitidae Cushman, 1927. *Cushman Foundation Special Publication*, No. 34, pp. 1–55.

Revsbech, N.P., Sorensen, J., Blackburn, T.H. and Lomholt, J.P. (1980) Distribution of oxygen in marine sediments measured with microelectrodes. *Limnology and Oceanography*, **25**, 403–11.

Rhoads, D.C. and Morse, J.W. (1971) Evolutionary and ecologic significance of oxygen-deficient marine basins. *Lethaia*, **4**, 41328.

Rhoads, D.C. and Stanley, D.J. (1965) Biogenic graded bedding. *Journal of Sedimentary Petrology*, **35**, 956–63.

Rhumbler, L. (1894) Beiträge zur kenntnis der Rhizopoden

References

II. *Saccammina sphaerica* M. Sars. *Zeitschrift für Wissenschaftliche Zoologie*, **57**, 433–617.

Rhumbler, L. (1911) Die Foraminiferen (Thalamophoren) der Plankton Expedition, Pt. I, Die allgemeinen Organizationsverhaltnisse der Foraminiferen, Lipsius and Tisher, Kiel und Leipzig.

Rice, D.L. and Rhoads, D.C. (1989) Early diagenesis of organic matter and the nutritional value of sediment, in *Ecology of Marine Deposit Feeders*, (eds G. Lopez, G. Taghon and J. Levinton), **31**, Springer-Verlag, Berlin, pp. 59–97.

Richter, F.M. and DePaolo, D.J. (1988) Diagenesis and Sr isotopic evolution of seawater using data from DSDP 590B and 575. *Earth and Planetary Science Letters*, **90**, 382–94.

Richter, G. (1961) Beobachtungen zur Ökologie einiger Foraminiferen des Jade-Gebietes. *Natur und Volk*, **91**, 163–70.

Richter, G. (1964) Zur Ökologie der Foraminiferen. II. Lebensraum und Lebensweise von *Nonion depressulum*, *Elphidium excavatum*, *Elphidium selseyense*. *Natur und Museum*, **94**, 421–30.

Riebesell, U. and Wolf-Gladrow, D. (1995) Growth limits on phytoplankton. *Nature*, **373**, 28.

Robbins, J.A. (1982) Stratigraphic and dynamic effects of sediment reworking by Great Lakes zoobenthos. *Hydrobiologia*, **92**, 611–22.

Robbins, J.A. (1986) A model for particle-selective transport of tracers in sediments with conveyor belt deposit feeders. *Journal of Geophysical Research*, **91**, 8542–58.

Robinson, E. (1969) Coiling directions in planktonic foraminifera from the coastal group of Jamaica. *Transactions of the Gulf Coast Association of Geological Societies*, **19**, 73–107.

Rögl, F. (1985) Late Oligocene and Miocene planktic foraminifera of the Central Paratethys, in *Plankton Stratigraphy*, (eds H.M. Bolli, J.B. Saunders and K. Perch-Nielsen), Cambridge University Press, pp. 315–28.

Rögl, F. and Hansen, H.J. (1984) *Foraminifera Described by Fichtel & Moll in 1798 – a Revision of Testacea Microscopica*, Ferdinand Berger & Söhne, Vienna.

Rohling, E.J. (1994) Glacial conditions in the Red Sea. *Paleoceanography*, **9**, 653–60.

Rohling, E.J. and Bigg, G.R. (1998) Paleosalinity and $\delta^{18}O$: a critical assessment. *Journal of Geophysical Research*, **103** (C1), 1307–18.

Rohling, E.J., Fenton, M., Jorissen, F.J. *et al.* (1998) Magnitudes of sea-level lowstands of the past 500,000 years. *Nature*, **394**, 162–5.

Rohling, E.J., Jorissen, F.J. and De Stigter, H.C. (1997) 200 Year interruption of Holocene sapropel formation in the eastern Mediterranean. *Journal of Micropaleontology*, **16**, 97–108.

Romanek, C.S., Grossman, E.L. and Morse, J.W. (1992) Carbon isotopic fractionation in synthetic aragonite and calcite: effects of temperature and precipitation rate. *Geochimica et Cosmochimica Acta*, **56**, 419–30.

Rose, P.R. and Lidz, B.H. (1977) Diagnostic foraminiferal assemblages of shallow-water modern environments: south Florida and the Bahamas. *Sedimentia VI*, pp. 1–56.

Rosenberg, R. (1995) Benthic marine fauna structured by hydrodynamic processes and food availability. *Netherlands Journal of Sea Research*, **34**, 303–17.

Rosenthal, Y. and Boyle, E.A. (1993) Factors controlling the fluoride content of planktonic foraminifera: An evaluation of its paleoceanographic utility. *Geochimica et Cosmochimica Acta*, **57**, 335–46.

Rosenthal, Y., Boyle, E.A. and Labeyrie, A. (1997a) Last glacial maximum paleochemistry and deepwater circulation in the Southern Ocean: Evidence from foraminiferal cadmium. *Paleoceanography*, **12**, 787–96.

Rosenthal, Y., Boyle, E.A. and Slowey, N. (1997b) Temperature control on the incorporation of Mg, Sr, F and Cd into benthic foraminiferal shells from Little Bahama Bank: prospects for thermocline paleoceanography. *Geochimica et Cosmochimica Acta*, **61**, 3633–43.

Rosoff, D.B. and Corliss, B.H. (1992) An analysis of Recent deep-sea benthic foraminiferal morphotypes from the Norwegian and Greenland seas. *Palaeogeography, Palaeoclimatology and Palaeoecology*, **91**, 13–20.

Ross, C.A. (1972) Biology and ecology of *Marginopora vertebralis* (Foraminiferida), Great Barrier Reef. *Journal of Protozoology*, **19**, 181–92.

Ross, C.A. and Haman, D. (1989) Suprageneric ranges of Foraminiferida. *Journal of Foraminiferal Research*, **19**, 72–83.

Röttger, R. (1972) Die Kultur von *Heterostegina depressa* (Foraminifera: Nummulitidae). *Marine Biology*, **15**, 150–9.

Röttger, R. (1973) Die Ektoplasmahulle von *Heterostegina depressa* (Foraminifera, Nummulitidae). *Marine Biology*, **21**, 127–38.

Röttger, R. (1974) Larger foraminifera: Reproduction and early stages of development in *Heterostegina depressa*. *Journal of Protozoology*, **25**, 41–4.

Röttger, R. and Berger, W. (1972) Benthic foraminifera: morphology and growth in clone cultures of *Heterostegina depressa*. *Marine Biology*, **26**, 5–12.

Röttger, R. (1976) Ecological observations of *Heterostegina depressa* (Foraminifera, Nummulitidae) in the laboratory and in its natural habitat. *Maritime Sediments Special Publication*, **1**, 75–9.

Röttger, R. (1978) Unusual multiple fission in the gamont of the larger Foraminiferan *Heterostegina depressa* (Rhizopoda). *Journal of Protozoology*, **25**, 41–4.

Röttger, R., Dettmering, C., Krüger, R. *et al.* (1998) Gametes in nummulitids (Foraminifera) *Journal of Foraminiferal Research*, **28** (4), 345–8.

Röttger, R., Fladung, M., Schmaljohann, R. *et al.* (1986) A new hypothesis: The so-called megalospheric schizont of the larger foraminifer *Heterostegina depressa* d'Orbigny, 1826, is a separate species. *Journal of Foraminiferal Research*, **16**, 141–9.

References

Röttger, R. and Hallock, P. (1982) Shape trends in *Heterostegina depressa* (Protozoa, Foraminiferida). *Journal of Foraminiferal Research*, **12**, 197–204.

Röttger, R. and Krüger, R. (1990) Observations on the biology of Calcarinidae (Foraminiferida). *Marine Biology*, **106**, 419–25.

Röttger, R., Krüger, R. and De Rijk, S. (1990) Trimorphism in Foraminifera (Protozoa): Verification of an old hypothesis. *European Journal of Protistology*, **25**, 226–8.

Röttger, R. and Spindler, M. (1976) Development of *Heterostegina depressa* individuals (Foraminifera, Nummulitidae) in laboratory cultures. *Maritime Sediments Special Publication*, **1**, 81–7.

Röttger, R., Spindler, M., Schmaljohann, R. *et al.* (1984) Functions of the canal system in the rotaliid foraminifera *Heterostegina depressa*. *Nature*, **309**, 789–91. Erratum note (1985): *Nature*, **315**, 77.

Rowe, G. and Menzies, R. (1969) Zonation of larger benthic invertebrates in the deep sea off the Carolinas. *Deep-Sea Research*, **16**, 531–7.

Rowe, G., Polloni, P. and Haedrich, R. (1982) The deep sea macrobenthos on the continental margin of the northwest Atlantic Ocean. *Deep-Sea Research*, **29**, 257–78.

Rowe, G., Polloni, P. and Horner, S. (1974) Benthic biomass estimates from the northwestern Atlantic Ocean and the northern Gulf of Mexico. *Deep-Sea Research*, **21**, 641–50.

Rowe, G., Smith, S., Falkowski, P. *et al.* (1986) Do continental shelves export organic matter? *Nature*, **324**, 559–61.

Rozanski, K. (1985) Deuterium and oxygen-18 in European groundwaters: links to atmospheric circulation in the past. *Chemical Geology (Isotope Geoscience Section)*, **52**, 349–63.

Rozanski, K., Araguas-Araguas, L. and Gonfiantini, R. (1993) Isotopic patterns in modern global precipitation, in *Climate Change in Continental Isotopic Records*, (eds P.K. Swart, K.C. Lohmann, J. McKenzie and S. Savin), *Geophysical Monograph Series*, **78**, American Geophysical Union, Washington DC, pp. 1–36.

Rozanski, K., Sonntag, C. and Münnich, K.O. (1982) Factors controlling stable isotope composition of European precipitation. *Tellus*, **34**, 142–50.

Rubinin, A.I. (1983) Evaluation of balance among hydrocarbon and chlorine hyfrocarbond in seas, in *Investigations of Oceans and Seas*, Gidrometeoizdat, Moscow, pp. 203–12.

Ruddiman, W.F. (1977) Investigations of Quaternary Climate based on Planktonic Foraminifera, in *Oceanographic Micropaleontology*, (ed A.T.S. Ramsay), Academic Press, London, pp. 101–62.

Ruddiman, W.F. and Glover, L.K. (1972) Vertical mixing of ice-rafted volcanic ash in North Atlantic sediments. *Geological Society of America Bulletin*, **83**, 2817–36.

Ruddiman, W.F., Jones, G.A., Peng, T-H. *et al.* (1980) Tests for size and shape dependency in deep-sea mixing. *Sedimentary Geology*, **25**, 257–76.

Russell, A.D., Emerson, S., Mix, A.C. and Peterson, L.C. (1996) The use of foraminiferal U/Ca as an indicator of changes in seawater uranium content. *Paleoceanography*, **11**, 649–63.

Russell, A.D., Emerson, S., Nelson, B.K. *et al.* (1994) Uranium in foraminiferal calcite as a recorder of seawater uranium concentrations. *Geochimica et Cosmochimica Acta*, **58**, 671–81.

Rutgers van der Loeff, M.M. (1990) Oxygen in pore waters of deep-sea sediments. *Philosophical Transactions of the Royal Society of London*, **A331**, 69–84.

Ryther, J.H. (1963) Geographic variations in productivity, in *The Sea*, Vol 2, (ed M.N. Hill), Interscience, New York, pp. 347–80.

Sachs, H.M., Webb, T. and Clark, D.R. (1977) Paleoecological transfer functions. *Annual Review of Earth and Planetary Sciences*, **5**, 159–78.

Sadler, P.M. and Strauss, D.J. (1990) Estimation of completeness of stratigraphical sections using empirical data and theoretical models. *Journal of the Geological Society of London*, **147**, 471–85.

Saffert, H. and Thomas, E. (1998) Living foraminifera and total populations in salt marsh peat cores: Kelsey Marsh (Clinton, CT) and the Great Marshes (Barnstable, MA). *Marine Micropaleontology*, **33**, 175–202.

Saidova, Kh. M. (1957) Kolichestvennoe raspredelenie foraminifer v Okotskom More. *Doklady Akademiia Nauk SSSR*, **114**, 1302–5.

Saito, T. (1976) Geologic significance of coiling direction in the planktonic foraminifer *Pulleniatina*. *Geology*, **4**, 305–9.

Saito, T., Thompson, P.R. and Breger, D. (1981) *Systematic index of Recent and Pleistocene planktonic Foraminifera*, University of Tokyo Press.

Sanders, H. (1968) Marine benthic diversity: a comparative study. *American Naturalist*, **102**, 243–82.

Sandon, H. (1934) Pseudopodial movements of Foraminifera. *Nature*, **133**, 761–2.

Santschi, P.H. (1988) Factors controlling the biogeochemical cycles of trace elements in fresh and coastal marine waters as revealed by artificial radioisotopes. *Limnology and Oceanography*, **33**, 848–66.

Sanyal, A., Hemming, N.G., Broecker, W.S. *et al.* (1996) Oceanic pH control on the boron isotopic composition of foraminifera: Evidence from culture experiments. *Paleoceanography*, **11**, 513–7.

Sanyal, A., Hemming, N.G., Hanson, G.N. and Broecker, W.S. (1995) Evidence for a higher pH in the glacial ocean from boron isotopes in foraminifera. *Nature*, **373**, 234–6.

Saraswati, P.K. (1995) Biometry of early Oligocene *Lepidocyclina* from Kutch, India. *Marine Micropaleontology*, **26**, 303–11.

Sarnthein, M., Jansen, E., Weinelt, M. *et al.* (1995) Variations in Atlantic surface ocean paleoceanography, 50°–80°N: a time-slice record of the last 30,000 years. *Paleoceanography*, **10**, 1063–94.

Sarnthein, M., Winn, K., Duplessy, J.C. and Fontugne, M.R.

(1988) Global variations of surface water productivity in low and mid latitudes: Influence on CO_2 reservoirs of the deep ocean and atmosphere during the last 21,000 years. *Paleoceanography*, **3**, 361–99.

Saunders, J.B. (1958) Recent Foraminifera in mangrove swamps and river estuaries and their fossil counterparts in Trinidad. *Micropaleontology*, **4**, 79–92.

Sautter, L.R. and Thunell, R.C. (1991) Seasonal variability in the $\delta^{18}O$ and $\delta^{13}C$ of planktonic foraminifera from an upwelling environment: sediment trap results from the San Pedro Basin, Southern California bight. *Paleoceanography*, **6**, 307–34.

Savin, S.M. and Douglas, R.G. (1973) Stable isotope and magnesium geochemistry of recent planktonic foraminifera from the south Pacific. *Geological Society of America Bulletin*, **84**, 2327–42.

Savin, S.M., Douglas, R.G., Keller, G. *et al.* (1981) Miocene benthic foraminiferal isotope records: a synthesis. *Marine Micropaleontology*, **6**, 423 50.

Savin, S.M., Douglas, R.G. and Stehli, F.G. (1975) Tertiary marine paleotemperatures. *Geological Society of America Bulletin*, **86**, 1499–1510.

Savin, S.M. and Woodruff, F. (1990) Isotopic evidence for temperature and productivity in the Tertiary oceans, in *Phosphate Deposits of the World, v. 3, Neogene to Modern Phosphorites*, (eds W.C. Burnett and S.R. Riggs), Cambridge University Press, Cambridge, pp. 241–59.

Schafer, C.T. (1968) *Distribution, Pollution Response, Temporal Variation of Foraminifera and Sedimentation in Western Long Island Sound and Adjacent Nearshore Areas*, Unpublished Ph.D. thesis, New York University, New York.

Schafer, C.T. (1970a) Studies of benthic foraminifera in Restigouche Estuary: Faunal distribution patterns near pollution sources. *Maritime Sediments*, **6**, 121–34.

Schafer, C.T. (1970b) Pollution and benthonic foraminifera species diversity in Long Island Sound. *Food and Agricultural Organization Technical Conference on Marine Pollution and Its Effects on Living Resources and Fishing, Rome, Italy, Abstracts Volume*, p. 14.

Schafer, C.T. (1971a) Distribution patterns of benthonic foraminifera near pollution sources in the Restigouche Estuary, New Brunswick. *Second National Coastal and Shallow Water Research Conference, University of Delaware, Newark, Abstracts Volume*, p. 197.

Schafer, C.T. (1971b) Sampling and spatial distribution of benthonic foraminifera. *Limnology and Oceanography*, **16**, 944–51.

Schafer, C.T. (1973) Distribution of foraminifera near pollution sources in Chaleur Bay. *Water, Air and Soil Pollution*, **2**, 219–33.

Schafer, C.T. (1975) Benthonic foraminifera as pollution indicators. *5th Indian Micropaleontology Colloquium, February 1975, Abstracts Volume*.

Schafer, C.T. (1982) Foraminiferal colonization of an offshore dump site in Chaleur Bay, New Brunswick, Canada. *Journal of Foraminiferal Research*, **12**, 317–26.

Schafer, C.T. (1992) Sedimentation-foraminifera-pollution relationships in the North Arm of the Saguenay Fiord. *M. La Montagne Institute, Mt. Joli, Quebec (March 1992), Abstracts Volume*.

Schafer, C.T. and Cole, F.E. (1974) Distribution of benthic foraminifera: Their use in delimiting local near shore environments. *Geological Survey of Canada, Paper 74-30*, 103–8.

Schafer, C.T. and Cole, F.E. (1978) Distribution of foraminifera in Chaleur Bay, St. Lawrence. *Geological Survey of Canada Paper 77-30*, 55 pp.

Schafer, C.T. and Cole, F.E. (1982) Living benthic foraminifera distributions on the continental slope and rise east of Newfoundland, Canada. *Geological Society of America Bulletin*, **93**, 207–17.

Schafer, C.T. and Cole, F.E. (1986) Reconnaissance survey of benthonic foraminifera from Baffin Island fiord environments. *Arctic*, **39**, 232–9.

Schafer, C.T. and Cole, F.E. (1995) Marine habitat recovery in the Saguenay Fiord, Canada: the legacy of environmental contamination. *Proceedings of the OCEANS 95 Conference, San Diego, October 9–12*, pp. 925–40.

Schafer, C.T., Collins, E.S. and Smith, J.N. (1991) Relationship of foraminifera and thecamoebian distributions to sediments contaminated by pulp mill effluent: Saguenay Fiord, Quebec, Canada. *Marine Micropaleontology*, **17**, 255–83.

Schafer, C.T., Scott, D.B. and Medioli, F. (1993) Modification of local seafloor environments by aquaculture operations: temporal changes reflected by benthonic foraminifera assemblages. *GSC Forum, January 1993*.

Schafer, C.T. and Sen Gupta, B.K. (1969) Foraminiferal ecology in polluted estuaries of New Brunswick and Maine. *Atlantic Oceanographic Laboratory, Bedford Institute, Dartmouth, N.S., Canada, Report*, 69–1, 24 pp.

Schafer, C.T., Wagner, F.J.E. and Ferguson, C. (1975) Occurrence of foraminifera, molluscs, and ostracods adjacent to the industrialized shoreline of Canso Strait, Nova Scotia. *Water, Air, Soil Pollution*, **5**, 79–96.

Schafer, C.T., Winters, G.V., Scott, D.B. *et al.* (1995) Survey of living foraminifera and polychaete populations at some Canadian aquaculture sites: Potential for impact mapping and monitoring. *Journal of Foraminiferal Research*, **25**, 236–59.

Schaudinn, F. (1895) Uber den Dimorphismus bei Foraminiferen. *Sitzungsberichte der Gesellschaft naturforschender Freunde zu Berlin*, **5**, 87–97.

Schiffelbein, P. (1984) Effect of benthic mixing on the information content of deep-sea stratigraphic signals. *Nature*, **311**, 651–3.

Schiffelbein, P. (1985) Extracting the benthic mixing impulse response function: A constrained deconvolution technique. *Marine Geology*, **64**, 313–36.

Schiffelbein, P. (1986) The interpretation of stable isotopes in deep-sea sediments: An error analysis case study. *Marine Geology*, **70**, 313–20.

Schmidt, G.A. (1998) Oxygen 18 variations in a global ocean model. *Geophysical Research Letters*, **25**, 1201–04.

References

Schmiedl, G. and Mackensen, A. (1997) Late Quaternary paleoproductivity and deep water circulation in the eastern South Atlantic Ocean: Evidence from benthic foraminifera. *Palaeogeography, Palaeoclimatology, Palaeoecology*, **130**, 43–80.

Schmiedl, G., Mackensen, A. and Muller, P. (1997) Recent benthic foraminifera from the eastern South Atlantic Ocean: dependence on food supply and water masses. *Marine Micropaleontology*, **32**, 249–88.

Schnitker, D. (1971) Distribution of foraminifera on the North Carolina continental shelf. *Tulane Studies in Geology and Paleontology*, **8**, 169–215.

Schnitker, D. (1974a) Ecotypic variation in *Ammonia beccarii* (Linné). *Journal of Foraminiferal Research*, **4**, 217–23.

Schnitker, D. (1974b) West Atlantic abyssal circulation during the past 120,000 years. *Nature*, **248**, 385–7.

Schnitker, D. (1980) Quaternary deep-sea benthic foraminifers and bottom water masses. *Annual Reviews of Earth and Planetary Sciences*, **8**, 343–70.

Schnitker, D. (1994) Deep-sea benthic foraminifers: Food and bottom water masses, in *Carbon Cycling in the Glacial Ocean: Constraints on the Ocean's Role in Global Change*, (eds R. Zahn et al.), Springer-Verlag, Berlin, pp. 539–53.

Schott, W. (1935) Die Foraminiferen in dem aquatorialen Teil des atlantischen Oceans. *Deutsche Atlantische Expedition 'Meteor' 1925–1927, Wissenschaftliche Ergebnisse*, **3**, 43–134.

Schröder-Adams, C.J., Cole, F.E., Medioli, F.S. et al. (1990) Recent Arctic shelf foraminifera: seasonally ice-covered vs. perennially ice covered areas. *Journal of Foraminiferal Research*, **20**, 8–36.

Schweitzer, P.N. and Lohmann G.P. (1991) Ontogeny and habitat of modern menardiiform planktonic foraminifera. *Journal of Foraminiferal Research*, **21** (4), 332–46.

Scott, D.B. (1976a) Quantitative studies of marsh foraminiferal patterns in southern California and their application to Holocene stratigraphic problems, in *First International Symposium on Benthic Foraminifera of Continental Margins, Part A: Ecology and Biology*, (eds C.T. Schafer and B.R. Pelletier), *Maritime Sediments*, Special Publication No. 1, pp. 153–70.

Scott, D.B. (1976b) Brackish water Foraminifera from southern California and description of *Polysaccammina ipohalina* n. gen. n. sp. *Journal of Foraminiferal Research*, **6**, 312–21.

Scott, D.B., Collins, E.S., Duggan, J. et al. (1996) Pacific Rim marsh foraminiferal distributions: Implications for sea-level studies. *Journal of Coastal Research*, **12**, 850–61.

Scott, D.B., Collins, E.S. and Tobin, R. (1997) Historical reconstruction of impact histories from several sites on the east coast of North America using benthic foraminifera as indicators. *Estuarine Research Federation annual meeting in Providence, Rhode Island, October 1997, Abstracts Volume*, p. 165.

Scott, D.B. and Medioli, F.S. (1978) Vertical zonations of marsh foraminifera as accurate indicators of former sea-levels. *Nature*, **272**, 528–31.

Scott, D.B. and Medioli, F.S. (1980a) Quantitative studies of marsh foraminiferal distributions in Nova Scotia: Implications for sea level studies. *Cushman Foundation for Foraminiferal Research Special Publication*, No. 17, pp. 1–58.

Scott, D.B. and Medioli, F.S. (1980b) Living vs. total foraminiferal populations: their relative usefulness in paleoecology. *Journal of Paleontology*, **54**, 814–31.

Scott, D.B. and Medioli, F.S. (1986) Foraminifera as sea-level indicators, in *Sea-Level Research: A Manual for the Collection and Evaluation of Data*, (ed O. van de Plassche), Geo Books, Norwich, U.K, pp. 435–55.

Scott, D.B., Schafer, C.T., Honig, C. and Younger, D.C. (1995) Temporal variations of benthonic foraminiferal assemblages under or near aquaculture operations: documentation of impact history. *Journal of Foraminiferal Research*, **25**, 224–35.

Scott, D.B., Schafer, C.T. and Medioli, F. (1980) Eastern Canadian estuarine foraminifera: A framework for comparison. *Journal of Foraminiferal Research*, **10**, 205–34.

Scott, D.B., Schnack, E.J., Ferrero, L. et al. (1990) Recent marsh foraminifera from the east coast of South America: Comparison to the Northern Hemisphere, in *Paleoecology, Biostratigraphy, Paleoceanography, and Taxonomy of Agglutinated Foraminifera*, (eds C. Hemleben, M.A. Kaminsky, W. Kuhnt and D.B. Scott), Kluwer Academic Publishers, Dordrecht, pp. 717–37.

Scott, D.B., Suter, J.R. and Kosters, E.C. (1991) Marsh Foraminifera and arcellaceans of the lower Mississippi Delta: Controls on spatial distributions. *Micropaleontology*, **37**, 1–11.

Scott, D.K. and Leckie, R.M. (1990) Foraminiferal zonation of the Great Sippewisset Salt Marsh (Falmouth, Massachusetts). *Journal of Foraminiferal Research*, **20**, 248–66.

Scott, G.H. (1972) Biometry of the foraminiferal shell, in *Foraminifera*, v. 1, (eds R.H. Hedley and C.G. Adams), Academic press, London, pp. 55–153.

Seiglie, G.A. (1964) Significacion de los foraminiferos anormales de la Laguna de Unare. *Lagena*, **1**, 6.

Seiglie, G.A. (1966) Distribution of foraminifers in the sediments of Araya-Los Testigos shelf and upper slope. *Caribbean Journal of Science*, **6**, 93–117.

Seiglie, G.A. (1968) Foraminiferal assemblages as indicators of high organic carbon content in sediments and of polluted waters. *American Association of Petroleum Geologists Bulletin*, **52**, 2231–41.

Seiglie, G.A. (1971) A preliminary note on the relationship

References

between foraminifers and pollution in two Puerto Rican bays. *Caribbean Journal of Science*, **11**, 93–8.

Seiglie, G.A. (1973) Pyritization in living foraminifera. *Journal of Foraminiferal Research*, **3**, 1–6.

Seiglie, G.A. (1975) Foraminifers of Guayanilla Bay and their use as Environmental indicators. *Revista Espanola de Micropaleontologia*, **7**, 453–87.

Seilacher, A. (1970) Arbeitskonzept zur Konstruktions-Morphologie. *Lethaia*, **3**, 393–6.

Sen Gupta, B.K. (1972) Distribution of Holocene benthonic foraminifera on the Atlantic continental shelf of North America. *24th International Geological Congress, Montreal, Proceedings*, Section 8, 125–34.

Sen Gupta, B.K. (1977) Depth distribution of modern benthic foraminifera on continental shelves of the World Ocean. *Indian Journal of Earth Sciences*, **4**, 60–83.

Sen Gupta, B.K. (1988) Water mass relation of the benthic foraminifer *Cibicides wuellerstorfi* in the eastern Caribbean Sea. *Bulletin de l'Institut de Géologie du Bassin d'Aquitaine (Bordeaux)*, **44**, 23–32.

Sen Gupta, B.K. (1989) Morphology and generic placement of the foraminifer *Anomalina' wuellerstorfi* Schwager. *Journal of Paleontology*, **63**, 146–58.

Sen Gupta, B.K. and Aharon, P. (1994) Benthic foraminifera of bathyal hydrocarbon vents of the Gulf of Mexico: Initial report on communities and stable isotopes. *Geo-Marine Letters*, **14**, 88–96.

Sen Gupta, B.K. and Hayes, W.B. (1979) Recognition of Holocene benthic foraminiferal facies by recurrent group analysis. *Journal of Foraminiferal Research*, **9**, 233–45.

Sen Gupta, B.K. and Kilbourne, R.T. (1974) Diversity of benthic foraminifera on the Georgia continental shelf. *Geological Society of America Bulletin*, **85**, 969–72.

Sen Gupta, B.K. and Kilbourne, R.T. (1976) Depth distribution of benthic foraminifera on the Georgia continental shelf, in *First International Symposium on Benthic Foraminifera of Continental Margins, Part A: Ecology and Biology*, (eds C.T. Schafer and B.R. Pelletier), *Maritime Sediments*, Special Publication No. 1, pp. 25–38.

Sen Gupta, B.K., Lee, R. and May, M. (1981) Upwelling and an unusual assemblage of benthic foraminifera on the northern Florida continental slope. *Journal of Paleontology*, **55**, 853–7.

Sen Gupta, B.K. and Machain-Castillo, M.L. (1993) Benthic foraminifera in oxygen-poor habitats. *Marine Micropaleontology*, **20**, 183–201.

Sen Gupta, B.K., Platon, E., Bernhard, J.M. and Aharon, P. (1997) Foraminiferal colonization of hydrocarbon-seep bacterial mats and underlying sediment, Gulf of Mexico slope. *Journal of Foraminiferal Research*, **27**, 292–300.

Sen Gupta, B.K. and Schafer, C.T. (1973) Holocene benthonic foraminifera in leeward bays of St. Lucia, West Indies. *Micropaleontology*, **19**, 341–65.

Sen Gupta, B.K., Turner, R.E. and Rabalais, N.N. (1996) Seasonal oxygen depletion in continental-shelf waters of Louisiana: Historical record of benthic foraminifers. *Geology*, **24**, 227–30.

Sepkoski, J.J. (1974) Quantified coefficients of association and measurements of similarity. *Mathematical Geology*, **6**, 135–52.

Setty, M.G.A.P. (1976) The relative sensitivity of benthic foraminifera in the polluted marine environment of Cola Bay, Goa. *Proceedings of VI Indian Colloquium in Micropaleontology and Stratigraphy, Banaras*, pp. 225–34.

Setty, M.G.A.P. (1982) Pollution effects monitoring with foraminifera as indices in the Thana Greek, Bombay Area. *International Journal of Environmental Studies*, **18**, 205–9.

Setty, M.G.A.P. and Nigam, R. (1980) Foraminifera as indicators of pollution in the marine environment of the west coast of India. *26th International Geological Congress, Paris, Abstracts Volume 2*, p. 541.

Setty, M.G.A.P. and Nigam, R. (1982) Foraminiferal assemblages and organic carbon relationship in benthic marine ecosystem of western Indian continental shelf. *Indian Journal of Marine Sciences*, **11**, 225–32.

Setty, M.G.A.P. and Nigam, R. (1984) Benthic foraminifera as pollution indices in the Marine Environment of the West Coast of India. *Riv. It. Paleont. Strat.*, **9**, 421–46.

Setty, M.G.A.P., Nigam, R. and Faterpenkar, A.D. (1983) An aberrant *Spiroloculina* sp. from recent sediments off Bombay-Daman, west coast of India Mahasagar. *Bulletin of National Institute of Oceanography (Goa)*, **16**, 77–9.

Severin, K.P. (1987a) Spatial and temporal variation of *Marginopora vertebralis* on seagrass in Papua New Guinea during a six week period. *Micropaleontology*, **33**, 368–77.

Severin, K.P. (1987b) Laboratory observations of the rate of subsurface movement of a small miliolid foraminifer. *Journal of Foraminiferal Research*, **17**, 110–6.

Severin, K.P. and Erskian, M.G. (1981) Laboratory experiments on the vertical movement of *Quinqueloculina impressa* Reuss through sand. *Journal of Foraminiferal Research*, **11**, 133–6.

Severin, K.P. and Lipps, J.H. (1989) The weight-volume relationship of the test of *Alveolinella quoyi*: Implications for the taphonomy of large fusiform foraminifera. *Lethaia*, **22**, 1–12.

Shackleton, N.J. (1974) Attainment of isotopic equilibrium between ocean water and the benthonic foraminifera genus *Uvigerina*: isotopic changes in the ocean during the last glacial. *CNRS, Colloques Internationals*, **219**, 203–9.

Shackleton, N.J. (1977a) ^{13}C in *Uvigerina*: tropical rainforest history and the equatorial Pacific carbonate dissolution cycles, in *Fate of Fossil Fuel CO_2 in the Oceans*, (eds N. Anderson and A. Malahof), Plenum, New York, pp. 401–27

Shackleton, N.J. (1977b) The oxygen isotope stratigraphic record of the Late Pleistocene. *Philosophical Transactions of the Royal Society, London, B*, **280**, 169–82.

Shackleton, N.J. (1987) Oxygen isotopes, ice volume and sea-level. *Quaternary Science Reviews*, **6**, 183–90.

Shackleton, N.J., Corfield, R.M. and Hall, M.A. (1985)

References

Shackleton, N.J. and Kennett, J.P. (1975) Paleotemperature history of the Cenozoic and the initiation of Antarctic glaciation: oxygen and carbon isotope analyses in DSDP sites 277, 279, and 281. *Initial Reports of the Deep Sea Drilling Project*, **29**, 743–55.

Shackleton, N.J. and Opdyke, N.D. (1973) Oxygen isotope and paleomagnetic stratigraphy of equatorial Pacific core V28–238: oxygen isotope temperatures and ice volumes on a 105 and 106 year scale. *Quaternary Research*, **3**, 39–55.

Shackleton, N.J, Wiseman, J.D.H. and Buckley, H.A. (1973) Non-equilibrium isotopic fractionation between seawater and planktonic foraminiferal tests. *Nature*, **242**, 177–9.

Shannon, R.D. (1976) Revised effective ionic radii and systematic studies of interatomic distances in halides and chalcogenides. *Acta Crystallographica*, **A32**, 751–67.

Sharifi, A.R. (1991) *Heavy Metal Pollution and its Effects on Recent Foraminiferids from Southampton Water, Southern England, U.K.* Unpublished Ph.D. thesis, University of Southampton.

Sharifi, A.R., Croudace, I.W. and Austin, R.L. (1991) Benthic foraminiferids as pollution indicators in Southampton Water, Southern England. *Journal of Micropalaeontology*, **10**, 109–13.

Sharma, P., Gardner, L.R., Moore, W.S. and Bollinger, M.S. (1987) Sedimentation and bioturbation in a salt marsh as revealed by ^{210}Pb, ^{137}Cs, and ^{7}Be studies. *Limnology and Oceanography*, **32**, 313–26.

Shi, G.R. (1993) Multivariate data analysis in palaeoecology and palaeobiogeography; a review. *Palaeogeography, Palaeoclimatology, Palaeoecology*, **105**, 199–234.

Shick, J.M., Lasser, M.P. and Jokiel, P.L. (1996) Effects of ultraviolet radiation on corals and other coral reef organisms. *Global Change Biology*, **2**, 527–45.

Shirayama, Y. (1984) Vertical distribution of meiobenthos in the sediment profile in bathyal, abyssal and hadal deep sea systems of the western Pacific. *Oceanologica Acta*, **7**, 123–9.

Shroba, C.S. (1993) Taphonomic features of benthic foraminifera in a temperate setting: Experimental and field observations on the role of abrasion, solution and microboring in the destruction of foraminiferal tests. *Palaios*, **8**, 250–66.

Signor, P.W. and Lipps, J.H. (1982) Sampling bias, gradual extinction patterns and catastrophes in the fossil record, in *Geological Implications of Impacts of Large Asteroids and Comets on the Earth*, (eds L.T. Silver and P.H. Schulz), Geological Society of America Special Paper 190, Boulder, Colorado, pp. 291–6.

Silva, K., Corliss, B., Rathburn, A. and Thunell, R. (1996) Seasonality of living benthic foraminifera from the San Pedro Basin, California borderland. *Journal of Foraminiferal Research*, **26**, 71–93.

Silver, M.W., Shanks, A.L. and Trent, J.D. (1978) Marine snow; microplankton habitat, a source of small-scale patchyness in pelagic populations. *Science*, **201** (4353), 371–3.

Simmons, M.D., BouDagher-Fadel, M.K., Banner, F.T. and Whittaker, J.E. (1997) The Jurassic Favusellacea, the earliest Globigerinina, in *The Early Evolutionary History of Planktonic Foraminifera*, (eds M.K. BouDagher-Fadel, F.T. Banner and J.E. Whittaker), Chapman & Hall, London, pp. 17–30.

Simon, W. (1986) *Mathematical Techniques for Biology and Medicine*, New York, Dover.

Simpson, G.G. (1953) *Evolution and Geography*, Condon Lectures, Oregon State System of Higher Education, Eugene, Oregon, 64 pp.

Sjoerdsma, P. and van der Zwaan, G. (1992) Simulating the effect of changing organic flux and oxygen content on the distribution of benthic foraminifera. *Marine Micropaleontology*, **19**, 163–80.

Smart, C.W., King, S.C., Gooday, A.J. et al. (1994) A benthic foraminiferal proxy of pulsed organic matter palaeofluxes. *Marine Micropaleontology*, **23**, 89–99.

Smith, C.R. (1994) Tempo and mode in deep-sea benthic ecology: punctuated equilibrium revisited. *Palaios*, **9**, 3–13.

Smith, C.R and Baco, A.R. (1997) Whale-fall communities on the northwest Pacific Slope: Succession and Food-Web structure. *Unpublished Abstracts, Eighth Deep-Sea Biology Symposium, Monterey, CA, September, 1997*, pp. 111.

Smith, C., Hoover, R., Doan, S. et al. (1996) Phytodetritus at the abyssal seafloor across 10° of latitude in the central equatorial Pacific. *Deep-Sea Research*, **43**, 1309–38.

Smith, J.N. and Schafer, C.T. (1984) Bioturbation processes in continental slope and rise sediments delineated by Pb-210, microfossil and textural indicators. *Journal of Marine Research*, **42**, 1117–45.

Smith, K. (1987) Food energy supply and demand: A discrepancy between particulate organic carbon flux and sediment community oxygen consumption in the deep ocean. *Limnology and Oceanography*, **32**, 201–20.

Smith, P.B. (1964) Ecology of benthic species: Recent Foraminifera off Central America. *U.S. Geological Survey Professional Paper*, **429-B**, 1–51.

Smith, R.C. and Baker, K.S. (1979) Penetration of UV-B and biologically-effective dose-rates in natural waters. *Photochemistry and Photobiology*, **29**, 311–23.

Smith, R.K. (1970) Late glacial foraminifera from southeast Alaska and British Columbia and a world-wide high northern latitude shallow-water faunal province. *Archives des Sciences, Genève*, **23**, 675–702.

Smith, R.K. (1987) Fossilization potential in modern shallow-water benthic foraminiferal assemblages. *Journal of Foraminiferal Research*, **17**, 117–22.

Smith, R.M. and Patterson, D.J. (1986) Analyses of heliozoan interrelationships: An example of the potentials and limitations of ultrastructural approaches to the study of protistan phylogeny. *Proceedings of the Royal Society of London, Series B*, **227**, 325–66.

Smout, A.H. (1954) *Lower Tertiary Foraminifera of the Quatar Peninsula*, British Museum (Natural History), London.

Sneath, P.H.A. and Sokal, R.R. (1973) *Numerical Taxonomy*, W.H. Freeman, San Francisco.

Snyder, S.W., Hale, W.R. and Kontrovitz, M. (1990a) Distributional patterns of modern benthic foraminifera on the Washington continental shelf. *Micropaleontology*, **36**, 245–58.

Snyder, S.W., Hale, W.R. and Kontrovitz, M. (1990b) Assessment of postmortem transportation of modern benthic foraminifera of the Washington continental shelf. *Micropaleontology*, **36**, 259–82.

Sollas, W.J. (1921) On *Saccammina carteri* Brady and the minute structure of the foraminiferal shell. *Geological Society of London, Quarterly Journal*, **77**, 193–212.

Song, Y., Black, R.G. and Lipps, J.H. (1994) Morphological optimization in the largest living Foraminifera: Implications from finite element analysis. *Paleobiology*, **20**, 14–26.

Speer, J.A. (1983) Crystal chemistry and phase relations of orthorhombic carbonates, in *Carbonates: Mineralogy and Chemistry*, (ed R.J. Reeder), Mineralogical society of America, Washington, D.C., pp. 145–90.

Speijer, R.P., van der Zwaan, G.J. and Schmitz, B. (1996) The impact of Paleocene/Eocene boundary events on middle neritic benthic foraminiferal assemblages from Egypt. *Marine Micropaleontology*, **28**, 99–132.

Spero, H.J. (1987) Symbiosis in the planktonic foraminifer, *Orbulina universa*, and the isolation of its symbiotic dinoflagellate, *Gymnodinium beii* sp. nov. *Journal of Phycology*, **23**, 307–17.

Spero, H.J. (1992) Do planktic foraminifera accurately record shifts in the carbon isotopic composition of sea water ΣCO2? *Marine Micropaleontology*, **19**, 275–85.

Spero, H.J., Bijma, J., Lea, D.W. and Bemis, B.E. (1997) Effect of seawater carbonate concentration on foraminiferal carbon and oxygen isotopes. *Nature*, **390**, 497–500.

Spero, H.J. and Lea, D.W. (1993) Intraspecific stable isotope variability in the planktonic foraminifer *Globigerinoides sacculifer*: results from laboratory experiments. *Marine Micropaleontology*, **22**, 221–34.

Spero, H.J and Lea, D.W. (1996) Experimental determination of stable isotope variability in *Globigerina bulloides*: implications for paleoceanographic reconstructions. *Marine Micropaleontology*, **28**, 231–46.

Spero, H.J., Lerche, I. and Williams, D.F. (1991) Opening the carbon isotope 'vital effect' black box, 2, quantitative model for interpreting foraminiferal carbon isotope data. *Paleoceanography*, **6**, 639–55.

Spero, H.J. and Parker, S.L. (1985) Photosynthesis in the symbiotic planktonic foraminifer *Orbulina universa* and its potential contribution to oceanic primary productivity. *Journal of Foraminiferal Research*, **15**, 273–81.

Spero, H.J. and Williams, D.F. (1988) Extracting environmental information from planktonic foraminiferal $\delta^{13}C$ data. *Nature*, **335**, 717–9.

Spies, R.B. and Davis, P.H. (1979) The infaunal benthos of a natural oil seep in the Santa Barbara Channel. *Marine Biology*, **50**, 227–37.

Spindler, M. and Dickmann, G.S. (1986) Distribution and abundance of the planktonic foraminifer *Neogloboquadrina pachyderma* in sea ice of the Weddell Sea (Antarctica). *Polar Biology*, **5**, 1–7.

Spindler, M. and Hemleben, C. (1980) Symbionts in planktonic foraminifera (Protozoa). *Endocytobiology, Endosymbiosis and Cell Biology*, **1**, 133–40.

Spivack, A.J., You, C.-F. and Smith, H.J. (1993) Foraminiferal boron isotope ratios as a proxy for surface ocean pH over the past 21 Myr. *Nature*, **363**, 149–51.

Srinivasan, M.S. and Azmi, R.J. (1978) Coiling direction in planktonic foraminifera and its value in correlation. *The National Geographical Journal of India*, **24** (Pt. 3–4), 99–106.

Stanley, S.M. (1979) *Macroevolution: Pattern and Process*, Freeman and Co.

Stanley, S.M. (1990) Delayed recovery and the spacing of major extinctions. *Paleobiology*, **16** (4), 401–14.

Stanley, S.M., Wetmore K.L. and Kennett J.P. (1988) Macroevolutionary differences between the two major clades of Neogene planktonic foraminifera. *Paleobiology*, **14** (3), 235–49.

Stapleton, R.P. (1973) Ultrastructure of some tests of some Recent Foraminifera. *Palaeontographica*, pt. A, **142**, 16–49.

Stehli, F.G., Douglas, R.G. and Kafescioglu, I.A. (1972) Models for the evolution of planktonic foraminifera, in *Models in Paleobiology*, (ed T.J.M. Schopf), Freeman, Cooper and Co., San Francisco.

Stehli, F.G., Douglas, R.G. and Newell, N.D. (1969) Generation and Maintenance of Gradients in Taxonomic Diversity. *Science*, **164**, 947–9.

Stevens, S.S. (1946) On the theory of scales of measurement. *Science*, **103**, 677–80.

Stewart, M.K. (1975) Stable isotope fractionation due to evaporation and isotopic exchange of falling waterdrops: applications to atmospheric processes and evaporation of lakes. *Journal of Geophysical Research*, **80**, 1133–46.

Stoecker, D.K. (1998) Conceptual models of mixotrophy in planktonic protists and some ecological and evolutionary implications. *European Journal of Protistology*, **34**, 281–90.

Stoll, H.M. and Schrag, D.P. (1998) Effects of Quaternary sea level cycles on strontium in seawater. *Geochimica et Cosmochimica Acta*, **62**, 1107–18.

Stott, L., Hayden, T. and Griffith, J. (1996) Benthic foraminifera at the Los Angeles County Whites Point outfall revisited. *Journal of Foraminiferal Research*, **26**, 357–68.

Strain, P.M. and Tan, F.C. (1993) Seasonal evolution of oxygen isotope-salinity relationships in high-latitude surface waters. *Journal of Geophysical Research*, **98**, 14589–98.

References

Streeter, S.S. (1972) Living benthonic Foraminifera of the Gulf of California, a factor analysis of Phleger's (1964) data. *Micropaleontology*, **18**, 64–73.

Streeter, S.S. (1973) Bottom water and benthonic foraminifera in the North Atlantic—glacial-interglacial contrasts. *Quaternary Research*, **3**, 131–41.

Stubbles, S.J. (1993) Recent benthic Foraminiferida as indicators of pollution in Restronguet Creek, Cornwall. *Proceedings of the Ussher Society*, **8**, 200–4.

Stubbles, S.J., Green, J.C., Hart, M. and Williams, C.I. (1996a) The ecological and paleoecological implications of the presence and absence of data: Evidence from benthic foraminifera. *Annual Conference of the Ussher Society*, pp. 54–62.

Stubbles, S.J., Hart, M., Williams, C.I. and Green, J.C. (1996b) Response of foraminifera to presence of heavy metal contamination and acid mine drainage. *Minerals, metals, and the environment II' conference, Institution of Mining and Metallurgy, Prague, September 3–6, 1996*, pp. 217–35.

Suchanek, T.H. (1993) Oil impacts on marine invertebrate populations and communities. *American Zoologist*, **33**, 510–23.

Sugihara, G. and May, R.M. (1990) Applications of fractals in ecology. *Trends in Ecology and Evolution*, **5**, 79–86.

Swart, P.K (1983) Carbon and oxygen isotope fractionation in scleractinian corals: a review. *Earth-Science Reviews*, **19**, 51–80.

Swart, P.K., Burns, S.J. and Leder, J.J. (1991) Fractionation of the stable isotopes of oxygen and carbon in carbon dioxide during the reaction of calcite with phosphoric acid as a function of temperature and technique. *Chemical Geology (Isotope Geoscience Section)*, **86**, 89–96.

Szmant, A.M. and Forrester, A. (1996) Water column and sediment nitrogen and phosphorus distribution patterns in the Florida Keys, USA. *Coral Reefs*, **15**, 21–41.

Talge, H.K. and Hallock, P. (1995) Cytological examination of symbiont loss in benthic foraminifera, *Amphistegina gibbosa*. *Marine Micropaleontology*, **26**, 107–13.

Talge, H.K., Williams, D.E., Hallock, P. and Harney, J.N. (1997) Symbiont loss in reef foraminifera: consequences for affected populations. *Proceedings, 8th International Coral Reef Symposium*, Panama, **1**, 589–94.

Tan, F.C. (1989) Stable carbon isotopes in dissolved inorganic carbon in marine and estuarine environments, in *Handbook of environmental isotope geochemistry*, v. 3A, (eds P. Fritz and J.C. Fontes), Elsevier, Amsterdam, pp. 171–90.

Tapley, S. (1969) Foraminiferal analysis of the Miramichi Estuary. *Maritime Sediments*, **5**, 30–39.

Tappan, H. and Loeblich, A.R. (1982) Granuloreticulosa, in *Synopsis and Classification of Living Organisms*, v. 1, (ed S.P. Parker), McGraw-Hill, New York, pp. 527–52.

Tappan, H. and Loeblich, A.R. (1988) Foraminiferal evolution, diversification and extinction. *Journal of Paleontology*, **62**, 695–714.

Tarutani, T., Clayton, R.N. and Mayeda, T.K. (1969) The effect of polymorphism and magnesium substitution on oxygen isotope fractionation between calcium carbonate and water. *Geochimica et Cosmochimica Acta*, **33**, 987–96.

Taylor, D.L. and Wang, Y.-L. (eds) (1989) Fluorescent Microscopy of Living Cells in Culture. *Methods in Cell Biology*, **29**, 5–339.

Taylor, K.C., Hammer, C.U., Alley, R.B. *et al*. (1993) Electrical conductivity measurements from the GISP2 and GRIP Greenland ice cores. *Nature*, **366**, 549–52.

Teal, J.M. (1996) Salt marshes: They offer diversity of habitats. *Oceanus*, **39**, 13–6.

ter Kuile, B. (1991) Mechanisms for calcification and carbon cycling in algal symbiont-bearing foraminifera, in *Biology of Foraminifera*, (eds J.J. Lee and O.R. Anderson), Academic Press, New York, pp. 73–89.

ter Kuile, B. and Erez, J. (1984) *In situ* growth rate experiments on the symbiont-bearing foraminifera *Amphistegina lobifera* and *Amphisorus hemprichii*. *Journal of Foraminiferal Research*, **14**, 262–76.

ter Kuile, B. and Erez, J. (1987) Uptake of inorganic carbon and internal carbon cycling in benthonic symbiont-bearing Foraminifera. *Marine Biology*, **94**, 499–510.

ter Kuile, B., Erez, J and Lee, J.J. (1987) The role of feeding in the metabolism of larger, symbiotic foraminifera. *Symbiosis*, **4**, 335–50.

Thiede, J. (1971) Variations in coiling ratios of Holocene planktonic foraminifera. *Deep-Sea Research*, **18**, 823–31.

Thiel, H. (1975) The size structure of the deep-sea benthos. *Internationale Revue ges. Hydrobiologie*, **60**, 575–606.

Thiel, H. (1983) Meiobenthos and nannobenthos of the deep sea, in *The Sea*, v. 8, *Deep Sea Biology*, (ed G. Rowe), Wiley Interscience, New York, pp. 167–230.

Thiel, H., Pfannkuche, O., Schriever, G. *et al*. (1989) Phytodetritus on the deep-sea floor in a central oceanic region of the northeast Atlantic. *Biological Oceanography*, **6**, 203–9.

Thiery, R. (1982) Environmental instability and community diversity. *Biological Reviews*, **57**, 671–710.

Thistle, D. (1981) Natural physical disturbance and communities of marine soft bottoms. *Marine Ecology Progress Series*, **6**, 223–8.

Thistle, D. and Eckman, J. (1990) The effect of a biologically produced structure on the benthic copepods of a deep sea site. *Deep-Sea Research*, **37**, 541–54.

Thomas, E. and Gooday, A.J. (1996) Cenozoic deep-sea benthic foraminifera: Tracers for changes in oceanic productivity. *Geology*, **42**, 355–8.

Thomas, E. and Varekamp, J.C. (1991) Paleo-environmental analyses of marsh sequences (Clinton, Connecticut): Evidence for punctuated rise in sealevel during the latest Holocene. *Journal of Coastal Research Special Issue*, **11**, 125–58.

Thompson, P.R., Bé, A.W.H., Duplessy J. and Shackleton, N.J. (1979) Disappearance of pink-pigmented Globigerinoides ruber at 120,000 yr BP in the Indian and Pacific Oceans. *Nature*, **280**, 354–8.

References

Thomsen, L. and Altenbach, A.V. (1993) Vertical and areal distribution of foraminiferal abundance and biomass in microhabitats around inhabited tubes of marine echiurids. *Marine Micropaleontology*, **20**, 303–9.

Thorne, R.F. (1972) Major disjunctions in the geographic range of seed plants. *Quarterly Review of Biology*, **47**, 365–411.

Thunell, R.C. (1976) Optimum indices of calcium carbonate dissolution in deep-sea sediments. *Geology*, **4**, 525–8.

Thunell, R.C. (1981) Cenozoic paleotemperature changes and planktonic foraminiferal speciation. *Nature*, **289**, 670–2.

Thunell, R.C., Anderson, D., Gellar, D. and Qingmin, M. (1994) Sea-surface temperature estimates for the tropical western Pacific during the last glaciation and their implications for the Pacific Warm Pool. *Quaternary Research*, **41**, 255–64.

Thunell R.C. and Belyea, P. (1982) Neogene planktonic foraminiferal biogeography of the Atlantic Ocean. *Micropaleontology*, **28** (4), 381–98.

Thunell, R.C. and Honjo, S. (1981) Calcite dissolution and the modification of planktonic foraminiferal assemblages. *Marine Micropaleontology*, **6** (2), 169–82.

Thunell, R.C., Williams, D.F. and Kennett, J.P. (1977) Late Quaternary Paleoclimatology, Stratigraphy and Sapropel History in Eastern Mediterranean Deep Sea Sediments. *Marine Micropaleontology*, **2**, 371–88.

Todd, R. and Brönnimann, P. (1957) Recent Foraminifera and Thecamoebina from the eastern Gulf of Paria, Trinidad. *Cushman Foundation for Foraminiferal Research Special Publication*, No. 3, pp. 1–43.

Toler, S.K. and Hallock, P. (1998) Shell malformation in stressed *Amphistegina* populations: relation to biomineralization and paleoenvironmental potential. *Marine Micropaleontology*, **34**, 107–15.

Towe, K.M., Berthold, W.-U. and Appleman, D.E. (1977) The crystallography of *Patellina corrugata* Williamson: A-axes preferred orientation. *Journal of Foraminiferal Research*, **7**, 58–61.

Towe, K.M. and Cifelli, R. (1967) Wall ultrastructure in the calcareous Foraminifera: crystallographic aspects and a model for calcification. *Journal of Paleontology*, **41**, 742–62.

Travis, J.L. and Allen, R.D. (1981) Studies on the motility of the Foraminifera. 1. Ultrastructure of the reticulopodial network of *Allogromia laticollaris* (Arnold). *Journal of Cell Biology*, **90**, 211–21.

Travis, J.L. and Bowser, S.S. (1986a) A new model for reticulopodial motility and shape: Evidence for a microtubule-based motor and an actin skeleton. *Cell Motility and the Cytoskeleton*, **6**, 2–14.

Travis, J.L. and Bowser, S.S. (1986b) Microtubule-dependent reticulopodial motility: Is there a role for actin? *Cell Motility and the Cytoskeleton*, **6**, 146–52.

Travis, J.L. and Bowser, S.S. (1988) Optical approaches to the study of foraminiferan motility. *Cell Motility and the Cytoskeleton*, **10**, 126–36.

Travis, J.L. and Bowser, S.S. (1991) The motility of Foraminifera, in *Biology of the Foraminifera*, (eds J.J. Lee and O.R. Anderson), Academic Press, London, pp. 91–155.

Turner, R.E. and Rabalais, N.N. (1994) Coastal eutrophication near the Mississippi River delta. *Nature*, **368**, 619–21.

Tyler, P. (1995) Conditions for the existence of life at the deep-sea floor: an update. *Oceanography and Marine Biology: an annual review*, **33**, 221–44.

Tyson, R.V. and Pearson, T.H. (1991) Modern and ancient continental shelf anoxia: An overview, in *Modern and Ancient Continental Shelf Anoxia*, (eds R.V. Tyson and T.H. Pearson), Geological Society of London Special Publication, No. 58, pp. 1–24.

Urey, H.C. (1947) The thermodynamic properties of isotopic substances. *Journal of the Chemical Society*, pt. 1, 562–81.

Usdowski, E. and Hoefs, J. (1993) Oxygen isotope exchange between carbonic acid, bicarbonate, carbonate, and water: a re-examination of the data of McCrea (1950) and an expression for the overall partitioning of oxygen isotopes between the carbonate species and water. *Geochimica et Cosmochimica Acta*, **57**, 3815–8.

Valentine, J.W. (1966) Numerical analysis of marine molluscan ranges on the extratropical northeastern Pacific shelf. *Limnology and Oceanography*, **11**, 198–211.

Valentine, J.W. (1968) The evolution of ecological units above the population level. *Journal of Paleontology*, **42**, 253–67.

Valentine, P.C. (1976) Zoogeography of Holocene Ostracoda off western North America and paleoclimatic implications. *U.S. Geological Survey Professional Paper*, **916**, 1–47.

Valiela, I. (1995) *Marine Ecological Processes*, 2nd Ed., Springer-Verlag, New York.

Van de Plassche, O. (1991) Late Holocene sea-level fluctuations on the shore of Connecticut inferred from transgressive and regressive overlap boundaries in salt-marsh deposits. *Journal of Coastal Research Special Issue*, **11**, 159–79.

Van der Zwaan, G. (1982) Paleo-oceanographical reconstructions by means of Foraminifera. *Bulletin Societe de Geologie de France*, **24** (3), 589–96.

Van der Zwaan, G.J. and Jorissen, F.J. (1991) Biofacial patterns in river-induced shelf anoxia, in *Modern and Ancient Continental Shelf Anoxia*, (eds R.V. Tyson and T.H. Pearson), Geological Society of London Special Publication, No. 58, pp. 65–82.

Van der Zwaan, G., Jorissen, F. and de Stigter, H. (1990) The depth dependency of planktonic/benthic foraminiferal ratios: Constraints and applications. *Marine Geology*, **95**, 1–16.

van Eijden, A.J.M. (1995) Morphology and relative frequency of planktonic foraminiferal species in relation to oxygen isotopically inferred depth habitats. *Palaeogeography, Palaeoclimatology, Palaeoecology*, **113**, 267–301.

van Geen, A., Fairbanks, R.G., Dartnell, P. *et al.* (1996)

References

Ventilation changes in the Northeast Pacific during the last deglaciation. *Paleoceanography*, **11**, 519–28.

van Geen, A., Hornberger, M.I., Fuller, C.C. *et al.* (1993) A record of cadmium contamination in the water column of San Francisco Bay from Cd/Ca ratios in foraminifera. *Geological Society of America, Annual Meeting Abstracts with Programs*, p. 137.

van Geen, A. and Husby, D.M. (1996) Cadmium in the California Current system – tracer of past and present upwelling. *Journal of Geophysical Research – Oceans*, **101**, 3489–507.

van Geen, A., Luoma, S.N., Fuller, C.C. *et al.* (1992) Evidence from Cd/Ca ratios in foraminifera for greater upwelling off California 4,000 years ago. *Nature*, **358**, 54–6.

Van Straaten, L.M.J.U. (1952) Biogenic textures and the formation of shell beds in the Dutch Wadden Sea. *Koninklijke Nederlandse Akademie van Wetenschappen, Proceedings, Series B, Physical Sciences*, **55**, 500–16.

Varekamp, J.C. and Thomas, E. (1998) Climate change and the rise and fall of sea level over the millennium. *EOS, Transactions of American Geophysical Union*, **79**, 69.

Varekamp, J.C., Thomas, E. and Van de Plassche, O. (1992) Relative sea-level rise and climate change over the last 1500 years. *Terra Nova*, **4**, 293–304.

Varshney, P.K., Govindan, K., Gaikwad, U.D. and Desai, B.N. (1988) Macrobenthos off Versova (Bombay), West Coast of India, in relation to environmental conditions. *Indian Journal of Marine Sciences*, **17** (3), 222–7.

Vasicec, M. (1953) Zmeny vzajemneho pomeru levotocivych a pravotocivych jedincu foraminifery *Globorotalia scitula* (Brady) ajejich vyuziti vi stratigrafi. *Ustredni Ustav Geologicky Sbornik*, **20**, 1–76.

Vella, P. (1974) Coiling ratios in *Neogloboquadrina pachyderma* (Ehrenberg): variations in different size fractions. *Geological Society of America Bulletin*, **85** (9), 1421–4.

Vénec-Peyré, M.T. (1981) Les Foraminifères et la pollution: etude de la microfaune de la Cale du Dourduff (Embochure de la Riviere de Morlaix). *Cahiers de Biologie Marine*, **22**, 25–33.

Vénec-Peyré, M.T. (1984) Les Foraminifères et le milieu étude de trois écosystèmes. *Benthos '83, April 1983, Pau – France*, pp. 573–81.

Vergnaud-Grazzini, C. (1985) Mediterranean Late Cenozoic stable isotope record: stratigraphic and paleoclimatic implications, in *Geological Evolution of the Mediterranean Basin*, (eds D.J. Stanley and F.C. Wezel), Springer-Verlag, New York, pp. 413–51.

Vermeij, G.J. (1989) Geographical restriction as a guide to the causes of extinction: the case of the cold northern oceans during the Neogene. *Paleobiology*, **15** (4), 335–56.

Vermeij, G.J. (1993) Biogeography of recently existing marine species: implications for conservation. *Conservation Biology*, **7**, 391–7.

Versteeg, D.J. and Shorter, S.J. (1992) Effect of organic carbon on the uptake and toxicity of quaternary ammonium compounds to the fathead minnow, *Pimephales promelas*. *Environmental Toxicology and Chemistry*, **11**, 571–80.

Vickerman, K. (1992) The diversity and ecological significance of Protozoa. *Biodiversity and Conservation*, **1**, 334–41.

Viela, C.G. (1995) Ecology of Quaternary benthic foraminiferal assemblages on the Amazon shelf, Northern Brazil. *Geo-Marine Letters*, **15**, 199–203.

Vilks, G. (1989) Ecology of recent Foraminifera on the Canadian continental shelf of the Arctic Ocean, in *The Arctic Seas: Climatology, Oceanography, Geology and Biology*, (ed Y. Herman), Van Nostrand Reinhold, New York, 497–569.

Vincent, E. and Berger, W.H. (1981) Planktonic foraminifera and their use in paleoceanography, in *The Sea*, v. 7, *The Oceanic Lithosphere*, (ed C. Emiliani), J. Wiley and Sons, New York, pp. 1025–119

Vincent, E. and Berger, W.H. (1985) Carbon dioxide and polar cooling in the Miocene: the Monterey hypothesis, in *The Carbon Cycle and Atmospheric CO_2: Natural Variations Archaean to Present*, (eds. E.T. Sundquist and W.S. Broecker), *Geophysical monograph series*, **32**, American Geophysical Union, Washington DC, pp. 455–68.

Vincent, E., Killingley, J.S. and Berger, W.H. (1981) Stable isotope composition of benthic foraminifera from the equatorial Pacific. *Nature*, **289**, 639–43.

Vinot-Bertouille, A.C. and Duplessy, J.C. (1973) Individual isotopic fractionation of carbon and oxygen in benthic foraminifera. *Earth and Planetary Science Letters*, **18**, 247–52.

Vitousek, P.M., Mooney, H.A., Lubshenco, J. and Melillo, J.M. (1997) Human domination of Earth's ecosystems. *Science*, **277**, 494–9.

von Damm, K.L., Edmond, J.M., Grant, B. *et al.* (1985) Chemistry of submarine hydrothermal solutions at 21°N, East Pacific Rise. *Geochimica et Cosmochimica Acta*, **49**, 2197–220.

Wallace, A.R. (1878) *Tropical Nature and Other Essays*, Macmillan, London.

Walter, L.M. and Burton, E.A. (1990) Dissolution of recent platform carbonate sediments in marine pore fluids. *American Journal of Science*, **290**, 601–43.

Walton, W.R. (1964) Recent foraminiferal ecology and paleoecology, in *Approaches to Paleoecology*, (eds J. Imbrie and N.D. Newell), John Wiley, New York, pp. 151–237.

Wang, P., Zhang, J. and Min, Q. (1985) Distribution of foraminifera in surface sediments of the East China Sea, in *Marine Micropaleontology of China*, (ed P. Wang), China Ocean Press, Beijing, pp. 34–69.

Warnke, G.L. and Abbott, R.T. (1961) *Caribbean Seashells*, Livingstone Publishing Co., Narberth, Pennsylvania.

Watkins, J.G. (1961) Foraminiferal ecology around the Orange County, California, ocean sewer outfall. *Micropaleontology*, **7**, 199–206.

Watling, L. (1988) Small-scale features of marine sediments and their importance to the study of deposit-feeding. *Marine Ecology Progress Series*, **47**, 135–44.

References

Watson, R.T., Rodhe, H., Oeschger, H. and Siegenthaler, U. (1990) Greenhouse gases and aerosols, in *Climate Change The IPCC Scientific Assessment*, (eds J.T. Houghton, G.J. Jenkins and J.J. Ephraums), Cambridge University Press, Cambridge, pp. 1–40.

Weber, J.N. and Woodhead, P.J.J. (1970) Carbon and oxygen isotope fractionation in the skeletal carbonate of reef building corals. *Chemical Geology*, **6**, 93–117.

Wefer, G. and Berger, W.H. (1991) Isotope paleontology: growth and composition of extant calcareous species. *Marine Geology*, **100**, 207–48.

Wefer, G. and Fischer, G. (1993) Seasonal patterns of vertical particle flux in equatorial and coastal upwelling areas of the eastern Atlantic. *Deep-Sea Research*, **40** (8), 1613–45.

Wefer, G., Heinze, P.M. and Berger, W.H. (1994) Clues to ancient methane release. *Nature*, **369**, 282.

Wehmiller, J.F., York, L.L. and Bart, M.L. (1995) Amino acid racemization geochronology of reworked Quaternary mollusks on U. S. Atlantic coast beaches: Implications for chronostratigraphy, taphonomy, and coastal sediment transport. *Marine Geology*, **124**, 303–37.

Wei, K.Y. and Kennett, J.P. (1983) Nonconstant extinction rates in Neogene planktonic foraminifera. *Nature*, **305**, 218–20.

Wei, K.Y. and Kennett, J.P. (1986) Taxonomic evolution of Neogene planktonic foraminifera and paleoceanographic relations. *Paleoceanography*, **1** (1), 67–84.

Weinberg, J.R. (1991) Rates of movement and sedimentary traces of deep-sea foraminifera and Mollusca in the laboratory. *Journal of Foraminiferal Research*, **21**, 213–7.

Weiner, S. (1986) Organization of extracellularly mineralized tissues: A comparative study of biological crystal growth. *CRC Critical Reviews Biochemistry*, **220**, 365–408.

Weiner, S. and Erez, J. (1984) Organic matrix of the shell of the foraminifer *Heterostegina depressa*. *Journal of Foraminiferal Research*, **14**, 206–12.

Weiss, R.F., Östlund, H.G. and Craig, H. (1979) Geochemical studies of the Weddell Sea. *Deep-Sea Research*, **26A**, 1093–1120.

Welnhofer, E.A. and Travis, J.L. (1996) In vivo microtubule dynamics during experimentally induced conversions between tubulin assembly states in *Allogromia laticollaris*. *Cell Motility and the Cytoskeleton*, **34**, 81–94.

Wester, P.W. and Vos, J.G. (1994) Toxicological pathology in laboratory fish: an evaluation with two species and various environmental contaminants. *Ecotoxicology*, **3**, 21–44.

Westerhausen, L., Poynter, J., Eglinton, G. *et al.* (1993) Marine and terrigenous origin of organic matter in modern sediments of the equatorial East Atlantic: the C-13 and molecular record. *Deep-Sea Research*, **40**, 1087–121.

Wetmore, K.L. (1988) Burrowing and sediment movement by benthic Foraminifera, as shown by time-lapse cinematography. *Revue de Paléobiologie*, **2**, 921–7.

Wetmore, K.L. (1998) Patterns of test growth after breakage – evidence for differences in developmental controls, in *International Symposium of Foraminifera, Forams '98, Monterrey, Mexico, Proceedings and Abstracts with Programs*, (eds J.F. Longoria and M.A. Gamper), Sociedad Mexicana de Paleontologia, A.C., p. 112.

Wheatcroft, R.A. (1990) Preservation potential of sedimentary event layers. *Geology*, **18**, 843–5.

Wheatcroft, R.A. (1992) Experimental tests for particle size-dependent bioturbation in the deep ocean. *Limnology and Oceanography*, **37**, 90–104.

Wheatcroft, R.A. and Jumars, P.A. (1987) Statistical re-analysis for size dependency in deep-sea mixing. *Marine Geology*, **77**, 157–63.

Wheatcroft, R.A., Jumars, P.A., Smith, C.R. and Nowell, A.R.M. (1990) A mechanistic view of the particulate biodiffusion coefficient: step lengths, rest periods and transport directions. *Journal of Marine Research*, **48**, 177–207.

Wheeler, C.W. and Aharon, P. (1991) Mid-oceanic carbonate platforms as oceanic dipsticks: Examples from the Pacific. *Coral Reefs*, **10**, 101–14.

Whitcomb, N.J. (1977) *Effects of Oil Pollution on Selected Species of Benthic Foraminifera from the Lower York River, Virginia*, Unpublished M.S. thesis, Duke University, Durham, North Carolina.

Whitcomb, N.J. (1978) Effects of oil pollution upon selected species of benthic foraminiferids from the lower York River, Virginia. *Geological Society of America Annual Meeting, Abstracts with Programs*, p. A 515.

Whitehead, J.M. and McMinn, A. (1997) Paleodepth determination from Antarctic benthic diatom assemblages. *Marine Micropaleontology*, **29**, 301–18.

Widmark, J.G.V. (1995) Multiple deep-water sources and trophic regimes in the latest Cretaceous deep sea; evidence from benthic foraminifera. *Marine Micropaleontology*, **26**, 361–84.

Wiebe, P.H. and Holland, W.R. (1968) Plankton patchiness: effects on repeated net tows. *Limnology and Oceanography*, **2**, 315–21.

Wilde, G.L. (1965) Abnormal growth conditions in fusulinids. *Contributions from the Cushman Foundation for Foraminiferal Research*, **16**, 121–4.

Williams, D.E., Hallock, P., Talge, H.K. *et al.* (1997) Responses of *Amphistegina gibbosa* populations in the Florida Keys (U.S.A.) to a multi-year stress event (1991–1996). *Journal of Foraminiferal Research*, **27**, 264–9.

Williams, D.F., Bé, A.W.H. and Fairbanks, R.G. (1981) Seasonal isotopic variations in living planktonic foraminifera from Bermuda plankton tows. *Palaeogeography, Palaeoclimatology, Palaeoecology*, **33**, 71–102.

Williams, H.F.L. (1989) Foraminiferal zonations on the Fraser River delta and their application to paleoenvironmental interpretations. *Palaeogeography, Palaeoclimatology, Palaeoecology*, **73**, 39–50.

Williams, H.F.L. (1994) Intertidal benthic foraminiferal bio-

References

Williams, J., Higginson, J.J. and Rohrbough, J.D. (1968) *Oceanic Surface Currents*, Oxford University Press, New York.

Winter, F.W. (1907) Zur Kenntnis der Thalamophoren. I. Untersuchung über Peneroplis pertusus (Forskål). *Archiv für Protistenkunde*, **10**, 1–113.

Wood, A. (1949) The structure of the wall of the test in the Foraminifera: its value in classification. *Quarterly Journal of the Geological Society of London*, **104**, 229–55.

Woodruff, F. (1985) Changes in Miocene deep-sea benthic foraminiferal distribution in the Pacific Ocean: Relationship to paleoceanography. *Geological Society of America Memoir*, **163**, 131–75.

Woodruff, F. and Savin, S.M. (1989) Miocene deepwater oceanography. *Paleoceanography*, **4**, 87–140.

Woodruff, F., Savin, S.M. and Douglas, R.G. (1980) Biological fractionation of oxygen and carbon isotopes by recent benthic foraminifera. *Marine Micropaleontology*, **5**, 3–11.

Woodward, S.P. (1856) *A Manual of the Mollusca, or, a Rudimentary Treatise of Recent and Fossil Shells*, John Weale, London.

Wray, C.G., Langer, M.R., DeSalle, R. *et al.* (1995) Origin of the foraminifera. *Proceedings of the National Academy of Sciences, U.S.A.* **92**, 141–5.

Wright, R.C. (1968) Miliolidae (Foraminiferos) recientes del estuario del Rio Quequen Grande (Prov. De Bs. As.). *Revista Museum Argentino Cienc. Nat., Hidrobiol.*, **2** (7), 225–56.

Wright, S.T. (1942) Statistical genetics and evolution. *Bulletin of the American Mathematical Society*, **48**, 223–46.

Yanko, V. (1989) *Quaternary Foraminifera of the Southern Seas of the USSR – Pontian-Caspian Region: Classification, Ecology, History, Environmental Reconstructions*, Unpubl. D. Sc. thesis, Moscow University, (in Russian).

Yanko, V. (1990a) Quaternary foraminifera of the Pontian-Caspian region. *Paleontological Journal*, **1**, 18–26 (in Russian).

Yanko, V. (1990b) Stratigraphy and paleogeography of marine Pleistocene and Holocene deposits of the southern seas of the USSR. *Mem. Soc. Geol. Ital.*, **44**, 167–87.

Yanko, V. (1993) The response of benthic foraminifera to pollution along Mediterranean coast of Israel. *Geological Society of America Annual Meeting, Abstracts with Programs*, p. A137.

Yanko, V. (1994) Problems in paleoceanography in the eastern Mediterranean: Late Quaternary foraminifera as a basis for tracing pollution sources. *Israeli Ministry of Science, Final Report #343294*, 275 pp.

Yanko, V. (1995) Benthic foraminifera as indicators of pollution in the eastern Mediterranean. *Rapport du XXXIVe Congres de la CIESM, Valletta-Malta*, p. 118.

Yanko, V. (ed) (1995) Benthic foraminifera as indicators of heavy metals pollution – a new kind of biological monitoring for the Mediterranean Sea. *European Commission, Program Avicenne, Annual Report, # AVI CT92–0007*, 270 pp.

Yanko, V. (1996a) Use of benthic foraminifera for the monitoring of trace metals pollution along northern Israeli shelf. *Second International Symposium on Eastern Mediterranean Geology, Jerusalem-Israel, Abstracts Volume*, p. 27.

Yanko, V. (1996b) Benthic foraminifera as indicators of heavy metals, fuel ash and domestic sewage pollution. *The Ecosystem of the Gulf of Aqaba in Relation to the Enhanced Economical Development and the Peace Process~III. Eilat-Israel, Abstracts Volume*.

Yanko, V. (ed) (1996) Benthic foraminifera as indicators of heavy metals pollution – a new kind of biological monitoring for the Mediterranean Sea. *European Commission, Program Avicenne, Final Report, # AVI CT92–0007*, 167 pp.

Yanko, V. (1997) Benthic foraminifera as bioindicators of stress environment: anthropogenic problems – foraminiferal solution. *First International Conference on Applications of Micropaleontology in Environmental Sciences, June 15–20, 1997, Tel Aviv, Israel, Program and Abstracts*, p. 117.

Yanko, V. (1998) Recent foraminifera of the Black Sea, the Sea of Azov, the Caspian Sea, and the Aral Sea, in *Forams '98 (International Symposium on Foraminifera) Proceedings and Abstracts*, (eds J.F. Longoria and M.A. Gamper), Special Publication, Sociedad Mexicana de Paleontologia, pp. 116–7.

Yanko, V., Ahmad, M. and Kaminski, M. (1998) Morphological deformities of benthic foraminiferal tests in response to pollution by heavy metals: implications for pollution monitoring. *Journal of Foraminiferal Research*, **28**, 177–200.

Yanko, V., Arnold, A. and Bresler V. (1995) Morphological abnormalities in foraminiferal tests: response to heavy metal pollution along the Israeli coast, eastern Mediterranean. *Geological Society of America Annual Meeting, Abstracts with Programs*, p. A244.

Yanko, V., Bresler, V. and Hallock, P. (1994a) Defense and transport systems against xenobiotics in some benthic foraminifera. *Israeli Journal of Zoology*, **40**, 114.

Yanko V., Cita, M.B., Meric, E. *et al.* (1994b) Study of the eastern Mediterranean coastal environment: The framework of the Avicenne International Program. *Annual Symp. on the eastern Mediterranean Margin of Israel, Haifa-Israel, Abstracts Volume*, pp. 25–7.

Yanko, V. and Flexer A. (1991) Benthic foraminiferal assemblages as indicators of pollution (on example of the north-western shelf of the Black Sea). *Third Annual Symposium on the Mediterranean margin of Israel, Institute Oceanography and Limnology, Haifa-Israel, Abstracts Volume*, 5 pp.

Yanko, V. and Flexer A. (1992) Microfauna as possible indicators of hydrocarbon Seepages. Method for oil-gas trap reconnaissance. *Israel Geological Society Annual Meeting, Ashkelon-Israel, Abstracts Volume*, pp. 169–70.

References

Yanko, V., Flexer A., Kress, N. et al (1992) Benthic Foraminifera as indicators of heavy metal pollution in Israel's eastern Mediterranean margin. *French-Israeli Symposium on The Continental Margin of the Mediterranean Sea*, pp. 73–9.

Yanko, V. and Kravchuk, O. (1992) Morphology and anatomy of framboidal iron sulfides in foraminiferal tests and marine sediments. *Israel Geological Society Annual Meeting, Ashkelon-Israel, Abstracts Volume*, pp. 171–2.

Yanko, V. and Kravchuk, O. (1996) Geoecological situation and specifics of sedimentation process in Haifa Bay (in Russian), in *Geoecology of Recreation Zones of Ukraine*, (ed M. Tolstoy), 'Astroprint', pp. 174–6.

Yanko, V. and Kronfeld, J. (1992) Low and high magnesian calcitic tests of benthic foraminifera chemically mirror morphological deformations. *IV International Conference on Paleoceanography, Kiel-Germany, Abstracts Volume*, p. 308.

Yanko, V. and Kronfeld, J. (1993) Trace metal pollution affects the carbonate chemistry of benthic foraminiferal shell. *Israel Society for Ecology and Environmental Quality Sciences, 24th Annual Meeting, Tel Aviv, Israel, Abstracts Volume.*

Yanko, V., Kronfeld, J. and Flexer, A. (1994c) Response of benthic foraminifera to various pollution sources: Implications for pollution monitoring. *Journal of Foraminiferal Research*, **24**, 1–17.

Yanko, V.V. and Troitskaja, T.S. (1987) *Pozdnechetverticnie foraminiferi Chernogo Morja*, Nauka, Moscow.

Zachos, J.C., Scott, L.D. and Lohmann, K.C. (1994) Evolution of early Cenozoic marine temperatures. *Paleoceanography*, **9**, 353–87.

Zahn, R., Winn, K. and Sarnthein, M. (1986) Benthic foraminiferal $\delta^{13}C$ and accumulation rates of organic carbon: *Uvigerina peregrina* group and *Cibicidoides wuellerstorfi*. *Paleoceanography*, **1**, 27–42.

Zalesny, E. R. (1959) Foraminiferal ecology of Santa Monica Bay, California. *Micropaleontology*, **5**, 101–26.

Zaninetti, L., Brönnimann, P., Dias-Brito, D. et al. (1979) Distribution écologique des foraminifères dans la Mangrove d'Acupe, État de Bahia, Brésil. *Notes de Laboratoire de Paléontologie de l'Université de Genève*, **4**, 1–17.

Zech, L. (1964) Zytochemische Messungen an den Zellkernen der Foraminiferen *Patellina corrugata* und *Rotaliella Heterocaryotica*. *Archiv für Protistenkunde*, **107**, 295–330.

Zhang, L., Liddell, W.D. and Martin, R.E. (1993) Hydraulic properties of foraminifera from shallow-water siliciclastic environments: A possible transport indicator in the stratigraphic record. *Geological Society of America Annual Meeting Abstracts with Programs*, **25**, A428.

Zieman, J.C. and Zieman, R.T. (1989) The ecology of seagrass meadows of the west coast of Florida: A community profile. *U.S. Fish and Wildlife Service Biological Report*, **85** (7.25), 155 pp.

Zinsmeister, W.J. and Feldmann, R.M. (1984) Cenozoic high latitude heterochroneity of southern hemisphere marine faunas. *Science*, **224**, 281–3.

Zumwalt, G.S. and DeLaca, T.E. (1980) Utilization of brachiopod feeding currents by epizoic Foraminifera. *Journal of Paleontology*, **54**, 477–84.

General Index

abnormal tests
 chemistry, 232
 morphology, 226–231, Fig. 13.2
 pollution as cause, 226–230
abrasion, in taphonomy, 285–286, 292
Acadian fauna/province, 99–100
adenosine triphosphate, *see* ATP
Adriatic Sea, 204, Table 12.2
advection, water, 5, 119, 120, 245
agamont, 48, 49, 51, 52, 54, 55, Fig. 3.14
Alabama, 150
Alaska, 100, 102, 152, 154
Aleutian fauna/province, 98, 100
alkali metals, 276
alkalinity, 127, 131, 134, 171, 247, 260, 269, 284–285, 287, 290
ALSCAL, 83
alternation of generations, 4, 37, 48–49, 51, 54, Table 3.1
Amazon Shelf, 156
amino acid racemization, dating technique, 286, 287
anaerobic, 162, 163, 166, 172, 178, 184, 201, 211, 231
analysis of variance (ANOVA), 85
angular data, 72
anlage, 45, 46, 47, 232, Fig. 3.10
anoxia/anoxic, 43, 142, 154, 163, 164, 166, 167, 171, 176, 178, 183, 196, 198, 201–214, 215, 216, Fig. 10.2, Tables 12.1, 12.2
Antarctic
 Bottom Water (AABW), 5, 186
 fauna/province, 94, 100
 seas, 45, 83, 94, 98, 100, 109, 154, 184, 186, 209, 210, 269
anthropogenic effects, 137–139, 184, 201, 204, 215, 276, 287, Table 12.2; *see also* pollution
antitropicality, 117
apogamic, 51, 52, Table 3.1
apparent oxygen utilization, 253
aquaculture, 204
 foraminiferal response, 220–222
Arabian Sea, 212, 247, Table 12.2
aragonite, 4, 15, 17, 19, 22, 32, 33, 58, 59, 65–67, 138, 248, 253, 255, 262, 265, 267, 274, 286
aragonitic wall, *see* wall, aragonitic
Arctic
 fauna/province, 94, 97, 98, 100, Fig. 6.3
 Ocean, 94, 97, 98, 100, 111, 154, 184
Argentina, 153
Atlantic
 Northern Inner Shelf fauna/province, 98, 100, Figs. 6.3, 6.4
 Northern Outer Shelf and Slope fauna/province, 100, Figs. 6.3, 6.4
 Ocean, 5, 94, 97, 98, 100, 102, 109, 111, 116, 117, 118, 119, 120, 121, 129, 132, 134, 139, 143, 153–154, 155, 182, 183, 186, 188, 192, 195, 218, 239, 260, 267, 269, 274, 294, Figs. 11.2, 11.3
 Southern Shelf fauna/province, 99, 100, Figs. 6.3, 6.4

atmospheric CO_2, 252

GENERAL INDEX

atmospheric vapor, 243–244, Fig. 14.3
ATP, 39, 125, 207, 209
Australia, 134, 135, 136, 139, 156, 158
autogamous, 53, 54

bacteria, 6, 39, 40, 42, 43, 126, 132, 136, 162, 163, 168, 172, 174, 177, 178, 181, 185, 195, 198, 203, 207, 210, 217, 221, 225, 231, Fig. 12.5, Table 12.2
bacterial mat/film, 6, 132, 168–169, 203, 207
Bahamas, 98, 135, 158
Baja California, Table 12.2
Baltic Sea, 150
barium, 267–269, Figs. 15.1, 15.3, Table 15.1
Belau, 130, 133, 135
Berger-Heath bioturbation model, see bioturbation, Berger-Heath (box) model
Bermuda, 94
bilamellar wall, see wall, bilamellar
binary fission, 51, 52, Table 3.1
biodiffusion, 282
bioerosion, 285, 286, 292
biogeographic province, 5, 6, 96, 153–154
biogeography, 93–102, 103–122, Figs. 6.1–6.4, 7.3, 7.4, 7.6
bioturbation, 164, 171, 172, 174, 178, 209, 281–285, 287, 288, 289, 290, 292, 295, 297
analytical versus numerical models, 295–296
Berger-Heath (box) model, 282–284, 293, 294, 295
Guinasso-Schink model, 282, 288, 295
pore-water chemistry, 284–285, 292
size-selective feeding, 284
bipolarity, 117
birds, transport by, 152–153
Black Sea, 108, 152, 218, 223, 226, 231, Fig. 9.5
boron, 273, Fig. 15.1, Table 15.1
Brazil, 148, 150, 153, 156, 157
British Columbia, 146
budding, 51, 52, Table 3.1

C_3 and C_4 plants, 252
cadmium, 259, 260, 266–267, Figs. 15.1–15.3, Table 15.1
calcification, 44, 45–48, 58, 59, 67, 124, 126–129, 134, 135, 137, 139, 176, 177, 228, 230, 231, 232, 234, 247, 248, 253, 254, 256, 257, 260–261, 262, 270, 276
calcite
dissolution, 33, 104, 106, 129, 137, 186, 215, 221, 226, 267, 269, 285–286, 287, 289, 292–295, gametogenic, 247
high-Mg, 19, 22, 27, 33, 58, 131, 134, Fig. 2.8

incorporation of trace elements, 261–264 spicules, 15, 19, 22, 28, 33, 57–58, Figs. 2.9, 4.1
calcium, 259, 261–262, Fig. 15.1, Table 15.1
California, 149
borderland basins, Table 12.2
continental slope, Table 12.2
Californian fauna/province, 98, Fig. 6.3
Cambrian, 3, 33, 37
Canada, 146, 149, 154, 156, 184, 221
canal system, 32, 61, 63, 64, 65, 131, 132, 133, Figs. 4.6, 4.11, 4.15
Cape Hatteras, faunal boundary, 153–154
carbon cycle, see global carbon cycle
carbon isotopes, 6, 164–165, 176–177, 239, 241–242, 248–255, 257, Figs. 14.4–14.6, Tables 14.1, 14.3
disequilibrium, 253–254
fractionation, 253–255
global shifts, 252–253
gradients, 249–252
carbon–14 dating, see radiocarbon dating
carbonate ion concentration, 247–248, 255
carbonate production, 123, 129, 138
Carboniferous, 33
Caribbean Sea, 5, 94, 97, 98, 105, 129, 130, 131, 132, 133, 134–135, 136, 155, 156, 157, 218, Table 8.1
carnivory, 39, 42, 44
Carolinian fauna/province, 99, Fig. 6.3
Caspian Sea, 218, 223
catalase, Fig. 12.5
Cenozoic, 102, 108, 114, 115, 116–117, 121, 259
centers of origin, 100–102
Challenger expedition/report, 5, 10, 94
chamber formation/construction, 45–48, 57–70, Figs. 3.10, 4.1–4.17
chamber wall, see wall
Chesapeake Bay, 149, 158, 204
China, 134
chloroplast, 43, 45, 123, 139, 210–211, Figs. 8.2, 12.5
classification, 7–36, Figs. 2.1–2.11, Tables 2.1–2.3
by Brady, 10
by Carpenter et al., 10
by Cushman, 11–14
by d'Orbigny, 7, 10, 18
by Galloway, 11
by Haynes, Table 2.2
by Jones, 10
by Lee, Table 2.2
by Lister, 10
by Loeblich and Tappan, 14, 15–19, Fig. 2.7, Table 2.2
by Rauzer-Chernousova and Fursenko, 15
by Reiss, 15

GENERAL INDEX

by Reuss, 10
revised (Loeblich and Tappan), 16–33, Figs. 2.8, 2.9, Table 2.2
clathrates, 248, 258
cluster analysis (CA), 74–77, 80, 96, 97, Fig. 5.1
CO_2
 atmospheric, 252
 metabolic, 246, 254, 255
coal and fuel ash pollution, foraminiferal response, 225
coastal marsh, *see* salt marsh
coccolithophorids, 284
coefficient, 76, 77, 84, 85
cold-water benthic faunas, 94, Figs. 6.1, 6.2
Colombia, 148
communalities, 80
compaction of sediments, 295, 296
competition, 172–174, 197
Connecticut, 147
conservative elements, 260–261
copper, 276, Fig. 15.1, Table 15.1
coral reefs, 133, 138, 139, 156–157
Cortez fauna/province, 98
Cretaceous, 17, 19, 27, 32, 33, 102, 114, 121
currents, effect on latitudinal provinces, 112, 119
cyst, 39, 40, 42, 45, 46, 47, 209
cytology, effect of pollution, 230–231, 232–234

dysoxia/dysoxic, 171, 177, 178, 202–209, 211–216, Fig. 10.2, Tables 12.1, 12.2

East African fauna/province, 94
East Indian fauna/province, 94
ecotone, planktonic, 119
Ecuador, 148
eigenvalue, 77, 78, 79, 82, Table 5.2
eigenvector, 77–82, 83
Elphidium-Ammonia association, 155
El Salvador, Table 12.2
encystment, *see* cyst
endemism, 5, 96, 114, Fig. 7.6
endoplasmic reticulum, 211, Fig. 12.5
English Channel, 154–155
Eocene, 33, 59, 138, 296
epifluorescence microscopy, 207, Fig. 12.4
estuaries and lagoons, 138, 148–153, 183, 212, 214, 218, 219, 221, 223, 224, 226, 228
euclidean distance, 76, 77, 83
euphotic/photic zone, 39, 42, 43, 45, 108, 109, 110, 124, 130, 132, 133, 161, 181, 182, 197, 211, 293
eutrophication, 138, 201, 204, 216, 221
evaporation, 242–243, Fig. 14.2
extinction, 33, 103, 114, 115, 116, 118, 121, 122, 172, 217, 234, 282–283, 287, 296, 297

$\delta^{13}C$ gradients, 249–252
data transformation, types of, Table 5.1
deconvolution, sedimentary signals, 295–296
deep-water age, 251–252
deformity, pollution as cause, *see* abnormal tests, pollution as a cause
dendrogram, 74, 76, 77, Fig. 5.1
deposit feeding, 39, 42
depth distribution/zonation, 4, 97, 100, 109–111, 114, 130, 131–135, 153–155, 156, 157, 183, 185, 196, 247, 255
diatom, 40, 42, 43, 44, 123, 124, 130, 134, 142, 171, 223, 225
dimorphism, 4, 48, 51, 54, 55, Table 3.1; *see also* alternation of generations
dinoflagellates, 123, 136–137, Figs. 8.2, 8.3
diploid, 48, 51
discriminant function analysis (DFA), 83–84, 192, Figs. 5.7, 11.6, Table 5.4
dispersal, 100–102, 117, 134, 152–153, 157, 158
dissolved organic carbon (DOC), 39, 43
Drammensfjord, Table 12.2
dredging, foraminiferal response, 225–226
dysaerobic, 202

f ratio, 182
factor analysis (FA), 74, 77, 80–82
facultative anaerobes, 164, 207–209
fertilization, 48, 51, 53, 54, Table 3.1
filopodia, 38
first appearance datum (FAD), 284
Florida, 94, 98, 135, 138, 139, 148, 158, 186, 296
fluoride, 272–273, Fig. 15.1, Table 15.1
food supply, benthic foraminifers, 171–172, 196–197, Fig. 10.9
food vacuole, 39, Figs. 3.4, 3.7
food web/chain, 129, 181, 230
foraminal plate, 63–65, Fig. 4.12
foraminiferal assemblages in sediment, temporal resolution, 281–298, Figs. 16.1–16.6
foraminiferal preservation and temporal resolution
 carbonate sediments, 285–286, 294
 deep sea, 282, 284, 288, 289, 290, 292–295, 296, 297
 marshes, 287–290, 296, Fig. 16.5
 shelf and slope, 290–292, 297
 tidal flats, 286–287
foraminiferal response to pollution, *see* pollution, foraminiferal response
fractals, 296; *see also* rescaled-range analysis

GENERAL INDEX

France, 222
fresh-water Foraminifera, 153
Frierfjord, Table 12.2

gamete, 19, 23, 44, 48, 51, 52–53, 54, 55, 247, Table 3.1
 amoeboid, 19, 23, 52, 53, 54, Table 3.1
 biflagellated, 19, 23, 48, 52, 53, 54, Fig. 3.15, Table 3.1
 triflagellated, 52, 53, Table 3.1
gametogamous, 48, 52, 53, Table 3.1
gamic, 51, 52, Table 3.1
gamont, 48, 49, 51, 52, 53, 54, 55, Fig. 3.14, Table 3.1
gamontogamous, 53, 54, Table 3.1
gas-hydrates, 248
gene flow and planktonic biogeography, 113, 116, 117, 119
genotypes, biogeography of, 119
Georgia, 72, 87, 145, 146, 147, 155
global carbon cycle, 248–249, Figs. 14.4, 14.6
global change, 116, 137–139, 287, Fig. 8.5
glycolysis, 211
glycosaminoglycans, 45, 128
Grand Banks, 87, 100
granular wall, *see* wall, granular
granuloreticulopodia, 18, 37, *see also* reticulopodia
grazing, 39, 40, 43
Great Barrier Reef, 156
Greece, 222
green algae, 123, 134–135, 138
growth, 45–48
Guinasso-Schink bioturbation model, *see* bioturbation, Guinasso-Schink model
Gulf of Aqaba, 129–130, 132, 133, 136, 156, 157
Gulf of California, 83, 287, Table 12.2
Gulf of Maine, 192
Gulf of Mexico, 82, 97, 98, 100, 146, 151, 155, 156, 158, 186, 196, 197, 204, 214, 216, 218, 284, 290, Figs. 6.3, 6.4, 12.6, Table 12.2
 hydrocarbon seeps, 98, 100, Figs. 6.3, 6.4
 Inner Shelf fauna/province, 98, 100, Figs. 6.3, 6.4
 Outer Shelf and Slope fauna/province, 100, Figs. 6.3, 6.4
Gulf of Trieste, 155

haploid, 49, 51
Hawaii, 152
heavy metal pollution, foraminiferal response, 223–225
heteroscedasticity, 85
heterothalamy, 55

historical factors, 94, 103–104, 106, 110, 113–117, 120–121
Hudson River estuary, 151
hydrocarbon pollution, foraminiferal response, 222–223
hydrocarbon seep/vent, 6, 203, Fig. 12.6, Table 12.2
hydrogen sulfide, 152, 161, 203, 207, 209, 210, 211, 215, 223, 231, Fig. 12.3
hydrogenosome, 211
hydrothermal vent, 6
hypersaline environments, 106, 135, 151, 158
hypoxic, 202

ice volume, 239, 244–245
imperforate wall, *see* wall, imperforate
India, 151, 223, 225
Indian Ocean, 94, 109–118, 132, 133, 136, 156, 158, 183, 186, 198, 218, 239, 270, 293
Indo-Pacific area, 94, 129, 130, 131, 132, 133, 134, 135, 136, Table 8.1
inner continental shelves, 5, 98, 100, 110, 153–156, Figs. 6.3, 6.4
inner organic lining (IOL), 45, 46, Fig. 3.11
instar, 62
interlocular spaces, 61–63, Figs. 4.7, 4.8
Ireland, 94
iron, 276, Fig. 15.1, Table 15.1
isotope fractionation, 241, 242, *see also* under carbon isotopes and oxygen isotopes
isotope stratigraphy, 239, Fig. 14.1
Israel, 129–130, 132, 133, 136, 156, 157, 184, 221, 225
Italy, 151, 155, 175, 216, 224, 228
iterative evolution, 114, 115, 121

Japan, 153, 156, Table 12.2
Jurassic, 19, 32, 66, 117

Kendall's horseshoe, 78
Kriging, 72, 88, 89

lagoons, *see* estuaries and lagoons
lamellar wall, *see* wall, lamellar
larger foraminifers, 42, 43, 123, 129–136, 137–139, 156, 158, Figs. 8.1, 8.4, 8.5, Table 8.1
last appearance datum (LAD), 284
life cycle, 38, 48–55, Fig. 3.14, Table 3.1
life position, 40, 168–169, 207, Fig. 12.4
linear regression, 83
lithium, 273, Fig. 15.1, Table 15.1
loadings, 77, 78, 79, 80, 83, 86
Louisiana, 146, 150, 222, 290, Table 12.2

GENERAL INDEX

Lusitanian fauna/province, 94
lysocline, 104, 267, 269, 292, 294

macrofaunal province, 98–99
Madang Lagoon, 212, 214
magnesium, 259, 260, 270–272, Figs. 15.1, 15.4, Table 15.1
Maine, 102, 143, 146, Fig. 9.3
manganese, 260, 275, Fig. 15.1, Table 15.1
mangrove swamps, 148, Fig. 9.1
marginal marine environments, 141–159, Figs. 9.1–9.6, Table 9.1
marsh, *see* salt marsh
Massachusetts, 143–145, 146
mating types, 54
McMurdo Sound, 154, Table 12.2
Mediterranean
  fauna/province, 94
  Sea, 38, 94, 107, 108, 152, 155, 157, 171, 178, 186, 218, 221, 224, 226, 256
megalospheric test, 48, 51, 54, Table 3.1
meiosis, 48–49, 51, 52, 54
metabolic CO_2, 246, 254, 255
metabolic rate, 246, 254
Mexico, 151
microaerophiles, 202, 211, 214
microelectrode, 207, Fig. 12.3
microhabitat, 5, 6, 37, 43, 145, 146–148, 161–179, 192, 196, 197, 198, 204–207, 253, 256, 257, 292, 295, Figs. 10.1–10.9
microoxic, 202
microspheric test, 48, 51, 54, Table 3.1
microtubules, 38, 39
microxia/microxic, 163, 171, 177, 178, 201–209, 211–216, Tables 12.1, 12.2
Miocene, 33, 102, 116, 134, 186, 252, 288
Mississippi River delta, 138, 186, 290
mitochondria, 39, 45, 70, 211, 214, 225, 233, Fig. 12.5
mixotrophic nutrition, 129
monocrystalline wall, *see* wall, monocrystalline
monolamellar test, 45, 46
monolamellar wall, *see* wall, monolamellar
Monte Carlo technique, 77
Monterey Formation, 252
Moorea, 212
morphogenesis, 45–48
morphogroup/morphotype, 6, 117, 119, 121, 174–176, 190–192, 196, 215
morphological deformities, distribution, 226–230
multicollinearity, 85
multidimensional scaling (MDS), 74, 82–83, Fig. 5.6
multiple broods, 52

neodymium, 274–275, Fig. 15.1, Table 15.1
  isotopes, 274–275
Neogene, 102, 114, 116
New York Bight, 204
New Zealand, 148, 149, 152, 156, 185, Fig. 9.4
nitrate, 163, 172, 182, 251, Fig. 10.8
non-lamellar wall, *see* wall, non-lamellar
North Atlantic Deep Water (NADW), 5, 186, 266, 269
North Sea, 155, 207, 222
Norway, 186, 196, 204, 215, 224, 228, Fig. 12.6, Table 12.2
Nova Scotia, 149, Table 12.2
Nova Scotian fauna/province, 100
nuclear dimorphism, 51, 54, Table 3.1
nutrients, 43, 106, 108, 110, 117, 120, 124–126, 129, 130, 137–138, 142, 156, 203, 204, 216, 221, 222, 223, 225, 231, 252, 257, 259, 260, 265–269

Okinawa, 130, 134
Oligocene, 59, 274, 288, 296
OMZ, *see* Oxygen Minimum Zone
ontogeny, 11, 109, 111, 246, 255, 256
opportunism, response to pollution, 226
ordinary least squares (OLS), 85
Ordovician, 33
Oregon, 83
Oregonian fauna/province, 98, Fig. 6.3
organic carbon supply, 181–182
organic matter, 2, 5, 40, 43, 57, 124, 128, 129, 134, 161, 162, 163, 171, 172, 176, 177, 178, 179, 181, 182, 183, 184, 185, 186, 188, 192, 194, 195, 196, 197, 198, 219, 220, 231, 233, 248, 249, 250, 252, 254, 264, 284, 286, 287, 290, 292, 293
  degradation, 40, 162–163, 172, 178, 188
  flux to the seafloor, 163, 178, 182–183, 192–193
  seasonality, 192–193
  labile, 5, 163, 171, 172, 178, 182, 183, 184, 185, 190, 194, 195, 196, 197, 198, 290
organic median layer, 59
Orinoco-Paria shelf, 204
Oslo Fjord, Fig. 12.6
oxic, 152, 162, 163, 164, 166, 174, 177, 178, 179, 196, 202, 203, 215, 290, Fig. 10.2, Tables 12.1, 12.2
oxidation, in sediment, 184, 285, 287, 289, 292, 293
oxygen
  bottom water, 5, 43, 45, 171, 177–179, 185, 186, 190, 201–204
  isotopes, 6, 239–248, 259, 262, 288, Figs. 14.1–14.3, Tables 14.1, 14.2
    disequilibrium, 246
    fractionation, 241, 242, 243, 245–248

GENERAL INDEX

Oxygen Minimum Zone (OMZ), 5, 190, 202–203, 212, 215, 254, Figs. 12.2, 12.6, Table 12.2

Pacific Ocean, 94, 97, 98, 109, 111, 117, 118, 129, 130, 131, 132, 133, 134, 136, 139, 155, 156, 158, 182, 183, 186, 188, 190, 198, 218, 239, 260, 267, 269, 274, 294, 295, Fig. 11.3, Table 8.1
Pacific Rim, 146, Table 9.1
paleoceanography, 6, 114, 130, 164–165, 176, 177–179, 185, 216, 239, 242, 256, 259, 260, 266, 270, 275–276, 292
Paleogene, 33, 79, 114, 131
Paleozoic, 33, 48, 157
Panama Isthmus, 117, 118
Panamanian fauna/province, 94, 98, Fig. 6.3
Papua New Guinea, 158, 212
parallel evolution, 15
parasitism, 39, 42–43
particle reactive elements, 261
patchiness of distribution, 114, 118, 120, 146, 153, 196
pathogenesis, 230–231
Pearson's correlation coefficient, 76, 77
peduncle, 38
Permian, 67, 114
peroxisome, 211, Fig. 12.5
Persian Gulf, 158
Peru-Chile Trench, Table 12.2
pesticides, foraminiferal response, 225
pH, 218, 222, 223, 248, 253, 262, 264, 269, 273
phosphate, 108, 109, 185, 186, 251, 259, 260, 266
photic levels, 108, 109, 110, 117, 221, 226
photic zone, see euphotic/photic zone
photosynthesis, 44–45, 123, 124–126, 128, 129, 135, 137, 139, 248, 249, 254–255, Fig. 14.4
phytodetritus, 5, 39, 42, 172, 177, 179, 183, 195, 197, 198
phytodetritus feeders, 172, 179
planktonic/benthic (P/B) ratio, 188–190
planktonic foraminifers, 3, 6, 10, 15, 19, 22, 23, 37, 42, 43, 44, 46, 47, 48, 52, 65, 70, 103–122, 123, 129, 136–137, 139, 188, 221, 239, 245, 246, 247, 253, 256, 257, 264, 266, 267, 269, 270, 272, 273, 276, 290, 292, 293, 294, 295, Figs. 2.5, 2.8, 7.1–7.4, 7.6
abundance, 104, 105, 106, 108–109
biogeography, 103–122, Figs. 7.3, 7.4, 7.6
diversity gradient, 103, 111–117, 121
genetic isolation, 114, 116, 118–119, 120
plasmotomy, 52, 53
plastogamy, 52, 53

Pleistocene, 102, 117, 239, 286, 287
Pliocene, 116, 117, 118, 134
Po Delta, 216
polar ordination, 87, 88
pollution, 6, 183–185, 215, 217–231, Figs. 13.1, 13.2, Table 13.1
effect on test texture, 230
foraminiferal response, 220–232, Fig. 13.2
research strategies for foraminiferal studies, 218–220
study locations, 218
ponticuli, 61, 65, Fig. 4.8
pore (test), 45, 46, 48, 55, Figs. 3.11, 3.12, 3.16
formation of, 58, 59, 69–70
size, 107–108, 214, Fig. 7.1
pore water (sediment), 5, 126, 143, 146, 169, 171, 176, 177, 178, 183, 186, 196, 207, 210, 246, 248, 261, 267, 275, 281–285, 292, 297
postoxic, 202, 209, Table 12.1
predation, 172–174
pressure, see water pressure
primary organic lining, 46
principal components analysis (PCA), 74, 77, 78–80, Figs. 5.2–5.5, 11.3, Tables 5.2, 5.3
productivity, 5, 108, 109, 110, 113, 120, 141, 142, 165, 176, 178, 182, 183, 184, 185, 186, 187, 188, 189, 190, 192, 193, 196, 197, 198, 199, 203, 220, 222, 249–252, 266, 290, 292, 295, Figs. 11.4, 11.5
proloculus, 48, 52, 54, 55
pseudopodia, 4, 7, 18, 37, 38–39, 40, 42, 45, 46, 47, 70, 132, 137, 156, 211, 214, Figs. 2.2, 3.1–3.3, 3.6
pseudopores, 70
Puerto Rico, 148
pulp and paper-mill pollution, foraminiferal response, 222
pycnocline, 107, 110, 117, 120
pyrite, 290
pyritization, as response to pollution, 231

Q-mode, 74, 76, 77, 78, 79, 80, 82, 83, 86, 87

R-mode, 74, 76, 77, 78, 79, 80, 82, 83, 86, 87
racemization, amino acid dating technique, 286, 287
radial wall, see wall, radial
radioactive waste, foraminiferal response, 225
radiocarbon dating, 286, 292, 293, 294, 296
rare earth elements, 276
recurrent group analysis, 87
red algae, 123, 135
Red Sea, 94, 256

GENERAL INDEX

reproduction, effect of pollution, 223, 225, 231–232
rescaled-range analysis, 296–297
respiration, 38, 39, 129, 182, 197, 202, 223, 225, 247, 249–251, 254
reticulopodia, 4, 18, 38, 39, Figs. 2.2, 3.6; *see also* pseudopodia
retral processes, 61, Fig. 4.8
reworking, 283, 284, 286, 287, 294
rhizopod, 37–38
Rose Bengal stain, 69–70, 155, 156, 166, 204, 212, 215, Table 12.2
Russian River estuary, 149

Sagami Bay, Table 12.2
salinity, 4, 5, 6, 106, 108, 109, 110, 113, 131, 134, 135, 136, 141, 143, 146, 148, 149, 150, 151, 152, 153, 155, 158, 183, 186, 218, 221, 226, 230, 231, 233, 239, 257, 264, 269, 272, Fig. 9.4
salt marsh, 141–148, 287–290, Figs. 9.1–9.3, Table 9.1
 grasses, 141, 142
Foraminifera
 as sea-level indicators, 146–148, 287–290, Fig. 16.5
 taphonomy, 146, 148, 287–290, Fig. 16.5
 widespread agglutinated species, 143, Fig. 9.2, Table 9.1
 zonation, 143–148
 organic matter, 142
 productivity, 142
 sediment, 142–143
San Diego Trough, Table 12.2
San Nicolas Basin, Table 12.2
San Pedro Basin, Table 12.2
Santa Barbara Basin, 45, 171, 207, 210, 214, 215, Figs. 7.2, 12.6, Table 12.2
Santa Catalina Basin, Table 12.2
Santa Cruz Basin, Table 12.2
Santa Monica Basin, Table 12.2
sapropel, 108, 171, 178
sarcode, 7, 38
schizont, 51, 54, Fig. 3.14
scores, 77, 79, 80, 83, 86, Figs. 5.3–5.5, 5.7, 11.3
scree plot, 78, 79, 80, Fig. 5.2
sea ice, 109, 184, 245
sea level, 137, 144, 146, 148, 239, 287, 289, 290, 292, 296, 297
seagrass, 135, 136, 157–158
sediment-water interface (SWI), 5, 40, 161–163, 164, 169, 171, 172, 175, 176–177, 178, 183, 190, 202, 212, 220, 284, 287, 290, 292, 293, 294, 296
Senegal, 155

sewage, foraminiferal response, 183–184, 185, 220–222
shell repair, 48
siliceous wall, *see* wall, siliceous
SLINK, 76, 77
sodium, 259, Fig. 15.1, Table 15.1
Sorby Principle, 286
South Carolina, 72
South China Sea, Table 12.2
Southern Ocean, 269
species
 diversity, 3, 87, 100, 103, 104, 108, 111–117, 119, 120, 121, 122, 129–130, 151–152, 153–154, 184, 194, 195, 197, 215–216, 217, 218, 221, 222, 223, 224, 225, 228, Figs. 9.5, 9.6
 duration, 121
 origination, 100–102, 104, 114–115
 pairs, 48
 standing stock, 108, 109, 166, 171, 174, 184, 188
 step-wise regression, 85, Fig. 5.9, Table 5.6
St. Lucia, 157
stratigraphic sections, continuity, 297
stratigraphic signal inputs, reconstruction, 295–296
strontium, 259, 272, 273–274, Figs. 15.1, 15.4, 15.5, Table 15.1
 isotopes, 273–274, Fig. 15.5
suboxic, 196, 202, 261, 273, 275, 290
subsutural canals, 61–63, Figs. 4.10, 4.11
sulfate reduction, 163, 172, 284, 287, 290
Sulu Sea, 177, Table 12.2
Sumatra, 148
surface mixed layer, sediments, 281, 282, 284, 285, 288, 290, 292, 293, 294, 295, Figs. 16.1, 16.2
Surian fauna/province, 98
suspension feeding, 39, 40, 43
Sweden, 150, 194
symbiont, 70, 123–124, 129, 246–247, 254–255, 256, Figs. 8.2, 12.5, Table 8.1
symbiosis, 43, 123, 124–129, 131, 135, 136, 137, 210

Tanner Basin, Table 12.2
taphonomic grade, 287
taphonomy, 33, 146–148, 184, 188, 190, 197, 215, 220, 221, 281–297, Figs. 16.1–16.6
temperature, 5, 6, 94, 100, 102, 105, 106–108, 110, 113, 114, 116, 117, 118, 136, 139, 142, 148, 149, 153, 155, 166, 183, 186, 218, 221, 225, 233, 239, 241, 245, 246, 247, 248, 253, 256, 260, 262, 264, 269, 270, 272, 276, 293, Fig. 14.5
test wall, *see* wall
Texas, 146, 150, 290
thermal pollution, foraminiferal response, 225

time-averaging, 281, 286, 287, 290, 292, 296–297, Fig. 16.6
circumvention, 296–297
scale, 296
toothplate, 15, 16, 19, 22, 29, 65
total organic carbon (TOC), 186, 224
trace elements, 259–276, Figs. 15.1–15.5, Table 15.1
abundance, 265
analysis, 264–265
as chemical proxies, 273
as diagenetic proxies, 275
as nutrient proxies, 265–266, Fig. 15.3
as paleoceanographic proxies, 260, 265–266, 269–270, 273
as physical proxies, 269–270
biological factors, 262, 264
culture studies, 262–264
incorporation, 261
thermodynamics, 261–262
transfer function, 86, 105–106, Fig. 5.8, Table 5.5
transition metals, 275–276
trend surface analysis, 86, 88
Triassic, 33
trimorphism, 51–52, Table 3.1
Trinidad, 148
trophic mechanisms, 39–45
Tunisia, 158

ultrastructure, 39, 45, 46, 58, 59, 67, 209–211, 230
umbilical cover plates, 63–65, Figs. 4.5, 4.6, 4.12–4.14
UPGMA, 76, 77
upwelling, 109, 112, 114, 118, 120, 252, 267, 276
uranium, 273, Fig. 15.1, Table 15.1
U.S. Gulf Coast, estuaries, 150

vanadium, 273, Fig. 15.1, Table 15.1
VARIMAX, 78, 79
Venice, 151
vertical distribution of species, substrate, 168–174, Figs. 10.3–10.8
vicariance, 102, 117
Virginian fauna/province, 100
vital effect, shell geochemistry, 6, 111, 254, 262, 286

wall
aragonitic, 15, 17, 19, 22, 32, 33, 65–67, Fig. 2.8
bilamellar, 15, 19, 22, 28, 30, 32, 46, 59–60, 66, 67–69, Figs. 2.8, 4.3, 4.4, 4.17
granular, 14, 15, 29, 30, 31, 59, Fig. 2.6
imperforate, 10, 14, 23, 26, 27, 28, 30, 33, 35, 58
lamellar, 22, 58–69
monocrystalline, 58
monolamellar, 15, 19, 22, 28, 59, Figs. 2.8, 4.2
non-lamellar, 58
radial, 14, 15, 29, 30, 31, 32, 35, 59, Figs. 2.5, 2.6
siliceous, 16–17, 18, 19, 32, 35, Fig. 2.8
Ward's minimum variance, 76, 77
warm-water benthic faunas, 94, 102, Figs. 6.1, 6.2
water mass, 5, 97, 100, 102
water pressure, 260, 267, 269, 272
West African fauna/province, 94
West Indian (Caribbean) fauna/province, 94, 98, 100, 102
Western Caroline Islands, 130, 134–135
western Africa, 151, 155, 186, Fig. 11.1

xanthosomes, 39, 40

Yucatan, 98

zinc, 275–276, Fig. 15.1, Table 15.1

Taxonomic Index

FORAMINIFERA

Acervulina, 31
A. inhaerens, 157
Acervulinacea, 31
Acervulinidae, 31
Adelosina cliarensis, 230, Fig. 13.2
A. intricata, Fig. 13.2
A. pulchella, Fig. 13.2
Adercotryma, 26, 214
A. glomerata, 209, Table 12.2
Agathistègues, Fig 2.3
Alabaminella weddellensis, 179, 192
Alliatina, 33
Allogromia, 23, 38
A. laticollaris, 48, 49, 52, 53, 54, 223, Fig. 2.9, Table 3.1
Allogromiida, 18, 19, 23, 33, Figs. 2.8, 2.9, Tables 2.2, 2.3
Allogromiidae, 19, 208, 209, 212, 215, Table 2.1
Allogromina, 15, Fig. 2.7
Allomorphina, 31
Alveolinacea, 28
Alveolinella, 28, 156
A. quoyi, 134, Fig. 8.1, Table 8.1
Alveolinellidae, Table 2.1
Alveolinidae, 28, 43, 123, 129, 134, Table 8.1
Alveophragmium, 26
Ammoastuta, 26, 150
Ammobaculites, 26, 149, 150, 158
A. crassus, 149, 224, Table 13.1

A. exiguus, Table 9.1
A. salsus, Table 13.1
Ammocibicides, 26
Ammodiscacea, 15, 23
Ammodiscidae, 23, Table 2.1
Ammodiscus, 11, 23, 212, Fig. 2.9
A. gullmarensis, Table 12.2
Ammoflintina, 23
Ammoglobigerina, 26
Ammolagena, 23
Ammomarginulina, 26
A. fluvialis, 151, Table 13.1
Ammomassilina, 27
Ammonia, 32, 38, 63, 64, 68, 149, 151, 153, 154, 155, 212, 224, Fig. 4.12
A. annectens, Table 13.1
A. beccarii, 42, 143, 148, 149, 151, 154, 155, 208, 212, 223, 289, Figs. 2.9, 9.4, Tables 9.1, 13.1
A. caspica, Table 13.1
A. dentata, Table 13.1
A. parkinsoniana, 143, 145, 151, 212, 214, 216, Fig. 12.6, Table 12.2
A. sobrina, Table 13.1
A. tepida, 45, 51, 54, 145, 148, 151, 155, 157, 223, 226, 230, 231, 232, Figs. 3.10, 3.12, 13.2, Tables 3.1, 13.1
Ammosphaeroidinidae, 26
Ammotium, 26, 148, 150
A. cassis, 149, 150, 214
A. fragile, 149, Fig. 9.4

TAXONOMIC INDEX

A. salsum, 143, 145, 148, 151, 289, Figs. 9.2, 9.3, Table 9.1
Amphicoryna, 28, Fig. 2.4
Amphisorus, 28, 70, 136
A. hemprichii, 46, 136, 157, Fig. 8.2, Table 8.1
Amphistegina, 31, 69, 70, 126, 128, 131–132, 139, 156, 157, 158, 286, 294, Fig. 2.1, Tables 2.1, 8.1
A. bicirculata, 132
A. gibbosa, 42, 51, 131–132, Table 3.1
A. lessonii, 79, 131–132, 134, 156, 157, Fig. 8.1
A. lobifera, 46, 131–132, 156, 230–231, Table 13.1
A. papillosa, 132
A. radiata, 132
Amphisteginidae, 31, 43, 124, 129, 131–132, Fig. 8.4, Table 8.1
Androsina, 135
A. lucasi, 135, 158
Angulogerina, 29
Annulopatellina, 30
Annulopatellinacea, 30
Annulopatellinidae, 30
Anomalinidae, Table 2.1
Anomalinoides, Fig. 2.1
Archaias, 28, 126, 135, 286, Fig. 2.1
A. angulatus, 135, 157, 158, 285, 286, Figs. 8.1, 8.2
Archaiasinae, 123, 129, 134, Table 8.1
Arenoparrella, 26, 148
A. mexicana, 143, 145, 147, 148, 290, Fig. 9.2
Articulina, 28
Assilina, 133
A. ammonoides, 133
Astacolus, 28, Fig. 2.1
Asterigerina, 31, 61, Fig. 4.9
A. carinata, 155
Asterigerinacea, 31, Fig. 2.1
Asterigerinidae, 31, 123
Asterorotalia, 32
Astrammina rara, 42, 45, 52, Fig. 2.2
Astrononion, 31, 63, 212, Fig. 4.14, Table 12.2
A. gallowayi, 154
Astrorhiza, 23
A. limicola, 40, 42, 208, 212, 214
Astrorhizacea, 23
Astrorhizida, 19, 23, 33, Figs. 2.8, 2.9, Tables 2.2, 2.3
Astrorhizidae, 10, 23, Table 2.1
Ataxophragmiacea, 26
Baculogypsina, 32, 133, 156
B. sphaerulata, 133, 156, Table 8.1
Baculogypsinoides, 133, Table 8.1
B. spinosus, Table 8.1
Baggina, 30

Bagginidae, 30
Bathysiphon, 23, 212
B. filiformis, 185, Table 12.2
Bdelloidina, 26
Beella, 32
B. digitata, Fig. 7.3
Berggrenia, 32
Bigenerina, 27
Biloculinella, 27
Bolivina, 29, 151, 174, 177, 212, 214, Fig. 9.4
B. albatrossi, Fig. 12.6, Table 12.2
B. argentea, Table 12.2
B. dilatata, 174, Table 12.2
B. interjuncta, Table 12.2
B. lowmani, Fig. 2.9
B. ordinaria, Table 12.2
B. pacifica, Table 12.2
B. rankini, Table 12.2
B. seminuda, 216, Table 12.2
B. spathulata, 174, Table 12.2
B. spissa, Table 12.2
B. subadvena, Table 12.2
B. subaenariensis, Table 12.2
B. vaughani, Table 13.1
Bolivinacea, 29
Bolivinellidae, 29
Bolivinella, 29
Bolivinita, 29
Bolivinitacea, 29
Bolivinitidae, 29
Bolivinopsis, 214
B. cubensis, Table 12.2
Bolliella, 32
B. adamsi, Fig. 7.3
Borelis, 28, 134, 156, 157, Fig. 2.1
B. pulchra, 134
Brizalina, 212, Table 12.2
B. pseudopunctata, 154
B. striatula, 155
Broeckina, 135
B. discoidea, 135
B. orbitolitoides, 135
Buccella frigida, 149, Fig. 9.4, Table 13.1
B. inusitata, 154
B. mansfieldi, 287
Bulimina, 7, 29, 155, 174, 177, 212
B. aculeata, 169, 192, Table 12.2
B. alazanensis, 5, 192, Fig. 11.5
B. elongata, Table 12.2
B. exilis, Table 12.2
B. inflata, 174

TAXONOMIC INDEX

B. marginata, 169, 174, 183, 192, 207–208, 209, Figs. 10.7, 10.8, 12.6, Table 12.2
B. marginata denudata, Table 13.1
B. mexicana, 193, Fig. 11.5
B. striata, Table 13.1
B. subornata, Table 13.1
B. translucens, Fig. 11.5
Buliminacea, 15, 29, 35
Buliminella, 29, 212
B. elegantissima, 155, 183, Table 13.1
B. morgani, 216, Table 12.2
B. tenuata, 210, 211, Figs. 12.5, 12.6, Table 12.2
Buliminellidae, 29
Buliminida, 16, 17, 19, 33, 35, 59–60, 65, Figs. 2.8, 2.9, Tables 2.2, 2.3
Buliminidae, 11, 29, Table 2.1

Calcarina, 32, 133, 136, 156, Fig. 2.1, Table 8.1
C. gaudichaudii, 133, Fig. 8.1
C. hispida, Fig. 8.2
C. spengleri, 156
Calcarinidae, 42, 43, 124, 126, 129, 131, 133–134, Fig. 8.4, Tables 2.1, 8.1
Calcituba, 27
C. decorata, 79
C. polymorpha, 46, 47, 52, 58
Camerinidae, Table 2.1
Cancris, 30, 212, Fig. 2.1
C. inaequalis, Table 12.2
Candeina, 32
C. nitida, 110, Fig. 7.3
Candeinidae, 32, 136
Carpenteria proteiformis, 156
Carterina, 28, 57, Fig. 4.1
C. spiculotesta, 57, Fig. 2.9
Carterinacea, 15
Carterinida, 18, 22, 28, 33, 57, Figs. 2.8, 2.9, Tables 2.2, 2.3
Carterinidae, 28
Carterinina, Fig. 2.7
Cassidulina, 29, 35, 212
C. crassa, Fig. 2.6
C. hooperi, 192
C. laevigata, 5, 79, 192, Table 12.2
C. neocarinata, Table 12.2
C. reniforme, 154
Cassidulinacea, 15, 29, 35
Cassidulinidae, 29, 35, Table 2.1
Cassidulinoides, 29, 212
C. porrectus, 209, Table 12.2
Ceratobulimina, 32, 66
Ceratobuliminacea, 32

Ceratobuliminidae, 32
Chiloguembelinidae, 32
Chilostomella, 31, 154, 177, 214, 215, Fig. 3.11
C. oolina, 212, Table 12.2
C. ovoidea, 212, 214, Fig. 12.6, Table 12.2
Chilostomellacea, 31, Fig. 2.1
Chilostomellidae, 31, 212, Table 2.1
Cibicides, 31, 60, 80, 158, 224, Figs. 2.1, 15.4
C. advenum, 230, Table 13.1
C. aknerianus, Table 13.1
C. floridanus, 79
C. kullenbergi, Fig. 15.2
C. lobatulus, 154
C. refulgens, 43, 80
C. wuellerstorfi, 5, 40, 175, 176, 177, 179, 192, 254, Fig. 15.2
Cibicididae, 31
Cibicidoides, 31, 174, 176, 248, 254
Clavatorella, 32
Clavulina, 7, 27
Conicospirillinoides, 32
Cornuloculina, 27
Cornuspira, 11, 27
Cornuspiracea, 27
Cornuspiramia, 157
Cornuspiridae, 17, 27
Coscinophragmatacea, 26
Coscinophragmatidae, 26
Cribrobigenerina, 27
Cribroelphidium, 32
C. poeyanum, 155
C. translucens, 224, Table 13.1
Cribrospiroloculina, 27
Cribrostomoides, 26, 214
C. crassimargo, 149
C. jeffreysii, 154, 155, Table 12.2
C. wiesneri, Table 12.2
Cribrothalammina alba, 45, 55, Figs. 3.1, 3.2, 3.4, 3.16, Table 3.1
Cristellaria, Fig. 2.4
Crithionina, 23
Cruciloculina, 27
Cushmanella, 33, 66
Cyclammina, 26
Cyclamminidae, 26
Cyclocibicides, 31, 157
Cycloclypeus, 32, 69, 133
C. carpenteri, 48, 133, Table 8.1
Cycloforina villafranca, Fig. 13.2
Cyclorbiculina, 28, 135, Table 8.1
C. compressa, 135, 157
Cyclostègues, 7, Fig. 2.3

TAXONOMIC INDEX

Cylindrogullmia alba, 52
Cymbaloporetta, 31
Cymbaloporidae, 31, Table 2.1
Delosina, 29
Delosinacea, 29
Delosinidae, 29
Dendritina, 28, 135, Fig. 2.1, Table 8.1
Dendrotuba, 23
Dentalina, 28, Fig. 2.4
D. albatrossi, Fig. 2.9
D. pauperata, Fig. 4.2
Dimorphina, Fig. 2.4
Discocyclinidae, Table 2.1
Discorbacea, 30, 35, Fig. 2.1
Discorbidae, 30
Discorbinella, 30
Discorbinellacea, 30
Discorbinellidae, 30
Discorbis, 30, 35
D. columbiensis, 184, Table 13.1
D. mediterranensis, 52, 54, Table 3.1
D. ornatissima, 54
D. patelliformis, 52, 53, Table 3.1
D. pulvinata, 53–54
D. vilardeboanus, 43, 49, Table 3.1
Discospirina, 27
Discospirinacea, 27
Discospirinidae, 27
Dyocibicides, 31

Edentostomina, 27
E. cultrata, 212
Eggerella, 27, 214, Table 12.2
E. advena, 149, 154, Fig. 13.2, Table 13.1
E. scabra, 208, Table 12.2
Eggerellidae, 27
Eggerelloides scabrus, 155, Table 13.1
Ehrenbergina, 29
Eilohedra, 30
Ellipsodimidae, Table 2.1
Ellipsoglandulina, 29
Ellipsolagenidae, 28
Elphidiella, 32, 63, Fig. 4.10
E. arctica, Fig. 4.11
Elphidiidae, 32, 35, 44, 59
Elphidium, 4, 32, 35, 38, 61, 63, 64, 150, 151, 153, 154, 155, 156, 158, 212, 224, 287, Figs. 1.1, 2.1, 4.8, Table 9.1
E. advenum, 155, Fig. 9.4
E. articulatum, 155, Table 13.1
E. bartletti, Table 13.1

E. batialis, 156
E. caspicum, Table 13.1
E. charlottiensis, Fig. 9.4
E. clavatum/incertum group, Table 13.1
E. craticulatum, 63, Fig. 4.15
E. crispum, 40, 42, 48, 49, 51, 54, 156, 287, Table 3.1
E. discoidale, 156
E. excavatum, 148, 149, 154, 155, 156, 208, 212, 216, Fig. 9.4, Tables 12.2, 13.1
E. granosum, 155
E. gunteri, 151, 155
E. incertum, 209
E. lidoense, Table 13.1
E. margaritaceum, Table 13.1
E. norvangi, Table 13.1
E. orbiculare, Table 13.1
E. poeyanum, 157, Table 13.1
E. translucens, Table 13.1
E. williamsoni, 143, 149
Enallostègues, Fig. 2.3
Entosolenia marginata, 42
Epistomariidae, 31
Epistomina, 66
Epistominella, 30, 212, 214
E. exigua, 5, 154, 155, 179, 192, Table 12.2
E. pusilla, 192
E. smithi, Table 12.2
E. vitrea, 155, Table 12.2
Epistominidae, 32
Eponidacea, 35
Eponides, 30, 35, Fig. 2.1
Eponididae, 30
E. antillarum, 79

Favusellacea, 19, 22, 32, Fig. 2.8
Fischerina, 27
Fischerinidae, 27, Table 2.1
Fissurina, 28
F. marginata, 42, 52, Table 3.1
Floresina amphiphaga, 42, 52
Florilus boueanum, Table 13.1
F. grateloupii, Table 13.1
F. scaphus, Table 13.1
Fontbotia, 176, 254
Foraminiiferea, 16, 18
Fondicularia, 28, Fig. 2.4
Fursenkoina, 29, 192, 212
F. apertura, Table 12.2
F. bramletti, Table 12.2
F. cornuta, 211, Table 12.2

TAXONOMIC INDEX

F. pontoni, Table 13.1
F. seminuda, Table 12.2
Fursenkoinacea, 29
Fursenkoinidae, 29
Fusulinida, 18, 19, 22, 27, 33, 48, Figs. 2.8, 2.9, Table 2.2
Fusulinidae, Table 2.1
Fusulinina, 15, Fig. 2.7

Gallitellia, 32, 33
Gaudryina, 26
Gavelinellidae, 31
Gavelinopsis, 30, 35, 212
G. translucens, Fig. 12.6, Table 12.2
Glabratella, 30
G. lauriei, 79
G. sulcata, 51, 52, 54, Table 3.1
Glabratellacea, 30
Glabratellidae, 30
Glandulina, 28, Fig. 2.4
Glandulinidae, 28
Globigerina, 7, 32, Fig. 2.5
G. bulloides, 108, 110, 117, 246, 248, 254, 267, Figs. 7.3, 15.2
G. calida, 110
G. diplostoma, 119
G. falconensis, Fig. 7.3
G. juvenilis, 119
G. adamsi, 110, 117
G. aequilateralis, 42, 110, 255, Fig. 7.3
G. calida, Fig. 7.3
G. quinqueloba, 108, Fig. 7.3
G. radians, 119
G. rosacea, 119
G. rubescens, Fig. 7.3
G. subcretacea, 119
G. trilocularis, 119
Globigerinacea, 15, 19, 32
Globigerinella, 32
Globigerinida, 10, 19, 22, 32, 33, 43, 59–60, 123, 124, 136, Figs. 2.8, 2.9, Tables 2.2, 2.3
Globigerinidae, 10, 32, 126, Table 2.1
Globigerinina, Fig. 2.7
Globigerinita glutinata, 110, Fig. 7.3
G. uvula, 108, Fig. 7.3
Globigerinoides, 32
G. conglobatus, Fig. 7.3
G. cyclostomus, 119
G. ruber, 24, 108, 118, 267, 293, Figs. 2.9, 7.3, 15.4
G. sacculifer, 48, 109, 246, 247, 254, 255, 267, Figs. 7.3, 15.4
G. suleki, 119

G. tenellus, Fig. 7.3
G. triloba, Fig. 7.3
Globobulimina, 29, 164, 168, 169, 171, 176, 177, 212, 214, 215, Figs. 10.3, 10.7, 11.5
G. affinis, 169, Figs. 10.7, 10.8, Table 12.2
G. hoeglundi, Table 12.2
G. pacifica, 42, Figs. 3.7, 12.6, Table 12.2
Globocassidulina, 29, 154, 212
G. biora, 154, 209, 210, Table 12.2
G. subglobosa, 192, Fig. 11.5
Globoquadrina conglomerata, 110, 117, Fig. 7.3
Globorotalia, 32
G. canariensis, 119
G. crassaformis, 255, Fig. 7.3
G. cultrata, 118, 121
G. hirsuta, 46, Fig. 7.3
G. inflata, 111, 117, 119, 255, Fig. 7.3
G. menardii, 42, 46, 117, 247, 255, 293, Figs. 7.3, 15.4
G. punctulata, 119
G. scitula, Fig. 7.3
G. seiglei, 119
G. theyeri, 117
G. truncatulinoides, 46, 107, 117, 255, 293, Fig. 7.3
G. tumida, 255, Fig. 7.3
Globorotaliacea, 19, 32
Globorotaliidae, 32, 136, Table 2.1
Globorotaloides hexagonus, 117, Fig. 7.3
Globotextularia, 26
Globotextulariidae, 26
Globulina, 28, Fig. 2.4
Gloiogullmia eurystoma, 211, 212
Glomospira, 23
Goesella, 27
Gordiospira, 27
Granuloreticulosa, 18
Gromidae, 10
Guembelitriidae, 32, 33
Guppyella, 26
Guttulina, 28, Fig. 2.4
Gypsina, 31
Gyroidina, 31
Gyroidinoides, 31

Halyphysema tumanowiczii, 52
Hanseniscа, 31
Hantkeninidae, Table 2.1
Hanzawaia, 31, Fig. 2.1
H. concentrica, 155
Haplophragmiacea, 26
Haplophragmoides, 26, 148, Table 9.1
H. manilaensis, 143, Fig. 9.3, Table 9.1
H. wilberti, 147, 149, Fig. 9.4, Table 9.1

TAXONOMIC INDEX

Haplophragmoididae, 26
Hastigerina, 32
H. involuta, 119
H. pelagica, 42, 65, 110, 136, Figs. 4.17, 7.3
Hastigerinella digitata, 110
Hastigerinidae, 32, 136
Hastigerinopsis, 32
Hauerina, 27
Hauerinidae, 27
Haynesina, 31
H. depressula, 155, Fig. 9.4, Tables 9.1, 13.1
H. germanica, 143, 145, Table 13.1
H. orbiculare, 149
Helenina, 30
H. anderseni, 68, 149, Fig. 9.4
Heleninidae, 30
Hélicostègues, 10, Fig. 2.3
Hemigordiopsacea, 27
Hemigordiopsidae, 17, 27
Hemisphaeramminidae, 23
Heromallenia, 30
Heronallenidae, 30
Heterocyclina tuberculata, 133
Heterohelicacea, 19, 32
Heterohelicidae, Table 2.1
Heterostegina, 32, 69, 156, Table 8.1
H. antillarum, 133, Table 8.1
H. depressa, 44, 48, 51, 126, 132, 133, 134, Fig. 8.1, Table 3.1
H. operculinoides, 133
Heterotheca lobata, 55, Table 3.1
Hippocrepina, 23
Hippocrepinacea, 17, 23
Hippocrepinidae, 23
H. pacifica, 169, 216, Figs. 10.5, 10.7, Table 12.2
Hopkinsina, 29, 212
Hormosina, 26
Hormosinacea, 23
Hormosinidae, 23
H. elegans, 168, 248, 253, 255, Fig. 10.7
Homotrema, 31
H. rubra, 156
Homotrematidae, 31
Hopkinsina, 29, 212
Hospitella, 23
Hyalinea, 31
Hyperammina, 23
Hyperamminidae, Table 2.1
Hyrrokkin sarcophaga, 43

Involutinida, 17, 19, 22, 32, 33, 35, Figs. 2.8, 2.9, Tables 2.2, 2.3

Involutinina, 17–18, Fig. 2.7
Ioanella, 30
Iridia, 23
I. lucida, 51, Table 3.1
Islandiella, 29, 35
I. algida, Fig. 2.6
I. islandica, 154

Jaculella, 23
Jadammina, 26
J. macrescens, 143, 144, 145, 146, 147, 149, 289, 290, Figs. 9.2, 9.3, 9.4
J. macrescens forma macrescence, 143, Table 9.1
J. macrescens forma polystoma, 143, Table 9.1

Karreria, 31
Karreriella, 27
Karreriidae, 31
Keramosphaeridae, 28, Table 2.1
Komokia, 23
Komokiacea, 23
Komokiidae, 23

Laevipeneroplis, 135, Table 8.1
L. malayensis, 134–135, Table 8.1
L. proteus, 135, Fig. 8.1
Lagena, 28, 35, 151, 224, Fig. 2.4
Lagenammina, 23
Lagenida, 19, 22, 28, 59, 224, Figs. 2.1, 2.8, 2.9, Tables 2.2, 2.3
Lagenidae, 10, 28, Fig. 2.4, Table 2.1
Lagenina, Fig. 2.7
Lagynidae, 19, 23
Lagynoidea, 26
Laryngosigma, 28
Laterostomella, 32
Laticarinina, 30
Lenticulina, 28, Fig. 2.1
Lepidocyclina elephantina, 37
Liebusella, 26
Lingulina, 28, 59, Fig. 2.4
Lituola, 26
Lituolacea, 15, 26
Lituolida, 19, 22, 23, 33, Figs. 2.8, 2.9, Tables 2.2, 2.3
Lituolidae, 10, 26, Table 2.1
Lituotuba, 26
Lituotubidae, 26
Loftusiacea, 26
Loftusiidae, Table 2.1
Loxostomatacea, 16, 29
Loxostomum, 33, 212
L. pseudobeyrichi, Table 12.2

TAXONOMIC INDEX

Marginopora, 28, 128, 136, 156, 158, Table 8.1
M. vertebralis, 136, 156, 158, 286, Fig. 3.8
Marginulina, 28, Fig. 2.4
Martinottiella, 27
M. communis, 80, 83, Table 13.1
Massilina, 27
Meandrospira, 27
Melonis, 31, 174, Fig. 2.1
M. barleeanus, 5, 169, 192, Figs. 10.4, 10.7, 10.8, 11.5
M. pompilioides, 61, 193, Figs. 4.5, 4.6, 11.5
M. zaandami, 5, 83
Metarotaliella parva, 53, Table 3.1
M. simplex, 53, Table 3.1
M. tuvaluensis, 43
Miliammellus, 16, 33
M. legis, Fig. 2.9
Miliammina, 23, 148, 150, 153
M. earlandi, Table 13.1
M. fusca, 143, 145, 146, 147, 148, 149, 151, 153, Figs. 9.2, 9.3, 9.4, Tables 9.1, 13.1
Miliolacea, 27
Miliolida, 16–17, 18, 19, 22, 27, 33, 43, 46, 58, 153, 154, Figs. 2.1, 2.8, 2.9, Tables 2.2, 2.3
Miliolidae, 10, 28, Table 2.1
Miliolina, 15, 16, Fig. 2.7
Miliolinella, 27
M. circularis, 158
M. subrotunda, 155, Table 13.1
M. warreni, Fig. 2.9
Miniacina, 31, 157
M. miniacea, 156
Miogypsinidae, Table 2.1
Mississippina, 30
Mississippinidae, 30
Monalysidium, 28, 135
M. sollasi, Table 8.1
Monostègues, 7, 35, Fig. 2.3
Monothalamea, 35
Myxotheca, 23, 35, 45, Fig. 3.9
M. arenilega, 55, Table 3.1

Nautilus, 7
Nemogulmia longevariabilis, 52, 211, 212, Table 3.1
Neoconorbina, 30
Neoeponides, 30
Neogloboquadrina, 32
N. dutertrei, 108, 110, 247, 255, Figs. 7.3, 8.2, 15.4
N. pachyderma, 109, 110, 117, 267, Figs. 7.3, 15.4
N. pachyderma forma *superficiaria*, 108
Neorotalia, 133
N. calcar, 133, Table 8.1
Neoschwagerinidae, Table 2.1

Neusinidae, Table 2.1
Nodobacullariella, 27
Nodogenerina, 30
Nodophthalmidium, 27
Nodosaria, 28, Fig. 2.4
N. subsoluta, Fig. 4.2
Nodosariacea, 15, 28, Fig. 2.1
Nodosariida, Table 2.2
Nodosariidae, 28
Nodulina, 23
Nonion, 31, Fig. 2.1
N. boueanum, Table 13.1
N. grateloupi, 212, Tables 12.2, 13.1
N. labradoricum, 61
N. tisburyensis, 153
Nonionacea, 31, 35, Fig. 2.1
Nonionella, 31, 175, 184
N. atlantica, 155
N. stella, 175, 210, 211, 212, 214, 215, Figs. 12.5, 12.6, Table 12.2
N. turgida, 155, 175, 208, 212, Table 12.2
Nonionellina, 31
N. labradorica, 210, 212, Fig. 12.6
Nonionidae, 31, 44, 212, Table 2.1
Normanina, 23
Notodendrodes, 23
N. antarctikos, 43, 154
Notodendrodidae, 17, 23
Nouria, 26
N. polymorphinoides, 155
Nouriidae, 26
Nubecularia, 27, 157
Nubeculariacea, 27
Nubeculariidae, 27
Nummulinidae, 10
Nummulitacea, 32, Fig. 2.1
Nummulites, Fig. 2.1
N. venosus, 52, 53, 133, Table 8.1
Nummulitida, 156
Nummulitidae, 30, 43, 48, 51, 52, 53, 65, 124, 126, 132–133, Fig. 8.4, Table 8.1
Nuttallides, 31
N. umbonifera, 5, 294, Figs. 11.5, 15.2

Oolina, 28
Operculina, 32, 69
Ophiotuba, 23
Ophthalmidiidae, 27, Table 2.1
Orbitoidacea, 15
Orbitoididae, Table 2.1
Orbitolinidae, Table 2.1
Orbulina, 32

TAXONOMIC INDEX

O. universa, 42, 108, 110, 137, 247, 254, 255, Figs. 7.3, 8.2, 8.3, 15.2
Orcadia, 32
Oridorsalidae, 31
Oridorsalis, 31
Osangularia, 31, 212
O. culter, Table 12.2
O. rugosa, Table 12.2
Osangulariidae, 31
Ovammina opaca, 52, 55, Table 3.1
Ozawaia, 32

Palmerinella, 31
Pararotalia, 32
P. spinigera, Fig. 13.2
Parasorites, 28, 134, 135, Table 8.1
P. discoidea, 135
P. orbitolitoides, 134, 157, Table 8.1
Paratrochammina, 214
P. antarctica, Table 12.2
Parrellina, 32
Patellina, 28, 58, 69
P. corrugata, 48, 49, 51, 53, 54, 55, Table 3.1
Patellinella inconspicua, Fig. 9.4
Patellinidae, 28
Paumotua, 30
Pavonina, 29
Pavoninidae, 29
Pegidia, 30
Pegidiidae, 30, Table 2.1
Pelosina, 23
P. arborescens, 40, 208, 212, 214, Figs. 3.5, 3.7
Peneroplidae, 28, 43, 123, 129, 134, 135, Table 8.1
Peneroplis, 28, 38, 126, 135, 157, 158, Fig. 2.1, Table 8.1
P. pertusus, 42, 135, Fig. 8.2
P. planatus, 135, 156, 158, Fig. 13.2
P. elegans, Fig. 8.1
Pileolina tabernacularis, 155
Placopsilina, 26
Placopsilinidae, 26, Table 2.1
Planispirillina, 32
P. papillosa, Fig. 2.9
Planispirillinidae, 17, 18, 32
Planispirina, 27
Planorbulina, 157
P. acervalis, 286
P. mediterranensis, 155
Planorbulinacea, 30, Fig. 2.1
Planorbulinidae, 31, Table 2.1
Planularia, Fig. 2.1
Planulina, 31, 176, 212, 254

P. ariminensis, 40, 179, Table 12.2
P. exorna, 155
Planulinidae, 30
Pleurostomella, 29
Pleurostomellacea, 29
Pleurostomellidae, 29
Polymorphina, 28, 154, 212, Fig. 2.4, Table 12.2
Polymorphinacea, 28
Polymorphinidae, 28, Fig. 2.4, Table 12.2
Polysaccammina hyperhalina, 145, Table 9.1
Polystomella crispum, 40, 48
Polythalamea, 35
Poroeponides, 30, 224
Porosononion martkobi, 231
Protelphidium paralium, Table 13.1
Protista, 18
Protoctista, 3, 18
Psammatodendron, 23
Psammophaga simplora, 52
Psammosphaera, 23, 153, 212, 215
P. bowmanni, 209, Table 12.2
P. parva, Table 12.2
Psammosphaeridae, 23
Pseudogaudryina, 27
Pseudogaudryinidae, 27
Pseudonodosinella, 26
Pseudoparrellidae, 30
Pseudorotalia, 61, 68, Figs. 4.7, 4.13
Pseudothurammina limnetis, 149, Fig. 9.3, Table 9.1
P. subgranulata, 230, Table 13.1
Pseudotriloculina, 212
Ptychomiliola separans, 155
Pullenia, 31
Pulleniatina, 32
P. obliquiloculata, 42, 110, 118, 255, Fig. 7.3
Pulleniatinidae, 32, 136
Puteolina, 134
P. malayensis, 134
Pyrgo, 27, 157
Pyrulina, Fig. 2.4

Quadrimorphina, 31
Quadrimorphinidae, 31
Quinqueloculina, 27, 216, 157, 158, 224, Fig. 9.4
Q. jugosa, 79, 83
Q. lamarckiana, 155, 157
Q. lata, 154
Q. rhodiensis, Table 13.1
Q. seminulum, 208, 212, Table 13.1
Q. stalkeri, 212, 216

Ramulina, 28, Fig. 2.4
Rectobolivina, 29

TAXONOMIC INDEX

Rectuwigerina, 29
Recurvoides, 26, 214, Table 12.2
Remaneica, 26
Remaneicacea, 26
Remaneicidae, 26
Reophacidae, Table 2.1
Reophax, 23, 212
R. arctica, 149, Table 13.1
R. bilocularis, Table 12.2
R. curtus, 79
R. dentaliniformis, 154, Table 12.2
R. excentricus, Table 12.2
R. gracilis, Table 12.2
R. moniliforme, Fig. 9.4
R. nana, 146, 155, Table 9.1
R. subdentaliniformis, 209
Reticulomyxa, 37
Reussella, 29
Reussellidae, 29
Rhabdammina, 23
Rhabdamminidae, 23
Rhizammina, 23, 212
R. irregularis, Table 12.2
Rhizamminidae, Table 2.1
Rimulina, 28
Robertina, 32
Robertinacea, 15, 32
Robertinida, 17, 19, 22, 33, 65–67, Figs. 2.8, 2.9, Tables 2.2, 2.3
Robertinidae, 33
Robertinina, 17, Fig. 2.7
Robertinoides, 33
R. charlottensis, Fig. 2.9
Robulus, Fig. 2.4
Rosalina, 30, 35, 157, 212
R. bertheloti, 79, 83
R. columbiensis, Table 12.2
R. floridana, 45, 46, 47, 48, 67, 69, 80
R. floridensis, 83
Rosalinidae, 30
Rotaliacea, 15, 31, 35, Fig. 2.1
Rotalidium annectens, 151
Rotaliella elatiana, 43, 55, Table 3.1
R. heterocaryotica, 49, 51, 53, Table 3.1
R. roscoffensis, 53, 54, Table 3.1
Rotaliellidae, 44–45
Rotalida, 16, 17, 19, 22, 30, 33, 43, 59–60, Figs. 2.1, 2.8, 2.9, Tables 2.2, 2.3
Rotaliidae, 10, 31, Table 2.1
Rotalina, 15, 16, Fig. 2.7
Rotorbinella rosea, 157
Rubratella intermedia, 53, Table 3.1

Rupertianella, 28
Rupertiidae, Table 2.1
Rupertina stabilis, 40
Rutherfordoides cornuta, Table 13.1
Rzehakinacea, 23
Rzehakinidae, 23

Saccaminidae, 208
Saccammina, 23, 35, 212
S. alba, 52, 55, Table 3.1
S. atlantica, 149
S. comprima, Fig. 2.9, Table 12.2
S. sphaerica, 52, 55
Saccamminidae, 23, Table 2.1
Saccorhiza, 23, 212, Table 12.2
S. ramosa, 42
Sagrina, 29
Saracenaria, 28, Fig. 2.4
Schlumbergerella, 133
S. floresiana, Table 8.1
Seabrookia, 28
Sidebottomina, 33
Sigmavirgulina, 29
Sigmoilina, 27
Sigmoilopsis, 27
Sigmomorphina, 28
Silicinidae, Table 2.1
Silicoloculinida, 16, 17, 19, 22, 33, 35, Figs. 2.8, 2.9, Tables 2.2, 2.3
Silicoloculinidae, 33
Silicoloculinina, 16, Fig. 2.7
Siphogenerina, 29
Siphogenerinoididae, 29
Siphonaperta, 27
S. sabulosa, 79
Siphonina, 30
Siphoninacea, 30
Siphoninidae, 30
Siphonodosaria, 30
Siphotextularia, 27
S. affinis, Fig. 2.9
Siphotrochammina lobata, 146
Soritacea, 28, Fig. 2.1
Sorites, 28, 126, 136, 157, 158, Table 8.1
S. marginalis, 157, 158
S. orbiculus, 136, 156, 157, Fig. 8.1
Soritidae, 28, 43, 123, Fig. 8.4
Soritinae, 123, 129, 136, 157, 158
Sphaeroidina, 30
S. bulloides, 193, Fig. 11.5
Sphaeroidinella, 32
S. dehiscens, 110, Fig. 7.3

Sphaeroidinidae, 30
Spirillina, 11, 28, Fig. 2.9
S. vivipara, 28, 48, 53, 54, Table 3.1
Spirillinacea, 15
Spirillinida, 17, 19, 22, 28, 58, Figs. 2.8, 2.9, Tables 2.2, 2.3
Spirillinidae, 28
Spirillinina, Fig. 2.7
Spirolina hamelini, 158
Spiroloculina, 27, 224
S. atlantica, 83
S. attenuata, 212
S. excavata, Table 13.1
S. hyalina, 47, 51, 58, Fig. 3.3, Table 3.1
Spiroloculinidae, 27
Spiroplectammina, 26, 212–214
S. biformis, 154, 216, Tables 12.2, 13.1
S. earlandi, Fig. 12.6, Table 12.2
Spiroplectamminacea, 26
Spiroplectamminidae, 26
Spiroplectinella sagittula, 155
S. wrighti, 155
Squamulina, 27, 35
Squamulinacea, 27
Squamulinidae, 27
Stainforthia, 29, 212
S. fusiformis, 155, 207–208, 209, 211, 214, Fig. 12.6, Tables 12.2, 13.1
Stainforthiidae, 29
Stetsonia, 30
Stichostegues, Fig. 2.3
Stilostomella, 30
S. antillea, 80
Stilostomellacea, 29
Stilostomellidae, 30
Stomatorbina, 30, 60
Suggrunda, 33, 212
S. eckisi, Table 12.2
Tappanella, 28
Tawitawia, 27
Technitella, 23, 212, Table 12.2
T. legumen, 52
Tenuitella, 32
Textularia, 27, 158, 214, Table 12.2
T. agglutinans, 79
T. candeiana, 47
T. conica, 79, 157
T. earlandi, Fig 9.4
T. kattegatensis, Table 12.2
T. palustris, 146
T. torquata, 154

Textulariacea, 26
Textulariella, 26
Textulariellidae, 26
Textulariida, 18, 22, 26, Figs. 2.8, 2.9, Tables 2.2, 2.3
Textulariidae, 10, 11, 27, Table 2.1
Textulariina, 15, Fig. 2.7
Textularinae, 10
Tinophodella, 32
Tipotrocha, 26
T. comprimata, 143, 144, 145, 146, Figs. 9.2, 9.3
Triloculina, 27, 38, 157, 158, 224
Tolypammina, 212
T. vagans, 154, Table 12.2
Tretomphalus bulloides, Table 3.1
Trifarina, 29, 212
T. bradyi, Table 12.2
T. barnardi, 48
T. affinis, 155
T. brevidentata, Table 13.1
T. marioni, Fig. 13.2, Table 13.1
T. oblonga, 145, Figs. 3.13, 3.15
Tritaxis, 26
Triticities, 27
T. secalicus, Fig. 2.9
T. nana, Fig. 2.9
T. ochracea, 154
T. pacifica, Fig. 12.6, Tables 12.2, 13.1
T. hadai, 153
T. inflata, 143, 144, 145, 146, 147, 149, 289, Figs. 9.2, 9.3, 9.4, Tables 9.1, 13.1
Trochammina, 26, 148, 153, 214, Table 12.2
T. globigeriniformis, Table 12.2
Trochamminacea, 26
Trochamminida, 19, 22, 26, Figs. 2.8, 2.9, Tables 2.2, 2.3
Trochamminidae, 26, Table 2.1
Trochamminita salsa, 149, Fig. 9.4, Table 9.1
Trochamminoides, 26
Trocholinopsis, 32
Tubinella, 28
Tubinellidae, 28
Tubinoidea, 10
Turborotalia, 32
Turrilina, 59
Turrilinacea, 29

Uvigerina, 29, 176, 177, 192, 212, 248, Figs. 11.5, 15.2
U. akitaensis, Table 12.2
U. bassensis, 154, 209
U. curticosta, Table 12.2
U. dirupta, Table 13.1

TAXONOMIC INDEX

U. juncea, Table 12.2
U. laevis, Table 12.2
U. peregrina, 42, 168, 171, 174, 177, 185, Figs. 10.4, 10.7, 11.5, Tables 12.2, 13.1
Uvigerinidae, 29

Vaginulina, 28, Fig. 2.4
Vaginulinidae, 28
Valvulineria, 212
V. mexicana, Table 12.2
Valvulinidae, 27, Table 2.1
Verneuilinacea, 26
Verneuilinidae, 26, Table 2.1
Verneuilinulla, 214, Table 12.2
Vertebralina, 27, 157
V. striata, Fig. 13.2
Victoriellidae, Table 2.1
Virgulinella, 29
Virgulinellidae, 29
Vitrewebbina, Fig. 2.4
Vulbulina, 26

Webbinella, 28, 157
Wiesnerella, 27

OTHER TAXA

Acrostichum, 141
Adamussium colbecki, 41
Artemia, 42
Arthrocnemum, 141
Avicennia, 141

Bacillariophyceae, 123, Table 8.1
Beggiatoa, 203, 207, 212, Fig. 12.4
Belemnitella americana, 241

Chione, 287
Chlamydomonas hedleyi, 135, Fig. 8.2

C. provasoli, 135
Chlorophyta, 43, 123, 129, 135
Chrysophyceae, 123, 136–137, Fig. 8.2, Table 8.1
Crassostrea gigas, 230
Cymodocea, 157

Drosera anglica, 152

Enteromorpha, 41

Gromia, 36, 212
G. oviformis, 36
Gymnodinium béii, 42, 137, Fig. 8.2

Halimeda, 156
Halophila, 158

Juncus, 141

Nitzschia panduriformis, Fig. 8.2

Plantango, 141
Porphyridium, 135
P. purpureum, 135, Fig. 8.2
Posidonia, 157
Puccinellia, 142
Pyrrophyceae, 123, Table 8.1

Rhizophora, 141
Rhodophyta, 43, 123, 135, Fig. 8.2, Table 8.1

Salicornia, 141
Spartina, 141, 142
S. alterniflora, 144, 288
Symbiodinium, Fig. 8.2

Thalassia, 136, 158

Zostera, 157

Made in the USA
Lexington, KY
28 August 2010